HANDBOOK OF BUSINESS LETTERS
Third Edition

HANDBOOK OF BUSINESS LETTERS
Third Edition

by L.E. Frailey

Revised by Susan P. Mamchak
and Steven R. Mamchak

PRENTICE HALL
Englewood Cliffs, New Jersey 07632

Prentice-Hall International (UK) Limited, *London*
Prentice-Hall of Australia Pty. Limited, *Sydney*
Prentice-Hall Canada, Inc., *Toronto*
Prentice-Hall Hispanoamericana, S.A., *Mexico*
Prentice-Hall of India Private Limited, *New Delhi*
Prentice-Hall of Japan, Inc., *Tokyo*
Simon & Schuster Asia Pte. Ltd., *Singapore*
Editora Prentice-Hall do Brasil, Ltda., *Rio de Janeiro*

10 9 8 7 6

10 9 8 7 6 5 4   PBK

Library of Congress Cataloging-in-Publication Data

Frailey, L. E. (Lester Eugene)
    Handbook of business letters / by L.E. Frailey; revised by Susan
P. Mamchak and Steven R. Mamchak.—3rd ed.
        p.   cm.
    Includes index.
    ISBN 0-13-376005-7
    1. Commercial correspondence—Handbooks, manuals, etc. 2. Letter
-writing—Handbooks, manuals, etc. 3. Business writing—Handbooks,
manuals, etc. I. Mamchak, Susan P. II. Mamchak, Steven R.
III. Title.
HF5721.F67 1988
651.7'5—dc 19   88-25377
                                                              CIP

ISBN 0-13-376005-7

ISBN 0-13-382003-3 PBK

PRENTICE HALL
BUSINESS & PROFESSIONAL DIVISION
A division of Simon & Schuster
Englewood Cliffs, New Jersey 07632

Printed in the United States of America

REVISORS' PREFACE TO THE THIRD EDITION

When L. E. "Cy" Frailey first shared his insights on business-letter writing, it was in the late 1940s, and *Handbook of Business Letters* gained immediate respect as one of the best books of its type. L. E. Frailey, an acclaimed expert in business communications and author of numerous company letter compaigns, had stocked his book with hundreds and hundreds of pieces of dynamic, practical, and highly useable material. The success of the book was assured, and, by the 1950s, *Handbook of Business Letters* was a classic—*the* definitive book on corporate correspondence.

Fully realizing that song-writer/poet Bob Dylan was right when he wrote, "The times, they are a-changin'," L. E. Frailey, in the 1960s, began the painstaking work of making the best even better. Consequently, the next decade saw continued and unparalleled success for *Handbook of Business Letters, Revised Edition.* Business writers everywhere were using the powerful, profitable, and precise guidelines that filled every page. By the 1980s, no office library of *any* business was considered complete without a copy of *Handbook of Business Letters.*

Remarkably, the book *grew* in popularity with each *passing year.* As we all realize, however, the years have a way of passing without much notice. That dear friend you see every day hasn't changed a hair in 30 years—or has he? That wonderful mate with whom you share that Golden Anniversary remains *exactly* the same as on that bright morning you married—right? Well...perhaps not quite. A few pounds have been added here and there; a touch of gray has appeared at the temples; the twinkling, laughing eyes look out at the world through bi-(or is it "tri-"?) focals. Does that alter the person's value to us? Is that person any the less worthy of our respect? Of course not!

This is precisely how we, the revisors, and Prentice Hall, the publisher, feel about L. E. Frailey's work. Throughout this revision, we paid careful attention to the details with which he filled each page. Each illustrated point was enhanced and brought even closer for your scrutiny. Whenever practically possible, the language of other eras was maintained to enhance the sense of history the book deserves—for, make no mistake, this *Handbook* has seen and includes vital coverage of every major milestone in 20th Century business—from pre-war depression to post-war boom; from neighborhood, family-operated companies to multi-national conglomerates; from coal deliveries to electronic mail.

For all of this, there is a timeless elegance of thought and conveyed knowledge from which each era has benefited.

So, what did *we* do? We did what L. E. Frailey would have done were he here to carry on. We talked to the business people who are now writing the letters for modern companies; we consulted the experts who are following in L. E. Frailey's footsteps and teaching others; we investigated the current trends in such areas as letterhead design, letter formality, and terms of address. We made certain that the materials in this revised edition were "now," and that they reflected modern American business communications at their best and most effective. Those outmoded or outdated items that L. E. Frailey himself called "Whiskers," we shaved. In short, we took each point and polished it as *he* would have—to help the business-letter "carpenters" of today build the strongest and most effective business communication possible.

So, welcome to the revised edition of *Handbook of Business Letters*. As you read on, you'll get a chuckle, you'll be deluged with brilliant and innovative ideas, you'll sharpen your personal knowledge of business communications of all types, and, perhaps most importantly, you'll *use* the knowledge in these pages to formulate letters that will be both effective and highly profitable for you and your business.

Now, *that* is something Cy Frailey would have loved!

Susan P. Mamchak
Steven R. Mamchak

ACKNOWLEDGMENTS

It is with deep gratitude that we acknowledge the valued contributions of some outstanding companies and services. Their assistance with this revised edition was vitally important in helping to keep this book both current and within the mainstream of modern American business practices.

Anderson Brothers, Inc.
Angostura International, LTD.
The Business Library of New Jersey
Criterion Music Co.
CSX Transportation
Darnell Corp.
Eastern Branch, Monmouth County Library
Empire Travel Corp.
The Folks
Fox River Paper
Greater Cleveland Growth Association, Research Dept.
Hickey Real Estate Agency
Mayfair-Lenox Hotel
Montgomery Ward
Neenah Paper
The Plaza Hotel
The Rylander Co.
South-Western Publishing.

Companies are run for and by people. The individuals with whom we dealt did a masterful job of representing their corporations as well as themselves. These particular people made our jobs easier, more pleasant, and, most importantly, guided us toward completeness and accuracy throughout the revision. Thank you all.

Walter Anderson; Dulcy Bunting; Anne Butler; Debbie De Silippo; Maryclaire Donovan; E. E. Edel; Michael Goldsen; Jean Godwin; Robert E. Hanson; Jamice Heashe; Helen Hickey; Charles Kruger; Raymond A. Linzer; Janet E. Martin; Betty Massey; Ingrid Pedersen; Dolores Recupero; Alice Rondazzo; Steven E. Rosenberg; James Saiter; Charles H. Thorne; Annette Toner; Patty Weir; and Darnell Yates.

Special thanks for permission to use the lyrics from the following:

"MAÑANA," Barbour & Lee, Copyright Criterion Music Co., 1948, 1976. Copyright Renewed 1976, Criterion Music Co. Used by permission.

A WORD ABOUT THE THIRD EDITION

Scores of new and revised sample letters form the heart of this Third Edition of L. E. Frailey's standard work in the business letter writing field. Many of the illustrative letters appearing in the previous edition have been revised or replaced by new letters, while others have stood the test of time and remain effective models.

The prime purpose of this revised edition has been to broaden the applications to types of letters, situations, and industries that did not exist when the first edition was published in 1948, and to retain to the fullest extent the direct and simple approach of the author with its emphasis on short words and brief sentences that has been so phenomenally useful in creating business-getting letters for large and small businesses in every type of industry.

AUTHOR'S PREFACE TO THE FIRST EDITION

Let's talk five minutes about this *Handbook!*

"In the past," I was just as much interested in letters, and what they could be made to do for business, as I am now. Even then I dreamed of one complete book which would give any executive and his secretary a simple, easy-to-read explanation of common-sense principles, and all the reference data needed to settle any questionable point with respect to letter mechanics.

The book I pictured would be concise and practical, but long enough to cover every kind of business correspondence; it would be helpful to sales managers, credit agents, personnel directors, chief executives, secretarial workers, and all the clerks who had to "talk on paper" or "take a letter." I wanted very much to write it then, but I realized that first must come years of experience and study, of actual testing for results...the accumulation of a great mass of case material. To be of any real value, the writing of such a book would take a long, long time.

I felt, the book just had to *grow.*

Nevertheless, knowing that someday I meant to do the job, I began then to keep my eyes open for anything that might help to make the various sections of the *Handbook* interesting and valuable. Fortunately, all through these years it has been my privilege to know many business executives, to work with many companies, and to gain a down-to-earth view of letter uses and problems. You *see*, I was *exposed* in a very practical way to the things that had to be known if my book were to become a reality.

Often, it has seemed that Providence was bringing me in contact with the people who could—and did—supply the practical, tested material which you will find on these pages. From business men and women who had to endure my lectures, from those enrolled in the Business Letter Clinics conducted in many cities, from workers in the companies where I reviewed correspondence, from students in my classes at Northwestern University, from the letter-experts with whom I became pleasantly acquainted...from all these and many other sources, a flood of letter-contributions came my way. Thus, the *Handbook* had many friends—it gained weight steadily.

The above explains why I do not regard myself as the sole author of this *Handbook of Business Letters*. On the contrary, thousands of generous business friends have helped to make it possible, and to them you and I owe a little bow of appreciation. They have helped to present you with information and suggestions based on practice, not theory. The things talked about are not what I *think* or *assume* about business letters; they represent the actual *experience* of many others like yourself who are constantly trying to make their letters do the best possible job.

The recorded results of experience...this I believe to be the only safe guide for one who dares to write a business book. Hence, I would not presume to talk to you about sales unless I, myself, had been a salesman; or about sales letters unless I, myself, had written successful sales letters. I would not presume to talk about credit problems unless I, myself, had wet my feet in trying to solve them. What right would I have to tell you, the head of a company, how to conduct a Better Letter Program unless I had practiced what I preached?

Yes, this is a practical book. There is nothing in it which will not hold water. For many years, I have been finding out why some letters pull and others flop. If that sounds like blowing my own horn, it is not so intended. It is simply that I have discovered many FACTS that *you* need to know about business letters, and you'll find them all in this volume.

The majority of the letters, the bulletins, and opinions were sent to me with permission to use them as I pleased. For others, permission was secured during the book's preparation. There are a few cases, however, where it has not been possible to identify the writer of the letter, or the company from which it originated. This is regrettable, but I did not believe that any business person would want a letter omitted which might help others to improve their dictation. Certainly, I have tried hard to render unto Caesar what is Caesar's due, and I ask the indulgence of anyone who has been inadvertently overlooked.

L. E. Frailey

TABLE OF CONTENTS

UNDERSTANDING HOW LETTERS SERVE BUSINESS

UNDERSTANDING HOW
LETTERS SERVE BUSINESS

1. WHY LETTERS MUST BE USED—AN OVERVIEW

Taking the place of personal contacts. Why should people complain about the letters they are forced to write in business? These fast-moving messengers who bear the U.S. Postal eagle do a job which no individual could do as cheaply. You pay what it takes to get them into the mailbox, and that is all. They get no salary, and turn in no expense account.

If you are a credit manager using letters, you can talk to a hundred, or a thousand, customers who owe your company money—on the same day, and without leaving your desk. If you are a sales manager, you can dictate one interesting, *"personalized"* form letter that will tell all your distributors about a new product—just the same as if you appeared personally on the same day in their stores. Letters conserve your time, and multiply your efforts, by taking the place of personal contacts. Letters are a great boon to business. They help to get things done.

Assisting as business expands. The larger the company, the wider the area it serves—the greater is the need for effective letters. The company which operates a local shoe store may be able to handle almost every communication need personally, with only a few letters. But, the multi-national corporation of shoe distribution centers could never get along without some efficient, inexpensive substitute for personal contacts. While, indeed, long distance calls, electronic mail, and commercial air time may get some of its messages across, it couldn't hope to rely on these expensive practices exclusively in the competitive, cost-conscious world of modern business. The written, individualized letter is still the key communication tool among the instruments of successful business growth. Letters conquer space. Letters make one minute do the work of many. Letters deserve more respect than they have had in business.

There was a time, of course, and not too far back, when letters were an exciting event. It didn't matter particularly how the letter was written. It was passed around, and always got attention. The only rule that seemed to prevail for letter-writing in those days was that it should be written in the driest possible manner, and in a language so still and formal that the true personality of the writer was completely hidden. Unfortunately, that rule was never abolished, and even now there are some who foolishly cling to it.

The awareness of change—the appreciation of up-to-date ways of doing business—are most important to anyone who aspires to become a successful writer. We gain nothing by imitating the past. Like life-styles and working conditions, the standards for a business letter have changed for the better. Why should any businessman use the same style for writing a letter as did his great-grandfather?

These are *modern* times! Many letters to write! Much to learn about *how* to write them!

2. A CHECKLIST OF THE MAJOR USES OF LETTERS

Guide to handling routine matters. A large part of the correspondence which passes back and forth in business is routine in nature. Letters of this type are usually short, and nobody expects them to be especially interesting or persuasive. In other words, routine letters don't try to influence human behavior, as would one to a salesman whose orders have fallen off, or as would another to a customer who has neglected too long the payment of a bill. There is no problem involved in the dictating of a routine letter, and for that reason the job is comparatively easy. For example, it requires no special skill to confirm an order. That is a routine matter which can be handled courteously in a few words. But if you must decline the order, and the customer is likely to be angry about it, then the letter situation is a problem far above routine level, and great skill is required to write the letter which will say "no" and still retain the goodwill of the customer.

The very simplicity of the job of dashing out a batch of routine letters also tends to set up a trap into which the writer may easily fall. The letters are sometimes too curt—too cold. They become contacts without a smile. They *could* help to win or hold goodwill, but they *don't*.

This tendency to serve the meat without the seasoning can represent a great loss to the company where it prevails. Since every friendly contact helps to maintain the right relationship between the company and the public it must serve to stay in business, why should any chance, no matter how small, to enhance the corporate image be disregarded? The letter-writer most valuable to the company is the person who makes *every* letter, routine or otherwise, a friendly, human message seasoned with a genuine will to serve. No letter can be considered so unimportant as to justify an indifferent job.

How to sell products and services. If any one type of letter were to be selected as most valuable in business, the *sales letter* probably would get the nod. Certainly, with the possible exception of some adjustment letters, it is the most difficult to write. As the name obviously implies, the object of the sales letter is to *sell*. If, for example, the letter is mailed to one thousand customers or prospects, its merit can be measured by the percentage of favorable replies.

Too many sales managers and executives still seem unaware of the fact that certain specific principles must be applied in the construction of a good sales letter, and that the percentage of "pull" will invariably depend on the writer's understanding of those principles, plus his ability to put them to work. The successful sales letter is neither the result of genius nor an act of Providence. There are *skills to master*, as will be explained later in this *Handbook*.

Since sales letters are used to develop orders, and thus have direct relation to profit, it must be the obligation of the sales manager, and even of the president, to make sure they are prepared in the way most likely to be effective. Any ignorance with respect to sales letter construction—any haste or carelessness in doing the job—will mean orders *lost* that might have been *gained*, and thus, a direct waste of possible profit dollars.

There are, of course, as shown in Sections 7 and 8, numerous kinds of sales letters—from those that come out at the end and ask for the order, to the more subtle ones that break the ice for future business. In every case, you are writing to a human being, seeking to impel a certain reaction, whether it be to sign and return the enclosed order-blank, or merely to make him say, "These people seem to know their business; while I don't need them now—let's keep them in mind for the future."

Although the number of sales letters mailed every year is truly enormous, a great many more could still be used to increase business. The smaller companies, and some of the larger ones, too, usually neglect this opportunity to keep people informed about the merchandise they have in stock. Except for the rare announcement of a sale, or of some special event such as moving to new quarters, you seldom get letters from the retailers serving your area. And yet, if used intelligently, sales letters will increase business for any vigorous company. This has been proven in every region of the country.

Establishing credit and collecting money. Few companies today can survive without effective machinery to insure the collection of oustanding debts and the prompt processing and checking of credit. In fact, many companies have either made this vital part of business life a separate in-house department or, in some cases, hired an outside agency to handle it for them. While in some instances, the credit department/ agency may deal with the customer in person, most communications are generally handled by letter.

Here again, a handicap exists for many credit agents because they disregard tested principles which would make their letters more effective. The best credit agents are both goodwill builders and money collectors. They work with the sales department and often find the way to place a sales "twist" in a letter about some credit situation. They are students of psychology, and expert letter-craftsmen. Agents have gained a fair concept of the principles of letter carpentry, and we are seeing less and less of old time collection methods where they started by calling the wayward customer a dead-beat, and then "worked up" to the point where they threatened the delinquent with legal action.

In the section of the *Handbook* devoted to credit and collections, you will find many fine letters to prove that credit agents in general are holding their own in comparison with those in other fields of business; but there are still too many money-collectors who believe, as in days of old, that a collection letter which sizzles with abuse is better than one which reasons with the customer.

Strategies for adjusting complaints and misunderstandings. Even in the best-managed company, where the customer relations policy is "fairplay and good manners," it is impossible to avoid an occasional tangle in the threads of business. No matter where the fault may rest, the company with long-pull vision will do everything possible to satisfy the customer. If the adjustment cannot be in the nature of a "yes," at least the effort is made to save face for the customer by making the "no" as gentle and painless as the adjustment manager can devise. The art of being able to smooth the ruffled feathers of a customer, of changing a frown to a smile, is one that seems better adapted to letters than to personal contacts. This, to be sure, is only a general statement, because there are exceptional cases where no letter could do the job.

The advantage of the letter adjustment over the personal one is that the writers can very carefully state their case from start to finish without the danger of an interruption which may take the argument off on a tangent, result in heated words back and forth, and conclude with the customer even more disturbed than before. The letter affords a better chance to place all the cards face-up on the table, and if the facts are stated in a friendly-game fashion, it is often surprising how neatly and completely the meeting of two minds can be reached. This job is not done so easily in a personal conversation.

Thus, we see that adjustments by letter not only save a lot of time, but also tend to eliminate the bickering which so often ends in the losing of the customer's goodwill. The aim, of course, is to assign the responsibility of handling complaints to people of good judgment who have the knack of writing friendly letters. Irrespective of whether they give all, give a part, or give not at all, their letter still carries a tone of consideration for the customers' point of view, and a sincere appreciation of their business.

Winning and holding goodwill. Naturally, it might be asked, "Why mention only goodwill letters as apart from all the other types? Isn't that one of the objectives in *any* business letter?" Quite true. Just as in one sense every employee of a company is a member of the sales department, so, in the same way, every letter should be a messenger of goodwill. But there are also those letters in business which are written for *no other purpose* than to make your customers feel they are important to your company, to show that a human relationship exists just as one person may be the friend of another. Such a letter is nothing more than the waving of a hand to someone across the street, and a "Hello there! How are you doing? We are interested in you and your business."

You could call these goodwill builders "unnecessary letters," and that's what they are if you think of business as a cold and formal thing in which there is no place or time for those little courtesies which help to make it warm and personal. Many executives hold a different opinion, however. They realize that competition is keen and that companies other than their own are often shooting for their customers. They think the time and effort well spent in sowing seeds of goodwill which may help to keep old customers in the fold and may round up some new ones.

In Section 10 of this *Handbook,* you will find many of these goodwill letters—messages of appreciation, of congratulation, of condolence— and you may judge for yourself how *you* would react to them. Certainly, if written at all, they must originate in a friendly company where the spirit of service is strong and genuine. Investigate the sales progress of any company committed to a letter-program for building customer goodwill, and you will surely find it a step in front of its competitors.

3. REVEALING LETTERS AS PART OF PUBLIC RELATIONS

Letters are *not* roses. When Gertrude Stein claimed, "A rose is a rose is a rose," some businesses interpreted this as meaning that all letters are like "roses." That is, if they all bear the company's letterhead, they will all convey the same company image to the public—automatically. This is so sadly not true. Often the good accomplished by the highly trained salesman is nullified by a letter-writer who has had no training at all. The salesman works hard to get a new customer for the company. A correspondent comes along with a tactless letter, and the customer is lost. Examples like these are countless, and they all result from the idea that a personal contact is different from one made by letter. That's all nonsense; words written are just as important as words spoken.

Letter-writing, unless it is of the lowest routine variety, is a psychological process. It involves the mastery of principles which are known and tested. When those principles are applied, success follows. The key is training. Every person who writes a letter to *anyone* in the name of your company must be fully aware of the proven strategies found in this *Handbook*. Care should be taken that all writers act as a team to promote the best image for your company. For every customer who is pleased by their contact, let there not be another ill-structured one which does not show your product or service in the best light. Train all writers—they *are* the company in the eyes of the public.

Let's talk. Aside from the principles that must be understood is the fact that a letter—a *good* letter—reflects the personality of the writer, which (needless to say) should be pleasing to the reader. In a good letter, a conversation is held. The reader must be made to forget that he is *reading* a letter. Instead, the writer has traveled on a piece of paper to *talk* to him—in exactly the same way that he would if he had appeared in person.

A letter is a personal contact. Never forget that. Why should it be anything else? There's a customer in California whose account is lagging. You can't go that far to talk about it, but you dictate a letter and ask him in a friendly way for a check. You can put the same smile in the words on paper that you would put in your voice if the customer were there in the same room with you.

There are many angles to the construction of various types of business letters, and it takes time and practice to master them. If your own letters have been dry and commonplace, you can add new life and vitality to the next batch by just trying to *talk* to the folks who are going to read what you have to say. Make them see your personality between the lines.

Your readers are human beings. After all, these folks—your readers—are not just *names*. They are *people*. They walk, talk, sleep, eat, gossip, worship, love, hate—just as you do.

Business consists of a multitude of human contacts—the clashing of opinions, the unity of desires—and making the sum total pleasant is the object of what we call "Public Relations." If the nature of these contacts determines the degree of goodwill earned and held by your company, then how can letters be ignored? Letters are part of public relations, and that means *human* relations. Two human beings with their heads together—you and your reader—that's all a letter is. At least, all it *should* be.

"The most effective letters," says a bulletin issued by the Household Finance Corporation, "are frank statements—messages from real people to other real people. They should be easy to read and easy to understand. They must be friendly and courteous. The often-stressed point that business letters should develop goodwill is…a principle of vital significance. Every letter involves a problem, and every problem has at least two sides: the customer's point of view, and that of the writer. It sometimes seems that these are opposed to each other, yet they usually are in harmony, because good business transactions are mutually profitable to the parties involved."

The idea that every contact in business tends to help or hurt in the molding of public relations was ably expressed in a letter written by the late L. A. Downs, president of the Illinois Central Railroad. He said:

> Cultivation of goodwill is not a departmental activity, but the work of the entire organization. Friends are made, or can be alienated by the operator who answers the telephone, the person who writes a letter, the clerk who sells a ticket or accepts a shipment; or, even through what is done or left undone by some member of the organization who does not come in direct contact with the public. *Every member of our company is a public relations worker,* and our reputation depends upon the skill with which each one does his part of the common task.

Speaking more directly of letters, Mr. Charles Kell, of the General American Life Insurance Company, said in one of his training bulletins: "It is foolish and wasteful for any organization to build at great expense a high…sales organization, and be indifferent to the counteraction resulting from letters that fail to follow through."

A letter about Movement 26402627X. There is no reason why a routine letter, if written by someone properly motivated toward the company, cannot *sell* as well as *tell*. In my collection of good letters is one which aptly illustrates this fact. It came from a secretary who cleverly handled a situation which every secretary encounters frequently.

> Dear _____,
> It will remind you that Illinois Central service extends far beyond our own rails when I tell you that Mr. Downs is calling on some of our shippers this week in California. As soon as he returns, I will show him your letter—and, of course, he will be glad to reply.

The situation was simple. All the secretary *had* to do was to explain why there would be a delay in the answer to the letter. Her boss was out of town. And that is exactly what the average secretary will tell you under the same circumstances. But this one was above average. She saw in this routine letter a chance to be a *salesman* for Illinois Central.

In contrast with the above example of sales co-operation, consider the story of a friend who inherited an old-style watch. It had been his great-grandfather's, and, of course, was big and amusing to see in these days of thin and elegant watches. But my friend soon discovered that this ancient time-piece faithfully kept on the job. So he said: "This is a remarkable watch. It may look old-fashioned, but the old boy still keeps perfect time. I am going to write to the company that made this watch, and give them the number. Maybe they can tell me how old it really is. Besides, they will be glad to know that one of their watches is still doing a good job."

There was a situation to excite anybody with an ounce of sales blood. The person who answered that letter had a lot more to work with than did the secretary whose boss was out of town. He had the chance to say, "Thanks for telling us about your old watch. It is still good for many years of perfect service. You see, that's the way our watches always have been made—to last throughout the years, and never cause any trouble."

But, my friend's letter fell into the hands of a—well, judge for yourself. He had all the chance in the world to *sell* as well as *tell*. But here is what he wrote:

> In response to your kind inquiry regarding *Movement* 26402627X, we wish to advise that our records show date of manufacture was July, 1886. We note your appreciation of our *product* and trust this information will be of some interest to you.

What a travesty of public relations, that such a letter could have been written! Not only was the language full of "whiskers" (see Section 2 of this *Handbook*) but the writer evidently didn't realize that his company sold *watches*. My friend had inherited a *Movement*—not a watch; and then it became a *product*. What about *your* wrist-movement? Does it keep good time?

The greatest fault of the letter, however, appears at the end— "and trust this information will be of some interest to *you*." Of interest to *him*? Why not of interest to the *company*?

Have we been too severe in our judgment of the person who wrote this routine letter? Well, perhaps so. Every day in business, thousands of other people are writing routine letters with no better realization of how they could create friendly contacts—winning goodwill for the companies where they originate, and helping to *sell* their services. Yes, the fault rests more with the company than with the individual. We cannot expect the employees to make the most of letter opportunities unless they are *taught* and motivated. Perhaps the boss of the secretary who wrote the preceding letter had talked to his secretary about the importance of letters; perhaps, from his own dynamic personality, she had absorbed some of his sales enthusiasm. Perhaps nobody at the watch company had ever pointed the right letter-way to the person who wrote so dully about "Movement 26402627X." After all, it is the responsibility of leadership to *lead*. Somebody must make the letter-writers in American business see the importance of what they are doing. Somebody must train—motivate—them.

Yes, letter contacts are part of the Public Relations Program. But this fact has little meaning until those who write the letters are conscious of it.

4. IDENTIFYING THE NEED FOR EXECUTIVE ATTENTION

Starting at the top. Almost without exception it is true that the best letters are being written, consistently, and throughout all departments, in those companies where chief executives take an active interest in the program. An ideal way for this interest to be shown is for the chief executives/managers to issue a message to all members of the staff. The message should clearly state how dedicated the company is to increasing the effectiveness of its written communications at all levels and in all positions—from the executive suites to the service offices. It is an unhappy condition when the majority of the letter-writers in a company are trying hard to write in an easy, natural, modern style, and letters of 1776 vintage continue to roll out of the executive offices.

This need of executive co-operation is so urgent that many competent communication experts will only accept an assignment to establish a better-letter program if they are assured that all those who write letters in the company, from top to bottom, are ready to do their part.

"Send me a copy." It is hardly possible that executives can be absolutely sure what kind of a letter-job is being done in their company unless they take an occasional inventory. This can best be done by asking that an extra copy be made of each letter written on a certain day or during a longer period. An examination of these copies will quickly reveal the weaknesses and strong points of the various letter-writers. Needless to say, one requisite for the people chosen to take the inventory is that they must already be thoroughly trained in the principles of good letter construction.

How the program can be carried out after the initial check of copies is discussed in Section 6, but obviously the better informed the chief executive is at the start with respect to what needs to be done, the better equipped he is to ask co-operation from those who look to him for leadership and example.

Securing maximum return per dollar cost. A very substantial reason for executive interest in the quality of the letters mailed from the staff is that they represent a major cost in the operation of the business. Because the average person tends to think of a letter in terms of the price of postage, a piece of paper, and an envelope, there often exists an astonishing indifference to the total yearly cost of sending out the necessary letters. As a result, many executives have no control over this expense, although they may be extremely cautious in approving other expenditures not nearly as large.

As in the operation of any other phase of the business, the chief executive has the right to insist that the cost of company letters be no higher than is necessary to secure the desired results.

Thus, a strange situation exists in many a company. The cost of the personal calls made by salesmen is measured down to a split penny, and every effort is made to hold it down. Dependent upon the type of business and the nature of the product, this cost per personal contact may represent a considerable line expense. Yes, a lot of time is spent checking these items—but in how many companies is the cost known for letter-calls? It is usually considered a part of the overhead, and hardly an item worth worrying about. Executives who feel that way are indeed headed for the suprise of their life—if and when they finally get the facts. Letters cost money—plenty of money—more than you might think.

What is the average cost of a business letter?—The truth. Fortunately, a number of intelligent surveys have been made to answer this question, and although the answer varies according to prevailing labor and material costs, it still remains an interesting, and perhaps surprising figure. Considering the dictator's time, stenographic cost, nonproductive labor, fixed charges, materials, mailing cost, and filing cost, the average cost for a letter is approximately $6.00.

A checklist of how savings can be made. By initiating an intelligent cost-cutting campaign, about 25 percent can be saved on each letter. How can this be done?

Today's modern communication methods make cost-reduction strategies as varied as the offices in which they're found. Industrywide communication changes have been coming continuously for the past five to ten years. Some of the major changes impacting cost are:

• less and less need for hard copy transmission and storage of intra-office information

• easy replication techniques for outgoing client/customer communications

• time spent in letter preparation is directly applied to transmission because of increased use of and access to word processing equipment by letter originators

While all seems in favor of saving through electronic mail, fax machines and mini/main frame/pc computers, the reality is that letters are still a cost item to business. Nowadays, instead of stenographer's time, dictating machines, and file cabinets, the moneys are being spent on needs analysis, terminals, and networks.

Yet with the impersonal machinery which increases costs, the savings gained by careful letter crafting is the best cost-reductive tool your company may have.

Longer than you've been alive! Assuming that everything possible has been done to hold down letter costs, there still remains the major saving achieved when letters are made to do a better job. This brings us back again to the stern necessity of making sure that every letter-writer understands and *applies* the known principles of good letter construction. Hence, the company must maintain a program through which these principles are *taught*, and follow a system of control that will offset the tendency of letter-writers to slip back into old habits or to become careless and indifferent when little or no attention is given to their handiwork. Lighting the fire which motivates letter-writers to do a better job is a sure step forward, but throughout the year someone must keep the fire burning.

As in the accomplishment of any other objective in business, a program for better letters will succeed in proportion to how completely it gains, in practice and spirit, the co-operation of *all* who write letters. A few old-timers, with minds closed to the possibility that their own letters might be improved, and outspoken in their criticism of the company program, may prove to be a serious obstruction to progress.

I well remember Mr. B., a sales manager in a large company where a concerted effort was being made to improve correspondence. Mr. B. wrote letters that were long, windy, and tiresome. Because of his lengthy service and high position, however, nobody felt qualified to step on his toes, or to suggest that he, too, might benefit by taking advantage of the company's better-letter program. Finally, the problem of Mr. B. was dumped in the lap of the president. The latter waited until a particularly bad example of Mr. B.'s letter-writing—a verbose sales letter which had failed to produce any business—crossed the desk. The president called Mr. B. and me in and the following conversation took place:

President: Mr. B., why don't you talk to Frailey about your next sales letter?

Mr. B.: Who, *me*?

President: Yes, why not? He has helped some of the other sales managers with their letters. Two heads are sometimes better than one, you know.

Mr. B.: Huh, that's ridiculous. Why *I've* been writing letters longer than you've been alive!

It makes no difference how *long* a man has been writing business letters. The point is, does he know *how* to put punch and pull in them? There are principles to master. This *Handbook* seeks to explain and illustrate what they are—and how you can use them.

There are many prestigious firms that have tackled the problem with persistence and have achieved gratifying results. There is no question but that in those organizations where the value of better letters has been recognized, and where an honest attempt has been made to motivate and train those who write them, the gain has far exceeded any imagined loss in time and cost.

The tragic toll of indifference. When we turn to those companies that continue to permit their letter-writers to shift for themselves, the picture is both dismal and discouraging. We know the cost of writing letters in business. We wonder how executives can continue to be indifferent to sales letters that do not sell, collection letters that do not collect, and adjustment letters that do not adjust. The principles of letter-writing are not difficult to master. Indifference to them takes a tragic toll which could very easily be avoided. The reaction to a business letter, as to a personal contact, may often persist for years. You never know when a poor letter may rise from the grave to haunt you or someone else who then becomes the victim of its misguided approach.

There's the memory of a young man who years ago was trying to sell rice for a Texas mill. It was the end of a hard week, and the orders had been scant. Ever hopeful, he went late one afternoon into the buyer's office of a grocery jobber. The buyer was cordial, and he poked his finger with interest into the various sample boxes. Finally he selected certain numbers and began to assemble the specifications for a carload of rice. The young man's heart beat faster. It was satisfying to know that he could send a good order to his company that night, instead of relaying the usual excuses.

Until that moment, the buyer had not been concerned with the name of the mill. Then he frowned. Leaving his office, he returned in a few minutes with a letter which was yellow and brittle with age. It had been written 30 years before, as the young man soon found out, by the credit manager of the mill he represented. And this is what the buyer said: "Young man, I am sorry, but you may tear up that order. Here is a letter which I received 30 years ago from your company. I have been in business a long time, and this is the most insulting letter that I ever had to read. I was a little pressed for cash at the time, but I wasn't a dead-beat or a thief. In Texas, an unpaid bill is not an excuse for discourtesy. I wouldn't care to deal with your mill, sir. Please don't call on me again."

The young man learned the hard way how important a business letter can be. You see, this is a true story. The young man wrote this *Handbook*.

5. ASSAYING THE VALUE OF KNOWING HOW

Seeing the importance to the individual. Knowing how to write good business letters is an asset in any career. With the increasing importance of letters, and the growing recognition that they help or hurt company objectives, it may even be said that the individual who lacks a thorough knowledge of letter-principles is seriously handicapped in building a successful career. Other qualities being equal, the capable letter-writer is more likely to win promotion than someone who has neglected to acquire the same knowledge and skill. More and more in the future, the person who can "talk on paper" to a customer or prospect in a friendly, forceful way will be marked as extremely valuable to the company and will progress accordingly.

If this be true, and it is, then why should any person who hopes to advance in business be indifferent to the importance of letters, or fail to utilize any and every opportunity to become an expert letter-carpenter? If the company provides this opportunity, the problem is simple. If not, the individual may create it—there are schools to attend, books to read, and others to study who have already mastered the art. The road is not barred to anyone who has an adequate knowledge of language and its usage.

College education not required. Unlike many other fields of human endeavor—medicine, law, engineering, chemistry—where advanced education is necessary, you do not need to be a college graduate to master the principles of letter-writing. Average intelligence, common sense, and the right mental attitude—plus the willingness to accept and apply the suggestions offered in this and other books—are the chief essentials. Once you know *what* you are trying to do, and *how* it should be done, the rest is accomplished by on-the-job practice.

Out of your own experience, you begin to compare results. You thought sales letters A and B were equally good. You prepared them carefully, using the formula of the Star, the Chain, and the Hook (Section 3). But when results were counted, letter A proved to be top notch and letter B only mediocre. Why? When you are able to spot the reason, you are a more seasoned letter-writer. You grow in skill as you play the game.

The news gets around. The individual who masters the art of writing a good letter does not remain unnoticed for long. Skill is respected, and you hear it said "_____ can help with that letter...see _____..._____ writes the best letters in the company." The news gets around, and soon your ability reaches executive ears. You are tagged as one worth watching. Your chances for promotion are enhanced.

Need of winners. Almost any individual in business can learn to write better-than-average letters. The slogan for success (see Section 2) is "Relax...be natural...just talk." Beyond this capacity for letting your hair down and being your everyday natural self, however, there are certain skills and qualities which are needed in the preparation of effective business letters. Although these are discussed more fully in later chapters, a preview will do no harm:

1. You cannot very well dictate a good letter unless you can put words together into correct sentences; that skill involves a workable knowledge of grammar, and a vocabulary sufficiently large to express any thought you wish to convey.

2. It cannot be stated too often—there are certain tested principles which must be mastered, both for general letter-writing and for specific types such as sales, collection, and adjustment. There is nothing about the learning of these principles to frighten anybody—but you *must know them.*

3. No one can successfully serve a company with the head but not the heart. Loyalty breeds an enthusiasm which is reflected in the letters that you dictate. In plain words, unless you like your company and your job you should quit.

4. The more you know about the products of your company and the nature of the services rendered, the better you are equipped to talk about them in a letter. This is especially true of situations where sales and complaints are involved. The good letter-writers do not sit in a vacuum and remain indifferent to what goes on about them. Instead they know how the company's products are made and why they are good. Consequently, they can write with enthusiasm about them—and that gives them *power* which otherwise they would lack.

5. A genuine liking for people is a "must." If the objective is to make every letter a cordial contact, then the writer must *feel* cordial. Any insincere friendliness would instantly be sensed by the reader. A liking for people leads to an understanding of human nature. You understand their problems and their point of view, and because you "talk their language" you are accepted as a friend even when you must say "no."

6. Imagination is a valuable asset to the letter-writer. Many think of it as a vague "something" which one must be born with. This is not strictly true, although certain people seem more endowed than others. Imagination is basically the taking of images (memories of experiences) from the mind where they have been stored, and creating from them new combinations or mental pictures. Thus, in a practical sense, and that's as far as we need to go, the businessman is using imagination when he *looks ahead.* Perhaps a new building is to be erected. He imagines first of all the uses to which it may be put, and then considers how it should be designed to achieve these uses. Another thinks of the company's radio or television program under preparation. He imagines the folks who will be listening or watching—their habits and desires— then he seeks to slant the program to fit the mental picture he has formed. Imagination gives color and life to a letter. It can be cultivated more easily than you think.

7. Whether a sense of humor is inherited, acquired, or both, can be left to the psychologists. Certainly, it may be described as a mental attitude which enables one to take the good and bad of life not too

seriously; in that sense it would seem worthy of cultivation. Humor in a letter is desirable when not overdone. No reader, for example, wants to feel that his problem has not been taken seriously, nor does he want to be the *object* of the fun. On the other hand, it has been proven frequently that a dash of humor can improve a letter's pull. Later in this *Handbook* you will encounter many successful letters in which there is a smile or even an outright laugh. You, too, will enjoy them, as surely as did the original readers.

8. Even though the mention of another quality essential to success as a letter-writer might seem to come from the pulpit rather than the desk of a businessman, the fact remains that moral stability is necessary in the handling of all forms of public relations. Letters reflect the character of the writers. Customers and prospects are placed in the mood for favorable reaction when they feel they are reading the words of honest, impartial, dependable people. Of course, in business there are always some who think they are smart enough to pull the wool over the customer's eyes. Such writers fool only themselves. Good, ethical writers place their cards face-up on the table. They play the game fairly; they practice the Golden Rule.

With all these qualities in mind, let us begin our building of effective business letters.

HANDLING BUSINESS LETTER LANGUAGE

HANDLING BUSINESS LETTER LANGUAGE

1. MAKING HUMAN CONTACT ACROSS SPACE

Putting "people" on paper. As explained in the previous section, an effective business letter is a personal contact between two human beings. To save time and to cross space quickly, writers of the letters put on paper a message which otherwise they would prefer to deliver in person; thus a conversation begins. Writers have "first say," but they may, and often do invite the reader to reply. As the letters pass back and forth, the two persons *talk* to each other until there is a meeting of minds, or, for lack of it, the conversation ends.

People who write with a sense of personal contact have a better chance to make what they say interesting and convincing than the ones who feel they are "writing letters." The good dictator says, "I want to talk to this person about paying his bill." The poor dictator is more likely to say, "I must write a letter about this delinquent account." Both dictate for the same purpose, but the first is mentally stepping into the shoes of the person who later will be reading what he says, while the other stays in his own office, physically *and* mentally.

If you want to write successful letters, always keep in mind that you are going to talk across space. In reality, you put your thoughts on paper, then you jump into an envelope and travel to where the reader lives or works. Out you pop with a friendly handclasp, ready to tell your readers why they should give you an order, or pay their past-due bills, or merely that you like them a lot as customers, and will continue to serve them the best that you can. No matter what you talk *about*, the language you use is the same as if you had met them on the street, at home, or in the office.

Contrary to what some may believe, as revealed by their colorless and tiresome letters, there is no special language for business—unless "special" means making an extra effort to be natural, so that the reader will be warmed by your friendly personality and feel that a likable human being has paused to chat with him. True, you want your sentences to be grammatically correct and free from slang or profanity—you are not on the golf course, or riding to work—nevertheless you are not using a *different* language. You are only dressing it up a little bit.

Of course, you do get letters in which the writers seem to think they are "on parade." Maybe they are thinking about the "dignity of business," or perhaps they have been taught that letters should be cold and formal—cold as an oyster, formal as an English butler. People who feel like that about letters are more to be pitied than blamed. They haven't an equal chance in competition with other letter-writers who practice the rule, "Relax...be natural...just talk." They are hopelessly handicapped by their stiff or stilted language. They can't possibly be accepted as friendly human beings or win favor by what they say. The reader simply yawns, and walks away.

"One of the family." The executives of your company don't want letter contacts to be cold and formal. They know that the most loyal customer is the one who feels like "one of the family." The following letter, amusing though it may be, illustrates the point. It was mailed by a lady in Michigan to an employee of Montgomery Ward in Chicago.

Ever since receiving your letter, and the enclosed refund check, I have worn a grin like that of the Cheshire cat. Perhaps you'll see the joke if I tell you.

A number of years ago, I visited a friend in Illinois. One day we came home to find her landlady dressed all in black, with her nose all red from weeping. She could hardly control her grief as she read us an item in the paper. Her friend, her *personal* friend (sob), one of the firm, one of the head officers of Montgomery Ward, was *dead*.

No, she had never seen him. But he did (sob) write her the loveliest letters! Ever since that time that a mistake had been made in one of her orders, and she had written about it! He (sob) had answered *personally*, and he had made them correct the mistake, and he had told her that he would attend to her letters and orders *himself!* And now (sob-sob) he was *dead*.

And did we think it would be all right if she sent some flowers? She had some lovely marigolds and zinnias in her garden.

And now *I've* got a "personal friend." I can picture you as that

old lady did *her* friend, trotting around from department to department, giving your "personal attention" to the selection of my boy's bike, choosing the best hammer for Joe, and picking out just the right frypan for my niece's wedding!
Please don't die, Miss B. What shoud I do without you? And I have no marigolds or zinnias.

Yes, we can smile at the lady pictured in the letter. And so did the mother from Michigan! But beneath the story is a fact important to the success of any business. When a person can write letters in such a cordial way that the customer feels a "personal friend" is speaking, then a great good has been accomplished for the company. The relationship may often endure throughout the years and spread to friends and relatives, so that many, many sales are developed—and all from a few friendly letters.

Avoiding language barriers. Since the language used in a business letter largely determines how successfully a human contact is made with the reader, common sense tells us that we should examine our letters carefully to make sure that we have no language habits hindering the effectiveness of the contact. Bad habits in word usage do exist, and any one of them may be a barrier that tends to hold writer and reader apart.

Unfortunately, some of the guilty letter-writers meet with a cold eye any suggestion that their style could be improved. Indignantly they reply, "This is the way we've always done it"—a condition of mental obsolescence for which there is no cure—and they keep on dictating letters that confuse or repel their readers. For example, here is a monstrosity in words which was actually mailed from the head office of an insurance company to a policyholder in North Carolina.

Surrender of the policy is permissible only within the days attendant the grace period, in compliance with the citation relevant options accruing to the policy. We are estopped from acquiescing to a surrender prior to the policy's anniversary date.
We are confident that an investigation relevant the incorporation of this feature will substantiate that the policies are not at variance with policies of other insurance companies.

Fine letter, isn't it? So easy to read—a friendly contact with a customer! Can't you see the smiling face of the writer between the lines? How pleased that North Carolinian must have been! That insurance company was fortunate to have on hand a letter-expert who knew how to hold the goodwill of a policyholder.

You think so? Nonsense! Of course you do not. Could there be a poorer attempt to contact a policyholder? By what strange and distorted concept was the writer driven? Where did he get the idea that a business letter should display as many big words as possible? Was he just a beginner trying to show his wisdom, or, worse, an experienced account representative who believed heart and soul in the "dignity" of business?

Apparently, the policyholder had written to the company, and requested the surrender of a policy. The answer was "No." A little word with two letters would have done the job, but what did the insurance company say? "We are estopped from acquiescing"—how much more impressive! Say those words aloud—"estopped from acquiescing"! Maybe they sound pretty but they certainly don't belong in a business letter. How *could* any human being talk to another in such a strange lingo?

You see, the writer of that letter had formed one of the bad language habits which become barriers between writer and reader. The fault was "goozling." We will hear more about it later in this section of the *Handbook*.

2. GROOMING THE OLD-TIME "WHISKERS"

Using word combinations of ancient vintage. Because in the early days of our nation letters were mostly used for formal purposes, the language was very cold and stilted. Those were the days when you might have ended a letter with, "Your obedient servant," or, "We beg to remain, dear Sirs, Faithfully yours." And of course the whole of your letter would have contained many other equally stilted phrases. Such word combinations are far removed from the natural, informal language which adds interest and personality to the modern letter.

However, before you criticize too severely the writers of these early letters, you must remember that the social customs of the upper class were much more formal than they are today. The language which seems so amusing to us now was actually *used* in high society. You see, they were partly, at least, following our modern rule for letter-writing—*Write as you talk*. The people of the middle and lower classes had little necessity for letters, and their use in business was the exception rather than the rule.

Today, many of the old customs have vanished. These are modern times of careless informality that tend to break down class distinctions and bring people together on a basis of free and easy living. The modern tempo is to be *natural*—in dress, in speech, in all other human relationships.

The "whiskers" linger on. With all these changes from the old days to the new, you would scarcely expect to find some business people still using the language of 1776 in their letters. For some strange, unexplainable reason, however, the stilted phrases of yesterday are frequently encountered, although they make impossible that friendly person contact which, as we have seen, is the aim of any good business letter. For example, here are some sentences taken from the copies of letters mailed recently:

We *herewith take the liberty* of acknowledging your letter *of recent date.*
Attached hereto, you will *please find same.*
Thanking you very kindly, we *beg to remain,*
In reply to your letter of *the 21st instant,* we *would wish to state,*
Trusting you will be in a position to do *same, we are,*
Your favor has duly come to hand, and *we beg to advise,*

The italicized phrases are *not* the language of modern speech. They are throwbacks—as obsolete and old-fashioned as candle-light or the pump in the village square. The most serious charge against them is that such phrases tend to destroy rather than help the chances of a business letter to succeed. You cannot possibly talk in a friendly, natural way with such stiff-shirt language. One's true personality is hidden just as a face might be with a two-week-old beard. And that's why I call them "Whiskers"—colorless word combinations, embalmed with cold formality—barriers which keep you and your reader utterly apart.

But call them what you will—whiskers, rubber-stamps, stilted phrases—they are taboo in business letters. They make an easy job hard. They throttle personality. They destroy goodwill. They *lessen results.* For this last reason, if for no other, there is nothing good that can be said for Whiskers. Common sense tells us we should do nothing to interfere with the chief objectives of business; namely, to win public acceptance, cultivate goodwill, sell goods, and make a profit. Whiskers obstruct these objectives. Why should any businessman cling to them?

If you think that a mountain is being made out of a molehill, and that actually very few whiskers are found in modern business correspondence, you are as wrong as wrong can be. Look at the morning mail which comes to any office and you will find a certain percentage of letters done in the style and spirit of quill-pen days. Here are three, taken from thousands I have collected.

Answering your esteemed favor of recent date, which has been duly received and contents noted, we wish to kindly advise that according to our records, your policy went forth in your direction on the 28th instant.

Pursuant to your question about premiums, we would wish to state that the writer has referred same to our Mr. Jones, who will write to you in due course of time or in the very near future.

Trusting this letter will come to hand, we beg to remain,

We regret to learn from your esteemed communication that you were unable to favor us with your recent order on which we had the pleasure of quoting, inasmuch as you found it to your advantage to place your order elsewhere at this time.

However, we appreciate your kind indulgence, and trust when you are again in the market that we will have the pleasure of receiving your valued inquiry. At that time, we will endeavor to submit prices and samples to merit our receiving your valued order.

Thanking you for the courtesies extended Mr. Black, and awaiting your further commands at all times with interest, we remain,

While the exegesis of downward economic indicators were duly noted in your gracious missive of Tuesday last, we humbly regret that our authority in this matter does not permit any surety on our part per se as to the change you so magnanimously offered.

Please accept our deepest regrets for unfortunate surcease of this matter. We stand ever at your service.

No doubt the writers of those three letters are pleasant people. At home, in the office, they may attract others to them by the warmth of their personalities. But from the way they have written, we have the right to picture three very old men, severe-eyed and white-bearded, clothed in the attire of the last century, seated on high stools, and laboriously writing with quill pens. As full of language freaks as these letters are, perhaps the prize of all is the statement in the first of them— "Your policy went forth in your direction." What a blessing! At least *that* was aimed at the reader.

Good until the bottom drops out. Can you imagine yourself, or any other human being of our times, *talking* the language of those letters? Would any lover say, "Darling, I wish to state, I'll be over at eight"? Or, later in the evening, on the sofa, say, "I beg to advise, it's time to arise"?

On leaving home this morning, did Mr. Businessman say to his wife as he kissed her good-bye, "With respect to the information duly received that you will serve corned-beef and cabbage tonight, I take great pleasure in advising that I will be on hand to partake of same"?

What if your company had received a request that a salesman call with information about a certain product? Would the salesman begin the interview as follows: "In reply to your kind request of recent date, I hand you herewith a sample of the product you mentioned. We will appreciate your kind indulgence in giving same your esteemed consideration." No, you have never heard whisker-talk from a salesman. It wouldn't get any orders.

If people do not use these moth-eaten old phrases in speech, why *do* they use them in their letters?

A truly remarkable example of what Whiskers can do to a letter is the following application for a job. The young man who wrote it was resourceful. He had read William H. Danforth's famous book, *I Dare You*, the theme of which is that we set our own ceilings in life—and can go as far as we dare to think we can. This young man made a clever attempt to dare the author who dared *him*. Here is his letter:

Dear Mr. Danforth,
I have just finished reading your wonderful book, *I Dare You*, and so I am daring myself to write you this letter.
I am 19 years old, and have had only one year in high school, but I am trying to make up for that by studying at night. Right now, I am making $50.00 a week in a grocery store. My dad is out of work, and I am trying to help support him and my sister, but $50.00 doesn't go very far.
Now, Mr. Danforth, that is my story, and *I dare you* to give me a better job, and if you have no opening for me in your company, then *I dare you* to find one.
Thanking you very kindly, and hoping to hear from you in the near future, I remain,
Yours very truly,

As you read that letter, you can't help but feel the personality of a person who seems to be made of good stuff, and is worthy of the job he is after. The language most of the way is natural. You can almost hear the young fellow *talking*. And then the bottom drops out!

Had he stopped without the last paragraph, the ending would have been strong and impelling. You could hardly devise a better close than "Then *I dare you* to find one."

But what happened? Who knows? Perhaps the young man had written his letter and then handed it to some older person. "Do you think this letter will get me the job?" he probably asked.

If we are guessing right, that tradition-bound sage handed the letter back saying, "Well, now it needs a better ending—something more businesslike—I'll show you what I mean."

No matter why the letter happened to end so sourly, you will agree that the whole effect was spoiled by the bromides in the closing sentence. Until then, we heard the voice of an ambitious young man, fighting to lift himself by the bootstraps. Then his voice is gone, and we have instead some sounds from the musty past.

"Whiskers" here, there, everywhere. It takes very little thought to dictate a letter when one's mind is merely a file for clichés. Without any effort, the dictator can say, "We have your letter of," or "Thanking you in advance, we remain." These and similar canned expressions can be used over and over again. It's the lazy way to write, but like anything else that comes too easily, the result is nothing to brag about. Canned letters lack the tang and flavor of those served fresh for each occasion.

Fortunately, there are in America many letter-writers who are fighting to eliminate the formal language which still appears in business correspondence and eventually this united effort may win. We can only hope for the best. One of the crusaders, Harold P. McQueen of Chicago, has cited the following example in which "Squibbs," a bookkeeper, had received a large check in full payment for a purchase made by a new customer. Squibbs rightly felt that the situation deserved a letter of thanks and this is the one she wrote:

> We beg to acknowledge receipt of your check No. 3433 in the amount of $5,550 in payment of our invoice dated June 7th, for which please accept our thanks.
> Enclosed please find receipted bill for your files.
> Trusting we may be favored with your future orders, we remain,

The facts in this case were no different from those in thousands of others. The bookkeeper was really grateful for the check. A genuine glow of appreciation warmed her heart. Her intentions were good. She wanted to thank the customer, and no doubt thought her letter did a fine job. In the words of Mr. McQueen, however, "it was too much like throwing a cold blanket over the whole pleasant transaction." Too much whisker-talk!

So this was the revision which was sent:

> Of course we are always glad to get checks in the mail, but with yours, which arrived this morning, came an added bonus. Your prompt payment seemed to say that you were satisfied with our service.

Your attitude makes our jobs a pleasure. This letter speaks for every one of us who had the delight of meeting and working with you on this order. We all look forward to repeating the experience again and again.

If 100 new customers were asked which of these two letters pleased them more, how do you suppose they would vote?

It would be incorrect to say that old-time, shopworn phrases are used more frequently in certain types of business and professions, and that other occupations are practically immune to whiskers. Although we know of no surveys that point to such a conclusion, offhand it seems you do encounter more whiskers in the letters of politicians, lawyers, traffic clerks, government employees, and purchasing agents, than in the letters of sales managers, personnel directors, advertising managers, credit accountants, and executives. As you would expect, older people with 20, 30, or 40 years' service are more likely to use stilted language than are younger ones who have not been subjected to the habits and traditions of earlier days in business. In companies where better-letter programs have been operating for a number of years, much progress has been made, with the result that only a few die-hards continue to use cut-and-dried, canned lingo.

In general, though, whiskers may be found here, there, and everywhere that letters are written. Why this foolish and wasteful language habit is so difficult to eradicate is impossible to explain. In hundreds of books, magazine articles, and speeches, business people have been told why they should make their letters personal, human, and natural. They nod their heads in assent, then later dictate sentences like these:

> We wish to advise consideration would not be in order at the present time. We crave your indulgence in this respect, and regret our inability to authorize gratis replacement in this instance. (From the desk of an executive in the automobile industry.)

> We beg to acknowledge receipt of your communication, and under separate cover we are forwarding forthwith additional copies. We trust this action has your esteemed approval and beg to remain. (Dictated by an advertising manager)

> Anticipating our thanks for a reply at your earliest convenience, which we trust will be soon in our hands, we are. (A president was father to this one)

In compliance with your request of the 24th, I transmit herewith a blank voucher for pension due you. (United States Pension Agent)

We have, therefore, checked and approved same and are returning herewith one copy to you, and are retaining the other and oblige. (A purchasing agent claims it)

You have seen how whisker-talk tends to hide personality and mechanize letters. The sentences just quoted are from the letters of six different business people, but read them aloud, and you would swear that they were dictated by the same person. How could such language, under any circumstances, create the illusion of *personal* contact? The reader is chilled by a conglomeration of words which sound more as if they came from a robot than from a person.

So much for the worn-out, hackneyed expressions so often seen in business letters—whiskers, rubber-stamps, chestnuts, call them what you please. They are sleeping pills which defeat the aim of making every letter a warm, *personal contact* with the reader.

The following list includes most of these bromides; make sure you avoid them:

You Don't Talk This Way
(Letter-Whiskers)

according to our records
acknowledge receipt of
acknowledge with pleasure
acknowledging yours of

as captioned above
as per
as regards
as stated above
assuring you of

at all times
at an early date
at hand
at the present time
at the present writing
at this time
at your convenience

attached hereto
attached herewith
attached please find

awaiting your further wishes
awaiting your order
awaiting your reply

beg to acknowledge
beg to advise
beg to assure
beg to call your attention
beg to confirm
beg to state
beg to suggest

carefully noted
check to cover
complying with your request
concerning yours of
contents noted
contents duly noted
continued patronage

deem (for think)
desire to state

due to the fact
duly noted

enclosed find
enclosed herewith
enclosed please find
esteemed favor
esteemed order
esteemed request

favor us with your order
favor us with your reply
for your files
for your information

hand you herewith
has come to hand
have before us
hereby advise
hereby insist
herewith enclose
herewith find
herewith please find
hoping for your order
hoping to receive

I am (ending last sentence)
I beg to advise
I have your letter of
I trust
in accordance with
in answer to same
in answer to yours
in conclusion would state
in connection therewith
in due course
in due course of time
in re
in reference to
in receipt of
in reply would advise
in reply would wish
in response to yours
in the amount of
in the near future
in this connection

kind indulgence
kind order
kindly advice
kindly be advised
kindly confirm same

looking forward to

may we suggest
may we hope to receive
meets your approval

of above date
order has gone forward
our Mr.—
our line
our records show

per
permit us to remind
please accept
please advise (be advised)
please find herewith
please find enclosed
please note
please rest assured
please return same
pleasure of a reply
proximo (prox.)
pursuant to

re
recent date
referring to yours of
regarding the matter
regarding the above
regarding said order
regarding yours
regret to advise
regret to inform
regret to state

said (the said regulation)
same (regarding same)
soliciting your advice
soliciting your indulgence
soliciting your patronage

take pleasure in
take the liberty of
thank you kindly
thanking you in anticipation
thanking you in advance
thanking you kindly
the writer
this is to acknowledge
this is to advise
trusting to have
trusting to receive same

ultimo (ult.)
under separate cover
up to this writing

valued favor
valued order
valued patronage

we are (ending last sentence)
we are pleased to advise
we are pleased to note
we have before us
we remain (ending last
    sentence)

we take pleasure in advising
we trust
wish to advise
with to state
with kindest regards
with reference to
with your kind permission
would advise
would state
would wish to

your esteemed order
your favor has come to hand
your future patronage
your kind indulgence
your letter of even date
your letter of recent date
your Mr. —
your valued patronage
yours of even date
yours of recent date
yours duly received
yours kindly
yours with regard to above
yours with respect to same

Carefully check your letters to make them as "clean-shaven" as can be.

3. PUNCTURING THE POMPOSITY OF PACHYDERMAL PROSE

Plying the gentle art of "goozling." Remembering that the aim of a business letter is to make a personal contact in the simplest way possible—using the words of everyday speech, and just *talking* to the reader—it can readily be understood how the purpose is defeated when writers allow themselves to be pompous or verbose. The gentle art of "goozling" may please the vanity of the person who is good at it, but it retards rather than speeds the effectiveness of his or her letters.

Do you ever "goozle"? Don't reply too quickly, as did a man in Kansas City who was attending a Letter-Clinic. He said: "You bet, I love to guzzle." "Goozle" is the word, not guzzle. You won't find it in the dictionary, but since it was invented by a college professor in Boston, its social standing is very good. New words, you know, are constantly forcing their way into our language, and we predict that "goozling" is here to stay. Certainly, it seems to describe a serious letter-writing fault as neatly as *any* word could.

"Goozling" is the language-habit of a "goozler." And what, you may ask, is he?

Identifying "goozlers." "Goozlers" are people who never use a short word if they know a long one of the same or similar meaning. You encounter "goozlers" in all walks of life–politicans, preachers, novelists, commentators, speakers—yes, *and letter-writers*. They are harmless and often mean well, but others consider them awful bores. Perhaps "goozling" is an obsession—a little bit of it leads to more and more.

When the habit is in advanced stages, the "goozlers" may be so proficient in the use of imposing words that only they, and they alone, can understand what they are trying to say. Even when the meaning is still vaguely recognizable, the "goozlers" have made such a spectacle of themselves that few take them seriously. In fact, "goozling" can be so silly that there are many examples that are passed around for their joke value:

> Individuals who sequester themselves within silicon-based domiciles ought to refrain from the hurling of petrous projectiles.
> (People who live in glass houses shouldn't throw stones.)

> One should never calculate ones pullets prior to their maturation.
> (Don't count your chickens before they hatch.)

Put this down as a truth for the writing of any kind of copy that seeks to influence human behavior—letters, advertisements, editorials, and all the rest—simple, *short* words do the best job. It may be great sport to "goozle," but it is not a pastime that gets results.

For example, not long ago an "ad" in one of the most popular magazines aimed to arouse interest in hats for men. At the top was the picture of a man and a woman in a flashy sportscar. That was okay. The picture got attention, and, of course, the man was wearing one of the good-looking hats. He was glancing in the rear view mirror, and the first line of copy read: "Is that trooper following us with arresting intent?"

Do you ever call a traffic policeman a "trooper"? No, you might call him an "officer," but the chances are you would say, "cop." And if you feared that soon you would be halted at the curb, with a ticket coming up, would you ask the girl with you, "Are we being followed with *arresting intent*"? You would not. And do you think that artificial jargon would ever help to sell hats?

"Goozling" in business letters. Strange, isn't it, how folks can distort the King's English, once their minds are set to the job? Consider the following extracts from business letters—word for word as actually dictated and mailed:

> "We have now heard from your doctor, and the condition which *necessitated operative procedure...*" Credit for this choice bit of "goozling" goes to the Claim Examiner of a big insurance company. Probably he meant the lady needed an operation.

> "Realizing the obvious advantages of personal intercourse over this inadequate correspondence form, and truly conscientious in the belief that association would result in mutual benefit..." It seems that this applicant for a job was trying to say it would be much better to get together and talk things over."

> "May we express satisfaction in our confidence that your own experience leads you to agree that at this holiday season, we all have a very real basis for the traditional spirit of happiness and goodwill—a more genuine basis and more nearly up to par, than for several years past...especially in view of still better things in store."
> "We hope that the enclosed is excusably appropriate, in connection with the sentiments we express...Certainly it connotes a substantial contribution to the efficiency now requisite for prosperity."
> "But regardless of anything else, please accept our most sincere wishes for a prosperous and satisfactory year."

In the above light and merry holiday message, there is one sentence which stands out like a sore thumb. The writer deserves at least an "Oscar" for superlative "goozling." Read it again—"It connotes a substantial contribution to the efficiency now requisite for prosperity." Ho, hum!

One more example of "goozling" and then you may turn to a more cheerful subject. The paragraph below opened a sales letter mailed to several thousand potential buyers. The writer had high hopes of getting some business with the letter. It produced not a single reply. Since then, no doubt, the company has been very bitter about sales letters. We could give you the entire letter, but there is no point in punishing you unnecessarily. Anyway, it is hardly possible that any of the original readers went beyond the first paragraph.

Okay! Here it is—the start of a sales letter, done in the very best "goozle."

From conversations with our clients in diversified lines of business, we have assimilated the impression that buying has reduced existing inventories to the point that their replacement cannot long be deferred, and that the enhancement of grain accumulations has corrected conditions in territories of the commonwealth where for an extensive buying period buying power has been greatly restricted, and the restoration of which is about to be reflected in the acceleration of trade activity.

Now, there *is* a mouthful of choice "goozling." It is doubtful if at the beginning you know what the writer had on his mind; the result is utter chaos—in your own. But we wouldn't for the world ask that you read and understand such a mumble-jumble of words. If you dug *deep* into that long sentence of overweight language, you would find that the writer was trying to say, "In my opinion, this is the time to buy."

When less is more. Here is an experiment you will find most enlightening. Buy two magazines: one of the cheap, lurid variety, and the other of top rank. Remember that those who write for the cheap magazine are paid very little for a story, while those able to sell their efforts to the good magazine receive a high reward. Now, examine the language used in the two periodicals. Do you find any difference? Yes, indeed. The writer who gets very little for his efforts is the one who takes a wild fling with big words. The good writer is more discreet. Occasionally he may use a big word for special effect, but on the whole he writes very simply. You see, the best writers know the power of short words—and this is true of all kinds of copy—speeches, advertising, and letters.

This statement is made with no thought of slighting the value of a large vocabulary. Words are writers' tools. The more they have at their command, the better equipped they are to express various shades of meaning. However, they never use a word of many syllables unless there is a *good reason* for it. They know they are talking to another person—they want their message to be easily understood, so they make it just as simple as they can without sacrificing vitality or interest. They are trying to place *thoughts* in their reader's minds, and avoid any confusion in reception.

A few words from Lincoln. You know how high in literature ranks the address made by Abraham Lincoln at Gettysburg. It has been printed in all the major languages of the world, and many scholars say it is the most eloquent speech ever made by a President of the United

States. And why? Well, not only is this address remarkable for its brevity, but it contains a great truth for those who aspire to influence human behavior or thought by the written or spoken word. Lincoln had a message to give to his audience. He wanted to make it as simple and direct as possible. He wanted those who were there that day to remember what he had said.

The address contained just 268 words. That alone should put to shame some of our modern politicians who love to break forth with long outbursts of "sweet wind," but of even greater significance is the fact that 196 of those words contained just one syllable. Furthermore, only 20 words in the speech had more than two syllables. In short, on that day Lincoln's percentage of one-syllable words was 73 plus—almost three words out of every four.

Here is the lesson for letter-writers in that speech—keep *high* the percentage of one-syllable words.

Perhaps you are saying that nothing can be proven with only one example. You are wondering what the result would be if the same test were applied to Lincoln's correspondence. Well, that's a good question. Let's see. Following are quotations from his letters written during the Civil War years. In analyzing the percentage of one-syllable words we will not count the names of people or places.

> *To General Hooker:* If the head of Lee's army is at Martinsburg and the tail of it on the plank road between Fredericksburg and Chancellorsville, the animal must be slim somewhere. Could you not break him?
>
> (86% one-syllable words)
>
> *To General Meade:* Do not lean a hair's breadth against your own feelings, or your judgment of the public service, on the idea of gratifying me.
>
> (69% one-syllable words)
>
> *To General Grant:* General Sheridan says, "If the thing be pressed I think that Lee will surrender." Let the thing be pressed.
>
> (93% one-syllable words)

Not counting the proper nouns, since Lincoln had no control over them, there are a total of 67 words in the above quotations from his letters. Fifty-five are one-syllable words. Hence, a percentage of 82.1 is the "batting average," several points higher than that of the Gettysburg Address. Abraham Lincoln knew the power of simplicity. He *used short words*—and where in the record of human correspondence can you find letters of greater weight?

Three letters in five words. An amusing example of what short words can be made to do is filed at an insurance company. It seems that a policyholder had allowed his policy to lapse, so he got the form letter which endeavors to recover lost sheep. Being a polite fellow, but perhaps a busy one, the policyholder took a red pencil and answered the form letter with one word—"NO."

Entering into the spirit of the game, the dictator for the insurance company went back with two words—"WHY NOT?"

Once more the former policyholder rose to the occasion—"NEW PLAN."

No...Why not?...New Plan—three letters with a total of five words. Who can produce a better evidence of simplicity? Was it not Alexander Pope who wrote: "Words are like leaves; and where they most abound much fruit of sense beneath is rarely found"?

In the *Beloit Daily News* there once appeared an editorial which many a letter-writer could well afford to read twice. Here it is, in part:

> They tell a story around newspaper offices of a very young and enthusiastic reporter who once dashed back to the city room after covering a spectacular fire.
>
> He crouched over his typewriter, tense, prepared to turn himself loose with everything he had, almost overcome by the excitement which he was about to transmit to his expectant readers.
>
> Feverishly, he rapped out a couple of words on the typewriter. He scowled at them, shook his head, and crossed them out. He tapped out two or three words on a fresh sheet, scowled again, and made a third start. He was fairly quivering with the excitement of this grand and dazzling story he had to write, and he was on the point of exploding because he could not seem to turn it into a narrative worthy of the occasion.
>
> There sat watching him a wise veteran who had been writing big stories since the Great Flood. Seeing the cub's difficulty, he came over to offer this profound bit of advice.
> "Just put down *one little word after another*."

"One little word after another!" There you have it—the secret which the most effective letter-writers have kept to themselves. At least, it must seem so, or why is this simple but sure-fire formula so often ignored? The big-word complex is still with us, and thousands and thousands of business letters continue to pay the penalty of lessened results.

Checking your percentage of one-syllable words. What if your letters were put under the microscope, as was done a moment ago with the address and letters of Abraham Lincoln? What is *your* percentage of one-syllable words? Probably you cannot answer that question because you never have thought to make the test, but it is extremely important that you do find out.

Take ten letters you have dictated recently. Make a random selection rather than one which might help to produce a favorable figure. You want to know the truth. Carefully count all the words, skipping only the proper names. Go back a second time, and count all the one-syllable words. Divide the larger sum (all the words) into the smaller sum (those of one syllable) and there you have it—your percentage.

This analysis may take a couple of hours—depending on the length of your ten letters—but it will give you a tangible idea of whether or not your letter-language is simple or "goozled." There is no way of saying what the *exact* dividing line should be, but an analysis of many, many letters makes it reasonable to conclude that 70 percent is close to the right figure. Letters with that percentage of one-syllable words, or higher, if not carried to the extreme, are usually easy to understand, and their chances of success enhanced. Letters with a lower percentage tend to be heavy and ineffective. Certainly, if your own test produces a figure of 60 or lower, you have a bad language-habit, and it is imperative that you begin to correct it. Your letters simply will not do the best job if handicapped with a cumbersome load of big words.

The finest letter-writers are critics of their own work. They take time off now and then to review copies of their own letters. They want to be sure that what they say is simple and direct. Moreover, they have a friendly, curious eye on the letters that pass over their desk. They keep folders of letters for various purposes—just as some people collect postage stamps or coins. They are often able to draw an idea from their collection to use in their own dictation. Letter-writing becomes a hobby as well as daily business—something vital and interesting rather than a necessary chore to be done.

This, perhaps, was the thought of the late newspaper man, Don Marquis, when he composed the rhyme:

> Webster has the words and I
> Pick them up from where they lie;
> Here a word and there a word—
> It's so easy, 'tis absurd;
> I merely range them in a row,
> Webster's done the work you know;
> Word follows word, till, inch by inch,

> I have a column. What a cinch!
> I take the words that Webster penned
> And merely lay them end to end.

Newspaper writers generally lean on short words. You don't have to read a newspaper story twice to get the meaning. Do you suppose short words help to give this little rhyme zest and "oomph"? Let's give it the one-syllable-word-percentage test. Omitting "Webster," a proper noun, we have 63 other words, and only 6 are words of more than one syllable. Ninety percent is the answer. Once again we see it doesn't take a sledge hammer to drive a tack.

Overcoming long sentences. Since the object of your business letter is to present your thoughts to the reader in a way that can be easily understood, common sense tells you that long and complicated sentences will defeat that purpose. Periods are like resting places spotted at frequent intervals on a difficult mountain path. They allow the reader to pause and grasp what *has* been said before he is asked to absorb something more. Sentences that run on like a babbling brook soon confuse the reader, and the confusion increases until at the end he cannot remember the beginning. Read the following sentence at normal speed, and judge if you clearly understand the thought when you finally reach the period.

> We are willing to consider an extension of the arrangement to cover the other branches, but feel that such an arrangement should be made with the Doe organization, similar to the one at Reading, or if the Smith Grocery Company can suggest any definite ways in which they can give us special support and a substantial increase on their outside jobbing business, then we might be able to justify considering a joint arrangement to be made with the Doe organization and the Smith Company based on total purchases of the two combines, the agreement to be based on our being given distribution in all Doe stores, special push by store managers and employees, displays of our products in the stores, special featuring of them in the Doe newspaper advertising, and also special pushing and support by the Smith Company, including a showing of substantial increase in volume at each point over the corresponding period for the previous year, in return for which after the end of the year, we would remit to each branch giving us such support and showing such increase 5 percent on the net amount of their purchases.

This is not a sample merely constructed to prove a point. It was actually dictated one day by a businessperson who must have had great faith in the psychic power of the reader. To understand what the sentence says, an ordinary person would have to go back and take it apart, piece by piece. Finally, by dint of much effort, he or she might emerge with the meaning, but what right has any writer to impose such a task on the reader of his letter? Unless the reader were a member of the same organization, and *had* to decipher the puzzle, the letter would surely be filed promptly, and with disgust, in the wastebasket.

If you think the above could never happen again, consider another sentence lifted from an actual business letter.

> Now the item of October 21, which you show as the balance due you, is in order, but there is a reason for holding it up, and you are fully aware of the fact that this shipment of printing was prepared without our instructions and shipped to the customer, and you admitted that it was an error in your manufacturing department in getting these out before you had authority to proceed, and you will recall that the customer cancelled this order and sent us a new order, but unfortunately, you had already shipped it, and we have been trying to get the customer's permission to bill it and get him to use the order ever since shipment was made, and now we are passing the invoice through, giving the customer December 1 dating in order to get him to use the order, and we are dating your invoice as of December 1, which we trust is satisfactory and will take care of the item mentioned.

You see, once again there has been an attempt to cram into one stretch of thinking far more than the average human mind can take. Instead of inserting periods now and then so that the reader might consolidate what had been said, this business person wrote "and"... "and"... "and." Now, notice what these periods would have done.

> The item of October 21, which you show as the balance due you is correct, but there is a reason for holding it up. You are fully aware that this printing was prepared and shipped to the customer without our instructions. You admitted that it was an error in your manufacturing department in getting the printing out before you had authority to proceed.
> You will also recall that the customer cancelled the order, and sent us a new one. Ever since the shipment was made, we have been trying to get the customer's permission to bill it. Now we are giving him December 1 dating in order to get him to use the order. Hence, we are also dating your invoice December 1. This we think should be satisfactory to you.

A few minor changes in wording and the periods have made the copy much easier to understand. The language is still more weighty than need be, but at least the reader has been given a fair chance of meeting the writer halfway. As the eminent letter-master Robert R. Aurner, once stated, "The period is the stop sign in the traffic control of thought. Learn to respect it exactly as you would a stoplight in traffic."

Going to extremes. Although you are told that long sentences, in proportion to their number and length, tend to reduce the effectiveness of a business letter, you should not be inspired to run amuck in the opposite direction, either. Sentences can be chopped up so drastically that a letter full of them moves along haltingly in a series of "huffs and puffs." Though you should not impose on the intelligence of your reader with sentences that run on and on like Old Man River, neither is it suggested that you approach your reader as if he were a moron. You frequently encounter business letters done in the style of a fourth-grade language book—an experience which is both dull and irritating. Furthermore, it must be remembered that some writers can compose long sentences which take the reader to the end with no confusion or loss of meaning.

After all is said and done, you must accept the suggestions in this *Handbook* with common sense, and avoid both extremes. You know that simplicity carries great power. You may attain it without the loss of color and personality which makes one letter stand out above the rest. What you are after is a certain "flow" of language which will carry your reader along *smoothly*, as a boat is carried by the current of a swift-moving stream. "Smoothly," is the key word. It is accomplished neither by sentences so short that the reader is jerked from one thought to another, nor by long spasms of expression which leave him without a clear understanding of the meaning.

4. SHUNNING THE USE OF UNNECESSARY WORDS

When the "sweet wind" blows. For at least two reasons, it is foolish to use more words than are needed to convey the thought of a business letter. First, you know that letters cost money. It is pure waste to make them longer than they need to be—more words to dictate, more words to type, more wear on equipment. Second, verbose language is "sweet wind" that makes a letter spineless and ineffective. Many letter-writers blissfully waste words and know it not. Let us examine some of the more common forms of verbosity, so that you will not fall into the same traps. Read the following letter:

Will you please let us take this opportunity to congratulate you upon the opening of your new drug store. We wish it every possible measure of success, and we believe that with your unusual experience, integrity, reputation, and business ability, it will even surpass your highest expectations.

It is also our desire to use this letter as an entering wedge, bringing to your attention the 60 or more well-known and effective products of this company which have been on the market for many years and which have proven their merit. We want to serve you through your favored distributor, and if you have not already stocked many of the Doe products, we shall be glad to make it to your advantage to do so. Give us the name of your distributor and we shall lend every effort toward serving you in the very best possible manner.

It gives us a great deal of pleasure to point out that Lone Wolf and Little Bear products are the best sellers, being especially good in meeting consumer requirements in each and every instance, and enjoying a ready sale. We beg to suggest that you take advantage of the ready sale of these items.

We are taking the liberty of enclosing our latest price list which gives you all the information you will require in ordering this profitable merchandise, and we assure you that at all times we hold ourselves in readiness to be of real service to you. We hope to be favored with your business.

When you have time to take a few minutes from the daily rush of business and its exacting requirements, we shall be glad to know how the store is progressing. May we call attention to the fact that your orders will receive our prompt and very best attention.

Perhaps at first reading even you did not realize how much this letter is padded with unnecessary words. The following revision is not changed in sequence of thought, and nothing of importance is left out. But the "sweet wind" has been red-penciled.

We congratulate you on the opening of your new drug store. We believe that with your experience and business ability, it will pass your highest expectations.

The 60 well-known and effective products of this company have been on the market for many years, and have proven their merit. If you already have not stocked many of the Doe products, we shall be glad to make it to your advantage to do so. Give us the name of your distributor, and we shall lend every effort toward serving you.

Lone Wolf and Little Bear products are the best sellers, being especially good in meeting consumer requirements. We suggest that you take advantage of their ready sale.

We are enclosing our latest price list which gives you all the information required in ordering this profitable merchandise. We ask to be favored with your business.

We shall be glad to know how the store is progressing. Your orders will receive our very best attention.

To be sure, the diluted version is still not a good sales letter, if you measure it as directed in Section 7. Nothing has been changed or added to make it good, but most of the useless padding is gone. The two copies do the same job, poor as it may be—but there is one striking difference. The original letter contains 313 words, as compared to 162 words in the revised form. Thus, 151 words are blotted out as unnecessary— "sweet wind."

The same letter at half the cost. Always a leader in the fight for better letters in American business has been the Dartnell Corporation of Chicago. In one of the Dartnell bulletins appeared this very fine example of how a windy letter may be trimmed to do a better job. First, you will read the original, which the bulletin calls, "a good biography, but a costly letter to produce," and then the revision made by Cameron McPherson— "the same idea, better stated, in fewer words, at half the cost."

Dear _____,

Please excuse me for writing you personally. It has been my experience that there are mighty few difficulties that cannot be overcome, mighty few differences that cannot be adjusted when the two parties sit down and talk things over.

I would love to walk into your store this morning and have a chat with you. I know you would greet me courteously and treat me fairly, but since I can't see you personally, let's talk it over.

What I want to talk about is your account with the Eastern Specialty Company of $125. Before I do so, however, excuse me please, while I talk for just a little bit about myself. I am living in New York but I am not a New Yorker. I am from "Down South" myself. I have traveled in every Southern state; yes, I guess I have been in every Southern county. I have made my home in the South, I have even followed a mule, plowing corn on an Alabama plantation. I have managed a commissary, have owned and operated my own retail business, in fact I have done pretty much the same thing you are doing, I know your business problems and your local conditions.

When your order was received, it was I who put OK on it.

Now I am in trouble. The Company has sent you statements, they have written you letters, but so far they don't seem to be getting very far in collecting your account. Just what is the matter? Can't we get together? The Company wants to do the right thing by you, and I wish you would look on me as your friend and believe me when I tell you that if there is anything you want done that is fair to good business principles, I am here to help you.

I would be mighty well pleased if you would send me a check by the next mail. If you can't pay all your account, send a part payment and see if we can't get everything fixed up. We will advertise for you if your goods aren't selling well; we will make an exchange for you if you have something that doesn't sell as well as some other item.

I am counting on your reply and I am sure you won't disappoint me.

Your first reaction to this long letter may not be favorable. The language is natural, and the approach of one southerner to another has some merit. But before you pass final judgment, compare the letter with Mr. McPherson's revision.

Dear _____,

I am writing you personally because it has been my experience that there are mighty few difficulties that can't be adjusted when the two parties sit down and talk things over.

What I want to talk about is your account with the Eastern Specialty Company for $125. It so happens that I am from "Down South" myself, and when your order came in, I put my OK on it without a minute's hesitation, because I know that the people down there are all right.

But now I am in trouble because the company tells me that you haven't paid any attention to our statements and letters.

Let's get together on this. We'll meet you halfway. If your goods aren't selling, we will advertise for you or make an exchange if you have some slow sellers.

At any rate, send me your check for $50 by the 15th, if you can't send the full amount. Then we will see what we can do to help you get the rest.

There is just as much "meat" in the second letter as in the first, but the unnecessary trimmings have been scrapped. The Southerner-to-Southerner approach is still used, but without all the gory details.

Moreover, because of its restraint, the second letter seems to carry a tone of sincerity which the first one lacked.

There is no end to the verbose letters that could be cited to prove that they are far too common in business correspondence. Here's another of the same dreary vintage. The words in italics are those which pad the letter for no good reason.

Dear _____,

Naturally we, *just as any other progressive manufacturer, strive for and much* prefer bouquets *and encomiums* to censure. But *we welcome frank statements, such as you have made and* thank you for telling us exactly what you think of Jamisonian quality.

Particularly do we consider, *seriously,* your comments, because we know *that your schooling and reputation have been of such high standard that you could justifiably be and probably are recognized as an art critic of proved repute and renown. As we understand it,* you have designed *and created* for the most prominent New York producers *and have engaged in other masterful creative and designing works,* too numerous to mention.

It would be unnatural then if your ideas in design were not of the highest possible expectancy. Incidentally, you have dealt with moneyed clients, where price was no object and was quite secondary to the creation of, and the desire to have and own something so different from the usual that even the ordinary layman would, at a casual glance, appreciate the difference in cost and value.

But Jamisonian Lamps are *manufactured and* designed to occupy a place in the home where price must of *necessity* be considered first, *last, and all times. There is a vast potential and found market for Jamisonians as evidenced by sales, testimonials, and statistics on average income.* We could not claim, *however,* that Jamisonian Lamps would add to the *setting and* beauty of the Rockefeller, Morgan, or Whitney mansions. *They would, we admit, be out of place.*

So, far be it from us to attempt *in any way* to sell you on the sales *and customer satisfaction* possibilities of Jamisonians in your Miami Beach or New York studios. Neither can it be said that *our sales policy was high pressured or that* we made claims which were *exaggerated and* unfounded.... The only thing we can offer *at all* is that you return the Jamisonians to our factory, *even though we have always been strict advocates of a non-consignment policy.*

Every day, in America, business letters are written that go around and around the mulberry bush, but this one really makes the circle so completely it is wondered the writer did not perish of exhaustion. How much of the letter remains if we omit the italicized words?

Dear _____,

Naturally, we prefer bouquets to censure. But we thank you for telling us exactly what you think of Jamisonian quality.
Particularly do we consider your comments because we know you have designed for the most prominent New York producers, too numerous to mention.

But Jamisonian Lamps are designed to occupy a place in the home of the man where price must be considered first. We could not claim that Jamisonian Lamps would add to the beauty of the Rockefeller, Morgan, or Whitney mansions.

So, far be it from us to attempt to sell you on the sales possibilities of Jamisonians in your Miami Beach or New York studios. Neither can it be said that we made claims which were unfounded. The only thing we can offer is that you return the Jamisonians to our factory.

Remarkable, isn't it, how that very poor letter becomes almost a good one, when we simply remove the excess weight? Nothing was changed—nothing removed except a lot of excess words. The thought remains the same, but in a form much easier to take.

Repetition, redundancy, and recapping—the wrong 3 "R's." It is surprising how many overstuffed phrases you will find in business correspondence, once you start to look for them. The cause may be the monkey-see, monkey-do tendency of the human race to form little language habits which are shared by all—a simple device to avoid original thinking.

Why should a letter-writer speak of "*past* experience," or "*final* completion," or "the *month* of July"? The italicized words are *totally* unnecessary. All experience from which we form judgments is *past*. The completion of a project must be *final*. July is a *month*, and can be nothing else. Things unnecessary must be *totally* so.

And here are some more of the padded phrases so often used in business letters:

It came *at a time* when we were busy.
Leather depreciates *in value* slowly.
During *the year of* 1964.
It will cost *the sum of* $100.
At a meeting *held* in Philadelphia.
We will ship these shoes *at a* later *date*.
In about two weeks' *time*.

This mistake *first* began due to a misunderstanding.
A *certain* person by the name of Bill Jones.
The *close* proximity of these two incidents.
It happened at *the hour of* noon.
We see some good in both *of them.*
In *the city of* Columbus.
The body is made *out* of steel.
Tracing the *course of the* campaign.
Perhaps it may be that you are reluctant.
Our uniform *and invariable* rule is.
Somebody *or other* must be responsible.
We are now *engaged in* building a new plant.
By *means of* this device we are able.
The radio sells for *a price of* $200.

Read the preceding lines without the italicized words—nothing has been lost in meaning or effectivenss. Hence, those words must be unnecessary. On and on we could go with similar examples—over-stuffed phrases which have become habitual in oral and written speech.

Remember the story of the man who read the directions given by his doctor, "Take one pill every three hours"? He promptly doubled the dose on the assumption that if one pill was good for him, two would be twice as beneficial. Perhaps it is the same reasoning that impels some writers to "double" in their letters. They think that if one word does the job, two should do it better. So they dictate, "it is *evident* and *apparent* that our position is *just* and *fair*," or "we *insist* and *demand* that this bill be paid." In their minds, the use of the two words gains added emphasis, but the truth is that they drag out the thought and tend to make it *less* effective.

This practice of "doubling" can do no good in any kind of writing. People who aim to make their letters simple, direct, and persuasive should avoid a habit so easily acquired and so hard to break. Consider the following New Year's letter.

Dear ——————,

Out of the fullness of a warm heart...I want to extend to you and yours my *sincere* and *earnest* good wishes for a Happy and Prosperous New Year.

The last few years have taught us many lessons...the *first* and *foremost* being a new understanding of life's values...to *appraise* and *determine* what, after all, are really worthwhile things.

Topping the list on such an inventory are our friends ... acquired through *experiences together* and *contacts* in a civic, business and a social way...with a record in review of their *deeds, actions,* and human qualities.

I am happy to have your name on my list of such friends.

May I express the hope that you, like many others, are approaching the New Year with a feeling of *optimism* and *encouragement.*

Strange, isn't it, how the writer "doubled" in a vain effort to stress his sentiments?

Sincere and earnest.	Experiences together and contacts.
First and foremost.	Deeds and actions.
Appraise and determine.	Optimism and encouragement.

But before you condemn this one person too severely—he or she may have let the spirit of the New Year inflate his or her letter-language—examine the correspondence that comes over your desk. You will surely find thousands of similar examples.

How long should a letter be? In urging the use of concise language in your business letters, there has been no intention of setting up any exact limitation with respect to the length of the conversation you may have with your reader. When Abraham Lincoln was asked how long a man's legs should be, he replied "long enough to reach the ground." If you should ask how long a business letter should be, the answer is "long enough to do the job." The use of unnecessary words is pure waste. The inflation of a letter with "sweet wind" is another form of lost motion. Every letter problem has its own set of facts and conditions. To omit anything which might help a letter to accomplish its purpose is obviously a mistake; to drag a letter out longer than it needs to be is just as unwise.

Brevity is commendable if your letter covers all of the ground that needs to be covered. Just what that ground is, you must decide, remembering that a lengthy letter tends to increase the hazard that the reader may become tired and leave you "waiting at the church."

In some companies the false notion exists that no letter should be longer than one page. Sometimes that limitation is even made obligatory. You will agree that the notion is absurd. Certain sales letters, for example, could not possibly do a good job in one page. The only safe rule to follow is that you handle your subject with restraint and caution, and resist the temptation to run wild with points of no real importance to your reader. As you will discover in the next section of this *Handbook,* a letter of any consequence deserves analysis of the facts which make it necessary—the selection of those points that should be treated, and *how* it is best to present them. Good letters are *planned* before they are written. And if that plan can be carried out in a short letter, fine! If it takes several pages, then let your letter be long. *Do the job.* Do it *right.* The length is inconsequential.

A friend once wrote to a Chicago newspaper. He delivered a long tirade against something the editor had written. Promptly, he received this reply, "Sorry! We'll try to do better." That was a very short letter which did the job neatly.

The president of an oil company in Texas wrote a letter to one of our large corporations, complaining about what was thought to be an unfair sales practice. The reply came back, signed by an official of the corporation, "You have been misinformed. We do not sell as you have outlined in your letter." That short letter did a very poor job. The president of the oil company resented the curt dismissal of his complaint. He deserved a more detailed explanation presented in a more courteous manner. He was a potential customer of the corporation but his goodwill was lost.

A letter soliciting subscriptions to *Fortune* magazine ran four pages. Another of the same length tried to interest young people in taking a correspondence course in hotel management. Both of these letters did a complete sales job. They were four pages long because they *had* to be. After all, the length of your letter depends on the nature of the particular problem. You can be too brief—you can be too "windy." Good judgment determines what must be said. Certainly there are language faults that stretch a letter longer than is necessary. You have seen what some of them are. Avoid them.

5. CRITIQUING OTHER LANGUAGE FAULTS

Using word pets. Letter-writers, like other craftsmen, must guard constantly against falling into ruts. There is always the danger of growing stale, so that what you write lacks the desired color and originality. Nothing contributes more to such a lamentable condition than the adoption of a number of word pets—words that you use over and over again until they become so habitual that you do not realize how cut-and-dried your writing appears. Mention this fault to almost any secretary, and her eyes will twinkle as she thinks of certain words and phrases which she types day after day.

To be sure, it may be unimportant that the one who types the letters is bored by these repetitions, but customers, too, may feel their deadly monotony.

"Glad to say?!?" The above brings to mind the rather amusing case of a clerk who wrote many letters daily for one of our large manufacturers. Somewhere in his business career he had been impressed with the fact that every letter should start on a cheerful note, so he had fallen into the habit of leading off with, "We are happy to tell you." This was bad enough in those letters where the introduction jibed with the rest, but it was especially vicious when the news that followed was unwelcome. A check of his letters one day brought to light the following rather startling assertions:

> We are happy to tell you that the merchandise you ordered for your Easter Sale will not be ready to ship until a month later.

> We are happy to tell you that we cannot allow credit for the merchandise you returned.

You can imagine how the customers getting these two letters must have exploded—to meet with such glee over their bad luck. A more extensive check of the clerk's correspondence revealed that "We are happy to tell you," was a language pet he never failed to take for a walk. Good news or bad news got the same introduction—he was always happy to hand it out.

A review of letters used by another company also brought to light word pets not so destructive as the other man's pride and joy, but just as tiresome to read. One of them was "out of suspense" and another, "held in abeyance." It was surprising how many things—claims, policies, letters—were either coming out, or still held in. Files, too, were beloved in this company. Here is one of the letters:

> We are trying to close as many of our pending *files* as we can. If the above case is now closed, we would appreciate your returning the *file* so that we may close our pending *file*, or bring before us such information as will place our *file* up-to-date.

"Our records" and "your records" also got a great play in the letters of the company. "According to our records, the grace period will expire next Monday," one letter would say, and the next, "The enclosed copy is for your records." But "records" are necessary in any company, and why can't they be taken for granted? Wouldn't the job be done just as well, or much better, by simply saying, "The grace period will expire next Monday," or "The enclosed copy is yours"? Customers have no special interest in the records you keep—but they are interested in the information supplied from them.

"We await your advice, with every good intention," was the ancient language pet of another writer. Every letter to which a reply was expected closed in the same dismal way. Another benevolent correspondent was very fond of signing off with, "Thanking you kindly, and with best wishes," even though the part that came before was quite often blunt and domineering.

Of course we understand that lawyers are trained to speak with caution. But this one in Wisconsin seems especially diffident as he leads his "pet" by the leash.

> I sincerely regret to advise that I do not feel that I am in just the position at the *present time* to make you the report as to the enclosed, for certain reasons. However, it may be at some *future time* I may be in the position to make such a report, and as aforesaid, I regret indeed just at the *present time* I really do not feel in the position to give you the requested information for certain reasons, that I would prefer not to state, just at the *present time*.

You might call that lawyer "time-minded," from the way he toys with the word. He also has another favorite word combination, "in the position."

"Splittingly yours." From a company in New York, you get the following example of word repetition.

> We are sorry that the roll is not satisfactory for the reason that it *splits*.
>
> In this connection, we examined the sample, and find that same *splits*. On this heavy weight it is impossible to guarantee it not to *split to some extent*. We can ship you another roll, but it is possible that it would *split* too. The reason is that it is so thick and has a tendency to *split*.
>
> However, it may be that another roll may not *split*. Does the entire roll *split*? You may of course return the roll if you find this *split* throughout.

This writer had a little pet named Split.

Many writers use the same words or combinations forever because they are in a rut and are too lazy to climb out of it. Others have slipped into the groove without realizing it. Certain writers are forced into the habit by a limited vocabulary. Members of this last group may know only one word for various shades of meaning, whereas you might have a separate word to match each shade.

For example, you know that *flowers* have *fragrance*, that *cigars* have *aroma*, that *perfumes* have *scent*, that *gases* have *odor*—but to the people whose vocabulary is small, all of these things might simply *smell*. If they wanted to describe an especially disagreeable odor, you know the word they would use. Yes, it "stinks." Sometimes, you hear people of great education and social standing use the same word to describe a play, or a book, or a song, but it seems a pity that those who know better should be so careless.

It is the people with the limited vocabulary to whom lips are *ruby*, teeth are like *pearls*, and the party a *howling* success. If they are businessmen, they may write about the *cordial* invitation, the *stirring* speech, or the *painstaking* effort to improve a product. You can't very well criticize folks who do the best they can with what they have, nor should you expect their letters to be as colorful and interesting as are the letters of those who can draw on a comfortable vocabulary account.

A limited vocabulary is *not* a hopeless handicap, however. If you feel that yours is too small, you *can* make it bigger. Fifteen to thirty minutes a day devoted to vocabulary building will produce amazing results in a year. For reference, any good dictionary will do, and *Roget's Thesaurus* will serve as a textbook. Reading books, magazines, and newspapers, with an eye for any word which you do not understand, is also very helpful. Once you have mastered the meaning and spelling of a new word, *use* it a sufficient number of times to make it a permanent part of your vocabulary. This may sound like a lot of work, but nothing worthwhile comes easy. When you see your word-chest filling up, the study will become more of a pleasure than a chore. Your letters will take on new life and vitality. Just as a carpenter would be handicapped without an adequate number of tools, so will you always be hindered without an ample and flexible vocabulary.

Avoiding red-pepper words. The power of a single word to ruin a business letter is well known to the experts. Sometimes, the trouble-maker is obviously ill-chosen—as when a collection letter insinuates the reader is a dead-beat or a chiseler—but often it may appear innocent until the psychology of its use is understood. The collection letter might say, "So far you have ignored our bills and letters." That doesn't appear at first thought to be a tactless statement, but it does carry the insinuation that the reader is one who *ignores* his obligations. In the same way, "We have not had the *courtesy* of a reply," insinuates that the reader is discourteous. Either of the two words is humiliating in inverse proportion to the thickness of the customer's skin. Why disparage people when trying to appeal to their better selves.?

Even the harmless little word "should" may arouse an undesirable reaction in your reader's mind. As children, most of us have been told thousands of times what we *should* or *should not* do. Our parents and our teachers have used the word to imply that we were falling short of the expected standard of performance. "Johnny," said the customer's mother, "you *should* know better than to track mud into the house"—and then years later you come along and say to the same man, "John Doe, you should know better than to ask for this unearned discount."

There are many similar words—okay if used cautiously, but little atomic bombs when they tend to irritate through some thoughtless insinuation. Always remember in your letter-writing—never use a word that might humiliate or belittle the reader.

Examining examples from business letters. We couldn't begin to list all of these red-pepper words. You must constantly be on guard against them, as they have a way of sneaking into a letter, and then popping up to cause trouble. Here are a few more examples taken from actual business letters:

"We do not understand your *failure* to pay this bill." The insinuation is that the customer cannot be trusted to meet his obligations. Moreover, "failure" is a negative word. We want our name and actions associated with success.

"Your *complaint* about the damaged shipment of flour will have our careful attention." Thus, you say the reader is one who "complains." He dislikes the insinuation. This word should be banned from business letters. There need be no Complaint Department; "Adjustment" Department is better. "Customers' Service" Department is tops.

"We have your letter in which you *claim* two cases of spoiled peas were included in the shipment." When you use "claim" in this sense, you are really insinuating, "You say it is so, but we have our doubts."

"Frankly, we are *surprised* to see you take this attitude after we have tried so hard to please you." You feel very much abused, and the customer is being dastardly. Of course, your "surprise" is humiliating.

"It seems *strange* that no other customer has mentioned this fault in our product." You are implying that this one customer is unreasonable, or he would climb on the band wagon with all the others.

"We didn't think you were the *type* to misunderstand our intentions." You mean you didn't think so before, but you do now. Who wants to be a "type" anyway?

"There will always be leaders and *plodders* on our sales force, although I would much rather see everyone a big success, and making lots of money." That's sweet of you, Salesmanager, but the person who read your letter was far down the line—one of the "plodders."

"You can't *fairly* blame us for the railroad's carelessness." His letter did blame you. He said your shipping cases were too light. Therefore, you have called him "unfair."

"Certainly, you *know* that we did not offer you any such concession." Well, he told you that you did. You are saying, therefore, that he must be a "bald-faced liar."

"This corrects the *mistake you made* in the amount of the check due us." Why remind anyone of their "mistake"? Help them save face with, "This balances your account, and thanks for your cooperation."

"In years past, you *used to be* one of our most loyal customers." The good old days are gone; if he "used to be" loyal, then he isn't any more.

"At *least*, we think we are entitled to know why you have stopped buying." Get out your crying towel. The customer isn't treating you right. The very least he could do would be to explain his peculiar conduct.

"It appears that you are *disgruntled* about the remark made by our clerk, but surely *you can't expect* us to know what goes on, every minute in our store." Obviously, you seem to be saying your customer is easily disgruntled. He should be more considerate, the old bear!

"*Please understand*, that *we* are still willing to met you halfway." Not only are you "bossy" with "please understand," but you also insinuate the customer is not a good sport. *We* are still willing (see the pretty halo), but he is not.

"*Others* continue to buy and make money on our goods, while you still *procrastinate*." The comparison does not favor the prospect. "Others" are smart, but he is dumb. What could be expected of one who puts things off—a "procrastinator"?

"Come, let's end this *childish* argument." A fighting word. You will never end an argument by calling the other fellow "childish."

"Your order was shipped in twenty-four hours. We try to give the same fast service to a *small* buyer, as we would to a large one." What a lucky peewee he is to be served by a company so big-hearted. The insinuation is that the customer's business doesn't amount to much.

"Although we could *ethically* deny your request, you may return the goods." A humiliating sentence— "ethically" is the stinger. The implication is that he was *not* ethical in making the request.

"Do you *fumble* the sales inquiries that come your way?" Who admires a "fumbler"? The question is insulting.

"We have the answer to your heating *problem*." This is a common beginning in sales letters, and a bad one. Taking for granted that he *has* a "problem" is irritating.

"You can't keep up with competition, using *antiquated* methods and equipment." The company using this letter sold only equipment but the writer for good measure included methods in the slam. You may think a customer is "antiquated" but keep the secret to yourself.

The above examples which show how to destroy goodwill by one or two words are by no means exceptional; you see them frequently in business letters. They are not intentional, but they bore deep, and never fail to irritate.

One word too many. The tone of the following letter is not bad. The writer is trying to remain friendly, even though the debt is old. But there is one insinuating word—a thoughtless dash of red-pepper.

Supposing a man owed you a few dollars, and they were long past due. What would you do about it?

Would you threaten to sue him? Would you assume he was a dead-beat? Would you put him on your blacklist, so that hereafter all orders would be shipped C.O.D.?

I don't know what to do about your account, because when one gets as old as yours, some action has to be taken.

You've been a mighty good customer of ours, so we don't want to do anything drastic; at least, until we hear from you. But we must ask that you do something about clearing up this balance at once.

If there is a red-pepper word in that letter, you would expect to find a quick reference to it in the customer's reply. And that was the first sentence! "Surely by this time you must know that we are NOT *dead-beats*." Yes, out popped that provoking term—and there was trouble.

A matter of policy. Probably the word most frequently used in denying requests is "policy." It is literally worked to death. "We regret to advise that it is not our policy to ship in less than case lots"..."Please excuse us, but a policy of long standing in our company makes it impossible to go along with you"..."Our policy is well understood by the trade, and we can make no exceptions." Some businessmen take this easy way of hiding behind a word.

"Policy" means nothing to a customer unless the *reason* for it is understood. Merely to say that you cannot do something because a "policy" prevents it is both irritating and inadequate. Although "policy" may be logical, your reader is entitled to an explanation. This involves more thought in writing the letter, but there is no other way to satisfy the reader and retain his goodwill. If the "policy" won't stand explanation, it is only a subterfuge—as the reader will think when you hide behind it.

The problem of avoiding these red-pepper words is largely psychological. The best solution is to put yourself in the place of the reader, and to contemplate his possible reactions in the light of what your own would be. The letter-writer who holds to the Golden Rule will seldom use an irritating word.

Using slang in business letters. You can ask, "How much is two times two?" and the answer is "four." It is the only answer, and final and absolute. But ask, "Is slang permissible in business letters?" and the answer is, "It all depends,"—which is no more satisfactory than to ask for a date and get the same reply.

Webster defines slang as: The specialized vocabulary and idioms...the purpose of which was to disguise from outsiders the meaning of what was said; the words and idioms of those in the same work, way of life, etc.; now called shoptalk; argot; jargon; coined words.

Since clear, personal communication between letter-writers and their readers is the goal of this *Handbook*, it seems obvious that slang would have no place in a well-constructed business letter. Certainly, if we use Webster's first definition this is true. The customers are vital to any corporate success and to make them feel that they are outsiders who can be trusted with plain, understandable language can only alienate them.

Webster's second definition, however, begins to weaken this argument. When the salesmanagers write to their salesmen, in-words of the business make their letters more precise in their impact. The staff and the managers are on the same team.

Webster's third definition admits that our written and spoken language is alive and constantly growing; the slang words of today may be found in the dictionaries of tomorrow. New technologies have given our language many words that are clearly understood, even though they are "coined"—entry-level position (beginning), VCR (video cassette recorder), floppy disk (computer software). These words are so common that they do not impede communication and allow a friendly, human touch to appear in otherwise cold and formal business correspondence.

James C. Fernald, author of several books on grammar, was of another opinion concerning slang.*

> It should be said that among the multitude of slang words and phrases, there are in each generation a few that meet a real need of the language, and win their way to acceptance. Dean Swift, in 1750, objected to the words *sham, banter, bubble, mob,* and *shuffle,* all of which have become approved English.

> Make sure that there is a real need for that word or phrase. If it has genuine merit, it will not be hurt by objection and criticism, while our caution will save our language from the inroad of a host of worthless adventurers.

> The safe rule is this: slang is never to be used except with care and intent, knowing it to be slang, believing it to be expressive for the immediate purpose, and when no better word or phrase equally forcible can be substituted.

So there you have the "pro and con" for slang, about as well as it could be stated. If you think a slang word or phrase—not vulgar or inane—will help your letter, go ahead—use it. But watch carefully that the practice does not become a habit in which you spread slang all over the page. An overdose of slang makes many a letter a joke, and a fool of the writer.

You will agree that there are many breeds of slang, and they don't all rate the same kennel. Phrases like "on the spot," or "out on a limb," or "level with me," are both useful and natural.

> "Joe, I am sorry if this report puts you *on the spot,* but we just must have it by Tuesday."

> "It's this way, Mr. Graham. I personally OK'd an open shipment of this order, and now with the bill still unpaid, I am *out on a limb.*"

> "John, there is no need of kidding ourselves about your sales record this year. But in the past, you were always a winner. So, why don't you *level with me* and tell me what's wrong?"

Each of those slang phrases helped to make the language more interesting and natural. They are phrases commonly used in speech, and thus they tend to create the person-to-person effect you are after. They are not vulgar or inelegant. These words stir the imagination and

---

* Reprinted by permission from *Expressive English* by James C. Fernald, copyrighted by Funk & Wagnalls Company, New York.

create a mental picture which formal language could not achieve in so few words.

But, there are slang words which make a business letter sound like a schoolboy's note to a friend.

> You failed us, and, *by golly,* we had so much faith in you too! We were sure and confident that *you,* of all people, would keep your word.

> To be perfectly frank, we feel *"kinda"* blue about it. And that's why we are writing this personal letter, so you will understand how we feel.

> But you can cheer us up—and here's how: Send your remittance *now.*

> I'll be a holy Pink Toed Prophet if I don't believe you have forgotten me entirely.

> Gosh! I surely would be happy if you'd send me a little change to sort of renew your account and relieve me of a few financial burdens. Honest, I need some help, so be a good sport and loosen up a bit.

> The entire amount is $15.40. All or any will help. Thanks. Can I have it right away, please?

In both of these letters, the writers were trying for a tone of personal cordiality. Like the golfers who press for distance and dub their shots, they tried too hard. Words such as "Golly" and "Gosh" just don't seem to belong in the vocabulary of grown-ups, especially in business. A prophet with pink toes may be a spectacular fellow, but you would expect to find him in a storybook for children, not in a business letter. Equally distasteful are such distortions as "kinda," "sorta," and "wotta."

Samples of the more inelegant slang words are "lousy," "nuts," and "guts." These may have a place in a sales manager's letter to the staff, or in a letter to a friendly dealer who favors that kind of talk. Usually such slang is dangerous, because you never know whom it may offend. Thus, you are better off not to use it. As Mr. Fernald wrote, "The burden of proof is always against the slang expression." Keep to the safe side. Use slang cautiously; when in doubt—*don't.*

Keeping profanity out of business letters. It is hardly possible to think of any situation where profanity will improve a business letter. This is so obvious that the question of its use needs no discussion. The answer is No! Admitting there may be many times when you *feel* the need of a healthy cuss-word in writing to a cantankerous customer or a lazy salesman, you can't afford to yield to temptation. Let's keep our letters clean.

Perhaps worse than the cuss-words are the attempts to soften their shock that we see in business correspondence— "*Wotinhel*" for "*What in hell*," or "*Heluva*" for "*Hell of a*," or others of the same breed. This is a childish way of fooling nobody.

Taboo profanity. There are plenty of chances for it—without putting it into your letters.

LEARNING THE ART OF BUSINESS LETTER CARPENTRY

1. CHARTING THE FLIGHT

2. BLUEPRINT FOR LETTER-BUILDING

LEARNING THE ART OF BUSINESS LETTER CARPENTRY

1. CHARTING THE FLIGHT

Before the letter comes the plan. Anything worthwhile in life or business deserves to be planned before it is done. As one popular sales slogan goes, "Plan the work, then work the plan." Certainly, a leap in the dark seldom lands you on the desired spot. It is much better to *see* first where you are leaping.

Only routine, repetitive actions can be carried out without a plan, and even they required intelligent direction in the beginning. The reward for repetitive work is usually meager. The bonus is found where there are problems to solve, and is awarded to those able to think them through. Everything important to business must be planned. Advertising is planned. Products are planned. Sales are planned. Production is planned. Policies are planned. And letters, too, are planned in those companies where an honest effort is being made to avoid waste, and to gain the best possible results.

Not like the grasshopper. Unfortunately, there are still people in business who are "too busy" to do an intelligent letter job. Their chief aim is to dictate as much as possible in a given period of time. You hear them say proudly, "I got rid of 100 letters today." They do not realize that they might better have served their company by writing 50 letters with more thought about their purpose and how to accomplish results. These slam-bang letter-writers are like grasshoppers—good on distance but poor on direction. It is much more commendable to plan and write ten collection letters that bring back $4,000, than to dash off 20 collection letters that bring back only $2,000. Which is more valuable to your company, a sales letter that pulls 20 per cent in orders, even if you took a day to plan and write it, or a sales letter dashed off in 15 minutes that pulls only 2 per cent?

What if you were a sales manager and had to announce a cut in commission rate? By hard thinking, you might be able to write the letter which would satisfy your sales force that the cut was necessary and fair to them; or you could just hand out the bad news with no regard for their point of view, and let them figure out for themselves why the cut had been made. The second letter would take less time to write, but would it be better? No; salesmanagers always have the problem of keeping morale at a high pitch. They would surely take time to write the letter that might cushion the shock.

Relating time to importance. Often when a group of writers are reminded that letters must be planned, one of them will exclaim, "That may be true theoretically, but it wouldn't work for me. If I took time to plan every letter I dictate, I couldn't do anything else." This person is really not thinking very straight. Nobody intends that you should go into mental contortions over every letter that you write. Many of the situations handled by correspondence are so similar that one approach serves for all. Others are so simple that they present no real problem. It takes very little planning to write to customers, thanking them for their orders, and telling when they will be shipped. Of course, you might think of something else to add that would warm the customers' hearts, and lead to other orders—and the extra planning would surely be worthwhile. Even when letter-problems are more complicated, experience is a big help. The planning of one successful letter develops a certain skill and understanding that carries over to the next. Thus, if each day you take time to *think* before you write, the job tends to be less and less difficult. You grow in power. Eventually, you become a letter-craftsman, and the steps you take to plan your letters are not nearly so hard as they were when you were still struggling to master the art.

The time one can afford to give to planning a letter depends, basically, on the nature of the problem, and how important it is to the company that the perfect solution be found. For example, the promotion manager of a Western corporation recently mailed a sales letter that in a very short time brought in orders amounting to over $300,000. When complimented, he said: "It was no miracle. I simply had to work real hard on the letter to get every word right. I did nothing else for ten days but work on it— couldn't sleep for thinking about it. You see, I *took time to make sure* the letter would do the job."

The letter-writer just quoted is one of America's best. He works as deftly as a surgeon and his output of copy is far above average, for he dictates very rapidly. In preparing that one sales message, however, he made no attempt to hurry. Instead, he was willing to sweat for ten days— "to make sure the letter would do the job." Each of those days spent in planning paid back to the company more than $30,000 of new business.

Learn to regulate your pace. Give each letter-problem the time and attention it deserves. A little planning for little problems! Big planning for big problems! But plan...plan...plan.

The first step: avoiding the "so what" letter. Knowing exactly what you mean to accomplish is the first step in planning a business letter. Obviously, unless this *purpose* is crystal-clear in the writer's mind, it will certainly not be clear in the reader's. Confusion breeds nothing more orderly than itself.

No doubt you have received letters that read well enough, but when you got to the end, you said, "Well, so what?" And that's a good name for letters that take you no place— "so what" letters. Reading them is like holding the bag in a snipe-hunt—nothing happens. Millions of dollars are wasted every year by letters that seem to have no clearly defined purpose. Apparently, nothing is expected of the readers—at least, nothing is asked. A good example is the one which follows. It was intended to be a sales letter, probably, but no order was requested. Or was the thought merely to keep the company name before the reader? We don't know. Maybe the writer was just as nonplussed.

Dear_____,

It may be hot—

when you read this letter, so we'll make it short and comfortable. We won't omit sending it, because that would be just like missing a friendly call.

Maybe you'll be "in conference" when this letter reaches you. Along about this time of the year, many big businessmen are. But if you stick around long enough, you'll find them coming back with a bag of clubs.

Which is perfectly all right! American businessmen have found it pays to play—as well as work. It's a good habit, although it would have been frowned on 50 years ago when this business of making boxes was first founded.

Times do change. And habits too. But the fundamental principles of success don't.

A good product—in our case, boxes—cartons—containers—a sincere service, and courtesy to the customer always—insures success.

We've found it so!

The letter has a few points in its favor. The language is natural—no "whiskers." The words are short, so that the flow is fast—no "goozling." The mention and approval of golf as the businessman's relaxation may rub a "soft spot" and thus tend to bring reader and writer together. There's a very gentle plug for the boxes and service, but just when you would expect a request for reader action, the writer signs off.

"We've found it so," says the writer.

"So what?" asks the reader.

Here, as you will discover later in this section, a good story may help to get a letter off to a good start. It serves as an appetizer, and whets the reader's taste for the "meat" which is to follow. But here's a letter which is *all* appetizer—no soup, no meat, no vegetables, no salad, no dessert. True, the writer finally slaps on a postscript in which there is a very mild request for business. Was that the primary purpose he had in mind, or was it merely to amuse his customer? If the latter, the story might backfire, for puzzles can be irritating unless they are easily solved by the customer.

> Dear————,
>
> There were three men on their way to a Kentucky Derby named Taylor, King, and Jones, who are an attorney, a salesman, and an adjustor, but not respectively.
>
> On the train with them were three credit men: a Mr. Taylor, a Mr. King, and a Mr. Jones.
>
> CONSIDER THE FOLLOWING:
>   1. Mr. King lives in New York.
>   2. The attorney lives halfway between Chicago and New York.
>   3. Mr. Jones earns $30,000 a year.
>   4. Taylor beat the salesman at poker.
>   5. The attorney's nearest neighbor, one of the credit men, earns exactly three times as much as the attorney who earns $65,000 a year.
>   6. The credit man whose name is the same as the attorney's lives in Chicago.
>
> Now then, WHO IS THE ADJUSTOR?
>
> P.S. If you can't find the solution...or want a confirmation...drop me a memo. If you have a claim to place for collection...call on the————Co.

In an amusing contrast (to us, if not to the writer) is a letter from a man sentenced to liquidation, and with only one last hope. There is little doubt of the writer's purpose. He wanted action, and he wanted it quickly. "Dear Governor," he wrote, "They are fixin' to hang me on Thursday—and here it is Tuesday." That was certainly to the point. There was nothing "so what" about it. A good business letter avoids any confusion and makes the most of the time the reader takes to read it.

How to handle your mail. If you read and mark a letter correctly, the purpose of the reply is more easily established. Many business correspondents make the mistake of taking a quick peep at the morning mail, and then shoving it aside for later handling. This involves a second reading, which often could be avoided. The most efficient businessmen reduce their letter-writing as much as possible to a one-time operation.

Each letter is read thoroughly, and the points that must be covered in the reply are marked with a red pencil. In many cases, where the facts are already known, the reply can be dictated immediately. No time is lost, and the marked passages establish purpose. Even when it is necessary to defer the reply for the lack of needed information, a second careful reading of the letter is not required. The writer simply picks it up and looks at the red marks.

This use of a red pencil as you read your mail, and the immediate reply to as many letters as possible, are two habits that will save time and also enhance your reputation as a writer who gets things done without fuss or bother.

Declaring the purpose to yourself. It is hardly possible that anyone would question the first step in planning a business letter, or for that matter, any other kind of a letter. When you know the "why" of any task, you proceed without lost motion to the "how" it may best be done. It is seldom necessary to rewrite a letter when your purpose is clearly understood at the start. Unprepared writers are forced to do things over; hence, smart dictators have another habit that helps them keep their letters on target. They mentally survey the letter-job they are about to do, and *to themselves declare the purpose for which they are writing.*

For example, you might say to yourself, "I am writing this letter...

• *to make this dealer understand that the goods substituted were superior in quality to those he ordered*—that we were trying to do him a favor so that he would not be caught short of merchandise during his sale.

• *to prove to this salesman that the new territory he has been asked to take is better than the old one*—that the change is a promotion and not unfair as he now thinks.

• *to explain that we cannot grant a concession to one buyer unless it were available to the rest*—to deny his request in such a way that he will respect us all the more.

- *to show this customer why he should pay this bill before it is placed in the hands of the lawyers*—to talk to him as a friend, even though he must be told we will wait only ten days longer.

- *to find out why this customer stopped buying from us six months ago*—to make him feel we really appreciated his business, and sincerely want the privilege of serving him again.

- *to thank this prospect for the time he gave our salesman, even though he didn't buy*—to win goodwill for the company, and a better reception for the salesman on his next call.

- *to tell this merchant whose store was destroyed by fire not to worry about his account with us*—to ask him how we may help to re-establish his business.

- *to refuse the request of this minister that we contribute goods for the church bazaar*—to make him understand the reason, and to keep his friendship.

- *to acknowledge our mistake in filling the order and to say we are sorry*—to do this without using a crying-towel, or attempting to give any excuses or alibis.

It doesn't matter what the situation is—how simple or complicated it may be. The declaration of purpose before you begin to dictate will help immensely to clarify your thinking, and to produce the letter that moves straight to the intended objective.

The second step: getting all the facts. To write a business letter, knowing you are not fully informed but thinking you may bluff it through, is both foolish and unpardonable. No only is "face" lost with the reader, but the chances are you will be asked for a better explanation. You have to get the facts anyway, and then you have written two letters where one would have sufficed.

When people talk across space to a reader, surely and positively, because they know what they are talking about, their words carry power and conviction. We all respect facts. We quickly lose confidence in anyone who, through ignorance or laziness, seems unsure of his own ground.

Fortunately, most of the facts needed to handle business correspondence are easily available. If you are a clerk in the credit department who is about to write about a past-due bill, you can review the copies of previous letters to the same customer. If you are in the sales department and are asked a technical question about a new product or a piece of machinery, you can get the answer from the director of research or the chief engineer. Practically everything done in a company is a matter of record. The correspondent who aims for the top will keep informed with respect to the methods, products, and policies of the organization.

The facts we need to know are seldom withheld from us. And the greater your knowledge, the greater your power as a letter-writer!

Lack of facts defeat a letter's purpose. Perhaps you do not know how to play chess. You have heard that it is a very difficult game, to be mastered only after years of study. Well, now you can easily become an expert. In two short paragraphs, the following letter tells you how to play—"through to the finer points." It was written by a clerk in one of the big mail-order houses. The customer had purchased a set of chessmen, and then had written for instructions for playing the game. Here is what clerk Whataguesser told her:

Dear_____,

We do not have any special directions printed for playing chess, but I would suggest that you take one chessman and move it from the bottom to the center, following the game through to the finer points.

The first party that fills in the top of the board wins the game. We assure you, that if you follow these instructions carefully, you will be able to play the game to your full satisfaction.

Could such a letter be genuine? Yes, indeed. It was dictated and typed, but fortunately a supervisor in the mail-order house caught the rascal before it got into the mail bag. The clerk perhaps thought he was smart to be able to write something about which he knew absolutely nothing. Smart enough, no doubt, to lose his job!

It has been mentioned how the abuse of facts, or the lack of them, tends to destroy reader confidence. It does more than that. Usually, the letter fails utterly to accomplish its purpose. Examine the opening and closing paragraphs of a letter mailed to the alumni of a Big Ten University by the circulation editor of the campus newspaper.

We are in the midst of the football season again—that most glamorous time of the entire college year....

Don't pass up this intensely interesting period. Follow the teams from day to day in the columns of the Daily_____.

The parts of the letter omitted were neither too good nor too bad, but whoever approved the mailing overlooked one important fact. "We are in the midst of the football season—follow the teams from day to day," appealed the circulation manager. Had he declared the purpose of his letter, no doubt it would have been "to convince the alumni that they should keep in touch with the football team this fall by subscribing to our student newspaper."

But—and it's a sad *but*—the letter was dated November 29, and the last football game of the season had been played the week before. The thrills used as bait for the reader's money had ceased to exist until another year—a simple fact that made the letter worthless.

This failure to change with the calendar is no rare accident in the business world. It is easy to prepare a form letter, start it going, check results for a while, and then continue sending it long after the things it talks about have ended or lost their appeal.

From the president of one of Chicago's hotels came a nicely worded holiday message to a friend. The use of a rubber stamp for the president's signature contradicted the personal tone of the copy, yet the recipient was graciously thanked for the many times he had stopped at the hotel, and heartily invited to make it his Chicago home on every future visit. The letter would have made a fine impression, except for one fact that didn't hold water. The reader had *never* been a guest of that hotel. This made everything in the letter sound insincere.

"Scratching the wrong back" in business correspondence is always a dangerous practice. The readers know they are getting a letter meant for somebody else, or at least not for them. Their opinion of the company goes down instead of up. After a few similar experiences, they become suspicious of all goodwill letters.

A very beautiful letter of condolence once came to Mrs. L.E. Frailey. The writer's choice of words was magnificent, and the whole effect would have been quite comforting, had it not been for one error. You see, the purpose of the letter, as revealed toward the end, was to sell the lady a tombstone for her husband's grave—a purpose which the latter deemed absolutely unnecessary and somewhat belittling.

Another letter equally wide of its mark, and thus only a waste of effort and postage, was one that began, "You do not need to be bald any longer." This would have been good news, perhaps, to one whose head was smooth, but not to the recipient. Gray hair, yes! But bald—what an unfounded suggestion!

Know what you are talking about, and shoot at the right target; otherwise, the backfire can be terrific.

When right and left hands work apart. Another form of factual inaccuracy in letters is that caused by lack of coordination between people or departments in the same company. For example, the promotion editor of a publishing house writes, "I am really disturbed that we have not heard from you concerning your renewal." Then she sweeps into a long, and somewhat windy exposition of the fine features which the former subscriber has been missing. The close is an urge for immediate action—"You surely cannot afford to delay any longer. We will expect and appreciate your renewal this week."

The letter so far is not too weak, but there follows a startling postscript "If you *have* renewed," it says, "please disregard this letter." The writer admits lack of teamwork between herself and the subscription editor—or else she is just too lazy to find out whether or not the renewal has been received. In either event, she is taking advantage of the reader's time by asking him to wade through a long letter, only to confess it may have been unnecessary.

A somewhat more obliging fellow is the president of a company. He, too, is shooting in the dark, but he admits it in the first paragraph.

> We have been mighty busy lately, and have not had time to check up your name with our order list to see if you have sent us your order, but we expect to do so soon. If you already have sent us your order, you do not need to pay any attention to this letter.

Evidently, the confession of ignorance weighs heavily in this executive's mind, for toward the end of his letter, he again returns to the subject.

> I am sorry we have not had time to check up your name with our order list, as you probably have sent us your order already, or expect to do so soon. If you haven't, let us hear from you promptly.

The reaction to such a flabby excuse for inefficiency could scarcely be good. Twice the president says he has been "too busy" to "check up" (why *up*?) the reader's name. What he really admits is ignorance of a fact needed, and obtainable, before the letter was written.

The American public has been led to expect efficient performance in big business. Anything short of that is a confession of weakness that undermines faith and interferes with progress. To plan a successful business letter, it is necessary to have or to *get* all facts related to the subject. Facts win respect. Facts build confidence. Be sure you have them.

The third step: visualizing the reader. Know your purpose, know the facts, know your reader. When this third step is taken, the letter is beginning to "jell" in your mind. You can now think of what may be said in terms of the man or woman who is going to read it. The point that might be most persuasive to reader Jones might fall far short if presented to reader Smith. Certain groups of people, bound together by similar living habits, occupations, and cultural levels, will tend to be receptive to the same suggestions—and that fact is important in planning a form letter—but the psychologists tell us no two individuals are exactly alike, or susceptible to the same arguments or reasons. Hence, the best letter will always be the one that is custom-built to fit the particular reader.

This seeking to approach the readers where they may be vulnerable, this rubbing of their "soft spots," is fundamental in the planning of a business letter. The expert learns to *look through the readers' eyes*, to understand their likes and dislikes, and to share their emotions. "It is a rare and priceless asset," says a famous copywriter, "when people dictating a letter can *project* themselves two or three days hence and imagine they are just now reading their own letter." When you are able to do that, your own opinions and valuations fade into the background. It is what the readers think, or want, or like, that counts. They are the ones who must be pleased. The more you know about them the better are your chances of gaining a favorable reaction.

Forming a mental image. Business correspondents who are about to dictate a batch of letters will, of course, encounter various degrees of difficulty in visualizing the readers. If they happen to know dealer Brown personally, the problem is comparatively easy. Success then depends on a knowledge of human nature, and an understanding of Brown's personality; but they still must see through Brown's eyes rather than their own. Some people are better judges of human nature than others, but this is a valuable asset to all letter-writers.

Dealer Martin, next on the list, may be only the name of a customer to the dictator, but certain facts about Martin are learned indirectly. He must be progressive and up-to-date or he would not stand near the top in sales among the several hundred dealers. The correspondence file reveals that Martin pays his bills promptly, that his relations with the sales department always have been friendly, that one of his sons went to Yale, that he was once mayor of his city. Gradually, the mental image of dealer Martin begins to form. His letters, too, are revealing. They indicate a sense of humor, a capacity for seeing both sides of a moot question, but also a well-defined stubbornness once Martin has declared his point of view. His letters frequently mention seeing a football game, playing golf, or something about his bowling average. It is plain he is the athletic type, at least he is keenly interested in sports.

You might ask, "Who would take time to study previous correspondence just to answer one letter?" The truthful answer is that many letter-writers *never* do it, some because they are "too busy," and others because they are too lazy. No one is recommending that such a plan be followed in answering *all* letters. But if you sat at your desk one morning, with a letter from dealer Martin in your hand, wondering what to say because a situation has developed which may break the business relationship—if that were true, wouldn't you want to get from Martin's file all of the help it might give you? The people who push aside any plan that involves a little extra effort are those unable to differentiate between a routine situation and one in which there is a real problem to solve. You cannot take all of the principles of letter-writing too literally—they are to be applied when and if they are necessary.

There can be no question, however, about the advantage of visualizing your reader. Even if the mental image is not perfect or complete, it seems to place the two of you in the same room. The person becomes not just a name, but a human being. You can *talk* to him as you would face-to-face. And you know from previous sections of this *Handbook,* that *talking* is the secret of writing an effective letter. The mediocre letter-writer says, "I must clean up this correspondence today." The good letter-writer says, "Now I must talk with all these people."

Visualizing the stranger. Of course, many business letters go to unknown persons—one from another state wants to know about a product, a London broker inquires about sales possibilities in England, a lady doesn't like a program because it frightens her children. In such cases the mental images are bound to be vague, although an individual may often reveal things about himself in his letter. Beyond those hints, when they are present, the dictator has only his knowledge of human nature and of certain characteristics.

An equally difficult task in forming the right mental image is the preparation of the form letter that may be sent to thousands of people in all parts of the country. Here, writers, can only set up in their mind what appears to be the typical reader, and then plan their message for that composite individual. They know they cannot influence everybody on their list favorably, but they aim for a favorable reaction from the largest possible number. When the list is occupational, such as teachers, lawyers, or funeral directors, the image of the typical reader is more readily formed. This is also true when those who will receive the form letter have allied interests—sales representatives, club members, labor groups, business executives, and all the others you can recall.

The fourth step: choosing the right ammunition. Down the fairway goes the professional golfer to the place where the next shot is to be made. The caddy is waiting with the usual big bag of clubs. To one who has never played the game, it looks foolish to carry so many, but the caddy doesn't complain. He knows every one of those clubs has a purpose, and the winning of the purse might well depend on the selection of the right one for a particular shot. He wants his golfer to win.

So now the shot must be made. The "pro" surveys the position of the ball, the distance to the green, and the obstacles to be avoided. Finally, the decision is made. "Four iron," he says. The caddy looks worried, for the green looks far away, but he knows better than to blink an eyelid. "Crack!" The head of the club cuts a path through the sod and lifts the ball on its course. Just over the trap—the caddy holds his breath! Up toward the cup rolls the ball, and stops short only a few inches.

Down the fairway they go again, the boy and his hero. "Wish I could hit a shot like that," the former exclaims. "Wasn't me," the "pro" replies. "I just happened to take the right club."

The explanation of the golfer could just as well be that of the letter-writers who have received a favorable reply. "Wasn't *me*," they might say, "I just happened to select the right appeal." You see, the first three steps in planning a letter all contribute to the fourth.

First, know the purpose—that's wanting to reach the green in one shot. Second, know the facts—that's studying the position of the ball, the distance, the obstacles. Third, visualize the reader—that's the mental image of the ball in flight. Fourth, choose the best appeal—that's taking the "right club from the bag." Each step is important, but they all cooperate to produce the desired result.

The situations to be handled in golf or letter-writing are never quite the same. To reach other greens no farther away, the golfers may one time take a spoon because they need loft to clear some trees, or another time they may take a jigger for a bullet-shot under the branches. To gain a reply with an order, the letter-writers may one time use "economy" to overcome the resistance of a tight-fisted prospect, and another time they may use "style" to whet the desire of a customer who counts not the cost.

For every reader or prospect, you are likely to find a different combination of "soft spots"—the things or benefits or reasons to which they are most vulnerable. Knowing *what* to say to *whom* and *when* is part of the planning of a business letter.

How letter-writers probe for "soft spots." Most business correspondents take this fourth step in letter-planning, even though they often seem to ignore the others. You seldom read a sales letter, for example, without noting how the writer appears to be trying to "cash in" on what he thinks to be some point of vulnerability in his reader.

Examine the following quotations:

> You know, the Irish are an impulsive race. Take me for example. I was born on the 14th of March. Now if I hadn't been in such a hurry to see what was goin' on in the world, I could have waited three days longer. Then I could have shared the 17th with St. Patrick. And that would have been a great honor for both of us.

> (There's a good bit of Irish wit and blarney in this door-opener. It's appeal is very strong, but only when mailed to an Irishman.)

> Did you know that 20 years ago there were four Sealyham champions in one litter? This is a record unsurpassed by any other breed except Springer Spaniels.

> (Sent to a man who had seven Sealyhams, the letter obviously hits a "soft spot," and, of course, the appeal would be even greater to a lover of Springer Spaniels.)

> Sometimes we get a steak that's a little tough, but we like steak, and there isn't any better steak available—so we take a firm grip on the knife and fork and bear down.

> Business is sometimes like that. Conditions are not always the best, but it's beyond us to change them. Still, we can get some of that business if we take hold of the knife and fork, and really cut in.

> (Probably steak is a magic word. Thus, the letter gets off to a good start. It would backfire, though, in the hands of one who did not eat steak.)

> A young telegraph operator had no money, and his salary was so small he could hardly make ends meet. But he decided that he had to risk some of that scant salary if ever he was to get anywhere. So he bought $5 worth of postage stamps, and in his spare time penned letters to other telegraphers along the line, telling them about a low-priced watch he could get for them at a low price.

> Soon he began to get orders, and as each one came in, he sent part of the money to a watch factory with orders to deliver the watch direct to the buyer, and then he put the rest of the money into more postage stamps. Before many months, he was making so much money selling watches that he gave up his job to build a business by mail. That telegraph operator's name was Sears, and you know the business he founded.

(The appeal, and it runs throughout the letter, is to the desire for more money—leading the reader to wonder if he, too, might become another Sears.)

Here is a letter that seeks to create business for a landscape gardener. For lack of any request for action at the end, it might be called a "so what" letter, were you not told it was one of a series sent to the same man. Thus, the purpose was to remind rather than to sell.

Dear_____,

Let's talk your language for a moment.

In a certain room in your factory is a hide. Sooner or later it will be placed in the show-window of a high class store, in the form of a pair of shoes. Master craftsmen will have transformed it into a pair of the finest shoes made—Doe shoes.

A thousand things have happened to it—things it has taken a lifetime to learn. Cheaper shoes are made—but none that are less expensive—for you tell me they will outlast two ordinary pairs. They are the best—made for the "man who cares."

The grounds around your new home are like that hide.

And like that hide, some master craftsman is going to change them into surroundings—simple, useful, attractive. A thousand things are going to happen to them—things that have taken a lifetime to learn. They must turn out to be the best—because they, too, belong to the "man who cares!"

Durability—snugness—elegance—poise—smoothness—these things are bound up in every pair of Doe shoes.

And those same things will make your grounds entirely satisfactory.

The appeal in that letter is to pride. The writer is saying, "You make the best shoes, and we do the best landscape gardening. Birds of a feather should get together."

The appeal to home-town pride. The person who first said, "There is no place like home," may have had an idea, one it would pay letter-writers to adopt more often than they do. There seems to be a streak of loyalty in human beings that make them stand up for their hometowns, though they be as humble as Dogpatch or Toonerville. Thus, when writers of business letters are able, without exaggeration, to work in a "plug" for the reader's home, they are using an old appeal that helps to break the ice. For example:

Dear_____,

Boston once held a tea party. There was objection to an exorbitant tax on a cargo of tea, you will remember, so it was dumped overboard.

Is Boston today less quick to throw overboard anything that carries too high a tax?

Waste is a form of tax. If there is a way to dump that tax, naturally you are for it.

Paper-carded belt hooks are from 10 per cent to 25 per cent wasteful. That waste tax is avoided by the use of improved Safety Belt Hooks, with Steel Binder Bars, to which there is no waste. Safety Belt Hooks also make smoother, longer-lived joints.

The literature and notebook enclosed tell the story. You can get Safety Belt Hooks and Lacers from the Boston dealers named below. If there are others you prefer to deal with, any one of them will get Safety products for you.

Evidently, in the above letter, the writer was not using the home-town appeal by accident, for it appears in his messages to prospects and dealers in other cities.

Dear_____,

Here is the information requested, and we think something is about ready to explode down there in your fine town in the way of orders.

We say fine town, not as a bit of flattery, but because I vividly remember spending a week in Houston during the International Rotary Convention. If your sales punch down in Houston matches your hospitality, you should decidedly go places with Safety Hooks and Lacers.

There is...

Dear_____,

A Philadelphian, one Benjamin Franklin by name, had more to say about waste than perhaps any other man who ever lived in Philadelphia, or elsewhere.

With such a tradition, the folks of Philadelphia ought to be about as thrifty as folks come anywhere. If we are right, then you will be very much interested in the next paragraph.

Paper-carded belt hooks are from 10 per cent to 25 per cent wasteful. That waste is...

The sincerity of plain talking. The next letter is one in which there is no beating of bushes or sounding of trumpets. The writer uses plain speech that is both convincing and refreshing. The appeal is, "We will treat you right," and you feel it is sincere.

Dear———,

We don't give rare coins but there's more than one way to get your money's worth out of a used car.

The idea that a certain dealer is about to sprout wings, and make things heavenly for used car buyers has been going the rounds so long that it rattles. The reason we give our customers their money's worth isn't because we are so big-hearted we can't help it. If you want to know the reason, it is because we want to stay in business.

The Mrs. has her mind set on sending our boy, Charlie, to college. If he is like I am, it will be wasted, but the Mrs. says he isn't and that's that.

I haven't enough money to retire on and I can't stand to loaf when anybody is looking; and we have such big show windows that people are always looking. So, for those reasons, I figure my best bet is to treat buyers right so they will come back, and tell others they got a good deal from Jimmy Davies.

Right now, I have some cars that are worth looking into. You won't find any rare dimes under the cushions—I look for them myself—but you will get all you bargain for.

I'd like to show you the Dodge Charlie Brooks traded in last week—*XXX* takes it and you cannot take as long as you like to pay for it. No terms beyond *XX* months go here.

As we recall, this letter was lathed by letter carpenter Vic Knight. Whether or not it sold the Dodge is not recorded. Nevertheless, the appeal is strong to those who are tired of high-sounding but empty promises.

A letter that tickles the funny bone. Appealing to the reader's sense of humor is a device often used to win acceptance for a business letter. The following example (Figure 3-1) was used by The Plaza, a New York City hotel. It really does a double job; it entertains the reader while putting across a sales message.

Use of "scare copy" as appeal for action. One of the major motives for human behavior is fear. People buy many things to protect themselves against hazards that may be real or imaginary. Hence, the use of "scare copy" is frequently seen in advertising and sales. A picture of

Figure 3-1

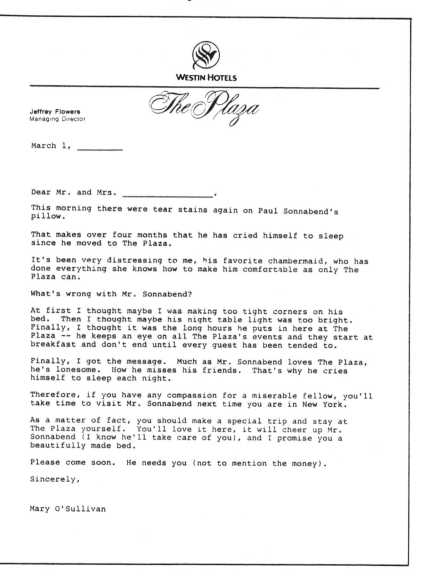

WESTIN HOTELS

The Plaza

Jeffrey Flowers
Managing Director

March 1, _____

Dear Mr. and Mrs. _____,

This morning there were tear stains again on Paul Sonnabend's pillow.

That makes over four months that he has cried himself to sleep since he moved to The Plaza.

It's been very distressing to me, his favorite chambermaid, who has done everything she knows how to make him comfortable as only The Plaza can.

What's wrong with Mr. Sonnabend?

At first I thought maybe I was making too tight corners on his bed. Then I thought maybe his night table light was too bright. Finally, I thought it was the long hours he puts in here at The Plaza -- he keeps an eye on all The Plaza's events and they start at breakfast and don't end until every guest has been tended to.

Finally, I got the message. Much as Mr. Sonnabend loves The Plaza, he's lonesome. How he misses his friends. That's why he cries himself to sleep each night.

Therefore, if you have any compassion for a miserable fellow, you'll take time to visit Mr. Sonnabend next time you are in New York.

As a matter of fact, you should make a special trip and stay at The Plaza yourself. You'll love it here, it will cheer up Mr. Sonnabend (I know he'll take care of you), and I promise you a beautifully made bed.

Please come soon. He needs you (not to mention the money).

Sincerely,

Mary O'Sullivan

some horrible automobile accident, with a description of all the gory details, may influence you to buy tires with a patented safety tread, or an insurance policy that would pay your hospital bills. A story about the consequences of poor nutrition and/or exercise may send you running out to enroll in a diet plan or an exercise program. Check your own buying habits, and you will be surprised to find how many of them are the result of the desire to protect yourself against poverty, sickness, and other forms of catastrophe. Check the letters that you get, and you will be surprised to find how many of them use fear as the major appeal.

Perhaps there is no emotion more universally shared than the dread of old age, particularly the fear that it may catch us unprepared to live without the aid of charity. To be sure, this is a fear that may vary in degree among different individuals and groups, but few of us are entirely free from it. For the purpose of example only, let's take one aimed at teachers. This group is employed at the discretion of a local school board. See how fear of retirement is used to sell a personal pension.

Dear_____,

It was Thursday evening—a closed school board meeting was in session. There had been a lot of spirited discussion, and all items had been disposed of—except one. Down at the bottom of the president's memo were but two words—"Miss Meridith."

To the School Board, it was merely another item of business routine, but to Miss Meridith it was a matter which affected her entire future.

The Board quickly decided: "She has served faithfully and well. She always has proved very capable, but she's getting a bit too old to teach. Her health isn't the best, and much as we regret it, she will have to be replaced."

The above incident is tragic, but not unusual. In fact, it is a typical experience which might be multiplied many times daily. And in all cases, the fate of the teacher hangs in the balance.

One of these days, perhaps, *your* name will be scrawled on the president's memo.

Right now, _____, that day seems far removed, but come it will, as it finally must to all in the teaching profession. Just how will the decision of the Board affect you?

With your earnings reduced, how will you live? Will you be compelled to throw yourself on the charity of friends or relatives—or will you mark the day as the beginning of a new era, bringing release from classroom duties, the thrills of a trip around the world, the opportunity to pursue a hobby, a future free from money worries?

Thousands of teachers already have adopted the Income Reserve Plan. Perhaps, it may appeal to you. But first we suggest you send for the free booklet, Money for the Wonderful Things You Crave."

The card will bring it to you quickly.

Is there anything unethical in the appeal to the fear of old age as used in the above letter? Certainly not! Even though the purpose is to sell an insurance plan, the result may be the solution of the schoolteacher's problem. In that sense, it offers an economic blessing.

Varying the appeal to find vulnerability. The approach just cited is obviously not the only one that could be used in a sales letter to teachers. If you were planning such a letter, your analysis of the individual or group might lead you to shoot from an entirely different angle—or, you might decide to test several appeals whose strength appeared about equal. Here, for example, are the opening paragraphs of three letters, mailed for the same purpose, but each probing a different possible soft spot.

Dear _____,

There's a little story of Joseph Conrad that every teacher will appreciate.

Long ago, when Conrad was a boy, he sat gazing at a map of the world. Suddenly, thrusting a grimy finger upon a colorful speck, the youngster exclaimed, "Some day I'm going there."

"Some day I'm going there!"

I wonder if there is a teacher in all the world, who hasn't said those very words! In teaching some bit of history or geography, you've felt an impelling desire to cast the book aside, and set forth on a joyous journey.

Hidden away in our hearts, we all have that dream of someday visiting those storied countries beyond the sea.

(*Appeal to the desire for travel*)

Dear _____,

A dear teacher I used to know, confided to me his fondest dream—to end his days in a cozy little cottage just over the hill from the school, where he could hear the bell...and never have to answer it at all. But to each of us there will come a time when we want to retire from active life, and take a well-earned rest. To solve that problem, we have devised a wonderful policy, just for you. It will assure your vine-clad cottage, with happy days for rest and relaxation.

(*Appeal to desire to get away from it all*)

Dear —————,

In that last quarter of an hour, after the students have gone home, and you are alone in the schoolroom, straightening up your desk....

...don't you sometimes stop and wonder what the future holds for you? Things are running pretty smoothly now. You really are enjoying your work. But what about the later years of life? Will you have to drudge along at the same old humdrum routine, just as so many older teachers of your acquaintance are doing?

Or will you be able to enjoy life, and make your cherished dreams come true?

Now—today—you have an opportunity to decide.

(*Appeal to desire for freedom in later years*)

Just as the quarterback of a football team may use different plays to test for soft spots in the opposing line, so is it often necessary for the letter-writers to try various appeals before they can be sure which is most effective. This can never safely be determined by opinion or guess. The only sure way to *know* is to test, and then test again.

An appeal to superstition. The soft spot you are seeking when you plan a business letter may not always be of the conventional variety. Instead, by mere intuition—or is it the help of Providence?—you may hit upon an unusual appeal that does the perfect job. A certain person— you may guess his identity—once sat in his St. Louis office, quite glum and discouraged. He was thumbing idly through the card file of customers, wondering what he might do to bring rain where there had been so much drought, when he happened to notice that an out-of-town order had been received several months previously on a Friday, the thirteenth. The calendar on the wall said that this very day was the second and only other Friday the thirteenth of the year. Had the young chap been wiser in the ways of the business world, he would have scorned the idea that the coincidence might develop an order. But he didn't know any better, so he hand-pecked on his typewriter the following "foolish" sales letter:

Dear —————,

I am not superstitious, but...

There are only two Friday, the thirteenths, appearing on this year's calendar.

On Friday, January the thirteenth, you gave me an order for a carload of Fancy Blue Rose Rice. I appreciated that order more than you knew, for it happened to be my first sale to an out-of-town jobber.

Now, here we are again at Friday the thirteenth, and I can't resist wondering if you are not ready to book another carload. I think I can persuade one of our mills to give you a price of 4 cents on the Fancy, and $3\frac{7}{8}$ cents on the Choice, f.o.b. mill, of course. And in the car could be placed a little Fancy Head Rice at about $6\frac{1}{4}$ cents!

The prices are right. Give me the specifications, and I *will* be superstitious all the rest of my life.

Many of the young man's friends have laughed at that letter, and when reminded that the only true test of a letter is whether or not it does the job, they have promptly replied, "Luck, my boy, just luck." Some have said "it couldn't happen," which may be true, except that it *did*.

Dear _____,

The writer's birthday was Friday, January the thirteenth.

While I have a stock of rice and a car in transit from Texas, I am going to give you an order for a car, for I know I can depend on you for quality. So enter me 225 bags Fancy Blue Rose, 75 bags Fancy Head, at prices you mentioned, and would prefer Texas; but that is up to you for quality.

I might say in passing that it is a pleasure for me to send you this order, for from your letter, I know it will be appreciated and happily executed.

Perhaps you may call the success of that letter a stroke of pure luck; but at least it proves that, contrary to popular thought, there *is* sentiment in business. The man who wrote the letter had the reputation of being a smart buyer, the last to let his heart influence his head. He was vulnerable to appreciation, though. He sensed that the young man needed the order, and he gladly came across. Did the birthday help? Maybe—let's not split hairs.

Be sure the appeal will not backfire. Sometimes a business letter may have the opposite effect from that intended. Basically, the appeal may be good, but it is handled in such a way that the reader is irritated rather than pleased. Consider this sales letter which presents a very necessary service, but not in the most tactful manner.

Dear _____,

When you decided on a midnight snack the other night and turned on the kitchen light only to find a few hundred roaches had the same idea—did you cuss under your breath, and say to yourself, "We've got to get rid of these ***!!! roaches"?

Maybe, you forgot the next morning, maybe it was too much trouble—maybe you didn't like the thought of a truck covered with signs such as "WE KILL LICE" rolling up in front of your house, so that your neighbors would know your troubles.

Now, through our personalized service, we not only rid your home of these obnoxious night prowlers, but we completely moth-proof all clothes closets, furniture, rugs, or garments that show signs of moth attack. Our service also eliminates water-bugs, ants, silverfish, etc., with no fuss, no muss—you and the insects are the only ones who will know we have been around—and the insects won't know it for long.

It is not necessary to leave your home. Our neat, well-trained men will call, do the work, and leave your premises spick-and-span. Our Home Service System is safe, noncontaminating to food, and is noninjurious to humans or animals.

Our price? Well, you will be amazed at the low cost.

Just mail the enclosed card, or phone _____, and a courteous representative will call with absolutely no obligation on your part.

Fundamentally, the appeal in this letter is sound. Roaches and other insects are not welcome in any home. If you happened to have any of these pests as uninvited guests, you certainly would be glad to know they could be eliminated so easily and so cheaply. The confidential treatment is also a good point. Roaches or bedbugs are nothing to be proud of, and you wouldn't want your neighbors to know they had moved in with you.

But the *backfire* comes from the way the writer of the letter overplayed his hand. He starts with the downright assumption that the prospect's kitchen is inhabited by roaches—not a few of them, but *hundreds*. He uses the appeal as a *fact* rather than a *possibility*. Hence, the prospect is humiliated. Particularly obnoxious is the reference later to "lice"—the most hated insect of them all. They are not mentioned as a fact, as were the roaches, but just the same there is an unpleasant insinuation that they, too, might be one of the prospect's "troubles."

The more tactful approach would have been to *start easy and work up*. Instead of the outright assertion that when the lights went on a few hundred roaches were there in the grandstand, ready to root for the hometeam, only the *possibility* of their being present should have been mentioned—and even then, not such a vast assembly of the pests. People look upon a roach as evidence of uncleanliness, and thus a reflection on their care of the home. A few roaches are bad enough, they figure—they could never stand an army of them. The letter should have started something like this:

> This is the time of the year when the war against roaches and other pets increases in fury. Where these little devils come from, nobody seems to know. When least expected, they appear in the most immaculate homes.

> Perhaps, so far, none of these unwelcome guests have moved in on you. And that's fine! You are lucky. But if, by chance, you have some of them around your house, you naturally want to get rid of them before they multiply and become even a greater nuisance.

> And that's where we come to the rescue. Not even your closest neighbor will know about it, but quickly, completely, we will liquidate the rascals.

In that introduction, there is nothing to offend or humiliate the readers. They are tactfully told that roaches and other pests (that would include the unmentionable lice) often appear in the most immaculate homes. The rest of the letter could be in the original form. Result? Success—much business!

Remember! *You can't win by insulting your reader.*

Avoid all possible irritants. There's an old and very wise saying, especially pertinent to letter-writers, "When in doubt, *don't.*" Unless you know your reader like a book, you run the chance of building your letter around an appeal that may offend rather than please him.

It is dangerous to mention politics, religion or race. A very good story might poke what seems to be innocent fun at the members of a certain faith, and what if it lands in the home of one of them? You might quote a saying of a Mexican, an Irishman, or an Italian, and have any one of those nationalities take it in the wrong way. It is far wiser not to take these chances in business letters. When in doubt, *don't.*

Even the reference to a physical attribute may rub salt in raw flesh. You have a laughable story about a bald-headed man. But it may not be so funny to one who is bald. You refer to a man who resembles a "bag of bones" and the reader has always been sensitive about being so thin. You write about the fat woman who wants to reduce but can't resist her pound of chocolates every day—and the letter is read by a lady in exactly the same plight.

You skate on thin ice when you voice a decided opinion on a controversial subject. You may detest rent control, but your reader thinks it is a fine plan. You may not like the wife of a President who frequently appears in public, but your reader may think she is wonderful. Reading the comics in the newspapers may seem a childish pastime to you, but what if your reader enjoys it? The purpose of your letter is to gain a meeting of minds. Why say anything that might interfere with that result?

Make the reader feel important. Contrary to the irritants just mentioned, it is often possible to "scratch the reader's back" by casual reference to some fact that he considers complimentary to himself. Of course, this cannot be done when writing to a total stranger. For example, any of the following phrases, or similar ones, might help to make the reader feel important.

"The research that made this product possible started back in the days when *you were playing football at Illinois.*"

"Your article in Sales Management makes me sure that your mind is open to any idea which might help to motivate your sales staff."

"The credit report on you and your business was *so outstanding* that we are puzzled not to receive your check."

"Because of *your leadership in civic activities,* we lean heavily on your opinion, which we know will be unbiased."

"Many people *like yourself,* serve others so generously that they overlook the protection which would take the sting out of old age."

"Any person who has *served three terms as mayor* must be an *enterprising merchant,* and the kind who wins friends by selling only quality products."

"We understand it is useless to talk business to anyone in *Columbus* during the week of a championship game, but now that the *Buckeyes have finished the season undefeated,* perhaps you can find time to tell us how you liked the samples."

"Surely, as people *of good judgment,* you and your partner do not always buy on the lowest price, *nor can you be fooled* by a product which looks better than it really is."

The compliments implied in the above passages are based on *facts* and could be offered *sincerely.* They are not to be confused with the silly flattery so often seen in business letters—those attempts to curry favor which the readers quickly resent.

The fifth step: coordinating the attack. Now the five steps to be taken in planning an important business letter can be listed. Please remember that the time devoted to them depends on the nature of the problem, and that many routine letter-situations may be "taken in stride," just as you mount and ride a bicycle, once the art is mastered.

1. Know your **purpose**
2. Get all the **facts**
3. **Visualize** your reader
4. Choose the best **appeal**
5. **Coordinate** the attack

To coordinate means putting your points together in the order or combination to gain the best possible effect. In other words, you decide how to play your cards to win the most tricks. You are like the general who is planning to attack a section of the enemy's line. The commanding officer knows that he will use infantry, planes, tanks, rockets, mortars, heavy guns, and other units, but he must coordinate them perfectly to achieve the breakthrough. In the business world, a clear communication breakthrough are good letter-writers. Having decided what the general letter-appeal shall be, and having decided what links to place in the Chain, they must still put the links together in the best combination to provide the most strength (see page 93).

Arranging your points. We doubt if average letter-writers give much thought to the *arrangement* of their points, and yet it is highly important that they should. They know, that they want: (1) to mention price because their figure is somewhat lower than their competitor's, (2) to talk about quality because it is at least equal to the best, (3) to emphasize style because they have a new design that they think will have great popular appeal. Price-quality-style! Those are their three aces, but what does it matter in what order they are presented to the reader?

By asking that question the letter writers have displayed an ignorance of psychological principles which go a long way in determining the final reaction—depending, of course, on how well they are understood and applied. One principle is that, in order to gain reader-attention, a very strong point should be used *first*. Another is that, when exposed to a number of items, we tend to remember the last one most vividly. Thus, the most convincing and action-impelling point should be offered *last*.

However, it is also true that at no place in the letter must the reader's interest be allowed to lag. This indicates that weak points, even when preceded and followed by strong ones, are *dangerous*. It is much better not to use them *at all* than to risk the reader's throwing the letter in the wastebasket and turning to something more interesting.

You see now, that the position of the person who is planning a letter is much the same as that of a lawyer who is planning a plea. Lawyers know they must start with a strong point to get favorable interest, and that they must end with the hammer blow which may obtain the right verdict. They are also faced with the problem of keeping the jury awake throughout their argument. They know, too, that a few strong points, forcefully presented, will have a better effect than a long list of points that tend to compete with each other in the listener's mind with the result—a little of everything, and nothing much of anything, is remembered. These are the facts that letter-writers also must understand!

If you ever have studied the formula for debate, you recognize its similarity to the above reasoning. When there are three speakers on a team, the arguments are reduced to three, each one strong and difficult to refute. These arguments are then assigned in the following order: the strongest to the last speaker, the second-strongest to the first speaker, and the second speaker gets what's left. Sometimes a very strong point is reserved for use in the last rebuttal, the thought being that it will impress the mind of each judge, even if earlier portions of the argument have been forgotten.

A case example. To understand how the capable letter-writer plans a coordinated attack to break down reader-resistance, consider the following hypothetical situation:

J. Jones, a real estate agent, has been asked to sell a small suburban property. Based on the present market, the owner's price is a little high, but the home has many advantages that may offset this one objection. Jones mentally reviews these sales points (Step Two, Get the Facts), and makes a list of them on a memo pad.

Easy transportation—a bus to the city every hour—four-lane express highway for automobiles.

Good neighborhood of first-class homes—served by all the utilities—free from noise and air pollution.

Beautiful site—more than 1 acre of land—large oak trees, many shrubs, ravine.

House designed by nationally known architect—plans won first prize in contest conducted by popular magazine—small and compact, with all modern conveniences.

Brick walls and tile roof, insulated—low cost for repair and maintenance—built by contractor with reputation for quality construction.

Two-car garage, with finished room and bath overhead—detached from the house.

Kennel for dogs, with three runs, at rear of the lot—disguised by brick wall which has climbing roses.

Rock garden, fish pool, and open-air oven.

House features large studio living room, two full baths, ultramodern kitchen, and basement recreation room with bar. Wood-burning fireplace.

Priced high at $_____, but owner will accept low down payment, and a long-term mortgage at only _____ per cent interest.

School one of the best in the area—special bus service for children.

Healthier place to live than in city—cooler in summer—always a nice breeze.

Five miles from 18-hole golf course—within walking distance of community shopping center.

Now the telephone rings. Cy Jerkins has heard about the suburban home. No, he isn't ready to look at it. His wife isn't too keen about living out there. No, he doesn't want to give in and see Jones. "Just give me the dope in a letter," says Mr. Jerkins, "and make it short—I'll let you know if we are interested."

Matching needs and benefits. Okay! Jones has a nibble, but it isn't a bite. What should the letter say to lure Mr. and Mrs. Jerkins to an inspection of the property? He begins to think about them (Step Three, Visualize the Reader) and what *they,* as apart from all other prospects, might want in a home (Step Four, Choose the Best Appeal).

It's all very simple. A sale is nothing more than *matching needs and benefits.* When you can do that, the sale is inevitable.

Jones knows a lot about Jerkins and his wife. That will save time. However, if they had been strangers, information would be needed before the letter could be written. How else could those unique advantages of the home be shown to fit their peculiar needs? Well, what *is* known about them?

Mr. and Mrs. Jerkins are renting a rather expensive apartment in the city. They are the type who spend most or all of their income. Mr. J. is a consultant on advertising and sales problems, and writes for both business and fiction magazines. Their only child is married and lives in the East. Mrs. J. has quite a reputation as a bridge player. They both play golf—and, yes—they belong to the club only 5 miles from the Oak Ridge home. Dogs? Of course! Didn't Jones read something in the paper last year about one of their Scotties winning "best in show"?

All right! Now Jones has the two mental pictures—of the home and all its advantages, and—of the prospects and their possible soft spots. He is ready to make the blend. "And make it short," Cy Jerkins had said. Obviously, Jones problem is to choose carefully a few of the points most likely to strike fire—that is the most effective plan for *all* sales letters.

Easy transportation? Not important. Both Mr. and Mrs. Jerkins have their own automobiles.

Good neighborhood? Well, maybe. Mr. and Mrs. Jerkins appear to entertain regularly. Nice area may impress their guests. But not in this letter.

Beautiful site? Yes, they are the kind to whom that will appeal.

Plans won first prize? Yes, indeed, Mrs. Jerkins will love that point.

Quality construction? No. They will probably take it for granted.

Two-car garage? A necessary point, but not worth emphasis. What's that? Wait a moment. Maybe that room over the garage would be a swell place for Cy Jerkins to write. Yes—use that.

Kennel? Wonderful. They show dogs.

Rock garden, pool, oven? No, they're not into flowers and swimming.

Large studio living room? Good for her bridge parties. *Recreation room with bar?* Fine! He especially will like that. What man wouldn't?

Low down-payment? Yes. The price will appeal to them, so long as they can swing the deal. Their monthly income is ample to meet the mortgage payments.

School bus? No. Their only child is an adult.

Healthier place to live? Doubtful. They are not seriously health-minded. The breeze might appeal. No. "When in doubt, *don't.*"

Golf course near? Yes, strong point. *Shopping center?* No.

There you are. Jones has completed Steps Three and Four. From all the points that *could* be used, he has chosen the following as most likely to please Mr. and Mrs. Cy Jerkins:

1. Beautiful site
2. Plans won first prize
3. Room over garage
4. Kennel

5. Large studio living room

6. Recreation room with bar

7. Low down payment and easy terms

8. Close to their golf club

Coordinating for best effect. Is Jones now ready to write the letter? No, not yet. Step Five has not been taken. He could just start with point number one at the head of the list and go right through to number eight, but only by sheer luck could that be the *best* combination.

Which of the eight points is the strongest? Not just for *any* prospect, but for Mr. and Mrs. Cy Jerkins? The decision calls for judgment, and you might not agree, but Jones' choice is number seven—low down payment and easy monthly terms. If the other points can make the Jerkins family want the home, they might ask themselves, "How can we possibly afford it?" Jones knows how, so he saves the answer to their question for a "clincher" at the end.

Okay! Which of the remaining points ranks next to number seven in strength of appeal? To Cy Jerkins alone, it might be number three. Perhaps for years he has dreamed of a hideaway place to work and write. Since Jones isn't sure about it, he can't afford to take a chance. No, he wants to start his letter with a point that will gain immediate acceptance from *both* husband and wife. He finally decides to appeal to their pride—a combination of number one and number two. Also, he thinks he may be able to work number eight into the first paragraph.

Thus, for the middle of Jones letter, Jones has left only the room over the garage, the kennel, the studio living room, and the recreation room. He decides on the combination 5-6-4-3. At last—Jones is ready to write. His plan has been carefully devised. Within the scope of his ability, he has prepared what seems to be the attack most likely to succeed.

> Prize winner on beautiful site, close to golf club
> Large studio living room
> Recreation room with bar
> Room over garage
> Kennel
> Low down payment and easy terms

Perhaps you are scowling. You say, "Who would take so much time and trouble, just to plan *one* business letter?" Well, the answer is "Who *wouldn't*?"—with so much at stake. The commission which Jones earns on a sale of property of this caliber could be several thousands of dollars. How about it now? Wouldn't *you* gladly spend an hour, a day, or a week, if that much money depended on the success of that one letter? Remember, the time you can afford to spend on one letter is determined by the nature of the problem, and the importance of getting it solved.

The letter that sold the home. So Jones writes the letter. He wonders if it should be mailed to the office of Cy Jerkins, or to his home; the latter seems best. He wants both husband and wife to read it together.

So much for this hypothetical example of planning a business letter. But what's a story without an end? Did the letter develop a sale? Well, we think it was mailed one morning and delivered that afternoon. At eight o'clock in the evening, Jones reached the promised land. Came a voice over the wire, "Thanks for your letter...Mrs. Jerkins and I are not much interested...but we'll meet you there at ten in the morning."

No, not much interested, but the following afternoon the contract was signed. Good news for all—even the pups.

What did Jones say in the letter? Well, you have the outline of points. Why don't you write it—something like this:

Dear_____,

I don't sell real estate. It's a lot more fun to find a perfect home, and then the people who *belong* in it—just as you folks surely do belong in the Oak Ridge home Mr. Jerkins asked me about.

When John Boardman, the famous architect, designed this prize-winning home—the one not far from your golf course— he must have visualized it set in an acre of trees and shrubs as it is now—and folks like you who would love it as much as he did when drawing the plans.

Mr. Jerkins said I must make this letter short, so I can't begin to explain all the charm of this magnificent little home. You'll have to see it to appreciate what I mean.

You, Mrs. Jerkins, will be delighted with the studio living room with its huge fireplace—plenty of space for a dozen bridge tables without crowding. And you, Mr. Jerkins, would surely be a proud host in the tiled recreation room with its unusual bar. Then over the garage—this is a secret—is the perfect place for you to write your stories. If you are like me, you always have wanted a hideaway. Every man needs one, and especially a writer like you.

Maybe, too, Mr. Boardman was thinking of folks like you—or he just loved dogs and couldn't imagine a real home without them—when he designed the kennel so cleverly hidden behind a brick wall covered with climbing roses.

Of course, there is always one thing that comes up in finding a home—the price and terms. They may not be important to you, but the owner will accept a very low down payment, and a mortgage for the balance with interest of only _____ per cent.

Will you do me a favor? When you read this letter—perhaps at dinner tonight—multiply many, many times in your mental image of this home the few things I have said about it. Then call me tonight, and say when you'll have the thrill of seeing it.

I've got the keys, and can meet you there any time tomorrow. Please do call me—(123) 456-7890—as I'll wait until you do.

Think before you write. Nothing worthwhile yields to human effort without a *plan*. The actual saying is easy. It's the planning *what* to say and *how* that determines how good your letter will be. When Abraham Lincoln was asked how he would write a speech if he had just fifteen minutes for the job, he replied, "Well, I would spend at least ten of the fifteen minutes planning what to write, and then I would use the last five minutes to write it."

Maybe it was a similar plan that Reverend Farmer used so successfully in his sermons. Rival ministers saw his results with great admiration. When questioned about his secret to success, he replied, "First, I tell them what I'm going to tell them; then I tell them; then, I tell them what I've told them." That's about it. That's working with a *plan*!

2. BLUEPRINT FOR LETTER-BUILDING

One skeleton that they all possess. In spite of the million and one variations in the blueprints from which business letters are constructed, there is one basic formula that all letters must follow, or else they are almost certainly doomed to fail. True, a writer may now and then risk another plan, but it rarely succeeds, and is then only the exception which proves the rule. Letters, like human beings; are built on a skeleton that has a striking similarity of form, although in "flesh and other attributes" they may seem totally unlike. No matter what kind of letters you write—sales, collection, or any of the others—you must always recognize the necessity of this "skeleton," and make sure it is there.

Many experts in the letter-world have devised figures of speech to describe this formula, skeleton, or whatever you may choose to call it. Even your grade-school teachers, when you were first being exposed to English Composition, had the formula in mind without a name for it, when they said that what you were trying to write must start with an Introduction, continue with a Body, and end with a Conclusion. They may have made plain to you the "why" of these three parts, but it is improbable that you understood then the psychological purpose of each part, or the connection of the whole procedure to influencing of human behavior.

The effectivenss of naming names. The names for the three steps in letter-construction which seem to have persisted the longest, and for that reason may be the best, were coined years ago by Dr. Frank W. Dignan. He was one of the pioneers who taught that letters should be simple, friendly, and natural, and was a master who helped to inspire this *Handbook*.

Dr. Dignan said that every letter needed first a "Star"—something to be said in the beginning that would quickly capture the attention of the readers. If this could be accomplished, he reasoned, then the readers would be willing to go on to find out what else the letter had to tell them. Without the Star, unless they had a personal reason for wanting to continue, the letter would be pushed aside and no matter how interesting the rest of it might be, it would never be read.

The second of the three parts, and the one which did the major job, Dr. Dignan called the "Chain"—a series of facts that would change the readers' casual attention to a real and sustained interest. This meant, of course, that each link—each fact—in the Chain had to be strong, for interest also can easily be interrupted, and when that happened, the readers would lose interest and the purpose of the letter would be lost.

Finally, said the master, a letter needs something to impel the desired action—a final urge that would make the readers send the check or buy the goods. This he called the "Hook." A Hook grabs and holds fast. The readers no longer can escape the issue. As they read through the Chain there was the danger that they might stop before the story had been told, but now they know what you want. They can still decide either way, but if the Hook is strong, they are inclined to say "Yes."

Take the following paragraph, put it on a small card and read it before you start your letter session—it is your key to success.

First, get the reader's favorable *attention*. Do it deliberately with an opening paragraph which is bright and brisk—the *Star*.

Second, follow quickly with a flow of facts, reasons, benefits, all selected and placed in the best order to transform attention to real *interest,* and finally to *desire*—that's the *Chain*.

Third, suggest *action*, and make it as easy as possible—the *Hook*.

Attention…interest…desire…action! There are the four psychological reactions in the mind of your readers, and they happen *in that order* as they take your letter from the envelope, begin to read, continue through the several paragraphs, and finally arrive at the last period. Obviously, it is a *progressive* process, each step paving the way for the next. Attention increases until it blends into interest. Interest deepens until desire is aroused. Desire, when strong and bold, leads to action. Hence, your letter is planned to stimulate those mental reactions, and each part does a *separate* job. If the Star does get favorable attention, nothing more should be expected of it. Developing interest and desire is the job of the Chain, but it does not reach for action. You still have a player on the bench with an eagle eye, and you use him to shoot the last winning basket. He is the Hook.

So you see the coordination between your efforts and the mental response of your readers. Cold, lukewarm, warm, hot—attention, interest, desire, action! The steps *must* be in that order.

Using the Star, the Chain, and the Hook. Although they deal with different situations, and have little affinity in either content or style, the following letters are all built on similar "skeletons." In each example, you can see how the writer has tried to lead the reader from

attention▸to interest▸to desire▸to ACTION.

The first is a sales letter mailed by the Pangborn Corporation, Hagerstown, Maryland.

IT'S THE LITTLE THINGS IN LIFE THAT COUNT

A cinder in the eye…

Gets more attention than a coal barge on the Ohio River. And a tiny pebble in his boot will cause a hunter more grief than a big bear.

Yes—it's the little things in life that count—that are important—that bring quickest reactions. (*End of the Star.*)

Take the blast cleaning division of a company, for instance. What could be more important than the operator's safety helmet, the air blast hose he uses, the nozzle, and the steel shot and grit? Yet these items are small—the "accessories" to the blast cleaning machines.

In June, July, and August, when the temperature reaches 92 degrees in the shade, what could be more important than the comfort, weight, and fresh air feed of your operator's blast helmet? Or the long wearing life of a *good* blast cleaning nozzle? Or the extra thickness of the rubber lining in the air blast hose?

Or the reliability of size, and the toughness and strength of the steel abrasives?

These are some of the little things in blast cleaning life that really count—that pays a tremendous return in satisfaction and production and profit, when they are *right*—and just as you want them. (*End of the Chain.*)

That's why we ask you to "come to Panghorn" now. For over forty years, we have specialized in providing the *best blast cleaning equipment and supplies*—and we will be happy to serve your needs now—promptly and carefully. Just drop us a note *today. (End of Hook.)*

The following letter was used to revive inactive customers. The Star supplies the theme for the whole message, and since the readers already knew about the products and services of the company, the Chain plays a minor role.

Dear _____,

I feel just like the man who dashed up to a hotel desk one evening—hat gone, and clothes all streaked with dirt.

"I want room 37," he shouted.

"But I can't give you room 37," said the clerk, after looking at the registry.

"I tell you, I want room 37," was the rising reply.

"But room 37 is taken. Mr. Johnson has the room." "Don't I know it? I'm Johnson. I just fell out of the window and I want to get back in again!" (*End of Star.*)

Yes, I feel something like that, and I want to get back in the room where you give out your orders for printing.

It's been a mighty long time since we've had the pleasure of serving you, Mr. Doe, and it certainly would make us happy to see your name back on our books.

Our equipment is modern and complete. We have both the facilities for doing good printing, and the will to give you the best of service. (*End of Chain.*)

There's a blotter enclosed with our telephone number on it in nice bold figures. Why not do unto us as you would unto Johnson. Give us a ring when you need your next printing job. (*End of Hook.*)

Collection letters, too, contain the Star, the Chain, and the Hook—first, something to put the readers in a good mood, then the reason why they should pay, and last, either a request for the money, or a statement of what will happen if they don't pay. The emphasis on the three steps varies considerably in collection letters—depending on the age of the unpaid account, and what the company intends to do about it.

Even short, routine letters can easily be fitted to the Star, the Chain, and the Hook, as is the following "reminder." The bill is not old, and there is no reason for a long letter. However, it starts gaily, states the necessary facts, and ends with a gentle request for action.

The Star to capture *attention*	The letter S is made up, as you know, of curved lines, but look what a straight and narrow path does for it...$.
The Chain to state the *facts*	And good old Uncle Sam will bring your check for $58, in payment of our January 31 invoice, straight to our door.
A Hook to ask *action*	Why not send it along, and then we'll all be happy.

There are only 57 words in the above letter, but some credit men would still insist it is far too long. They would ask one question—"Will you please send us your check for $58, in payment of your invoice of January 31?"—and call it a good job. Others, more reckless with their time, might add "Thank you," but nothing more. The difference in the effectiveness of the two letters could only be measured by *results*. If each of the two letters were sent to identical groups of 100 customers, which would pull the highest percentage of checks, and in the shortest time? Personally, we vote for the longer one, because it is the more interesting.

Relating length to difficulty. "Long enough to do the job," is how long a business letter should be (Section 2), but certainly the problem of holding reader-interest becomes more difficult as the length increases. No matter how many pages a letter may run, the Star and the Hook tend to remain short. The burden of keeping interest alive falls upon the Chain. Every point added is another link, and the letter-writers are ever reminded of the adage, "A chain is only as strong as it's weakest link." They hate to omit a point that might help their cause, and yet they know that when the readers are bored, the cause is lost.

Some of the best *longer letters* seen in business correspondence are those that seek to obtain magazine subscriptions. The writers probably wish they could do the job in a few short paragraphs, but they know that mention of one or two points about a magazine will not heat the water to a boil. They are forced to tell a longer story, even at the risk of letting the fire go out. That hazard, of course, they fight hard and cleverly to avoid.

The Hook impels action. Some letters in business ask for no reply, and are purely routine in nature—acknowledgments of orders, carriers of checks, expressions of goodwill, answers containing requested information, and others. Most of the important ones—those written to sell, or collect, or adjust—do reach out for a favorable response. No matter how interesting and convincing such a letter may be, you will agree it is wasted unless the desired reader-reaction is attained. Many letters, like race horses, get away from the post beautifully, lead most of the way, but falter coming down the stretch. The cause of their failure is the weakness of the Hook.

There is an old saying, often heard in sales meetings, that "the way to get an order is to *ask* for it." This thought neatly fits all business letters in which an attempt is made to influence human behavior. To get action, you must *ask* for it. Furthermore, you must ask with the implied confidence that a favorable reply is expected. The end of your letter is not the place for timidity or lack of faith. Assuming that you *believe* what has been said in the Chain, and that what you are asking is to the benefit of the reader, why should anything else but the desired reaction be expected?

The situation at the end of the letter is quite different from what it was at the beginning. First, you had to get the readers' attention. They were indifferent. You had to pull something out of the bag that would quicken their pulses, make them willing to continue. Then you presented fact after fact (link after link) to arouse interest and build desire. Hence, if the Chain was strong and convincing, the readers are thinking as you think when it comes time for the Hook. They are ready to go along with you, and do not resent being "told" as they would have earlier in the letter. Often, they stand on top of the fence, but need a little "push" to make them jump in the right direction. That's your job, and the "how" of it is to be explained later in this section.

Which key unlocks success? Sometimes, the question is asked, "Which is the most important in writing a successful business letter—the Star, the Chain, or the Hook?" Well, which does you the most good—breakfast, luncheon, or dinner? The difficulty in rating the comparative importance of the three parts is that each does a *separate* job, and each must be judged by a separate set of standards. If one of the three parts is poorly constructed, then the whole letter is a failure. The three parts team together to score the touchdown; one opens a hole in the line, one blocks, and the other carries the ball. *All* are important.

To be sure, the *first* job is to open the hole in the line. That's done by the Star. Unless the hole is there, the blocker and the ball-carrier are stopped. But if the blocker fails to get his man, or if the ball is fumbled, the play still fails. So you see why the Star, the Chain, and the Hook cannot be rated comparatively. Each part is an independent function that contributes to the success of the whole.

We have chosen the figure of speech used by Dr. Dignan as the one that best describes the three parts of a business letter. There are others with which you may wish to be familiar, however. One of the experts compares the writing of an effective letter to a successful flight in an airplane. First comes the take-off—getting the reader's attention. Once in the air, the pilot follows his course as swiftly as possible—the time when interest is quickened, and desire awakened. Finally, comes the landing, end of the flight—request for action. The analogy is good, because each of the three operations is quite different from the others—just as the three parts of a business letter are different in function, and in the skills needed to complete them.

In the Dartnell publication, *American Business,* the writing of a business letter was once compared to setting off a giant firecracker. The description was as follows:

The flame of the match is the opening paragraph. It gets the readers' attention—makes them want to see what is going to happen next. Once lit, the fuse should burn steadily. The flame is carried along to that exciting moment when it reaches the powder.

Well, so must the interest of the readers be carried along to the end of the letter. Back in the days when we were kids, you can remember the suspense of those few seconds while the fuse was burning. There must be the same suspense in a letter. A defective fuse means that the flame stops burning. Sometimes, in the middle of a letter, the readers' interest is also extinguished.

And finally, the cracker is fired. Bang! It is the climax of an interesting experience. But the crackers don't always explode. Some fizzle and sputter—others are complete duds. So it is with the closing paragraphs of a business letter. They either go off with a bang, or they fizzle. The readers are either sold, or they are lost.

Flame—fuse—fire! Those are the three steps in writing a business letter.

Another comparison, more applicable to sales letters than to the others, is the one of the five "Ps." The idea is that the writer of a business letter must in the following order—please, picture, prove, promise, and push. This conforms very well with the other comparisons.

Please........get **Attention**
Picture ⎫   **Interest**
Prove   ⎬ .... to
Promise⎭   **Desire**
Push.........**Action**

Okay! You have seen that there are three parts in a business letter; that all combine to do the job, but that each is quite different in function and the manner of execution. Naturally, your mind now turns to "how." *How* is attention gained? *How* are interest and desire developed? *How* is action impelled?

3. HOW TO GET READERS' ATTENTION

Value of the first impression. One of America's leading letter authorities, Frank H. Roy, told letter-writers: "A letter to the reader is a great deal like a conversation. A letter drags just like a conversation that is dull unless there is some spirit and life in the opening paragraph. The question with most of us is—'How can I liven up my starting paragraph? What appeal can I use that will be so interesting the reader wants to go on?' The first impression your reader gets from your letter is very important. You can open the door graciously or you can slam it in his face, and all you can say in your remaining paragraphs will be of little value."

Mr. Roy is absolutely on the beam. First impressions, by personal contact or by letter, are extremely important. You are introduced to a stranger, and before he utters a word, an impression has been formed which will tend to persist as long as you know him. You pull a letter out of an envelope, and before a line has been read, you have formed an impression of its general appearance which may influence, favorably or otherwise, your final reaction. Then, that first quick impression is strengthened or weakened by what you read in the first paragraph.

There are many factors that contribute to the appearance of a business letter—the quality of the paper, the design and printing of the letterhead, the way it is typed, the signature—but they will be explained in Section 4. What we want to know now is *in what ways, in the beginning of a letter, can attention be captured?*

"Get off to a flying start." This is the advice of William H. Butterfield, the author of numerous books on business correspondence. In one of them, he writes: "If all the preliminary steps have been handled effectively, the reader approaches the first sentence with at least a spark of casual interest. The opening sentence applies the fuel that either ignites the spark or smothers it. The application must be immediate, too, for the average reader allows a letter only a few seconds in which to prove its interest to him. This means that the lead-off sentence must 'click.'"

In the book, *Modern Business English,* by Babenroth and Parkhurst, we read: "The purpose of the first sentence is to win the reader's attention. Upon its power to interest him depends his willingness to read further....The attention-getter must be brief, attractive, and appropriate. Because a long paragraph is heavy and uninviting, the first paragraph should always be short."

People rarely throw a letter away without reading a word, *unless* they recognize the letterhead, guess what it is about, and from previous correspondence are utterly indifferent to the content. Usually there is an element of curiosity that forces them to take at least a quick peep at the opening paragraph. If they find something there of interest to them they are likely to continue. If not, another letter has died in infancy—another postage stamp has been used in vain. As Butterfield says, only a few seconds will decide what happens. You get them quick, or you get them not at all.

A poor place for "whiskers." In view of this necessity for a fast start—something to change casual attention to at least a small degree of interest—it must be apparent that "whiskers", as you saw them in Section 2, are strictly taboo in the Star of a business letter. Who would not yawn on reading, "Your kind favor of recent date has duly come to hand," or "With reference to your esteemed communication, we would wish to state"? Who would go a word further?

> "We have your favored epistle of the 21st instant, and have read same with considerable embarrassment."

> "I have just read your letter—and is my face red!"

Which of those two opening sentences would arouse the most interest? Which would be most likely to spur the reader on? If you have no special design for capturing interest, at least be sure to remember the slogan—"Relax...be natural...just talk."

Taking advantage of previous contacts. In those cases where you know your readers, or have had previous contacts with them by letter or in person, there may often be a mutual interest that tends to get the letter off to a good start. "It doesn't seem possible that two years have passed since we took time off at the Milwaukee convention to bowl together—but I still remember how you pinned my ears back." A sentence like that would be sure to get you off to a flying start, but it wouldn't have been so good had the readers' ears been pinned instead of yours. Nevertheless, any contact which has been pleasant is quite useful as an attention-winner.

> Your letters always make good reading—that last one was great!

> Hello, Mr. Gordon. Remember me? We met last week at the University Club, and you told me about your dogs, and all the ribbons they have won.

> Our mutual friend, George Davis, wants the three of us to play golf together soon. In the meantime, I need your opinion on a problem in our business.

> Last summer, when I camped near Nisswa, in Minnesota, your son was my guide on several fishing trips. I have never seen anyone cast as well as he does. One day we were talking about your business and mine. Bob thought we should get together.

To be sure, it requires no particular skill to start a letter, when the gate is already wide open. On the other hand, when these personal contacts are available, it would be foolish not to take advantage of them.

A tip from newspaper reporters. When you know your letter is going to an individual or group that should be interested in the contents—if time is taken to digest them—newspaper reporters have a plan which you could well afford to copy. In the first paragraph of most news stories an effort is made to summarize all that is to follow. This is called the "lead" and it contains the five "W's"—Who, What, When, Where, and Why. Thus, the lead is really a preview of the story, and the reader goes on to get the details.

> This morning at 9 o'clock (WHEN), crazed with jealousy (WHY), John Doe, local dentist (WHO), returned to his former home at 1010 West Broad Street (WHERE), and killed his ex-wife with a hatchet (WHAT).

That's newspaper style, and it can be very effective in starting certain kinds of business letters. Suppose the head of a retail organization wants to announce a sale in a letter to customers. She believes the values are outstanding, and that any reader is sure to be interested if she takes time to read about them. To assure that happy circumstance, it seems best to hand out the good news just as quickly as possible.

> Beginning next Monday morning, and as long as they last (WHEN), in order to clear out shelves for summer stock (WHY), the Carlson Company (WHO), at all of our six stores in

the Twin Cities (WHERE), will set all remaining winter shoes at exactly half-price (WHAT).

Details about the sale, that it was only for old customers who brought the letter with them, and something about the types and brands available, could follow later. The biggest inducement—Half-Price—can be counted on to arouse interest, especially in old customers who have been buying shoes at the Carlson stores and know their quality.

Use of a question. There is something about a question that seems to demand an answer. This fact is well known to speakers and teachers. When they see a yawn coming up, they simply ask the offender a question. In that way, he is quickly brought back to the world of reality. It's an excellent, excellent method of getting attention, and it works just as well for the letter-writer.

Of course, there are questions and questions, and like everything else pertaining to business letters, they need to be used with intelligence and discretion. Merely to ask a question, tell a story, or state an interesting fact, knowing there is little or no connection between what you are saying and the "meat" of the letter, is an insult to the reader. You are then merely a trickster, and even if you gain momentary attention, it will surely be lost when the reader discovers you have "taken him for a ride."

But when appropriate to the subject matter, in keeping with good taste, and not "wild and woolly," a question can capture immediate attention, and help to hold it as the meaning develops. Here are a few attention-getters that might induce you to keep on reading. They are all taken from successful business letters:

"People do the darndest things, don't they?"...Yes, you agree, but just what in particular was done this time?—I'll read to find out.

"Do you know that if you were to take one penny, and double your money each day for 30 days, you would then have more than $5 million?"...No, you probably didn't, but the thought is pleasant. You may even start figuring to see if it is true.

"Can you keep a secret for $500?"...You bet, but he had better not be kidding. I'll read on to find out.

"Can fish tell one color from another?"...Well, if not, why do fishermen carry all those colored flies and gadgets?

"Would you think a man could make a million dollars selling onion plants by mail?"...No, I wouldn't, but maybe this fellow had a secret for getting rich that I should know.

"Do you know what a dozen eggs, a quart of milk, or a loaf of bread will cost next month, next year, or in half a century?"...No, but if this fellow does, you would like to be cut in on the secret.

"Wouldn't you like, with our compliments, to have a new road map which tells you at a glance the best routes between thousands of cities in the United States and Canada?"...Yes, I would. I'll read on to find how to get one.

Probably all of those questions got favorable attention, but you couldn't tell whether or not there was an appropriate connection with what followed. Figure 3-2 depicts the whole of the letter which started with the rather vague but interesting question, "People do the darndest things, don't they?" Stop, and read that letter now.

All right, what's the verdict? Is there a logical tie-up between the Star and what followed? Well, yes, but you have to reason it out. The man shot another fellow for kissing his wife, although he had neglected that goodwill gesture for five years. In the same way, the two business executives were angry at the disloyal customers who also had been neglected. Really, you are supposed to think, neither wife nor customer was very much to blame. If you feel inclined to call the connection far-fetched, don't overlook the fact that the letter *did* do a successful job.

There was one question among those quoted which had a double pull—"Can fish tell one color from another?" Fishermen are great people to talk about their favorite sport, and in the hands of one of them, the letter would be sure to arouse interest.

How to use interesting facts. One of the most deep-seated traits of human nature is curiosity. It is often said that a reporter must have a nose for news. In our opinion, all people have it. They especially like to hear about facts they did not know before—unusual facts—anything to relieve what might otherwise be the monotony of everyday existence. If this were not so, why are the gossip columnists so popular? Why do people flock to the museums, read travel books about strange places, or go miles out of their way to see a natural phenomenon? Yes, we all have a bump of curiosity big as a mountain, if only it could be seen.

It is this thirst to be informed, to pry into things we do not understand, that has lifted mankind above the level of other animals. The cow doesn't seem to care what other cows are doing. She chews her cud complacently all day long and is no wiser at the end than at the beginning. The sow wallows in the mud, and is content to stay there. Human beings look about for new worlds to conquer. They are never quite so happy as when they contemplate something out of the ordinary,

Figure 3-2

October 3, ____

Dear _____ ,

People do the darndest things, don't they?

We know a man who hadn't even kissed his wife in five years...and then shot another man who did.

While this may seem strange, a few days ago I heard two business-men complaining because their customers weren't very loyal. You know, switching to competitors, changing distributors, cancelling long-standing supply orders. Yet, neither of those executives had ever thought to thank their customers for their business or even wish them "Happy Holidays!"

Maybe loyalty and friendship are supposed to work only one way. But I always felt that people couldn't expect to receive friend-ship unless they gave friendship.

That's why I feel that a warm, personal, whole-hearted message to customers at the Holidays is one of the best investments any firm can make. They're more susceptible to overtures of friendship; more inclined to take the wish for what it is...a sincere expres-sion of good will and appreciation.

In the last few years, our organization has helped hundreds of businesses plan and prepare seasonal greetings to customers -- greetings that stand out in the minds of people who receive them.

This year your customers will appreciate knowing that you look upon them as something more than just animated signs. Let us help you prepare a really outstanding Holiday message to them. We are ready to start any time that you give us the word. Just call or drop the enclosed card in the mail.

Cordially yours,

BURGESS-BECKWITH, INC., 426 South Sixth Street, Minneapolis, Minnesota

or when they reflect on some choice bit of information that later they can proudly pass on to others.

If you agree that the above is true, then you understand why letter-writers so often begin their messages with a few bizarre notes—statements of unusual or not commonly known facts to satisfy the instinctive craving for news which they know is shared by all their readers. Sometimes, the fact is offered plain and without sauce, sometimes it takes the form of a story, but, either way, the effect is to gain reader-interest. They may feel pleased to have had such a choice piece of information. They return the favor by going on with the letter. But, woe to the writer if the fact used as bait is *not* new to the readers, or *not* interesting. Then they are bored and their opinion of the writer promptly falls below zero.

Here are some factual Stars:

> You can do it in the rain without an umbrella—in a hovel, a palace, or under a weeping willow. It is the supreme luxury, enjoyed by the poor and the rich. It starts revolutions, wars, tyrannies, banks, businesses, explorations—and *stops* them.

> It is the beginning and end of civilization. They can abolish the movies, the stage, dinner parties, art galleries, musical instruments, and you'd still have it.

> It is God's greatest gift to mankind...

> (The next word gave away the secret. Are you curious?)

> "He is not worth his salt."

> Our word "salary" and its definitions—wages, pay, stipend, compensation—were derived from the Latin word, "salarium," which means "of salt." In the days of Caesar, the Roman soldiers received part of their pay in salt. Hence the saying—"He is not worth his salt."

> (Interesting. And how would you like this payment plan?)

> Sportsmen the world over will never forget Black Gold, winner of the Kentucky Derby way back in 1924. In size he was a peewee, but there never ran a thoroughbred with a bigger heart. And yet, it isn't his victory in the Derby that gave Black Gold immortality.

> Many years have passed since he went to the post for his last race, but strong men who were at the track that day are not ashamed of tears when they tell you what happened.

> Coming down the stretch...

> (To lovers of the Sport of Kings, this is an especially interesting Star, but any reader would continue to find out what happened "coming down the stretch.")

> In the South Sea Islands, deep-chested natives dive time after time, bringing up great handfuls of oysters in the hope that some of them may contain pearls.

> There is no way of telling which oysters *do* bear pearls, and the oysters themselves are strangely silent. A diver may work for

hours without acquiring more than the basis for a stew. But the law of averages dictates that every so often he *will* find a pearl...and the more oysters he brings up the more pearls he will find.

Your business, like ours, is based on that old law of averages. (A Star used for a letter stressing the importance of continuous contacts with possible buyers.)

Interesting facts to fit various letter-situations are valuable but hard to acquire on the spur of the moment. A fine plan is to keep a notebook in which facts for future possible use are recorded. Every business correspondent should have a scrapbook of such material. You never know when it will provide the inspiration for a good letter.

Interesting stories make good Stars. Most people are story-minded. You often see them huddled in the office, on the street, while a new one is being told. It is all right to take advantage of this human interest, *providing* your story is fresh, not "off-color," and that it is suited for the message of the rest of the letter. If the story does not comply with these requirements, the reader's reaction will be negative, and more harm than good is done by the letter.

For example, consider the following letter inviting dealers to attend a meeting:

Dear Dealer,

A farmer planned to surprise his wife. He bought a new suit of clothes, a new hat, and a new pair of shoes, carefully placing the bundle under the buggy seat.

On the way home he pulled up beside the river, tied his horse, took off his old clothes, and threw them in. After a good swim, he enthusiastically reached for his new togs. *They were gone.* Shaking his head, he climbed into his buggy and said, "Well, we will *surprise* her anyhow."

There will be a *worthwhile surprise* in store for you at the Springfield Dealers' School on November 19th and 20th. With any number of new ideas and new sales plans to create profits for you, the program will be of real growth calibre.

The return of the attached card *with your signature* will assure your firm representation at every session.

Was the story used in this letter a good one? Did it tie in with what followed? Well, "no" to both questions. The story is hopelessly dated and has no relevance in a modern business letter. Moreover, the only connection between it and the Chain is the far-fetched play on the word "surprise"; the farmer's wife would be surprised—so will the reader if he attends the meetings.

This one is somewhat better. It was used as a follow-up to prospects who had ignored previous letters. The author was Colman O'Shaughnessy.

Dear _____,

Val Briggens once stood in the heart of Times Square selling $5 bills for $2.98. They were real honest-to-goodness $5 bills—complete with Abe Lincoln's picture and the Treasury Secretary's signature. But there were no sales.

You can't fool New Yorkers.

And we haven't been able to fool you into inquiring about our low envelope prices.

Our prices on open-end catalog envelopes *are* unbelievably low. But we do make a lot of sales because a lot of people know we have our own paper mill, a large improved factory, and they know we have the lowest possible selling cost. In short, they know *why* our prices are the lowest they find anywhere.

In a letter like this, it's hard for me to back up my low price statement with specific figures—for I don't know what envelopes you use, or in what quantities you order.

But I would very much like to show you. If you'll just take samples of your present envelopes, mark them with the quantities you usually order, and put the whole business in the enclosed postage-paid envelope, I'll shoot you figures by return mail.

And when you see the high quality of our samples, you'll have the surprise of your envelope life.

This story has a clever Star. Furthermore, it illustrates a point made in the rest of the letter. The reader has been turning *his* back on a good thing, just as did the New Yorkers.

The technique of starting business letters to capture reader attention—a device *deliberately* used by the experts—is demonstrated in some more Stars taken from contacts with prospects.

The wife of the Consul to Timbuktu dressed for dinner in her silver-sequin gown...but it was all wasted on the desert air...no one there to admire her beauty...no dances to grace...just a thousand natives and one loving husband. She was all dressed up—and no place to go.

But your products will go places, and be *seen*, and be *eaten*. Dressed in X-ama coverings, they will sparkle appetizingly— and stay that way.

. . . . .

Remember the three sisters—Faith, Hope, and Charity?

Faith and Hope went off to the big city, and they came back wearing rings on their fingers and mink on their shoulders. But when little Charity met them at the station, *she* had a sable coat, three strings of pearls, six diamond bracelets, and money in the bank. For Charity began at home.

That's the best place to begin, if you want to make yourself a little present in savings. Right at home—on the things you buy and use every day.

. . . . .

Just suppose...

...as you are sitting at your desk now I came in to ask you for a position. And suppose I needed a shave, and my suit wasn't pressed, and my shoes were muddy—what chance would I have? I might be a world-beater, but I surely wouldn't *look* it.

First impressions are hard to change. They're often wrong but they last a long, long time.

What sort of first impression does your catalog make?

Today, Miss Susie Jones read one of your ads. And she liked it. She thought the pictures were terrific. The copy moved her, and she honestly wanted to buy your product.

But Susie couldn't buy. Susie is in the State Reform School.

Of course, there aren't many Susies. But she, as an individual, represents waste advertising circulation—which brings me to my little sales talk. We have an advertising medium which has *no* waste circulation.

. . . . .

She walked out of the store...

...and continued shopping along the street. She stopped to look at the window displays. After going into several stores, she took a bus home.

Who was she? I don't know her name, but she bought several items at one of the stores. They were put in a handsomely printed bag—and she carried this bag as she continued on her shopping tour.

How many people saw that bag, and...

All these Stars were intended to sell. If you are going to adapt or use them, consider their appropriateness for *your* readers. Without this analysis, the Star might not shine as well for you.

Because of their universal appeal, if they are interesting and to the point, Stars of the story type seem to work well, especially for sales letters. You can see how the following could, followed by a strong Chain, land the readers happily on the Hook.

> A certain gentleman, fishin' in a river down in Mississippi, pulled in his line and was surprised to find a minnow on the hook. Disappointed, he tugged a bottle of white mule from his pocket, took a pull, and then poured some on the tiny fish.
>
> Almost instantly, it flopped overboard, and his line went taut. After a 15-minute battle, he got it back in the boat again, and would you believe it, that minnow had a 5-pound bass by the throat.
>
> •   •   •   •   •
>
> Two frogs found themselves in a can of cream being shipped to the city. Both struggled to get out. One gave up, but the other kept on agitating in the hope he would find some means of escape. The end of the journey found one frog dead at the bottom of the can, the other sitting alive on a raft of butter.

Clever, and oh, so effective.

Good taste sells; bad, repels. Although there is little to be said for the "dignity of business," as contemplated by stiff-shirted businessmen who use "Whiskers" in their letters and who consider a smile in them very much out of place, yet discretion and good taste must still be used in the selection of the story.

There is a wide gap between that which is really funny, and that which only attempts to be. Be sure that you know the difference. If you are not *sure* about the use of a story, remember—"When in doubt, *don't.*"

The big question—"Does it FIT?" As you have already noted, it is folly to drag a story into a letter, merely in the hope of getting attention when you know it has little or no connection with the subject matter. The big question is—*does it fit?* For example, when Vic Knight was promoting the use of classified ads for a western newspaper, he sent the following letter to prospects. Not only is the opening story amusing, but it also fits in nicely with Mr. Knight's assertion that he does not intend to exaggerate what the ads will do.

> Dear _____,
>
> They tell the story of an Alaskan sourdough miner who struck a mountain of pay dirt, and came to Seattle to go on a spree.

He walked into a cafe and ordered $25 worth of bacon and eggs, bragging about how much Alaskans could eat.

The waiter, who was a proud Texan, turned up his nose and said, "Well then, you'll have to order more than that. We don't serve *half*-portions."

This just illustrates the point that no matter how strong a fellow goes, there's always someone who is ready to go him one better. So, if I *said* the *Review-Chronicle* classified ads were the best poultry medium on earth, somebody else would *say* they had a better way to advertise chicks, hatching eggs, or breeding stock.

"No, *talk* doesn't prove anything. But the fact is that rising sales figures show that the successful poultry men advertising in the *Review-Chronicle* are getting even more profits.

How about you?

If you are looking for more orders and greater profits, the *Review-Chronicle* classified ads will help you find them.

We don't serve *half*-portions in results here. If that seems like just talk, make us prove it. Try a few classified ads in the *Review-Chronicle,* and find out what they *can* and *will* do for you."

When a story really "fits" in a letter-drama, it doesn't appear in the first act, and then never again. Instead, as the letter progresses, you will find the point of the story reappearing, as it does in the last paragraph of the *Review-Chronicle* mailing.

Okay! What about this letter, used to sell used cars? Is the Star a good one? Does it "fit" what follows?

Dear _____,

The used car problem you hear so much about reminds me of the man 35 years old who married a child 5 years old. He was then seven times as old as his wife. Five years later he was 40 and she was 10—he was four times as old. Twenty years more, and he was 60, and she was 30—he was then only twice as old.

The question is, "How long would they have to live together to be the same age?"

Used car sales have been coming closer to new car sales right along. Already, they amount to more in number of cars sold, and it's not impossible that this year they will be almost the same in dollars and cents.

We've simply got to get rid of 100 used cars this month. If you'll help us solve our used car problem by buying any car in our stock, we'll give you a free auto license, and 50 gallons of gas.

You can drive any car you select for five days before the deal is closed.

Why not look them over today?

Did the story capture your attention? Doubtful. Is it in keeping with good taste? The thought of a middle-aged man marrying a girl of five is repugnant, even if only imaginary. Does the story fit? Is their a logical connection between point of story and point of the attempted sale? No!

All right! Now examine the next letter. It also starts with a story of the humorous type. Is this story acceptable? Is there continuity between it and what follows? These are some of the questions you must ask yourself when judging the effectiveness of a letter-introduction. It's better to form your own opinions than always to be told. Put this letter through the wringer. How does it come out?

When the lead-horse does most of the work. There is always the danger in using a story for the Star that the writer will become so engrossed in the telling that insufficient time is devoted to the subject matter which should pull most of the load. Then the letter becomes dwarf-like, with a huge head and very short legs.

Dear _____,

You may have known the salesman who met a fellow canvasser and said that he had just called at a house where a nudist party was in session.

"I knocked at the door and out came the nudist butler."

"How did you know it was the butler?" asked his friend.

"Well," was the reply, "I knew it wasn't the maid."

That same sort of an attitude is oftentimes an excellent way to judge a good Direct Mail Piece. Given even limited facts, the smart businessmen will make certain decisions.

It isn't just what you say but what you don't say that many times makes an impression in a sales letter.

An especially created Direct Mail Campaign can tell your story simply and effectively. It will do so, at less cost, than any other personalized method.

If you have a sales problem, large or small, in which we can be of assistance why not call us? We'll be happy to offer suggestions. No obligation, of course. Just phone (123) 456-7890. Thank you.

Yes, stories are good ammunition for the letter-writer. They *do* get attention. But when you use one, be sure it is *worth* the telling—that the point *does* fit the message you are trying to put across. One last reminder, when you are visualizing your readers be sure to keep their feelings and tastes in mind. If the story can even possibly offend or rankle them—don't use it. Again, when in doubt, *don't.*

The power of famous names. There is little doubt that most human beings are hero-worshippers. Thus the name of a great statesman, of a beloved author, or of any famous personage in history, may help to win reader-attention for a business letter. See how effective these famous Stars are!

Mark Twain at one time was a newspaper editor. One day a subscriber wrote that he had found a spider in the folds of his paper. He wanted to know if this was good or bad luck. Twain replied:

"Finding a spider in your paper was neither good luck nor bad luck for you. The spider was merely looking over our paper to see which merchant is not advertising, so that he can go to that store, spin a web across the door, and live a life of undisturbed peace afterward."

So it is today in...

Columbus never did know where he was going, and when he got back home, he didn't know where he had been. You'll remember, too, he made the trip on borrowed money.

Many men in business today don't seem to know...

"Allure" is the same today as it was when *Cleopatra,* the sexy lady of Egypt, kept the Nile boys in a romantic doze. Femininity is still the stock-in-trade of women.

Feminine products are...

Robert Bruce, hiding in a cave, watched a spider spinning and climbing a web. Time after time the web broke, but always the spider began spinning and climbing again, until at last he reached his goal.

Watching this determined fellow, Bruce got renewed courage, emerged from his hiding place, and started his successful "comeback" to the throne of Scotland. Perhaps he or one of his followers coined the old maxim: "If at first you don't succeed— try, try again."

You can see, therefore, how we can't simply sit back and...

There's a big difference between confidence and conceit. When *Babe Ruth,* in that World Series game, laughed at the crowd, and pointed to the exact place where he would hit the ball into the bleachers, maybe that was conceit in your book, but not in mine.

You see, Babe hit the ball just where he had said he would—for a home-run.

A lot of folks I know could stand...

Names have great power in proportion, of course, to how well they are known, and the particular individual's attention to them. It is hardly possible to think of *any* name that will win a favorable reception from *everybody*. Impossible as it may seem, there are people who know nothing of Babe Ruth, and as time passes, there will be more of them. In the imagination of many men, Cleopatra still holds her own with the beauties of Hollywood—and long after some of the latter have been forgotten, she will still live on. But to one who has never heard of "Cleo," the name of Sophie Glutz would mean as much.

Use of an interesting quotation. Many a business letter gets off to a flying start with a quotation that makes the readers nod their heads, or it may merely amuse them. Unlike stories, the statements of interesting people do not seem to suffer from repetition. The value of a story decreases rapidly with each telling, but this is not true of a proverb, a poem, or a striking utterance by some speaker or writer. If the quotation is one that the readers know and *like,* the use of it establishes a bond of mutual appreciation. Hence, in your scrapbook of possible material for business letters, reserve one section for quotations. You may be surprised how one of them will come to your rescue in a hurried moment.

Insurance agent Rupert L. Mills of Peoria, Illinois, used a Chinese proverb to good advantage in the following letter. Notice that toward the end he repeats the quotation for a better "fit."

Dear _____,

There's an old and bitingly truthful Chinese proverb that says:

"Man who sits with open mouth waits
long time for roast goose to fly in."

If we want the good things of life for ourselves or those who look to us for support, the only way to obtain those good things is to *get busy and go after them.*

Now, one of the eternally good things in life, but one that few enjoy, is peace of mind. There is no more comforting thought in the world than this: the complete certainty that when we grow too old to work, we can retire and enjoy a steady monthly income which is recession-proof, inflation-proof, and guaranteed to last as long as we do.

Just ponder that blessing a moment—the knowledge that when you want to quit work and spend your sunset years in leisurely independence, you will be able to do so—*without fail*. If you could have that positive assurance *now*, wouldn't it remove those aggravating worries that flit through your mind every time you indulge in some financial "splurge" with today's hard-earned dollars? With the *future* safe, the *present* is far, far sweeter to enjoy.

But unless you *do something* about those years ahead, you will be very much like the chap who "sits with open mouth waiting for roast goose to fly in." Future prosperity must be planned in advance. We cannot put off indefinitely the business of getting started on our program of personal independence. The longer we delay our start, the harder the task will be.

For your own peace of mind, I'm hoping that after reading this letter, you'll decide *today* to do something for your eventual comfort, while there's still time to do it properly and completely. This letterhead tells you how you can get in touch with me, so that I can show you the ideal, guaranteed way to financial security.

This letter has a homespun tone that carries considerable conviction. It seems that one man has placed a friendly hand on the shoulder of another. "Don't wait for the roast goose to fly in," he says. "Come, let me help you while there is still time."

Let's see that scrapbook we were talking about. A real estate salesman wants to write a letter about the joys of home ownership. Is there a quotation in your book that might help him? Here's one—"When you buy a *house* it becomes a *home*." And what about those others?

"HOME—a world of strife shut out, a world of love shut in."
"HOME—where Heaven touches earth."
"HOME—where we grumble the most and are treated the best."
"HOME—the only place on earth where the faults of humanity are hidden under the sweet mantle of charity."

Any one of those quotations, could be used as the Star in a letter to sell homes. The sentiment expressed in them is appropriate. It wouldn't do for selling locomotives, cement, or filing cabinets, but people are sentimental about owning their own homes. For this particular purpose, a serious quotation is much better than a humorous one. In fact, for *all* general letter-purposes that is likely to be true.

Use humorous quotations with caution. It is much easier to start a letter with something serious, of good attention value, and continue in the same tone, than to first make the reader laugh and then face the problem of bringing him back to the plane of sober contemplation. Besides, the situation becomes hopeless if the reader *doesn't* laugh.

There are all kinds of humor, and what strikes one person as funny may leave another person cold. For example, here's a letter which begins:

> You have heard what one big toe said to the other big toe— don't look now, but I think there's a couple of heels following me.

Is that funny? For some readers it could be a perfect opening—for others it might fail to even get a smile. Choose your audience.

The following are a little more subtle, and for that reason, not counting others, you would no doubt rate them higher in humorous appeal.

> "We know of no sadder case than that of the young man who joined the Navy to see the world, and then spent four years in a submarine."

> You often hear it said: "Watch your Ps and Qs." Well, I've got to watch them. That's my job. You see, I'm a proofreader.

> Mark Twain once said, "Always do right. This will gratify some people, and astonish the rest."

> "They licked their platters clean."

> I am a cook—a very good cook. I know this for two reasons: First, my taste tells me. Second, like the people in the fairy story, my customers "lick their platters clean." (From a letter applying for a job in a company cafeteria. The chef *got* it.)

Touching the "soft spot." Earlier in this section, we saw how various appeals may be used to influence reader-response. Moreover, we agreed that no two individuals are likely to react in exactly the same way to the same appeal. Thus, the letter-writer considers each reader as a separate problem, and seeks a point of vulnerability—a soft spot—that might be entirely different if he were writing to someone else.

When the soft spot is known, the logical place to begin talking about it is in the Star, otherwise you may play your ace too late—after the reader has pushed the letter aside. To list all of the special interests to which various individuals may give attention is impossible, but you know the wide range they cover—sports, one of the sciences, collectors' items, any of the arts, dogs, horses, amateur theatricals, gardening, and many others. Sometimes the weakness, if it can be called that, may be the love of gin-rummy, or fine food or wine, or even certain designer clothes, but whatever it may be, a reference to it can be the opening wedge for a successful letter. To be sure, this reference must be made in good taste, and not appear as a blatant attempt to curry favor, but when that requirement is met, there can be no wrong in talking to the reader about the one thing in which there is an interest. And thus many a strong Star is developed. As each new piece of information is learned about a customer, add another reference for a future Star. In a very short time, you will have a wealth of these gems to draw upon. Also, there are many fine books on the market to help you find just that right quote or story.

Don't tip your hand too soon. Remember that the purpose of the Star—the *one thing* it is supposed to do—is to capture favorable *attention*. This is a separate job, quite apart from what must be accomplished later. It is a Star when the reader is sufficiently interested to continue, but should not come so soon in the letter that the reader is expected to take immediate action. That comes later, when the reasons to *increase* interest have been offered in the Chain. By then, the readers should be ready for action, but seldom before.

With these facts in mind, you can realize the danger of exposing the real purpose of the letter before interest has been deepened, or desire created. This is especially true when readers are asked to buy something they had no thought of buying, or to give their time to a cause in which they have had no previous interest. By letting the cat out of the bag too quickly, readers are put on guard and become much harder to persuade. They know what you want, and you have taken the chances that they will either stop, or continue in a negative mood.

For example, a publisher begins a letter in the following very dull and revealing way:

Announcing the Publication of _____'s

AN INTRODUCTION TO PUBLIC SPEAKING

Here is an eminently practical text which includes quantities of new information *not* contained in any other book.

In the very first sentence, the purpose of the letter is made known. If directed only to a list of people who buy everything published about public speaking, perhaps no harm has been done. But everyone else would know immediately that they are about to be asked to buy a book, and they know that *before* anything has been said to make them *want* the book. The letter defies the principle of letter carpentry which says that the reader must be led *progressively* from *attention* to *interest* to *desire* to *action,* and the steps must not be taken in any other order.

More early cats. Many, many business letters are wasted because they suggest action before readers are *prepared* for it—they go into the wastebasket for this one reason, although in other respects the proposition may be inviting and the arguments convincing. The letters from which the following Stars were taken are not at all bad when the whole of them is viewed, but the cat came out of the bag too early. The readers were jolted to action before they had read all the fine reasons which might have appealed to them had they only been approached less abruptly.

> When you buy the policy I am going to tell you about, your worries about retirement are "gone with the wind."

> (Oh-oh—trying to sell insurance! My good friend, Mr. Waste-paper Basket, here's something for you.)

> May I suggest to you the convenience of a standing order for our country sausage and hickory-smoked bacon?

> (Thanks for the suggestion, but no sale. It costs too much to buy food by mail.)

> May we send you, at our risk and expense, a get-acquainted shipment of the most distinctive and most delicious food products that ever graced your table?

> ("At our risk and expense"—some catch in that. What's he talking about anyway—"food products" take in a lot of territory. No, my friend, you may *not* send me.)

Remember this point about the Star—*don't let the cat out of the bag too soon.* It is a costly mistake often made by letter-writers, but now you know better. Be sure to avoid this trap. Keep the readers guessing. Curiosity breeds interest. Get them ready for action before you ask for it.

Three steps to starting routine letters. Even though the job is simple, as when no reply is expected or no particular problem involved, it is still worthwhile to start a routine letter in a natural and interesting manner. This tends to be accomplished when the writer forgets any false ideas about the "dignity of business," and just sits down to *talk* to the reader as if they were both in the same room. However, there are three little tricks of the trade, used by the best letter-carpenters, and you should know them.

First. Make the opening sentence short—just as your greeting would be if you met a friend on the street. If the previous correspondence has been pleasant, and you feel that you know the writer in a personal way, you can go so far as to say, "Hello, Mr. Gordon"..."Good morning, Mr. Gordon"...or any other natural thing you might use in speech. Even if the relationship is somewhat formal, or there have been no previous letters, you can still start "free and easy" with such sentences as,

"You are right, Mrs. Jones."
"Thank you for writing about the bill, Mr. Doe."
"I am sorry, Mr. Black, that we let you down."
"Yes, indeed, Mr. Barton, you can have the map."
"Good news for you, Mr. Sickle!"
"Don't worry, Mrs. Fisher, we'll exchange the lamp."

The trick is to just start talking, as if the letter you are answering had been spoken, and you are now taking your turn in the conversation. This does away with the foolish practice, so often encountered in business letters, of *rehashing* what the other party has said before getting down to the reply. Why say to Mrs. Fisher, "We have received your letter of the 15th, in which you inform us that the lamp recently shipped to you was damaged in transit"? What a lot of nonsense that would be. Mrs. Fisher *knows* that you received her letter or else you could not be answering it. She does not care on what date it was written. She *knows* the lamp was damaged in transit or someplace. What she wants you to tell her is that the lamp will be exchanged for a new one.

There is not the slightest reason for a preface in a routine business reply letter. Don't waste any time telling *what* you are going to say, or referring to what the other fellow has already *said*. Just *begin*.

Dear ——————,

Your letter of March 8th, relative to John Doe's application for employment, shall now claim my attention.

From my personal knowledge of this young man, I am inclined to believe he will be fully competent if given a job within the limits of his capacity.

A pretty kettle of fish, isn't it? Why didn't the person who wrote the letter omit the first paragraph, and simply say, "From what I know about John Doe, I think he will make good in your company"?

Second. Personalize the opening sentence of a routine letter by including, when possible, the name of the reader. This is perfectly all right even for the first letter-contact. There is no discourtesy in the use of a person's name—in fact, it is more of a compliment. People rather like to hear their names pronounced, or to see them in print. It makes them feel important, and the use of the name in the opening sentence seems to put the letter on a conversational basis.

With this tip, there must go one caution: Do not *overdo* the practice. In a short letter of two or three paragraphs, one use of the reader's name is sufficient. In a longer letter, of one full page or more, the name might appear two or three times—but not any more. When overdone, the letter sounds flippant and contrived.

There are two main changes in terms of address in business correspondence. With the advent of more women working, the use of *Ms.* became the proper form for writing to a female whose marital status was unknown. Much care should be taken, in fact, when addressing blind letters, not to make an inadvertent sexist distinction. "Dear Sir," or "Dear Gentlemen," can easily offend the potential female customer. Rather, the modern approach is to use the position in the salutation— "Dear Plant Manager,"... "Dear Credit Officer,"... "Dear Buyer."

The second major break with tradition is the use of the reader's first name within the letter. A long-time association, a follow-up to a conversation or meeting, or an invitation to a business event are all now seen as perfectly appropriate situations for the first name usage. However, several words of caution. If in all previous communications, your reader has never permitted such familiarity, *do not* use it in a letter. Secondly, never use a reader's first name in the first written contact. To do so smacks not of friendliness but of off-handed casualness and flippancy. Wait—mutual respect will make this personal gesture more valid in the future. Finally, unless it is the policy of your company, or unless it has been specifically requested, never use a first name in a letter to a superior. While it is important to make warm, personal contact with your readers, respect for position and authority are still parts of acceptable business courtesy.

Third. Use a positive and pleasant word or phrase to launch this first sentence. Go as far as you possibly can in *agreeing* with what the reader has said in his letter to you. This is especially important in adjustment letters. Keep the bad news out of the first paragraph. Begin with

> Right you are, Mr. Underwood,
> Your letter is appreciated, Mrs. Garner,
> Yes, Mrs. Jones, we understand perfectly,
> Thanks a lot, John,
> You are very patient, Mrs. Gardner,
> You can count on us, Mary,
> Everything is okay, Mr. Bates,

or any other appropriate statement that may start a reaction of goodwill in the reader's mind. To be sure, if a request is to be refused later on, the opening sentence can hardly be, "You are absolutely right, Doctor Long," but the sting could be lessened with, "You have been so frank and fair in giving us your point of view, Doctor Long, that we are encouraged to put our cards face-up on the table in the same friendly spirit."

Use these three simple devices to personalize the first paragraphs of your own routine letters. You will be surprised and happy to see how they help to smooth the rough spots in human relations, and give what you write a warmth which may have been lacking.

So much for the more common ways of getting attention at the start of a business letter—the points of the Star. Here they are in final review:

1. Mention a previous contact
2. Use the "S.W. Paragraph Newspaper" Approach
3. Begin with a question
4. Relate an interesting fact
5. Share a good story
6. Refer to a famous person
7. Use a pertinent quotation
8. Touch a "soft spot"
9. Use the reader's name

There remains one more method—both spectacular—and effective—which deserves separate consideration. We will now see what it is.

4. GAINING ATTENTION WITH SHOWMANSHIP

Dramatizing the business letter. Somebody once said that all the world loves a parade. This love for anything out of the groove may simply be the rebellion of the human race against the monotony of everyday existence. At least, there can be no doubt that the average person likes a "show" and anything out of the ordinary quickly gets attention. This fact is well recognized in sales and advertising. This is not said in a spirit of criticism, for if one makes a living by influencing human behavior, then one must be aware of those things which trigger positive responses in prospects and customers.

Certainly, we know that a dramatized business letter, if the idea is really clever and interesting, may often out-pull one of the more conventional kinds. This has been proven many times by actual test and comparison, so that no matter what our personal opinion may be, we cannot afford to overlook or scorn a device that has made many a letter an outstanding producer. Like every other idea or method used in business correspondence, the so-called "stunt" letter can be very sweet or very sour, depending on the quality of the idea and how deftly it is carried out. While there may be some risks, when the idea clicks it is very impressive. The main difficulty is arriving at just the right dramatic impact so that your letter achieves the results you expect—dramatically.

But perhaps you are asking—"What *is* a dramatized letter?" Well, it is one in which an idea or thought is given *special prominence* by some illustrative or mechanical device that would not be used in the ordinary business letter typed in the usual way on the usual company letterhead.

No relation between cost and effectiveness. There is no end to the forms the special treatment may take in a dramatized letter. The idea may be quite simple and inexpensive, or it may be very elaborate and costly. Curiously enough, there seems to be no relationship between cost and effectiveness, as you might mail a dozen sales or collection letters, one each month for a year, and discover that the one which cost the least out-pulled all the others. The premium depends on the *originality* of the "stunt" used and on how aptly it fits the main purpose of the letter, *not* on what a big show it may make.

Figures 3-3 and 3-4 are dramatized letters once used by The Rylander Company of Chicago. One is so simple that practically no extra expense was involved. (See Figure 3-3.) The other gets away from

Figure 3-3

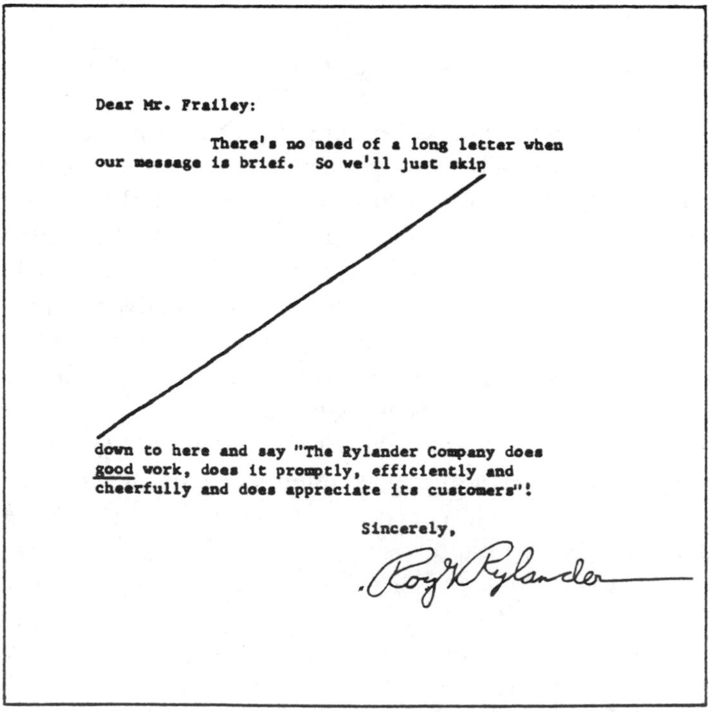

Dear Mr. Frailey:

There's no need of a long letter when our message is brief. So we'll just skip

down to here and say "The Rylander Company does good work, does it promptly, efficiently and cheerfully and does appreciate its customers"!

Sincerely,

Roy K Rylander

the regular company letterhead, and of course the postage stamp in the man's hand was an added cost. (See Figure 3-4.)

Figure 3-4

The other day a close friend of ours asked, "Say, just what does your organization do? You say your business is 'mail advertising service' : Just what does that mean?"

"That", we answered, "is a rather difficult question. So many steps are involved in the handling of direct mail, and our service is so closely tailored to the needs of each individual customer that there is almost no limit to the things we do.

"When a firm like yours, for example, needs help in developing more business by mail -- that's when we step into the picture.

"Often we supply names and addresses of likely prospects -- suggest ideas for letters or mailing pieces, compose the copy -- and draft layouts for presenting the sales story. We produce the finished material by any one of several processes ... multigraph, mimeograph, planograph or letter press.

"We serve many customers on a strictly mechanical production basis. Printinq is a big department with us, and our modern equipment helps us do unusually fine work, at a minimum of time and cost. We produce form letters that look freshly typed. We do typing of all kinds and handle mailings, small and large, with economy and dispatch.

"We even lick the stamps!

"When you give us an order, you use the particular part of our high- ly skilled organization and modern machinery that your job requires. And you pay only for the time spent on your job. That makes for economy and efficiency and workmanship of high quality."

That is the information we gave our friend ... and we're passing it on to you with the thought that you may not have known of the many ser- vices we render.

I hope you will find many ways in which we can serve you throughout the coming months. Call us. Our number is Franklin 5954.

Sincerely yours, .

Both of these Rylander letters used two-color printing, although this does not show in the reproduction. The second color was red—always strong in attracting attention. Only the line was red in the first letter; in the second, all parts were red except the typing. Neither could be called elaborate, but both were successful as business-builders.

Use of "gadget" to illustrate point. Many of the dramatized letters that you encounter are made more expensive by the addition of some object, usually in miniature, which is used to gain extra attention. This attention-pull decreases, however, with repetition of the idea. The first time you received a Christmas letter with a miniature Santa Claus attached, it was an interesting experience. But if by now, as with most people, you have had a dozen or more Christmas letters with similar attachments, you are more chilled than thrilled.

Some of these gadgets are so clumsily conceived and so far removed from the point of the letter that they fail the first, and all other times, to make a favorable impression. Let me give you a few examples. Although the gadgets cannot be attached to the pages of this *Handbook*, a description may suffice.

> The first is a letter with the caption, "You wouldn't drive a nail with a shovel." Then the first sentence reads, "It's the wrong tool for that kind of work—and efficiency demands the use of the right tool for each job."

> There are two attachments stuck to the paper with Scotch tape. How the letter got through the Post Office is a mystery. One of the attachments, as you would guess, is a nail about 2 inches long. The other is a miniature shovel about 4 inches long. The general effect of the idea is preposterous, and after the first sentence there is no more mention of the shovel or nail.

> Difficult to mail, clumsy to look at, no punch, no pull—another letter-idea gone wrong!

> "Cigars are on us—we've a new addition to our family," begins the second example. Stuck to the letter is a cigar, a match, and a piece of sandpaper. Everything so convenient!

> But, Oh, *what* a cigar! An anemic-looking, thin slab of tobacco, wrapped in cellophane.

> A paragraph in the third letter reads: "People aren't buying buggies any more—nor bustles—nor petticoats—nor corsets."

> The message in the letter is good. It urges the reader to forget old-time methods, and sell the modern way.

> But my, my—what an attachment!

At the top of the page are two rows of punched holes, and woven criss-cross in them is a corset string. The two ends, dangling out, are at least 5 feet long—the whole string must be about 5 yards.

It seems to be a form letter, and no doubt a considerable number were mailed. To punch the holes and weave in the corset string must have been quite a job. And what would be the effect on the reader who pulled the letter and the long string from the envelope?

Good? That's very doubtful. Corset strings and business somehow don't seem to mix.

A checklist for gadgets. When you feel the impulse to dramatize a letter, and your idea includes an attachment to help catch the fancy of your reader, ask yourself these questions: (1) Will the reader be favorably impressed by what I am going to do, or will he make fun of it?...(2) Is the dramatization just an attention-winner, or does it also give emphasis to the main purpose of my letter?...(3) Is the idea original with me, or have I borrowed one with which the reader might already be familiar?...(4) Is the idea practical, so that it can be prepared easily at not too great a cost, or is my enthusiasm overshadowing my good judgment of results logically to be expected?...(5) Can it be mailed?

If your dramatized letter-idea can survive those questions, then no doubt it is a good one. Go ahead—use it. It pays to get off the old path now and then, and when you do, you may be pleasantly surprised to find how green the grass is.

Good letter-carpenters never place so much dependence on a dramatic idea that they neglect the importance of the copy. In these stunt letters, the body text could stand alone if the showmanship were omitted. It is seldom intended that the dramatization should carry the whole load, or even the largest part of it. Instead, it is present to help win attention, to induce a smile or nod, and thus make the body of the letter do a better job.

Importance of dramatization varies. Since each letter problem is distinct from all others, it is impossible to set forth any fixed rules for dramatization, or to consider the importance of showmanship as anything but relative. If the letter answers the questions asked a moment ago, it will quite likely succeed, but the dramatization may vary from being only an attention-getter, consistent with the general purpose, to being the central idea around which all of the copy revolves. Its importance rates high in some letters, but in the following sales message, prepared by Advertising Manager D. M. Sweet for *Successful Farming,* the little bell only illustrates the story.

Dear _____,

Advertising, in one form or another, is a necessity for the life of business, not for just a month or a year—but always.

One day, a salesman seeking advertising for a local paper called on the village grocer. He was surprised when the gray-haired proprietor said, "Nothing doing. I've been established 50 years, and I've never advertised."

"What is that building on the hill?" asked the salesman.
"The village church," said the grocer.
"Been there long?" asked the salesman.
"About 200 years."
"Well, they still ring the bell!"

You must keep "ringing the bell" at customers' doors year in and year out. And by no means forget that *farmers* represent a vast, moneyed market that can bring you rich returns....But it takes a *farm* publication to reach the farm market and it takes *successful farming* to reach *quality* farmers. *Successful farming* concentrates more of its circulation in the world's richest farming region—the "Heart"—than does any other farm magazine. That is where farmers are worth two for *one!*

You will agree that in Mr. Sweet's letter the miniature bell had a small role to play. But when the curtain went up, the bell did help to get reader attention, and later it added a little reality to the story of the church-bell. Just how much—if at all—the miniature bell contributed to the *pull* of the letter, nobody could say.

Figure 3-5

JUST A REMINDER
YOUR TV SERVICE
CONTRACT WILL SOON
EXPIRE—DON'T LET IT—

Nevertheless, it must be reasonable to assume that any illustrative idea in keeping with the theme of the letter, and helping to capture that important first-second attention, must be accorded some credit when the votes are counted.

You see in the letter with the bell, the "gadget" only illustrates something said in the copy. The text, without the bell, would be understood just as clearly by the readers.

Consider, also, the beginning of a dealer's letter for Hart Schaffner & Marx. The story used for the Star would stand alone, but the horseshoe (a miniature one attached to the page) commands instant attention, and thus helps the effectiveness of the copy.

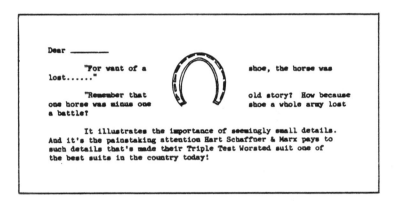

Using bold type, pictures, and color. As you have seen, there are several methods for introducing the luster of Stars to your letters. Here's another eye-catching technique. Look at the illustration in Figure 3-5. With that Star to lead off, you can just bet the Chain will tell the reader the advantages of *instant* renewal of the service contract. Using oversized type, or illustration, or even an actual reproduced photograph, are all Stars not to be overlooked.

When you combine several of these Star Methods, the possibilities for dramatizing your business letters become endless. Consider how dramatic certain sweepstakes promotions have been when the letters for entry have included a celebrity (The Power of Famous Names—Section 3) *and* his or her picture.

With the advent of color printing and computer-assisted graphics, more color is appearing in business correspondence. One must be cautious, however, not to turn a serious letter into a neon sign. But, used properly, in sales or promotionals, the effect can be dramatic and effective, indeed."

Letters where the "stunt" plays first fiddle. There are many ways to classify dramatized letters. One is to place them in two groups— letters similar to the above where the dramatization merely increases interest, and those in which it is woven into the copy, so that it could not possibly be omitted. For the second type, we may begin with a clever idea used by the circulation editor of *Life* magazine. The letter is dated March 4, and was typed on the back of the March 7th issue cover. The copy explains itself.

> I'm sorry—
>
> Sorry that I can't send you more than the cover of *Life* (because your subscription has expired)...
>
> Sorry that you are going to miss seeing all the exciting, important news stories pictured in this issue...
>
> But let me send you *all* of *Life*.
>
> I will gladly pay the postage on the enclosed renewal card to save your missing another issue of *Life*.
>
> Sign the card and mail it today—and I will re-enter your subscription without a break.

You can imagine the reaction of the subscribers. Because the "joke's on them" they might smile and hasten to sign the card. To be sure, there is also the chance they might not be the kind who enjoys a joke on somebody else, so that the unusual approach would anger rather than please them, but I doubt it. The important question is, would that dramatized letter, mailed to a large number of delinquent subscribers, bring more of them back than would a more conventional reminder? Yes, absolutely. It did so. However, good as the idea may be, it cannot continue to pull forever. Ideas lose power as they are copied, until eventually they are worthless.

Several years ago a most unusual eye-catcher was sent by a smart boutique to announce their summer swim fashions. You can guess the smiles and the sales that it brought.

The "gadget" used as the theme of the letter is a miniature pair of scissors attached to the page with a narrow strip of Scotch tape. The blades are slightly open, and are supposed to suggest two legs. The comparison is continued by the two round handles, which in a vague way complete the figure. The letter is shown in Figure 3-6.

Enclosing a stamp to increase the chance of a reply is one of the oldest devices, still going strong, in the letter-world. That the pull is strengthened, no one can doubt it. It doesn't seem honest to keep a stamp, so most people feel an obligation to do something with it. The following letter, used by *Time* magazine, dramatizes the use of the stamp and makes it play the leading role.

Figure 3-6

```
Dear _____,

Presenting                          Inspired by
the newest                          Laurender Fabrics
"SCISSORS"                          of the Islands,
SILHOUETTE                          Freeport, Bahamas


You'll cut a smashing figure this summer.  Chest out...tummy in...
silky wrap-arounds wide and flowing!  You'll find your silhouette
will look for all the world like a "scissors."

To help you achieve the "Scissors" silhouette, Laurender Fabrics of
the Islands has conceived some of the most devastating designs. So
clever are they that they'll sculpt your shape comfortably and in-
stantly.  (And you thought all your friends at the beach worked out
all year!)

This year's collection of Laurender Fabrics of the Islands swimwear
is now available for your inspection.  We've priced them so they
won't mangle your bank account.  So come in and pick out the ones
that will help you cut that ravishing swath at poolside.
```

Dear New Subscriber:

"Jones of Binghamton—he pays the freight."

Thus, some 50 years ago, proclaimed Jones' Scale Works at Binghamton, New York, to its prospective customers.

We know you want to pay the enclosed bill promptly—that you like to keep small bills off your desk and out of your morning's mail.

So here is the freight—prepaid—in anticipation of your willingness to mail your remittance today.

With thanks for your promptness and for your interest in *time*.

Even a couple of aspirin tablets can be made the heroes of a sale as shown by this letter from the files. The brand used was Bayer's, one of the advertised brands. The tablets were enclosed in a neatly imprinted, transparent envelope that seemed to have been furnished by the Bayer Company. Because of their prestige and utility value they could not fail to arouse favorable and quick attention. The letter was sent to credit managers by The Credit Clearing House Adjustment Corporation.

Dear _____,

'Tis widely advertised that should you be smitten with a headache, aspirins will relieve it. Two are enclosed.

But should that headache be the result of trouble with collections, then I unreservedly recommend our service—especially if you want to clear any old claims, hanging over from previous years.

For best results on "headache accounts," I prescribe the following treatment: At the very first symptom of an account turning sour, *get in touch with us*—our remedy consists of mail and personal persuasion. It's potent!

First, we send an ingenious *prestige or free demand letter*—it commands respect—and usually collects a substantial number of claims right off. If your account is reluctant, we send a trained expert—an adjuster skilled in winning respect, adroit in selling the idea of honoring obligations, practiced in the art of holding goodwill.

You'll find our service penetrating the most inaccessible places, liquidating the most complex situations, freeing your frozen accounts.

Yes, for "headaches," Bayer and Credit Clearing each is pre-eminent in its field. The acid test of experience proves it. We've never lost a patient.

Have your bookkeeper draw up a list of "Past Dues" for us. If we don't collect, you don't pay. If our *prestige or free demand letter* collects, you don't pay. If we collect with Personal Service, the fee's moderate.

You've everything to *win*—nothing to lose. Just *try us*.

The copy in that letter is above average—it shows the hand of a skilled "carpenter." The aspirin tablets were cleverly used to gain attention and were woven throughout the fabric of thought. The letter did a good job.

Using showmanship to sample the product. Among the very best of the dramatized letters used in business are those that manage to sample the company product, or some part of it. As all salesmen know, there is no better way to arouse interest in prospects than to get the thing being sold *in their hands*. The *feel* of an object creates a sense of possession. This is just plain sales psychology, which can sometimes be applied in a written contact as effectively as in an oral one.

In a sales letter used by the Badger Paper Mills in Wisconsin, attention is called to a sizeable little piece of spruce, enclosed in a glassine bag attached to the top of the page. "The paper on which this letter is written was once a chip like the one above. It is a piece of 100% American Northern Spruce, from which our Ta-Non-Ka Bond is made. The exclusive use of spruce fiber is one reason for Ta-Non-Ka's greater strength, higher white, and..."

Thus, the readers have for their inspection, not only a sample of the Bond being sold, but also a piece of the wood from which it is made. This is a simple but interesting demonstration, and certain to help the letter do its job.

Some companies are more favored than others in their ability to let a letter carry a sample of their craftsmanship. For example, a commercial photographer should have no problem in using a letter, containing a photograph, that will illustrate excellent quality photography. However, the subject of the photograph should not be so overpowering that the reader concentrates on the picture and forgets the letter. Even the passage of time cannot dim the classic effectiveness of this gem.

A masterpiece of "sampling." If letters were rated like Hollywood actors, one of the "Oscars" would surely have been awarded to the oriental rug sales presentation prepared by Norman Focht for importer Joseph M. Eways of Reading, Pennsylvania. In fact, if *any* letter *could* be called perfect, this one would closely approach that distinction. (See Figure 3-7.)

To this letter are clipped two pieces of yarn—one rust and one blue. As the letter tells you, the rust sample is machine-spun, but yarn like the blue is spun by hand "in far off Persia." From this simple explanation, the whole letter develops, and at the end the reader emerges with a most interesting conception of the value of oriental rugs. Can't you imagine the reader feeling the two samples, and seeing for himself how much stronger the one is than the other? This is *salesmanship* at its best, and yet the idea back of the dramatization is so simple and inexpensive that it puts to shame some of the other far more elaborate attempts that you see in the letters that cross your desk.

Another good job of sampling is that used by Montgomery Ward in a letter sent out by store managers, presumably to customers who had previously purchased fishing equipment. Clipped to the page was a card that carried short pieces of two of the fishing lines sold by the company. Again, we see a very simple idea, although it must have been very interesting to those who got the letter. The copy is good too.

Figure 3-7

Joseph M. Eways
IMPORTER OF ORIENTAL RUGS AND CARPETS
213 North Fifth St. Reading, Pa.

Dear Mr. Jones:

Just two little pieces of yarn -- but what an important story they tell you.

Pull the ends of the rust yarn and notice how the strands separate and fray easily. Now pull the blue yarn and notice the difference -- it will not fray!

The rust yarn was spun by machine. The blue yarn was spun by hand in far off Persia.

Genuine oriental rugs are made only with the hand spun yarn. The wool for this yarn comes from the backs of sheep which graze most of the year in the warm, sunny pastures of the lands across the sea. It is the extra strength of this wool and the skill of the hand weaver which enables the genuine oriental rug to hold its beauty for centuries.

I would like you to see the exceptional oriental rug in my shop which was hand-woven so firmly that there are as many as 400 knots to the square inch, compared to 200 knots in the average oriental rug.

I would like to show you some of the genuine Orientals which have journeyed thousands of miles across oceans and continents to reach my shop from far off lands. I can promise you one of the most pleasant half hours you have ever enjoyed, just "talking rugs" ... telling you some of the truly romantic legends behind these rugs and showing you the magnificent pieces which will add charm, distinction and character to your home.

Of course, you will not be under the slightest obligation. Either stop at the store the next time you are down town or telephone 2-3446 for an evening appointment if you wish.

Sincerely yours,

Joseph M. Eways
Joseph M. Eways

JME:LK

RUGS REPAIRED · CLEANED · STORED · PHONE 2-3446

Hello there, Sportsmen,

You have heard fish stories a-plenty—but just absorb this little bit of news I'm *casting* your way, and ten to one you will find fishing a greater pleasure than ever.

Guess I've a *reel* yearning for that "Wonderland" of rod and line—and sky and stream that's always fine. Maybe, it is simply that Ol' Spring is in the air.

But honestly, what's more thrilling than to land one of those glistening, nimble trout or scrappy bass? Well, fishermen, you know that high-grade tackle will help do this, and that's why I'm a little bit afraid of my own tackle. Noticed the other day my leaders were all stiff and dried out—a few of my lines beyond repair! Incidentally, how do you like these sample casting and fly lines?

Oh, yes, another thing—our sporting goods sales personnel and I have just looked over a new shipment of fishing tackle that we have on display. No kidding, it really looks good to me. Why not drop in some day this week and look it over? And if you don't see what you want in our display, I'll personally see that you get it direct from the manufacturer, at Ward's usual low prices.

Don't forget—the fishing season will be in full swing soon, and you'll be needing new tackle.

Other eye-openers in the Frailey collection. Of course, you realize the impossibility of hanging shark's teeth, wedding rings, or four-leaf clovers on the pages of a *Handbook*. Many dramatized letter-ideas simply defy reproduction in book form. However, here are a few brief descriptions of "gadget" letters that may stir your imagination:

"THE POWER OF A SHARK"...in big red letters; that is the caption of a letter used by the Wizard Company in St. Louis. Above the title is fastened a *real* shark's tooth. The letter begins:

The power of a shark is in its teeth. Nature keeps them sharp as you will find after examining the tooth attached. With teeth like this, a shark can sever a man's arm with one bite and a twist. The power of a shoe sale, too, is in the "teeth" that are put in it. The "teeth" are the "plus" that make the sale stick. Take Trimfoot—it's a natural "plus"...

"CONSIDER THE 'PEEP,' MR. JONES"...so starts a letter mailed by The Men's Shop in West Chester, Pennsylvania. Attached is a yellow cotton baby chick. The letter continues:

Along about this time each year, we see lots of pictures of this little fellow popping out of a cracked shell, and taking his first "peep" at a new world. He's a symbol of Easter, and he seems pretty happy about it.

Same way with a boy in a smart looking Spring suit—he's a symbol of Easter too, and...

"HERE'S A SHAMROCK"...is the logical salutation which gets a Saint Patrick's Day message off on the right foot. It was used by Leonard H.

Graves as a goodwill contact. The paper is green, and on it, over the typed letter, is the imprint of Mr. Graves' right hand. In one corner is a Shamrock, over which is tied a miniature clay pipe.

The letter isn't long. You may read the whole of it:

Here's a Shamrock, Mr. McNulty, and my right hand goes with it.

"Good Luck to You on Saint Patrick's Day in the Morning!"

My son overheard a conversation at school in which the "Luck of the Irish" was mentioned, so when I got home that night he asked: "Daddy, what made the Irish lucky?"

"The luck of the Irish, son," I said, "is due to the fact that they work hard, talk little, and always wear a Shamrock on Saint Patrick's Day."

So today, I'll be wearing a Shamrock and doing everything that a good Irishman is supposed to do on Saint Patrick's Day.

And I hope that you will wear the Shamrock, too, for I have a sneaking feeling that the "Luck of the Irish" is hovering near, and that the wishes and plans which are uppermost in your mind will become a reality.

P.S. Believe it or not, one way to have "Irish Luck" on your mailing pieces and letters is to have our Irish crowd write and produce them.

"A FEATHER IN YOUR CAP, MRS. FOX"...that's the beginning for a letter used by Kaufman's, in Reading, Pennsylvania. Attached is a red feather about 3 inches long. The copy begins:

Perhaps you didn't realize it, but all you owe us on your account is a small balance.

That certainly is a "feather in your cap," as the saying goes. You can feel proud of the way in which you have handled this charge account, and your credit always will be A-1 at Kaufman's.

Because of the sincere effort to meet your payments regularly, I am very happy to extend a special courtesy to you. You can purchase any additional furniture and...

"RIVER FISHIN'S BEST"...printed in large type, this is the title of a letter used by the magazine, *Down Beat*. The letter-head reveals a plump old fellow, with pipe and rod. A red string (real) runs from the end of the rod to the lower right-hand corner of the page. On the lower end, is tied a metal fish. To keep the string in place, both ends are clipped to the sheet. Says the letter:

"According to Old Timer, 'You got more chance of ketchin' somethin' in a river, cause more fish see your bait.'

"Old Timer's philosophy isn't new to music advertising people who also want to dangle their bait before the greatest number of prospects. They're river fishermen, too.

"Maybe that's why *Down Beat* carried more..."

"GETTING DOWN TO BRASS TACKS"...begins a letter used by Wurzburg Brothers, in Memphis, Tennessee. At the end of the first line of copy, two holes are punched about an inch apart. Into each is inserted a common brass paper fastener, head to the front. About as simple as any showmanship could be—but these old expressions are popular, and the dramatization of this one is quite effective. Here is how the letter starts:

"Getting Down to Brass Tacks"...it's your tag business we're after.

"Will you meet us halfway, and let us show you what we can offer on your tag requirements? It won't take..."

"HERE'S THE BRIGHT IDEA"...starts this letter used by the American Nickeloid Company, and to prove it's no joke, a disc of bright metal is attached—so bright you could almost use it for a mirror.

"Here's the Bright Idea"—try brilliant metal as it's used on this letter. Always distinctive, always...

Showmanship on the typewriter/word processor. The tools available to the letter-carpenter today are more varied than those that were in the offices of the past. Unless the executives of the past had very patient or extremely creative secretaries, anything tried outside the standard letter format was time-consuming and barely cost-effective. With today's expanded typewriters and word processors, however, anything conceived in modern letter-writers' minds can be brought to screen on paper. Adding accessories of color copies, with enlarging or reducing capabilities, line printers and light pens for sketches, the varied changes for using graphic showmanship are apparently endless.

For the purpose of this *Handbook*, I will show only a few examples of the ways these tools can be used by the good letter-writer. As you look at each example, consider that each served to handle a specific problem. Keep the purpose of each letter in mind as you adopt the technique to your next dramatic letter.

The typewriter. "There have long *been* many tricks taught on the typewriter in typing classes throughout the nation. Most of these Christmas trees, turkeys, forces of presidents, and such, were typed with XXX's instead of actual words. The reason was simple and effective—the picture was the purpose of the exercise, not any subsequent message. The good letter-carpenter should also be guided by this rule. No matter how clever the idea, if the readers cannot get your message, the letter has lost its purpose. Remember, when in doubt, *don't*.

Trick typing need not be formidable. The following letter, used by the Central Manufacturers Mutual Insurance Company, Van Wert, Ohio, took very little extra time to type, but it rates high as an attention-getter. Moreover, the words typed in the unusual way gain extra emphasis for their meaning.

                          g cost of living p
                n   i
               i   n
              s   n
Dear Policyholder,   i   e
Are you trying to keep the r   d down?
Then don't forget that when you insured your property in The Central you r
        e
       d
     u
      c
     e
            d the cost of your insurance protection considerably, because The Central as you know, pays dividends to policyholders.

Unusual typing is like billboard advertising which chiefly aims to make sure that certain products are *remembered* favorably, and to the exclusion of others. For such a purpose, the dramatically typed letter would seem to be perfect.

Anything *different* seems to attract attention; a commonplace request can be given a bit of color simply by typing the letter in an unusual way. The following inquiry (see Figure 3-8) to put a mailing list in order should have had more than ordinary pull because of the type format. It was used by Prentice Hall.

Figure 3-8

Dear _____,
We're trying
To bring our records
Up-to-date.

So—
Will you do us a favor
And slide the card
Out of the pocket
At the top of this sheet
And correct
Any misspelling of your name—
Change of address—
Addition to your zone number—
Or anything else that makes
Our present method of addressing you
Inaccurate.

EVEN IF THE LISTING IS CORRECT,
We'd appreciate it if you'd
Check the "OK" box,
And mail the card.

Thanks
Ever so much.
Just drop the card
In your outgoing mail.
The postage will be paid
By us.

The graphics copier. Whether actual drawings are reproduced or a graphics tablet is used, the results can be quite dramatic. Diagrams, graphs of many types, or illustrations can be made to make your readers want, first, to read on and then, to act as you wish them to act.

For those who think that copy is "everything" and who ridicule any form of showmanship as undignified and childish, I have an example that still remains somewhat of a sales letter mystery. A young lady who was contemplating a career in advertising decided to seek a connection with a good agency. Accordingly, she sent a mimeographed letter asking for an interview to 48 advertising executives. As you can see (Figure 3-9), the copy was trimmed to the bone, and the emphasis placed on the sketch of the "copy cub" at large.

Figure 3-9

Dear _____,

A "COPY CUB" WITH THE FOLLOWING QUALIFICA-
TIONS IS AT LARGE.

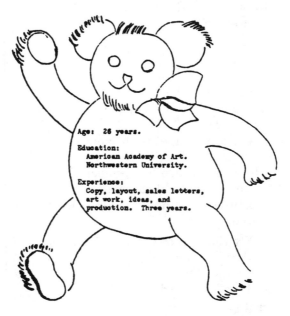

Age: 26 years.

Education:
American Academy of Art.
Northwestern University.

Experience:
Copy, layout, sales letters,
art work, ideas, and
production. Three years.

Won't you use the enclosed reply-card to give this ambitious,
hard-working, and capable young woman an interview?

(Signature)

It is doubtful that any of our letter experts would have predicted
success for that sales attempt. And who could blame them? Except that
the sketch may provoke a smile, what is left in the copy to make a big
impression on high-powered advertising people? But here's the mystery:
37 of these people took the trouble to reply, 18 granted the interview,
and three offered the girl a job. You couldn't ask for better success than
that with an application letter—shooting in the dark at total strangers.

Why did it pull so well? It is *different* from the usual run of tiresome
and stilted requests for employment that come in throughout the year.
You know the kind that start, "Having recently completed the secretarial course at King's Business College, the writer would appreciate an
interview relative to a position with your company." Then, as a rule,
there follows a blow-by-blow description of the applicant's education,
age, weight, height, church affiliation, disposition, and whatnot—
ending with reference to people who, of course, have been carefully

chosen as sure to be kind-hearted and complimentary. But this "copy cub" knew better than to bore her readers with facts that could be saved for the interview. Maybe the results are not so mysterious after all. The letter did a fine job, and who are we to discount success?

Keep your uses of electronic reproductions crisp, clever and to the point. Then, no matter what your interest, your results will be astounding. The key to success is making your showmanship fit your purpose.

Oversized letters and fliers. A very old idea for getting attention is the use of a letter or flier many times the customary size. These blowups are simple to make, and not expensive. The master copy is typed the usual way on the letterhead or plain paper, then enlarged. Naturally, the reader is startled to encounter such a giant in the ordinary run of his mail, and tends to be favorably impressed. Here is the copy on a BIG letter used by Eastin Pictures Co., of Davenport, Iowa. The size of the mailing sheet was four times that of an 8 ½ by 11 letterhead.

Dear _____,

What's the BIG idea?

We thought that 144-page catalog of ours was big enough to get your attention. But so far, neither the catalog nor our letters have brought any response from you.

Therefore, I'm writing you a really BIG letter this time, and it's about a really BIG day for you—the day you start your summer exhibit season with those outstanding Eastin Films.

Eastin Film alone has developed methods to maintain films in trouble-free running condition at all times. It is only here— week after week—that you get prints that are free from trouble-some breaks while showing—that are cleaned, with all surface oil, grit, and lint removed by our special process.

Eastin gives you more for your money in every way...full insurance...topnotch subjects...good prints...prompt, dependable delivery. Audiences from coast to coast applaud the title "Eastin Film," as identification of the finest in 16 mm and cassette entertainment.

Your BIG opening day will be the beginning of your BIG profit year with films from Eastin. Immediate booking means choice subjects. Don't delay. Shoot your order in today.

You can see how the BIG letter idea can easily be adapted to a thousand and one uses in business.

"I am afraid that my previous letters about your unpaid bill have been too small to get attention, so now I am writing to you in the BIGGEST way I know how."...(Credit Manager)

"This new product calls for BIG enthusiasm on the part of every salesman. It's your BIG opportunity for BIGGER income. Only a BIG letter like this could express how I feel about it."...(Sales Manager)

"This is a BIG way to tell you about the BIG campaign which begins next month in all the BIG magazines. It is the BIGGEST STORY every told to your customers about this, and it means BIG business for you."...(Advertising Manager)

"This is the BIG sale of the year—nothing held back. BIG values, BIG assortments to choose from, BIG savings for you! Everything BIG, except the prices."...(Retail Merchant)

"Best wishes to all of you for a BIG New Year. We have made BIG progress, in spite of BIG obstacles, and in that each of you has played a loyal part."...(President to employees)

"BIG news deserves a BIG announcement. The date is set for June 1, and a BIG night it is going to be. Nothing will be skimped or left out—BIG dinner, BIG entertainment, and your BIG chance to meet and hear our National President."...(Association Secretary)

Big mass media, too, are useful in similar ways. A good example (see Figure 3-10) is a message sent by Charles Kell when he was Western Life Director of Agencies; the layout on yellow paper was telegram-style, but titled differently.

Figure 3-10

Western Life
TREASURE-GRAM

ST. LOUIS, MO. FEBRUARY 20

MR. BILL BATES,
2470 ESTES AVE.,
CHICAGO, ILL.

HERE IS A BIG MESSAGE CONCERNING A BIG OPPORTUNITY. THE MESSAGE IS OURS BUT THE OPPORTUNITY IS YOURS. SIX WEEKS REMAIN IN WHICH YOU CAN WIN POINTS IN THE WESTERN LIFE GREAT TREASURE HUNT SALES CAMPAIGN. YOU HAVE 234 PRIZES FROM WHICH TO CHOOSE—MERCHANDISE EQUALED ONLY IN THE BEST DEPARTMENT STORES. THESE AWARDS ARE YOURS. IN ADDITION TO YOUR LIBERAL COMMISSIONS. SET YOUR GOAL FOR A BIG BUSINESS...THEN MAKE EVERY DAY COUNT. THE ENTIRE HOME OFFICE STAFF IS PULLING FOR YOU. GOOD LUCK.

CHARLES KELL
DIRECTOR OF AGENCIES

Oversize notices give the readers the feeling that something momentous is happening.

Be different, not difficult. When you reflect on these sample dramatized mailings, plus others of your own observation, it is evident that they all handle problems common in business correspondence, and that what they *say* is the same as it would have been if done in the conventional way. Dramatic messages are all inspired by the fact that human beings tend to give special attention to anything out of the ordinary. Thus, they do the same job as does an ordinary letter, but they do it in a *different* way.

This is fine, provided the difference is *pleasing* to the reader. In the effort to get out of a rut, we sometimes see the writer wandering too far from the groove, and the reader's reaction is not as intended. For instance, you may have received letters with facsimile checks printed on the upper third of the page, and folded in such a way that through the window envelopes they appear to be genuine. The first reaction is wonderful. You say, "A check…swell…now the baby gets a pair of new shoes." But alas, the check turns out to be a swindle. It is *like* the check you *would get* if you were smart enough to own a certain policy and unlucky enough to break your leg before it expired. Perhaps you don't mind this form of deception, but it does lift the readers up and then throw them down. The effectiveness of the idea is doubtful.

Another experience that never seems to please is the reception of a letter on which there is postage due. The victim feels that he is expected not only to read the letter but to pay for the privilege. This tribulation was given a new twist by a clever letter-writer in Davenport, Iowa. He sent his mailing out knowing that one penny would be collected at the point of delivery. When the reader opened the letter, he found a card inside on which was mounted one penny—and the words, "Here is the penny you just spent to get this message."

Yes, this was a novel form of showmanship, and we must give its "daddy" credit for originality. No doubt, some of the readers accepted the stunt as a good joke on them, but others probably thought a childish device had been used to get their attention. The latter reaction may also have been strengthened by the fact that there was no connection between the idea and the rest of the letter. The writer knew he was taking a chance with the prank, but went ahead anyway.

Using the same approach of a shock followed by immediate recovery is the letter once mailed to prospects by one of the leading insurance companies. When the readers pulled the letter from its envelope, the first thing they saw was an itemized bill from the "Emergency Hospital." If they knew that such a hospital did not exist, the reaction was not too disturbing. Otherwise, they must have felt a chill running up and down their spines. However, the first lines of the letter ended the panic—"The thought of such a bill, if presented to you, gives an awful jolt, doesn't it? We will take the burden of responsibility. Pay all such bills promptly and completely! A modern shock-absorber at your service!"

But again, what was the reader-reaction? Were those who received the "phoney" bill so impressed with the seriousness of what *could* happen that they wanted to know more about the prevention, or did they resent the trick used to get their attention? The reaction was probably split both ways—only the insurance company could tell us.

Among the doubtful forms of showmanship that may backfire is a letter used by a Chicago printing company. Figure 3-11 shows a part of it.

Figure 3-11

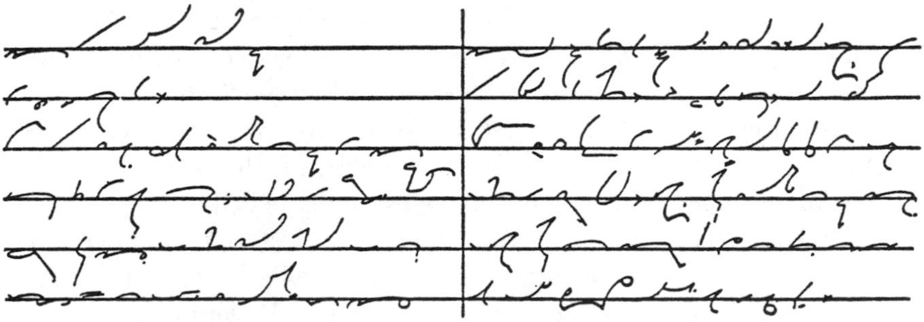

After several more paragraphs—the letter filled a page—there appears a postscript, typed in red: "You don't have to know shorthand nor even call your secretary to find out what this stenographic letter is all about—*just dip it in water.*" Now isn't that fine and dandy? People should take time to walk over to the drinking fountain and wet this letter. Of course, by chemical process the real letter will then be revealed. Can you imagine the readers enjoying such a damp experience? There they stand, with the wet sheet in their hands, and after the letter "magically appears," what do they do with the soggy thing?

Showing the personal touch. The passing from quill pen to typewriter was a great step forward in business correspondence, but it did eliminate a personal touch which only script possesses. To offset the coldness of a typewritten message, many letter-writers have the habit of adding a few words in longhand along with their signature. For example, on the bottom of the letter just signed, the credit manager may write "Please" or "Come on, friend Jones, let's get this thing settled." The salesmanager, on a letter to a dealer about some prosaic subject, may write, "Don't forget to bring your clubs on your next trip to the city," or "That is really a good buy, John."

The sight of the words in longhand is pleasing to the readers. They make them feel that they have received personal attention—that a cordial relationship has been recognized. It's a good idea to add a little warmth to the letter, but *not* when the addition in longhand is merely to take care of something forgotten in the dictation. A letter with scribbling all over the margins and at the top and bottom is most unsightly, and contributes nothing except the impression that the writer is both careless and lacking in pride.

No current support exists for hand-written business letters. However, the selling points of most text-editors and expanded typewriters is to personalize correspondence. It is to this purpose that we altered this section and replaced it with the rewrite.

With text masters and expanded typewriters, personalized letters are the norm today. By leaving proper spacing codes within the master letter, the reader's name can make each recipient feel special. No matter how routine the purpose of a letter, a personalized salutation and inserts will bring writers and readers closer. How often and when to use a person's name are always questions a good letter-writer asks. As we saw earlier in this section, times change and terms of address are keeping pace with them. A good rule-of-thumb to follow as to how often a reader's name should be incorporated in a letter—once for every three paragraphs of copy. Too many more than that and the impact is lost and the letter sounds insecure. Think in terms of a convention and decide when you, naturally, say the other person's name. It is usually when you want to place special emphasis on a particular point. So, too, with your letters.

Another word should be said here about using names. To be sure of not offending, use the reader's last name (i.e., Dr. Rogers) if you have never had physical or phone contact with the person. If, at that time, a first-name relationship was established or requested, your use of a first name is considered proper. If no familiarity is offered, *do not* become casual in your correspondence.

I have always kept in mind that the average business letter is not only seen by the intended readers, but it is often passed on to others. In cases where I know this is going to occur, I tend to keep the letter a little more formal, particularly in the salutation. Here is an example (Figure 3-12) of correspondence to a good friend who was an executive of a major manufacturing company. I knew the letter would be seen by members of his production staff.

Figure 3-12

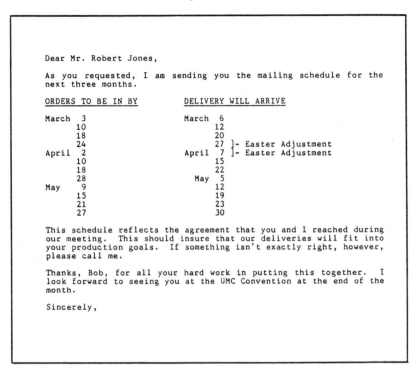

```
Dear Mr. Robert Jones,

As you requested, I am sending you the mailing schedule for the
next three months.

ORDERS TO BE IN BY          DELIVERY WILL ARRIVE

March   3                   March  6
       10                          12
       18                          20
       24                          27 ]- Easter Adjustment
April   2                   April  7 ]- Easter Adjustment
       10                          15
       18                          22
       28                   May    5
May     9                          12
       15                          19
       21                          23
       27                          30

This schedule reflects the agreement that you and I reached during
our meeting.  This should insure that our deliveries will fit into
your production goals.  If something isn't exactly right, however,
please call me.

Thanks, Bob, for all your hard work in putting this together.  I
look forward to seeing you at the UMC Convention at the end of the
month.

Sincerely,
```

In the same letter, sent to someone not known as well, "Robert" in the salutation would have been omitted. Also, "Bob" in the copy would have been replaced with "Mr. Jones."

Personalization is not only good showmanship—it's good communication.

More examples for good measure. The forms that showmanship may take in business letters are so numerous and so different that a whole volume of examples would only scratch the surface. You have seen that they may be good or bad, depending upon the originality of the idea, how appropriate it is to the subject matter of the letter, whether or not it is simple enough to be practical from the expense angle—and, most important of all, the final effect it has on the reader.

For good measure, you may conclude your survey of this device used to win attention by examining a few more examples (Figures 3-13, 3-14, and 3-15)—all of them good enough that we know the letters did a fine job for those who used them.

Figure 3-13

TIME IS RUNNING OUT ON YOUR LAUNDRY EQUIPMENT WARRANTY...PROTECT YOURSELF WITH A NEW SERVICE CONTRACT

Dear Customer:

Your one year free service and parts warranty on your automatic laundry equipment is about to expire. We think it highly important for you to extend this protection with a Montgomery Wards Service Contract. This low cost, 12-month contract can really be a blessing. It covers all parts. labor charges and all service calls to your home necessary to maintain your equipment under normal use.

Why not safeguard your big investment and end all your service worries for the coming year. Even though your appliance is only one year old and was engineered to deliver dependable service...all automatic equipment is quite complex and its many parts are subject to the normal effects of usage.

So act today and make sure your protection does not lapse. Order your Service Contract now, before your warranty period ends and save the cost of an inspection call.

If you have a Credit Account at Montgomery Wards, you may add this purchase without a down payment. and usually without increasing your monthly payment.

For your convenience, we have enclosed an application form for your Montgomery Wards Laundry Equipment Service Contract. Just check the plan that fits your needs and the method of payment you wish to use. sign and forward the application to us in the self-addressed, postage paid envelope. You will receive your contract by return mail.

Yours very truly,

5. FORGING THE CHAIN TO BUILD DESIRE

Adding fuel to the fire. You will recall that the Chain of the business letter has the important job of taking the readers from a state of attention, caused by the Star, to one of increasing interest, so that they are *ready*-to act as the writer will suggest in the Hook. Thus, after the spark that starts the fire, the Chain comes along to add fuel—not only to keep the fire burning, but to make it burn more brightly.

The Chain, of course, is the body of the letter, and of necessity is usually much longer than either the Star or the Hook. This is true

Figure 3-14

Dear Customer:

Soon the warranty on your Montgomery Ward stereo equipment will expire. Why not S-T-R-E-T-C-H your coverage -- and your dollars -- with a Montgomery Ward Service Contract.

You can continue to enjoy beautiful music relaxed without a care in the world. With a Montgomery Ward Service Contract, the burden of repair expense and worry shifts from your shoulders to Montgomery Ward's. Your stereo is completely covered -- all parts and all labor. Remember -- you get unlimited service in your home regardless of the number of calls you may require, and it can't cost you one additional penny.

It's the modern approach to the care and maintenance of your fine systems. You plan ahead and budget your money, secure in the knowledge that there will be no unpleasant repair surprises for you. Doesn't it make sense to spend just a few pennies a day now, rather than be jolted by a major repair bill when you least expect it?

There are many features that make our contracts unusually attractive -- our nationwide service -- people who specialize in your particular equipment -- and a solid, money-back guarantee on your Service Contract. You will be delighted to join the thousands of Montgomery Ward customers who have responded enthusiastically to this new approach to repair service.

If you have a credit account at Montgomery Ward, you may add this purchase without a down payment and usually without increasing your monthly payment.

Take care of this right now. Sign the enclosed application form for a stereo Service Contract. Check the plan that fits your needs and the method of payment you wish to use. Forward the application to us in the addressed, post-paid envelope. You will receive your contract by return mail.

Yours very truly,

Montgomery Ward

Figure 3-15

WORLD EXPLORER CRUISES
S.S. UNIVERSE

Many cruises are guilty of discrimination. While the physical pleasure — eating, lounging around, etc. — are well taken care of, the intellectual pleasures are often sadly neglected.

Not on the S.S. Universe. On our Alaskan cruise one's mind will have as much fun as the rest of the body.

A 14-DAY CRUISE THAT'S LESS EXPENSIVE THAN SOME 7-DAY CRUISES.
Departure Date July 14 - Return July 28

THE CREW INCLUDES
FIVE PhD's AND
CLASSICAL MUSICIANS.

A MESSAGE FROM FELIX MOLZER, DIRECTOR OF MONMOUTH COUNTY ARTS COUNCIL

Because it is in keeping with our desire to make available to our community a broad scope of cultural and educational experiences, the Monmouth Arts Council is happy to sponsor this exciting Alaskan Cruise. You will be taken to the most wondrous sights in Alaska, and the geologists, anthropologists, and oceanographers on board will teach you all about the sights with films, lectures, and insights. Of course, you will also enjoy delicious food, classical musicians, dancing, variety shows, as well as all the other typical cruise activities.

As you may know, the council has embarked on an extensive renovation project. In a cooperative effort with the local business community to help the Monmouth Arts Council, Empire Travel Corporation has given us this opportunity to join them in helping ourselves and our community. If a minimum of 10 people participate in this cruise, at no additional cost to the participants, Empire Travel will contribute $200.00 per person to the Council's building fund. This contribution will be tax deductible to the participants. In addition, the Arts Council will place a plaque engraved with the participant's name on a newly redecorated seat at the theater.

I URGE YOU TO MAKE THIS A GIFT TO YOURSELVES AND TO THE COMMUNITY

If you would like to learn more about this cruise and this opportunity, join us at a cruise party held at the UNION HOUSE RESTAURANT, 11 Wharf Ave., Red Bank, on Thurs., Oct. 11 at 8 p.m.

Since we are going to serve refreshments and need to prepare in advance, we ask that you let us know if you can come. Please call Empire Travel.

because it takes time to parade before the readers the facts they must know if action is to be secured. The length cannot be avoided, as the readers will not jump directly from mere attention to favorable action, but it does present a serious problem for the letter-carpenter. This problem is that at some point, before all the facts can be marshaled and the whole story told, interest can be broken, and no more of the letter will be read. Hence, the facts in the Chain must be coordinated into a *swiftly flowing* message, with never a dull spot or let-up. Nothing is more important to the success of a business letter where action is to be requested than this "**FLOW**" from fact to fact—keeping readers' minds on the subject and giving them no chance to think of something else.

How can this be done? Well, the answer to that question is a major purpose of this *Handbook*, and suggestions appear at almost any place that you might stop to read. For example, letter-carpenters must construct their Chain with words, and so could not do the job unless they understood the language principles explained in Section 2. They must work with a plan (as emphasized in this Section) or surely the Chain will fall apart. They must also be familiar with letter-mechanics (Section 4), and if able to reflect a pleasing personality (Section 5), their chances of success will be increased. All through the other sections, matters important to the building of the Chain are set forth—some related more to one type of letter than another, but each having some connection with the major objective of making *every* letter do a good job.

Particularly in Section 7, How to Write the Sales Letter, you will find the Chain taken apart, and then put together again, and a survey of what can be done to make it strong, and of common mistakes that tend to make it weak. This information might, just as logically, be given in connection with the present analysis of the Star, the Chain, and the Hook, except that many of the points would need a second "airing" in connection with the sales letter, and there is no reason why you should be burdened with the repetition. So that the continuity of the formula will not be overlooked, however, here are a few examples of that fast "flow" which is so essential if the purpose of the Chain is to be accomplished.

How to fashion each link. A short letter in which the reader is carried along rapidly once he has passed the introduction is one used by LaSalle Extension University, Notice that it has a title instead of the usual salutation.

"LEGAL KINKS AND TRICKS IN BUSINESS"

On my desk is a booklet that should be yours. May I send it to you?

Other readers have called it the most human collection of real-life narratives about what can "go legally haywire" with perfectly good business situations that was ever put into so little space. My guess is you'll agree after you have read it. And if you do, it will more than justify my entirely selfish motive in offering it —namely, to place one more goodwill builder for our Institution and its work where it will be most appreciated.

Here are a few instances of the bill of fare offered. Don't they suggest how rich the booklet is in food for serious business reflection?

—the banker who should have written on his cuff, and didn't

—the outlawed million francs that Baron Rothschild collected

—the clubman who thought he had bought a $40,000 piece of real estate...only he hadn't

—the bank whose birthday mistake cost $6,000

—the coal company that had to pay $70 for a window it didn't break

—the jeweler who left his name on another man's check and paid $2,000 for the privilege

—the refinery that became an abandoned warehouse because a big executive "took something for granted"

—the $5,000 that Benjamin Franklin's will turned into $1,631,000...and so on.

Every day your own duties bring some aspect of the legal side of business to your attention; and if the subject of Law has ever appealed to you at all, I think you'll get an added "kick" out of this "Legal Kinks" booklet.

If you would like a copy, without obligation, simply return the enclosed card.

The Chain in this letter carpentered by L. R. Alwood is superb. The facts are fired with machine-gun speed. "The banker who should"...bang! "The outlawed million francs"...bang! "The clubman who thought"...bang! "The bank whose birthday—the coal company that had to pay"...bang, bang! "The jeweler who left"—"the refinery that became"—"the $5,000 that Benjamin Franklin"...bang, bang, bang! When a letter *moves so fast*, there is no time for the reader to think of quitting. More than 16 percent of those on the mailing list replied, asking for the booklet, so beyond any question, the letter was a big success.

However, there is no harm in wondering if that percentage might not have been higher, had two small changes been made—one in the Star and the other in the Hook. "On my desk is a booklet that should be yours." That is an interesting statement. The readers would promptly ask themselves, "What *kind* of a booklet?" But the question which follows seems to let the cat out of the bag—"*May* I send it to you?" So the readers could say, "There's a catch in this letter. He is asking my *permission* to send me the booklet." That *could* cause some people to stop reading, and who knows—perhaps it did.

The other possible error occurs in the Hook. As you will discover later in this section, "if" is a negative word when used in asking for action. "*IF* you would like a copy" means "perhaps you do, or perhaps you don't." The last sentence, then, would have been stronger had it read—"For *your* copy, simply return the enclosed card"—thus implying no doubt that the booklet *would* be wanted.

But why criticize success? Has anything ever been written that might not have been made better?

Another letter which rates high in letter "flow" is one used by Merrill M. Jackson, of Kansas City, Missouri. It is especially noteworthy for the short sentences, the simple language, the interesting introduction, and the pile-driver speed with which the links in the Chain are put together. Before the letter starts to develop interest, two cards are played to win attention—the mention of the dog, "Snooks," and of the famous book which so many people have read. Also, a small picture of "Snooks" is attached.

Good Morning Folks,

My friend,,, "Snooks" has never read Dale Carnegie's book—but she certainly knows how to make friends and influence people. She hasn't got a thing but a bark, a cute little wiggle, and a heap of curiosity. She has never met a stranger in her life. She has the idea that if she's friendly she will get along. It's quite an idea—for it makes her life pleasant. It brings her plenty of attention, car rides, and a good living.

Your ideas may do as well for you. For a good idea is the most potent thing on earth. An idea built Ford's business. Ideas built Katz and Luzier's. Ideas win wars. Here are a few brand new ideas that are building business today. Money making ideas! Ideas that are making jobs! Ted Ruhling of Independence, Missouri, has a new idea for fish stringers. He's selling loads of them.

George T. Cummings has a new portable vise, weighs less than 4 pounds. Can be carried in a tool kit, a car or a truck! It is stronger than any wrench. Everyone who sees it wants it. The artist who retouched the photo bought four. My foreman bought one. My wife bought one for her brother-in-law, who has a home workshop. Distributors are buying them 500 at a clip.

Brunson has a "fishing gadget." Attach it to the end of the line! The instant the fish nibbles, "Bingo" the hook is set. Fishermen are buying them as fast as Brunson can make them. Suppliers are flooding him with orders.

You may say, "Heck, those are all gadgets—nothing serious." Okay. My friend, Cheek, has an improved wheel-barrow. The only real improvement for years! The load is perfectly balanced. A simple release automatically dumps the load. This makes all present wheelbarrows obsolete. So I still say that ideas make business, make jobs, make money.

Maybe a new idea will help sell your deal. A new approach: it could be a premium deal! A cooperative advertising campaign! A house organ! A mail order campaign! Your dealers, agents, and distributors will need help. Perhaps your salesmen can't see them all. Direct-by-mail campaigns will help them.

There are many ways to use mail advertising. Why not find out just how it can help you? Our business is planning, writing, and producing effective mail campaigns. If you're too busy, we'll do the mailing. In fact, we'll take care of all the details for you—get your mailing list if you wish.

So, my friend, it's a good idea to call (123) 456-7890 and ask for Jackson—or drop the card in the mail

Yours Merrill-y,
Merrill M. Jackson

P.S. Printing by Jackson is a good idea, too. Have Jackson do yours. Fast automatic presses! Hurry-up service! Lowest prices!

"When you Advertise—Jacksonize"

Yes, there are faults in this letter. It's good that you are catching them. You are becoming a real letter-carpenter when you can. The twice used "my friend" might rub some readers the wrong way. But Mr. Jackson is not trying to curry favor. You would understand that if you knew him. He *feels* friendly. He writes as he talks. His personality is very much revealed in the letter, as you know by now it should be.

The postscript also is questionable. Postscripts usually are. This one tends to take the reader's mind from direct mail to run-of-the-mill printing. Thus it competes with the chief objective of the letter. This is not good sales psychology. Hammer on *one* thing—hammer it home. One big bullet shot from a rifle straight to the mark has much more power than a thousand pellets blown from a shot-gun. We'll concede that point. In this letter at least, the postscript does more harm than good.

But the Chain is a fast-stepper. It leads readers swiftly from one money-making idea to another. Subconsciously, they begin to visualize what a good idea might do for them. Because that mental image is pleasing, they may do as requested—mail the card or telephone. Anyway, they are more in the mood for action at the end of the Chain than at the beginning. The Chain has quickened interest—and that's its job.

Another possible fault is that the introduction about the dog and the book are only remotely related to the message that follows. Thus, the Star gets attention, as it must, but there is no "carry-over" to the Chain; probably "Snooks" was forgotten long before the letter ended.

But these are minor errors in carpentry. The Chain is strong. No doubt the letter brought business back to Jackson.

In later sections, you will hear much about the Chain. At present, we will turn our attention to the Hook.

6. SETTING THE HOOK FOR ACTION

Easy, easy does it—a guide to when and what. The Star gets attention. The Chain develops interest and desire. So at last, with those parts of the job completed, the letter-carpenters reach the climax of their efforts. It is time for the Hook—that confident, forceful ending which makes the letter a success.

As you know, it would be folly to call any one of the three parts more important than the others. But we can agree on the utter *finality* of the Hook. It is then that the reader says "yes" or "no." No second-shots are allowed. When the letter is signed, and leaves your office, the die is cast.

> The moving finger writes, and having writ
> Moves on: nor all thy piety nor wit
> Shall lure it back to cancel half a line,
> Nor all thy tears wash out a word of it.

Thus, thinking only of sequence, you could give the Hook the nod as critical. It is the part of the letter that either carries the ball over for the touchdown, or leaves it short of the goal. You have seen football teams that seemed able to do everything but score. They could march up and down the field at will, but couldn't produce that one final punch.

Well, many letters are like that. They start beautifully, sweep rapidly forward, and then stumble at the end. The trouble seems to be one of timidity—lack of confidence. Their carpenters work with precision until the time to ask for action—then they lose their nerve.

> We *hope* with the above facts in mind you will be favorably impressed with our proposition, and that we will soon receive your order.

> *If* you wish to give us a trial order, please be assured it will be appreciated.

> Now is the time when our customers are stocking for summer business. We *trust* you will join them by placing your requirements on the enclosed order blank.

> We appreciate your patience in reading this somewhat long letter, but it was necessary that you understand the many advantages of our service. *May* we now have the pleasure of sending our representative to see you?

In each of those flimsy Hooks, a negative word reveals that the writers are not at all sure of the reaction they are to get. These negative "fatal four" tend to defeat the purpose of any business letter.

> We **HOPE** you will be favorable impressed.

> **IF** you wish to give us a trial order.

> We **TRUST** you will join them.

> **MAY** we have the pleasure of sending our representative?

There they are, words that hold readers back at the very moment when they need a confident push forward—**HOPE, IF, TRUST,** and **MAY.** Never "hope" or "trust" for action. **KNOW** you are going to get it. Never say "if" or "may" because then you are confessing doubt in your own mind, and letting the readers decide what to do. Note the difference in these Hooks.

> *Weak* . . . ."We trust that this price will meet with your favor. Hoping to have the pleasure of shipping you the range soon, we remain, respectfully yours,"

> **Strong** . . . ."To save you time, a duplicate copy of this letter is enclosed. Just initial and return it to us, using the stamped envelope. You can then have the range to enjoy by the end of next week."

> *Weak* . . . ."Considering the quality of our line, we feel our prices are reasonable. If you

would like to have our salesman call with samples, please so advise."

Strong . . . . "When you buy our quality, you get more for your dollar than any other way. Jack Cook, a fellow you are going to like, will be around next Monday morning to show you samples, and service your order."

Weak . . . . "We feel you must realize this bill should be paid, as you have had the goods a long time and should appreciate our patience. If you agree this is only fair, we shall hope for a check soon."

Strong . . . . "There comes a time when patience is no longer a virtue, and the lawyers take over. Frankly, we now expect our money, and shall look for a check from you not later than Saturday."

Weak . . . . "If you will OK the card, we will gladly send you a copy of the bulletin. Trusting you will do this,"

Strong . . . . "Your copy of this interesting bulletin is waiting for you. Just OK and mail the card."

The difference in those Hooks is so apparent that it scarcely needs comment. The weak ones are very timid; they do not encourage *action*. The others are positive and confident; they *tell readers* what they are expected to do.

Perhaps you think this is too commanding—that such a positive tone might be resented. That means you are overlooking the psychological background of the Star, the Chain, and the Hook. Remember, at first the readers are cold and casual. The hold on them is quite easily broken. So you "start easy and work up"—seeking only to increase interest until it becomes desire. In the early part of the letter, you wouldn't dare tell the readers what to do. That would be the quickest way to lose them. But as you go from point to point, as the fire blazes higher, a psychological change occurs in readers' minds. They are now genuinely interested— they have confidence in what you are saying. They are more emotional—less rational. You can throw caution to the wind as you approach the Hook. It's time for "do" or "don't." The cat is out of the bag. The readers know what you want. *Ask for it.* Not with "if" or "may" or "trust" or "hope," but with every indication that you know the victory has been won.

You can soon convince yourself that the Hook demands a positive tone by examining the best sales letters that cross your desk. You will find without exception that courteously but firmly you are *told* what to do. Let's prove it. Here are the closing sentences of ten successful letters chosen at random. Notice how they all ask for action, without limitation or equivocation—and not one "if" or "hope" or "trust" or "may" in the whole lot!

*Keep this letter as your guarantee, and mail the handy card—today.

*Don't disappoint me—I shall expect your check by return mail.

*Put your check in the enclosed envelope, and mail it before you forget.

*Defy the summer slump by using the enclosed envelope.

*Return the card now while you have it on your mind.

*Our supply is limited—use the blank today.

*No satisfaction—no charge. Send no money. Simply mail the card.

*Come, come. Send a check immediately, so we can both stop worrying about this account.

*The minute you tell us what you will need, the best assortment will be reserved for you. But tell us today.

*Don't order your Spring stock until Bert Bemis gets to your store. He is worth waiting for, and will be in to take your order by the 15th.

No effort was made to sort these letters by purpose or style. If they are at all similar, it is because the writers were skilled in letter carpentry, and used the technique that they knew would get the best results.

Stilted endings break the charm. Remembering that the function of the hook is to get quick action before the readers have a chance to cool off, you can understand why "whiskers" are taboo in the close of a business letter. Many a letter, otherwise good, is spoiled when the writers, by force of habit, think they must sign off with one of the old-time conventional phrases.

The following letter is quite bright and interesting, except for the rather tepid conclusion.

Dear _____,

It's Springtime...glorious Springtime here in the mountains.......and that means handclasps, smiles, and greeting old acquaintances here at Sunrise Lodge. For at this marvelous season of the year many of our old friends visit us for a weekend, or a whole week of relaxation in the sublime beauty and restfulness of Spring in the famous Blue Ridge Mountains.

All nature seems to be saying "Welcome back to Sunrise Lodge" and with Easter coming so late this year you can spend a most enjoyable Easter weekend at Sunrise!

Our season will open on Friday, April 19th. Decide now to be among those present during the colorful Easter opening…renewing fond friendships here at Sunrise Lodge.

I have not missed a Springtime here in the mountains for 35 years, and I can't recall that the surrounding hills and valleys were ever more beautiful than they are this Spring. The vast panorama of nature's richest green and brown is a fairyland of enchanting colors. So you will surely enjoy your restful visit to Sunrise Lodge more than ever before.

Rates are very modest both by the week or daily.

Write to me immediately for your Easter reservations, or phone (123) 456-7890, and I will have everything in readiness for you.

[This is where the letter should have stopped. The urge for action has been made—and it is positive. But no, the writer was not content. So a new sentence drags in another sales point apart from Easter, and then a second sentence beginning with "May" spoils the positive urge for action even further.]

You *might* also let me make reservations now to assure your favorite room for your summer vacation.

May I have the pleasure of hearing from you in the near future?

There is absolutely nothing that can be said in favor of stilted, moth-eaten language when used *any* place in a business letter. You have seen that in our discussion in Section 2, and you will never be guilty of the practice in your own letters. But these old-time "whiskers" are particularly harmful at the time when action is being requested. The readers have been carefully nursed along through the early stages of attention and interest. As the Hook is reached, they are close to saying "yes" as they will ever be, but they are still undecided, torn between desire and caution. And then, at this extremely delicate point in the psychological process, along comes a sentence so stiff and meaningless that the effect is like pouring a glass of ice-water down the readers' backs. That is exactly what happened in the letter selling Sunrise

Lodge. The climax was reached in "and I will have everything in readiness for you." That was a confident assertion. The writer *expected* favorable reaction. Period! So it would have seemed that the letter stopped there. But then came the glass of ice-water—*"May* I have the pleasure of hearing from you in the near future?"

So often you hear it said: "I never know what to say at the end of my letters," as if when the job is done there still must be a final flourish. This is nonsense, but it probably explains why so many business letters are handicapped by a totally unnecessary closing sentence. The time to stop is when you've "had your say." Anything additional is superfluous, and only tends to chill the interest you have worked so hard to develop in the mind of the reader. If you, too, are one of those who "never know what to say" to finish off your letters, here is the answer to your problem. It's quite simple—say *nothing.* To prove that's good advice, consider this final example—the close of a letter soliciting club memberships.

It costs nothing to be one of us. You simply pay $30 a year, and get 12 good meals for your money. There is nothing more to spend. So fill out the application blank, and return it with your check. Do this right away, so you can be with us next Wednesday.

Not a bad Hook, is it? The job is done. Put away your tools, letter-carpenter; you will probably get the check, and greet a new member next Wednesday. But wait a minute. What's this strange stuff you have added?

Thanking you for your kind consideration of the advantages of membership in our organization, and trusting you will see your way clear to acceptance of this invitation, we remain, yours very truly,

Ho, hum, fiddle-de-dum! Another letter spoiled by that impulse to add just a little bit more. And what a contrast there is between the tone of the first paragraph, and the second. Could it possibly be the same person who wrote both of those paragraphs? Why not? You see numerous examples of the same sort in everyday business correspondence.

How to avoid the divided urge. It is a trait of human nature that if people are told to do one thing, they may go ahead and do it, but if given the choice of two things, they are quite likely to do neither. An understanding of this fact will prevent a very common mistake in closing business letters—the divided urge for action. The following

Hook taken from a collection letter illustrates the common fault of a divided appeal:

> Five dollars a week will clean up the balance in one year. If you cannot make payments that large, then send us $3 every week—or, start with $1 if that's the best you can do. At least, it is only fair that you should write us when you will start to reduce this debt.

All right, what has the credit agent told the reader? Pay $5 a week, or $3, or $1—or at least write and tell us when you will start paying. With such a divided plea, to which of the four suggestions is the debtor likely to respond? Probably none of them.

Examine these three closings:

> Let me tell you more about the convenience and comfort, the time and money-saving advantages of—service. Just return the enclosed card, marked for my personal attention—or call your local office, any hotel, or travel agency for full information.
>
> • • • • • • •
>
> Don't lose a minute. Write us a letter, or send the enclosed card right now. If you are not ready to decide now, then please drop in to see us the next time you are in our city.
>
> • • • • • • •
>
> And now, during March only, you can save 5%. Simply give us your order now, for delivery as late as March 30, if you wish. See your painter right away if you want his advice, or I will be glad to call and tell you exactly what paint your home should have. Phone (123) 456-7890. Or the enclosed card mailed will take care of everything.

In none of these three Hooks is suggested action specific or impelling. Instead, the many suggestions tend to confuse readers, so that no *one best thing* is left for them to do. Thus, the situation facing you as a letter-carpenter as you decide what action to urge is somewhat the same as when you use your garden hose. You may turn the nozzle to produce a strong stream of water that lands with force on a small spot, or you may turn it to produce a fine spray, which gently covers a wide area with no immediate effect. It is the single, forceful stream that does the best job in the Hook. Of the many forms of action that might be requested in closing any letter, there should be one that stands out above the rest as probably the most acceptable to the reader. Concentrate your power of persuasion on that *specific* suggestion. Remember this point, because it is very important. Beware of the divided urge.

Using "dated" action. Here is a tip for letter-writers which is in no sense experimental or untried. It *works*. When used in your letters it *will* increase their pull. This simple device adds power to collection letters, sales letters, follow-up letters, or any other letters that ask for reader reaction. It has been thoroughly tried and tested. Use *dated action.*

What *is* dated action? Well, instead of telling your readers what to do in a general or vague fashion, as so often happens in business letters, *set a time limit.* Tell them *when* the reply is expected.

*We will expect this check not later than *next* Saturday.

*An *immediate reply by airmail* will enable us to ship your order day after tomorrow.

*We must hear from you by *June 1.*

*Doctor, in order to handle this claim promptly for your patient, it will be necessary to have your preliminary report by the *end of this week.*

*Joe, be sure to give us this information along with the Daily Sales Record that you mail us *Thursday evening.*

*This letter leaves for your city this evening. By using the enclosed stamped airmail envelope, you can get your reply back to us on *Friday.*

*The lawyers will be ready to take over week after next. You still have ten days—until *December 31*—to spare yourself this trouble.

There is something about a *dated* request for action that makes it preferable to the one which goes at the job in a more general way.

*Please let us have your reply at your *earliest convenience.*

*Your *prompt* reaction to this proposition will be appreciated.

*We shall expect to receive this report in the *near future.*

*A check *without delay* is necessary to put your account in proper order.

*Return the order blank *soon* so that no sales will be lost.

Such generalities sound all right, but apparently they do not prod a reader to quick action. In fact, do they *ask* for it? How early *is* "earliest convenience"? How near *is* the "near future"? How soon is *"soon"*? You see, generalities are hard to pin down. To 100 people you can say, "not later than June 1," and they all know exactly how much time has been allowed. To the same group, "in the near future," might be interpreted in many ways, depending on the disposition and time-habits of each individual. Furthermore, when a *specific date* is suggested, the obligation of meeting that date tends to form in the readers' minds. It is something definite to remember. They have been told what to do and *when*. Quite often, they *do* it.

In this connection, the experience of an insurance company in Massachusetts is enlightening. One of the thorns in the flesh of this company was the time it took to get reports from examining physicians who were located all over the country. By test, over a three-month period, it was determined that after a certain blank was mailed, it was necessary, on the average, to follow up each doctor 3.7 times by letter to get the blank back to the home office. In the department handling these follow-ups, eight full-time workers were employed. Only generalities were used to ask for action, such as "We know you are busy, doctor, but won't you please get this blank back to us as *soon as possible?*"

Then it was decided to try *dated* action. All of the closing paragraphs in the follow-up letters were revised accordingly. The department head was willing to give the idea a trial, but he was quite sure it would make no difference. That opinion, however, he was very happy to change after another three-month test. With the action *dated*, the same follow-up letters were reduced to an average of 2.1 times per blank mailed. Not only were three workers transferred from the department, but clients with claims were given quicker service.

When preparing the Hook for your next letter—sales, collection, or otherwise—be sure to ask for *dated* action. Say **when** it is expected.

Making the action easy. Probably it is true that human beings tend to follow the path of least resistance. Hence, in asking for action at the close of a business letter, common sense tells us to spare the reader as much time and bother as possible. How often are we tempted to say "yes" after reading a fast-moving, interesting letter, only to hesitate and then push it aside because at the end we are asked to fill out a long blank, answer a questionnaire, or just go to the bother of replying by letter? How often, on the other hand, do we say "yes" because there is only a card to sign, with the postage taken care of—nothing to do but put the thing in the mail?

The majority of the people you meet will tell you that they don't like to write letters, and perhaps this is understandable when you remember that nine steps must be taken to dictate and mail one. Do you doubt that? Well, count them:

1. Dictate, or write in longhand
2. Type it
3. Proofread for errors
4. Add the signature

5. Fold and enclose
6. Seal the envelope
7. Address it
8. Fix the stamp
9. Mail

Just a lot of little things to do, except the dictation or writing, but a ten-to-twenty-minute job just the same, and big enough to cause many a letter never to be answered.

You are, of course, familiar with the devices used by letter-carpenters to make action easy. The most common is an already-addressed card that needs only initials or signature. When the postage is prepaid that's all the better. The enclosing of a stamped and addressed envelope is another action-producer, especially if genuine United States postage stamps are used instead of the permit privilege. Receiving a stamp is, to most people, no different than receiving the equivalent in money. How, then, can an honest person keep the stamp and not reply? Of course, it can be argued that the reader didn't ask for the stamp, and is not bound to return it. That is true, but nevertheless there does seem to be a moral obligation to *use* the stamp.

Another very good plan for easing the reader's burden in making the expected reply is to tell the reader, "Just *initial* a copy of this letter, put it in the stamped envelope, and it will come back to us in a jiffy." A busy person appreciates such an act of consideration. He or she initials the copy, hands it with the envelope to a secretary, and the reader's part of the job is done.

When order blanks are enclosed, they should be made as "short and sweet" as possible, with specifications already typed in, unless these are subject to the will of the reader.

Requesting that a telephone number be called, easy as the task may be, is not always a suggestion that wins favorable response. Some people shrink from a telephone call for fear that pressure may be put on them when the connection is made. We know of no test to prove it, but in our opinion a letter asking that a card be returned will usually outpull one asking for telephone calls.

In comparative analysis, the value of these plans to make action *easy* must depend on such variable factors as the nature of the problem at hand, the relationship between writer and reader, and those other conditions which are never fixed or static. The letter-carpenter builds to fit the particular time and need.

SECTION 4

HOW TO USE
BUSINESS LETTER MECHANICS

5. DEVICES FOR MAKING READING EASIER

HOW TO USE BUSINESS LETTER MECHANICS

In the previous section when we had the Star under the microscope, we found that letters, like people, make a first impression which may or may not be helpful when the final effect is weighed. Since the factors which contribute to this first impression can be controlled, and may be as perfect as you are willing to make them, they can very properly be called the "mechanics" of letter-writing. There is no reason in the world why the correspondence of any company cannot enjoy the advantages of a good-looking letterhead, precision typing, and those other features that help to present a pleasing appearance. Anything short of this ideal can only be attributed to the indifference or ignorance of those responsible.

Furthermore, the attainment of distinction in appearance is not an item of great expense, because it may often cost just as much to prepare and mail sloppy, unattractive letters as those others which reflect pride and quality. True, the initial expense of a fine letterhead, designed and printed by craftsmen, may be higher than that of one which is cheap and commonplace, but the difference is many times offset by the better reception it is sure to get. The other factors, mostly in the hand of the typist, have no expense angle, and depend simply on the standard of performance which is considered acceptable. It costs no more to type 50 good-looking letters than to type 50 inferior ones. In fact, secretaries who take pride in their work are more likely to exceed the production of the ones who are careless.

We may therefore agree that the appearance of a company's letters depends largely on the attitude of those executives who have the authority to set the standards and to insist that they be met. If the president, the department head, and the dictator are not sufficiently interested to make sure that the letters reflect the same quality claimed for the company's products, then obviously the standards will be low and the performance inferior. But when you encounter an organization where the crusade for better letters has adequate leadership, plus the willingness to supply modern equipment, it is sure to follow that those of the rank and file are encouraged to do their best to keep in step.

It is hard to understand why any business executive would *not* want the letters of the company to make a pleasant first and *last* impression. When we remember, as was explained in Section 1, that letters are definitely a part of public relations, we realize that any indifference toward them is a form of business negligence. This, of course, is a condition not found in business as a whole, although there are still many lamentable examples of companies handicapping their own public relations with letters written on old-fashioned letterheads, typed in a slam-bang manner, and giving off an odor of indifference.

"Costly thy raiment as thy purse can buy...rich but not gaudy...for the apparel oft proclaims the man," said Polonius to his son. "Costly thy letters as thy purse can buy...rich but not gaudy...for the appearance oft proclaims the company," says Good Judgment to the business executive. (See Figures 4-1 through 4-8 as examples of thoughtfully designed, modern letterheads, that favorably reflect each company's respective image.)

1. ENHANCING THE APPEARANCE OF THE TYPED LETTER

Checking details. The best of letterheads on the finest paper cannot be held entirely responsible for first impressions. The reader sees everything on the page, and each part has something to say about whether or not the whole appearance is pleasing. These factors are, of course, far more variable than that of the letterhead. Once the latter is designed and processed, it stays the same, but a typist may turn out one beautiful letter, and then an ugly one, depending on the mood of the moment and how faithfully there is an adherence to excellence. The attitude, too, of the person for whom the typist works helps to determine whether all of the letters will appear neat and in good proportion, for it is true that most people perform only as *expected*, and seldom any better.

Frankly, a survey of the mechanical features that contribute to the appearance of a business letter cannot possibly be as interesting as some of the other aspects of letter carpentry, but they are all important, and should be understood if a high level of quality is to be attained. A

Figure 4-1

KNAPP COMMUNICATIONS
CORPORATION
5900 WILSHIRE BLVD.
LOS ANGELES, CA 90036
TELEPHONE: (213) 937-5486

Figure 4-2

FLOOD & ASSOCIATES, INC.
3782 Cerritos Avenue
Los Alamitos, California 90720
213 594-8625

Figure 4-3

BY APPOINTMENT
TO HER MAJESTY THE QUEEN
SUPPLIERS OF SMOKERS REQUISITES
ALFRED DUNHILL LTD LONDON

ALFRED DUNHILL OF LONDON, INC.

11 EAST 26TH STREET, NEW YORK, N. Y. 10010

PHONE 212-481-6900 · CABLES·SALAAMS·NEWYORK · TELEX·422843

Figure 4-4

Figure 4-5

JACKSON BREWERY DEVELOPMENT CORPORATION
100 Conti Street • New Orleans, Louisiana 70130 • (504) 581-4082

Figure 4-6

THE MOORINGS
At Clarksville. A Condominium.

Represented exclusively by Brandermill Realty
Post Office Box 58275, Raleigh, North Carolina 27658 (919) 876-1081

Figure 4-7

Colorado Springs Symphony Post Office Box 1692 Colorado Springs. Co. 80901 (303) 633-4611
Charles A. Ansbacher, Music Director and Conductor   Beatrice W. Vradenburg. Manager

Figure 4-8

ATTORNEYS AT LAW

BOLLIGER HAMPTON & TARLOW
A PROFESSIONAL CORPORATION

RALPH BOLLIGER
LEWIS B. HAMPTON
ARTHUR L. TARLOW
JOHN S. CAVANAGH
BRUCE L. SCHAFER
E. ANDREW JORDAN
KATHERINE M. ZELKO
WILLIAM R. CAFFEE

1600 S.W. CEDAR HILLS BLVD.
SUITE 102
PORTLAND, OREGON 97225
TELEPHONE (503) 641-7171
TELECOPIER: (503) 641-2991

dictator must know what the letters should look like, what will help, and what will not, before proper instructions can be given to the secretary or transcriber. Moreover, quality-consciousness, every day, must be present—for the moment zeal falters, the level of performance is apt to sink.

As you know, among the several persons who contribute to the success of a business letter, the cycle is quite clear. The advertising manager usually plans the letterhead and selects the paper. Next, an artist makes the layout, an executive approves the design, a printer does the processing, and, finally, the dictator places thoughts onto a tape or directly across the table into the notebook of the stenographer. Usually the dictator never *sees* the letter until it comes back ready for signature. Someone else must be depended upon for attention to all those *little things* which will help make the letter attractive, and in harmony with the letterhead. That *someone* is the typist.

Typing and much more. There was a day not so long ago when the only requirements for a typist were a working machine, clean ribbons, and a method of erasing errors. However, as one secretary told me recently, a degree in electrical engineering, data processing, or computer service is needed to work in some offices today.

With the advent of the electrical typewriter, the job of typing became easier *and* harder. The mechanical aid eliminated the problem of uneven "touch" and increased both speech and clarity. Later, correction capabilities even took care of "clean" copy. But with each new improvement came another button, sequence, or method with which the secretary had to become familiar. The sale of typewriters now needed a training course to facilitate their use.

By the late 1970s, computers and word processors were common office machinery. Again, the secretary was expected to use this equipment effectively and flawlessly. Learning time was expanded as the business of letter-writing became crowded with tapes, hard discs, library management techniques, and data storage.

Letter-writing mechanics can be seen as a multi-step process which effective executives must fully understand and coordinate. Here, at a glance, are the main tools they must handle:

1. Selecting the word processing equipment best suited to the company's needs.
2. Furnishing proper working conditions for the equipment and its use.
3. Training and/or hiring personnel to efficiently operate it.
4. Overseeing letter production to ensure the quality, consistency, and appeal.

The selection is fairly easy. Any reputable office machine company will assist a business in buying the equipment that will best suit its needs. If your business does 20 letters a day, two reports a week, and maybe four or five special tasks a month, any good office typing system should be fine; if your output is a hundred times that in all areas and more besides, more elaborate equipment is a necessity.

Good lighting, desks and chairs at the proper height, and sufficient room for work layout are all essential in furnishing proper working conditions. Remember, once letters are finished they must be stored. Just as important as producing the letter is the quick retrieval of it. File cabinets, disk storage boxes, and/or tape racks are vital.

No equipment can produce a letter. A *person* does the work. The more complicated the letter production process, the more training the secretarial assistants must have. For your office staff, one more training session may be needed. Be sure to sit in on their sessions yourself. You will learn the working capabilities of *all* the equipment you have available. This will allow you flexibility in your correspondence and make you aware of what can and cannot be done easily by the typist.

The person ultimately responsible for the letter is the one who signs it. Nothing should leave your hand until it represents the best of your company. As we have said before, the letter *is* your company to its reader. Check each one carefully.

Placing the letter on the page. From experience in typing many letters, it is easy to judge accurately how much space on the page a letter is going to take. With this forecast, the typist is able to "frame" any letter so that the margins are about the same width—narrow margins for long letters, and wide margins for short ones. The letter, Figure 4-9, is about as near a work of art as any letter could be. An amateur typist might spend an hour trying to "frame" a letter so perfectly, but to this expert it must have been only a small incident in a busy day. The same Monarch letter, Figure 4-10, retyped for comparison, has lost the impression of quality. With the narrow margins, and the high position on the page, it looks top-heavy, and like any other of the many letters that are dashed off with no regard for "harmonious proportion" on the page.

Does such a small thing make a real difference? Oh, yes. How a business letter *looks,* and what it speaks for, before a word of the message is read, is vital. An impression of quality carries over to the products or services offered by the company. To pull the first example from the envelope, to sense at first glance the care and pride in its preparation, is to make one feel that the insurance sold by the company *must* be of the same fine quality.

Figure 4-9. A Letter Perfectly Framed on the Page

PARTICIPATING - NON PARTICIPATING LIFE · NON-CANCELLABLE HEALTH AND ACCIDENT INSURANCE

Monarch
LIFE INSURANCE COMPANY

SPRINGFIELD, MASSACHUSETTS

October 17, 19——

Mr. L. E. Frailey
1053 North Shore Avenue
Chicago, Illinois

My dear Cy:

Thanks a lot for your letter. If I have contributed
anything to the present-day thinking, I am happy.

In summarizing briefly this particular experience,
I think of the story that is told of Mark Twain's
first visit to the Atlantic Ocean. As he stood
looking out upon miles of water before him, his
host asked,

   "What do you think of our ocean, Mr. Clemens?"

To which Mr. Clemens replied,

   "It seems to be a huge success."

Tell Mary I am happy to have acquired another booster
and I hope that my friend, Joe Behan did not tire her
out. He is a remarkable man, has a host of friends
and an unlimited faculty for spreading good cheer.
It was nice to see you both, even if it was for only
a short time.

Hope this finds you well and may the enthusiasm,
originality and capacity for friendship of Frailey &
Associates continue to spread their beams of light.

               Sincerely yours,

CWY/HW
                           President

Formatting a letter. When it comes to arranging the various parts
of a business letter on the page, there is no one form that might be called
"best." The decision depends on the personal taste of the person for
whom the letters are typed, and the only limitation is that of consistency.
For example, if indented paragraphs are preferred, then they *all* must

Figure 4-10. Copy of Same Letter in Top-Heavy Position

PARTICIPATING - NON PARTICIPATING LIFE · NON-CANCELLABLE HEALTH AND ACCIDENT INSURANCE

Monarch
LIFE INSURANCE COMPANY
SPRINGFIELD, MASSACHUSETTS

October 17, 19——

Mr. L. E. Frailey
1053 North Shore Avenue
Chicago, Illinois

My dear Cy:

Thanks a lot for your letter. If I have contributed anything to the present day thinking, I am happy.

In summarizing briefly this particular experience, I think of the story that is told of Mark Twain's first visit to the Atlantic Ocean. As he stood looking out upon miles of water before him, his host asked,

"What do you think of our ocean, Mr. Clemens?"

To which Mr. Clemens replied,

"It seems to be a huge success."

Tell Mary I am happy to have acquired another booster and I hope that my friend, Joe Behan did not tire her out. He is a remarkable man, has a host of friends and an unlimited faculty for spreading good cheer. It was nice to see you both, even if it was for only a short time.

Hope this finds you well and may the enthusiasm, originality and capacity for friendship of Frailey & Associates continue to spread their beams of light.

Sincerely yours,

CWY/HW

President

be indented, and with the same number of spaces. It is not uncommon to see a very wide indentation in the opening paragraph, and a smaller one for the others, but this in our opinion is not pleasing to the eye, and there is no reason to justify it.

Surveying the letter to be typed on the page, the typist is conscious of one major part—the body—and several accessories. Not all accessories are used in every letter, but they may include:

The date	The complimentary close
Name of recipient	Name of writer
Job title	Job title
Full address	Name of company
The salutation	Initials of writer and typist
Reference or identification line	Enclosure line
Copy to line	Postscript

For the use of these various items, certain forms have been established by utility and custom, and we shall investigate what they are. It must be plain that they need to be assembled on the page in a format that is both practical and orderly. What that format is to be depends on the judgment and good taste of the individual responsible. It may be set by the person who writes the letters, or, in other cases, by company regulation. The latter is the best practice since it results in uniformity in style, and is the format considered "best" by the supervisor, or the executives of the firm. Certainly it is not a decision that should be left to the typist.

Let us see what some of the more common forms are like. There are others, of course, because some of the more adventuresome letter-carpenters are always experimenting with new ways of doing things. Here we will concern ourselves only with the forms generally accepted by busines which, of course, represent 99 percent of all the letters written.

So far as we know, no one has attempted to tabulate the use of these current formats in percentages, but it is our guess that the one most popular today is the *blocked* letter. This is the form in which all of the body lines start even with the lefthand margin, with only the date line, the complimentary close, and the identification of the writer, title, and company, remaining on the right half of the page. There are no indented lines to start each paragraph, or in the part which carries the recipient's title, company, and address. The effect, as illustrated in Figure 4-11, is both substantial and appealing. I happen to think it is the best looking of all the forms now in use.

Figure 4-11. A Blocked Letter

 PRENTICE HALL

BUSINESS & PROFESSIONAL BOOK DIVISION

June 29, 19--

Mrs. William Lynch
Columbus Hospital Service Association
P. O. Box 1896
Columbus, Ohio

Dear Mrs. Lynch:

It is always a pleasure to hear from those who have read and used
our books. I hope that I can give you some help.

Although our secretarial books do not have any sections concerned
with house organs as such, the section on preparing material for
the printer in COMPLETE SECRETARY'S HANDBOOK by Doris and Miller
should be of some help in proofreading and publishing the paper.

Prentice-Hall's PUBLIC RELATIONS HANDBOOK, edited by Philip Lesly,
contains a section on the employee house organ, suggesting how
to set it up, how to make the dummy, and giving recommendations
to the editor on style and format. The main body of the book,
however, is devoted to public relations. I suggest you see the
book at your local bookstore or library and see whether or not
it will fill your needs.

Good luck with your monthly bulletin.

Sincerely,

Barbara Nelson, Editor

bs

Simon & Schuster Reference Group

Prentice Hall Building, Englewood Cliffs, NJ 07632 (201) 592-2000

A third style, and once standard in business, is one with indented lines, as displayed in Figure 4-12. Probably it has retained its popularity because many people like the appearance of the indentations.

Figure 4-12

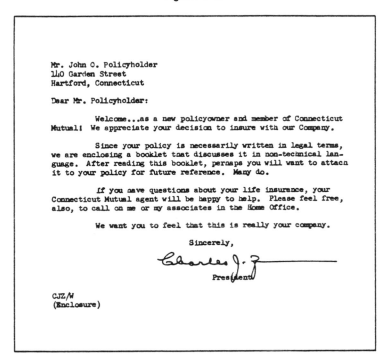

In some blocked letters, the practice is that all items start from the lefthand side. An example of the "all blocked" format is shown in Figure 4-13.

There seems to be no established practice with respect to the number of spaces before an indented line begins. Some use three spaces, some five, some ten, and others go almost to the center of the page before typing the start of the indented line. These variations are merely a matter of personal taste, and no one can say that one is better than the rest. After all, inasmuch as the indentations are used to improve the appearance of the typed letter, it is the job of those responsible to decide *what* number of spaces look best.

Figure 4-13. "All-Blocked" Style

```
Miss Frances Bailey
F. W. Fitch Company
304 15th Street
Des Moines, Iowa

Dear Miss Bailey:

It is a real pleasure to have you in Mr. Frailey's letter
writing class.

"Doc" Frailey is going to dispense a thousand dollars' worth
of good, usable ideas on business letters during the next
seven weeks.

He is a famous "doctor" for curing the pains, aches, and bruises
caused by poor letters.  For years Frailey has run a "clinic"
for pale and puny letters, and his fame has grown by leaps and
bounds until today he is "tops" in the letter writing field.

Here is an A.I.B. souvenir pencil.  Make a note that you have
a date at A.I.B. the next seven Wednesday nights.

The class is now going--and going places.  Come early, if you
can, and get acquainted.

I wish you increasing, continued success in your business,
and pleasant personal progress.

Sincerely yours,

Keith Fenton

KEITH FENTON

KF:MLH
```

The worst of all the styles, as we view them, is the one displayed in Figure 4-14. Every line in the body of the message is indented except the beginnings of paragraphs. To be sure, this format has the merit of gaining special attention, since it differs so widely from the others, but we doubt very much if the final reaction is favorable. To gain the reader's attention by trick typing is one thing; to please with it is another.

Placing the date line. The general custom is to place the date line of a business letter on the upper righthand side of the page, so that it stands two or more spaces below the printed letterhead.

It cannot be set forth as an absolute rule that the date line *must* be in the above-described position; in the "all-blocked" style, as we said, it starts on the *left*. Here again, we face a decision which depends more on personal judgment, and the willingness to go along with prevailing custom, than it does on any implacable authority which cannot be

Figure 4-14

May 15, 19--

Mr. John Taylor
111 East Main Street
Kansas City, Missouri.

Dear John:

I was in Chicago the other day for the purpose of giving a talk to the executives of one of the banks, and while there I asked Miss Underwood to find out where you were. Her letter received today gave me the above address.

The principal reason I wanted your address was to send you mine in order that I might not miss seeing you if you happened through Denver any time soon. They are having a big real estate confab here this week, but insist that you are not on the program.

During these past years I have often thought of you. Our friendship has been worth a great deal to me, and I hope that someday we may have the opportunity of sitting down to "sorta" lick the chops of memory together.

I am still a bachelor and my brother and I have just taken over some bachelor quarters. That means you have a place to stay when you are here. Please remember me to the wife.

Sincerely,

---

broken. In some cases, and particularly those where the design of the letterhead favors the variation, you run across date lines which are centered on the page immediately below the name of the city and state. For example, the position of the date line on a Continental Can Company letter dating back several years (See Figure 4-15) seems to be a good one, and better from the appearance angle than if it had been typed in the customary spot, to the right.

Neither is it reasonable to establish, as some letter manuals do, any exact number of spaces that the date line should be typed below the letterhead. If the body of the letter is short and, to gain the best

Figure 4-15. A Letter with Date Line Centered on the Page

CONTINENTAL CAN COMPANY, Inc.

C

CONTINENTAL CAN BUILDING
100 EAST 42ND STREET
NEW YORK 17, N. Y.

CABLE ADDRESS
"CONTINCAN, NEW YORK"

February 24, 19__

Mr. John Doe
1234 Broadway
New York 34, N.Y.

Dear Mr. Doe:

Thank you for your recent inquiry concerning employment
possibilities with Continental Can Company.

We have considered your training and interests carefully
as they relate to our immediate requirements and, unfortunately,
have concluded that we are not in a position at this moment to
offer you anything that would utilize your background to full
advantage.

Your interest in Continental Can, however, is sincerely
appreciated and you may be assured we will contact you if
any openings for which you qualify should subsequently come
to our attention.

Sincerely yours,

CONTINENTAL CAN COMPANY, INC.

L.R. Hamilton
Director of Recruitment

LH:ml

appearance, it is dropped down to the center of the page, the date line may well be dropped with it.

After the figure or figures designating the day of the month, the comma should follow immediately. It is unnecessary, and may be considered wrong, to use *nd, rd, st,* or *th.*

Wrong:	*Right:*
April 1st	April 1
March 3rd	March 3
July 20th	July 20
August 2nd	August 2

In the above examples, the periods were omitted at the end of the date lines, although they just as properly could have been used; the decision depends on whether the punctuation of the name and address lines is "open" or "closed."

It is not thought good form to abbreviate the name of the month, or to substitute a figure for it.

Wrong:	*Right:*
Feb. 1, 1999	February 1, 1999
Feb. l, 99	
2-1-99	
2/1/99	

It was once customary to use words instead of figures for the year and day of the month.

Variations in the date line. The great majority of date lines are typed in the sequence of month, day, and year. This is purely a matter of custom, as it would appear more logical to start with the smallest unit (the day) and proceed to the largest (the year). The latter is the form officially used by the military services. Some letter-writers evidently agree with this logic, as you now and then encounter a date line typed in the following order.

25 September 1999 *instead of* September 25, 1999

When this newer form is used, and there is not the slightest objection to it, no punctuation is needed. The punctuation automatically becomes "open" for the inside address and signature lines.

That the form of the date line is not fixed, except by custom, is proved by the numerous attempts made to make it more interesting or ornamental. Often, the variation serves some special purpose for the company, as to call attention to an anniversary year. Other times it may simply represent the desire of the writer to get out of the groove and do something different. To ban such a device on the ground that it takes more time to type or read, seems rather like splitting hairs, as anything done to improve the appearance or effectiveness of a business letter can only be judged by whether or not the results are worth the time and effort.

The forms taken by these date line variations are too numerous for description. Some seem within the bounds of good taste; others, too "wild and woolly." The latter, of course, do not merit your approval, but there are always those who dislike *any* departure from the conventional standard even though it may be good.

These examples are typical of special date lines typed in forms that get away from the conventional. Since the first job of a business letter is to get attention, it may be that in their small way they support that purpose. At least, they are different, and not unpleasing to the eye. After all, there is no law that says this part of a letter must be typed on one line or in any certain position—nor is it a breach of business etiquette to use variety. The forms commonly seen have been developed by custom, and none are fixed or unchangeable.

August
26
1999

26
August
1999

August 26
1 9 9 9

Five More Days
26 August 1999
Clearance Sale

2. SIMPLIFYING THE INSIDE ADDRESS.

Making letter handling easy. The lines that identify and locate the recipient are called the "inside address," and in content they should be exactly the same as those on the envelope which tell Uncle Sam to whom and where the delivery is to be made. The "rules" governing their use are given below, but again it is well to remember that in some respects they merely represent the preference of the majority of letter-writers, while those of the minority often take liberties with them.

The chief benefit of the inside address is to the company served by the writer of the letter, since it gives the information necessary for filing and future reference. Inasmuch as the recipients are thoroughly acquainted with their own address, it would seem foolish to type it under their name, were it not for the utility purpose of recording it on the copy.

All right, here are the things to remember in connection with the inside address. Call them rules, if you wish, for they tend to create orderliness and uniformity when coordinated with similar conventions that govern the handling of the salutation, the complimentary close, and the other parts of the typed letter.

1. Choosing the best position. It is the first line of the inside address which determines what the margin shall be on the left side of the page. The whole appearance of the letter is influenced by how well the typist is able to select the position which will leave the right amount of space for the other parts, and thus achieve that "harmony of proportion" so necessary if the best possible impression is to be made.

The exact spot where the first letter of the first word is to be typed, as "M" in "Mr. John D. Doe," depends on the length of the copy that is to be balanced on the page. If the letter is a short one, the inside address may be started several spaces below the date line, but even if the letter is long, a minimum of two spaces is considered necessary to avoid the appearance of overcrowding. In the same way, the width of the margin may be varied, but should never be less than 1 inch. It is much better to run the letter to a second page than to disregard these two minimums in an effort to squeeze more on the one page than it should carry.

The lines of the inside address should always be single-spaced and blocked. The first line of the inside address and the salutation are aligned with all the lines in the body which are not indented.

2. Selecting a punctuation style. The oldest method of punctuating the inside address is to place a comma at the end of each line except the last, which ends with a period. This is called "closed" punctuation, in contrast with the "open" style in which no marks are used at the end of any of the lines—except when the name of a company ends with an abbreviated word.

The punctuation of the date line determines whether that of the inside address is to be "closed" or "open," since the form used in both of these parts must *agree*.

May 9, 1999.

	Mr. John Jones, Secretary,
	Jones Costume Co.,
	234 East Gay Street,
(Closed)	Decatur, Illinois.
	62525

Dear Mr. Jones:

May 9, 1999

	Mr. John Jones, Secretary
	Jones Costume Co.
	234 East Gay Street
(Open)	Decatur, Illinois
	62525

Dear Mr. Jones:

Two facts need to be remembered in connection with the punctuation of the inside address. The first is that no matter which form is used, open or closed, the salutation is commonly followed with a colon or a comma. The second is that "open" does not mean any of the punctuation marks can be omitted *except* at the end of the lines.

Also notice that in the second line of the first example, the word "company" could not be spelled out to agree with Secretary, Street, and Illinois, because the abbreviated form is part of the official firm name.

In the second example, which was open, the abbreviation, "Co." had to be punctuated with the period, although the comma was omitted to agree with the other line endings. This illustrates a law which in all cases must be followed—it is not permissible to alter in any way the established form of a firm or association name. If a word is abbreviated, or if & is used for *and*, the typing must conform.

Blueprint for content. The simple rule for the make-up of the inside address is that it should contain everything necessary for the easy delivery of the letter, a duplicate of the address on the envelope, and that it should give proper recognition of title when the recipient holds a position of importance in the company. In typing the sequence of lines, the practice is to start with the smallest item and work down to the largest—name, title, company, street address or box number, city, state, and zip code. Also, if the letter is going outside the United States, the name of the country would come last.

To be sure, not all of these items appear in every inside address. If the letter is dictated to an individual, and the contents are personal, the name of the company or association is not used unless it is necessary as a guide to delivery.

The shortest form of all is that of two lines—name, city, state, and zip code—as when the letter is going to some very small village where the street address is not needed, or to a public official whose address is well known to post office authorities. A none-too-popular example of the latter is, Internal Revenue, Detroit, Michigan."

Here are examples, in the order of their complexity.

Mrs. Doris George
Walker, West Virginia 26180

Mr. John Q. Public,
Rural Route 2,
LaGrange, Indiana 46761

Mr. Jonathan Doe,
505 Oregon Street,
Rollins, Montana
59931

The Purina Mills
Seventh and Gratiot Streets,
St. Louis, Missouri
63116

Dr. W. B. Black, Treasurer,
The Continental Corporation,
10 Rut Road,
North Conway, New Hampshire
03860

Mr. Frank Hesselroth, Manager,
Advertising & Sales Executives Club,
913 Baltimore Avenue,
Waterbury, Connecticut
06710

Mr. James Doe,
Superintendent of Maintenance,
The Buckeye Building,
42 East Gay Street,
Tempe, Arizona
85281

Mr. Oscar Merriwell, President,
Springfield Advertising Club,
Petterson and Hogart,
987 Washington Avenue,
Portland, Oregon
97231

Mrs. Morgana Hanford Goodfellow,
Assistant to the Vice-President
Johnstown Construction Company,
4454 Riverside Road,
Cleveland, Ohio 44101

Mrs. Burton Maxwell McPherson,
Chairman, Entertainment Committee,
Sales & Advertising Club,
McPherson, Mack, and Monihan,
333 Grandville Avenue,
Grand Rapids, Michigan 49500

To avoid the formidable appearance of the six-line address, it is desirable to place the name and title of the individual on the first line, but this is not always possible—see last address above. Had the first and second lines been combined, the one line would have stretched across the page to a point below the date line; moreover, it would have appeared off balance with the rest of the inside address.

Just how far across the page the first line of the inside address may properly reach is a debatable question of no great importance. As in all matters which influence the appearance of a typed letter, the aim is to make the best possible impression, but what determines "best" is often a matter of opinion. Some letter authorities say that the first line of the inside address should not reach beyond the center of the page. Roughly, this is probably as good a guide as any, although no harm is done if the line happens to exceed that point by a few spaces.

To keep the first line within the limitation of half the page, one of the leading experts, William H. Butterfield, approves the "carryover" of part of the line to the space below. According to Butterfield, "if this is done, the continuation should be indented five spaces when the paragraphs of the letter body are not indented, and the same amount as the paragraphs when the latter are indented." He gives the following examples:

> Dr. Edward J. Bell, Director
> Department of Aeronautical
>   Engineering
> The University of Oklahoma
> Norman, Oklahoma 73019
>
> Dear Sir:
>
> We have given much thought to your suggestion…
>
> Professor Carol Brighton
> Massachusetts Institute of
>   Technology
> Cambridge Station
> Boston, Massachusetts 02139
>
> Dear Professor Brighton:
>
> It was a pleasure to hear from you regarding…

Always remember to include the proper zip code. This speeds the letter toward delivery. If you're not sure of the proper zip code, there are several fine Zip Code Directories on the market. They are invaluable, yet inexpensive, tools.

4. Adding numbers. The use of a sign or word before a street number is taboo in the inside address. The number can stand on its own legs.

> *Wrong:*   Mrs. Jacob Goldman,
>   #3561 Lindell Boulevard,
>   Louisville, Kentucky
>   40201

Wrong:	Mrs. Jacob Goldman, No. 3561 Lindell Boulevard, Louisville, Kentucky 40201
Right:	Mrs. Jacob Goldman, 3561 Lindell Boulevard, Louisville, Kentucky 40201

When the numeric names of streets and avenues are composed of single numbers, they should be spelled; when composed of compound numbers, use the figures.

Wrong:	Seventy-third Street
Right:	73rd Street or 73 Street
Wrong:	4th Avenue
Right:	Fourth Avenue

A possible exception to the above rule is created in those cities where numbers and words are used to identify streets and avenues of the same names, as "4th Street," and "Fourth Avenue"—the one thoroughfare usually running east and west, and the other north and south. In such cases, the typist uses the forms established by the city, as otherwise there might be confusion in delivery.

5. Using abbreviations. To an extent, the use of abbreviations in the inside address of a business letter is dictated by custom, or by the personal inclination of the writer or company. You should never abbreviate the name of a city. Even when "to do or not to do" is a matter of choice, the fact still remains that most typed words look better when *not* abbreviated, and nothing is gained by the shortened forms except a little saving of space and time. Certainly, good taste decrees *consistency* in the one direction or the other.

Wrong:	Mr. John T. Williamson, 1876 Parkview *Avenue,* Atlanta, *GA,* 31702
Right:	Mr. John T. Williamson, 1876 Parkview *Avenue,* Atlanta, *Georgia* 31702
Right:	Mr. John T. Williamson, 1876 Parkview *Ave.,* Atlanta, *GA* 31702

In general, the abbreviations used may be grouped in three classes: obligatory, customary, and permissible. Those in the last group are left to the choice of the writer, but it is not wise to disregard those in the second group dictated by custom. Those in the first group may not under any circumstances be spelled out.

(a) Abbreviations that *must* be used in both the outside and the inside address are those already fixed in the official name of the company or association as indicated on their letterhead. Even though the abbreviated word may not appeal to the writer of the letter, and he would much prefer to see it spelled out, there still remains no choice. This also is true of the substitution of the sign & for *and*. While not technically an abbreviation, it may logically be included with the others, such as *Co.* for *Company,* and *Corp.* for *Corporation.*

(b) There are many of the abbreviations so firmly established by custom that they should not be tampered with. For example, the use of *Mister* instead of the abbreviated form would be rather sure to attract unfavorable attention, and thus in its small way detract from the success of the letter. These abbreviations established by custom are listed below:

*Straight address: Mr., Mrs., Ms., Messers., Esq., Jr., Sr., Dr.

*Professional/Official acknowledgement: C.P.A., Ph.D., D.D.S., M.D.

*Trade associations: A.A.A., N.A.M., A.F. of L., N.E.A., A.S.C.A.P.

*Associations, Honors and Distinctions: D.A.R., B.P.O.E., U.S.O., V.F.W., U.S.N., USMC., ret.

*Titles: Rev., Hon., Pres., Sec., Tres.

*Postal indicators: Rt., P.O. Box, F.O.B., UPS

(c) The abbreviations left to choice are many. For example:

*Titles: Prof., Rev., Hon., Sen.

*State Names: NJ, WY, AZ, MI, IL, TX

*Location/Address: St., Blvd., Ave.

As previously stated, these abbreviations in the flexible group are best when used only for a good reason, such as to shorten a long line in the inside address.

A few additional facts should be understood with respect to abbreviations in the inside address.

(a) When the person addressed holds more than one degree, indicate only the highest, unless there are two or more in different fields of endeavor.

Wrong: Professor Albert S. Jones, A.B., A.M., Ph.D.
Right: Albert S. Jones, Ph.D.
Right: Asa B. Underwood, A.M., LL.D.

(b) When only the last name is known, it is considered discourteous to abbreviate the title.

Wrong: Prof. Bagby...Dr. Schreiner
Right: Professor Bagby...Doctor Schreiner

(c) If the last name only is used, the word *Reverend* should be followed by *Mr.*—or *Dr.* if the clergyman is a D.D. It is customary to abbreviate this word, unless preceded by *The*.

Wrong: Rev. Boardman
           Reverend Boardman
Right: Rev. Mr. Boardman
           Rev. Dr. Boardman
           Rev. James Boardman
           The Reverend Mr. Boardman
           The Reverend Doctor Boardman
           The Reverend James Boardman

(d) The use of the word *Honorable* and its abbreviation is the same as that of *Reverend*.

Wrong: Hon. Bricker
           Honorable Bricker
Right: Hon. Mr. Bricker
           Hon. John W. Bricker
           The Honorable John W. Bricker
           The Honorable Mr. Bricker

(e) The word *Esquire* or its abbreviation is sometimes used after the names of prominent attorneys or other high-ranking professionals who do not have other titles. The custom dates back to early days and is fast fading in popularity. When a title precedes the name, the use of the word or its abbreviation is not permitted.

Wrong: Mr. L. E. Mackie, Esq.
Right: L. E. Mackie, Esq.
Wrong: Dr. Claude Minton, Esq.

(f) The use of *Messrs.* is not permissible in addressing companies or associations with impersonal names. It is okay for a company where the names in the title represent men, or men and women.

Wrong: Messrs. General Electric Company
           Messrs. Illinois Central System

Right: General Electric Company
              Illinois Central System

Right: Messrs. Brown, Brown, and Brown
              Messrs. Marrison Parks and Bros.
              Messrs. Wollett and Kirby

(g) A widow should be addressed as *Mrs.*—and socially she continues to be known by her husband's name. In legal and financial affairs, however, her given name is substituted.

Socially: Mrs. Abner Carter
Legally: Mrs. Julia Carter

(h) A divorced woman may continue to use her husband's full name, or a combination of his and her surnames. However, if she has legally resumed her maiden name, she may be addressed as Miss or Ms.

Right: Mrs. Andrew H. Bronson
Wrong: Mrs. Bernice Bronson
Right: Mrs. Baker Bronson
Right: Miss Bernice Baker (if legal)
Right: Ms. Bernice Baker (if legal)

6. Checklist for capitalization. Prevailing customs for capitalization within the inside address are as follows. Some are a matter of correct English practice, others are rules developed by common usage.

Capitalize—

(a) Initials, given names, and surnames.

(b) All words and abbreviations in the names of companies, trade associations, and other organizations, *except* conjunctions, prepositions, and articles. However, an *exception* to the exception is that an article must be capitalized if it starts a line.

Right: Empire Service Corporation
              The Brokers' Institute
              Baker, Brown, and Buggins, Inc.
              The City of Columbus

(c) Names of thoroughfares, and words that describe direction.

Right: 22 East Gay Street
              431 West Fifth Avenue
              33 Park Terrace
              5676 Oleotangy Boulevard

(d) Words to indicate post office delivery, and rural mail routes.

Right: Post Office Box 99
P.O. Box 333, Station B
A.P.O., Ft. Sam Houston
Rural Route 3

(e) Names of buildings, and units in them.

Right: The Buckeye Building
Room 777, Federal Insurance Building
Apartment D, the Park Plaza
Suite BB, Jefferson Hotel

(f) Names of cities, counties, territories, provinces, states, nations, and their abbreviations.

Right: Columbus, Franklin County, Ohio 43216
Washington, D.C. 20001

(g) Abbreviations for degrees and other official designations.

(h) Titles and designations of rank or position, such as Miss, Mrs., Ms., Mr., Professor, Dr., Reverend, Messrs., Secretary, Vice-President, Chairman of the Board, Manager, Editor, Personnel Director, and the others. When the title consists of more than one word, all are capitalized except articles, conjunctions, and prepositions.

(i) Names of divisions or departments within an organization or company, except for articles, conjunctions, and prepositions.

Right: Department of Finance
Maintenance and Repair Division
Committee for City Planning

7. The attention line. Considerable difference of thought exists in the business letter world with respect to the necessity of the attention line and where it should be placed. It is discussed here, in connection with the inside address, because it is my opinion that nine out of ten of the attention lines encountered in business correspondence could just as well, or better, have been omitted. I see no reason, at least generally, why a letter should be addressed to a company, and then bounced back into the lap of an individual through an attention line. Why not address the letter to the individual, followed by the name of the company? This is a controversial question, and after you have examined the evidence on both sides, you may make your own decision as to which plan you prefer.

John Doe, for example, is about to write a letter, with a check enclosed, to the Canary Cracker Company. He would have sent the money sooner, but an argument has been going on as to whether or not he is entitled to a special discount he thought he would get. Several letters have passed back and forth between John Doe and Robert Black, Credit Manager of the cracker company.

Okay, that is the simple background, and here is the problem faced by John Doe. Obviously, he owes the money to Canary Cracker Company, but all of his correspondence has been with Mr. Black. How shall his letter be directed? That is the point where the opinion of business people and letter experts seems to split. One group says that John Doe should write to the company, and ask that his letter be called to the attention of Robert Black. The other side says that is nonsense. Mr. Black's delegated responsibility in the company is understood. He is the Credit Manager. He *represents* the company, and has authority to make decisions. Why go around and around the mulberry bush? Write to Black direct.

Well, if you want to get into the fight, take off your coat. You are welcome. Here are the two ways John Doe might address his letter.

With *Attention* *Line*	Canary Cracker Company Main Street at Drexel Hijinks, Colorado 80022 Attention Robert Black

Gentlemen:

The *Direct* *Approach*	Mr. Robert Black, Credit Manager Canary Cracker Company Main Street at Drexel Hijinks, Colorado 80022

Dear Mr. Black

If one looks with impartiality at both sides of the question, it is apparent that the attention line can at times serve a useful purpose. The chief objection is that it adds a formal touch to the appearance of the letter, and thus works against the major aim of making every letter a personal contact betwen writer and reader. Furthermore, it seems that some businessmen fall into the habit of using the attention line a lot more often than is necessary. But if there are circumstances which make its use advisable, as when some legal question is involved, or when the name of the head of a department is unknown, the attention line merits approval. However, it is safe to say that the attention line is declining in popularity.

Sometimes the need is also felt for a reference line, such as the order number, the file number, or the subject of the letter being answered. In a consideration of the appearance of the letter, and the necessity for keeping it as simple as possible, it is much better when the letter does not need to be cluttered with any of these special items; when absolutely necessary, the following position is recommended.

Mr. John B. Duffy
Iowa Mail Company
343 Chapel Avenue
Davenport, Iowa 52805

Re: Order #7889

Dear Mr. Duffy,

The lawn mower which you billed on the above order number
is being returned today because...

Sometimes, to facilitate the handling of mail, large organizations *ask* that an identifying number or initials be mentioned when the reply to a letter is dictated. This leaves writers no choice but to follow instructions, as otherwise their letters may not get to the right party, or receive prompt attention. There are also companies that ask, on their letterheads, that all mail be directed to the company, rather than to any individual in it. Here again, writers should accept the fact that there must be a reason for the request, and comply with it.

8. The importance of proper names. Accuracy in the use of names is a most important requisite for the inside address, as well as any other place in the letter or on the envelope. Individuals hold high respect for their name; and want nobody to take liberties with them. Furthermore, they have selected for their own use the form which they like best, and any variation by others is likely to irritate them. They expect you to spell the words correctly, to use the right initials, and they don't like any combination to which they are not accustomed. Offhand, you might think that any error which does not interfere with the delivery of the letter must be a small thing to worry about, but that is not true. It is discourteous to write any part of an individual's name incorrectly, and doing so is quite likely to hinder the success of the letter. For example:

John D. Jones does not appreciate being addressed as John B. Jones.

Marie Ashton-Smith wants her lineage known or she wouldn't use the hyphenated surname. Don't write to her as Marie Smith or she might take insult.

J. Alphonse Goodfellow has some reason sufficient to himself for not spelling out the first name. Even though you knew it to be James, it would be unwise to address him as James Alphonse.

Wm. H. Warren likes the abbreviation for William. Then why take the chance of displeasing him by spelling out the name?

L. E. "Cy" Frailey may look like a funny way for a fellow to sign his name, and probably it is. But go along with him. He likes it, so humor the codger.

If Mrs. Boone uses the signature Mrs. Marshall V. Boone, III, then that's your cue. Address her the same way.

There may be no real reason for John Jacob Heinbaugh to place "Jr." after his name, because you know his father is dead and there could be no confusion in delivery of his mail. But follow his lead. His signature carries the "Jr."—respect his preference.

When replying to another person's letter, the signature is your guide—*if* you can read it. Of course, if the name seems to have been written in a wild frenzy by a contortionist, you may not be able to decipher it. Usually, the problem is solved by the name typed on the signature line. A further difficulty may arise at this point, however. The typed signature may be more formal than the swiggly lines you couldn't read. The best rule of thanks is—don't guess. If you can't make out the handwritten signature, address your letter as it appears typed.

Other times, the letter may be going to an individual as the first contact, and only the last name is known. For such a predicament, the solution may be found in the telephone book, the city directory, *Who's Who*, or some other national compilation of names and titles. Or, it may be that someone else in the company has had previous correspondence with the same individual. It is surprising how much information the files of an organization may produce for those who will turn to them.

Accuracy in writing company names is also important, as any error indicates lack of familiarity with the company, and it may detract, in the mind of the reader, from the good impression which the writer wants to make. There is seldom any excuse for a mistake of this kind, as usually there is a letterhead available which carries the correct form.

With a letterhead before you, there is no problem. When in Rome, do as the Romans do. What you might like, if the firm were yours, is of no consequence. Your typist must type the name exactly as it is used by the company.

The variations in name forms are numerous, and that requires alertness in copying the style of each particular company. Some begin with *The,* and others do not. Some prefer abbreviations such as *Inc.,* *Corp.,* and *Co.,* and others like these words spelled out. In a sequence of surnames, some firms use a comma preceding *and,* and others omit it.

The Pierce Brokerage Company

Union Clothing Company

Bates and Gerry, Incorporated

John C. Featherweight, Inc.

The Dartnell Corporation

The American Mutual Benefit Corp.

James W. Underwood Company

The Universal Motor Co.

Baker, Jones, Brown, and Bean

Walker, Bechtel, Doe & Flesh

When the exact form of the company or organization name is not known and there seems to be no way to check it, you may use the forms considered best. This would mean, with respect to the variations illustrated above, that you would use *The* when the rest of the name permits; spell out Incorporated, Corporation, and Company; and not use the comma between the last two names of the sequence. But these choices would endure only until the official forms became known. After that, you would properly frame the inside address to conform with company usage.

Street names should be spelled exactly as they exist, although sometimes this rule is disregarded. For example, *St. Louis* is the official form for that city, and not Saint Louis.

In connection with street names, there are the words which designate direction, and when space permits, they should not be abbreviated. Usually, the qualifying word appears after the number and before the generic name, but when placed last in the line it should be preceded by a comma.

999 *North* High Street
3232 *East* Broad Street
121 *South* Parkview Drive
4996 S.E. Connecticut Avenue (Abbreviated to conserve space)
3333 Grand Avenue, North
237 Lindell Street, East
6543 Tchoupitoulas Street, S.W. (Abbreviated to conserve space)

When a street number immediately follows a house number, confusion must be avoided by one of two devices. Either the space between the numbers should be doubled, or a comma should be placed between them. Of course, there is no problem when a word standing for direction appears between the two numbers.

656 32 Street
656, 32 Street
924 East 15 Avenue

For corner addresses, it is often customary in business to use the names of the intersecting thoroughfares, omitting numbers. If both are of the same type—streets, avenues, roads—the designating word may be used only once in the plural form. If they differ in type, both of the designating words must be used.

Right: Grant and McKinley Streets
Wrong: Grant Street and McKinley Street
Right: Lee Avenue at Clay Street
Wrong: Lee and Clay

Earlier in this section, other facts related to the street address were covered. It would help to review them in connection with the material just presented.

The title *Miss* is used only when it is the preferred one of the receiver or when the letter is going to a very young girl; even girls in their teens have become accustomed to being addressed as "Ms.". One of the problems which used to confront business letter articles of the past has been solved with the common title of "Ms.". When the writers did not know the marital status or age of their contact, errors were always possible. Sometimes the methods were overlooked and caused no damage to either party, but when the contact aimed at influencing behavior, the stumbling block created by incorrect addressing became insurmountable.

The policies of some companies still cause letter mechanics concern. When you receive a letter from "B.L. Garner, Credit Manager," for example, you may be at a loss as to how to properly address your reply. In order to promote equality, this company may have a policy of using only initials for their personnel. This certainly does not help you. If you cannot determine whether B.L. is male or female, take a chance on "Mr.". The odds are in your favor. If B.L. turns out to be a female who would prefer Ms., she will most likely tell you in your next contact with her; if not, no harm has come to your relationship.

Women in business is common practice today. The proper forms of address is part of the imperative knowledge of the good letter-writer. A woman is *not* addressed by a title conferred on her husband.

Wrong: Mrs. Professor J.B. Maynard
    Mrs. Dr. Wayne Brooks

Right: Mrs. J.B. Maynard
              Mrs. Wayne Brooks

However, any titles which *she* has received are used *in addressing* her. All rules of address are the same as applied to her male counterpart. The only present exception are the formal address used for women holding political or professional office. Here the title of Madame is added to the position she holds, such as, Madame Chairman, Madame President, etc. For letter style, see below.

Inside Address	Salutation
The Honorable Clara B. Jones	Madam,
Sam Rayburn Office Building	Dear Madam,
Washington, DC 20001	Dear Representative Jones,

It will greatly simplify your understanding of titles and their uses if you will think of them with respect to the major groups into which they may be classified. The rules for each group are limited by tradition and custom, so that modern letter-writers are forced to obey conventions and formalities which are a hindrance to the general objective of making every letter a natural, personal contact.

For your convenience, check the chart below for specific specialized forms of address.

ADDRESS AND SALUTATION FORMS FOR INDIVIDUALS OF RANK

(When two or more forms are suggested for the same title, they are listed in the order of decreasing formality. To complete address, the street and number, and the names of city and state, need to be added.)

Personage/Title	Salutation
Abbot	
The Right Reverend Abbot Denn,	Right Reverend and dear Abbot,
O.S.B. (or other initials of the Order)	Dear Father Abbot,
Admiral, Full, Fleet	
The Admiral of the Navy of the United States	Dear Sir

Admiral Jonathan Doe
Chief of Naval Operations   Dear Admiral Doe,

Alderman
Alderman James B. Noon   Dear Sir,

           Dear Alderman Noon,

Ambassador (American)
His Excellency   Sir,
The American Ambassador to
 Great Britain   Your Excellency,

The American Embassy
London, England   Dear Mr. Ambassador,
The Honorable Carl Reid
The American Ambassador to
 Great Britian

Ambassador (Foreign)
His Excellency   Sir,
The Ambassador of the
 French Republic   Excellency,
French Embassy
Washington, D.C.   Your Excellency,

His Excellency
M. René Lenoir
Ambassador of the French
 Republic

Archbishop
Most Reverend Albert B. Dean Your Excellency,

           Your Grace,

Archdeacon
The Venerable the
 Archdeacon of Philadelphia Venerable Sir,
The Venerable Woodson Ware,
 Archdeacon of Philadelphia

Assemblyman
    The Honorable Walter B.
        Goon   Dear Sir:
    Member of Assembly   My dear Mr. Goon,
    Assemblyman Walter B. Goon   Dear Mr. Goon,

Assistant Secretary (Cabinet)
    The Assistant Secretary of the
        War Department   Sir,

                          (My) Dear Sir,
    The Honorable Russell C. Doe   My dear Mr. Doe,
      Assistant Secretary of the   Dear Mr. Doe,
      War Department   (*Never* Mr. Secretary,)

Associate Justice of the Supreme
      Court
    The Honorable William H.
      Black   Sir,

    Associate Justice of the
      Supreme Court   Mr. Justice,
    The Honorable William H.
      Black   Your Honor,
    Justice, Supreme Court of the
      United States   My dear Mr. Justice,
    Mr. William H. Black   My dear Justice Black,
      United States Supreme
      Court   Dear Justice Black,

Attorney General
    (See Cabinet Officer)

Baron
    The Lord Scarborough   Sir,

                          Dear Lord Scarborough,

Baroness
    The Lady Scarborough   Madam,

                          Dear Lady Scarborough,

Baronet
    Sir James Kinsman, Bart.   Sir,
Bishop (Methodist)
    The Reverend Bishop Carl
      Crew   Dear Sir,
    Bishop of the Eastern Area   My dear Bishop Crew,

                                         Dear Bishop Crew,

Bishop (Protestant Episcopal)
    The Right Reverend Samuel
      Seabury   Right Reverend and dear Sir,
    Bishop of Cleveland   My dear Bishop Seabury,

Bishop (Roman Catholic)
    The Most Reverend James
      Bartley   Your Excellency,
    Bishop of Baltimore
    The Most Reverend Bishop
      Bartley   My dear Bishop,

Bishop (Anglican)
    The Right Reverend the Lord
      Bishop of (name of
      bishopric)   My Lord Bishop,
                                         My Lord,

    The Lord Bishop of (name of
      bishopric)

Bishop (Scottish)
    The Right Reverend Bishop   Right Reverend Sir,
    James B. McPherson

Brigadier General
    Brigadier General   Dear Sir,
    Arthur C. Clandleman   Dear General Clandleman,

Cabinet Officer

The Honorable the Secretary of Agriculture (or War, State, Commerce, etc.)	Sir,
	Dear Sir,
The Honorable the Postmaster General (or Attorney General).	Dear (My dear) Mr. Secretary, (Postmaster General, Attorney General)

Cadet

Cadet Harrison Slagle	Dear Sir,
	Dear Cadet Slagle,
	Dear Mr. Slagle,

Canon

The Very Reverend Canon Walter Woodsberl	Very Reverend Canon,
The Very Reverend Walter Canon Woodsberl	My dear (or Dear) Canon Woodsberl,

Captain

Captain William Fahnestock United States Army (or Navy or Marine Corps)	Dear Sir,
	Dear Captain Fahnestock,

Cardinal

His Eminence, Frank, Cardinal Cantell	Your Eminence,
His Eminence Cardinal Cantell	My Lord Cardinal, (to those of foreign countries)

Cardinal (if also Archbishop)

His Eminence the Cardinal, Archbishop of Baltimore	Your Eminence,
His Eminence Cardinal Smythe, Archbishop of Baltimore	

Chargé d' Affaires
   The Chargé d' Affaires of
      Mexico   Sir,
   Mr. Salico Gonzoles   Dear Sir,
   Chargé d' Affaires   My dear Mr. Gonzoles, (or use
                            title if there is one—
                            hereditary, military, or naval)

   John Shrewsbury, Esquire
   Chargé d' Affaires

Chief Justice of the United States
   The Honorable John W. Bates   Sir,
   Chief Justice of the Supreme
      Court of the United States   Mr. Chief Justice,
   Chief Justice Bates   My dear Mr. Justice,
   United States Supreme Court   Dear Justice Bates,
   The Chief Justice of the
      United States

Chief of Police
   Frank Minton   Dear Sir,
   Chief of Police   Dear Chief Minton,

Clergyman
   The Reverend Donald Beard   Reverend Sir,
   Reverend Dr. Donald Beard   My dear Sir,
   (If Doctor of Divinity)   My dear Mr. Beard,Dear Mr.
                          Beard,

                          Dear Dr. Beard,

Clerk of the House (or *Senate*)
   The Honorable James Pierce   Dear Sir,
   Clerk of the House (or Senate) My dear Mr. Pierce,

                          Dear Mr. Pierce,

Colonel
   Colonel Gerard B. Goodman   Dear Sir,
   United States Army (or
      Marine Corps)   Dear Colonel Goodman,

Commander

Commander B.C. Winters	Dear Sir,
United States Navy	Dear Commander Winters,

Commissioner of a Bureau

The Honorable William Dorset	Sir,
Commissioner of the Bureau of Education	Dear Sir,
Department of Interior	My dear Mr. Dorset,

Comptroller of the Currency

The Honorable Robert C. Roberts	Sir,
Comptroller of the Currency	Dear Sir,
	My dear Mr. Roberts,

Congressman

The Honorable Howard Reamer	Sir,
House of Representatives	
The Honorable Howard Reamer	Dear Sir,
Representative in Congress, (when away from Washington)	My dear Congressman Reamer,
Representative Howard Reamer	Dear Representative Reamer,
House of Representatives	Dear Mr. Reamer,

Congresswoman

The Honorable Clara O. Booth	Dear Madam,
House of Representatives	
The Honorable Clara O. Booth	Dear Representative Booth,
Representative in Congress (When away from Washington)	My dear Miss Booth,
Representative Clara O. Booth	
House of Representatives	

Consul
 Mr. Richard D. Mann   Dear Sir,
 Consul of the United States of
  America   Dear Mr. Consul,
            My dear Mr. Mann,

Corporal
 Corporal Charles Hayes   Dear Sir,
 United States Army or United
  States Marine Corps   Dear Mr. Hayes,

Countess
 The Countess of Sheffield Madam,

            Dear Lady Sheffield,

Dean (Ecclesiastical)
 The Very Reverend the Dean
  of St. Joseph's   Sir,
 The Very Reverend Dean
  George Conant   Very Reverend Sir,

            Very Reverend Father (Roman
             Catholic),

Dean (Graduate School or
 College)
 Dean Casper Millwright   Dear Sir,
 School of Commerce   Dear Dean Millwright,

Diplomat

 (See Ambassador, Chargé d'
  Affaires, Minister. For
  diplomats of lower rank, use
  the common forms of
  address, unless they have
  military, naval, or
  hereditary titles.)

Duchess
The Duchess of Ashleigh   Madam,

Dear Duchess of Ashleigh,

Duke
The Duke of Ashleigh   Sir,

Dear Duke of Ashleigh,

Earl
The Earl of Scofield   Sir,

Dear Lord Scofield,

Ensign
Ensign E. W. Brown   Dear Sir,
United States Navy   Dear Mr. Brown,

Envoy
(See Minister, Diplomatic)

General
General Henry S. Hatch   Sir,
United States Army   Dear Sir,

Dear General Hatch,

Governor
His Excellency   Your Excellency,
The Governor of Ohio   Sir,
The Honorable the Governor
 of Ohio   Dear Sir,
The Honorable John W.
 Bricker   My dear Governor Bricker,
Governor of Ohio

Judge
The Honorable Harold
 Lemming   Dear Sir,
United States District Judge   Dear Judge Lemming,
The Honorable Amy O'Neil   Dear Madam,
Judge of the Circuit Court   Dear Judge O'Neil,

Knight
    Sir James Parkersdam   Sir,

                                    Dear Sir James,

Lawyer
    Mr. Carl Benbow   Dear Sir,
    Attorney at Law   My dear Mr. Benbow,

                                    Dear Mr. Benbow,

Lieutenant
    Lieutenant Ralph Maloney   Dear Sir,
    United States Army   Dear Mr. Maloney,

Lieutenant Colonel
    Lieutenant Colonel John Beam Dear Sir,
    United States Army   Dear Colonel Beam,
  (Omit the *Lieutenant* in the Salutation.)

Lieutenant Commander
    Lieutenant Commander C. O.
      Blue   Dear Sir,
    United States Navy   Dear Mr. Blue,
  (The salutation to a naval officer of or below the rank of
  Lieutenant Commander should not refer to his title. Use *Mr.*)

Lieutenant General
    Lieutenant General Casey Shea Dear Sir,

                                    Dear General Shea,
  (Omit the *Lieutenant* in the Salutation.)

Lieutenant Governor
    The Honorable Hiram B.
      Snooks   Sir,
    Lieutenant Governor of
      Arizona   Dear Sir,

                                    My dear Mr. Snooks,

Major
Major Robert C. Wolling   Dear Sir,
United States Army   Dear Major Wolling,

Major General
Major General T.T. Thaad   Dear Sir,
United States Army   Dear General Thaad,
(Omit the *Major* in the Salutation.)

Marchioness
Marchioness of Huntleigh   Madam,

     Dear Lady Huntleigh,

Marquis
The Marquis of Huntleigh   Sir,

     Dear Lord Huntleigh,

Master in Chancery
Honorable Hugo B. Bauman   Dear Sir,
Master in Chancery of the
    Circuit Court   Dear Judge Bauman,

Mayor
The Mayor of the City of
    Chicago   Sir,

The Honorable Anton J. Kelly   Dear Sir,
Mayor of the City of Chicago   My dear Mr. Mayor,

     Dear Mayor Kelly,

Midshipman
Midshipman E. C. Obear   Dear Sir,
United States Navy   Dear Mr. Obear,

Minister (Diplomatic)
The Spanish Minister   Your Excellency,
The Spanish Legation
Washington, D.C.   Sir,

His Excellency A. B. Coe
Minister of the United States
   of America
Madrid, Spain

My dear Mr. Minister,

Minister (Religious)
   (See Clergyman; Priest, Rabbi)

Monk
   (See Priest)

Monsignor
   The Right Reverend
   Monsignor Malcomb McComb

The Right Reverend and dear
   Monsignor,
The Right Reverend Monsignor
   Malcomb McComb,
My dear Monsignor McComb,

Mother Superior
   The Reverend Mother
      Superior
   Convent of the Sacred Heart
   Mother Mary Louise, Superior
   Convent of the Sacred Heart
   Reverend Mother Mary Louise
   (Plus initials of the order)

Reverend Mother,
Dear Madam,

My dear Reverend Mother,
Dear Mother Mary Louise,

Nun
   Sister Mary Angelica

Reverend Sister,

Dear Sister Mary Angelica,

Pope
   His Holiness Pope John Paul
      II

Most Holy Father,

Your Holiness,

Postmaster General
   (See Cabinet Officer)

President (College or *University)*
President Robert Lee Jones   Dear Sir,
Ohio University   My dear President Jones,

Robert Lee Jones LL.D.
President, Ohio University
  (Use initials of only the highest
  degree, unless in different
  fields)

Very Reverend Robert Lee
  Jones   Very Reverend and dear Father,
Loyola University
  (If a Catholic College)

President (State Senate)
The Honorable John Doe,
  President   Sir,
The Senate of Oklahoma

President (United States Senate)
The Honorable the President
  of the Senate of the United   Sir,
  States
The Honorable James J. James
President of the Senate
Washington, D.C.

President of the United States
The President of the United
  States   Sir,
The President   My dear Mr. President,
The White House   Dear Mr. President,

Priest (Roman Catholic)
The Reverend Father Harold
  Harms   Reverend Father,
  (Plus initials of the Order)   Dear Father Harms,
  (Above are regular forms;
  note exceptions below.)

Benedictine, Cistercian, or *Canon*
   Regular
     The Very Reverend Dom
       Harold Harms   Reverend Father,
       (Plus initials of the Order) Dear Father Harms,

Carthusian
     The Venerable Father Harold
       Harms, O. Cart.   Venerable Father,

                         Dear Father Harms,

Secular
     The Reverend Harold Harms   Reverend Sir,

       (Plus initials of the Order) Dear Sir,

                         Dear Father Harms,

Priest (Episcopal)
     Reverend Hector M. Heath   Dear Father Heath,

Professor
     Mr. Robert C. Wilcox   Dear Sir,
     Professor Robert C. Wilcox   Dear Professor Wilcox,
     Dr. Robert C. Wilcox   Dear Dr. Wilcox,
       (If he holds the degree)
     The Reverend Professor   My dear Sir,
     Harold D. Esper   Dear Professor Esper,
     The Reverend Harold D.
       Esper D.D.
       (If he holds the degree)

Rabbi
     Rabbi Jacob Solomon   Reverend Sir,
     The Reverend Jacob Solomon   Dear Sir,
     Dr. Jacob Solomon   My dear Rabbi Solomon,

                         Dear Doctor Solomon,

Representative
    (See Congressman)

Secretary of Agriculture, Commerce,
    War, etc.
    (See Cabinet Officer)

Secretary to the President
The Honorable John Doe	Sir,
Secretary to the President	
The White House	Dear Sir,
	Dear Mr. Doe,

Senator (United States or State)
Senator Alvin E. Tobin	Sir,
The Honorable Alvin E. Tobin	Dear Sir,
United States Senate	My dear Senator Tobin,
The Honorable Luther Mack	
Senate of North Carolina	Dear Senator Mack,

Sergeant
Sergeant Terry McGuire	Dear Sir,
U.S. Army or U.S. Marine	
Corps or	Dear Mr. McGuire,
U.S. Air Force	

Sister of Religious Order
The Reverend Sister Mary	
Louise	My dear Sister,
Sister Mary Louise	
(Plus initials of Order)	Dear Sister Mary Louise,

Speaker of the House
The Honorable the Speaker	Dear Sir,
House of Representatives	My dear Mr. Speaker,
The Honorable William Potts	
Speaker of the House of	
Representatives	Dear Mr. Speaker,

Undersecretary of State
 The Undersecretary of State Sir,
 The Honorable Ralph Richey Dear Sir,
 Undersecretary of State
           My dear Mr. Richey,

Vice Admiral and *Rear Admiral*
 Vice Admiral Carl Garner Dear Sir,
 Rear Admiral John Case
 United States Navy   Dear Admiral Garner,

           Dear Admiral Case,

Vice-Consul
 (Same forms as Consul)

Vice President of the United States
 The Vice President   Sir,
 Washington, D.C.   My dear Mr. Vice President,
 The Honorable John Doe
 Vice President of the United Dear Mr. Vice President,
  States   Dear Mr. Doe,

Viscount
 The Viscount Huntleigh Sir,

           Dear Lord Huntleigh,

Viscountess
 The Viscountess Huntleigh Madam,

           Dear Lady Huntleigh,

Note: The above list includes positions of rank most likely to confront the business letter-writer, but it is not intended to be complete. When two or more forms of address are suggested for the same person of title, any one of them may be accepted as correct. The suggested salutations are only those most commonly used. Any of them are correct, but the more informal ones are recommended.

When you write letters, you must make the people feel that you intended to write just to them. This is done by paying careful attention to the proper use of their names and titles.

9. Applying titles. No one has to go through life without a title, even though the four most common lack the distinction of rarity. They are, of course, *Mr., Mrs., Ms.,* and *Miss,* the first two being abbreviations of *Mister* and *Mistress.* Only the abbreviations are ever used in business correspondence, but their acceptance is so wide that to omit them, when no other higher title is sanctioned, is not considered good taste.

Any man may be addressed as *Mr.,* and any woman as *Ms.* if she is married, single, a widow, or a divorcee. As explained previously, a married woman uses her title in connection with the full name of her husband, but a widow also has the choice of substituting her given name for that of her departed husband. If the choice is known to the letter writer, he properly complies with her wishes.

Married:	Mrs. Albert K. Kissell
Widow:	Mrs. Albert K. Kissell, or
	Mrs. Mary Anne Kissell
Divorcee:	Mrs. Mackey Kissell (husband's surname)
	Mrs. Mary Ann Mackey (maiden name)
	Ms. Mary Anne Mackey (as before wedding)

3. EXAMINING THE SALUTATION AND COMPLIMENTARY CLOSE

Shaking hands in letter form. When you walk into a man's office, come down to the breakfast table, or meet an acquaintance on the street, your natural impulse is to extend some form of greeting. You say, "Good morning," or "Hello," or "How do you do?" and the other person would consider you rude if you didn't.

This is exactly what happens in the business letter when you write the salutation. You are greeting the other party before starting the message to be presented in the body of the letter. The ice is broken, and your reader sits back to see what you have to say.

Unfortunately, the greetings used in business letters are not nearly as natural or friendly as those used in personal contacts. Instead, they have been so standardized by custom, in stiff and stilted forms, that little warmth is left in them. This is especially true of the salutations considered proper for persons of rank. They are cut and dried, and serve no good purpose except to satisfy the demands of established custom. To omit them would be called an act of discourtesy and might offend the "bigwigs" to whom the letters are addressed, yet few writers feel that they add in any way to what they are trying to accomplish.

For this reason, no doubt, a revolution against the salutation has been under way for several years in certain business organizations, including some of our largest companies. They have gone so far as to omit entirely the salutation in their letters, and most of the pioneers who have led this crusade will tell you that there has been no loss of goodwill or effectiveness as a result of the bold departure. Whether or not the idea of this omission appeals to you is beside the question. At least, it is at work in business circles, and you should know about it. The number of companies that omit the salutation seems definitely to be increasing, too.

For example, the salutation is not used in letters mailed from one of the nation's largest utilities. Instead, the reader's name is used in the first sentence of each letter, with a tone of cordiality which more than takes the place of the missing salutation. Thus, these letters begin: "Yes, indeed, Mrs. Leary, we will be glad to turn on the gas for you at your new home next Saturday," or "Thanks, Mrs. Bailey, for your letter about the April bill," or "As you requested, Mr. Gordon, we are enclosing an itemized list of your gas bills for last year." These sentences, we think, do a better job in getting the letters started pleasantly, than would the conventional salutations of "Dear Sir," or "Dear Madam," or "Dear Mrs. Bailey." After all, the letters of this company have been remarkably successful in building customer goodwill, although no one can say how much the omission of the salutation has contributed to that accomplishment.

How does a business letter look without a salutation? Well, see Figure 4-16.

Would the omission of the salutation in such a friendly letter make any difference in its reception by the customer? Frankly, the answer to that question is a matter of opinion. You may draw your own conclusion.

In the meantime, consider the various aspects of the salutation, as it is still commonly used in American business letters:

1. Where does it go? The salutation should be typed two or more spaces below the last line of the inside address; it helps to establish the lefthand margin of the letter. The preferred number of spaces is two, since otherwise the inside address seems to dangle apart from the rest of the letter. However, when window envelopes are used, it is sometimes expedient to increase the number of spaces, and the same device is used by some letter-writers for very short letters. The great majority, however, favor the two-space separation, and it probably results in the best

Figure 4-16

July 6, 19XX

Mrs. James C. Wood,
4961 South Wabash Avenue,
Chicago, Illinois 60615

Yes, you are right. Your check for $15.86 paid in full your bills for July and August. You owe us nothing, Mrs. Wood.

We want you to know that we have appreciated having you as a customer, and we hope you will enjoy your new home in Joliet.

Should you later return to Chicago, we will be happy to have the privilege of serving you again. Your credit will remain very good with us, for you have been very prompt in meeting every obligation.

Sincerely,

appearance. For those letters where the inside address is placed below the body, the salutation is typed several spaces below the date line, but of course on the left side of the page. The actual number of spaces depends on the length of the letter and the judgment of the writer.

2. Who and how many. The salutation may be singular or plural, depending on the nature of the first line of the inside address. It should be singular if the letter is sent to one individual, and plural if to a company, organization, a box number, any group such as a board of directors or a committee, or to more than one individual.

The most common plural forms are *Gentlemen* and *Ladies*. The first word, of course, is used in letters going to companies, or associated persons, as a committee or partnership, where the heads are either all men, or a combination of men and women. The other word is used when the company or group consists entirely of women. When there is any doubt, the masculine word should be used.

In military and official correspondence, but preferably in no other kind, *Sir* or *Sirs* is a correct salutation. It is a very formal and uninviting greeting and has nothing at all to recommend it for business letters, not even when combined with *Dear* or *My Dear*.

Obviously, a letter to a company or group is more formal in nature than one to an individual, and for the latter considerably more freedom is allowed in choosing the appropriate salutation; the selection will depend on previous relationships between writer and reader and the contents of the message, which may be "strictly business," or semi-personal. In today's business correspondence, salutations run a wide gamut from formal to personal, and the only problem is that of using the one which best fits the particular situation.

This range in choice for salutations to an individual runs from "cold to warm," and covers a lot of ground, but the following are typical:

Sir   My dear Carl,
Dear Sir,   Dear Carl,
My dear Sir,

Dear Mr. Blake,
My dear Mr. Blake,

Another form not often seen, but which seems to have an added warmth, is that in which both given and surname are used—"My dear Carl Blake." Then there are the other more personal forms allowable only when the relationship is very friendly, and of long standing. Among them are:

Dear friend,   Hello, Carl,
Dear friend Carl,   Thanks, Carl,
Good morning, Carl,   Right you are, Carl.

Because of the extreme informality, the salutations just mentioned are only a sample of the many variations which these nontraditional greetings may take. On the whole, their use is dangerous, and for that reason, not recommended for everyday business correspondence. On the other hand, they do come closer to the greetings exchanged in speech, and when appropriate they help to make the letter a personal contact.

Salutations to ladies follow the same pattern as those for men. In the order of decreasing formality, they include:

Madam,   My dear Phyllis,
Dear Madam,   Dear Phyllis,
Dear Mrs. Blake,
Dear Ms. Blake,

When the title *Dr.* is used in the salutation, it takes the place of *Mr.* The same is true of *Professor* or its abbreviation. Otherwise, letters to doctors or professors run the same gamut of decreasing formality, except that the more personal forms of greeting seem to be used less frequently—perhaps because some writers are awed in approaching men of such importance:

My dear Sir,	My dear Professor Roe,
Dear Sir,	Dear Professor Roe,
My dear Dr. Battin,	My dear Emanuel,
Dear Dr. Battin,	Dear Emanuel,
My dear Fred,	
Dear Fred,	

The words, *Honorable, Reverend* and *Esquire,* are not used in the salutation, even though they appear in the inside address. If he holds a doctor's degree, a clergyman with the title of *Reverend* should be addressed as *Dr.* in the salutation. If he does not hold a degree, the proper word is *Mr.* The use of a clergyman's surname with *Dear* or *My dear* is not considered good taste. Do not say in the salutation, *Dear Worthsbey* or *My dear Worthsbey.* When the relationship is extremely personal, however, you may correctly address the clergyman by his first name—*Dear Harold* or *My dear Harold.*

My dear Sir,	Dear Dr. Worthsbey,
Dear Sir,	Dear Mr. Worthsbey,
My dear Dr. Worthsbey,	My dear Harold,
My dear Mr Worthsbey,	Dear Harold,

For *Esquire,* substitute *Mr.* in the salutation. Thus, the proper form is *Dear Mr. Mills,* and not *Dear Esq. Mills* or *Dear Esquire.* In connection with the last mentioned error, it should be noted that no title should be used in a salutation without the surname. It is just as wrong to say, *Dear Doctor, Dear Reverend,* or *My dear Professor.* Use, instead,

Dear Doctor Merkle,	Dear Reverend Harms,
My dear Professor Pate,	

Occasionally, business letter-writers omit *Dear* or *My dear* in the salutation, and simply use the reader's name and title—*Mr. John Baker* or *Dr. Arthur Jones;* even the first name is sometimes omitted—*Mr. Baker* or *Dr. Jones.* Since the authorities disapprove the practice, you cannot afford to copy it, but it is easy to understand the motive. One of the great inconsistencies in all forms of correspondence, and especially in that for business purposes, is the use of the word *Dear* in any of the common forms. It is, for example, hard to justify a word of affection in a greeting from one business person to another. John Bates and Oscar Prine may never have met, and yet Mr. Bates says to his secretary, "Take a letter to Oscar Prine...*Dear* Mr. Prine." Credit Manager Elaine Smith writes to a customer that her patience is exhausted, and that unless a check is soon forthcoming legal action will be taken. But she still says, *"Dear* Sir." The clerk in a mailorder house writes to a woman in North Dakota, and though he knows her not, he says, *"Dear* Mrs. Malstrom." Customs and propriety keep these inconsistencies in our letters and a good letter-writer continues to use them.

In the salutation of a business letter it is not permissible to substitute a designation of rank or position for a name, title, or for both. A similar designation after the name of the individual is also taboo.

> *Wrong:* Dear Comptroller:
> My dear Mr. Comptroller:
> Dear Comptroller Williams:
> *Right:* Dear Mr. Williams,
> *Wrong:* Dear Mr. Williams, Comptroller:
> My dear Mr. Lait, President:
> Dear Mrs. Brown, D.A.R.:
> *Right:* Dear Mr. Williams,
> My dear Mrs. Brown,

Some authorities object to the salutation, *Dear Friend,* but under certain circumstances, I see no objection to it. If the man to whom you are writing *is* a friend, why not address him as such? Certainly, the use of the word cannot be as illogical as that of *Dear.* Moreover, it does not stretch the imagination too greatly to think of even a customer as a friend—and for some form letters to customers of longstanding, the term does not seem too farfetched or unreasonable.

3. Using abbreviations. The only titles that may properly be abbreviated in the salutation are *Mr., Mrs.,* and *Dr.* Particularly offensive are such contractions as *Gents* for *Gentlemen,* or in lesser degree, *D'r* for *Doctor.* We can think of no better way for letter-writers to label themselves as ignoramuses than to address a company or group as "Dear Gents," although now and then this monstrosity is met in business correspondence. The title *Messrs.* or feminine version *Mmes.* should not be used as a salutation, or as any part of one.

> *Wrong:* Messrs:
> Mmes.:
> Messrs. Bailey and Bailey:
> Mmes. Helen Rupert, Inc.:
> *Right:* Gentlemen,
> Ladies,

4. Remembering capitalization. There are four things to remember in connection with capitalization in the salutation of a business letter. Always use capitals for: *Sir* and *Madam,* given names and surnames, titles, and the first word.

A *don't* for good measure is that the word "dear" is never capitalized unless it starts the line.

Wrong: My Dear Miss Jones:
Right: Dear Miss Jones,

Ending with the complimentary close. It is not difficult to understand why below the body of practically all business letters there is added the phrase rather aptly called the "complimentary close." That's exactly what it is—a parting gesture from the writer of the letter to the reader. Just as you feel the impulse to end a conversation with "Good-by now" or "Thanks a lot," so does a letter seem to require some similar courtesy to avoid too abrupt an ending—"Yours very truly," "Sincerely yours," or one of the other commonly used expressions.

With the motive for the custom there can be no serious objection, since anything that might tend to humanize a letter-contact must be accepted as quite worthwhile and desirable. But when you remember that the same set of stock phrases are used over and over millions of times every year, you must concede that the complimentary close adds very little warmth to a business letter. It is simply another of the conventions which has come down from the past, and is quite likely to persist for no better reason than "this is the way we've always done it."

To prove that the complimentary close is merely a convention to be taken as a matter of course, try to remember which of the customary phrases was used in the very last business letter that came to your attention. Was it "Yours very truly," "Cordially yours," or just *what* was it? Probably you haven't the slightest idea what the words were, and that is no reflection on your memory. It was there, as you would expect it to be, but you paid no attention to it. We think that is what happens 99 times out of 100 when business letters are read. The complimentary close is taken for granted, and adds nothing to the message in the body of the letter.

Does this mean that the practice might just as well be discontinued? Well, it has been by some companies, and those responsible tell us there has been no criticism from those receiving the letters. The reason is possibly that business-contacts are less likely to be formal and traditional than in other fields of human relations. Business people, writing to customers and prospects, are less bound by custom than they would be if writing to a high government official or to some other important individual of title.

However, the complimentary close is commonly accepted as a necessary part of the business letter, and so long as the majority of our companies continue to use it, you must understand the rules which govern its form and content as approved by the authorities for different letter situations. Certainly, we do recommend that when choice is offered between the formal and informal forms, that you use the latter.

This leaning toward informality in the complimentary close is strictly in keeping with the modern trend with respect to other aspects of the business letter—the turning away from old-fashioned, stilted phrases, the growing preference for the more intimate forms of salutation, and the general effort to write as we *talk*. Already, the most extreme formal forms of the complimentary close, as seen in the letters of our forefathers, have passed into the letter limbo. We no longer encounter letters ending with "Your obedient servant," "Yours faithfully, Sir" or those other equally cold and exaggerated forms so common in the past.

There are three main factors for the letter-builder to consider when using the complimentary close. Let's look carefully at each of them.

1. Position on page. Usually, the complimentary close is typed two spaces below the last line of the body of the letter, but there is no hard-fast rule that it must be in exactly that position. On the contrary, when the letter is very short, a better appearance may be gained by dropping the complimentary close a greater number of spaces. When this is done, however, more space should be allowed for separating the other parts of the letter, as otherwise the complimentary close would seem to dangle alone and remote from the rest of the structure.

The line ordinarily starts a few spaces to the left of the vertical center of the page, and in that position it tends to balance best with the inside address at the top. Here again, the choice of the starting point depends more on the judgment of the typist or dictator, than on any rule that says where it must be marked. You have noted, perhaps, the practice followed by some letter-mechanics of starting the complimentary close in line with the lefthand margin. The American Institute of Business letter from my file (see Figure 4-17) illustrates this point. One must admit that the general appearance of the letter is both interesting and pleasing.

No matter what the starting place of the complimentary close, it should never extend beyond the line made by the righthand margin.

2. The common forms. Although there are no rules to tell you exactly what form the complimentary close should take for a particular letter, common sense suggests that in the degree of formality it should

Figure 4-17. Complimentary Close and Signature Blocked at Left

Mr. L. E. Frailey
1053 North Shore Avenue
Chicago, Illinois

Dear Cy:

When I received your file on your letter writing clinics, I was
rather disappointed in the puny efforts of some of those advertising geniuses.

Now I have labored and brought forth a mouse. Let me know what
you think of my efforts. Of course, I don't care what you think--
if it doesn't get results it won't be worth a dime.

The point is that you are to speak to the group on Wednesday morning, June 15, at nine o'clock. I hope you will rouse the Rock
Island engineer and see that he gets you here on time. If there
is any slip-up on this, it will be my most embarrassing situation
in all the twenty-nine years of my life.

Get yourself a glass cage and stay in it until June 15.

If this clinic "clicks," it will be an annual affair.

May I have your reaction to all this activity?

Very sincerely yours,

Keith Fenton

KEITH FENTON

KF:CW

conform with the salutation which has been selected as most appropriate for the individual who is to receive the letter. For example, in a letter to a well-known business acquaintance or friend it would be absurd to greet him with "Dear Mr. Carter," or "Dear John," and then sign off with "Very respectfully yours." In like manner, it would be just as inconsistent to begin with a blunt "Sir," and then conclude with "Cordially yours." At least the latter fault is not condoned by modern practice, though, frankly, I think cordiality should always be welcome.

As you may have guessed, I don't have too much sympathy with the inherited conventions that tend to stiffen and make unnatural the tone of a business letter. However, we must recognize that these conventions exist, and that they are followed by the great majority of letter-writers, including even those who strive to make the body of their letters human and conversational. Hence, it is well that you should be familiar with the forms of the complimentary close that are commonly used, particularly with their respective degree of formality.

The most formal of them all are those that were used by our ancestors. Fortunately, these have just about disappeared from business correspondence, although it is surprising to note one book of high authority recommending that a letter to the President of the United States should close with, "I have the honor to remain, Sir, Your most obedient servant," the last four words being the complimentary close. Frankly, we do not think that even our President expects such servility from one of his citizens. For that reason, we do not propose to include such forms in the list below which contains, in the order of their formality, the phrases now in common use.

Very respectfully yours,	Very sincerely yours,
Yours very respectfully,	Yours very sincerely,
Respectfully yours,	Sincerely yours,
Yours respectfully,	Yours sincerely,
Respectfully,	Sincerely,
Very truly yours,	Very cordially yours,
Yours very truly,	Yours very cordially,
Truly yours,	Cordially yours,
Yours truly,	Yours cordially,
	Cordially,

The above list includes all of the forms recommended by the authorities, but they shut their eyes to many variations which are seen every day in business correspondence. Some are the more intimate forms used by business friends, and others are suggested by special occasions. For example, here are a few typical ones taken from incoming mail:

> Yours with appreciation,
> Best regards,
> Gratefully yours,
> Always a Buckeye,
> Your Texas friend,

While we realize that these forms may be too personal for general use, there can surely be no harm in them when a friendly relationship exists between writer and recipient. In fact, they have a human touch which would be entirely lacking in any of the old cut-and-dried forms. If one person has done a favor for another, why shouldn't the latter end the thank-you letter with "Yours with appreciation"? "The complimentary close," writes one of the best authorities, "is to a business letter what the expression 'Goodby' is to a conversation." All right, agreed! Then why not make it *conversation?* Not in all letters! Unfortunately, no. If the letter goes to a stranger, to a mere acquaintance, to someone of higher rank, then drag out the proper formality. But there are many occasions in business, when we can be as natural in saying "Goodby" as we would be in speech.

3. Rules to remember. Following are facts about the complimentary close that the business letter-writer needs to know.

(a) Capitalize the first word only.
Wrong: Yours Very Respectfully,
Right: Yours very respectfully,

(b) The last word should be followed with a comma. Even if open punctuation is used for other units of the letter, the comma should be used.

Wrong: Sincerely
Right: Sincerely,

(c) Do not abbreviate in the complimentary close.
Wrong: Yrs. very truly,
           Respy, yrs.,
           S'c'ly yrs.,
Right: Yours very truly,
           Respectfully yours,
           Sincerely yours,

Since there is such latitude in choosing a complimentary close, it is impossible to create a chart for appropriateness such as the one for salutations. Even if you were to look at all the letters crossing your desk in a month, no absolute conclusion, or propriety could be reached. The best thought we have on the subject is that the complimentary close should conform with the whole *feeling* of the letter. If the letter has been formed and/or directed to a person of high rank, the complimentary close should also be respectful. If the whole tone of the letter has been left light and free, the complimentary close can be equally as informal and friendly. Let your own common sense guide you. When you remember that the purpose of all letters is to establish personal contact, then each part of the letter, even the complimentary close, becomes important.

4. EXAMINING SIGNATURES AND OTHER NOTATIONS

What's in a name? The signature on a business letter is far more important than it might seem at first thought. It not only serves to place responsibility for what has been said in the letter, but also may add or detract from the general appearance of the whole ensemble. It may also be assumed that the reader has the right to know, easily and without the slightest inconvenience, to whom the signature belongs, and how it is spelled. Thus, we have the simple "must" that either the written name and initials should be legible without question of doubt, or they should be duplicated by the typist. In the latter case, the writer can have as much fun as he wants in signing his name; otherwise, the slightest inconvenience to the reader in trying to decipher a signature is inexcusable. Any thought that this comment is superfluous may be canceled by an inspection of the "cockeyed" signatures in Figure 4-18. They were taken from business letters where no other means was supplied to identify the writers—nothing on the letterheads, and no duplications in type. In each case, the writers signed their name in a way to indicate that they had swallowed a hornet, and the readers were left to decipher the spelling as best they could.

The rules that govern the position and content of the signature are far from ironclad. They are based on prevailing custom, the will of the individual, and the practice of the company as may be ordered in the correspondence manual. Some serve a utility purpose, and others are merely a reflection of what seems to be common sense and good judgment. You are not forced to follow these rules as they are set forth below, but you cannot "go wrong" in doing so. They represent the opinion of the leading authorities, and for that reason may be accepted with confidence:

1. Determining the position. Usually, the signature on a business letter consists of three or more lines—the name of the company, the name of the writer in longhand, and the typed copy of the writer's name, with designation of department or title. These lines are arranged in an orderly fashion, somewhat similar to those in the inside address and salutation. The best appearance is gained when no one of these lines extends far beyond the others. One line may be sufficient for name and title if both are short, or two lines may be necessary to keep the entire signature in harmonious proportion.

If the first line is typed, it may be dropped two spaces below the complimentary close, to agree with the space allowed between paragraphs and between the other letter units. However, if greater space has been allotted between these other units, the same should be true of the space between complimentary close and first line of the signature. Particular care should be taken to allow sufficient space for the longhand signature of the writer.* It may be from three to six spaces,

---

* All longhand signatures are shown here in italics.

depending on the size of the name as it is customarily penned. Some people write with generous flourishes; others with minute precision. The typist soon learns how much space is required.

When two lines are typed consecutively, they should be single-spaced for two reasons. First, to save space, and second, because they look better that way.

Figure 4-18

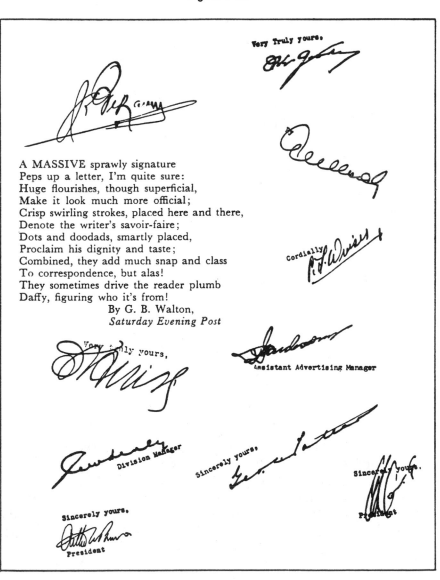

A MASSIVE sprawly signature
Peps up a letter, I'm quite sure:
Huge flourishes, though superficial,
Make it look much more official;
Crisp swirling strokes, placed here and there,
Denote the writer's savoir-faire;
Dots and doodads, smartly placed,
Proclaim his dignity and taste;
Combined, they add much snap and class
To correspondence, but alas!
They sometimes drive the reader plumb
Daffy, figuring who it's from!
                    By G. B. Walton,
                    Saturday Evening Post

Not Good This Way	Cordially yours, The Doe Supply Company *Albert S. Grace* Albert S. Grace Advertising Manager
Okay with Last Two Lines Single- Spaced	Cordially yours, The Doe Supply Company *Albert S. Grace* Albert S. Grace Advertising Manager

In the opinion of most letter experts, the signature lines make the best appearance when *blocked,* starting at the same distance from the left edge of the page as does the complimentary close. In every case, this should be done when the other parts of the letter are arranged in the blocked form.

> Very cordially yours,
> Caldwell Processing Co.
> *Leslie J. Caldwell*
> Leslie J. Caldwell
> Director of Personnel

This blocking of the signature is recommended, even when the other parts of the letter are indented, with the exception that the lines no longer start even with the first word in the complimentary close. The one indention assures consistency with the general form of the letter.

> Very cordially yours,
> Caldwell Processing Co.
> *Leslie J. Caldwell*
> Leslie J. Caldwell
> Director of Personnel

One rule for the position of the signature which should never be disregarded is that none of the lines should reach beyond the righthand margin of the page. This creates a problem for the letter-writer and typist when one of the lines is extremely long and cannot be broken. In such a case, the long line cannot be blocked with the rest of the signature, and still kept from stepping over the righthand margin. Hence, some other form must be followed.

Very truly yours,
   Blue Bonnet Oil Co.
   MaryAnn Williams
   MaryAnn Williams
Assistant Superintendent of Production

Most Sincerely yours,
Larson Lithograph and Printing Company
   James C. Donovan
   James C. Donovan
   Credit Manager

While neither of the above solutions to the problem of the unusually long line present the neat, orderly appearance of a pure block, they are probably as good as the circumstances will permit. As has been said, the signature rules are not ironclad, and when two of them oppose each other the best compromise must be left to the judgment of the sender.

Of course, another possible solution to the problem is the one illustrated on page 223. The unorthodox alignment of the signature with the lefthand margin, allows considerably more space for any overstuffed line.

2. Varying the content. The simplest of all forms for the signature is the one in which only the pen-written name of the writer appears. It looks best and is best, unless additional information is necessary or desired by the company. This form is also especially appropriate in correspondence between business friends; the titles, being understood, do not require repetition which would only be an indication of vanity. In such cases, the writer assumes full responsibility for the message in the letter as there is no company name coupled with his own.

Yours cordially,
   John E. Doe

Another form almost as simple is the one where the name is typed as well as pen-written. This also looks good, and is a courteous procedure when the writers know their signatures are not easily deciphered. The typed copy of the name is unnecessary if it also appears on the letterhead. The only exception to this rule is when the letterhead also contains in printed form the names of several other officials. This forces readers to study the list of names to see which one compares most closely with the written signature—an inconvenience to which they should not be subjected. Again, since the company name does not appear in this form, the assumption is that the writers assume responsibility in a personal way for what they have said.

> Yours cordially,
> *Howard H. Wainwright*
> Howard H. Wainwright

Sometimes a two-line signature consists of the pen-written name plus a typed line giving the title or department. This form is often desirable in business, as it helps the reader to understand the source of the information received, or the authority of the writer in supplying it. Thus, if Mrs. O'Brien has written to a mail-order house about the poor performance of her new stove, she may have more confidence in the suggestions offered in the reply if it is identified as coming from the "Chief Engineer," rather than just from a name which might belong to a mere clerk whose job it was to handle any complaint. In similar fashion, a collection letter with only a name at the bottom might not carry as much weight as if that name were designated as belonging to the Treasurer. Or, a letter identified as coming from the Vice President in Charge of Sales might make a customer feel more important than one coming from an unknown member of the Sales Department, whose position or authority is not stated. You can think of many other situations where the mention of title or department strengthens the effect of a business letter.

> Yours very truly,   Very truly yours,
> *Oscar Bauman*   *Charles Gast*
> Chief Engineer   Charles Gast, Treasurer
>   Sincerely yours,
>   *Carrie C. Goode*
>   Service Department

In one of the preceding examples, it was possible to place both title and typed copy of the pen-written name on the same line. But when this results in too much length, so that the signature is thrown off-balance, a three-line form becomes necessary.

> Yours very truly,
> *Arlene C. Wood*
> Arlene C. Wood
> Advertising Manager

> Cordially yours,
> *Malcomb Hennapenny Bates*
> Malcomb Hennapenny Bates
> Superintendent

So far, we have inspected only the signature forms that do not include the name of the company or organization. When the latter is included, the procedure becomes more complicated. Not only are more lines usually required, but several problems present themselves with respect to the position of the company line, and just how it is to be typed. For example, note the different treatments of the following four-line signature.

(a) *Company name first*

Very truly yours,
The Cameron Rug Company
Russell T. Geho
Russell T. Geho
Sales Manager

(b) *Same, all capitals*

Very truly yours,
THE CAMERON RUG COMPANY
Russell T. Geho
Russell T. Geho
Sales Manager

(c) *Writer's name first*

Very truly yours,
Russell T. Geho
Russell T. Geho
Sales Manager
Cameron Rug Company

(d) *Same position but company name all capitals*

Very truly yours,
Russell T. Geho
Russell T. Geho
Sales Manager
CAMERON RUG COMPANY

These four forms for the same signature illustrate two problems. The first is where the name shall be typed, and it is inconsequential. The people in authority may decide whether or not they want the company name to have the added display gained by all capitals. Once the decision is made, however, it should be adhered to in all departments and by all individuals. A company should develop a style for its correspondence, and not let every dictator do as they please, which results in lack of uniformity and no style at all. Particularly is the last point true with respect to the second problem—in what position the company line shall be placed. If there seems to be a good reason for having it precede the name of the individual (examples *a* and *b*), then the form should be followed in all of the company letters.

The point of difference between the two positions is largely one of determining the responsibility for the content of the letter. If the company name is typed first, then the implication to the reader is that the company has stated the facts, and the individual who signs the letter has acted in the capacity of interpreter or transmitter. Thus, the concept of complete company responsibility gains greater emphasis than when the individual's name comes first, and he seems to speak for himself.

The question of whether or not the company name shall be used at all in the signature may be influenced by the inclination of the executive in charge of such matters, or sometimes by the more urgent factor of necessity. If the letter is typed on a blank sheet of paper, which could hardly happen in an organization of any prestige or importance, then obviously the company name must appear in the signature, unless the subject matter is purely personal, and the writer is acting strictly for himself. In the vast majority of letter situations there is a letterhead to tell the reader plainly the source of the message. When this is true, the company name in the signature is only a repetition, and may be considered as unnecessary. The person receiving a letter on the stationery of *Blank & Blank, Inc.,* and signed by *John Doe, President,* hasn't the slightest doubt as to the identity of the organization of which Mr. Doe is the head. Neither would a reader question the authority to act for the company of a person who signed as Credit Manager or Sales Manager.

A signature of more than four lines does not enhance the appearance of the entire letter—in fact, it tends to have the opposite effect—but sometimes the long form is necessary. For example, this is true when both title and department need to be mentioned.

(a) *Better balanced with company name placed first*

Sincerely yours,
PARAMONT MOTOR COMPANY
Horace P. Oliver
Horace P. Oliver
Assistant Superintendent
Used Car Department

(b) *The four consecutive lines look awkward*

Cordially yours,
Teresa S. Fritsche
Teresa S. Fritsche
Manager Experimental Farm
Research Department
BRUNSON FEED MILLS

So far as is reasonable and possible, the best procedure in determining signature forms is to keep them simple and short by eliminating all unnecessary information.

3. Choosing the correct punctuation. As with the date line and inside address, the punctuation of the signature may be either *open* or *closed,* but the form used must agree with the other units. Hence, the punctuation of the date line sets the style for the rest of the letter. Remember, however, that the complimentary close is *not* a part of the signature, although it teams closely with it. The complimentary close ends with a comma, no matter which of the two punctuation forms is used for the other parts. In contrast, the pen-written name of the writer has no punctuation mark following it in either form, unless an abbreviation concludes the name:

(a) *Open punctuation*   Sincerely yours,
             McNULTY & MINTON, INC.
             John Selby Graham
             John Selby Graham
             Sales Manager
             Textile Division

(b) *Closed punctuation*   Sincerely yours,
             McNULTY & MINTON, INC.,
             John Selby Graham
             John Selby Graham,
             Sales Manager,
             Textile Division.

(c) *Open punctuation*   Yours very truly,
             Barbara Gore
             Barbara Gore, Secretary
             The Battin Company

(d) *Closed punctuation*   Yours very truly,
             Barbara Gore
             Barbara Gore, Secretary,
             The Battin Company.

4. Using abbreviations. In the preceding example (*a*), the word *incorporated* was abbreviated in the signature because in that form it was a part of the official company name. There can be no deviation from this rule—as the name stands on the letterhead, so it must appear in the signature. On the contrary, personal names, with certain exceptions, should not be abbreviated. The authorities do not approve such contractions as *Geo.* for *George* or *Vin.* for *Vincent,* but there are occasions when an exception must be conceded. For example, we know of one great business leader whose first given name is *William,* but for more than 50 years he has used the contraction, *Wm.* To suggest to this individual that he should start signing his letters with the full name, *William,* would surely be the height of absurdity.

The abbreviations, *Jr.* and *Sr.* have become so standardized by common use that they also are exceptions to the rule. It is very seldom that the longer forms are ever seen in personal signatures. Approved, too, are initials, although the preference is for at least one of the given names to be spelled out. Thus, *James C. Hardy* undoubtedly has a more balanced appearance when written or typed in the signature of a business letter, than does *J.C. Hardy*. However, if an individual prefers to use both initials, it may be considered his personal business, and no one has the right to criticize the practice.

Designations of position and departments should not be abbreviated. For example, *Advertising Manager* should never be typed *Adv. Mgr.*—*Circulation Department* should never be typed *Circ. Dept.*

5. Checking the rules of capitalization. The following rules apply to capitalization in the various signature forms.

Capitalize—

(a) All initials, given names, and surnames.

(b) All words designating title or position, except prepositions, conjunctions, and articles. The latter, however, should be capitalized if they begin the title or position.

Wrong: Sales manager
 Director Of Personnel
 Assistant to the treasurer
 the Grand Marshal

Right: Sales Manager
 Director of Personnel
 Assistant to the Treasurer
 The Grand Marshal

(c) Abbreviations *Jr., Sr.,* and *Mrs.,* and the designation *Ms.*

(d) All words and abbreviations in the name of a company or association, except prepositions, conjunctions, and articles. The latter, however, should be capitalized when they begin the name.

(e) All words in the names of departments, except prepositions, conjunctions, and articles. The latter, however, are capitalized if they begin the name.

Wrong: National association of real estate boards
 Department of traffic control
 Credit And Collection Division

Right: National Association of Real Estate Boards
 Department of Traffic Control
 Credit and Collection Division

6. Signatures for women. Nothing has changed the world of business as has had the influx of women. When women first began to appear in positions of high rank, the rules for properly signing a letter were chaotic and inconsistent. Some companies refused to let their female employees use anything that would indicate to the recipients that this practice is foolish and unnecessary.

All of the signature practices discussed for male personnel apply to their female counterparts as well. There are, however, two special instances when a woman's signature line may need to be special. These are:

a) When the signer is acting on behalf of her husband, the typed signature usually carries her full married name. She may wish to alter the formality by using her handwritten given name.

Right: Sincerely,
          Shirley Johnson
          Mrs. William S. Johnson, Jr.

Right: Very truly yours,
          Mrs. Robert Tyton
          Mrs. Robert Tyton

b) When the signer particularly wishes to indicate her sex to her readers. This is often done in sales letters. Here, certain rules of custom apply. If a woman is single, or acting in her own right, she generally uses Ms. on the signature line; if she is widowed or divorced, she may use Mrs. along with her given name. It is considered improper for a married woman to do so, since custom has shown that her given name indicates the current absence of a husband.

Wrong: Mrs. Barbara Dean
              (married)

Right: Ms. Barbara Dean
              (single)

Right: Ms. Barbara Dean
              (married)

Preferred: Mrs. Gertrude Simpson
              (widowed)

*Also
Correct:*   Mrs. Marshall Simpson
              (widowed)

Preferred: Mrs. Jacqueline Alban
              (divorced)

*Also
Correct:*   Mrs. Charles Alban
              (divorced)

The key to proper signing is consistency. Whatever method has been adopted, should be adhered to at all times.

7. Looking at other suggestions. Although the discussion so far covers the major points with regard to the signature in the business letter, there are other important facts that should be recognized. They are:

(a) If it helps to harmonize with the general appearance of the letter, there is no objection to a color other than black for the pen-written name. However, very bright colors such as red, orange, or yellow often detract from the letter and should be avoided.

(b) Once, the use of a rubber stamp to affix the individual's name was quite common. This practice is no longer considered good form, and it also weakens the message of the letter by making it seem too casual.

(c) Titles should never appear on the same line with the pen-written signature, either before or after the individual's name. They are bad form if typed this way, but especially uncouth if written in ink along with the name.

(d) People signing letters should remember the appearance value of their signatures. They should not write over the other lines, or at an angle. They should also stay within the limits of the space provided, and not allow the name to stick out beyond the righthand margin.

A very bad habit, but one often followed in business letters, is the attempt to avoid responsibility for what has been said in the body of the letter (or for the errors that a reading might detect) by the addition of a qualifying statement such as, "Dictated but not read," or "Signed but not corrected." The readers have the right to resent such a sloppy and careless device, and their opinion of both writer and letter may justifiably be negative. When it is impossible to check or sign a dictated letter, the initials of the pinch-hitter should appear below the pen-written name, and in some cases a postscript by the secretary or typist may explain why the situation required special handling.

With initials of the pinch-hitter	Very truly yours, *John B. Whittier B.E.F.* John B. Whittier Advertising Manager
With postscript signed by the secretary	Very truly yours, *Harry S. Wheatley* Harry S. Wheatley

P.S. Mr. Wheatley left for Toronto before this letter could be typed. To avoid any inconvenience to you, he asked me to sign and mail it for him.

> *Julia Groves*
> Secretary to Mr. Wheatley

Identification devices. It is a business custom to place certain coded information below the signature lines and aligned with the lefthand margin. In some cases this serves a useful purpose, but in others it might just as well be omitted. This statement clashes with some of the authorities who insist that these identification marks are always necessary. There are others who believe to the contrary, however. I cannot recall one single instance in my years of business experience when I made any practical use of the identification symbols, although during that stretch of time I have handled many thousands of letters. Yet it is desirable that we keep our minds open toward any practice pertaining to business correspondence. When there is a sound *reason* for an identification line, as there may well be for certain companies, then there can be no objection to it. When the reason does not exist, as frequently it doesn't, then it becomes only another thing to clutter the page, serving no good purpose for the company which mails the letter, and certainly none for the person who receives it.

What *are* these identification symbols, and why do they rate such a controversial paragraph? Usually they consist of the initials of the person who dictated the letter, of the person who typed it, and sometimes, also of a third person for whom the letter was dictated, and who usurps the privilege of signing it. You know, initials like these: LEF/CM. Deciphered, they mean that Luther Elijah Flesh dictated the letter, and the secretary, Crystal Mooch, typed it.

All right! You know that symbols like those just cited are generally encountered in the lower lefthand corner of business letters. But why? What's the *reason* for putting them there? "The identification line," says one of the nation's best letter-authorities, "provides an easy, accurate, and inconspicuous means of recording the identity of the dictator and transcriber. Its use enables a business organization to ascertain the identity of either individual by merely consulting the correspondence file."

With half of that definition at least, there must be complete agreement. Probably the secretary could not, in many cases, be identified any other way. The initials, coming last of course, are a sort of trade-mark, and perhaps she takes pride in seeing them on the letters that she types. Also, because of those initials, she can be quickly brought on the carpet if she has made an error in typing embarrassing to the company.

Okay, so far, so good! But what about the initials of the dictator? If under the pen-written signature, the name is typed, then what purpose is gained by repeating initials in the identification line? Our authority says that they facilitate identification by merely consulting the correspondence file. In other words, a glance at the initials on the copy quickly puts a finger on the writer. Yes, that is true. But why isn't it just as easy to look at the name typed under the pen-written signature?

Of course, if the name of the writer is *not* typed under the space left for the penned signature, then we have a very *good* reason for the identification line.

Sticking to our premise of accepting the initials or name of the dictator in the identification line when there is a good *reason* for it, we must admit the necessity when a third party enters the picture, as the one who signs the letter even though he did not write it. For example, in some companies the practice still prevails of having all letters dictated within a department signed by the highest in authority. Thus, all collection letters are signed by the Credit Manager, all sales letters by the Sales Manager, and similarly throughout all the company units. This means that if the company is large, a number of subordinates may dictate the letters signed by one person. The idea is to give each letter importance in the mind of the reader, since it apparently comes from the "top," but except for this questionable advantage, the practice has nothing to recommend it. Under such a condition, there is less incentive for superior dictation, and the company surely loses more than it gains.

From what has been said about the identification line, the following policy is presented as being, in our opinion, the most consistent and logical:

1. Let the initials of the typist always be displayed—for reference purposes, and for whatever beneficial effect it may have on morale.

2. If the same person dictates and signs the letter, use only one identification form—either the typed name under the signature or in full with the secretary's initials. But don't do both.

3. If the dictator does not sign the letter, then let his initials or name appear in the identification line.

Although some authorities may not agree with this policy, which is surely their privilege, we believe it will hold water with the majority of individuals who have had considerable business experience.

Using other notations. It is sometimes considered desirable, outside of the body of the letter, to call the reader's attention to some special feature of the mailing, such as the presence of an enclosure, the sending of an extra copy to some other individual, or some particular form of handling. These notations are customarily placed in line with the lefthand margin and below the identification marks; the number of spaces depends on the length of the letter and your own judgment.

It is not always necessary to refer in this special way to an enclosure, but usually the plan has merit. For example, in a large company where all letters are folded and prepared for mailing in a centralized department, the word *Enclosure* tells the clerk that something besides the letter-page is intended to go into the envelope. Thus, the simple device helps to reduce the possibility of error.

Another benefit is to the recipient of the letter. The word calls his attention to the fact that something extra accompanies the letter. You probably have had the experience of removing a letter from the envelope and overlooking an enclosure. If it was a check, you no doubt were put to considerable inconvenience in getting a duplicate. Had the word *Enclosure* been plainly typed on the page, or better still, the words, *Check Enclosed,* the catastrophe would have been prevented.

The preferred position of an enclosure notation is immediately below the identification line. It may be abbreviated, but commands more attention if spelled out. If there are two or more enclosures, the fact is also indicated either by word or numeral. Here are some of the forms commonly used.

RCHunter/wv	MH/mj
Enclosure	Enclosures 2
GAF/fc	Carl F. Lunt: ad
2 Encls.	Check Enclosed

J.J. Cartwell/ing
Enclosure:
Mortgage

In the same manner, the notation may call attention to a special form of mailing.

MLFahnestock/lef	KIUtterbach/or
Registered mail	Special delivery

JSC/grt
AIR MAIL

When the writer wishes the reader to know that a copy of the letter is being mailed to another individual, a notation to that effect is placed in line with the lefthand margin. To give it special emphasis, the notation is usually the last item typed on the page, and if possible, a few spaces removed from any other items. The full name and title of the individual is typed.

Very truly yours,
The Maxwell Company
J.H. Cambleton
Sales Manager

JHC/ac
Copy: John Doe

Cordially yours,
Luther G. Long
Luther G. Long
Credit Manager

LGL/mlf
Copy: Alice Dill

Sincerely,
R. C. Bellwether
Advertising Director

RCB/mjk
Copies to:
James Duncan
R.L. Defoe

Sometimes, for good reason, the writer of the letter does not wish the recipient to know that other individuals are getting copies. Then the notation is placed only on the file copy. To make it more conspicuous, the position generally preferred is at the top of the page several spaces above the inside address.

Viewing the postscript. Opinion as to the value of the postscript in the business letter is divided—some think it serves a useful purpose, and others believe it should never be used. The latter hold that anything that needs mention can be adequately covered in the body of the letter, and that the postscript is merely evidence of careless preparation and thinking. We believe this is true in the great majority of cases, as it is very easy to overlook a point until the main part of the letter has been dictated, and then say, "Oh, yes, put this in a postscript." This, of course, is inexcusable. Possibly if all postscripts were outlawed, better letters would be the result.

When *purposely* used, the postscript gets a spotlight position which gives an emphasis to its content that might otherwise be rather difficult to attain. It is a device often used with powerful effect in the sales letter, and we hardly think it should be ruled out completely. It does not particularly injure the appearance of a letter, certainly to no greater degree than some of the other notations we have been surveying. However, postscripts should never be longer than a few words, or the one argument of gaining special attention is eliminated.

When a postscript is used, the common practice is to place the initials, P.S., in line with the lefthand margin, and two or more spaces below the last line of the signature. This puts it ahead of the identification initials, but occasionally you see the positions reversed. The message of the postscript should follow on the same line as the P.S., and should be punctuated like any sentence. As justified by those who cling to it, the postscript highlights some special fact. It may be a repetition of something told in the body of the letter, or something in the nature of a digression from the general message.

P.S. Remember—June 2—don't fail us.

P.S. Confidentially, you will save money by ordering before August 1. You can guess the reason.

P.S. I saw Joe Warner yesterday. He spoke highly of your hospitality.

P.S. It hurt me to have to write this letter, Jim. Please try to understand my position.

We see no harm in postscripts of the above variety, but you may decide for yourself whether or not to use them. Be sure you do it *purposely*, and not as an afterthought.

Devices to gain emphasis. To capture special attention for a word or phrase, several devices are commonly used. One is to underscore, another is to use all capitals, and a third is to type the word or phrase in a different typing element (italic, script, etc.). There are other methods, such as circling the desired part of the letter, drawing a hand or arrow that points to it, or placing a cross in the margin with a red pencil, but in general these are messy in appearance and cannot be recommended. Your opinion, however, of any of these devices must be tempered by the results which they attain.

The two devices used the most, and sometimes in combination, are underscoring and capitalization. Consider the following examples.

Underscored:	This is the first time we have made such a liberal offer, and we do not expect ever to repeat it. You actually <u>save two dollars,</u> and you cannot afford to delay, as only the <u>first thousand</u> who reply will be accepted.
With Capitals:	This is the first time we have made such a liberal offer, and we do not expect ever to repeat it. You actually SAVE TWO DOLLARS,

and you cannot afford to delay, as only the
FIRST THOUSAND who reply will be
accepted.

Combination: This is the first time we have made such a
liberal offer, and we do not expect ever to
repeat it. You actually <u>SAVE TWO DOLLARS,</u>
and you cannot afford to delay, as only the
<u>FIRST THOUSAND</u> who reply will be
accepted.

A comparison of the above three paragraphs will prove that the
underscored words stand out more boldly than do those capitalized. In
the same way, the combination of both gains still greater force as an eye-
catcher. A further step would be typing the words in red ink. However,
there is one caution to be remembered about the use of these devices.
When you *overdo* them, they tend to irritate more than please. Furthermore, if too many words and phrases are underscored or capitalized,
the purpose of the device is defeated, since all of the parts emphasized
compete for attention against each other. This is illustrated when we
increase the underscoring and capitalization in the third of the above
examples.

Overdone: This is <u>THE FIRST TIME</u> we have made such
a <u>LIBERAL OFFER</u>, and we do not expect ever
to repeat it. You actually <u>SAVE TWO DOL-
LARS</u>, and you <u>CANNOT AFFORD TO
DELAY</u>, as only the <u>FIRST THOUSAND</u> who
reply will be <u>ACCEPTED</u>.

Only confusion is created with so many words emphasized. In fact,
it is questionable which parts stand out the most—those highlighted, or
those left untouched. The letter in Figure 4-19 is an example of
emphasis sought with considerable restraint. Only three words are
capitalized, but as paragraph starters they hold special prominence.
Incidentally, the writer, Mr. Robert Stone, is a highly successful sales
letter-writer, and you will notice that he uses a postscript for a thought
connected with the body of his message but somewhat remote from it.

One last thought on emphasis devices: One practice used today is
accomplished with boldfaced type. Standard office machines have this
effective capability at the typist's fingertips. Just remember that over-
use means under-power.

How to prepare second sheets. When two or more pages are
necessary for a business letter, the second page should be typed on
exactly the same paper as that used in the official company stationery. It

Figure 4-19

2518 Gunnison St.
Chicago, Illinois

May 16, 19__

Mr. L.E. Frailey
22 W. Monroe
Chicago, Illinois

Dear Mr. Frailey:

STAR: Best of luck to you in your new
location. I'm sure that it will make
it possible for you to go stronger than
ever.

CHAIN: I phoned you at your old address
the other day and the operator gave me a
Glen Ellyn phone number. I called there
and was told that you had set up an office
here in Chicago.

In the first paragraph, I wished you the
best of luck. Guess you don't really need
this since "Smooth Sailing Frailey" really
knows his stuff.

HOOK: Please call me at my office, phone
Armitage 4255, and I'll give you a Safety
Kit free.

A Frailey Student,

P.S. If you fail to call me, you will shatter
all my confidence in the Frailey Star-Chain-
Hook method.

is a poor form of economy to have a special paper of inferior quality and weight for the extra pages, even though the practice is not uncommon. The saving is inconsequential, and certainly the effect on the average reader is negative.

Custom varies as to what the notation on the second sheet shall be. Usually it consists simply of the numeral 2, in parentheses, typed about four spaces below the top of the page. If on the left side of the page, the designation also sets the margin line, which should be of the same width as on the first page.

There are those who like dashes with the number, and we won't split hairs about that. If -2- looks better to them than (2), or if they prefer *Page Two* to the numeral, that's okay, too. There does seem to be good reason for adding two other items—the name of the recipient, and the date. In the event the second sheet was detached from the first (perhaps in the mailing department where incoming letters are received), this additional information becomes valuable. Just how the three items are to be placed on the page is a matter of personal preference, but the following form is both attractive and consistent with the position of the name and date on the first page.

(2)

Mr. James A. Cook   November 1, 19XX

In transcribing a letter, the typist sometimes finds that the body has taken all of the first page and only complimentary close and signature remain. This results in an odd-looking second page. The letter should be retyped and spaced so that at least one full sentence appears on the second page. After making a few of these major corrections, the typist soon learns to plan ahead.

Secretaries are, of course, important members of the team which gets out the daily run of business letters. They are the ones who actually put the letter on the page.

Some of the hints given under the following heading may prove useful to secretaries facing the task of presenting a business letter in its best possible format.

5. DEVICES FOR MAKING READING EASIER

Practical paragraphing. We have noted that short words and short sentences tend to improve the effectiveness of a business letter because they impose less strain on the reader's mind than do long words and long sentences. In like manner, the thought is easier to absorb if the paragraphs are not too formidable, and so constructed that each one covers a separate and complete unit of the message. The readers know at the beginning of each paragraph that the previous division of thought has been completed and that they are about to be presented with a new one. Of course, this is true only when the paragraphing has been done by a competent and logical thinker. A paragraph composed of unrelated material causes confusion, and hinders the assimilation of the central thought.

The chief responsibility for the arrangement of paragraphs in logical and compact form belongs to the writers. If they have planned their letters properly, they know what points they intend to present, and in what order. When one point has been thoroughly covered, they are ready to say "new paragraph," and proceed to the next, which will present a new point, completely and without digression. However, if the point is complex and requires lengthy discussion, the writers face the choice of using a long paragraph, or breaking the thought into several paragraphs to cover separate sub-points. The choice of several shorter paragraphs is preferable, since a lengthy one is tiresome to the eye and tends to repel the readers before they have started to read the letter.

Placing the burden of responsibility on the writers does not mean, however, that competent secretaries have no part in proper paragraphing. When they notice that the writers have forgotten to signal a new paragraph, they may make the division in the copy which they type. Moreover, some dictators make no pretense of indicating paragraph beginnings. In this case, even though it cannot be approved as the best practice, the secretaries must do the best they can to make the paragraphs presentable and logically cut to the pattern of what seems to have been the dictator's intention.

We have seen paragraphs that filled an entire page of typing, and many more that ran a half page or longer. This indicates both careless and loose thinking on the part of the dictator, and a lack of skill on the part of the typist or secretary. The influence of these long paragraphs cannot possibly be favorable. They tell the reader that the letter is going to be difficult to read, and they set up a negative mental attitude which puts the writer behind the eight ball at the very start. This fact is well recognized by the majority of business letter-writers, and the modern trend is toward paragraphs that will not impose on the eye or mind of the reader. Sometimes the tendency is overdone, with each paragraph consisting of a single sentence or a couple of short ones. This succession of small bits of copy is just as objectionable as the other extreme. Hence, you will gain the best results by sticking to the middle of the road, and making your paragraphs neither *too long* nor *too short*.

One factor influencing length of paragraphs is the nature of the message in the letter. Certain phases of business, for example, are more technical and complicated than others. The paragraphs in a sales or adjustment letter might be expected to run somewhat longer than in a letter which merely thanks a customer for an order or asks when a bill is to be paid.

One writer may be able to use longer paragraphs, and make them easier to read, than can another. As in all other aspects of business letter-writing, paragraphing should take into consideration the probable reading habits and intellectual status of the individual to whom the letter is addressed. Generally, you may be sure that it is better to write short paragraphs than long ones—no matter who the potential reader may happen to be.

Highlighting special material. In many business letters there are certain facts or figures that the writer particularly wants the reader to remember. In such cases, the special material may be highlighted by contrasting forms of indentation, by tabulation, or by some other similar method. Facts buried in the middle of a paragraph are much more likely to be overlooked by the reader than when they are given a more prominent display. For example, consider the different typings of the following letter to a salesman. (See Figures 4-20 and 4-21.)

Figure 4-20

Dear Jimmy,

First, let me tell you that I am much pleased with the way you have taken hold in your new territory. If you keep on at the same pace, there is a big bonus assured for you at the end of the year. Your success gives me personal satisfaction, because as you know there was some opposition to your appointment on account of your youth.

During the coming week, I want you to spend a day in Cairo. Talk to John Doe, president of the Doe Implement Company, and see if you can revive his business. He was a steady buyer until last December, when he suddenly left us cold. Probably something happened to displease him, although I cannot think what it could be. Also, while in Cairo, see old man Roe again. You said last month that he would make a substantial payment on his account, but nothing has happened. Be courteous, but make it plain that we are about ready to call on the lawyers to get our money. In Centralia, be sure to get the contract signed with Black and Black. You seem confident this business will jell, but from my own field experience I can tell you that no order is any good until the buyer puts his John Hancock on the dotted line.

Here in the office, we are going ahead with plans for the national convention. This will be your first, and I know you will get a tremendous kick out of it. By the way, if you want a room reservation, don't neglect returning the card to Hotel Jefferson—the one sent to you three weeks ago. If you overlooked doing this, it will be your hard luck as there won't be a chance to get a room after you arrive.

Again, Jimmy, I compliment you on your efforts. You may not be satisfied to see your name twenty-ninth on the list, but that is a fine rating for a beginner, and I have no doubt before the year is over, you will be crowding the leaders.

Report to me on the matters I have mentioned.

Sincerely,

Probably, Jimmy was pleased with the letter from his boss. But in addition to the compliments, it contains certain instructions which are more or less covered up in the body of the message. Without any major changes in wording, these instructions could have been highlighted by the following form of typing:

Figure 4-21

Dear Jimmy,

First, let me tell you that I am much pleased with the way you have taken hold in your new territory. If you keep on at the same pace, there is a big bonus assured for you at the end of the year. Your success gives me personal satisfaction, because as you know there was some opposition to your appointment on account of your youth.

Jimmy, along with your other calls, here are three things I want you to do this coming week:

1. Talk to John Doe, president of the Doe Implement Company, in Cairo, and find out why he stopped buying from us last December. An order from him will be another feather in your cap.

2. While in Cairo, also see old man Roe again. He has not made the substantial payment, as promised to you last month. Be courteous, but make it plain we are ready to call on the lawyers to get our money.

3. In Centralia, be sure to get the contract signed with Black and Black. An order is never an order until the buyer's John Hancock goes on the dotted line.

Be sure to report to me on these three special assignments by the end of the week.

Here in the office, we are going ahead with plans for the national convention. This will be your first, and I know you will get a tremendous kick out of it. By the way, if you want a room reservation,

don't neglect returning the card
to Hotel Jefferson—the one sent
to you three weeks ago.

If you overlook doing this, it will be your hard luck, as there won't be a chance to get a room after you arrive.

Again, Jimmy, I compliment you on your efforts. You may not be satisfied to see your name twenty-ninth on the list, but that is a fine rating for a beginner, and I have no doubt before the year is over you will be crowding the leaders.

Sincerely,

Your eye tells you that numbering and indenting the three points gives them a special emphasis they did not have in the first version of the letter. In the same way, the indention highlights the reference to the room reservation. With these assignments so prominently displayed, Jimmy is not likely to forget or neglect them.

Explanatory material presented in tabulated form is usually easier to read and understand than when worked into the body of paragraphs. For example, compare Figures 4-22 and 4-23 that follow:

Figure 4-22

Thank you, Mrs. Doe, for writing, and for the payment of $5.00 to apply against your unpaid bills. We appreciate the effort you are making to bring your account up-to-date, and your offer to send us another payment of $5.00 in two weeks is quite satisfactory.

The total amount which you still owe is $16.35, and not $14.00 as mentioned in your letter. The difference of $2.35 is the amount of the March bill, which you thought was paid. The confusion, no doubt, is caused by the fact that both the February and March bills were for the same amount. The receipt you enclosed covered the February bill, but left the one for March still unpaid.

Since the first of January, you have made four payments: $3.42 against the January bill; $2.35 against the February bill; $3.29 against the April bill; and your latest payment of $5.00. This is a total of $14.06.

During the same period, the following bills have been issued: January, $3.42; February, $2.35; March $2.35; April, $3.29; May, $4.01; June, $3.17; July, $3.99; August, $4.10; and September, $3.73—a total of $30.41.

Thus when you deduct the total paid from the total billed, there is a balance of $16.35 still due.

We hope these figures are clear to you, Mrs. Doe, but if you have any question to ask about them, we will be very glad to answer it. It was nice to know that your husband has now recovered after his long illness, and that he has found such a good job.

Cordially,

The above letter (Figure 4-22) is about as clear as any exposition could be, but the many figures make the deciphering a slow process. When these figures are tabulated (as in Figure 4-23) the job is much simpler.

Figure 4-23

Thank you, Mrs. Doe, for writing, and for the payment of $5.00 to apply against your unpaid bills. We appreciate the effort you are making to bring your account up-to-date, and your offer to send us another payment of $5.00 in two weeks is quite satisfactory.

The total amount which you still owe is $16.35, and not $14.00 as mentioned in your letter. The difference of $2.35 is the amount of the March bill, which you thought was paid. The confusion, no doubt, is caused by the fact that both the February and March bills were for the same amount. The receipt you enclosed covered the February bill, but left the one for March still unpaid.

Bills			*Payments*
January	$3.42	$3.42	Paid February 2
February	$2.35	$2.35	" March 22
March	$2.35	$3.29	" May 6
April	$3.29	$5.00	" November 6
May	$4.01		
June	$3.17	$14.06	Total
July	$3.99		
August	$4.10		
September	$3.73		
Total	$30.41		
Less	$14.06		
$16.35	The amount you still owe.		

We hope these figures are clear to you, Mrs. Doe, but if you have any question to ask about them, we will be very glad to answer it. It is nice to know that your husband has now recovered after his long illness, and that he has found such a good job.

Cordially,

Obviously, this second version of the letter is easier and quicker to read. It could hardly be misunderstood. Business letter-writers should use these and similar forms of typing to clarify the letter's message, and to put emphasis on items that deserve it.

Another method of highlighting material is the use of *exclamation marks.* These may be used to close a word, a group of words, or a full sentence when the thought is more emotional or dramatic than the ordinary sentence carries. When not overdone, its use adds spice and color to business writing, especially in advertising copy and sales letters. With the exclamation mark, the writer can vary the monotony of conventional sentence forms, and thus create extra interest in the minds of the readers. Unfortunately, the majority of businessmen make small use of this punctuation mark probably because they have not learned what it can do for them.

Listen a few minutes to conversation on the street, in the office, or anyplace where people meet, and you will agree that everyday speech is not made up of a steady sweep of full-rounded sentences. Far from it! Instead, in between the sentences are numerous exclamations, couched in single words or short phrases, adding life and interest to what might otherwise be rather dull language. Well, if we are still sticking to our major premise—that we should write as we *talk*—*why* shouldn't our letters have some of the same atmosphere? What's wrong with a word or phrase interjected in the flow of thought that makes the letter sound like a person *talking?* What's wrong, for that matter, with a dash of emotion? Is there anything so phlegmatic or academic about business that one connected with it cannot be natural, interesting, often excitable? If you think business is immune to emotion, watch sales managers as they near the end of a quarter, with a fighting chance of making quota; watch advertising directors as they contemplate the million dollars they have risked on the new campaign, wondering if their judgments were sound. The "dignity of business" is only a pose—a thin shell which hides situations, experiences, frustrations, and ambitions, as dramatic as any you will encounter in other walks of life.

Yes, we cast our vote for the exclamation mark, and the kind of business language which makes it necessary. Look at Figure 4-24.

From the above letter written by a sales manager—he got a telegram to tear up the resignation—you can see how handy exclamation marks can be. *All right, Joe! Nonsense! Yours! Okay! Sure! Listen! No argument about this, Joe! You know it! Good luck!* None of those words or phrases *had to be* in the sales manager's letter, but don't they add naturalness and power to it?

Figure 4-24

All right, Joe! You say you are discouraged, and you will be solving a problem for me by quitting. Nonsense! You never have been a problem to me in all these ten years we have worked together. Nobody here in the office wants you to quit, Joe. Nobody has been discouraged about *you*.

But there *is* a problem, Joe. Yours! It's in your own mind, and either it will lick you, or you will lick it.

We have no room for men who get discouraged, and start to pity themselves. You are right about that. If you really have lost your grip, if your blood has changed to water—okay! But I never expected to see the day when Joe Doe's guts ran out—when he couldn't take the rough spots with the smooth.

Sure! You can quit, or you can be your old self again, and tell me to tear up this foolish resignation. But I'm not telling you *what* to do. The problem is in your lap, Joe—with a swell wife and three kids sitting on the sidelines to see how you solve it.

Listen! You go fishing next week at our expense. We owe you that for all the ten years you have fought the good fight and never weakened. So, go ahead, and see if you are too discouraged to catch a few big ones.

No argument about this, Joe! When you get back, write me your final decision. I still want you around. You know it! But you'll have to get those bugs out of your bonnet.

It's you in the driver's seat, Joe. Good luck!

Of course, you may be saying that the situation of the salesman wanting to resign is naturally emotional, and not a fair sample of the more prosaic things generally handled in business letters. Yes, that is a very good comment. It is true that salesman Joe Doe left himself wide open to the personal language used by his sales manager. Most letter-situations in business are far less dramatic, but even if dry-as-dust, can't they be handled in a human, conversational manner? Here are a few examples of how dynamic the use of the exclamation mark can be:

Please! Won't you sit down right *now* and write us a check? We know the amount of your bill is small, but with several thousand other customers also holding out on us, the size of the total might surprise you.

We did appreciate this first order, and wanted so much to please you. *Is my face red!*

Right you are! Your June bill is paid. The check and our letter must have crossed in the mail. *Sorry!* Please excuse us for the trouble we have caused you.

Good news for you! Effective July 1, you will be entitled to an extra discount of 5 per cent.

Listen! We cannot sell your products unless you keep us supplied. Where is the shipment you said we could count on last week? We aren't angry. But it's bad business to change our customers over to your feed, and then run short. *Please!* Get on your horse, and give him the whip.

There you are! Even the run-of-the-mill letters can be made to sound as one person talking to another. There's a lot of power in an exclamatory word or phrase.

Other methods of highlighting material will be found in Sections 3, 7, 9, and 14. These techniques include the use of large capital letters for emphasis, color-writing, illustrative devices, and various other forms of showmanship.

Throughout this section we have explored many aspects of business letter mechanics. Each point, from designing a letterhead to the appearance of the typed product, from the presentation of address forms to signatures, from readability to dramatic emphasis, has been thoroughly reviewed. You can see how effectively you can use each facet to make your best impression on your readers.

Now, let us go into using your personality to enhance reader contact.

PUTTING PERSONALITY IN BUSINESS LETTERS

PUTTING PERSONALITY IN BUSINESS LETTERS

1. WHAT MAKES A LETTER INTERESTING?

Reflecting your personality. You do not need to be told that some writers manage to make themselves more interesting than others. Among those from whom you get letters, no doubt two or three are especially favored, and when one of them is represented in a newly arrived batch of mail, you push everything else aside until the message is read. But why? Why are these writers able to do what others cannot? Is there some one quality in their letters that makes them outstanding? Is it a quality that anyone might attain if you only knew how?

Well, yes. There is no reason why most business letters should be so dry, so dull, so colorless. There is no mystery about an interesting letter. It simply reflects more of the *friendly personality* of the writer than do messages which are lifeless, cold, and stiff. In the interesting letter you hear people *talking,* and you feel the smile between the lines. They aren't trying to be clever, nor are they doing anything purposely to attract attention to themselves, but you sense that they are there with you, and the warmth of their presence is a pleasant experience that you miss in the letters which seem to be only a collection of words.

Of course, in some letters the subject material is in itself more interesting than in others. That gives the writers a running start. Generally speaking, sales letters talk about more exciting things than do collection letters; letters about advertising have more interesting content than letters about traffic. But these advantages in nature of material, or the lack of them, make little difference to the writers who have the gift of *putting themselves* in their message. Personality is a quality that has few limitations. Certainly, you must admit the truth of that statement, for you have read letters about simple, routine matters that made you smile, and you felt attracted to the writers; and in contrary fashion, you have read letters that had every chance to be interesting, but left you cold and yawning.

Examining the meaning of the word. Before we go any further in talking about *personality* in the business letter, we should define its meaning. In the broadest sense, every individual has a personality, although it may not be pleasing. This fact is brought out in Webster's definition.

> *Personality* 1. Quality or state of being personal, or of being a person; personal existence or identity. 2. That which constitutes distinction of person; individuality; as, a *striking personality.* 3. A personal being; a person. 4. Quality of relating to a particular person, esp. disparagingly or hostilely; as, *vulgar personality.* 5. A personal remark, esp. one disparaging or offensive;—usually in pl.; as, to indulge in *personalities.*

It is the second of the five definitions which comes closest to what we mean when we offer *personality* as a quality to be desired in the business letter. We want "distinction of person" to be evident in the dictated words; and more than that, distinction of a likable, *friendly* person.

If you still lean to making business letters as short as possible, countless examples could be cited to prove that brevity and interest are not incompatible. Remember?

> Dear Governor: They are fixing to hang me on Thursday, and here it is Tuesday.
>
> .   .   .   .
>
> Will you please send me the name of a good lawyer in your town? I may have to sue you.
>
> .   .   .   .
>
> Yes, John Doe did work for us several weeks. When he left, we were satisfied.

None of the examples just cited are letters in the conventional style. Instead, the writers dared to get out of the groove and to express themselves as they would in ordinary speech. People like things which are *different*—shoes cut in a new way, a breakfast food unlike any they have eaten before, a play with a fresh plot. They also are receptive to a new approach in letters. At least, this must have been Miles Kimball's thought when he dared the following unusual collection letter (Figure 5-1). He had a lot of small accounts to collect, and several of the customary conventional appeals had failed. There was nothing much to lose in trying something entirely different, even though he hesitated at the last moment to mail a message so remote from the "dignity" of business. But out it went.

Figure 5-1

Dear _____,

The worst has happened! Elmer, our treasurer, has found out about your account, and is threatening to write you a letter.

As a friend of yours, I implore you to pay now before it is too late! People who get Elmer's collection letters never recover. We hide the Accounts Receivable Ledger from him, but sometimes he finds it and gets out of control. If you realized the horror of it, you would mail your check at once. If you had seen the pitiful results as we know them! Young men prematurely aged, and strong men broken—babbling in a corner through palsied fingers. It is hideous!

Usually, Elmer's letters result in 40 percent collections and 60 percent suicides. He may have other words in his vocabulary besides "sue," "legal action," and the unrepeatables, but no one has heard him use any since the spring of 1928.

Elmer's old mother (who has been in a sanitarium since he was seven) tells us that he was a happy, normal boy until he was five. Then a neighbor child persuaded him to trade two old pennies for one shiny new one. When Elmer found out he'd been hornswoggled, the change came over night. He earned his first dime drowning kittens, worked in a slaughter house when he was 14, and is now treasurer of our company. He is president of the League for Restoration of the Death Penalty, and has filed a standing application for the job of public Hangman.

You see the situation. I like people, and I just can't stand the thought of having Elmer destroy your will to live. So please, for your own sake and the sake of my conscience, mail your check today for the $17.65 owing to us—or you may get a letter from Elmer—God forbid!

Miles Kimball, one-time president of Direct Mail Associates, Inc., Oshkosh, Wisconsin, had used many collection letters in his business career. But never one so shockingly different. Before you join those who could not tolerate anything so unconventional, consider also the fact that this letter outpulled by a wide margin all of the others that had been mailed by the company over a period of many years. Why? Perhaps because people like to be amused. Perhaps *humor* in some intangible way is connected with *personality* in a business letter.

Another example, of similar vein, is the celebrated letter written by a prominent business executive to the manager of a large Chicago hotel. In condensed form, here is the correspondence between the two men:

Dear _____,

Upon making the customary room inspection after a guest's departure, our housekeeper advises that two brown woolen blankets, replacement value $15 each, were missing from the room you occupied....Guests frequently, we find, in their haste inadvertently place such items in their effects and, of course, return same when discovered.

The accusation, politely made in the guise of "inadvertently," would have angered the average human being. But the executive to whom it was mailed was more of a philosopher. He realized, no doubt, that hotels do suffer considerable loss because of the "haste" of certain guests. Anyway, his reply is a classic in funpoking; it bubbles over with the calm personality of a man who chooses to see the humorous side of the experience rather than to write back in righteous indignation.

Dear _____,

I am desolate to learn that you have guests who are so absent-minded. I suppose that passengers on railroad trains are apt to carry off a locomotive or a few hundred feet of rails. Or a visitor to a zoo may take an elephant or a rhinoceros, con-cealing same in a sack of peanuts after removing the nuts (replacement value of $.25).

It happened that I needed all the drawer space you so thoughtfully provided. The blankets in question occupied the bottom drawer of the dresser, and I wanted to put some white shirts (replacement value of $6.50 each) there, so I lifted said blankets (replacement value of $15 each) and placed them on a chair. Later, I handed the same blankets to the maid, telling her in gentlemanly language to get them the hell out of there.

If you'll take the trouble to count all the blankets in your esteemed establishment, you'll find them all present.

Very truly yours,

P.S. By the way, have you counted your elevators lately?

Thus confronted with a guest who refused to take his first letter too seriously, the manager of the hotel removed his stiff shirt, and did his best to write a second letter in the same spirit. You need not be bothered with the whole of it, but from the following paragraph you can see how different is the language—how much more human is the writer.

> Dear _____,
>
> Yes, we do a lot of counting around here. I've counted the elevators. What I want to count now is more important to me. I want to keep on counting you as a friend of the _____ hotel....As the song says, "Let's Call the Whole Thing Off."

Perhaps by now you are beginning to catch the meaning of "personality" as it may be expressed in business letters. It is not something that can be weighed, or counted, or painted; nor is it ever manifested twice in exactly the same manner. The latter is impossible because no two persons are exactly alike, and *personality* as nearly as I can describe it, is the reflection of people—their dispositions, their mental attitudes, their feelings towards the world in which they live, and the other human beings in it. All of this sounds intangible, but it isn't really. A letter gives out personality when you forget it *is* a letter—when you feel the *presence* of the writers, and hear them *talking* to you.

2. HOW TO EXPRESS YOUR OWN PERSONALITY

Loosening your belt. In an earlier chapter of this *Handbook* you were urged never to think about writing letters. Instead, you were to say, "Today I must *talk* to these people." And if from these many pages only one idea were to be culled, the one of *talking* and not writing is probably most valuable. The chief reason why so many letters—the great majority of letters—are dull and uninteresting, is because those who write them cannot shake off the concept that they are preparing something to be *read,* rather than *talking* to other human beings. The difference in these two approaches is so wide and radical that the one produces letters dry as dust; the other, letters which sparkle with human personality.

Hence, if you wish *your* letters to be interesting—to reflect *your* friendly personality—the first requisite is that you adjust your own mental attitude toward the job. Take off your necktie, loosen your belt. Forget the silly formalities. Sit down, and be comfortable. Remember the slogan: "Relax—be natural—just TALK." If your letters are drab and colorless, it isn't because *you* lack personality. It is because you keep it bottled, so that not a drop can escape to lighten your words, or to make you sound like the friendly, interesting person that you really are. You can't express your real personality when using the stilted language of 1776. You can't make your letters vital and human while sitting behind your desk with the same austere dignity that you may affect in a box at the grand opera.

Good manners are as necessary in writing letters as in any other human relationship. We do not mean that you should wisecrack, try to "show off," or that you should write a letter in the same spirit that you might shoot a game of pool. On the other hand, neither do we think that business relationships need to be any more formal than those of everyday, decent, pleasant living. The people who are to read your next letter are just other human beings—like your neighbors, your friends, or your colleagues. They don't want you to slap their backs on the first acquaintance; neither do they want you to talk as if they were old fuddy-duddies, allergic to a smile. Maybe you are saying, "But their letters to me were cold and formal...*I* must go back at them in the same way." Why must you? Perhaps they learned to write letters in the old school. They don't know any other way. Must you keep your personality undercover because someone else does? No. Keep your letters on a high plane of courtesy. Write with respect, but *be yourself.* Relax...be natural...just *talk.* There is no logical reason for assuming a personality that is false—no reason why you should be cold and formal in a letter, if in reality you are not that kind of a person.

Homey language helps. In the writer's scrapbook is an old clipping titled "Every letter ought to make a friend." The author's name has been lost along the way, but his comments are pertinent to the subject of our quest—how to put personality in a business letter. Read what he says about Bill Galloway:

> When Bill Galloway was president of a farm implement company in Waterloo, Iowa, he made a fortune for himself and others because he knew how to write a good letter. I think Bill's chief qualifications for letter writing were that he *knew* people, and *liked* people.

> Galloway never wrote a form letter. He could always find time to *talk* to a farmer. Every letter, even though the same copy would go to a hundred thousand farmers, was a personal letter to him. Bill was a great believer in friendliness. Even in form letters he could manage to put in some personal touch.

> One time he had some letterheads printed with a picture of his office building in the upper righthand corner. One of his favorite stunts was to draw a crude cross in ink over one window. Under this cross he would write, "Here is where I sit."

> That simple cross-mark and phrase added a friendly note to a letter which made a deep impression on farmers. They were

accustomed to doing business in a personal way. The idea made Bill into a human being who reached out from the envelope and shook hands with every reader.

There are homey words in our everyday language, and combinations of words, which seem to fit the pattern of the average, commonplace, likable human being. When used in business letters, they contribute a personal touch which helps to bring reader and writer on the same plane. You know these expressions, because you use them every day—that's water over the dam...he would give you his last shirt...let's take the bull by the horns...don't swap horses in midstream...you can't burn a candle at both ends...and the thousands of others which make our language interesting even though they may not be favored in college classrooms. The power of these homespun expressions is generated by the fact that they are mutually understood. Average Americans are suspicious of "fancy" language; they like best the common words that are a part of their own vocabulary. *Folks,* for example, is a word with great popular appeal. When you *talk to folks*—or about *folks*—you are really writing a persuasive letter.

Adding the personal touch. An old and effective device used by letter-writers to season the meat of their message, is the addition of a sentence or two of a personal nature. Usually, these "extras" are typed near the end of the letter, but sometimes they are written in ink at the time the writer signs the letter. For example, here are three of these personal touches taken from letters dictated for the Jefferson Standard Life Insurance Company, of Greensboro, North Carolina. The subject matter in the three letters was not very dynamic, as it included references to policies, rates, premiums, and the like; but the sentences thrown in for good measure help to give the message life and personality.

> *In a letter to an agent in California:* What about letting me know how you like the Golden State. Have you crashed the movies yet?
>
> *To an agent in Augusta, Georgia:* I enjoyed visiting in your office Friday morning, and I hope it will not be my last visit to your beautiful city.
>
> *To a policyholder:* We enjoyed having you with us yesterday. Come to see us again.

None of these letters actually *needed* these personal touches. In a business way, they would have done their job had the digressions been omitted, and a little time could have been saved by sticking strictly to the subject. But who would say that the time taken to personalize the letters was wasted?

One expert once stated that "nine letters out of ten can be improved by a human touch at the close." We agree heartily. Except when used for a very formal occasion, there seems to be no sensible reason why the human touch will not improve any business letter.

Using the readers' names. The value of working the readers' names into the body of a letter has already been mentioned. It is also one of the ways that personality is gained. In speech, we use over and over again the name of the people to whom we are talking. While this must be done with more restraint in letters, it is still one of the simplest methods of making the readers feel that their identities as individuals are recognized. In his book, *Goodwill Letters That Build Business,* William H. Butterfield says: "Every normal person likes to be noticed, not as a name in the company ledger, but as a flesh-and-blood human being. Mr. John Q. Public is proud of his individual identity; so he is complimented and flattered when a personal letter makes him feel that someone has noticed his existence and appreciates his patronage.... Any evidence of office routine is a death blow to letter tone, and it kills the reader's enthusiasm instantly. He realizes that he is not being written to as John Smith or William Jones, but merely as one of the firm's customers."

Then Mr. Butterfield tells how destructive to the personal tone is the robot-like reference to company records. And to that comment, amen! Human beings never want to feel that they are merely a matter of record—names in the file of customers. Nevertheless, thousands of business letters are written every day with the deadly, impersonal beginning, "According to our records." What does this indicate to the reader? Why, simply that someone in the company has been going through the files, and happened to see a name as one who hadn't been buying recently; or as one to whom, for some other reason, a letter might be written.

Think of your readers as *people,* not *names.* Address them directly, and without any explanation or apology. To be sure, every company has records, and from them may come the impulse to write to a particular person. But don't *tell them* that the kick-off was prompted by seeing their name in the file. "According to our records," writes the promotion manager, "you have been giving us the cold shoulder." What a ridiculous thing to say to a former customer! She knows you have not missed her as an individual. She knows, too, that none of the clerks have remarked about her not being in the store. How did you know she had stopped buying? You told her in the first four words. The records said she had not used her charge account. How differently the letter would have sounded had the start been, "Mrs. Wilson, you haven't used your charge account in the last six months, and we are getting concerned about you. Will you do us a favor? Write and tell us what happened; or better still, come in and let us serve you again."

This last letter begins with the customer's *name*. That makes her feel important. Then it gives the fact that she has not used her charge account. That warms her ego—she has been missed. Finally, a favor is asked. That is especially pleasing. She, Sheila Wilson, can do a big company a favor. All of this is a matter of psychology, but what are business relationships if not psychological? The more you recognize that fact, the better your letters will be.

Don't overplay your hand. As has been explained previously, the personal tone *can* be exaggerated in a business letter, and in proportion to how deeply the writer falls into that trap, the less sincere it seems. Simply telling you that a letter is improved by the direct use of the reader's name in the body does not mean that you should use it with sickening frequency:

> Thanks for your check, *Mr. Doe*. We were glad to hear how pleased you are with the shipment, and that makes us wonder, *Mr. Doe*, when we may expect another order. Please remember, we are here to serve you, *Mr. Doe*. And believe us, *Mr. Doe*, we do appreciate your business.

The use of John Doe's name four times in one paragraph would be absurd, and no doubt more offensive to him than to use it not at all. Nobody likes to be bombarded with his own name. Doing so makes the letter sound flippant and insincere. Stick to the middle of the road. Let your readers know that they are recognized by name. Use it once or twice in the letter, but not so often as to sound like a ward politician out for votes.

The use of nicknames without benefit of authority can be particularly obnoxious. No one has the right to address another individual with such familiarity unless a friendly relationship has been established, and in sufficient degree to warrant doing so. Any step beyond this limitation is bad manners, and quite likely to be resented. Consider, for example, the absurdity of the letter which was addressed, "Dear Si," and closed with the postscript, "Did I spell your nickname correctly?" Certainly, if the spelling were not known to the writer, he could not claim a friendship that would sanction the nickname's use.

3. HOW TO SPOTLIGHT THE READER

More YOU and less WE. Some business letters make us wonder if the writers were not thinking more about themselves than about their readers. They are full to the brim with *I* and *We,* but contain hardly a drop of *You.* This is fundamentally so wrong an approach that it would seem apparent to anybody. But you know from your own observation how often in business writing the reader is forced to play second-fiddle. For example, note in Figure 5-2 how the emphasis is placed on the

Figure 5-2

Dear Friend:

(We) are pleased to announce that (we) have been appointed distributors of Doe Feeds in this area.

(We) recognized the ever-growing demand for feeds of superior and proven quality, which would enable (us) to help you lower production costs, whether it was to produce MILK, EGGS, PORK, or BEEF. That is why (we) chose Doe Feeds.

(We) have no hesitancy in recommending Doe Feeds, because they are backed by over 25 years of successful experience. Strict laboratory control of the completed ration, as well as the careful selection of ingredients from which they are made, give uniform, dependable results at all times.

(Our) line is complete in livestock and poultry feeds.

(We) receive Doe Feeds each week from Doe's modern mill. (We) would appreciate your visiting (our) store the next time you are in town, and letting (us) show you how YOU CAN SAVE MONEY ON YOUR FEED PURCHASES and MAKE MORE MONEY BY FEEDING DOE FEEDS.

Sincerely,

company. Four paragraphs beginning with *We,* and the fifth, with *Our.* The purpose of the letter is to bring buyers to the dealer's store, and we cannot believe the writer meant to take the play away from the prospective customers. That is exactly what it does, though.

The personality expressed in the above letter is selfish and egotistical. The writer is "blowing his own horn" and quite happy to be doing it. He isn't really thinking about the money the readers of his letter can make by using Doe Feeds; instead, he is contemplating the money *he* is going to make with the new account. In the first four paragraphs, the reader gets the call only once. In contrast to the one *you* in the middle of the second paragraph, there are five *we's*. At the very end of the letter, *you* and *your* get a better break, but long before he reads that far, the recipient's sense of importance has been rudely shattered. We doubt very much if this letter pulled many prospects to the store. It never had a chance, because the spotlight was turned on the wrong fellow.

Another letter with the emphasis just as badly placed is the four-liner below. The person who got it wrote in the margin: "Give this letter to Frailey as a letter that should never have been written. Look at the first word of each line. This is truly a horrible example."

> Gentlemen,
>
> **We** are returning herewith Connecticut policy #1887, which
> **we** have signed, consenting to the assignment of interest.
> **We** regret that it was necessary for you to return it to
> us for this signature.

Letters that star the reader. Turning to the more pleasant side of the We-You problem, notice in the following letter, Figure 5-3, how the reader is given the center of the stage—the place where the reader always belongs. It was written by advertising manager Martin F. Maher, of the Florsheim Shoe Company, in an effort to win cooperation of dealers in a direct mail campaign:

Figure 5-3

Gentlemen,

We know that this time of year finds *you* very busy, and that's why we are reluctant to bother *you* again about a detail that may seem small to *you*, but one that can have a marked influence on *your* Spring Florsheim business.

We are holding 1180 Florsheim "Styles of the Times" booklets, all addressed to *your* mailing list, and properly imprinted with *your* store name; and we think it important that *you* give us mailing instructions as soon as possible.

It is now the first of May and *you* are getting into *your* spring selling season, and Florsheim Style Booklets should prove a helpful aid.

For *your* convenience, a business reply envelope is enclosed. All *you* have to do is to indicate at the foot of this letter the date on which *you* want these booklets mailed from Chicago.

Throughout this Florsheim letter, the reader is allowed to play the leading role. He is made to feel that the request made of him is for his own benefit. Mr. Maher knew that mailing the booklets would help Florsheim, but he appears more eager to help the dealer.

Robert Ray Aurner, maestro of letters, says in his interesting text, *Effective Business Correspondence:*

> There is one person in whom your reader will forever be most interested. That is *himself.* From this fact is drawn one of the important principles of business writing: Take the "You" attitude. You have heard the saying, "Put yourself in his shoes." That applies here. Talk about the reader, and you are discussing the most interesting thing in the world—to him. Make his interests, his wishes, his preferences, his hopes as nearly as possible yours. See, if you can, what he sees, through his eyes. Assume his viewpoint. Interpret your business through his sight channel, and you reinforce your appeal with the motive power of his self-centered attention. In your imagination take up your position beside him, look back at yourself, and ask, "What would I like to have myself say if I were over here with my reader instead of in my own office?"
>
> > To sell John Smith
> > What John Smith buys,
> > You must *see* John Smith
> > With John Smith's eyes.
>
> Thus runs a convenient little verse that contains both rhyme and reason. It applies to every business relationship.

To see through your readers' eyes, to talk their language, to present your message in the light of their thinking—this is the field from which you must take off, if your letter is to possess that intangible something we call *interesting personality.*

It's a matter of mental attitude. Keeping out of the rut called *We* is not difficult, once the business letter-writers grasp the fundamental fact that to gain favorable acceptance for what they say they must *please their readers.* On the other hand, it is only natural that we should take for granted that others react as we do. This fallacy, coupled with the sense of our own importance, leads us with lamentable ease away from the *You* approach. It is a temptation against which we must ever be on guard if we wish our letters to attain maximum results—and of course we do.

The determining factor with respect to whether or not you are able to meet your readers on their own ground, is your own mental attitude. "The psychological fallacy," said William James, "is the almost universal tendency of people to think that others see a problem as they do themselves. On the contrary, they see the problem from one angle, you from another. Your duty is to see clearly, and understand both points of view."

Although some authorities do not approve the *practice,* we see no harm in the writers of letters revealing themselves as *individuals,* speaking for themselves or for the company they represent. This means there is no objection to the use of the pronoun *I,* but it must never be allowed to "steal the show" so that the readers, cast in the leading role, are forced to yield their favored position. However, this can hardly happen as long as the writers hold steadfastly to their readers' points of view, and do not prattle about things as they, themselves, happen to see them.

The use of *We* instead of *I,* which in many companies is a law that must be obeyed, is another odd custom we seem to have inherited from earlier writers. When a business writer speaks wholly for the company, as in telling a customer, "We will ship your order tomorrow," obviously he should not speak for himself. On the other hand, if he means to see personally that the order is shipped, why shouldn't he say, "I will personally look after this order, and you can be sure we will ship it tomorrow"? Thus, in the same sentence, both *I* and *We* properly appear, and logically there is no reason why they shouldn't. The idea that business writers must always speak in the sense of "We, the King," seems utter nonsense. Certainly, the insistence on *We* to the exclusion of *I* in all cases is a barrier to the goal of "writing as you talk"; writers cannot be their natural selves if they must forever cancel their presence as individuals.

In the insurance letter, (Figure 5-4), the writer often uses the pronoun *I.* Although the purpose is to get the policy reinstated for the company, it is nevertheless plain that the writer is responsible. Surely the letter would lose much of its human, friendly personality if it started, "*We* feel a little like Bill Stebbins," and continued in the same impersonal manner.

All right, what do you think? Would that letter have been as natural and interesting if the writer had hidden his personality by using *we's* instead of *I's*?

4. ADDING SAUCE TO SEASON THE LETTER

The world loves a cheerful writer. You remember, of course, the old adage, "Laugh and the world laughs with you; weep and you weep

Figure 5-4

Dear _____,

I feel a little like Bill Stebbins. At plain and fancy cussing, Bill could outdo anyone in Blair County. On even ordinary occasions, Bill could turn the air blue—with provocation, he just about singed your ears!

One day, Bill was hurrying to deliver ripe peaches in his old pickup truck when he hit a huge pothole. The tailgate snapped and the carload of peaches filled the roadway. People who saw, gasped and, with fingers in their ears, waited for the expletive explosion.

Bill got out, surveyed the squashed mess, and slowly shook his head. Turning to the assembled citizenry, he said quietly: "Now, I know what you're expecting, folks—but, honestly, I'm not equal to the occasion."

To date, I've written you several letters about your lapsed Reliance Life Policy, something you need and should take care of. I hate to see you lose it, because I know you'll always regret doing it. But I've never had a word from you. I guess I'm like Bill—"not equal to the occasion."

Won't you either send in the completed health certificate, or at least write on the back of this letter: "It's all right, old-timer; you've done your part," and shoot it on to me, so I can get this matter off my conscience? I'll certainly appreciate it.

alone." There's truth in it. The most interesting letter-writers seem to have the knack of seasoning the meat of their message with a little sauce of humor. Thus, the reader not only sees the face between the lines, but on that face is a friendly smile, sometimes even a chuckle.

And why should it not be so? When you step into a room, crowded with strangers, are you not immediately drawn to those of cheerful manner; repelled by those who appear glum and distant? Isn't it only common sense that the same people might make the same impressions in their letters? In your own business experience, have you not responded more freely to the salesperson of pleasing personality than to the one who is blunt, argumentative, or gloomy? Isn't it only reasonable to think that the letter-writers who can make their readers smile a little bit will get better results than the ones who curtly state their case, and end with abrupt "Yours very truly"? It doesn't matter what the purpose of the letter may be—to sell, to collect, to correct an error, to build goodwill—it may still reflect a smiling personality, and is more likely to succeed when it does. The following examples, serving various needs of business, are proof of the pudding.

Applying humor to adjustment letters. Handling the complaint of a customer is always a ticklish problem. Writers lose face by being too apologetic; they offend by taking the matter too lightly. The best place to stand is near the middle of the road: sorry, but not begging for mercy; eager to make a fair adjustment, but not wasting any time in useless explanation; disturbed, but not without poise. Figure 5-5 is an example of how to handle this dilemma.

Figure 5-5

Dear _____,

Your letter of December 6 blasted me right out of my chair and into the circulation records—a distance of 20 feet and probably the longest non-stop circulation hop on record.

En route I grabbed the plaid two-peak Sherlock Holmes cap, polished off the magnifying glass, and yelled lustily for Watson. However, the case didn't prove to be as baffling as the "Study in Scarlet," because we quickly located the source of the crime. That's too bad, too, because I was all ready to say in a loud voice, "Why doesn't somebody tell me these things?"

Here is the post mortem. I tried to locate you by sending copies of the October and November issues to your old address, hoping somebody would put your new address on them and forward them to you. This neighborly act did not take place, so then I tried to locate you through the *National Sportsman*, and they were sportsmen enough to send the letter on; but by the time your reply arrived it was November 1, and the December issue had been made up and sent out. But the change was made on our galleys so we could send you future copies and promotional material.

After 20 years of seeing accidents like this happen, I just refuse to tear my hair out anymore. As a matter of fact, there is very little of it left; but in accordance with good circulation custom, I will either send you the copies missed or extend your subscription for that number of copies, and leave it up to you to advise the number of them. October, November, and December issues came back.

However, if you feel that personal persecution has been perpetuated with malice aforethought, and alienated your original interest, I will cancel and refund. You're the customer in this case, and whatever you say goes.

Kindest regards and greetings from one c.m. to another!

In that letter, John H. Reerdon, then circulation director for *Popular Photography,* was neither too abject nor too blunt. To soothe the feelings of his angry customer, he chose the man-to-man approach summarized by the closing sentence, "Greetings from one c.m. to another." In other words, he said in a friendly, half-humorous way, "You should understand how these mistakes can happen, because we are both circulation managers." The approach was successful, as it brought back a friendly letter from the customer.

The next exhibit, Figure 5-6, is a reply made to an outraged customer who had received a nasty collection letter, although his account was fully paid. This situation, which occurs too frequently in business, has put gray hairs in the heads of many credit managers.

Figure 5-6

Dear _____,

On April 1, one year, my staff got me with a great practical joke. They rigged a bucket of "water" over my office door. You can just picture my surprise, then fright, and then relieved laughter as the "water" proved to be confetti.

That's sort of what I'd like to do to the *competitor* who wrote that outrageous collection letter to you. It must have been a competitor. It couldn't possibly be genuine, because certainly this business was not built by calling customers names.

The dumbest person on our payroll, in all our 63 years, wouldn't have written that letter. Certainly, nobody would write it when the bill had not been *paid* four months, because we've got the best bookkeeping system since Noah checked the passenger list for the Ark. It just couldn't have happened here.

So-o-o, the explanation is that some competitor of ours wants your business, and plans to heckle you by writing letters and signing our names. Please let me know who the first competitor is that calls and asks for your business. I'll run right over and set up the "bucket trick"—this time with real water.

Yes, that was a dangerous letter to write, for it could have backfired if the customer had taken it seriously. Evidently the writer was sure of his reader and could predict the reaction. The result was a reply in the same spirit, and a satisfied customer. In fact, Mr. Adams liked the letter so much that he commented. "This fellow's sense of humor kept my business for his company." And "that" must have been its purpose!

Now we will climb over the fence, and read a letter of complaint, quite unlike the usual sort that rant and rave. It was written to the superintendent of the Franklin Freight Lines by a lady who had a large bump of humor, and could laugh at her own troubles—a more effective way to get them removed than to loose a tirade of abuse.

Dear _____,

Short of strapping my belongings to my frail back and striding up Highway 101 to San Francisco, I'm beginning to believe there's no tougher way to get hold of them than through your lines.

Things are loused up for sure now. I'm leaving here on Monday, December 14th, and will not return until Tuesday, December 22nd. Unless the things can be delivered before next Monday, it looks like we'll have a dizzy Christmas.

If you try to pry open the doors and deposit them while I'm away, there won't be anyone here to pay you. Not that I feel like it right now.

Your Frisco office seems to be staffed by persons of bad temper and subnormal intelligence.

First, they refused to take the order; second, after the fifth vain call I am still unable to persuade them to jot down my phone number. Now really, I can remember the not-too-distant day when men *fought* over my phone number, and blood flowed freely.

Today's call to the Frisco office was typical.

I phone. A female answers and cuts me off. I wait ten minutes. I hang up. I phone back. She says, "Did you want something?" (Do I want something? Of course!) I say, yes, and explain my business. She gives me Mr. Smith. Mr. Smith listens ten minutes before explaining he is the wrong guy, and I really want Mr. Jones. I say I don't want Mr. Jones—I only want some sense to the whole thing.

Mr. Jones, after an interval of 12 minutes, deigns to answer the phone. He will not, however, deign to (a) take down any instructions, (b) jot down my phone number, or (c) do anything. I explain that you suggested it, and he implies that the Frisco office is far, far above the Los Angeles office. So you, George, will have to attach the phone number and instructions firmly to my trunk, and hope for the best.

My mother and father live at 654 Hunters Drive. Their home, a large brown house in need of paint, is located at the corner of Hunter and West, if that is any help.

Before removing the things from the garage, please ask one of my parents to instruct your men. The whole darned family stores things in Mother's garage, and I don't want any of Aunt Maggie's old junk. The items I *do* are:

1 filled, locked trunk (labeled *JRC*)
1 couch (brown with white stripes)
1 coffee table (brass)
1 chest of drawers (heavy and labeled JRC, too)

There are four pieces in all, unless you have me confused too. We live in a firetrap located at 0000 Sacramento Street, San Francisco. Do not ring the bell. It is dead and nothing happens. I've begged my husband to fix the darned thing, but he only hides behind his paper and says "wump."

Enter the CENTER door (painted red). Take the long flight of steps to the extreme right. On the top floor, turn to the left and continue to third floor back. That's us—Apartment 33. I'll admit it's a bother to climb all those steps, and my husband nearly broke his neck when he came in the other morning from a Legion meeting, but the rent is cheap.

Now, George, I'm awfully easy to please, but I do have my little whims, so will you indulge me just this once. You see, people have an unhappy way of delivering things out in the street to me. This is where I do *not* want them, so I demand that the Frisco office send me a second brawny back to help the driver lug my chattels up these 56 steps.

Now, are we straightened out? I understand the charge is $48.00 per hour. Try to keep it cheap, huh? You've cost me so much already in phone calls and postage that I'm considering sending *you* a bill.

I'm not really angry, George, because this is the way things always happen to me. I was even born in a taxi.

Have a good Christmas—and if you help, maybe I will too.

Admitted that the above letter is longer than it needs to be, and that the intimate tone would not be appropriate in the average business letter, there is no doubt but that the lady reveals a personality which is both delightful and strongly tinged with a sense of humor. The comment made by the party who contributed the letter was, "Incidentally, the lady got prompt delivery!" It did the job, which is the best that can be said of any business communication.

Writing interesting routine letters. No matter what the business letter talks about, or how routine in nature it may be, there is no reason why it cannot contain a dash of personality. The following are run-of-the-mill illustrations: a letter about a check gone astray and a request for glossy prints. Even though the subjects are not life-or-death, the writers manage to season them with a smile.

(1)

Gentlemen,

The invoice which we received had not the slightest intimation of where we should send it. We scanned it on both sides with much precision, and even applied a match to it to see if, by some chance, you had used invisible ink.

After much deliberation, we took a shot at Evansville, but a miss is as good as a mile and the check, which we crave to spend, was returned to us as is evidenced by the envelope.

Now you may be a large concern and think that everyone down in these hills, even I, should know where to address your mail; but it seems that even Uncle Sam was somewhat befuddled, and this alleviates my inferiority complex in no infinitesimal manner.

We have gone to great pains to make this remittance to you; and if, by the time it does reach you, we have disintegrated to dust, please don't blame us.

(2)

Dear _____,

I was greatly intrigued by your latest letter.

The purpose of this letter is to ask if you could forward me several 8 x 10 glossy prints of your handsome fizzog.

I feel that displaying your "Rogues' Gallery" photograph will do more to kill the sale of the film we're showing than anything else, but after all, we must give you a little break on the publicity.

Nothing remarkable about those two letters, was there? Nobody expects every routine business letter, done in a jiffy and without special thought, to be a precious gem. Nevertheless, in each of those letters a real human being seems to be *talking*—a friendly person with a sense of humor.

5. WINNING WAYS IN SALES LETTERS

Personality sells. Sales letter-writers have at least two advantages over those who handle other types of correspondence, when it comes to making them express personality: the subject matter is naturally more interesting, and they are expected to spend more time on them. In the section two steps ahead, How to Write the Sales Letter, you will find many samples of the masters' skill which are interesting to the "last drop." It is not difficult for writers of imagination to *relax, be natural, just talk,* when explaining the merit of products or services which themselves have plenty of "oomph." They have a big edge over their associates who must write about traffic regulations, unearned discounts, shipping specifications, and other matters no more exciting. You would think that every sales letter would sparkle with the personal touch, but as you will also find out in Section 7, this is not always true.

In no other kind of business letter-writing is it so important that the personality of the writer be expressed. The urge to buy is usually more emotional than rational. You are swayed by the enthusiasm of the clerk in the store where you are trying on a new hat more than you are by the reasons why the hat may be worth the price. If that enthusiasm is lacking, you probably walk out without the hat. The problem of sales letter-writers are much the same as that of people behind the counter. They must make their prospects feel that they are proud of the thing they are talking about; that they themselves would like to own it, or already do.

Three letters to sell. Examples of winning sales through personality illustrate how well this technique can work. Figure 5-7 is a clever hook to sales; Figure 5-8 passes along information with humor. The approach is pure slapstick comedy, but it probably made many readers laugh. You may decide for yourself whether or not you like these out-of-the-rut sales attempts, but at least you will concede they are not deficient in personality.

Boyd's, St. Louis store of high standing, had considerable success with this Christmastime sales letter (Figure 5-7). It was mailed, of course, to wives of customers. The next letter (Figure 5-8), comes from Garden City. The wit is contagious and the Star, Chain, and Hook are spiced with more than a pinch of humor.

The pictures used in this mailing were genuine. Snapshots of customers were on file; they had been taken at the time of the first major purchase.

Examining the importance of tone. One danger novices face in trying to put their personalities in a sales letter is that they may exaggerate, so that the general tone becomes irritating to the reader. It is for this reason that beginners are reminded to be *natural* and *not to*

Figure 5-7

My dear and faithful companion,

This letter deals with a very ticklish subject. It concerns the Christmas gift you are going to select for me.

Last year you gave me a box of cigars, some screaming green and yellow seat-covers for my car, and a red leather volume of Love Lyrics.

The cigars broke Henry, our office porter, of his smoking habit; the seat-covers have been a source of real enjoyment to Uncle Nathan, who is color blind; and the Love Lyrics went over in a big way with little Patricia.

This letter I'll admit is a trifle cruel, but I am determined to help you avoid past mistakes.

Old age has made my golf bag unfit for further service; my trousers are fast giving up the ghost; I long for a set of matched irons. I wear a size 38 sweater, and 10½ hose. Dark blues, maroons, and golden browns are my best colors. I look terrific in maroon v-necks.

These are a few of the things I noticed the other day on the Fourth Floor Sports Gift Section at BOYD'S.

BOYD'S, by the way, is my favorite store. Need I say more?

Lovingly,

Your Lord and Master.

press for effects that under the pressure may seem artificial. There is hardly anything more irritating than a writer *trying* to be clever.

Furthermore, what may be a proper tone for a sales letter to one type of reader could be a very wrong tone for a sales letter to some other. Thus, one group of people might enjoy greatly a letter that would be considered too flippant by another. This fact takes us back to the necessary steps in planning an important letter. You will remember that two of the steps were (1) to visualize your readers and (2) choose the approach most likely to please them.

Never can we afford to forget that underneath all business writing certain psychological principles are always at work. Since no two individuals are exactly alike, then no two letters should be written in the same way if you hope to achieve the best results. This, to be sure, is only

Figure 5-8

Just as a reminder to the gentle-man whose picture appears on the left, my records show that he made his last purchase on—
July 4, 1776

Might I, with great humility, suggest to this gentleman, that if he will present himself at 325 E. Market Street, with his Social Security number, his driver's license, and his voter registration card, and insist on buying a lawn mower, edger, or hedge clipper—and if, after strict examination, I feel that he really is in need of one or more implements—it is possible that I might be bribed or persuaded, if caught in a weak moment, to allow him to select one or more implements that would prove to be a credit to both of us.

Under a recent ruling of the Supreme Court, I am not allowed to mention the very low prices of these items, which start at $7.50—the tools represent some of the finest domestic and imported values it is possible to get. This low price of $7.50 is made possible through our tremendous "No-Volume" business, and the extreme need for ready cash.

I have just received 50 beautiful stolen garden hoses, that would sell anywhere for at least $19.95 or more, but which, on account of the purchase price, I am tearfully and reluctantly offering for $9.95 each. Sales are limited to no more than six per customer—don't crowd, fellas!

You don't have to worry about parking here. There's plenty of parking space and it's *free*. During the month of May, we will discontinue stripping accessories from customers' cars. This service will be continued, however, after Labor Day, with several added features.

GARDENING NOTE—lawns with brown spots, hedges of uneven height, and weed-infested flower beds, will again be popular this season with conscientious landscapers.

says
"The Genial Garden Bandit"

an ideal to be talked about and never entirely attained, because no business letter-writer has the time to tackle everything he dictates as a psychological problem.

Nevertheless, the nearer the match between letter tone and reader individuality, the greater will be the sales pull.

Four with a flair. The four letters that follow are quite different in tone. Obviously, they were not intended for either the same types of readers or purposes. Let's look at the tone of each and try to determine why each was so successful.

(1) A letter to sell expertise.

In Figure 5-9, the writer, a fine men's tailor, sets a formal, courteous, and gentile tone.

Figure 5-9. This letter, Mailed to 200 Prospects, Gained 150 Orders for a London Tailor

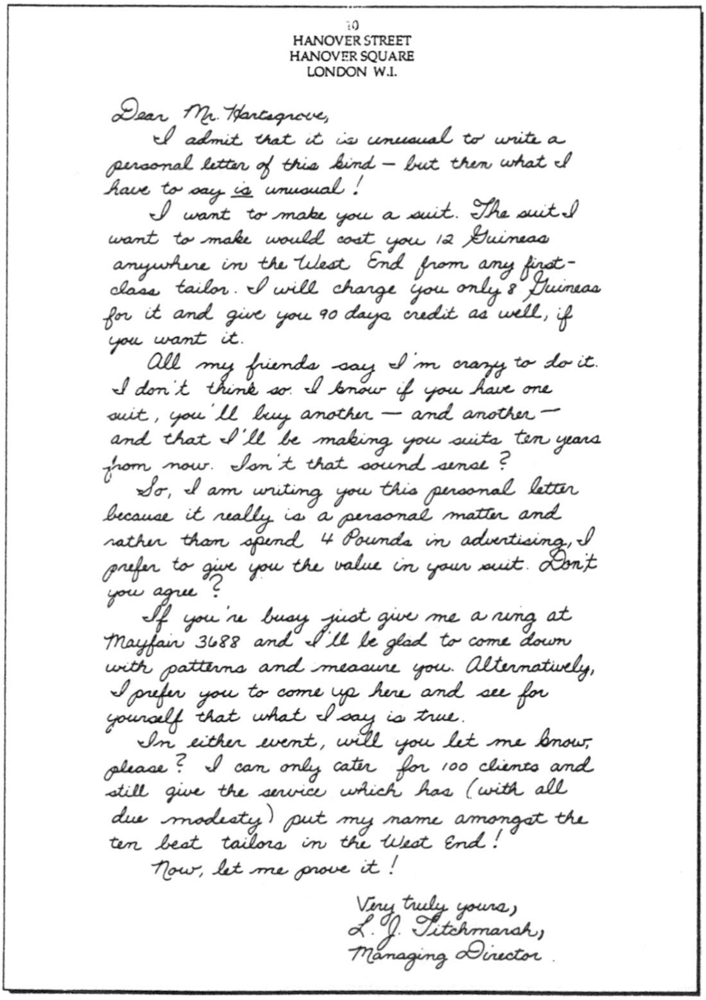

(2) A letter to sell advertising.

The next of the four letters of different tone is shown in Figure 5-10. It attempts to sell printing and advertising services to business executives. Notice the not too farfetched play on the writer's name in the complimentary close—"Merrill-y yours." Notice, too the unconventional salutation, "Good Morning Friend:" But the body of the letter contains no horse play. The writer is friendly, but not intimate. You can guess that the people on his list were of a different type than those on the list to get the clothing letter. Vary the tone to fit the intended readers. That's only sound sales psychology. If you think your reader likes brass instruments, get out your trumpet; if you think he likes stringed instruments, get out your violin.

Figure 5-10. A Cordial Contact Selling Cordial Contacts

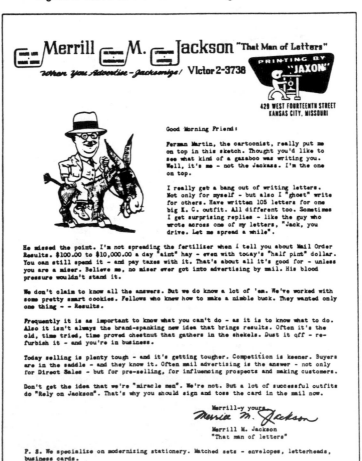

Letters to sell letters. A man of many years' experience in writing letters was Jack Carr, creator of *Cordial Contacts*—monthly mailings for companies to use in holding the goodwill of customers. In Figure 5-11, you see a Jack Carr letter to his own clients. The tone is lively and very informal. It would please a lot of people, but not *all* people. Of course, Carr, the expert writer, knew the limitations of the tone he used in all of his Cordial Contacts. But like printerman Jackson, he had specific types of readers in mind, and sought to match their moods.

Figure 5-11

If I remember rightly the Scotch poet Bobbie Burns wrote something about "the best laid plans of mice and men" often go haywire, or words to that effect.

And he hit the nail on the well-known head !

Consider my case for an example. I figured to leave the maddening marts of trade and commerce to fight it out for themselves, while I sought seclusion and rest in the shade of a sheltering palm on a Florida farm.

Of course, I wasn't going to stop work entirely. But you know what I mean, just do enough to live simply. Sort of a fifty-fifty basis, you might say. Half my time to my letters and half to my loafing.

Bet you've often thought you'd like to do the same.

But did it work out? Helno ! You see, I'd been making my monthly mailings for so many years that it had become a habit. And I couldn't seem to break it.

So I was silly enough to continue making my monthly mailings and now, instead of being able to take things easy like I planned, I'm so darned loaded up with orders for Cordial Contact Letters, I can't go fishing.

I'm warning you now like one friend to another. If you are planning to let down a little and take things easier, don't start making monthly mailings to your customers and prospects.

Why even this friendly little letter is likely to cause someone to send me an order. And —

That's the hell of it !

Mr. Carr's letter would probably fall flat if mailed to the customers of Mr. Vernon S. Porter, whose letter is reproduced in Figure 5-12. But to make it tit-for-tat, so would Mr. Porter's letter fall flat if mailed to those on Mr. Carr's list. Hence, we have another demonstration of our salient point—no letter-writer can hope to shoot at the moon and blast the whole of it. He must be content to aim for a certain slice, and use the ammunition most likely to hit the particular target.

All four of the sales letters cited have personality—but no two are of the same variety.

Figure 5-12. The Picture Helps to Personalize This Letter

S. MAW, SON & SONS, LTD

(G.P.O. Box No. 54)
7 to 12 ALDERSGATE STREET, LONDON, E.C. 1.

TELEPHONE:
NATIONAL 2488
(PRIVATE BRANCH EXCHANGE)
TELEGRAMS:
"ELEVEN, CENT.
LONDON"
CABLEGRAMS:
"ELEVEN, LONDON"

Directors:
MOWBRAY T MAW
ARTHUR T MAW
ALBERT F PORTER
VERNON S. PORTER
NORMAN M. PORTER

Manufacturers of
TOILET BRUSHWARE, TOILET PREPARATIONS, SURGICAL DRESSINGS
CLINICAL THERMOMETERS, DRUGGISTS' SUNDRIES, ETC. • SHOPFITTERS

FACTORIES: NEW BARNET, HACKNEY, HAGGERSTON

SEASONAL EXHIBITION OF CHRISTMAS MERCHANDISE,
GRAND HOTEL, BOURNEMOUTH. COMMENCING 8.10.

Dear ————,

We are pleased to advise you
that our special range of
Christmas Merchandise has had
a most encouraging reception
at the hands of the trade in
all parts of the country.

Special exhibitions have
already been held in such
centres as Birmingham, Glasgow,
Edinburgh, etc. at which
attendances and sales have broken all our
established records for many years.

In fact, we have had such a high degree of
interest, that it has been difficult to
attend to all customers on certain days,
despite the use of trained auxiliary staff.

We are writing to tell you that so far as
Mr. John Swan's exhibition at the Grand Hotel
is concerned, we have arranged for Mr. Phillips
of our Showroom Staff, to be in attendance with
him for the rest of the week, to ensure proper
service.

We are looking forward to a personal visit from
you, and if you can possibly telephone and make
an appointment, it would be of assistance to us,
but in any case you can be sure of the most
cordial welcome.

This is going to be a vintage year for Maw
Christmas Merchandise, and it promises to be the
finest season for our customers that they have
ever known.

We do hope that you will come along to our Stock-
room, so that you may judge for yourselves just
what we are doing to help you.

Wishing you the most successful Christmas you
have ever known, and thanking you for your
support,

Yours very truly,
S. MAW, SON & SONS LTD.

(VERNON S. PORTER)
MANAGING DIRECTOR.

REF: VSP/P

The "how" of it. Perhaps by now, through summary and review, we can devise a formula for injecting your writer's personality into your business letter; remember that anything so abstract and intangible cannot be reduced to an exact science. However, the following roadmarks may point in the right direction:

1. Try to begin with the concept of *talking,* not writing. Hold fast to this feeling of personal contact to the very end.

2. Use the language that is yours in everyday speech. Do not "press" or try to be clever. Relax. Be yourself.

3. Avoid the stilted expressions that make business writing stiff and colorless. Use, when you can, the homespun words like *folks, home,* and the others that have pleasant meaning to your readers.

4. Reflect good manners, rather than the "dignity" of business. There is no more dignity in business than in any other ordinary form of human activity.

5. Let the readers know they are being approached as fellow human beings. Call them by name a time or two. Add an "unnecessary" line about them, their city, a previous contact, or anything that may be of mutual interest.

6. Put the emphasis on *them.* Start sentences with *you*—avoid *we.* Interpret everything you talk about in terms of benefit to your reader—keep yourself and your company in the background as much as possible.

7. Keep in mind above all else that you must *please your readers.* See through their eyes, not your own.

8. Cultivate a sense of humor, but do not *force* for it. If you have to stop and think about something funny to say, by all means don't say it. But don't be afraid to unbend. A smile is a million times more inviting than a frown.

9. Try hard to make the tone of your letter fit the personality of your reader.

10. Never dictate when you are cross or irritable. To be friendly, you must *feel* friendly.

Sober contemplation of these 10 points brings one fact to mind which cannot be disregarded. Not every person in business is qualified to write letters. You cannot write in a friendly way unless you *are* friendly; you cannot make the readers feel you are interested in them unless you *feel* that interest; expressing a pleasing personality is impossible unless you *have* one. It may be that your letters have been cold although your heart is warm. If that is true, then your problem is simple.

Open the gate, and let the warmth flow out. But if at heart you are contentious, sarcastic, suspicious, unfriendly, keep the gate closed. You can't make a silk purse out of a sow's ear; you can't express a pleasing personality when there is none to express.

6. PROMOTING THE SPIRIT OF THE COMPANY

Expressing another personality. Business organizations, like the people in them, have personalities to express. Some are forbidingly cold; some are warm and attractive. Others, clinging to the fetish of "business is business," have the best of intentions toward their customers, but hide them behind a barrier of formality. The writers who serve an organization which is either cold, or appears to be, work under a severe handicap. If they write friendly, person-to-person letters, sometimes flavored with a touch of humor, they are quite likely to be called on the carpet and told their letters must stick strictly to the business at hand. This is lamentable, of course, as the very spirit which would help to get results is prohibited.

In the largest sense, the business correspondents write for their companies more than for themselves. This thought is expressed in the book, *Smooth Sailing Letters,* in the chapter called "A Pint of Molasses or a Barrel of Vinegar." The title, of course, refers to Abe Lincoln's familiar saying that a pint of molasses catches more flies than a barrel of vinegar. The application to business letters is quite obvious.

> It's the company that writes the letters—not you or me. And the company is bigger than any man or woman on the payroll. The company has just one purpose—to render an honest service and thereby reap an honest profit. Everything that helps the company to achieve that purpose is good—anything that works against that purpose is bad. There is no middle ground.
>
> What good could an angry, impudent, or sarcastic letter do the company? You could sock a fellow in the eye for calling you a liar. You wouldn't be much of a man if you didn't. But the company can never take a punch at a customer. Customers are the root of the business. Without customers, there would be no business. Without customers, there would be no job for you.

If the above sounds reasonable, then it must be conceded that letter-writers have a double purpose to attain; first, to express their own personalities in a pleasing way; second, to express the *spirit of goodwill* that exists in their company. To be sure, the second purpose is missing if the company spirit is not friendly. But we are not talking about exceptions. We believe the great majority of organizations that comprise

American business are genuinely eager to render an honest service. Some of them may not *express* goodwill as well as they could, but the spirit is there just the same.

A blueprint for "terrible" and "terrific." If you take time to study the letters that come your way, you no doubt are amazed at the two extremes which they often represent in helping or hurting public relations. It is difficult to understand how any business executive could have dictated the following letter, and then signed his name to it as general manager. The letter was written several years ago, and from the spirit reflected in it, we may assume the company is no longer in business.

Gentlemen,

You had a few shipments of our harmless active _____ _____. You have not purchased for a long time.

From our viewpoint there can be but one conclusion. You have no business, or, you do not know what _____ _____ is, or what it should be.

Manufacturing firms having brains leading them, use this _____, as we can prove by transportation records, so that we and our dealers are supplying more _____ consumers than those supplied by all other _____ producers combined.

The reordering goes on while you slumber.

However, we shall be glad to supply you when in the market.

If it were not such a horrible illustration of tactless writing, you could smile at that letter. After insulting the former customer by insinuating he is asleep and has no brains, the writer ends with "Very kindly." If you can find anything kind in the letter, you are a wizard. The spirit expressed is utterly selfish. The general manager is irritated because the customer stopped buying. He plainly says what he thinks of such stupidity.

Under no circumstances can business correspondents be justified in slapping back at a customer. The writers may have received a provoking letter; they may have good reason to resent it. But their job is not to add more fuel to the argument. They must, if possible, smooth the ruffled feathers; the old saying that a soft answer often turneth away wrath is true. Consider the very fine example that follows:

Dear _____,

Whatever you may say about us, you will not deny that we have developed an almost fiendish accuracy in treading on your toes. I won't insult your intelligence by giving you a lot of baloney about why these mistakes happened, or why they won't happen again. I can't even promise that.

But I will do my best to set things right, and I am sorry that you feel I am personally responsible for these blunders.

No doubt if I were in your shoes, I would echo your "Nuts to you" with vehemence. But I'm not—I am on the other side of the fence, and honestly you haven't left me a leg to stand on. Sorry, Jerry! But I hope you don't feel too angry to accept my sincere apologies, and best personal wishes.

You could hardly ask for a finer illustration of good letter writing than the above. It reveals a man of pleasing personality expressing the goodwill of his company—a spirit which carries on in spite of trying circumstances.

Pertinent points of personality: a summary. Throughout this section we have looked at the value of expressing your personality in writing business letters. You must keep in mind that you are a real human being, with likes and dislikes, talking in written form to other real human beings. Stiff, stilted, excessively formal letters kill the warmth of the friendly personal contact you desire.

Some key factors we discussed will help keep your letters lively, personal, and successful.

• Remember to use your readers' names occasionally—you are writing to *them* individually;

• Keep your letters friendly—even rough situations can be soothed with kind words;

• Smile as you write—an angry countenance will show through.

To make all your company's letters of the highest caliber, let's look at company letter planning.

SECTION 6

HOW TO CREATE A COMPANY BETTER LETTER PROGRAM

HOW TO CREATE A COMPANY BETTER LETTER PROGRAM

1. SETTING CONDITIONS NECESSARY FOR SUCCESS

Let it start at the top. Many companies in recent years have undertaken programs to improve letters. Some attained temporary results that were eventually nullified by lack of sustained effort. Others, equally successful at the start, have managed to keep the fire burning. But many fizzled, either from inadequate supervision or lack of executive backing. It is useless to consider a letter program in your company, in spite of the good it might accomplish, unless the top executives are thoroughly sold on the need, and will let it be known that cooperation is expected from all employees who have anything to do with company correspondence. This, of course, includes themselves, since cooperation does not permit exceptions.

An interesting example is the contrasting experiences of two companies that launched letter programs at about the same time, and under the same leader, who had been able to improve correspondence for many other organizations. There were many other similarities that make the comparison even more convincing. In both companies, the number of people handling letter writing totaled about 80, and the preponderance of the letters went to customers. No attention had been paid before to letter improvement, and those being written were stilted, curt, and often unfriendly.

Since the program and conditions in both cases were identical, it would seem that the results should have been just as gratifying for the one company than the other. This was far from what happened, however. Company A came through the program with flying colors. The improvement in the letters was so marked that even many customers remarked in a complimentary way about them. Sales letters produced more orders; collection letters brought back the money with less friction; complaints were handled more tactfully; the company felt an unmistakable improvement in public relations.

But the results in Company B were quite different. Some of the letter-writers improved, others did not. The program was carried out as agreed, but with lukewarm cooperation. At the end, nothing was done to keep it going. Here and there some individuals were doing a better job, but the majority slipped back quickly to their indifferent, and often rude, manner of writing. In a few months, no one would have known that a better letter program had ever been launched in that company. The results could hardly be called worth the effort.

Why did Company A succeed, and Company B fail, with the same letter program? Well, because of one very important reason. In Company A, the president and all of the other officials were highly interested. They set an example for every employee to imitate. They encouraged every letter-writer, regardless of position, to attend the meetings. The president announced the course in advance, and asked for complete cooperation. He said that his letters would be treated like any others, and that he and the other officials would attend the meetings. And they did, without exception.

In Company B, the attitude of top executives was the reverse. The program was placed in the charge of a junior department head, who probably was the one who had sold the need for better letters. Unfortunately, he was one of the poorest writers, and not popular among the other personnel. No announcement or call for teamwork came from the president's office; none of the officials appeared at any of the meetings. Of course, their letters were not put through the wringer. From the beginning, it was obvious that the program was intended to be only a school for down-the-line employees—and they resented the idea. They were expected to improve their letters, but the "biggins" in the company were immune to the treatment. Some department heads came to the meetings as observers, but a sure way to kill even this casual interest was to find a fault in their letters. Naturally, the program failed to gain a fraction of the results gained in Company A. The cause was lack of executive backing!

Viewing the inception of the program. The better letter program can originate in any department, but, as previously mentioned, it must have the interest of company officials to give it the impetus needed for success. For example, the idea for a better letter program in the New York Life Insurance Company was born in its public relations department. However, that is not an important fact. What was crucial to the success of this program was the backing it got from company executives.

This company has been in the forefront in the development of a better letter program.

If you are the one who wants to initiate the program, do some research first and you will be in a good position to make recommendations to your superior. The following memorandum was adapted from an actual one. See how well the initiator presented a well-thought-out program for his superior's consideration.

PROPOSED PROGRAM FOR IMPROVING COMPANY CORRESPONDENCE

There are two broad approaches to the problem of improving correspondence: By employing an outside agency to do a complete survey and wholesale revision of letters, as in the case of the ABC Company; or by developing a program from within the Company, as in the case of DEF Company. Among the objections to the first approach are the antagonisms and resistance which an outside organization is likely to encounter when dealing with department heads, the danger of reverting to old habits when the outside organization has completed its task, the fact that an outside organization would require considerable assistance and direction on the part of people within the Company, and expense.

It is recommended that the second approach be adopted, with this office taking on the task of developing a plan which would have the full-time attention of an expert writer.

The plan, in brief, would cover a broad, overall program for stimulating interest in better writing, and secondly, assistance and guidance for particular departments and individuals. The general principles and procedure, as outlined below, were developed after studying the experiences of other life insurance companies with this problem:

1. A course, consisting of six or seven one-hour lectures, to cover the general principles of how to write a better letter. The course would be given to groups of 15 or 20, generally from the same department at weekly intervals. This procedure has proven very successful at DEF company.
   a. Organize material and prepare lectures, which might be illustrated with slide film.
   b. Enroll members and deliver lectures.
   c. Provide summaries of each lecture.
   d. Prepare and provide study material.

2. Prepare, and send periodically, reminder follow-up bulletins to those who have taken the course, to keep them from

backsliding into old habits. Experience of other companies has indicated the advisability of this.

3. Enlist the cooperation of department heads. We feel that this may best be accomplished by having a particular department head recognize the need for better letters and come to us to assist him. In this way we could cooperate with the department head to find a satisfactory solution to the particular problem, and avoid the natural resistance which usually arises in these situations. It is not expected that they would hesitate asking for help when it becomes known that the top officers of the Company are interested in improving the quality and character of correspondence, and that there is a set-up to help department heads in this regard. As a good job is done in one department, we believe that word would get around and that there would be heavy demand for the service we would be ready to provide.

4. The procedure by departments might be as follows:
   a. Review an extensive file of letters and classify the various types of letters written in the department.
   b. Prepare model letters and guide paragraphs for the most common types of letters.
   c. Provide each letter-writer in the department with a correspondence manual on how to write good letters for that department.
   d. Review printed forms going to customers and agents, and suggest ways to improve them in appearance and phraseology.
   e. Work in close collaboration with the department head, lawyers, and actuaries in making all revisions.
   f. Counsel with individual letter-writers and show how particular letters can be improved.
   g. After completing the job in a particular department, inaugurate a system of periodic review to make certain high standards are maintained.

5. Review with the Committee on Procedures the relative advantages and disadvantages, from the viewpoints of economy, efficiency, and public relations, of individually typed letters, automatically typed letters, disc-stored letters with typewritten fill-in, printed letters with typewritten fill-in, and printed forms.

This program may seem rather ambitious and comprehensive, and obviously all of it cannot be accomplished immediately. DEF spent a full year developing a program before introducing it; and ABC employed a considerable staff of outside consultants who spent several years before completing a program of departmental correspondence manuals. It is certainly enough to occupy the full time of one person. As the program is new, it would probably be advisable for us to feel our way, especially in the beginning, to make certain we are on the right track, although the fundamental procedures and principles are based on the experience of other companies.

A plan so well thought out had to be approved, and it was. There are so many sound ideas presented in this memorandum that companies of all types and sizes can find some that are useful for their purposes.

Announcing the program. Since the logical next step in a better letter program is the announcement, it is important that a high-ranking executive sign this call-to-arms so that it is given the proper weight. The announcement should stress the purpose and importance of the program. Following is a letter that can be a guide for you.

As you know, letters written by the company to customers, agents, and the general public play an important part in determining the nature of public feeling toward the company and toward the business as a whole. Except for the agents, the only contact in many cases between a company and its customers is through written communications.

In view of the importance of the letters we write, the Public Relations Committee for some time has been trying to work out some way in which it could be helpful to those who have the responsibility of writing letters in the Home Office. As a result of this study, an "Effective Letters" program has been developed. It will include a series of round table conferences for those who write letters, review and analysis of individual letters, and consultation with the head of the department on correspondence problems.

The general plan will be administered by the Public Relations Department under Assistant Vice President Doe, and conducted by Ms. Jane Smith of the Department. Before joining the Company, Ms. Smith was a successful writer for leading national magazines, and has had considerable experience in the field of business letter-writing.

The program will be started one department at a time, and eventually it will cover all departments of the Company. Department heads wishing to take advantage of the Effective

Letters service should get in touch with Mr. Doe. He and Ms. Smith will be glad to explain the program in detail and work out plans to fit particular needs.

John Jones

Executive Vice President

Providing adequate leadership. If maximum results are to be secured, a necessary condition is the selection of qualified people to plan and supervise the program. As in any other similar undertaking, the net gain is sure to be in proportion to the knowledge and experience of the instructors, plus their ability to present their material in an interesting, practical manner. Some companies are blessed with such individuals within the organization, and those people can do the job as a part-time activity, which they are often glad to do if paid a bonus for the extra effort. Many of the bigger organizations, however, maintain full-time correspondence supervisors. This is the ideal set-up, and it pays high dividends to the company that can afford the cost.

Looking for outside help. When the company considers the cost of a full-time correspondence supervisor prohibitive, and there is no person in the organization ready to take over, the only alternative is to look outside for help. Fortunately, this alternative is not a restricted one. Many companies are located in cities where universities, colleges, and business schools offer good courses in letter composition.

In addition to the helpers that may be drawn from the college field, there are also a number of professional business letter consultants. Some of them conduct letter clinics in the larger cities. These are valuable in laying the groundwork in principles, and in motivating correspondents who lack the understanding of the relation between their letters and pleasant public relations.

Searching the company library. A business organization need not be large to maintain a library of books for the training of employees in various aspects of business. However, the number of companies offering this service is surprisingly small. There are several exceptionally good books on business letter-writing, and any person who handles correspondence should be encouraged to read them. Sometimes, a small group may be organized to study the same book, with weekly get-togethers for discussion, and a systematic application of the subject matter to the company's letter problems. Many a company school has started in this informal way. The average employee is receptive to the idea of self-improvement when those higher up provide the opportunity.

It is foolish for executives to say that they would like to see their letter-writers do a better job but that no means of training them are available. They may have to scratch here and there, but they can always come up with some kind of a letter program. It may not be the best in the world, but it will be better than nothing. If sincerely offered, with genuine executive encouragement, the results are bound to outweigh the cost in time or money.

Realizing the need for sustained effort. A lot of better-letter programs go up like a rocket, and fall like a dud. Someone in the company gets the idea that correspondence needs a shot in the arm, and sells a bill of goods to the chief executive. The stimulant may have been a letter that caused the company much embarrassment, or the person inspired may have heard about the results gained by some other organization. Anyway, the program is launched with the best talent available, and the company spares no cost in turning old methods upside-down. In some cases, the intentions are better than the procedure; results are negligible. In others, the immediate progress is even better than had been expected. The letter-writers are all doing a much better job. The executives agree the program is a swell idea—and then they promptly let go of it. Better letters are an accomplished fact in the company. They can now think of other things.

But that is not true. The minute the program is put on the shelf, it begins to lose its effectiveness. One by one the letter-writers return to their old bad habits. With nothing to keep them on the new trail, they soon return to the old and easier one. They, too, stop thinking about better letters. In the course of time, most of the progress is erased. And all for the lack of *sustained* effort.

This fall from proficiency and return to the old inferior way of doing things is common in business. Factory workers slip in quality and quantity of production unless the incentives to do good work are kept fresh and alive. Advertising copy tends to become impotent unless somebody continues to prod those who write it. Errors increase in the shipping department unless the work there is kept under continuous observation. It is just human nature to take the easy road when there is no one to lead the way on the hard road. No letter program will continue at maximum speed unless a competent driver stays at the wheel.

If this fact sounds discouraging, let it not be so. The bulk of the job is done when the letter-writers, and the others helping them, have mastered the principles of letter construction and have caught the idea that their output is directly connected with sales and public relations.

With that much accomplished, they *know how* to write effective letters. When they slip back to former bad writing habits, it is not because they don't know better, but because nobody continues to check their work, nor seems to care any longer whether it is good or poor. Thus, the incentive to fine performance is gone.

The companies that manage to keep the quality of their letters high throughout the years are those that maintain an adequate form of supervision. At regular intervals, and sometimes unexpectedly, copies are checked. Bulletins, too, are sent forth regularly to keep the principles alive and to present new ideas. Praise of good work is freely given, and now and then a prize is awarded to the writer of an especially good letter. Never are the writers allowed to forget either the principles or the need for their application to company correspondence. Thus, the program never dies—because somebody is around to keep it fresh and vital.

Using memos to keep interest high. As part of its program, a company should send announcements to department heads before the beginning of each course. Department heads are thereby reminded of the program and invited to submit names of employees who are interested in taking the course. The announcements, in memorandum form, should be clearly written and fully explain the program. The following memorandum is an example:

> Next month, we will begin another course in writing improvement as part of our continuing Effective Letter Program. To help us do this, will you please send the names of those under your supervision you would like to be considered for training. Please submit the names by Monday, March 5, as follows:
>
> Type separately on 3×5 cards the name of the employee who will participate in the program:
>
> John Doe   (Group Classification)*
> Insurance Department
> Room   ,Extension #
> *Group Classification will be either 2A or 2B: "A" for those who will attend the 2 morning workshop meetings and "B" for those who will attend the afternoon sessions.

HOW DOES THE COURSE WORK?

The course will be given in the same manner as the most recent one, which was successfully concluded in February. Two lectures, based on the principles of effective business writing, will be followed by 26 weeks of copy analysis. That is, each week, trainees will submit copies of their letters, which will be analyzed and returned to them with comments. The "Effective

Letters" manual will be distributed. At the end of the program, we will send a progress report of each trainee's writing to his department head or division head.

WHO IS ELIGIBLE?

While the program concentrates on our special type of correspondence and is intended mainly to build goodwill through our letters, it is not restricted to those who write letters only. It is open to anyone who writes or is expected to write *in any media* as part of his job responsibility. Those who have had previous training are eligible. Only letters will be critiqued, however, not memorandums or reports—but the principles and skills learned will be useful in all kinds of writing. If the writers have no letters of their own to submit for evaluation, they will be asked to complete exercises that will be furnished them each week.

Enrollment is voluntary, of course, but it is expected that trainees—once enrolled—will do all assignments until the end of the course.

A report on the just-concluded program is in preparation and will be distributed soon.

Please send the names of your prospective trainees, on the 3×5 cards, by Monday, March 5, to Effective Letters Program, Room 3311. If the first evaluation of your writing shows that you have no need for training, we will notify you immediately to that effect.

After the names of employees who are going to take the course are submitted, the supervisor of the program should send a memorandum to the participants welcoming them to the course and restating the importance of better letters to the company. Included in this memorandum can be general information about the course. The following is an example:

Effective business letters are a vital part of our Company's public relations, and we are delighted to learn that you will participate in our Effective Letters Program. We know that you will find your assignments to be both interesting and useful.

The program consists of 2 major elements: Lecture-workshop meetings, and comments on your letters from expert writers and teachers.

LECTURE-WORKSHOP MEETINGS

There will be 2 of these meetings, conducted by a professor of Business Writing at New York University. He is the author of several books and articles and is a past president of the American Business Writing Association. Meetings will be held on the following days in the 13th Floor Conference Room.

	Group 2-A	*Group 2-B*
Friday, March 23	9:15 a.m.	2:00 p.m.
Friday, March 30	9:15 a.m.	2:00 p.m.

You will find your group classification underneath your room and tube number on the white slip at the top of this page. Please use this slip when submitting your first set of copies.

COMMENTS ON YOUR LETTERS

From now on, beginning the week of March 21, we would like you to make extra copies of all your letters, and to select *every week* the 5 that you think are the best, for comments. Your editor will comment upon how they conform to our principles of effective writing, and return them to you. Your editors will be Robert Cain and Lionel Dael, experienced editors in this field.

You will receive 6 months of such training—in 2 periods of 3 months each. This will involve 26 different sets of copies. The first period will begin the week of March 21 and end during the week of June 20.

NOTE: At the conclusion of the program, a progress report will be sent to your department head. To help us with this, we will need a sampling of your letters before the Program begins. Therefore, the copies you submit on March 21 will not be returned to you. However, the copies you submit on March 28 and thereafter will be returned to you with comments.

The program coordinator in your department has already let you know, or will soon let you know, the schedule he wishes to follow when he collects your copies. They will always be collected on the *same* day every week. Also, because comments are only a week apart, no late copies can be accepted; and no more than 5 copies can be submitted in any one week.

The copies with comments, will be folded and stapled and returned directly to you through sealed interoffice mail. In this way, the comments made will remain confidential between the instructor and yourself.

YOUR NAME SLIPS

At the first meeting, you will receive 15 slips containing your name and other information. Please clip (NOT STAPLE) one of these slips to your copies every week when your coordinator collects them. The same slip will be used to return the copies to you. (If you should lose these slips, please prepare new ones.)

We will have further information and materials about the program for you at the meetings. This material will be packaged, labeled with your name, and placed on tables at the side of the Conference Room. The material will be arranged in alphabetical order. As you enter the Conference Room, please pick up your material *before* taking your seat.

Meanwhile, if you have any questions, will you please get in touch with your program coordinator immediately.

We are looking forward to seeing you at our first meeting on Friday, March 23.

2. FIRST, THE LETTER AUDIT

Knowing where you stand. The logical beginning of any better-letter program is to take inventory of the letters currently mailed. In some companies, this job is done by more than one person. Other companies leave this to the program leader. By making this audit, the people in charge gain useful information to guide their steps. They find out the major faults of the company's correspondence as a whole, and focus in on the letter-writers who need the most attention. This is a necessary "first" because in no two companies will the same conditions prevail, and the program should be custom-built to fit the letters at hand.

This information is very simple to get. Several weeks before the program is to begin, a period is named during which extra copies of all letters are made for the program leader. These copies should be placed in folders: there should be a set for each correspondent, sufficient in number to give a fair sample of his work. The leader then proceeds to read and mark the copies, in preparation for a personal conference with each letter-writer. These conferences should be kept strictly between the leader and the letter-writer, as it encourages cooperation if the writers know their faults are not to be called to the attention of their colleagues. Inasmuch as some men and women are keenly sensitive about their faults, the program leaders need to search for good points in the copies as well as bad, even if they have to stretch their imagination a little bit to find something worthy of commendation.

Copies are audited throughout the entire course.

Future inventories: watching growth. At the end of the formal meetings and personal conferences, if the leaders really know their subject, considerable improvement should already be noted in the work of the various writers. A second audit is then necessary to know exactly how much ground has been gained. Based on this second analysis, a report to the executive responsible for the program is in order. This report can show by comparison the improvement made, and it may also call attention to certain individuals whose ability has been overlooked. The executive thus has a guide for the future selection of employees to handle important letter jobs. The report may also point to certain individuals who have not benefited by the program, and who are not likely ever to produce effective business letters. By transferring these persons to other jobs that do not involve letter writing, a benefit is created both for them and the company.

If an outside firm has been employed to head the program, the second audit of copies and the final report on the results is the signal for its departure. But while it has built the foundation for better letters in the company, and the principles are understood by all who write them, this is by no means the end of the job. If the gains are to be held, the letter audits must be continued indefinitely, preferably twice a year. The copies may be reviewed by someone in the company who has developed the inclination and ability for the job, or they may be sent to the outside firm who directed the initial stage of the program. These semiannual check-ups, coupled with the regular distribution of better-letter bulletins, should keep the program alive.

Training beginners. Because of the recurring turnover in personnel in the larger companies, one troublesome question pertaining to the letter-program is what to do about correspondents who are new on the job, and have not had the benefit of previous instruction. Of course, when their number is large enough to warrant the cost, the initial steps of the program can be repeated in a beginners' class, conducted either by the person in the company who has taken over the supervision of correspondence, or by the same outside firm who launched the program. It is also a good idea to save complete sets of bulletins for these beginners.

3. HOW TO CONDUCT THE MEETINGS

Checklist for the physical set-up. It is important that meetings for letter improvement be held in a place where interruptions or distractions can be avoided. If the company has a large conference or director's room, the problem is solved. Whatever the place selected, it should be apart from the rest of the business and free from noise, so that the program leader will have undivided attention. For example, one professional letter-consultant will never forget the conditions under which he was forced to operate in a certain company. Arriving for his first lecture, he was taken to an upper floor in the factory part of the building where a space had been cleared for the first and subsequent gatherings. On the other side of a temporary partition certain machines were pounding and thumping. The noise was so great that he had to shout to make himself heard. When he asked if the machines could not be stopped until after the session, one of the executives replied, "Certainly not, we are way behind in filling orders, and those machines must run night and day." You can imagine how successful the meetings were under those circumstances!

It is also important that those attending the meetings should be made as comfortable as possible. They should be provided with arm-chairs, or seated near tables so that notes can be taken. The instructors should have a rostrum on which to lay their papers, a large blackboard, and plenty of chalk. These may appear to be minor details, but unless someone looks after them the program will be hindered.

Planning and attendance: keys to success. The need for complete cooperation, so that every letter-writer attends every meeting, has been mentioned. Not only should they be expected to be there, but punctuality also needs to be stressed. It is distracting to the group members and to the instructor when persons arrive late or leave in the middle of a meeting to take telephone calls or for some other purpose.If a letter program is to be launched at all, it should be considered important enough to set aside everything else for it.

The material that will be covered at each meeting should be clearly outlined before the beginning of the course. How much should be covered will be dictated to a great extent by the needs of the company and by the program leader's preferences. The first two meetings in one company's program were devoted to the tone of a letter and to saying what you mean. You might decide to cover more or less, or to discuss something entirely different at your first meetings.

4. EMPLOYING DEVICES TO RATE LETTERS

Letters aren't steaks. A business letter cannot be rated as a piece of meat is weighed on the butcher's scale. There are too many factors that must be working in the right combination, too many psychological forces that may play on one reader with different effect than on another. Even the experts are often fooled in advance about a letter, calling *poor* the one that later gets fine results, and rating *good* the one that later turns out to be a flop. Nevertheless, there are evaluating devices that may be used with a reasonable percentage of accuracy. Even though they may at times miss their mark, they do have the great merit of forcing the writers to judge their letters with a more casual examination of the letters.

The trouble is that most people hastily read a letter they have written, consider the general effect, and then jump to the conclusion that it is good or bad. They do not stop to take the letter apart, or to view it from several angles, as the Rating Scale shown in Figure 6-1 requires them to do.

Rating your own letters. This scale places before you—one at a time—six major factors in the success of a letter. First, you are asked to consider only the *appearance* of the letter, and nothing else. If there is a fault in the letterhead, the position of the letter on the page, or the way it is typed, it should be noticed because you are concentrating only on appearance, and its importance is not overshadowed in your mind by your enthusiasm for something else.

Then, in sequence, but always only one factor at a time, you are led by the Rating Scale to a consideration of Language, Argument, Carpentry, Personality, and Spirit. When weighing the language of the letter, you have pushed aside the question of its appearance. And when you come to argument, language in turn takes a back seat. Hence, if there *is* a deficiency in any one of these six respects, you are more likely to spot it than if you had taken a once-over view of the whole.

The system of grading is simple. You are not asked to pare your judgment to a hair's breadth, as must be the case when a teacher says that one composition is worth a grade of 86 and another a grade of 87. Instead, when considering *appearance* you come up with one of four valuations, worth in points as follows:

If extremely good ....15 points
If better than average ....10 points
If questionable .... 5 points
If obviously poor .... 0 points

If you are willing to look at your letter with an impartial eye, you can tell very quickly which of the above four ratings it deserves on appearance. If "5" is the answer, then you know that from one angle the letter has a serious weakness. Probably, you decide immediately that it must be retyped, or that you will call your printer and have a new letterhead designed.

With the appearance graded, *language* takes its turn. Perhaps the words are short and expressive, the sentences neatly turned, with not a "whisker" to mar the naturalness of the message. Okay! No doubt the proper rating on language alone is 15 points. Or, if not that good, at least it rates above average—10 points.

When the last of the six points is reached, the points can be totaled, perhaps like this:

Appearance, better than average 10
Language, extremely good 15
Argument, questionable 5
Carpentry, better than average 10
Personality, extremely good 15
Spirit, better than average 10
    Total points 65

Figure 6-1

CY FRAILEY'S RATING SCALE FOR BUSINESS LETTERS		
	! = 15 + = 10 ? = 5 — = 0	Points
Appearance	How well is the letter groomed? Is the letterhead attractive without being wild? Does the letter sit nicely on the page? Is the typing good and free from erasures? Does the letter appeal to the eye as one easy to read?	
Language	Are the words short and natural? Would the average person know their meaning? Is the letter free from whiskers? Does it carry the distinction of simplicity? Is the language the same that the writer would use if he were talking to the reader?	
Argument	Has the story in the letter been well told? Do the facts seem complete? Is all the information presented that the reader needs? Does the letter "ring true"? Does the writer seem to know what he is talking about? Does the purpose of the letter stand out sharply?	
Carpentry	What kind of craftsman does the writer prove to be? Between the lines can you see the skeleton that all good letters must have? What about the Star, the Chain, and the Hook—are they all there? Do the paragraphs cling together? Does the story move along?	
Personality	Does the writer succeed in getting himself into the letter? Does he take the reader on an interesting journey? Does he get out of the rut of the commonplace? Does the letter sparkle with originality? Is the interest sustained from beginning to end?	
Spirit	Will the letter win goodwill for the company? Is it free from sarcasm, ridicule, anger, and bluster? Does the reader get the impression that he is being well served? Is it a letter the writer would be proud to show to the head of his company?	
Result	And now, beyond all of those six points, what general impression does the letter give? Does the writer seem to have accomplished his purpose? Does the letter do the job?	
	Final Rating	

Finally, when your rating is complete, and not before, there is one question to be answered, and it is the only time that the letter is considered as a whole. *Does this letter do the job?* If you sincerely think it *does*, then give your letter an additional 10 points. But if you have any doubt in answering the question—if you are not *sure* it does the job—no additional points are given. For example, it would not be consistent to say a letter does the job, if the argument in it has been rated questionable.

As can readily be seen, only what appears to be a perfect letter with not a flaw in any of the six qualities could receive a final rating of 100. Since perfection is rare in business correspondence, if you rated your own effort 100 you would do well to question your judgment, and repeat the procedure. On this Rating Scale, a total grade of 80 indicates a very good letter, although it might rate so low on just one point that a serious weakness would obviously demand correction. Little is to be gained by leniency in the evaluation of our own handiwork. Why should we fool ourselves?

Checking copies of letters. Copies of letters that are actually sent to customers can be submitted to an editor for appraisal and criticism. This practice is the backbone of the company better-letter program. The following (Figures 6-2 through 6-7), are examples of the type of comments that a letter-writer who is taking this course can expect:

Figure 6-2

EFFECTIVE LETTERS PROGRAM

NEW YORK LIFE INSURANCE COMPANY

Mary _____:

Welcome to the course.

I didn't think we were handling inter-office letters and memos, but since you sent them on I'll be glad to read them. First, I would like you to work on tightening up your prose—be concise, say what you must say in simple language. You'll find that writing becomes more effective when you get the message across in few words. And, it's obvious that a clear, concise letter reveals a writer who knows what she's talking about.

If you're interested in learning a bit more about the subtitles of syntax, you might read Plain Words, Their A B C, by Sir Ernest Gowers. It's interesting and has always helped me.

A Note From Your Editor: I have tried in my comments to reflect your Company's policy toward letter-writing. Always, I will put myself in your reader's place; if your letter seems ineffective to me, probably it will not satisfy your reader either. But sometimes, when I don't have the technical information relevant to a particular reply, my remarks may be inappropriate. If this should happen, I hope you will let me know.

Figure 6-3

Mary ———:

Who is the "she" mentioned in the Tripp letter? Is Dr. Howard
a woman? Then why didn't you give the reader a clearer idea of
this. When you use a personal pronoun the antecedent must be clear.
Where is the antecedent to "she"?

I think you could be clearer in your letters. You tend to get
caught up in medical jargon. Re-read your letters, and rewrite them
if they're not clear.

The Barrett letter is a little better. But, even here, you use
starchy expressions: "in reference to" (about); "shall advise you
further".

Sir Ernest Gowers gives one good rule you might follow:
"Use words with precise meanings rather than vague ones."

Figure 6-4

Mary ———:

Your letters are improving. The tone is getting friendlier, and
you are writing with more clarity.

"Forward" is one of the words classified under the heading "Non-
conversational", which we try to avoid in writing letters.

"The above" is jargon. Just say, "this policy", or "the item."

Be careful in using commas. They can be important in making
an idea clear, or in getting the wrong idea to the reader. There is
no set body of rules in punctuation. Writing changes, and the rules
change. If you can, read Strunk and White, The Essentials of Style,
on this subject.

Figure 6-5

Jane ———:

You can be more concise--and effective--in your letters, if you
try to avoid superfluous language. In the Bradley letter, you mention
"measured height" and "scaled weight." Isn't "height" always "measured?"
"Scaled" is also a superfluous word. Re-read the section in the
manual on how to "eschew surplusage."

"Furnished" (sent), "contact" (write), and "indicate" (state)
are non-conversational words--try to use more specific, friendlier
words.

Figure 6-6

```
Jane _____ :

     Try to be more concise in writing.  In the Avill letter, for
instance, notice the changes I made in the last paragraph:  "Please
let me know if you want this coverage..." is friendly and effective.
"Is desired..." is stiff.  And "outlined above..." is unnecessary--
and sounds like commercialese.

     "Prefer the familiar word to the far-fetched.  Prefer the con-
crete word to the abstract.  Prefer the single word to the circum-
locution."  These are a few of Fowler's rules.  Think about them.

     Isn't that jargon in par. 1 of the Vanel letter?
```

Figure 6-7

```
Jane _____ :

     I would like to give you one method of judging conversational and
non-conversational words.  You can "furnish" a home; but you can not
"furnish" a statement, you can only "read", "receive" or "send" one.
"Furnish a statement" is commercial, not popular, usage.

     "It may be necessary for us to," is a round-about way of saying
"we may have to...."  Why not use the latter.

     The second sentence in the Kucharski letter might be written in
a more direct manner:  "You said we were getting a statement from
Dr. M. Bernstein."

     It is a good idea to re-read the finished letter.  Then you might
not make typographical errors such as the two in the Bennett letter.
```

How to report results. Illustrated in Figure 6-8 is a progress report that can be sent by an instructor in the company program. It helps gauge the participant's progress, or lack of it, and describes in detail strong areas, weak areas, and areas where improvement has been made.

At the completion of the course, another evaluation tool can be used effectively. This is the questionnaire shown in Figure 6-9. All participants are given a copy, and asked for their opinions. Often a short memo explaining that the questionnaire is for the company's use only and need not be signed by the participants gets very accurate results.

Many companies have found a questionnaire to be helpful in keeping its better-letter program geared to the needs of the employees. For example, here are some excerpts from completed questionnaires on just two of the questions:

What Do You Consider to Be the Greatest Strength of This Program?

- In each case where the instructor made corrections or offered advice, I felt the suggestions were excellent. I wouldn't hesitate to follow his advice, and I feel he pointed out weaknesses.

Figure 6-8

Typical Instructor's Evaluation
Instructor's Evaluation of Trainee

Please complete in duplicate, and return no later than Tuesday, February 20th.

1. How many weekly comments did you return to this trainee during the 13-week period just completed? 13

2. How do this writer's letters compare with his letters written at the beginning of this 13-week period?

Now		*Then*	
Excellent		Excellent	
Better than Average	X	Better than Average	
Fair		Fair	X
Poor		Poor	

3. How would you describe the improvement, if any, in this writer's work since you began to work with him?

He was addicted to the use of stiff, formal language and wasted no time being friendly toward the reader. Lately, his style has begun to loosen up and his tone has been warmer, more personal. His improvement in tone has been particularly striking and he has maintained it consistently for the last 4 or 5 weeks. I feel that he has really grasped the concept of creating goodwill for the company with his letters.

4. What problems still appear to bother this writer?

He could loosen his style a little more. His phrases are still somewhat stiff and when in doubt, he often heads for some cliches.

- The effective letters manual and the professor's criticisms every week, I think, proved beneficial both to the company and particularly to the individual.

- The program has helped me to be more conversational in my writing. It has helped me to feel that the person to whom I am writing is actually present in the room. Lastly, I have learned to avoid cliches and other bad habits which I picked up in the past.

Figure 6-9

Effective Letters Questionnaire

1. Do you think that your writing has improved as a result of the program?

   Yes, very much _____

   Yes, a little _____

   Very little _____

   Not at all _____

2. Did you feel at the beginning of the program that your writing was relatively satisfactory? *Yes* _____ *No* _____.

3. Now that you have completed your carbon analysis, do you still feel that your writing was satisfactory at the beginning of the program? *Yes* _____ *No* _____.

4. If your writing has improved to any extent, in which of these areas did you find your training to be especially helpful?

   Writing more concisely _____

   Writing more conversationally _____

   Using passive voice less _____

   Avoiding clichés _____

   More aware of readers' interests _____

5. What do you consider to be the greatest strength of this program?

6. What was the greatest weakness of the program, if any?

7. Would you like more time to be devoted to any other aspects of writing? If so, which ones?

8. You had a different instructor for the last 13 weeks of the program. How would you compare the second instructor with the first one?

9. Do you think you could be helped by further training?

   Yes _____ *No* _____.

10. Any other comments?

11. Are you in Group A _____ or B _____ ? (check one)

   Please Return to:

   Director of Home Office Training

- Self-criticism can be very difficult and I think that the comments of an objective reader are valuable. I'm always interested to hear the impressions of a reader and to discover whether I have succeeded in conveying what I wanted to say, the way I want to say it.

- Two meetings at the beginning together with copy analysis so that we could tie in our own work with what was talked about at the meetings were very helpful.

Would You Like More Time to Be Devoted to Any Other Aspects of Writing? If So, Which Ones?

- No, I think criticism of the actual everyday letters that we write is most helpful.

- Yes, offer more substitutes for opening and closing sentences of the letters.

- No, the people who write to me in this jet age of ours have a greater interest in getting the word in a word, than they have in beauty of expression or purity of language. What I need most is writing ideas, those little touches which give life or color or force to a dull story. My instructors can teach me correct literary deportment. But they can't teach me how to "invent" ideas which will result in my writing letters with sentences that sing or sentences that succeed.

- Once-a-month lectures throughout the course would keep the course up-to-date by criticizing letters submitted during the course and give students an opportunity to ask questions that arose *after* the course started.

- The company does a lot of writing to their general offices. We write letters to the public, but write memos to offices. Can we have lessons on this subject? (Interoffice memos.)

Given such insightful views, a company can feel justified in the expense and time incurred with the programs. All aspects of business benefit—the writers, the company, and, most of all, the recipients of the better letters produced.

5. POSTING BETTER LETTER BULLETINS

Keeping the fire burning. Bulletins distributed with reasonable regularity help to keep a letter program alive; their value depends on how attractive the contents are made to those who receive them. As is true of messages to the sales staff, the first requisite of a bulletin to letter-writers is that it be *interesting*. If it contains nothing but a rehash of things the reader already knows, it is rather sure to suffer a quick burial in the wastebasket. Too often, the preparation of letter bulletins is left to someone with only a casual interest in the assignment; consequently, they are dashed off just before the deadline with little thought or care.

On the other hand, many companies have found letter bulletins a fine means of keeping their correspondents and secretaries on their toes, and the quality of the material in them is just as high as you will find in the best books on business correspondence.

Letter bulletins may be used for various purposes:

1. To illustrate faults in letter writing, and to explain principles.
2. To call attention to outstanding letters that have been written by certain employees, and thus to encourage similar work by others.
3. To quote interesting and helpful passages from books and magazine articles.
4. To promote interest in better letter contests—a very effective device in the general program.
5. To present new ideas, or old ones used by other companies.

While the above are major purposes for letter bulletins, there are others that may arise to meet the need of a particular company.

Above all other reasons for their use is the fact that they are an inexpensive method of keeping everybody letter-conscious. Thus, they serve in a way similar to the kind of advertising that is designed more to keep products before the public than to lead to their immediate sale.

Checklist of reminders. New York Life Insurance Company letter writers are asked not to mail their letters before checking seven important points. These points are put in question form on a card that is distributed at the end of the program. The card, reproduced here as Figure 6-10, can serve as a guide for other companies, both large and small, to help them formulate a similar checklist.

Two examples of practical bulletins. With the understanding that one illustration is worth a thousand words, the following bulletins, Figures 6-11 and 6-12 on pages 310-317, are given to show how valuable a resource they can be. The company, New York Life Insurance, Co., took the company letter-writing program seriously. The improvements were dramatic and these bulletins helped keep enthusiasm high and growth continuing.

Figure 6-10. Checklist of reminders.

DO NOT MAIL UNTIL

Before you mail a letter,
ask yourself these questions:

1. Is it **reader-oriented?** Have you considered the reader's interests?

2. Is it **tactful?** Are you courteous? Have you put yourself in the reader's place?

3. Is it **clear** and **concise?** Do your sentences generally contain no more than one main idea? Are these ideas linked with strong transitions? Do you avoid technical terms that may not be clear to your reader?

4. Is it **forceful** and **friendly?** Do you generally use a "personal" subject ("I" or "we" as opposed to "the Company")—and the active voice? Have you eliminated "negative" words?

5. Is it **conversational?** Do you avoid "commercialese" and "business English", and use words and phrases from your everyday speaking vocabulary?

6. Is it **helpful?** Have you anticipated and met the reader's needs? Have you given him useful information he may not have expected?

7. Have you affected your reader **agreeably?** Have you created **good will** for your Company?

If you can answer "yes" to each of these questions, you have written an "effective letter."

**Effective Letters Program
New York Life Insurance Company**

Figure 6-11, Page 1.

Afterthoughts and notes of interest to business correspondents, published bi-monthly as part of New York Life's continuing Effective Letters Program.

Effective Letters

BULLETIN

MARCH
APRIL

THE GENTLE ART OF SAYING "I'M SORRY"

It seems easier for most people to face death and taxes than to admit they've made a mistake. At least that's the impression we've gotten from a number of business letters that have come our way recently. For instance, the following letter which a friend of ours received from his insurance company:

> *Dear Mr. Green:*
>
> *Upon checking our records we noticed that we had charged you the wrong amount for the proportionate premium for December, 1959. The correct amount is $105.70. Since we only collected $103.67 our file and your records are incomplete. Would you please send us the difference in the two amounts which amounts to $2.03.*
>
> *In addition to this will you please sign the attached form so that our records will be corrected?*
>
> *Your attention to this matter will be greatly appreciated.*
>
> *Sincerely yours,*

Reduced to its simplest terms, the letter seems to be saying "We made a mistake. You straighten it out."

Then there's the relentless emphasis in this letter on "our records." It seems to us a safe bet that a reader doesn't care a whit about company housekeeping. Harping on "our records" or "our files" is not likely to impress him and is almost sure to irritate him. In this case, the reader knew the company wanted $2.03 because it was due, and not because "our files and your records are incomplete."

And what about the phrase "proportionate premium?" Most policy owners have little or no knowledge of insurance terms. Involved technical expressions are apt to baffle, or worse, annoy them.

Figure 6-11, Page 2.

Then there's the word *only*, first paragraph, third line. The phrase should read "collected only . . ." not "only collected . . ." Faulty grammar is not a cardinal sin perhaps, but it is surely a breach of etiquette, indicating disrespect for your reader as well as for your subject.

The final discourtesy was, according to our friend, "the perfect parting shot." The writer enclosed a self-addressed envelope — not stamped. Not only did he have to sign a form and send another check, he had to pay four cents to rectify a mistake he hadn't made in the first place.

Now, we're not saying this was an easy letter to write. It wasn't. But surely there are other ways to do it. Here's one way:

Dear Mr. Green:

We always appreciate the opportunity to be of service to our policy owners, but I'm sorry to tell you that last month we did you — and ourselves — a disservice. The correct amount of your December, 1959, premium was $105.70, and we billed you for only $103.67 a difference of $2.03.

May we ask you to sign the attached form and send it to us with your check for $2.03?

I'm certainly sorry to bother you with this, Mr. Green, but you can be sure we'll do our best to see that it doesn't happen again.

Sincerely,

This, plus a stamped envelope, might not send the reader into transports of joy, but surely it wouldn't set him smoldering, as the first one would — and did.

Being courteous takes more time, maybe, but it's time well spent, since discourteousness can lose for you and for your company the confidence of your reader. That's no small loss.

"Our representative will be in Chicago from March 14-18. Please look him up when you arrive at the convention; he will be manning our booth."
This is part of a letter which was dictated to a secretary. When she finished transcribing and typing it, she brought it to her boss for his signature. The last sentence read: "Please look him up when you arrive at the convention; he will be Manning R. Booth."

Figure 6-11, Page 3.

WHAT DOES THIS MEAN?

It has come to our attention that herbage, when observed in that section of enclosed ground being the property of an individual other than oneself, is ever of a more verdant hue.

AND THIS?

Inasmuch as dividends under your above-mentioned policy are payable under date of December 6, it is impossible for us to issue and forward our check in payment of such dividend until the due date, making it, therefore, impossible for you to pay your August, 1959, premium with the dividend to be payable on December 6, 1959.

THIS MEANS

The grass is always greener in the other fellow's yard.

AND THIS

I am sorry to tell you that we cannot apply your December, 1959 dividend toward your August, 1959 premium.

Figure 6-11, Page 4.

IT'S THE STYLE

As a general rule, italicize (or underline):

TITLES OF PUBLICATIONS:
>*The New York Times, Saturday Review, The Diary of Anne Frank*

Occasionally you will see titles of publications set off by quotation marks instead of italics. But the best practice is to reserve quotation marks for articles from publications, chapter headings from books, short stories, poems, quotes, and the like.

FOREIGN WORDS AND PHRASES:
>*e pluribus unum, vis à vis, Zeitgeist*

There are a number of words — *chauffeur, ballet, beau, cliché, opus, data, via, hoi polloi* — which, though certainly foreign, have been so incorporated into our language that they're no longer considered so. However, foreign words and phrases less well-known should always be italicized or underlined.

WORDS USED AS SUCH:
>"You have used *may* when you should have used *can.*"

You'll notice that in the example under foreign words and phrases we italicized those words which we said need no longer be italicized. That's because they were used not to represent concepts or ideas, but to represent words as such.

LETTERS USED AS SUCH:
>"The *p* in *ptarmigan* is not pronounced."

TITLES OF MUSICAL COMPOSITIONS, WORKS OF ART, NAMES OF SHIPS AND AIRCRAFT:
>Bach's *Jesu, Joy of Man's Desiring*
>Rodin's *The Thinker*
>*U.S.S. Missouri*
>*Columbine II*

FOR THE SAKE OF EMPHASIS:
>"Not only *can* we go, we *must* go."

On this point — a word of caution; too-frequent use of italics for the sake of emphasis defeats its own purpose. As Fowler, the distinguished compiler of *Modern English Usage* puts it, "To italicize whole sentences or large parts of them as a guarantee that some portion of what one has written is really worth attending to is a miserable confession that the rest is negligible."

Figure 6-12, Page 1.

Afterthoughts and notes of interest to business correspondents,
published bi-monthly as part of
New York Life's continuing Effective Letters Program.

Effective Letters

BULLETIN

NOVEMBER
DECEMBER

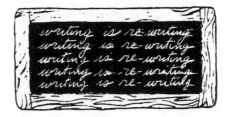

WRITING IS RE-WRITING

Mining a diamond does not produce an engagement ring any more than a random collection of facts produces a good letter. It is rewriting, the writer's refining process, that turns the raw material into the finished product. Let's look at an example of raw material:

Dear Mr. Jones:

We have received your inquiry of November 6. Regarding this inquiry, we would like to state that we are in no position to comply with your request, changing the method of premium payment on your above-numbered policy to the monthly basis, because the monthly premium must amount to at least the sum of $10 per month, inasmuch as the Company has found it impractical to issue policies with a monthly premium of less than this amount.

We might, however, make mention of the fact that your policy contains an Automatic Premium Loan clause and under this clause, unpaid premiums can be taken care of by loan provided there is sufficient cash value in your above policy to warrant doing so, and provided small repayments are made on your loan from time to time.

If it should be your desire to do this, kindly contact us and we shall be pleased to comply with your request.

Sincerely yours,

Figure 6-12, Page 2.

The raw material is there, but certain refinements seem to be in order. First of all, because the sentences are overloaded, the letter demands a second or even a third reading — hardly fair to the reader. So on the first rewrite, let's take out the linking words — *and, because, since, inasmuch as* — and make separate sentences out of what follows:

Dear Mr. Jones:

> We have received your inquiry of November 6. Regarding this inquiry, we would like to state that we are in no position to comply with your request, changing the method of premium payment on your above-numbered policy to the monthly basis. This is because the monthly premium must amount to at least the sum of $10 per month. You see, the Company has found it impractical to issue policies with a monthly premium of less than this amount.

> We might, however, make mention of the fact that your policy contains an Automatic Premium Loan clause. Under this clause, unpaid premiums can be taken care of by loan. This can be done provided there is sufficient cash value in your above policy to warrant doing so, and provided small repayments are made on your loan from time to time.

> If it should be your desire to do this, kindly contact us. We will be pleased to comply with your request.

Sincerely yours,

This seems to be a lot clearer. At least it can be better understood on first reading. But what about all the gingerbread — "We are in no position to," "We would like to state that," "If it should be your desire,"? A second rewrite could take care of those:

Dear Mr. Jones:

I am sorry to tell you that we cannot change ~~We have received your inquiry of November 6. Regarding this inquiry, we would like to state that we are in no position to comply with your request, changing~~ (the method of premium payment on your ~~above-numbered~~ policy to the monthly basis. This is because the monthly premium must amount to at least $10 ~~per~~ month. You see, the Company has found it impractical to issue policies with a monthly premium of less than this amount.

~~We might,~~ however, ~~make mention of the fact that~~ your policy contains an Automatic Premium Loan clause. Under this clause, unpaid premiums can be taken care of by loan. This can be done provided there is sufficient cash value in your above policy ~~to warrant doing so~~, and provided small repayments are made on your loan from time to time. *Let us know if you want us to do this, won't you?* ~~If it should be your desire to do this, kindly contact us. We shall be pleased to comply with your request~~ *It will be a pleasure to take care of it for you.*

Sincerely yours,

The language sounds more courteous and clear, but what about the order of the letter? Is the reader seeing first what's most important to him? What if it read like this:

Figure 6-12, Page 3.

Dear Mr. Jones:

Since your policy contains an Automatic Premium Loan clause, we can arrange to have your premiums paid by loan provided there is enough cash value in your policy. Then you can simply make repayments toward your loan and all will be in order.

I'm sorry that we cannot arrange to have you pay premiums on the monthly basis, as you asked, but monthly premiums must amount to at least $10. However, this Automatic Premium Loan arrangement will, in effect, accomplish the same thing.

Let us know if you want us to do this, won't you? It will be a pleasure to take care of it for you.

Sincerely yours,

Admittedly, such revisions take time, but with practice, rewriting becomes habitual and takes less and less time. It's part of the correspondent's job to be an editor, too.

Begin by relying, as we did here, on only 3 simple rules of editing:

1. Look for overloaded sentences. When you find words like *and, because, since, inasmuch as, which, for the reason that*, you can usually begin a new sentence at that point.

2. Look for words and phrases of traditional "Business English." Delete them and substitute the language of conversation.

3. Look at your reader. Arrange your material so that he will see first what is apt to interest him most.

WHAT DOES THIS MEAN?

It has been observed that an enclosing barrier, for the purpose of discouraging and preventing intrusion upon that which it encloses, tends to enhance the amicability of those whose property abuts on said barrier.

AND THIS

The current dividend notice from you has been received on which was indicated your election of option to have the existing and latest dividend under your above policy applied to reduce future premiums under this policy and we are pleased to advise that this, and further future dividends, in accordance with your election will be duly applied to reduce future premiums.

THIS MEANS

Good fences make good neighbors.

AND THIS

We'll be happy to apply your current and future dividends to reduce premiums on your policy, as you asked.

Figure 6-12, Page 4.

IT'S THE STYLE

Division of words should be avoided whenever possible, but when it's unavoidable, the following guides should help:

1. Divide according to pronunciation — in other words, make sure that the part of the word left at the end of the line will suggest the meaning and the sound of the whole word:

   pro-gress (noun), *prog-ress* (verb), *epi-taph, epit-ome*

2. Never divide words of one syllable:

   asked, named, strolled, height
       not
   ask-ed, nam-ed, strol-led, hei-ght

3. Never divide words with only 4 letters:

   only, also, into, open
       not
   on-ly, al-so, in-to, op-en

4. Never divide a syllable of only one letter:

   about, away, again, enough, mighty
       not
   a-bout, a-way, a-gain, e-nough, might-y

5. Usually divide compound words between the members:

   laundry-man, under-secretary, astro-naut

6. In verbs ending in *ing*, usually divide before *ing*:

   offer-ing, say-ing, danc-ing, ask-ing

   But there are exceptions; for example, words in which the consonant has been doubled before the ending:

   admit-ting, prefer-ring, stop-ping

7. When 2 different consonant letters appear together, or when a consonant letter is doubled, usually divide between rather than after them:

   sym-bol, fal-ter, abun-dance, advan-tage, exces-sive, dif-fer

   However, if this rule conflicts with Rule 1, Rule 1 takes precedence:

   demo-cratic, camp-ing, stick-ing

8. Never, ever, hyphenate at the end of the page.

6. REVIEWING OTHER DEVICES TO IMPROVE LETTERS

How to base contests on company letters. Probably more than any other nation, the people of America love competitive sports. This will to beat the other fellow can be made a powerful asset in a better-letter program by staging contests to see which letter-writer can excel the rest in solving a correspondence problem. The best results are obtained when actual situations, taken from the company's experience, are used to test the writers' skill. It may be a letter of complaint received from a customer, an attempt on the part of another to deduct an unearned discount, or any other real letter-problem that somebody in the company had to handle.

The procedure is simple. A copy of the letter that had to be answered——the more recent the better—is given to every letter-writer—or printed in the company bulletin. All who write letters may be requested to dictate their idea of a reply, or volunteers may be called. The weakness of the voluntary alternative is that only the better letter-writers are likely to try their hands at the problem, and thus those who need the practice most are self-eliminated.

Of course, a time limit is set for the replies to be returned to a certain party—the correspondence supervisor if there is one, or to anyone else who is directing the better-letter program. The ideal plan is to code the replies in some way so that the identity of the contestants is not revealed until after the prize-winner has been selected. The people heading the program may do the judging, or they may ask some outsider, who is an expert in business letter-writing, to serve in that capacity. First, second, and third selections are usually made.

The reward for winning need not be anything of great value—perhaps a new hat, a pen, or a good new book on letter writing. Cash prizes are not considered advisable, since the competition may become too bitter and losers may not accept their defeat gracefully. The highest reward for human achievement is not material. People will try just as hard for the honor of being first as for some gadget that may go with it. The important thing to remember, however, is that each winner in a contest should be publicly praised. It may be announced in another bulletin, at a meeting of the letter-class, or at some company function.

If the company has some kind of a school, with one or more classes in letter writing, a sequence of problems may be used, a new one assigned at each weekly meeting, and the winner of the previous contest announced.

Better letter contests, as briefly outlined above, serve at least three beneficial purposes: (1) since the letters to be answered are taken from all parts of the business, they give the contestants a better idea of what goes on outside their own department; (2) by coordinating training with the deep-seated thirst for competition, contests tend to make the training more interesting; and (3) they encourage the best kind of practice in letter writing, since each assignment represents an actual company experience.

Perhaps a fourth benefit that should have been mentioned is that often in the contests some hitherto unrecognized writer of ability comes to the foreground. The executives thus discover an asset in their personnel that later may be required to solve a manpower need.

Using correspondence manuals. Another helpful instrument in maintaining a high standard of correspondence, and for use as a reference guide, is the manual of information prepared by some companies for their letter-writers and typists. Since these manuals are assembled independently and slanted at the needs of the particular company, no two of them are ever found to be alike. Executives in charge of correspondence have their own preferences with respect to letter mechanics, and the manual they put together is sure to differ from the one in use in the company across the street. Generally, the contents include sample letters to show the forms writers are expected to follow, and information with respect to titles, punctuation, capitalization, abbreviation, and such other matters as the company may consider important. Perhaps the biggest value of the manual is that it assures consistency, so that all letters mailed from the company are similar in appearance and form.

The manual is usually prepared only in the larger companies where many letters are written, and where some one person devotes full time to keeping correspondence on a high level. Unfortunately, however, some of the manuals now in use do not reflect modern letter principles, and many of the rules they set forth are those of the hidebound past. In some cases this may be because they have been in existence a long time and never revised; in others, it simply means that they have been prepared by individuals not familiar with modern letter practice.

Correspondence manuals are also valuable in getting the newly hired typist or correspondent quickly acclimated to company letter-practices. In this sense, they are time-savers and mistake-eliminators. They cannot, however, take the place of personal training; nor do they provide the challenge to do better work which the novice gets from a well-directed letter program.

Reviewing the problems of form letters and paragraphs. A form letter is essentially no different from any other letter, except that it is mailed to more than one person, with the name and address of each recipient filled in at the top. When the fill-in is a perfect match with the part already prepared, the average reader does not realize that the same letter has been sent to other people. Unfortunately, however, the "perfect match" is more of an exception than the general rule, and this is the great weakness of the device. When the reader knows that he is only one of many to get the letter, much of its power is lost, since the effect is no greater than getting a circular or some piece of advertising.

Another weakness in the use of form letters is the failure to rewrite them at regular intervals. Result: They are no longer up-to-date, or they are mailed to the same individuals more than once. This, of course, creates a poor impression in the reader's mind, unless the purpose of the letter is purely routine, and the recipient does not care whether it is a form letter or not. For example, a form letter might be used to notify dealers that orders had been shipped. In this case, the only purpose of the message is to give information.

In spite of the fact that form letters are black sheep in the opinion of certain writers, and that some companies rarely use them, they do serve a useful purpose in business. If properly handled, there can be no logical objection to them; in fact, some form letters rate higher than those individually typed. The reason is that they are carefully tailored to fit certain situations, and often represent the best skill and thought available in the company. This is not likely to be true of the other letters, often written on the spur of the moment by various individuals of different abilities.

Another advantage of interest to the average business executive is the immense saving in time and money. In an hour or two, numerous copies of the form letter can be processed by photocopy machines, computer-driver printers, or word processors. The time spent in placing the names and addresses on them is only a fraction of what it would have been to type them individually. Furthermore, an even greater saving is the time it would have taken to write the letters personally. This time-saving not only leaves the typists and letter-writers free to do other work, but it represents a considerable reduction in cost—a fact no company can very well afford to disregard. What this reduction represents in actual money is difficult to estimate, since the possibilities in one organization for the use of form letters, and the nature of their content, may differ widely from those in another. However, it is safe to say that the average form letter costs, to prepare and mail, no more than one-fourth of what the same letter would cost if individually written and typed.

Except in a general way, it is difficult to state the uses of the form letter. It is quite satisfactory for repetitive and routine situations where no attempt is being made to slant the message at a particular reader. On the other hand, when the purpose is more important, or involves special circumstances, the use of a form letter cannot be approved. For sales letters, the form letter gets the green light only when it is necessary to contact a great many prospects quickly but little is known of their individual characteristics or buying habits.

Personalizing the form letter. Since we know the importance of making individuals feel they are getting a special letter prepared for them and nobody else, it is plain that the form letter should be made to appear as if it were a personal message. Whether or not this object is ethical you may decide for yourself, but it may be justified on the ground that the readers would still get the same message if it were individually written.

As we have pointed out, many of the form letters mailed in business would not fool a moron. The type of the name and address may not match the type of the body. The ink of the two parts may be of different shades. The spacing and alignment are often dead giveaways. Another fact to cause suspicion is the use of a salutation made to fit all those who are going to get the letter; the condition can easily be avoided by *not* including the saluation in the form part of the letter. Naturally, the letter is more likely to pass as personal if it starts "Dear Mr. Doe," than if it starts "Dear Friend," or in some other general way.

To personalize the form letter, several simple steps may be taken. Why they are ignored is hard to say, because there is no logical reason for handicapping a mailing any more than is necessary. You should, therefore, observe these steps:

1. Use a letterhead of good appearance, printed on paper of at least average quality—not a cheap substitute, poorly processed on thin paper, that any reader would know could not be the company's regular letterhead.

2. Use an envelope to match the paper. It will look better with the firm name neatly printed on it than it will blank.

3. Let the salutation be filled in by the typist, along with the name and address.

4. Insist that the fill-in be a perfect match with the rest of the letter. This means that the proper equipment must be provided, and that the work must be supervised.

5. See that the signature is personal, and affixed with ink. Processed signatures are easy to recognize. Never use a rubber stamp.

6. Mail the letter first-class. Seal it. Use regular postage stamps. This is not the cheapest method, but it is the best. Before you decide the cost is prohibitive, consider comparative results.

Today's office machines have made mass mailings of form letters much simpler. Every nationally known brand of machine has a required feature called "letter repeat" or "text memory" or "letter library." This quickly stated, allows the writer to place a letter in storage, and each time the letter is needed, retrieve it for mailing. Added memory and list capabilities even allow for frequently contacted readers' addresses to be retrieved and added at only the touch of a key. This takes more of the typist's time and adds to the expense, but the added touch of personalization may sometimes be more than worth the cost.

Do not turn a cold shoulder on form letters. Use them in their proper place, but use them *properly*. Make every one as much like an individually typed letter as possible. Form letters serve a useful purpose, but keep them up-to-date. Change the copy at *regular* intervals, not just when you happen to think about doing it.

Keeping an eye on the black sheep. Since form letters are just as important as any others, assuring that they are doing the best possible job is a logical part of a company's better-letter program. In those cases where an outside firm has been called in to start the program off, one of its chief duties is to examine the form letters currently in use, to suggest others that might be used, and to assist in such revisions as may be necessary.

The work does not stop with the departure of the expert, however, nor after the first house-cleaning is finished. At least four times a year the entire ensemble of form letters should be reviewed; most of them should be rewritten at least that often.

The fact that form letters are devised to take the place of those that are personally written does not mean that, like a piece of machinery, they can be left alone until they wear out. A great many companies make the mistake of thinking of form letters as a necessary evil—paying little attention to them, even though they may be giving a lot of attention to the improvement of general correspondence. Form letters are not black sheep unless the company treats them as such. They deserve better consideration than they usually get.

So with a good company letter program in place, the business-letter mechanic has the support, information, and incentive to raise the caliber of the material produced. Successful letters linked to successful businesses.

In the next section on sales, we will see how the foundations we have laid will bring the results we desire.

BLUEPRINT FOR STRENGTHENING THE SALES LETTER

BLUEPRINT FOR STRENGTHENING THE SALES LETTER

1. HOW TO CONSTRUCT A SALES LETTER

The supreme test of writer's skill. No letter written for business purposes can be called unimportant, but the relation of sales to profit makes the sales letter stand out above the rest. Furthermore, in the writing of the sales letter, the skill of the business correspondent is put to the greatest test.

Unfortunately, in many kinds of business writing it is not easy to *measure* results. For example, letters mailed to gain goodwill may do the job, but except in specific cases where evidence is developed, the exact accomplishment is still intangible. This is not true of the sales letter. It either sells or it does not, and the extent of the pull is known by the number of orders received. Thus sales letter-writers are always under fire. Unless the results of their efforts are considered satisfactory, they are quite likely to lose their job or be transferred to some other type of less difficult letter writing.

On the other hand, the reward for successful sales letter-writers are usually high. They are the people who are bringing orders to their company, and orders are precious. The greater the pull of their letters, the greater is their prestige. Besides, there is much personal satisfaction to be derived from the writing of a letter that does a good sales job. Out it goes to a list of prospects—or to just one important prospect—and then comes that period of waiting to see what the result will be. And then, the orders begin to come in—perhaps, lots of orders. What a thrill it is to be able to say, "This sales letter of mine had a pull of 10 per cent." Ten per cent is considered good in the average instance, but what if it is 20, 30, or even higher? Then, indeed, the writer's cup of joy runneth over.

Watching the letter carpenter at work. To get the most value out of this discussion of how to write the sales letter, a review of Section 3 is suggested. There, the principles of letter carpentry were explained as they apply to any kind of business correspondence in which an effort is made to influence human behavior—letters to collect money, letters to adjust complaints, letters to motivate salesmen, and all the others where the object is to get the reader to *do something* desired by the company. These principles of letter carpentry are broad enough to cover all business correspondence, with the possible exception of those that are merely routine and commonplace. Now we are going to narrow the arc of the spotlight, and see how they apply to the one type of business correspondence for which they hold the greatest importance—the sales letter.

No doubt you remember the necessary steps in planning a letter. They are especially important in the construction of the message that goes out looking for orders. First, determine clearly the *purpose* you want to accomplish. Second, know all the *facts*. Third, *visualize* your reader. Fourth, select the *appeals* to which he will most likely be vunerable; or, if there are to be many readers, the best appeals for the group. Fifth, *arrange* the arguments you plan to use in an order that encourages maximum continuity and conviction.

Remember to consider how the reader must be led carefully from *attention* to *interest* to *desire* to *action*: how fatal it is if that sequence of psychological reactions is changed or interrupted. For example, you know that action cannot successfully be induced until desire has been created; that increasing interest eventually creates desire; that getting attention is the first step toward arousing interest. You understand what happens when the writer lets the cat out of the bag too soon; when he begins so dully that no more of the letter is likely to be read; when his conclusion is not positive and impelling.

For accomplishing these psychological reactions in their proper order, you have a formula to follow—the Star, the Chain, and the Hook. The purpose of the Star is to stop the readers, so that they might go a little farther with you in the letter. The purpose of the Chain is to make them more and more interesting, until finally they want to do as you desired. The purpose of the Hook is to produce immediate favorable reaction—before desire begins to chill.

The construction of the Star is a separate problem from the

construction of the Chain or the Hook. For each of the three parts in the job there are different factors to consider, different principles to apply. Sample letters to illustrate strong and weak Stars, strong and weak Chains, strong and weak Hooks. There are definite ways to get attention, to build interest and desire, to impel action. Thus, by now you understand the use of the Star, the Chain, and the Hook for all *letters*. But here we are to apply the formula strictly to sales letters—the kind of business writing in which it is most needed, and where it exerts the greatest power.

Understanding the psychology of a sale. As the well-written sales letter travels its course, certain psychological changes take place in the mind of the prospect? To be sure, they have to *be* a prospect. The best sales letter ever written would not cause readers to buy a country estate if they already owned one or detested country life. People might be moved mightily by a letter presenting the merits of a Cadillac automobile, but if they have no money to buy one and couldn't get it, the presentation would be sheer waste. Wastage of this sort is to be expected in the use of any list of possible buyers. Some of them are not prospects because of their total inability or disinclination to buy.

But when the readers are potential buyers, it may be assumed that a change in mental reaction is usually taking place as they read from paragraph to paragraph. At first, they are politely indifferent—controlled by *reason*, and well-versed in all the objections that may exist. Moreover, they are strictly on the defensive against any effort to high-pressure them into action. Thus, if the positive urge appears too soon—as so often happens in sales letters—they are quite likely to be frightened or irritated, and into the wastebasket goes the letter.

On the other hand, if the readers are gently led from point to point, the things talked about may begin to appear in a new and pleasant light. This simply means that interest has quickened, and desire has begun to form. The readers by this time are not nearly as suspicious or as indifferent as in the beginning. Their reactions are colored with *emotion*. Objections are fading out.

You know how the application of the Star, the Chain, and the Hook, has brought about the above-described change in mental attitude. The chart in Figure 7-1 shows the thought sequence.

A study of this simple chart quickly reveals why so many sales letters flop. They do not *take time* to do a complete job. They expect and ask for action while the reader is still only cold or lukewarm toward the item or service for sale. They disregard the necessity of changing rational reactions to emotional reactions. They either do not use the Star, the

Figure 7-1

S T A R	Indifferent Cold Mildly attentive	Reactions are RATIONAL
C H A I N	Casual interest Lukewarm Deeper interest Visualization of benefit Begins to want Desire increases Objections pushed aside	Reactions are EMOTIONAL
H O O K	Ready for action Hot Needs only a push	

Chain, and the Hook, or they do it so awkwardly that the letter falls apart. Some fail for *lack* of a Star; others, for *lack* of a Hook. Some turn the formula upside down, revealing the purpose of the letter before the reader has had a chance to visualize benefits. Truly, this is not a formula to be tampered with, or one in which any of the three parts can be left out. You must take all of the four steps, and always in the same order.

First—Get ATTENTION. Think about nothing else. In what logical, appropriate way can you win a little favor at the start—enough that the reader is willing to read on? That is the job of the star. Nothing more. Just that.

Second—arouse INTEREST. A deeper and more sustained interest than you had at the start. This is the first job of the Chain. In this stage, you are not trying to make the sale—simply paving the way.

Third—build DESIRE. Desire comes as the natural result of increased interest. Make the reader see himself enjoying the benefits of your product or service. And that's the second job of the *Chain*. Now the sale is coming up. Your reader *wants* what you have to sell.

Fourth—impel ACTION. That means *ask* for it. Make it easy. That is a problem different from the rest. Think only of that. It's time for the hook.

Remember, you have four jobs to do in your sales letter, and no two of them are alike in purpose or technique. Take one at a time and concentrate on it alone. It's something like scoring a run in baseball. You go from first, to second, to third—each base reached means a problem solved. When you stand on first base, you have the reader's attention. But many a player gets no farther. Neither may you. If you get to second, you have aroused interest; if you get to third, you have built desire; if you cross home plate, you have stimulated action. The sale is made.

If you want to carry the analogy a point further, consider pitchers as your readers. When you go to the plate to bat against them, they know nothing of your proposition; they have no thought of buying what you have to sell. Their main object is to strike you out so that they can give their attention to something else. But step-by-step you wear them down. Each base that you advance stands only for temporary success. You may not arouse their interest—you are caught trying to go to second. You may get as far as third, but never score. You didn't completely overcome their resistance. You were close to success, but lacked the final drive that would have sent you home. A lot of sales letters die at third. Some have Hooks which are too weak; some have no Hooks at all.

Examples of sales letter carpentry. Now that we have discussed the theory of constructing sales letters, let us consider some actual examples taken from the business world. The first, Figure 7-2, is a letter that seeks to sell a merchandising plan to dealers in footwear. The very logical appeal is to the desire of the dealers to make more money. The Star opens with this appeal in a rather spectacular way which could hardly fail to get attention.

This sales letter to dealers did not waste any time in explaining the details of the plan; the agreement contained that information. Instead, the emphasis throughout the entire Chain was on what the plan would *do* for the dealer. The appeal would be of interest to any retail merchant—how to keep stock turning over and thus increase profits. Even the end of the Hook repeats that theme— "Thaw out those frozen dollars."

The letter shown in Figure 7-3 is an additional example of the effective use of the Star, the Chain, and the Hook in sales letters construction. The Hook is positive and courteous. "Either order card will start your subscription," says Mr. Westerfield. As you discovered in Section 3, the tone of this conclusion is correct, although it might offend

Figure 7-2

Dear _____,

You would be surprised, wouldn't you...

...if you walked into your store tomorrow morning, glanced at your shoe stock, and saw several fresh, green $5 bills hanging out from every box lid?

Money, as you know, has no value unless it is working. If you invest money in something that does not earn anything, it costs more money to leave it there. This is why a large group of our customers willingly go to a little extra time and effort to harness their shoe stocks with our Concentration Plan. This plan helps them drive those slow-moving shoes off the shelves. It spotlights every pair that should not be there.

In every carton of shoes on your shelves there is merchandise representing at least $35 per carton. It is your money that is invested. But, do you know definitely how many of those pairs have no right to remain on your shelves?

Our Stock Control System is a part of the Concentration Plan. Properly used, it will dig out all of those buried dollars that you can use to buy new shoes.

For what little time and effort you put into it, the Concentration Plan can earn mighty big dividends for you next year. Install it in January, and it will be operating smoothly when you commence selling spring shoes. It costs nothing except your willingness to start it and keep it going.

Please read the attached Concentration Plan agreement. Fill in the information on the second sheet and we will forward the necessary supplies and information. Thaw out those frozen dollars in your shoe stock. We will help you put them to work next year.

---

if used earlier in the letter. The end of your sales message is no time to lose your nerve with "If" or "May" or "Hope." These are negative words that betray your lack of confidence in your own sales message. Mr. Westerfield tells the readers what to do, and leaves no hint that he fears an unfavorable answer.

In this sales letter (Figure 7-4), the Star is a question which no doubt would be successful in getting the attention of many students just out of high school, unless they were already registered for a university course.

Figure 7-3

```
April 26, 19__


Dear Reader:


TIME, of course, is a magazine you know.  It's a favorite of
business and professional people; a prime source of news, a
powerful medium for advertising, a magazine that has earned
the respect (and readership) of the country's leadership com-
munity.

If you see only an occasional issue -- or receive it regularly
but don't always have a chance to read it thoroughly -- it's
our feeling that you're missing TIME's true value as a con-
tinuing service.

     Our suggestion: accept a trial subscription, delivered either
     to your home or office -- sample TIME for less than 50¢ an
     issue.  Put one of the two order cards in the outgoing mail
     now; if TIME disappoints you, cancel your subscription and
     we'll return the pro-rated balance of your payment.

If you'd like to know more about the news and the people who
shape it than you are ever likely to get out of just the daily
papers and the broadcast reports --

-- if you consider it worth your while to keep up with all
   the extra fields that TIME covers (art as well as sport) --

-- and if you're willing to take your news, not just in a bare
   recital of facts, but in a story told as thoughtful reporters
   and editors see it

... then accept our invitation to subscribe on a trial basis.

Formalities (like a bill) can wait until after you begin to
receive copies.  The order card enclosed will start your sub-
scription.


Cordially,



Putney Westerfield
Circulation Manager

PW:LM

Enclosed
```

But any letter mailed to a graduating class would be wasted on a certain percentage of the members.

The Chain continues the theme sounded in the first paragraph. The readers are told they don't have to worry about being idle—that in a short time they can enjoy a good income and be on the way to success while other students are still in college, or side-tracked in blind-alley jobs. The plan, they are told, has always worked for other high-school graduates—why not for them?

Figure 7-4

Letter from Moline Business College,
Signed by A.L. Due, Manager.

Dear Student,

Would you like to receive a nice salary check every week, soon after finishing high school; and to know that the future held for you opportunities for outstanding success?

If you are like most high school seniors, you have this picture in the back of your mind, but you are wondering WHEN and HOW you will be able to fulfill it.

There IS a way by which you can protect yourself against the uncertainties and idleness which face most young people; and assure yourself of pleasant and profitable employment...

And—best of all—it is a way which does NOT require from four to seven years of study, or a college investment of several thousand dollars. It builds towards life's greatest goal—financial independence—without demanding that you postpone your earning period for a long interval. You can enjoy a good income, make your parents proud of you, have money to spend in your younger years, and advance to substantial success—while other high school graduates are still going to college, waiting for "something to turn up," or are side-tracked in "blind alley" jobs.

There is nothing theoretical about this plan. It has worked for other high school graduates year after year—even during the darkest days of recession.

Today it provides one of the safest and surest methods by which high school graduates can win early success that it is possible to conceive.

Would you like to know more about it?

The enclosed card will bring you complete information, entirely without obligation. It requires no postage. It is ready to mail as soon as you fill in your name and address.

Then in the Hook, which begins with "Would you like to know more about it?" they are impelled to sign and return the enclosed card. The object of the letter is attained if the card comes back—a personal call will complete the enrollment.

Inspiring teamwork between Star and Hook. Although it is true that the functions of Star and Hook are quite different, and each is an independent problem for the sales letter-writer, they can be teamed to help gain the major objective. In this way, they perform like two players on a football team: the Star stops the reader with a momentary block; the Hook makes the tackle. Consider the Star and the Hook in Figure 7-5.

Figure 7-5

Dear _____,

On the high seas, there are none who enjoy a more enviable position than do the captain and officers of a great ocean liner. They represent the last word in navigation—on the high seas. When the liner nears port, a weather-beaten man whose oil-skins contrast sharply with the golden splendor of the ship's officers comes aboard.

He's the port pilot, whose job it is to bring the ship through the maze of harbor channels, buoys, lights, and congestion, to a safe berth.

The Chicago Elevated Advertising Company is comparable to the port pilot. We live in Chicago and are in intimate contact with local conditions and market information. We understand the current of preferences and prejudices. We are familiar with channels of distribution.

Our knowledge and experience regarding this one market is of inestimable value to those seeking safe anchorage for a worth-while product, in Chicago.

So when it's "cast off" for Chicago—just remember a satisfactory landing is made with greater assurance with a "port pilot" aboard.

Obviously, this letter was not intended to make an immediate sale. Its purpose was to drive home the one point that a local advertising firm is in the best position to understand its own market. Looking to future business, this one point might win the order, and it is very well illustrated in the story about the port pilot. But having used this story to get attention, the writer does not entirely discard it. Instead, the importance of "knowing the channels" is emphasized in the body of the letter, and the "port pilot" himself reappears in the conclusion. Thus, the story is the skeleton that holds together the flesh of the whole letter.

Emphasizing the need for balance. Since each of the three parts of the sales letter has an important job to do, it is generally poor procedure to let one part steal the show to the detriment of the other two. The following election letter (see Figure 7-6) used by a printing company illustrates the point. It has a very interesting introduction, based on the coming Derby in which donkey and elephant are to run. It also manages to echo the idea in the conclusion, but there is no balance of emphasis on the three parts, because the sales argument consists of exactly one sentence. Thus, the message consists of a fine Star, a fairly satisfactory Hook, and practically no Chain.

Figure 7-6

Dear Friend,

Here it is again, the grand old Election Derby, with the donkey and the elephant staging a whirlwind race before 200,000,000 enthusiastic citizens. Fireworks all along the way, with perhaps a bit of mud from a flying hoof now and then. What a race!

The man on the donkey lays on the leather, lashing the long-ear down the stretch. The elephant fights for the pole, running under the goad as a deputy jockey gets in some fancy hard-riding at the rear. Battle! Dynamite! Storm! But onlookers, hotter than a campaign speech, will cool down the minute the race is ended.

We have 14 salesmen, covering the entire state, at your service. Call on us and we will show more speed than you can get out of either the donkey or the elephant.

The italicized sentence is the Chain. The company has 14 salesmen to serve the reader. That's fine. But what about the service? Is it especially beneficial and outstanding?

In contrast, here is a sales letter (Figure 7-7) with a Chain and a Hook that could hardly be beaten, but with a Star so weak that it might bring about the demise of the message without any more reading. That would be a tragedy, for if the readers push past the dull generalities at the beginning, they go the rest of the way on a very interesting and persuasive journey. The lack of balance is in the Star. You wonder if the same person could possibly have written the other two parts:

Figure 7-7

Dear _____,

APPETIZING, HEALTHFUL, and SATISFYING—[here reader yawns].

This is the SKITLE—born in the shadows of Hollywood Hills and nurtured by famous movie stars.

Fiend of the waistline, easy to digest, and nemesis of hunger, SKITLE is a sandwich three times bigger than the low-born hamburger and five times as good.

Ground veal from itsy-bitsy baby calves snatched from clean, green pastures, garnished with mild dry-eyed onions, topped with blushing tomatoes, and a crunchy, spicy relish, all tucked in a big, oversized bun that's been toasted to a golden brown and—ah! You have a sublime creation—the SKITLE.

It's truly a meal in itself and all for a paltry 99 cents! You will want to try one, and as a get-acquainted offer we will furnish one for half the regular price. Here's how you do it:

Just bring this letter and a friend some time before the first of March. You order the first one, and the second will be on the house.

We're located at 4937 Main, on the east side of the street. There's lots of room to park your car and we stay open until 2:00 a.m.

Come up and see us some time. Bring your friend and the letter.

Cordially yours,

P.S. We have dandy chili, too.

It is the Hook in the sales letter that is most likely to get insufficient attention; at least, you will find a lot more letters slumping at the close than in the middle or beginning. This, of course, is unfortunate because the function of the Hook is to *complete* the job.

Figure 7-8 was written by a master in the use of words. In a novel and interesting way he sells the prestige of his company and the quality of its services. But where is the Hook?

You can see the lack of an urge to action in this cleverly written letter. The prospects may have been impressed by the message, favora-

Figure 7-8

Dear _____,

In Chicago, it's 75¢, no matter whether we ride in a new air-conditioned bus on Madison Street or the hottest, oldest model in the fleet—the price is established.

But *not so* when we think of operations; of clothing; of furniture—yes, and of landscape work!

"I'll remove your appendix for $875.00," says one physician. "Twelve hundred dollars is my charge," says another. "Milady's dress will cost her $35.00," declares the sign in the window, while across the street we see a similar-appearing creation for $85.00. The dining room set for $3,750.00 is laughed at by the table and chairs which claim to be "just as good" for $1,100.00.

So we shop around, pitting price against reliability, until at last we find the place where, in our judgment, they meet.

It will be the same with the work on your grounds: Sometime soon, after calm consideration, you'll select a company where price and reliability go hand in hand.

Before the first horse-drawn car left the barns; before modern medical science had come into being; and while milady in crinolines rode her carriage on the cobblestones of the Avenue, and furniture was still being made from the forests surrounding the swamp city of Chicago...

As far back as that, this company founded their business on the proposition that in all their work, price and reliability must travel together—and through the years they've proven trustworthy companions.

---

bly disposed toward the company—but what are they expected to *do about it*? Perhaps it was never intended to be a sales letter, but only a bit of promotion to pave the way for a salesman's personal call. In that sense, it would not be necessary to worry so much about the missing Hook.

A neatly balanced letter, with each of the three parts doing its share of the job, is one used by the Naylor Corporation (Figure 7-9) as a follow-up to a mailing of samples. This Star is especially appropriate, and would serve equally well for any follow-up letter.

Strive for balance in your own sales letters: let each part do its fair share of the work, with no one part overcrowding the others.

Figure 7-9

Dear Mr. Wilson,

Did you ever drop a stone over the edge of a cliff and wait for the echoing sound to come back to you?

If you heard nothing at all, then your curiosity really was aroused and you wanted to find out what was at the bottom of the cliff, and how deep it was.

We are in the same position today, but the stones we dropped were the samples of our Tap-A-Way set and Cash Register. They were dropped in your direction last July, and since then we have heard—nothing.

Frankly, the samples were sent to you to arouse interest in our line. If they have accomplished that purpose, we are human enough to want you to tell us so; and at the same time, to tell us what the chances are of your buying some of these items.

The enclosed literature tells the story of Naylor toys, and we invite you to read it, keeping in mind that these toys offer you a real merchandising opportunity. Hundreds of other department stores are arranging for Tap-A-Way demonstrations, and for promotion on the Earl Toy Register sales.

Now that a second stone has been dropped your way, we will listen intently for the echo. When can we count on getting your order?

Sending the undisguised form letter. Many attempts to sell by letter are directed to groups of prospects, rather than to separate individuals. This means that the sales message must be broad enough to cover all members of the group, even though by automatic name insertions and by other devices, an effort is made to make the letter seem to be a personal contact. Disguising the form letter is thus considered an innocent and justifiable deception by most sales letter-writers, although they realize the negative effect when the disguise is obvious.

Some writers, however, make no bones of using the form letter openly without trying in any way to hide it. In their opinion, if the letter is interesting and convincing, average readers don't care whether or not they are the only ones to get it. Of course, in taking this position, the users of the undisguised form letter save themselves considerable trouble. The need of a perfect fill-in is eliminated, and for the names of the readers an attention-pulling caption can be substituted. A good example is the letter reproduced in Figure 7-10.

Figure 7-10. Plainly a Form Letter, but Convincing Nevertheless

Dear Friend,

Try it. Sip it, taste it, sample it. Test drive it. Use it on a trial basis in the comfort of your own home. Appliances, cars, foods, gadgets -- everyone's doing it, we noticed, so why not ANAGRAMS?

Why not, we thought, give people a chance to sample _our_ wares -- have them sip and test drive our magazine and provide for their continued enjoyment if they like what they sample?

And so we devised our Quarter Plan, your risk-free satisfaction-guaranteed introduction to ANAGRAMS.

Send us $.25 and we'll rush you a copy of next month's ANAGRAMS. (It will be selling on the newsstands for $1.00.)

This will be our signal to send you the next 8 issues at $.25 apiece for which we will bill you later. If after inspecting the copy for which you sent your quarter, you decide you want no more, write "Cancel" across your bill. We'll stop service immediately and you'll be under no obligation whatever. Fair enough?

...

I think that on receipt of your first copy, you'll agree that never did 25 cents go out and bring back so much.

...

TAKE M.G. (MENTAL GYMNASTICS). ANAGRAMS carries the best available for two good reasons. First, ANAGRAMS' editors have a fondness for meaty, mind-expanding puzzles and they spare no effort in unearthing them. Second, ANAGRAMS has a tradition to uphold. Since its inception, ANAGRAMS has consistently provided the cream of intellectual exercises. Its puzzles, whether solvable in 5 minutes or 55, have caused its readers to applaud the high level of entertainment. And, once solved, these devilishly devised gems begged to be shared! ANAGRAMS readers claim they enjoy tickling their friends with their favorite M.G.s almost as much as figuring them out.

TAKE VARIETY. Whatever your interests -- logic puzzles, cryptograms, brain-teasers, word ladders, rebuses, mathematical anomalies, mysteries -- ANAGRAMS will serve you well. Yes, ANAGRAMS covers the full range of mind fun for the modern person who knows that leisure means more than beer, bowling, and boob-tube.

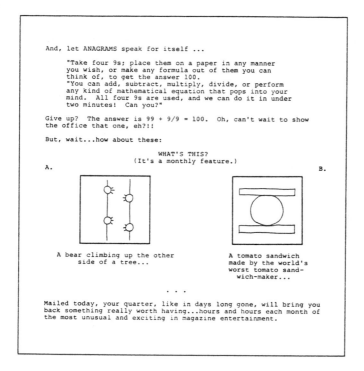

```
And, let ANAGRAMS speak for itself ...

        "Take four 9s; place them on a paper in any manner
        you wish, or make any formula out of them you can
        think of, to get the answer 100.
        "You can add, subtract, multiply, divide, or perform
        any kind of mathematical equation that pops into your
        mind.  All four 9s are used, and we can do it in under
        two minutes!  Can you?"

Give up?  The answer is 99 + 9/9 = 100.  Oh, can't wait to show
the office that one, eh?!!

But, wait...how about these:

                    WHAT'S THIS?
                (It's a monthly feature.)
A.                                                        B.
```

A bear climbing up the other
        side of a tree...

A tomato sandwich
made by the world's
worst tomato sand-
wich-maker...

```
                        . . .

Mailed today, your quarter, like in days long gone, will bring you
back something really worth having...hours and hours each month of
the most unusual and exciting in magazine entertainment.
```

2. CAPTURING SALES THROUGH SPECIFIC APPEALS

Exploring man and his inner self. From the time that he begins to be aware of the world about him, and perhaps even before, man is driven by inner forces which influence and direct the molding of his own personality, and his reactions to the things, people, ideas, opportunities, and beliefs he meets daily in his own world. Call these forces what you will—instincts, emotions, inherited tendencies, or those acquired—the fact remains that they are ever present, and must be understood by any person who seeks to influence human behavior, as, for instance, in a sales letter.

We have neither the inclination nor the ability to approach these inner motivating forces from the scientific viewpoint of learned people who may hold the highest degrees in psychology, philosophy, and sociology, and who know how to take people's emotional being apart and sometimes put it together again. That can never be the approach of practical business people, although it might be helpful could they use it. On the other hand, it may be best that they cannot, since too much emphasis on theory is not always constructive.

Even we know, however, the major inner forces by which our own lives are directed, and judgment and common sense tell us how one or more of the drives may be used to build a successful sales letter. The ability to select the right appeal for a given situation grows with time and experience. Psychology, in the language of the layman, is the study of human nature, and many a salesman who lacks a formal education, who might not even know how to spell the word, is a psychologist in practice if not in name.

You know—we all know—that *fear* is one of the forces which governs the actions of all human beings; never in the same degree, perhaps, but always present. To *protect* himself and his family, his business, or some group to which he belongs, against the things he *fears*, John Doe will buy insurance, vitamin pills, a football helmet for his boy, or new tires for his automobile. Thus, if the product or service to be presented in the sales letter guarantees protection against any of the evils that the reader fears, then that may be the major appeal which the writer should use. Never, however, will this appeal have the same effect on different individuals, or under different conditions. Knowing *when* a certain appeal may have the greatest effect, and when it may be disregarded as not the best for the particular occasion, is one of the skills of the expert letter-writer.

Why do people buy? The appeals that may be used in sales letters are numerous and varied. Often, too, the reason that leads to a sale is so small that only the buyers know why it was important to them. A home is sold because the wife of the buyer likes the color of the kitchen walls. A hat is sold because of a feather stuck in the band. A book is sold because the title sounds interesting. None of these reasons *appear* important, but they were to the buyers. Smart sales letter-writers look for these *little* things that may count *big* in the mind of a prospect. They don't care *why* the prospect feels that way—they are glad to find "*a peg to hang the sale on.*"

But aside from these unexplainable reasons why some people buy, clever sales letter-writers are well acquainted with the smaller number of major reasons that are common to *all* people, and they are alert to the possibility of using any one of them for a specific sales situation. They analyze their product or service to decide what benefits are supplied; they analyze their prospect to decide what needs or desires exist, knowing that if a benefit and a need can be matched, the sale is likely to follow.

What *are* the major forces that influence the thoughts and actions of the average human being? Well, *fear* has been mentioned. If protection against something feared is the major benefit, then protection is the thing to talk about in the letter. Another primary force which seems at work in every human being is *pride;* who among us all is entirely without it? Another is *love:* love for children; love for parents; love for animals; sometimes, love for self. *Loyalty, greed, hate, ambition*—you know the others. Even *sex* may be the "peg to hang the sale on," and often is in a sales letter. The point is that among these many possible appeals, there is always at least one most likely to have the greatest effect for a particular letter situation. The problem is to make the right selection.

Creating letters that appeal to fear. Much of the "scare copy" that you see commonly in advertising, and in some sale letters, is an insult to the intelligence of the reader. To be urged to buy some remedy which "might" cure a disease that "might" develop, is a form of high pressure which any reader has good right to resent. However, if the condition that the letter seeks to correct is common to mankind, and people have *reason to fear it,* then the writer is a benefactor and not a quack; the appeal is logical and its use is ethical.

There are many kinds of businesses whose services or products may properly be offered as protection to offset fear. The insurance companies, for example, have good reason to talk about the various forms of protection provided by their policies—and each form is the answer to something dreaded by the average individual. Hence, the sales letter that quickens one of these fears to the point of action has used an appeal as beneficial to the individual as to the company. In this sense, the letter in Figure 7-11 reminds the reader that men die and leave their families

Figure 7-11

a Mortgage Is a Wonderful Thing...

Do you have a mortgage? Most families couldn't enjoy living in their homes if there were no mortgages.

But mortgages are obligations that have to be paid. Right now you're paying on yours, and you fully expect to continue to meet your payments. But what would happen to your home - to your family - if you should suddenly be taken away?

We have the answer. It's a simple plan of life insurance that promises, in event of your death, to pay off the mortgage. It means that your family will have their home as you planned it. It means a home if they want to live in it, an asset if they want to sell it, an income if they want to rent it. It means all these things, for only about 1% of your mortgage annually.

Surprising? Yes, but it's true. Our representative, whose card is enclosed, will call on you within a few days to give you facts and figures.

homeless, but that no one need fear for their family's welfare if protected by the right kind of insurance policy.

Overcoming price objections. Companies that sell products or services of the highest quality are forever faced with price objections. "Too high," say the prospects—and unless they can be convinced that they are getting just as much or more for their dollar, they are quite likely to buy elsewhere. The individuals who do pay the extra amount for the extra quality are influenced by at least two of the inner forces we have been discussing—*pride,* and the *fear* that something cheaper may turn out to be unsatisfactory. Both of these appeals are often used by sales letter-writers—Figures 7-12 and 7-13 are excellent examples. Both

Figure 7-12

Dear_____ ,

I admit it is a temptation for you to go ahead and buy cheaper alfalfa seed than I have offered you. I used to be tempted to pay less and be able to sell for less myself.

But when I look over the wholesale offerings of cheap seed, my temptation is all gone. I would never have the nerve to sell it to my friends and customers. Mostly, it is a sorry lot of seed. Generally dull and small and wrinkled. None too clean. And nobody knows for sure how many weeds are in the lot.

Our alfalfa seed is big, plump seed. It has a bright, healthy color that you will recognize as fresh and full of vitality. It is cleaned, mighty carefully cleaned. All the chaffy stuff and all the light, small seeds are removed. They wouldn't grow, anyway. And it is absolutely free of noxious weeds.

In order to get the good heavy stand of alfalfa you want, you will have to sow from 15 per cent to 25 per cent more cheap seed than quality seed like ours. And you will have to take the weeds as they come, whether you like them or not.

Now, just figure it out for yourself. My price is higher. It ought to be. But when you figure it out you will need enough less of my quality seed to make up the difference and then some. Goodness knows, I like to see every man save money, but I never heard of one who saved any by planting seed because it was cheap.

That is pretty straight talk, but I believe you will appreciate it. Get good, honest seed, whether you send your order to me or to someone else.

If you like my kind of quality seed at a fair price, send your order along in the enclosed envelope. You will never regret it, and I will be glad to get your order and see another farmer on the right road.

Figure 7-13

Dear _____,

Let's sit down, figuratively speaking, and talk this thing over. I'll admit you've got reason enough to stand, but I think we'll get places quicker if we're comfortable.

It's a ticklish business, Charlie—this price business, and yet it's the most important item in your and my existence. It has been our contention all along that *price is part of printing.* A printer can break down his cost only to a certain point. He can allow so much for composition, ink, type, paper, and printing, but the one thing that no guy's been smart enough to figure is an arbitrary cost on *craftsmanship.*

I think all the heat's been raised on account of our refusing to do a job that we know in advance won't come up to our standards because of a too-low estimate. And, Charlie, there *is* a difference in good and bad printing even in the simplest jobs. Ed Boetcher will be glad to call and explain further our point of view on this matter.

But probably more important to you is again this angle of price and profit. You're in a good business. You've got clearly defined grades of meat and prices adjusted accordingly. For example, when a customer complains (maybe one of our employees for all we know) about a piece of beef liver being tough, you can always say that *calves* liver is a better kind of meat. While your beef liver is the best obtainable, it still doesn't compare with your calves liver. You carry both of them because some people like beef liver.

We only stock one kind of quality, Charlie, because it's our native cussedness to insist that people should only like the best. You and I have grown to be the biggest concerns in our respective fields around here. The quality of our efforts always has been high, and neither one of us intends to lower the standards that have earned us the reputation we now enjoy.

We do quite a bit of business with you, and we'd sure like to do this job. It'll be a bang-up one, too, I assure you.

of these letters are conspicuous for their person-to-person style, and both are extremely adroit in selling the wisdom of buying quality—the folly of buying cheap. Consider first, the letter by the seed seller.

You will look far and wide to find a sales letter that talks the reader's language any better than this one selling quality seed. In pile-driver fashion, one phrase after another hits the prospect between the eyes. No doubt you noticed them.

"never have the nerve to sell it"
"a sorry lot of seed"
"nobody knows how many weeds"
"they wouldn't grow anyway"
"take the weeds as they come"
"figure it out for yourself"
"price is higher—ought to be"
"whether you like them or not"
"make up the difference and then some"
"Goodness knows, I like to see"
"who saved because it was cheap"
"get good, honest seed"
"you will never regret it"
"another farmer on the right road"

You don't encounter any fancy words in that sales letter. But the language used is common sense talk, and so are the ideas. The man talking is a *friend*—he wants to put *another farmer on the right road.*

The printer in his letter to a long-time customer is just as direct and persuasive, but he talks to a business executive, not a farmer. The language isn't quite so homespun but it's still person-to-person.

Again, you have a letter full of simple but expressive phrases—the kind heard everywhere in everyday speech.

"and talk this thing over"
"a ticklish business, Charlie"
"price is but part of printing"
"no guy's been smart enough to figure"
"all the heat's been raised"
"And, Charlie, there *is* a difference"
"you're in a good business"
"is a better kind of meat"
"because some people like beef liver"
"it's our native cussedness"
"a bang-up one, too"

You notice that in this letter selling quality above price, the reader's own business is tactfully brought into the picture. Also, his name is used several times but not too often, although the men seem well-acquainted and the length of the letter permits the repetition.

Using a sample to prove quality. The following letter (Figure 7-14) was used by the Gates Rubber Company to sell garden hose to dealers. The appeal throughout is based on the quality of the product, with a sample sent along to prove it. Four hundred and fifty hardware dealers got the letter; orders were pulled for 14,700 feet of hose.

Figure 7-14

"Spring is just around the corner"—

Dealers with vision are NOW giving serious thought to their Garden hose requirements for the coming season. The Gates factory in Denver is prepared to solve this problem, and to help make this YOUR most profitable year.

Here is YOUR opportunity to deal direct and take advantage of factory prices, just as many other thoughtful buyers are doing. Complete stocks carried in our Denver and Chicago warehouses enable us to give prompt attention to your orders for Gates "factory fresh" Garden hose—the kind that gives your customers extra service *without* extra cost—the kind of service you want them to have.

The sample in the attached bag is our 2-braid Greenlawn DeLuxe Garden hose. Test it any way you want to. Twist it, try to tear it, try to chip the tough tube with your fingernail. Press the sides together and notice how quickly the hose springs back to its original shape. The attractive dark green cover with its deep corrugations insures long life and prevents cracking.

Each type of Gates Garden hose is THE outstanding value in its particular class, built to give maximum service; and you will be surprised at the moderate cost. Gates Garden hose is available in all sizes, in grades ranging from All Rubber to the Greenlawn DeLuxe—in black, red, and green.

Each brand is distinctively wrapped to make it stand out and attract your customers' attention—actually selling itself. Each length of standard braided hose carries its own guarantee tag, enabling your customers to see and feel the QUALITY.

The attached card requires no postage. Fill it in, and drop it in the mail-box. Without obligation to you, samples and quotations on our complete line of superior Garden hose will be sent to you immediately.

You will profit by dealing direct with us, so be sure to mail the card TODAY.

Garden hose is not a glamorous thing to talk about, since it serves only a utility purpose. Hence, the Gates writer wisely chose to pack the sales pitch with solid facts.

"This is the season when garden hose will sell."
"You can buy our quality hose at factory prices."
"The sample *proves* our claim to quality. Treat it rough. See how it fights back."
"Surprisingly low price for each grade."
"Wrapped to invite customer attention."
"Each length tagged to guarantee quality."

All of these facts are up the hardware dealer's alley. Supported by the sample, they could hardly fail to impel interest among those who had not already purchased seasonal requirements.

Hard-selling unseen quality. The job of the sales letter-writer is not nearly so difficult in talking about quality which is obvious as in talking about quality which is hidden. A sample of shirt material attached to a letter, can be seen and felt; it can be compared to other pieces of similar cloth. Gates invited various tests of their sample of garden hose; they knew quality could be demonstrated on the spot. The seed company's problem was not so simple. How can anyone looking at a handful of alfalfa seed *know* whether or not the seeds of weeds are included? Perhaps an expert could tell, but not the average farmer.

The quality of many products is revealed only in *use:* by their length of service; by performance; by comparison with results attained with other inferior makes. Two homes may stand side by side on the same street—both newly built, equally attractive in appearance and interior arrangement. They *look* alike, but they are not. The builder of one knew how to cut corners; how to cheapen construction in ways that would be hidden. The builder of the other used quality construction throughout. The one home will last 30 or 40 years longer than the other, but real estate agents who are trying to sell houses cannot wait that long to prove the fact. They must tell their prospects *how* the home was built: about the extra precautions to insure durability; about the quality of materials that went into the house, even though they are now concealed.

Unseen quality must be sold more consistently than that which is apparent. Buyers must be kept conscious of the values they are getting. Not always by letters that ask for orders, but at regular intervals new fuel must be added; otherwise, the customer may be lured into buying that which *seems* "just as good."

Appealing to personal pride. Most people like to put their best foot forward; they are receptive to anything of quality which may enhance their appearance or prestige. Of course, many merchants and manufacturers base their sales programs on this appeal to pride. Millions and millions of dollars are spent annually on advertising in an attempt to create an image of quality for certain brands, products, and services; and once these concepts of quality are established, the buying public gratifies its pride by paying a premium for better-known products. But these are the methods of the big corporations that have millions to spend for magazine ads, billboards, direct mail, and other forms of promotion. The smaller companies, the retailers, and certain types of service organizations may logically turn to sales and goodwill letters as the most inexpensive means of enhancing the quality of what they have to offer.

Any local company, if it is willing to take the trouble, may build a list of prospects and customers; without much ado, it can keep the list up-to-date. Letters can be sent to these people at regular intervals—announcements of new merchandise just received; the news of special sales; talks about goods to fit seasonal needs; or messages serving no other purpose than to keep the company's name and the quality of its products or services in the public consciousness.

Selling to pride in personal courage. You see, there is no end to the tangents pride may follow or to the appeals that it makes possible. Perhaps one of the most potent is pride in personal courage. People like to imagine themselves a combination of Tarzan, the Three Musketeers, and John Wayne. Any insinuation that they are quitters will either challenge them to prove they aren't, or send them snarling to lick the wound. Because one never knows what the reaction will be, the appeal is a dangerous weapon in the hands of the sales letter-writers. It may work, and it may not, depending on the ability of the reader to "take it."

In Figure 7-15, International Correspondence Schools used another appeal to pride.

So much for the various forms which the appeal to *pride* may take. There are many others of which you are conscious because they influence your own life. But there is another and more worthy inner force at work in human beings which we can contemplate with considerable pleasure.

Writing sales letters with appeal to love. Fortunately, man is not entirely selfish. In many of his activities and associations, *love* for others has a strong influence on what he thinks and does. This force is manifested in numerous ways—love for parents, love for children, love for friends, love for animals, and for others—and because of this love, he is often moved to protect them against misfortune. Thus, sales letter-writers in surveying their product or service, may often find therein a protection against the evils that man wishes to keep away from those he loves. It may be that the writers have a policy to provide monthly income for the prospect's spouse in the event of sudden death, or a food product that helps to keep children strong and free from colds, or even so small a thing as a powder that chases insects from a pet. In every case, if the offer is accepted, the motivating force is love of others, not love of self.

The chief danger in using the appeal to love is that writers may become so engrossed with their subject and its sentimental aspects that they overpaint the picture. People as a rule do not like to wear their hearts on their sleeves; they are moved by sincere sentiment, but turn away from abject sentimentality. Hence, the writers using this appeal should be careful not to "gush" or let their message become too "sticky." When this happens, a tone of exaggeration and insincerity creeps into the letter and its purpose is defeated.

Figure 7-15

THIS ...IS...FIGHTING...TALK

If you are a quitter you won't read this letter. But—

If you are not—if you have the courage to face facts—you want to know who is responsible for your not getting ahead faster.

Do you accept the challenge? All right—

It's YOU!

The person who *won't* be licked *can't* be licked.

The world is filled with people who *wish* something would happen. But it takes people of determination and purpose to *make* things happen.

Maybe you are making things happen for yourself and for your family. A lot of people like you, then, are making them happen faster by acquiring more practical training through International Correspondence Schools Courses.

If things are not happening, and if you are a fighter, you will do something about it!

You'll get the special training that fits you for advancement, and you'll go to a bigger job and better pay.

In your spare time, right at home, you can get the training you need. Through I.C.S. Courses thousands of other people have lifted themselves out of the rut into well-paid, responsible positions.

They're no better people than you. They had ambition and they seized opportunity.

Here's opportunity for you. Mark and mail the enclosed card. It will bring you news that can change the course of your whole life. Do it today.

The letter in Figure 7-16 used by St. Louis Union Trust Company, is written with restraint and tact. The incidents mentioned in the introduction are sufficient to arouse the protective instinct in those who received the message. No doubt, some of them were impelled to see this trust company about their wills.

No doubt you noted the strong Star in the above letter. The three concrete examples are powerful attention-getters. The readers naturally wonder if their own wills might contain similar flaws, or, if they have not made one, the urge is strong to do so.

Looking at a letter with double love appeal. Lovers of dogs can never understand why anyone else doesn't love them. To the great majority of people, any reference to these devoted tail-waggers is liable to receive immediate attention. The letter , Figure 7-17, serves a double purpose: it appeals to a woman, particularly if she is a dog lover, and if

Figure 7-16

Dear _____,

I know of a case where through a mistake a man's entire estate went to his wealthy brother-in-law, leaving his dependent parents in want.

In another case, a man worth $500,000 provided bequests of $75,000 in his will and left the residue to his children. When he died, he was worth barely enough to pay these bequests and his children received nothing. In a third case, a childless man worth $50,000 neglected to make a will, and consequently, his wife received but half his estate, the other half going to his brother.

These are but a few of many cases which have come to my attention in which an ample estate, for some reason, has failed to provide for those who should have benefited, or has been subject to heavy unnecessary loss. Some unfortunate provision in a will, the failure to make a will, or the mistake of an inexperienced executor, is the usual cause of such—often tragic—miscarriages of purpose.

If you haven't made a will, I urge you to do so without delay. If you have made a will, I suggest the advisability of reviewing it carefully.

In either case, you will find our booklet "Your Will" interesting and helpful. It is written in simple, nontechnical language and crammed full of information pertaining to estate matters of vital importance to people of means.

A return card is enclosed for your convenience in sending for a copy of this helpful booklet.

Figure 7-17

Dear _____,

Do your children love dogs?

Do you like dogs?

Does your husband like dogs?

The affectionate fellow that looks up wistfully at you and wags a doubtful tail—how could you help but love him?

But the boys can't keep a dog in the city. That is, *really* keep him.

It isn't safe to let him run, and he *must* run to be a happy, natural dog.

What if you had a real home in the suburbs where a dog can really live?

There's some satisfaction in being a dog in the suburbs. And there's some satisfaction in being a boy or girl.

Why not have a real home, where children can be children and dogs can be dogs, and you can all be free and happy together?

The cost? Nonsense! We have plans that will carry you safely and easily over the cost, whatever your income is.

Why not let us tell you about them? At least, you ought to *know*. Call us, or return the enclosed card, and our representative will call on you.

---

she isn't it still touches her desire to make her children happy. The message was used by Realtor G.K. Masterson of Philadelphia.

The buying bait: to save time or money. Numerous products and services have as buying bait a saving in time or money, or a combination of both. The sales letter-writers who are able to offer something of equal value at a lower cost are rather sure of success *if* they are able to *prove* the equality. In similar fashion, their chances are good if they have some convenience, such as a saving in time or labor, to talk about. This is simply because one of the inner forces in man is the craving to possess as much as he can with the least possible effort. This may be an unworthy trait of the human race, but you know it is present to some degree in practically all individuals.

Most of the inventions with which modern man is blessed are the result of this craving. If conservation of time and money had held no special meaning, we probably would still be using primitive machines and working from the rising to the setting of the sun. The first wheel was no doubt conceived by some savage whose back was tired from dragging heavy objects over the ground. He thought how much nicer it would be to push a lot less and move a lot faster. Be that as it may, a great many sales letters are based on a possible saving in one form or another. The message (see Figure 7-18), written for Augustine Office Communications, Inc., offers added comfort and convenience without any great drain on the prospects' purse—an appeal to which they may be very receptive. The letter starts with an interesting comparison—always an effective device for the Star.

Figure 7-18

Dear _____,

Two Bosses Went to the Office

One went in to start his day. He wasn't in the mood. He would rather have been getting in an early game of golf at his club. But this was out of the question. Messages, letters, and telephone calls were waiting—so down to the office he went.

What happened then?

First, he deciphered the overnight answering service's handwritten notes. Even his secretary couldn't always do that. Next he had to sit through a litany of "You must's..." and "You have to's..." and "Before 10, you will's..." from this same distraught lady. Usually, before he even finished with this, today's schedule, based on yesterday's demands, had begun. It isn't even 9:30, and he's behind! This day-after-day frustration can leave no doubt in our minds—the SCHEDULE is the BOSS.

Consider the second man. He also went to his office. But, what a difference! As he entered, his secretary handed him a printout of the day's amended schedule through lunch. At a glance, over that first cup of hot coffee, he could see who he had to see, call, or go to. All important items had been set off clearly, and all appointments were confirmed. In just a few moments, he had decided how *he* would spend his morning. A grateful smile passed his lips as he thought of his Augustine Communications Sales Representative.

Don't let the frantic pace of office mornings dominate your work life.

Find out now—before another day has passed—how little it really costs to enjoy an Augustine Office Communications System (AOCS) without work or worry. Call today for a FREE Office Communications Survey. This will produce an accurate estimate of exactly how much an AOCS will cost (and SAVE) for YOUR office—installed in your present office communications operation in only a few hours time.

Act now, while current rates are in effect.

The work and worry the Augustine letter talks about is real to the readers, it is trying to reach—hence, the appeal of sparing themselves in the future is tempting.

Another variation of this type of sales letter is the one that offers to spare the readers the expense and annoyance of some kind of unsatisfactory service. You know how often you have taken your car to a garage, and then taken it away later, wondering if the fault has been permanently corrected and if the bill you paid was fair and reasonable. You had no way of knowing the truth until the car was tested on the highways—because you couldn't stand around to see the work being done, and you had no way of checking it.

The company who sent the following letter very adroitly seized this common state of mental uncertainty and used it as a powerful appeal in their message (Figure 7-19). The readers are told that visitors are always welcome in the shop; that the mechanics are proud of their work and like to have it inspected. Note, too, how the name of a famous and beloved person is used in the Star to win attention.

Figure 7-19

Dear _____,

Mark Twain once remarked: "Always do right. This will gratify some people, and astonish the rest."

Perhaps that is one of the reasons our Service Department is so popular. Our aim is always to do right by our customers and their cars.

But there isn't any trick to that because our shop is well equipped to keep cars in perfect running condition. Moreso, we believe, than any other nonspecialized headquarters in the city.

The staff here are born mechanics. Visitors and customers are always welcome to thoroughly inspect their work. They don't attempt to hide it, because they are proud of it. Besides giving efficient service, they are mighty interested in seeing that you get friendly treatment. You'll feel at home here...and like it.

Starting with the first expert analysis of your car's trouble by Ed, the foreman, the mechanics want to give their best. And do.

So this, our first letter contact with you, is just a real friendly invitation for you to visit us. When your car is ill, let our doctors examine it. The diagnosis costs you nothing—obligates you to nothing.

The foregoing letter doubled business over the preceding month for the garage. It was written by a master sales letter-composer, C.D. Craddock.

Capitalizing on the appeal of something free. Watch the people leaving any kind of a business show, carrying bags full of give-aways, and you have tangible evidence of another deep-seated human desire. Perhaps it is fair to call it *greed*, but not in its baser forms. Many of the gadgets and samples in the bags are later tossed into the junk pile, but just the same it seems to be a commonly shared thrill to get something free.

This weakness in man, if you want to call it that, is frequently used by sales letter-writers, and by credit agents, as an approach to the sale. Although the readers might know that the cost of the bait is included in the sales price of the article or service, they still like to fool themselves with the idea they are not paying for it. This comment, however, is not intended as a criticism of the method, provided the buyers still get their money's worth.

A good illustration of the appeal at work is the letter shown in Figure 7-20 which was once used by Circulation Manager R.R. Rountree in an effort to get subscriptions to the magazine, *Advertising & Selling*. The book offered as an inducement, *My Life in Advertising* by Claude Hopkins, is extremely interesting and instructive. Those who took advantage of the offer were in no way deceived.

Because the subscription sales letter is fundamentally sound in construction, a review of its strong points should be helpful to any other sales correspondent. Notice:

1. That the appeal of getting something *free* is started in the first sentence, thus inviting the reader to continue.

2. That mention of the enclosed card early in the letter is an exception to the rule which says we should hold the Hook for the conclusion. In this case, the reader is only being urged to take something free, not to buy. That comes later.

3. That more than half of the letter is used to sell the free books. If the reader can be made to want the book first, he will be ready later to take the subscription also.

4. That a flock of big names are used to impress the reader with the author's importance. This as you know by now is a powerful sales device.

5. That the impression of author's importance is strengthened further by mention of the huge sums of money he has earned.

Figure 7-20

Dear _____,

I see that your name is not on the list of executives to whom we have mailed a copy of *My life in Advertising*—free.

I am sure you will not want to miss the outstanding advertising books of the last decade, so I urge you to mail the enclosed card promptly.

Claude Hopkins' autobiography relates his sensational career in advertising. He was personally responsible for many of advertising's greatest successes—Palmolive, Pepsodent, Edna Wallace Hopper, Puffed Wheat, etc. He wrote a single advertisement that brought in 1,460,000 coupons for Van Camp's Evaporated Milk. He tells you the inside story in his amazing book, *My Life in Advertising*.

He describes intimately his experience with Swifts, Liquozone, Studebaker, Schlitz beer, etc.

Mr. Hopkins earned as much as $185,000 in one year by writing advertisements. He was President of Lord & Thomas for seven years, and when he left he was receiving $120,000 per year for half of his time. He describes in detail why campaigns worked—why others failed. He tells the schemes he used—his methods of testing copy—why the public buys. His book is filled with facts and usable ideas that will be of tremendous value if you want *your* advertising to pay its way.

The question is—how can you get your copy of *My Life in Advertising* free?

The answer is—a copy will be sent to you without charge if you will authorize your subscription to *Advertising & Selling* on the enclosed card.

The combination of Hopkins' book and *Advertising & Selling* is an unbeatable bargain—one that will pay you dividends. The book will present ideas that you can use in your business right away. *Advertising & Selling* will bring you every other week adaptable ideas on all phases of advertising and sales: copy, media, markets, research, etc.

The supply of books is limited and this offer is limited to January 30. Make sure of your copy by using the enclosed card now.

6. That the author's ability is *proved* by the mention of the 1,460,000 coupons one of his ads brought back to Van Camp's Evaporated Milk.

7. That the reader is told how the ideas in the book are usable in his own business.

8. That before swinging to the discussion of the magazine, a second mention is made of the appeal— "your copy *free.*"

9. That the impetus developed by the sale of the book's value is not retarded by a too-long sale of the magazine. The writer chose to gamble on the pulling power of the book, and was too smart to let the reader's mind wander too far from it.

10. That quick action is impelled by mention of the limited number of books on hand.

Offering to solve financial problems. Another twist of the money appeal is that used by the personal loan companies. In a different sense, the soft spot touched is mankind's natural desire to free itself from worry. You know, of course, the argument on which practically all of these letters are based— "it is better to owe us a lump sum of $500 than to owe ten different people or companies sums of $50 each." Financially it may not seem that the people who take the large debt are any better off, especially if interest charges increase. However, they are spared the annoyance of being pursued by many bill collectors. A second advantage of the one debt is that it may be stretched over a longer payment period.

From the letters you have received from loan companies, it may not appear that they are overcrowded with expert correspondents. At least some of their collection letters could stand considerable improvement. The sales letter reproduced in Figure 7-21 has much that you may commend. It starts briskly with an observation which in many cases is likely to provoke the mental reaction, *yes.* It then mentions some of the common needs for money and concludes with a friendly offer of service. The language is talkative—mostly made up of short words. An interesting sentence is the one that says, "Let's talk turkey to eat turkey enjoyably." The message contains no exaggeration or insincerity. The writer does not pose as the big-hearted brother, as is too often the case in this type of a sales letter.

Outstanding appeals for fair play: Two examples. Asking the reader to apply the Golden Rule is an appeal more often found in collection letters than in sales letters. However, the justice of reciprocity can be made an effective sales argument— "I've been scratching your

Figure 7-21. The Cure for Financial Worries

GENERAL FINANCE LOAN COMPANY
1301 CENTRAL STREET·EVANSTON, ILLINOIS·UNiversity 9-9800

October 18, 19--

Mr. William J. Nelson
545 Bergen Boulevard
Ridgefield, New Jersey

Dear Mr. Nelson:

If you are like most of us, you will have urgent need for extra cash
right now.

Winter is drawing near and bringing with it a higher cost of living.
It's likely you will need cash for clothing, fuel oil, taxes, car
repairs, or emergencies. Perhaps you would like to reduce the payments on your car to have more of your income free for other things,
- with no payments to be made for thirty days.

You may arrange for a loan in person, by mail, or by telephone. You
may borrow on your signature, automobile, household security, personal
property or farm chattels. Your excellent credit record with us
entitles you to immediate action on any new request for cash.

Why face Fall and Old Man Winter with a lot of unpaid bills when it
is so easy to group them and have only one small amount to pay monthly?
Let's talk turkey now, and perhaps you can eat it more enjoyably next
month!

We'll be glad to serve you any time. If it isn't convenient for you
to come in during the day, drop around any Tuesday or Thursday evening
before 8:30.

Very truly yours,

GENERAL FINANCE LOAN COMPANY

Byron S. Coon
President

---

back, now you scratch mine." If offered tactfully, as in the following
message, the idea will sometimes produce the desired result; on the
other hand, if the appeal smacks of high-pressure it may do more harm
than good.

This, we think, is the right way to use it:

This income tax business gives me a pain in the neck. I have
been through my canceled checks half a dozen times, trying to
find some deductions.

I didn't have much luck with the deductions, but I did run
across a lot of checks payable to you. We've been trading with
your stores for years, because we like good merchandise and
you give good service.

We, also, have a service which is that of things pertaining to real estate. Our service here in Tulsa is selling, buying, renting, and leasing property.

When you or any of your organization need the help of a Realtor, it would be nice to have you call on us.

Written in such a polite manner, without insinuations or threats of withdrawing as a customer if business were not forthcoming, the above letter at least keeps the writer's name before the reader. It might lead to an immediate service; if not, it at least might develop goodwill looking to the future.

Getting away from business, you often encounter the Golden Rule as the major appeal in sales letters that reach out for charity or civic donations. The soft spot touched is the reader's better self: a spot which fortunately runs to larger size in some individuals than in others. Figure 7-22 is an excellent letter of this type—with an extremely interesting story for the Star.

Figure 7-22

Dear Mr. and Mrs. —————,

Have you ever heard the old fable about the villagers who each agreed to contribute a sack of grain for those of their neighborhood who were ill or poor?

A large vat was put in the village square where the sacks were to be emptied. The day appointed for the opening arrived; the villagers assembled; the vat cover was lifted.

It was empty. Each villager, thinking, "My grain will not be missed," had forgotten.

In a drawer in one of Glenwood's files stand 1,121 cards, the records of 1,121 people who know and believe in the worthwhileness of giving homeless, friendless boys a chance to become the right sort of men. But those 1,121 men and women, for one reason or another, have forgotten to send their checks; there is not only a blank space on each card, but a corresponding lack in Glenwood's treasury.

Your card is among the 1,121.

Please don't think that your contribution hasn't been missed—even though it may be a one-figure amount. No donation is too small to be helpful; none too small to be missed. All together, these donations accomplish a wonderful work.

Won't you please, remembering the story of the empty vat, send your check? We *need* it more than ever this year.

It is impossible to say how the 1,121 people responded to this letter, but one man who got a copy sent a check for double the amount of his pledge. When asked *why*, he replied, "Well, I had forgotten to send my check, even though I knew the good work that school does for boys—then that letter got under my skin. I made up my mind right on the spot to put at least two sacks of grain in that empty vat." In that case, then, it was the story that stirred the reader's imagination and goaded him to action—as good stories often do in sales letters.

Using an indirect appeal to customers. The letters we have been viewing, to see how they probed for soft spots, were slanted largely at prospects, rather than customers; they were after new business. Getting orders from customers is an entirely different job. It is not necessary to talk to them about the nature of the service or product, or to sell them on the reliability of the company. In a way, they are already members of the family; they will continue to buy as long as they feel satisfied, or until some other company lures them from the family circle.

Smart businesspeople, however, do not take customers for granted. They appreciate the necessity of keeping their goodwill, and many letters are written for no other purpose. And, of course, some of these goodwill letters properly reach for orders. Letters of this class are especially effective when signed by the company's president; they make the customer feel important. An example is the letter in Figure 7-23, one of many similar customer contacts made throughout the years by the Kalamazoo Vegetable Parchment Company.

You can be sure that several of Kalamazoo's customers took the gentle hint and sent in "another order."

3. WRITING POWERFUL SALES ARGUMENTS

Uniqueness: The point of difference. Blessed is the sales correspondent who has a "point of difference" to talk about in his letters. It may not be so important compared to other features of the product, but it still has special power to charm his readers. People are instinctively interested in anything new or different, and the desire to own the item is always potent.

What are these *points of difference?* Well, for years we've been told that one product's users had 25 per cent fewer cavities than those who didn't. Whether this was true or not, the sales figures from the product's manufacturer had 38 per cent more sales than its nearest competitor. The customer *believed* that the product made a difference and that's what counted.

Figure 7-23

Dear _____,

What the Business World
Needs Isn't a Better Five-Cent Cigar
But a Good Hearty Laugh

When we were youngsters on the farm, we devoted consider-able time to feeding chickens and hunting eggs.

One year, one of our chickens got the pip and it spread to the entire flock. We did not know at the time and we do not know now what caused the disease; but we do know that it spread until all of our egg producers were non producers, and they wobbled around the barnyard, glassy-eyed, and with their tail feathers dragging in the dust.

An old farmer told us to mix cayenne pepper with their feed and it worked wonders. In a short time they had pep instead of pip.

So, as the entire business world has been suffering with the pip for the past 12 months or more, we suggest that the pippers, instead of taking the cayenne pepper, indulge in a few hearty laughs occasionally. Having tried this remedy ourselves, we can testify to the fact that we have saved ourselves from a perfectly good nervous breakdown by substituting a good laugh for a glum look and a groan.

Sincerely yours,
Kalamazoo Vegetable Parchment Company
J. Kindleberger

P.S. Since dictating the above, our mill manager informs me that the biggest need of the mill just now is another order.

Some phrases appeal to points of difference:
- the only one of its kind that...
- the first to...
- tests show the —gets more...
- new, improved formula means more/less...

Also, appeals to unique features of a common product accent its point of difference. For example TV sets have been sold for years. Each manufacturer has stressed a point of difference with each new model. When we realize that a TV set is still a box with a picture in front, we can see how important emphasizing uniqueness must be. Larger screens, smaller screens, sharper picture, glare protection, portability have been used to show a point of difference.

Writers of sales letters should look long and hard for a *point of difference* to talk about. There are few products or services on the market that are not duplicated in many respects by others. Consider the various automobiles in the low-price range: they are so similar in price, quality, power, etc., that not one of those factors makes a strong sales argument. However, just one of these cars might have a new patented feature which would be a point of difference—something worth talking about. Or, it could be that the *appearance* of one make of car is far superior to the others.

Waste few words on arguments that your competitors can also use. Pound hard on something which is *yours,* and yours *alone.* Then you develop sales power—and nobody can stop you.

Proving by testimony. It sounds big and means little to say in a sales letter, "Thousands of famous men, whose names you would quickly recognize, have worn our shirts for years." That is a generality, pure and simple. Who *are* the famous men? Mention just two or three of them, and the statement immediately has power. Human beings are natural-born hero-worshipers. They are easily influenced by reference to people they have learned to admire. Quotations, of course, are even more powerful; but just the names will often give your letter the "teeth" that it needs.

The following letter in Figure 7-24, for example, would be far less convincing without the mention of certain highly respected customers. The use of these names makes the sales message a hundred times more convincing than if the writer had said "Many well known-companies use our labels."

The letter to poultrymen (Figure 7-25), which heralds the benefits of classified advertising, features three testimonials in a most interesting fashion. Each is tagged "RESULTS" with a golden egg to tie in with the introduction.

Inasmuch as those receiving the sales letter knew the spokesmen personally, the effect of what they say is bound to be considerable. A possible weakness in what is otherwise a strong message is the lack of any request for action. In other words, the letter has no Hook. Of course, the answer to that criticism may be that this letter is one of a series—the purpose being to build acceptance for the power of advertising in the two papers.

Figure 7-24

THE TABLET & TICKET CO.

BUILDING DIRECTORIES   LABELS, EMBOSSED TAGS
CHANGEABLE LETTER SIGNS   ADVERTISING SPECIALTIES

1021 WEST ADAMS STREET, CHICAGO 7, ILLINOIS

WILLSON SPIELMANN
President

John Brown Distilleries
Rockford, Illinois

Gentlemen:

We don't claim to know the first thing about liquor and we
can't guarantee you repeat business. But -- if it's new business you want, if you're looking for new customers to develop
into steady ones, here's a real tip for you.

Hiram Walker, the Schenley folks, Gooderman & Worts, Arrow,
Philip Blum, Paramount and others you know, are no longer experimenting on their labels. They know from experience that a
cleverly designed foil label creates sales and pays for itself
over and over again.

If you are not satisfied with your label and are open to suggestions, we will send you a collection of beautiful foil
label samples. Furthermore, if you wish, our Art Department
will reproduce any one of your labels on foil, through a
sketch. Then you can see exactly how your favorite brand
will appear dressed in a bright, attention-getting label produced through the Perfect-o-Cut embossed foil method.

Here is more good news, too. Modern equipment, plus quantity
production, has lowered costs, so that the finest foil label
costs surprisingly less than you would suppose.

Let us send you samples, or better yet, send us a sample of
your label, so we can submit a sketch.

No obligation to you, of course.

Very cordially yours,

Geo. L. Candler
THE TABLET & TICKET CO.

AREA CODE
312
Executive Offices: Chicago, Illinois.   HAymarket
NEW YORK, SAN FRANCISCO, LOS ANGELES, SEATTLE, PORTLAND, DALLAS, KANSAS CITY, ST. LOUIS, ST. PAUL, MILWAUKEE, DETROIT, BOSTON   1-3883

Figure 7-25. More About the Golden Egg

You've heard of the hen that laid the GOLDEN EGG

M. E. Atkinson
Hollywood Poultry Farm
Woodinville, Washington

Dear Mr. Atkinson:

The hen that laid the golden egg is an old story. So is
it an old story that Review-Chronicle Poultry Want Ads get results
for advertisers.

RESULTS H. Kincaid, Freshlaid Farm, Colfax, Washington
writes, "Your papers have played a very important part in selling the 4,000,000 chicks we
have hatched since we have been in the business."

RESULTS Elmer Tucker, Tucker's White Leghorn Farm,
Coeur d'Alene, Idaho, writes, "The combination
of morning Review and evening Chronicle gives
an ideal advertising medium that brings results."

RESULTS I. D. Casey, Walla Walla, Washington, Pacific
Northwest pioneer poultryman, writes, "Year after
year the Casey Hatchery has used the Spokesman-
Review and Chronicle Want Ads to sell poultry
with excellent results."

Of course, results are more interesting when you are the
person who is getting them and making the profit from the orders
Review-Chronicle Want Ads bring.

By starting a Review-Chronicle Want Ad now you can have a
RESULT story of your own to tell before long. The poultry business
is so much better than it was two or three years ago that there is
no comparison. People are ordering chicks and breeding stock. One
large hatchery is already booked to capacity for the entire season.

Review-Chronicle Want Ads will help you get your share of
the business.

Yours very truly,

THE SPOKESMAN-REVIEW and SPOKANE DAILY CHRONICLE

J. J. Tierney

Manager / Classified Advertising Division

Sometimes, the testimonial may be offered in the form of an interesting story, as is done in a sales letter to fire chiefs, composed by Advertising Manager W. E. Cox, of the Quaker City Rubber Company, Philadelphia. (See Figure 7-26.) The value of the story is increased because it describes the experience of another chief whose name is also mentioned.

Figure 7-26

Dear Chief —————,

Yeadon is a nice suburban town near Philadelphia. They are building there a new $800,000 municipal building. In the tower there's a fine new siren. It went off the other day. It's so loud and uses so much air it nearly blew the workmen off the tower. It was necessary for Wayne Ross, chief of the fire company, to go back to the smaller siren until the workmen finish the new building.

Give Chief Ross credit for installing a siren that will be heard in all sections of his town. His judgment was also good when it came to the selection of fire hose, for his town uses Quaker Fire Hose. He is in good company, for many intelligent fire chiefs all over the United States, from New York to small cities, use Quaker. They are free from the worry of bursting hose when the pressure gets high and action is at fever heat.

For over 50 years we have been building fire hose. The inside pages give you a graphic description of the largest single order for fire hose ever placed...and it was for Quaker.

Quaker Fire Hose is built by master craftsmen who realize their responsibility to humanity. I wish you could see the care exercised in the selection of the materials, the precision in compounding the rubber, the smoothness of the tube, and the uncanny accuracy of the machines in weaving the jacket, and finally, the rigid test and inspection to which every length is subjected. If you could take a trip through our plant, you'd say, "No wonder the larger cities buy Quaker Fire Hose."

We have an excellent little souvenir you'll be glad to possess. Something for nothing you say? Then beware! You have to work to earn this article. Easiest kind of a job though! Just fill out the enclosed card and mail it. No postage required. We'll be looking for the card. Hope you won't disappoint us.

This letter must be conceded a success, for it brought back orders totaling almost $7,000. Thus, we are again reminded that under the right circumstances letters may be as effective as salesmen; don't forget, too, that they are paid no salary.

The use of local testimony in selling is a powerful procedure, when and if the information is available to the writer. It takes time to assemble testimony of this kind, but the time is well spent. A prospect is far more impressed by the favorable experience of someone he knows locally, than by some generality like, "Many prominent executives in your city are using our protection," or, "Many housewives in your city are delighted with the cooking qualities of this stove." In contrast would be:

"Here are the names of the banks in your city using our blanket bond insurance." (Followed by list)

"Mrs. Doe, why not talk to Mrs. Oscar Judd, who lives in your block, about the cooking qualities of this stove? Six months ago, she purchased the same model and by now she knows from experience all its fine points."

Use testimony when you can. It will surely increase the pull of your sales letters.

Checklist for effectively using facts and figures. You will remember from Section 3 the necessary steps in planning a sales letter. The second point we examined then was to know the *facts*. The more facts you can parade in a sales letter the greater the conviction it will carry; keep in mind, of course, that facts should be interesting, pertinent to the subject, and directly or indirectly of benefit to the reader. As facts are piled one upon another, the presentation of the product or service seems to gain speed; an accumulation of power drives hard into the mind of the reader; until at the end, unable to resist such a combination of persuasive force, he is swept to the place where favorable action takes place.

What must happen is a mental process—when the facts are wisely chosen, interesting enough to induce reading, and move at a swift pace through the letter. Unfortunately, the result can be just the opposite, too. If the facts presented are *not* pertinent, are *not* interesting, and are *not* connected with the benefit being offered to the reader—if these things are true, the letter is sure to be dull, hard to read, and slow-moving. Many a sales message is doomed to failure by factual content either too remotely related to the subject, or because of the deadly, dry way it is handled.

Survey with an extremely critical eye all the facts you mean to use. Be sure they *help* your cause, and not *hurt* it. Put yourself in the shoes of the person who will read what you are going to dictate. Would *you* be impressed, interested, moved to action by these same facts? Can you present them from the *reader's* point of view, instead of glorifying the product, or satisfying company pride?

Figures put power in the following sales letter, Figure 7-27, mailed to prospects by Merrill E. Jackson—starting with the question, "You would hardly think that a person could make a million dollars selling onion plants by mail, would you?"

Figure 7-27

Good Morning,

You would hardly think that a person could make a million dollars selling onion plants by mail, would you?

Yet that is essentially what Clyde H. Melton of Texas has done in the past few years. He tried growing Bermuda onion plants and selling them to his neighbors. His finances permitted him to plant only a few acres, and at first his sales were made in person.

Then he tried mail advertising. It is said he has an investment of $3,500,000.00 in the Bermuda onion plants and the means of producing them. He frequently has four to five thousand acres of irrigated land planted exclusively in Bermuda onions. He has shipped as many as one hundred million plants a day. Seed for one crop were imported from an island off the coast of North Africa, and cost $375,000.00.

He started with a few dollars. He built a business that has gone into millions. It is another example of what can be done by mail advertising; by the right kind of copy, the right plan, and the right product—sent to the right people.

If onions can be sold successfully by mail, don't you think that your product can be successfully sold by mail too?

What it took to sell onions by mail was a well-formed plan with the right ideas and printing behind it. The same plans have sold hearses, caskets, cosmetics, raincoats, baby buggies, septic tanks—or what have you? Jackson's will be glad to submit a plan to sell your products, with money-making ideas behind it—ideas that have brought from $10,000 to $100,000 in sales per month to others.

There is no obligation to you. Just drop the enclosed card in the mail, and find out what we can suggest for your business. Then judge for yourself as to whether or not it will be as successful as the plan that sold onions.

Most people do not realize how much money they pay in rent over a period of years, but in the Realtor's letter in Figure 7-28, the figures tell the story to "Mary and John." Sixty thousand dollars wasted. "One house paid for—most people pay for *three!*"

Figure 7-28. Figures Used to Sell Home Ownership

OUR PHOTO FILES *Save You Miles*

DOUGLAS
VAN RIPER *INC.*
REALTOR & INSUROR

Douglas Van Riper
Chairman of the Board
Douglas M. Van Riper
President

154 PLANDOME ROAD
MANHASSET
LONG ISLAND

BROOKVILLE OFFICE
Northern Blvd. & Cedar Swamp Road

Dear Mary and John:

During the past ten years to my knowledge you have never paid less than $500 per month rent, and most of the time a higher amount than this. This means you have paid out approximately $60,000 for shelter during this period.

It's time to own your front door key!

As you know a tenant takes no credit on his income tax for rent, whereas if you are an owner, your mortgage interest and taxes are deductible, which would reflect a <u>great saving</u> on both federal and state income taxes. Furthermore, each month as you make a mortgage payment you add to the equity in your home and in a specified number of years you will own it outright. Pride of ownership not only for you but for your children will really pay dividends in satisfaction, security, prestige, and in many other ways. It pays to have your roots down.

Renters rarely retire. How true this is. Don't you think it's time you became a homeowner and enjoy the manifold blessings and benefits of homeownership?

I am sure if you analyze the situation you will find that you have almost paid for one house so far. Most people pay for three. Why not own one now? May we show you how easily this can be accomplished?

Cordially yours,

Douglas Van Riper:f

MEMBER OF LONG ISLAND AND MANHASSET REAL ESTATE BOARDS

You have seen in an earlier section how some companies manage to use their products in the construction of letterheads. Thus, while reading the letter the prospect *sees* the thing talked about. The use of samples in any form in a factual sales letter carries great conviction. The reader knows that the company has confidence in its own wares, and is not afraid to place evidence of quality in his hands for inspection. Naturally, the confidence of the company and its representatives carries over to the reader. This tends to increase the pull of the letter in a manner hardly possible otherwise. The quality talked about is a *fact* actually demonstrated, and not merely a word description.

Of course, the use of samples in letters is limited by the nature of the product. You cannot attach a can of peas or stewed tomatoes to a sales letter—or an outboard motor, a vacuum cleaner, or a furnace. But the use of many other products is not so restrictive. For example, in the following letter (Figure 7-29) the Ohio Rubber Company attempts to sell a safety flooring. The writer couldn't attach a large enough piece to prove how easy and safe the material is to walk on, but he could and does send along a sample two inches square. It is glued on the upper right hand corner of the letterhead—a visible proof of quality.

Figure 7-29

Dear _____,

That small square you see above is a sample of Orco Safety Flooring.

Try rubbing your thumb over it. Do you notice the resistance it gives? Well, imagine walking on an area covered with this material—you'd feel safe and it would be comfortable, too.

Your rubber heels have taught you that rubber is resilient—comfortable. You also know that you feel safe with them as well. We combine those natural qualities of rubber with wear-resisting abrasive Norton Alundum for extra safety, add an attractive color, and we get Orco Safety Flooring.

It is the best insurance against accidents due to falls that we know of.

And speaking of falls, I hope this request for payment of your past-due account for August, amounting to $15.00, does not fall into the discard. We imagine our first request for payment slipped your attention. This bit of Orco Safety Flooring is to prevent that, and to establish your interest in our new material. May we expect your check soon, and an inquiry regarding our new product?

Combination collection and sales letters are infrequently used in business. Perhaps there should be more of them!

Printing companies have a natural advantage in the use of samples in their sales letters. In the first place, the letterhead itself speaks for the quality of the business, although sometimes it does not speak as convincingly as it should. Also, it is easy for the printers or lithographers to enclose some evidence of their originality and skill. Blotters, for example, are doubly good; they serve a useful purpose as well as sample the company's work. Mailed once a month throughout the year, they keep the sender's name constantly before the prospect, as a blotter is something seldom discarded. Figure 7-30 includes such a reminder.

Figure 7-30

Dear _____,

Here's your March blotter.

It has been said, "Whichever way the wind doth blow, someone is glad to have it so." Well, we won't argue because we've been told that you can't sell and argue in the same breath, and we're supposed to make this letter SELL SOMETHING.

SELLING SOMETHING in our case naturally means printing, and the services pertaining thereto—so back to the blotter. The last two blotters we've sent to you portray a different technique in artwork; also, a little different type of printing. The art is what we call a free poster style. The printing is done from rubber plates, and is particularly adapted to the style of artwork for comparatively short runs.

Do you like it?

Perhaps you have something in mind that could be handled this way—a counter card, calendar, poster, label, blotter, placard, or any other item where masses of color and a small amount of detail work is desired. This economical process fits any of those needs.

To have more details as to cost and application to your job, USE THE CARD; or maybe you are considering another type of printing. We're still interested. Again, just use the card.

The reference to the blowing of the wind in the Star of the above letter was a tie-in with the illustration on the blotter—a man trying to hold his umbrella against a high wind. Another handy part of the blotter is a calendar for March. This mailing, one of a monthly series by the McCormick-Armstrong Company, of Wichita, Kansas, was made with excellent results.

4. DIRECTING SALES LETTERS TOWARD SPECIAL GROUPS

Visualizing the reader: the third step in planning. As you will recall, the third step in planning a business letter is to visualize the reader. Then, in the later steps, the arguments are selected that seem most likely to win that particular individual's favor. This procedure is of special importance in sales letters. The ability of the sales letter-writer to match approach and content with the mental reader-picture determines whether or not the letter is to succeed or fail.

Even when the sales letter is directed to *one* prospect, the problem of making the "match" is not simple, unless the writer knows the addressee's characteristics and buying habits. When the letter goes to a *number* of possible buyers, and must be slanted at them all collectively, then the problem is extremely difficult. Nevertheless, for certain groups in which the members are closely related in ways of living, type of work, degree of wealth, education, or other similar respects, it is usually possible to form a *composite* mental picture that may be used as a guide in preparing the letter.

Obviously, a sales message aimed at business executives should not use the same approach or arguments as might be appropriate in a letter about the same product or service to a group of clerical or factory workers. In the same way, the approach and content would differ in a letter to college professors and students; professional men and laymen; politicians of the liberal variety and those known to be conservative; and on through a thousand other comparisons. To be sure, we are citing average cases rather than exceptional ones. In any group mailing, there must be assumed to exist a certain percentage of waste—variations from the typical composite picture. All the sales letter-writer can do is touch as many of the group as possible by the appeal to common interests; to keep the percentage of "misses" as low as could humanly be expected.

The types of groups to which sales letters may be addressed are as numerous as the leaves on a tree, but they tend to become standardized for a specific company; at least, as to the number that must be approached. A company offering very expensive fur coats for men is not bothered about how to sell them to women or to customers in our southern states. A company publishing a so-called "high-brow" magazine is not likely to mail a sales letter to a list of teenagers. The manager of the health spa is not concerned with selling a course of weight training to elderly people. For each kind of product or service there are likely to be well-defined groups of potential buyers. What kind of people they are, and how they commonly react, tends to become known as the sales letter-writer continues on the job.

Probably, there is no greater degree of difference in buying habits, and the appeals that match them, than between men and women. The two letters that follow illustrate how this difference influenced the sales approach for exactly the same type of service.

1. The Letter to Women

Dear ——————,

Of course, her name is confidential, but she is one of the social leaders in our city—probably, quite well known to you. She came last week to have her eyes examined, and seldom in my 30 years' experience have I encountered such a pitiful example of visual neglect. You see, for a long time this lady had suspected the need of glasses, but she couldn't stand the thought of wearing them. She was afraid they would detract from her beauty.

So year after year, she had suffered with headaches, and nerves on edge. Once, fine embroidery had been her hobby, but she gave it up because she couldn't see the stitches. Even reading had been abandoned—the type would dance and blur after a page or two in any book. She finally gave up the struggle and came almost tearfully to ask my advice.

But the sad part of this story is that when I helped her select the glasses for her type of features, she was amazed to find they made her even more beautiful than before. All those years she could have been protecting her eyes without the slightest detraction from her physical charm.

I think a lot of women are like this—they suffer in silence because they do not know how cleverly nowadays glasses are custom-built for every style of beauty. Now, I don't mean that *you* are having the same experience, but I do know you will be glad that never will you have to worry about glasses spoiling your beauty. And if you will pardon me for saying so, there is no one who knows better than I do what glasses to recommend for each style of feminine personality.

In fact, stop in at my office on State Street any day next week, and I'll be glad to show you dozens of styles in glasses—how each one is designed to add charm to a different type of beauty. It's a demonstration in which you will be tremendously interested—so please do come next week.

That letter to women attempts to do only two things: first, remind the readers what dreadful things can happen if eyes are neglected; second, to answer the fear that glasses may detract from beauty. The second appeal, of course, plays the major role.

But what about men? Are they worried so much about glasses detracting from their appearance? Well, a few might have that objection, but certainly not the great majority. How *can* they, then, be induced to have their eyes examined?

2. The Letter to Men

Dear_____,

A businessman doesn't want to be bothered with a long letter...so I'll make this a short one.

Nowadays there is such a fine line between profit and loss, that all of us are constantly seeking ways to increase efficiency without increasing cost.

Has it ever occurred to you that your eyes have more to do with your efficiency on the job than any other factor over which you have control?

Strained or tired eyes sap vitality, foster sleepiness, and weaken the power to concentrate. And the strange part of it all is that you, yourself, can seldom tell when your eyes are causing these troubles.

But your efficiency is surely diminished.

The only way of assuring that your eyes are up to par is to have them examined about once a year. And we would like to perform that service.

If an examination shows that you need glasses, our reputation for dependability will guarantee the best. If you don't need glasses, we will be frank in telling you so.

But not knowing is not good business. Come in some day this week, and let us give you a quick but thorough examination. You couldn't make a better investment of the half hour it will take.

Women, glasses will not spoil your beauty. Men, protect your efficiency on the job. How widely apart are those two reasons for eye examinations; and yet, they are specifically chosen to hit their respective marks.

Examining other sales letters to women. It is not our intention to imply that the *only* thing of interest to women is their personal appearance. As a group, they are receptive to many other approaches—

the one most effective depending on the nature of the product or service being offered, their special interests, and their place in the social pattern. A woman may be attracted to a new food product because one of her chief delights is setting a good table; because it may contribute to her children's health; because it is something different to serve at parties; because she thinks her husband may like it; because it is reputed to be a good conditioner against old age; because it is better than some similar product she has been using; because it will save her time and money; because—oh, because of many other reasons. For a particular sales letter, the problem is to decide which of the many approaches has the greatest chance of touching the largest number of the group.

The following sales letters show how creative approaches can be found to pinpoint the interests of women. The first defined a typically "male" product, a set of power tools, in terms of female customers.

1. The New Set of Power Tools

Dear _____

> "The window it is leaking and the rain is coming in—
>   if someone doesn't fix it, I'll get soaked right to my skin!
> But if I wait another day, the rain will go away
> And who will need a window on such a sunny day!!"
> —Lee & Barbour © Criterion Music Co., 1948, 1976.

How many times has *"Mañana"* been the solution for repairs in your house? If you waited for *him* to do it, you'd drown. Why wait?

Masterson's Hardware understands your frustration. The answer is simple—get your own tools and do the darn job yourself! We've taken the guesswork out of selecting the tools you need—you tell us the job, we'll supply the tools. What's more we will show you how to use them safely and competently. Forget what *he* told you; it doesn't take a card in the Carpenters Union to hang a stormdoor or replace a broken porch step. Rickety bannisters, leaky drainpipes, broken tablelegs are not beyond your "dainty" grasp. Grab hold of a Masterson tool and have at it.

Come in this Saturday, May 3, and we'll be more than willing to let you tell us about all those jobs *he* won't do. You see, for the next 6 months, on the first Saturday of each month, we're holding "Mañana Day." You bring us the problem and *we'll* lick it. Let *him* go play golf—you'll manage quite well without *his* help—you and Masterson's tools, that is.

See you Saturday.

The pull on this gem was exceptional. The women arrived in droves, swapped complaints with other ladies who came in, and bought everything in sight.

The second appealed more seriously to a true feminine concern.

2. The Lion's Charity Party

Just for one minute, Mrs. Jones...

...picture yourself in THIS position with Christmas coming on—Suppose you were 21, a young wife and mother prematurely grown old with the worries and strife of life. Suppose you had a husband who tried his best, but was the victim of unfortunate circumstances and sometimes could not bring home enough food for the table. CHRISTMAS would be sad enough for you two, but you both would be old enough to understand and bravely "make the best of it."

But suppose you had a little girl, a good youngster, and as deserving of Santa's blessings as any other child. And as Christmas day draws near, you are both sorry for her because you do not want her to know how selfish and cruel the world can be.

If only this day of days would not have to be a meaningless, drab day for her, who has never had much cause to smile as other children smile.

Like other mothers in this sad position, you would find it hard to put your child to bed and know that there would be no Christmas for her.

Imagine then your utter happiness if, to your complete surprise, someone would notify you that your child was invited to attend the Lions' Club Christmas Party for deserving, underprivileged children—that she would enjoy a good warm dinner with all the trimmings—could sit on Santa's lap and get a few little toys and things to wear and fruit and candy that would bring her joy for many, many days to come.

Wouldn't you and your husband be thrilled, for her sake? Wouldn't you be thankful that the Welfare Committee of the Lions' Club had been so thoughtful? Of course you would, and you will want to help us make our Annual Christmas Party a grand success this year, by attending the special Lions' Bingo Party described on the attached sheet.

Your husband has been assigned ten tickets. *Please* help him sell them, and more, if possible. One of our members has already sold over 50 tickets to friends in bridge clubs, etc. The success of our Christmas Party this year depends largely upon the success of this Bingo Party which is being sponsored to raise additional funds. So please do your best, for the sake of the 65 unfortunate boys and girls we're going to entertain on December 23rd!

Appreciatively yours,

WELFARE COMMITTEE

The approaches of these two letters to women were certainly different. The basic appeal to certain attitudes and concerns was, however, very carefully tailored to only the ladies in the audience.

Slanting Letters at men. As we saw in the letters to women and to men about eye examinations, what may be a good approach to the one sex is not likely to be good for the other. It is true that men and women may be equally interested in the purchase of many things—a home, an automobile, tickets to take them on a vacation trip, membership in a book club, an insurance policy, and thousands of others. But the *reasons* that impel the purchase may be far apart. A sales letter to women about a vacation hotel might properly talk about the luxurious appointments, the social activities, the famous people who are frequent guests, and the facilities for working out; whereas to men, the things talked about might be the nearby trout-filled stream, the thick steaks served in the dining room, the poker room, the facilities for keeping in touch with the stock markets, and the easy access to the stadium where famous teams compete.

Furthermore, sales letters to men must differ in content and approach according to the nature of the respective group—their financial level, their social or political affiliation, their occupation, and the many other factors that might influence their reactions. For example, the following letter, used by Alexander Hamilton Institute (Figure 7-31) is directed at young men in business who have yet to reach high position. To *them*, the letter should have considerable appeal; to *executives* near the top, it would probably fall on barren soil.

The level on which the above sales letter travels is quite plain. It is trying to reach men in business who represent neither of the two extremes in attainment: neither the top executives nor the novices, but those in between who are mature enough to know what business is about, young enough to be reaching for greater success. The idea of letting the reader qualify himself to get the booklet is also worth noting. No young, upcoming businessman wants to be considered a boy— rather, he wants to see himself as a "mature man actively engaged in business." This clever appeal to vanity is well handled by the writer.

Figure 7-31

Dear _____

I once figured that I throw into my wastebasket every year at least $1,000.00 worth of literature which people send me in the mistaken notion that I have nothing to do but read.

You are probably in the same position.

I mention this frankly because we have just published, and are sending without cost to interested men, a booklet entitled "Forging Ahead in Business." It's rather unusual. Just as an insurance company, from its study of millions of men, can make a pretty shrewd guess as to how long you will live; so, from our 25 years of watching men promote themselves through business study, we have a good measure of just what an average man can accomplish in six months, 12 months, 18 months, and two years of definitely guided effort.

We have put the results of that experience into this booklet and I want to get a copy into the hands of every man who has a real reason to be interested in it. I don't want to feed anybody's waste basket.

Will you tell me frankly whether it's worthwhile to send this book to you?

Of course the book has a good deal to say about the work of this Institute, but it also deals with problems you are facing every day. We do not claim that the Institute meets every man's needs, but if you are on the lookout for broader business knowledge, then what we have to offer is invaluable to you.

The Institute has reached a point of national acceptance in the business world; its problem is not one of *recruiting* but of *selecting* the men who can get the most from its service in the shortest time. In this process of selecting we try to appeal only to mature men who are actively engaged in business. We have nothing to offer boys and can be of no service to men who are not keenly interested in business.

We want you to decide for yourself whether or not the booklet is intended for you. If you are not interested in business training, don't send for it. If you are seeking new ways to add to your knowledge of business, we want you to have a copy with our compliments. Simply fill in and mail the enclosed card and the booklet will reach you by return mail.

A moment ago you read Masterson Hardware's letter to women. Here is how Saks Fifth Avenue approaches men. The tone of the letter is light and pleasing, but still in good taste for business executives. The offer presented solves a problem which bothers many men near Christmas time. It must have brought orders to Saks.

Dear _____

We spent about 300 days getting thousands of rare gifts under one roof. We know that men appreciate them because they are rare and hard to find. Our only problem now is to bring together all the busy men who want them. But *this* is where our Gift Counselors come in.

The Gift Counselor, a fast-moving, quick-witted young person, is our "middle-man" between a store full of rare gifts, and the busy executive. You will find her, and her associates, in the Main Floor Foyer near the elevators. She will select the entire list of gifts for you, getting your official scrutiny on them all, have them wrapped and sent, and not budge the budget if you say so.

Call her—up to 6 p.m.—for an appointment, and you will find your Christmas shopping this year the most painless you ever did.

Another sales letter that seeks to solve the same shopping problem is one mailed to business firms and executives by Berea College Student Industries. (See Figure 7-32.) In the letter from Saks, the emphasis was on saving time for the busy executive; in this one, there is the added possibility of helping impoverished boys and girls get an education. As has been pointed out, a lot can be learned about business letter-writing by *comparing* the efforts of those working toward similar objectives. Which of these two sales letters developed the most business?

In writing a sales letter to executives, it is well to remember characteristics which they generally possess. Disregard of any one of these characteristics is likely to destroy the letter's chance for success.

1. They are interested in anything that will improve the operation of their business: the conservation of time or money; the speeding of production; new ideas or methods to better the quality of their products; anything that will smooth employee relations.
2. They have many responsibilities, and have no time of their own to waste in reading long-winded letters. This does not mean that they will react unfavorably to a long letter, provided it is direct, factual, and *worth* their attention.

Figure 7-32

Dear _____

Once a year we have a chance to write this kind of letter, and we get a big kick out of it. So here goes.

You know Berea's story—how we make it possible for 1,700 needy boys and girls to get an education by means of our Student Industries. No fancy frills here, just downright earnestness and hard work. You and your organization have had a part in this enterprise.

We can show our appreciation by extending to you our wholesale prices. And you can show your approval of Berea's work at this Christmas season to your own benefit and satisfaction.

How? Give to your preferred customers, to your own staff, or to your personal friends, a remembrance which comes from Berea. If you are racking your brain now for something different, give our suggestion an ear.

All we ask is that you allow your secretary or some volunteer to act as a clearing house. Orders can be pooled then, and we can make shipment economically.

And does this sound familiar? Please give us your orders as *early* as you can, specifying a later shipping date if you wish, so we can serve you as well as you have served us.

---

3. They are serious-minded, and expect to be met in the same spirit. Letters of too light a tone, such as might be sent to younger men, tend to irritate them and handicap the effectiveness of the letter.

4. They read quickly, and like their information in condensed form without unnecessary explanation. This means they appreciate simple language, and any other devices that help them to grasp the "meat" of the message—tabulations, summaries of facts, captions that lead them surely from one point to another.

While the characteristics listed above are for letters slanted at men, it is obvious that the principles apply to all businesspeople. No matter what the gender, an executive expects clarity, conciseness, and competence in the material that comes in the mail.

Look at the two letters that follow. They were used by the TelAutograph Corporation; the first pulled a 25 per cent response, and the second 15 per cent. The two mailings were separated by a three-week interval. Although a form-letter job, the first letter achieved some personalization by the fill-in of the reader's name at the beginning of the fourth paragraph.

1. The Opening Shot

We have just completed a job for you. We are now ready to submit, in folder form, the results of our experience in working with basic systems and procedures of a sizable cross-section of manufacturing companies. We invite you to accept copies without charge and without feeling obligated in any way.

These folders will prove valuable to you as a check on your own operations. They offer you a means of comparing your own systems with those of other plants. You'll find much helpful information in them that may enable you to cut corners in time and cost.

Our facts are based on actual in-the-plant surveys made by specially trained engineers—aided in many companies by executives like yourself. They represent our experience in a cross-section of plants, both small and large, differing widely in physical layouts, nature of products, and in volume of business.

Mr. Doe, other manufacturers of equipment such as your own have basically similar procedures. Of course, they vary in terminology and in scope for different types of business and for different plant sizes—simple in small plants and complex in large ones.

We present six basic systems: SALES ORDER ... PRODUCTION PLANNING AND SCHEDULING ... INSPECTION AND QUALITY CONTROL ... WAREHOUSING AND SHIPPING ... JOB COST ANALYSIS ... OFFICE RECORDS, CREDITS, AND CASHIERING. Each of these systems is discussed fully in an easy-to-read, graphically illustrated four-page folder. Three such folders are now ready to be placed in your hands.

SALES ORDER—Answers such questions as: What is the crucial test of an efficient sales order procedure? What are other companies doing to keep their hard-won customers from slipping through their fingers?—by insuring fast, errorless service on orders...avoiding slip-ups on delivery promises...handling unexpected delays and order changes easily and quickly.

PRODUCTION PLANNING AND SCHEDULING—Gives you a quick picture of a typical planning and scheduling system. Tells how companies have developed systems that enable them to plan production on a quick-turnover basis...how they get quick action on schedule changes...stop production on not-so-urgent stock items...make way for rush orders...and keep inventories at a minimum. Discusses management's problem of correlating the responsibilities of the production and sales departments.

INSPECTION AND QUALITY CONTROL—Show what other companies are doing to reduce their scrap losses, lower salvaging costs, hold down "off-standard" products, or "seconds," and eliminate production delays due to late reports from laboratories. Cites specific examples in six different types of industries.

Experiences summarized in folder form, analyzing the last three of the six procedures, are now "in work." These will be available to you in a short time. All have this single purpose—to help executives like yourself compare their present mode of operation with systems now in use in other companies.

Since we are sending these folders without charge or obligation, it occurs to us that you may want copies sent to several of your department heads or systems men—in addition to your own copies. Please feel free to requisition as many as you need.

To avoid unnecessary delays in getting them to you, we are enclosing a convenient requisition form. Please check which of the folders you desire for yourself, and which ones we should send to other people in your company. Slip this form into the stamped envelope attached and drop it into your outgoing mail.

2. The Follow-Up

A short time ago I wrote you in regard to several new folders we've prepared for free distribution to the management of a cross-section of manufacturing companies. As mentioned in my previous letter, these folders summarize our company's experience during many years past in working with basic manufacturing systems and procedures.

I firmly believe that you'll find these folders, as described in the leaflet enclosed, of great value. Each one represents a system common to your plant, to ours, and to the majority of all plants. These folders not only offer you a means of comparing your own operating procedures with those in other plants, but included is a considerable amount of helpful information designed to aid you in cutting time and cost in your operations.

Since I wrote you, we've received requests from hundreds of executives like yourself, manifesting great interest in our presentation of systems. We've supplied these men with copies, as well as their various department heads and systems analysts.

May I repeat my invitation to you to obtain copies of these folders. They will be sent to you without charge or obligation. We want you to feel perfectly free to request as many copies as you need—for yourself and for other men in your company responsible for basic operations.

A requisition form and stamped, addressed envelope are enclosed for your convenience in requesting copies. Please check which of the folders you desire, and which ones we should send to other members of your company. It will be a pleasure to see that they are sent without delay.

In this letter and the follow-up, signed by "W. F. Vieh, President," we have the practical demonstration of one executive talking to another. Obviously, Mr. Vieh should have known, and did, the language of his group. Both letters put the emphasis on things dearest to the heart of the average executive—methods, costs, how to cut corners. To younger people of less experience in business, these two messages would have been tiresome; to the executives *for whom intended,* they are just the opposite.

Offering to solve a problem. Shot-in-the-dark sales letters which assume the reader has a problem that the writer proposes to overcome can be extremely irritating. You have probably received letters which start, "Here is the answer to your fuel problem," or with some other equally brash statement. It may be that you are living in a hotel, or are blessed with the finest type of heating equipment—the writer puts the problem in your lap whether it belongs there or not. Unless the assumption happens to hit the mark, letters of this type promptly tell readers that they are only names on a list, and that the writer *hopes* they will be interested.

On the other hand, the approach may be quite all right if the problem is known to exist. The readers then feel that you have come to them with a helping hand, and they willingly continue to see just how valuable your assistance may turn out to be. For example, the program chairman of any business group is likely to welcome an offer to solve the problem of finding speakers or talent for entertainment. The following letter, Figure 7-33, does a very good job.

In the letter-situation just reviewed, the assumption of a problem was logical and not just a guess. The offer to solve it is pleasingly made, and sounds convincing.

Figure 7-33

Dear _____,

When you plan the entertainment for your coming convention, you naturally want the very best that your budget will afford.

You are eager to give your members something they will long remember and talk about.

But probably you are saying, "Where can I turn for talent? Who can be trusted not to let me down?"

Well, Ms. Fleming, that question is my cue. I've been helping other program chairmen with their shows for 15 years, and I can just as surely help you. It doesn't matter what kind of entertainment you want—musicians, dancers, singers, actors, magicians, novelty acts—I am able to give you the best. You can have your pick of local talent, or I can bring you artists from other cities who are tops in their specialty. And the cost in either case will be a lot lower than you may expect.

This isn't just an idle statement on my part. Many businessmen in Columbus will tell you that Bobby Warren knows *how* to plan and stage an entertainment which really goes over in a big way. You tell me what you want—how much you can spend—and I do the rest. You won't need to worry about the success of your show, or the danger of getting a lemon when you thought you had a plum.

A reply to this letter will bring me to your office any time you wish. I have pictures and press notices to show you that are very helpful in deciding what acts to use.

Please do give me the opportunity to give you the benefit of my experience. You will be under no obligation to follow my suggestions, but I *do* have ideas which will make your entertainment the best you have ever had.

Mastering letters to occupational groups. To approach effectively the members of a group engaged in the same kind of work or activity, sales-letter writers must have a reasonable knowledge of what they are doing, their special needs, and how the benefits of the product or service offered may touch their daily activities. The more they know about these things, the better able they are to select the best appeal for the particular problem. In a letter to army officers, H. N. Fisch, sales manager for H. J. Justin & Sons, used pride in immaculate appearance as the appeal because he knew that military men are especially receptive to it (Figure 7-34). Also, to gain their interest, he starts his letter with the story of Napoleon's reprimand after the battle of Jena.

Figure 7-34

Dear _____,

History tells us that Napoleon, recognized as the greatest military genius of his day, was a "stickler" in matters pertaining to the neatness of his officers and enlisted men, although he, himself, dressed rather slovenly.

Reviewing his troops after the battle of Jena. October 14, 1806, he severely reprimanded one of his higher officers because of the appearance of his uniform and his mud-bespattered boots. This officer, being next in command, first excused his appearance with the statement that the previous day had been a strenuous one, and he had not found time to clean up: then commented on the fact that the uniform of the great Napoleon was also rather disreputable.

The great General's reply is interesting: "Only Napoleon can afford to dress and do as Napoleon does." But I venture to suggest there is one thing that even Napoleon overlooked—the importance of setting a good example for those of lower rank.

On regular duty, as you so well realize, you dress properly to retain the respect of the personnel under your command. On the Parade Ground, in the Hotel Lobby, in the Reception Line, and among your fellow officers, you maintain the appearance of one who is interested in reflecting the dignity of the rank designated to you.

There isn't anything that improves the personal appearance of an officer as does a pair of neat, snappy, well-built boots. They are a mark of distinction, an insignia that pictures your pride of service to your country—and their selection means much to you.

The enclosed folder illustrates and describes some of Justin's finest boots; built to exacting specifications and bearing a trade-mark of 54 years of satisfactory dealings as your guarantee. Boots that are unsurpassed by any American or foreign makers.

Perhaps, you have been saying to yourself, "I really need a new pair of boots." With the attractive prices now in effect, this is decidedly the time to buy.

Perhaps you are thinking that this sales letter is interesting enough, but that it lacks evidence to prove the quality and attractiveness of the boots. That would be true were it not for the folder mentioned in the next to the last paragraph. In it, six steps in the making of Justin Boots are described, with pictures of different workmen illustrating each step. The copy with the "steps" is done in very human language, and helps to make the sale.

A strong feature of this copy describing boots in the making is the use of the workmen's names, and the telling of their many years of experience in the plant. And the personal touch is strengthened by the pictures of the men talked about!

In many cases, sales letter-writers have a strong argument in the story of how their product is manufactured, but the difficulty in using it is that the body of the letter becomes too long. Mr. Fisch got around this barrier by using the three-page, $8^{1}/_{2} \times 11$-inch folder—a device open to anyone with the same problem. The letter on the first page serves the purpose of getting the reader interested enough to look inside; the story there goes ahead to complete the sale. Actually, the Star and the Hook are in the letter; the bulk of the Chain appears on the inside pages.

Another sales message of the same type is one that was sent to school teachers by the Fidelity Investment Association, Wheeling, West Virginia. (See Figure 7-35.) The letter on the first page aims for attention and interest by telling the story of a teacher who is enjoying life in Florida because she followed the company's Income Reserve Plan. Then on the inside pages desire is awakened by additional copy and pictures. The whole would be too much for the ordinary letter form. The key-note of the inside sales copy is the caption: "When the zest for your job is lacking...when working days are over...GO *where* you please—when you please...there's nothing to prevent!" The choice of this appeal is evidence that the writer understood one of the biggest worries of the average school teacher—how to accumulate money for retirement, and to have enough to do some of the things that were impossible during the many classroom years.

Good as the letter is, it would not do the job if left to stand alone, for the Hook is merely a question and suggests no action. However, as was true of the letter to Army officers, the inside pages complete the job; also, this mailing is one of a series of three mailed by the company to teachers, and did not have to carry the entire load.

Examples of sales letters to different types of occupational groups are far too numerous for complete coverage in any business book, but the most important principle in preparing any of these messages is always the same—acquaint yourself with the problems of the particular

Figure 7-35

Dear _____,

Last winter—when a blizzard hit Chicago, Anne Andrus, Chicago school teacher, went to Florida.

You will be interested in the following paragraph from the letter she wrote to us from St. Petersburg.

"The reason I am able to bask in the sunshine all day with pleasant companions, surrounded by blossoming plants, growing fruits, and tropical birds, while your Northern newspapers are carrying headlines about zero weather, is because I adopted the Fidelity Plan some years ago...I do not attribute my good fortune to either wisdom or luck. It was because I felt that here was something that would compel me to save systematically. And while there were times when it pinched a bit, especially during the long summer vacations, I managed—and now I am thankful that I did."

What Anne Andrus did—you, too, can do! Only you will find it infinitely easier with the new and improved Income Reserve Plan, which calls for no deposits during the teachers' vacation season.

The Income Reserve Plan, sponsored by this 25-year-old, $27,000,000 company, is safe—simple—convenient. Accumulating money is made easy, almost automatic. And each month finds you nearer your financial goal.

If you've found it difficult to save in the past—if you are not satisfied with the money you have accumulated to date, isn't it time you gave the Income Reserve Plan your most earnest consideration?

group, and try to connect your sales message with one or more of them. You have seen how this was done in Figures 7-34 and 7-35.

When you wish to sell a universal product such as cars, boats, or, as in these examples (Figures 7-36 and 7-37), refrigerators to an occupational group, language is the key. Look at these two approaches and note the use of words and phrases commonly used by each prospective customer group.

Sales Letter to Doctors

Figure 7-36

Dear Doctor,

"QUIET ZONE," say the street signs in front of your hospitals. And even the most careless of us give heed.

"Absolute rest and quiet," you prescribe for your patients. And gradually, as we learn the value of silence elsewhere than in the sick room, we eliminate noise from our offices and our homes.

The kitchen can be in a "Quiet Zone," too. Clatter and noise need no longer go hand-in-hand with automatic refrigeration. Servel, the Gas Refrigerator, has changed all that.

Servel freezes with heat—without machinery—no noise, no loud starting and stopping. The chilling action is continuous—and silent. Servel produces constant, healthful cold, and ice cubes aplenty, with never a whisper of sound—and saves its price in food and ice.

Knowing as you do, doctor, all about the cost of operations, I believe you will be much interested in the cost of operation by Servel. I should like the opportunity of giving you (briefly, of course) this and some other facts about this remarkable refrigerator.

Will you mail the card, please, permitting me to call?

The above letter seeks to use the language of the medical man, and the comparisons are taken from his professional life. In Figure 7-37, the same company approaches lawyers in a different way—*their* way.

Unless they were teaching those subjects, the comparisons used in the letters to the experts in medicine and law would have little interest or significance in a sales message to college professors.

How to send letters to those of mutual interest. If your firm and that of your prospects are the same type of business, other approaches can be taken.

One of the best sequences of sales letters came from the desk of the late Henry P. Williams of Hart, Schaffner and Marx.

Sales Letter to Lawyers

Figure 7-37

Dear Sir,

Haven't you often heard of cases where the true facts were so inconceivable that the strongest sort of testimony was necessary to obtain a favorable verdict?

It is hard to believe that ice cubes can be made by heat, that a constant temperature of 50° and less can be maintained in a refrigerator without machinery of any kind. Yet Servel, the Gas Refrigerator, does just this. "Incredible," you'll say until you know the true facts in the case.

I want to tell you in very few words, as a good witness should, the story of Servel. I know you will find it amazingly interesting.

Will you return the enclosed card summoning me for questioning?

First Letter to Clothing Merchants—"Join Us"

Dear ＿＿＿＿＿＿,

You know how it is in business; there are a lot of people that you'd like to sell goods to who don't trade with you. Quite likely you can name a dozen, right in Indianapolis, just your kind of fellows, who don't come to you. You wish they would; you believe honestly that it would pay them to do so; and you'd like to know why they don't.

That's the way we feel about the good clothing men who don't buy our goods. We don't expect to sell everybody in the business; it wouldn't be a good thing if we did.

But your concern, somehow, seems to be our kind; we feel that, with a town like yours, and a trade like yours, and a business sense like yours, we ought to be working together to build up a fine trade for both of us.

Now, you know us; you know our goods. There's probably some reason why you're not buying them, and you know what it is. We wish you'd tell us what it is, very candidly. If we're "in wrong" we ought to be told, and if there's something here that's a good thing for you, then you ought to know about it.

Let's write a few letters to each other and see if we haven't some common ground of advantage.

Second Letter—"Why Didn't You Join Us?

Dear _____,

You had a letter from us the other day; it wasn't a circular letter either; it was "personal"; so is this one.

In that letter, which used up quite a good many words, we really asked just one simple question—Why don't you handle our goods? We put it much more delicately than that, but that's really what it amounts to.

Now we can't decently insist on your answering that question; but we'd like very much to have you answer it. You may have so good a reason for not selling Hart, Schaffner & Marx Novelties that when we know what it is we'll say, "You are right," and that will be the end of it.

But we're not going to be quite satisfied until you tell us. For fear you haven't our stamped envelope handy, we enclose another. Tell us very plainly.

Third Letter—If You Didn't Join Us, Maybe Something's Wrong. What Is It?

Dear _____,

The fact is, we really want to know, and you haven't told us yet—Why don't you handle Hart, Schaffner & Marx goods? Is there a good reason? Maybe you don't like the goods; maybe you don't like us.

You needn't feel that you are committing yourself to anything by answering our question: but we don't feel that we are being fair to ourselves unless we know why so good a concern as yours, and so good a concern as ours, are not on closer terms.

We don't want to bother you with calls; letters are really more convenient for both of us. But letters don't get anywhere unless the other fellow answers them. Drop us a line and tell us.

We doubt if a series of three sales letters ever was written that hammered on one thought so steadily as these for Hart, Schaffner & Marx. Mr. Williams evidently decided that his ace was the thought that two good concerns should be together. The quality of the goods made by this company needed no explanations or proof: his readers *knew* that. But, Mr. Williams must have thought, he could appeal to pride—the idea of two "champs" playing doubles together.

There are, of course, many bonds that tie people together besides those of trade, profession, or some other work connection. In fact, many of the activities people consider important are those in which they amuse themselves; sometimes they are even more important than those connected with earning their daily bread. All of these outside activities tend to bring people of a type together, although within the groups there may be some exceptions. You know what these groups are: golf players, particularly members of a specific club; bridge players, baseball players, football players, all kinds of groups interested in a certain sport; those of the same religious belief, and especially, of the same church; members of a business association, a fraternity or sorority; a little theatre, or a musical organization; even so thin a bond as owning the same kind of automobile, or smoking the same brand of cigar, may tend to develop mutuality of interest, and make those brought together open to a common sales appeal.

5. INCREASING PULL WITH SPECIAL INDUCEMENTS

Emphazing the role of the Hook. You have studied from the blueprint from which the letter-carpenters construct their sales message: starting with a Star to get attention; followed by a Chain to arouse interest and awaken desire; and ending with a Hook to impel action. You have seen many examples of successful letters built from this blueprint. It has been demonstrated that no one of the three steps in letter-construction can be called more important than the others, since each must do a job necessary to the success of the whole.

However, the Hook is the final blow; and unless it induces the desired result, the whole structure might just as well not have been erected. It is the climax of the sales presentation—the readers either do what they have been asked to do, or they do not. If their decision is unfavorable, the writer has no chance to continue the argument in an effort to change the reader's mind. Once the letter is mailed, nothing more can be done. There are no second shots in letter writing. The attempt succeeds or fails according to whether the readers say *"yes"* or *"no,"* and you are not with them when the decision is made.

You have seen, too, in Section 3, how the Hook must be constructed to attain the nearest possible chance of success: how the request for action must be offered in a confident and positive way; how such negative words as *if, may, hope,* and *trust* weaken the request; how the action suggested must be made as easy as possible for the reader; how *dating* the action will tend to increase the pull. All of these "hows" must be understood and applied if the letter is to have the maximum pull.

Assuming, however, that the writers have followed the principles, so that their Hook is fundamentally proper and sound, there are still other inducements that can be used to make the urge to action even more forceful. These special inducements in no way lessen the necessity of a correctly constructed Hook; they simply help it do its job.

Checklist for special inducements. In sales letters, particularly, there are numerous ways to increase the power of the Hook by offering special inducements. Not all of them, however, are suitable on every occasion; their use depends on the nature of the product or service, the type of people to whom the sales message is going, and the policy of the company. For example, one letter offered a free trial of the company's cigars; the reader could even smoke ten and then return the rest if he did not like them. But no fruit grower would be likely to ship a crate of oranges on the same basis—eat ten and return the rest if you don't like them. Spoilage would make such an offer too costly. Some products cannot even be guaranteed beyond date of delivery, or for a limited number of days, because control over their use or abuse is impossible once they reach the customer.

The following list is consequently offered only in a general way. Many are valid for most sales letters. Be selective in your use of ones that suit *your* purpose. Once you have reviewed the list, you may want to add others that are of particular value in *your* business.

(a) *Just sign and mail the card; we will bill you later.* This merely postpones the day of settlement, but the average human being worries less about the future than the present. Also, the offer gives the customer a chance to wiggle out if not satisfied.

(b) *You have nothing to lose; within ten days send us your payment, or return the goods.* This gives the buyer complete control of the situation. The inducement is not justified, however, if the percentage of returns is high. Of course, the allowed number of days may vary.

(c) *Enjoy it as you pay; take advantage of our easy terms.* The terms vary according to the will of the respective company, but the offer is tempting. Many people buy things on the installment plan that they could not buy for cash.

(d) *You take no risk; with the goods you will receive our unqualified Guarantee Certificate.* Of course, the guarantee may have strings tied to it, but the buyer still feels safer.

(e) *You get both for the price of one.* Everybody likes a bargain, and combination offers often impel action.

(f) *To show our appreciation for your order, we will include without charge, a handsome, sterling silver tie-clasp.* Premiums have helped to develop millions of dollars' worth of sales, both by mail and in order forms of selling. Often, the premium is offered only with full payment.

(g) *Be sure to send your order TODAY, as this offer will be withdrawn soon.* There is no great urge to action in this statement. How soon *is* soon?

(h) *Please hurry, as no orders can be accepted on these terms after July 31.* Here the time limit is definitely established, and the reader is more likely to believe the statement.

(i) *We have only 59 more to offer at this unusual price; do not delay in sending the card.* A limit in number seems more impressive than one in time. Always a strong urge to action.

(j) *Frankly, we want you as a customer, and to prove it, we will allow you a special discount of 10% on any order placed within two weeks.* Offers such as this have pulling power, but the special price—if genuine—sets a precedent that may cause trouble later.

(k) *Please rush the card back immediately, as the price positively goes up $10 on the first of next month.* Statements like this have caused many sales; also, much ill-will if the advance does not take place.

(l) *To prove we have not oversold this new open-air theatre, we enclose two complimentary tickets good any night next week.* Assuming the recipient would not otherwise visit the theatre, this inducement really costs nothing; the value is in the repeat visits that may follow.

(m) *All we ask is ten minutes of your time; our representative will also bring you a very useful reminder of his visit; it's yours whether you buy or not.* Not telling what the gift is makes the inducement more attractive; the reader agrees to find out.

(n) *We cannot tell you why, but confidentially, there is one special reason why you should not delay.* A good inducer if true; otherwise, not ethical.

The above list by no means covers all of the special inducements that you, yourself, may be offered in a month's batch of incoming letters; but there is no need to stretch it out any longer. Anybody who understands human nature will know *why* these inducements do help to get action. In some ways, man is a funny animal: he thinks it will be easier to pay later for what he can't pay now; he buys and hoards things that are scarce, even though he may not need them; he thinks he is getting a premium for nothing when common sense should tell him the cost is included in the price of the product. Thus, the appeals of *deferred payment, limited number, free gift,* and all the others are often used to put added power into sales letters.

How inducements sell: three examples. The following letters show how some of these special inducements have been used by various companies. Before we put them under a microscope, here is one important caution—*never let the buyers down* with any special reason for action. If a gift is offered, don't oversell it, causing the recipients to be disappointed when it gets in their hands; if the offer is limited in time or number, be sure to do exactly what you said would be done; if a free trial is the inducement, and the goods are returned, make no effort to high-pressure the buyers.

The first of the examples, Figure 7-38, is a sales letter used by the Neil Barron Fuel Company in Kansas City, Missouri. As a token of appreciation for orders received during the summer months, the readers are offered a beautiful colored etching, and to give some idea of its appearance, a miniature copy was clipped to the letter. The letter sounds sincere—the gift appears worthwhile. Thus, the inducement is of the best sort, and deserves our approval.

Figure 7-38

Dear _____,

I am writing this personal letter because I have a gift for you. You have admired beautiful etchings; particularly, those colorful types depicting rural life in the old country...the scene of a quiet English countryside, or one of a picturesque mill on the banks of a Dutch canal.

I have one of these etchings for you; tastefully created by the artist, Wettel, who is famous for his artistry in the field of etching. The size of the picture is 24×28 inches and I can truthfully say that it will grace the loveliest of living rooms, when properly framed. The retail price of this picture is from $15.00 to $25.00.

I want to ask a favor of you, and in asking this favor I can save you money. Most everyone knows that in the fuel business the months of July and August are rather slow periods as far as sales are concerned, and our firm is no exception. We want to make it worthwhile for you to order during these months.

If you will place an order for fuel for delivery during the months of July or August, you will receive our usual discounted summer price, which saves you from 12 cents to 25 cents per gallon; and, in addition, I will present you with one of the beautiful etchings described in the first part of this letter.

My supply of these etchings is limited; consequently, I am writing to only a small number of my preferred customers.

I have arranged with my salesmen to carry several of these pictures with them, and if you would like to see one before placing your order, I will be glad to have one left at your home for inspection. I know you will be more than pleased.

Call me today at chestnut 0-0000.

This letter, a winner of the Dartnell Gold Medal Award, contains three of the special inducements to action which have just been listed. First, it offers a nice gift with the order, and to make it seem truly worthwhile, the retail cost is mentioned—$15.00 to $25.00. Furthermore, the miniature copy is visible proof of value. Second, it tells the reader that the supply of etchings is limited. Third, it mentions the discounted summer price—a saving of 12 cents to 25 cents per gallon.

A considerably less valuable gift—but interesting to many people—is in Figure 7-39 offered by the Chicago eating place, Martini's. This was some time ago—the prices will have changed, but the letter doesn't need changing:

Figure 7-39

Dear Mr. _____,

Every day several people walk into our place, lay one of these letters down and say, "Now let's see if your food is as good as you say it is."

We'd like to have you put us on the spot that way. We know you'd soon be a regular customer like the rest of them and get real enjoyment out of our Italian home cooking.

There's boneless chicken, spaghetti, ravioli, green noodles, steaks, chops, roasts, served with sauces that you'll smack your lips over.

But no orchestras or fancy fixtures—just good food and good drinks—and to show you how easy the prices are—we serve a Chef's special dinner for $1.25—a regular dinner for $2.00—and at luncheon on weekdays we serve cocktails for 55¢.

On Sunday's we're closed so that we all have a little breathing spell and are ready to serve you better during the week.

That offer of mine still goes for you—I'm ready to buy the first introductory drink myself—I hope it will be soon.

To personalize this sales message still further, the signature is simply "Johnnie." Two special inducements help to power the sale—low prices, and the free drink. The idea brought many new customers to Martini's.

A few years ago, in the letter problem contest conducted by *Printed Salesmanship*, the following combination sales and Christmas message was submitted by Dorothy Marie Johnson, one of our better writers of business material and fiction. The special inducement to make the Hook more impelling is a discount of 5% during the month of December. Of course, not all writers can handle the King's English as gracefully as does Miss Johnson.

Dear ——————,

Your first sled—you thought there might be one, but you didn't see it by the tree, so you pretended for Dad's and Mother's sake that you didn't care at all. And then you found it in the dining room!

What do children remember longest—the things they had, or the things they wanted and never got?

Godwin's will help you play Santa Claus this year—not just with a red Santa Claus, though he's here too, but by making Christmas giving easier for you. Further on in this letter you'll learn of our gift to you.

Christmas is the time when you make up to your loved ones for the things they didn't have on other Christmas days, when grownup boys and girls get things to take the place of the tricycles and talking-dolls Santa Claus forgot in other years. Christmas is the time when you make dreams come true.

Your own dream comes true at Godwin's too, for every gift you give can come from here. The small, the large, the quaint, the beautiful—all these are here for you to choose. We've gathered from across the world the fruits of its people's labor. You'll want to spend a day or two in Godwin's. Your packages can be mailed direct from Godwin's post office; stamps and ribbons and tissue and wrappings are ready here.

But all these aisles and floors of useful and lovely things are lacking in this, that only you can furnish—the spirit of Christmas giving. Your gifts are waiting at Godwin's, but in your own heart alone is the priceless ingredient that you must wrap into each package. The gift without the giver is bare; yours must be wrapped with the invisible finery of human affection.

To make Christmas giving more pleasant, and because we want to show you our appreciation of a friendly relationship, we are presenting you with this card as our gift. It entitles you to a special Friendship Discount of 5% at any time during the month of December. It is good throughout the whole vast Santa Claus workshop of Godwin's store.

More than nineteen hundred years have passed since three wise men rode down to Bethlehem, but the spirit of giving has grown, not lessened, through them all. When Christmas morning dawns, may you, too, have...

A Very Merry Christmas

Yes, you are right. The letter was planned primarily for home mailing—to women with charge accounts at the store. The letter pulled very well because it was planned and executed well. The inducements were real and had genuine value to the readers. All these points enhanced its success.

How to use gifts as inducements. The sales letter used by the Kansas City fuel dealer, offering a $25.00 etching to those who would buy their fuel in the summer, was good because the reader could clearly understand the motive behind the gift. The dealer wanted orders, and said so. He did not start with an extravagant promise, which he later failed to keep. But not all sales letters offering gifts approach the readers so frankly. They lead them to believe they will get something absolutely free, letting them trip later on the strings attached to the offer.

Particularly obnoxious are those sales letters which begin: "Within five days, you will receive absolutely without charge or obligation a handsome, durable, efficient pen and pencil set which you will be very proud to own and show to your friends." Or, some similar form of deceptive palaver! Later, it turns out the set is free provided something else is purchased; meaning, if the readers are smart enough to figure it out, that what they pay for the one article includes the cost of the "free" one, plus a nice profit for the seller on the whole combination. This use of so-called free gifts was mentioned in our discussion of the Star (Section 3); it is equally taboo when used to impel action.

Quite different in color, and without the odor, are those sales letters in which the readers are offered the gift free-and-above-board and with the reason understood by both parties. The gift may be a prize in return for a purchase, or the payment of a bill; it may be a token of welcome to new residents, presented with the hope of gaining their goodwill; it may be in the nature of a sample of the product sold, or the service. Of course, nothing can be given away in business without being an item of expense, and thus a drain on profit—unless enough additional volume is created by the device so that the cost is more than offset by the extra business. In many types of selling, the premiums, discounts, large samples, souvenirs, and the like, more than pay their freight; in others, they do not. The decision as to their use is an executive responsibility. In any case, the sales letter-writer has no legitimate right to offer a gift under false colors. In one way or another, it is a device for getting business—and that's the way most readers understand it.

Consider, for example, the letters in Figures 7-40 and 7-41. The first one offers an attractive pencil. The second offers the parents of a new arrival free washing for one week; but could the baby's parents have any doubts as to the motive? The use of gifts, when genuine, are fine inducements to sales. Used carefully, they can do wonders for your sales campaigns.

6. STIRRING THE IMAGINATION IN SALES LETTERS

Imagination: the highest form of salesmanship. This section contains some of the finest letters we've presented so far. They are truly the work of the masters, and from them you may gain ideas that will be extremely helpful. Nevertheless, it is very difficult to say *why* they are so outstanding, or *how* the writers went about the job. Perhaps the common characteristic is that they succeed better than ordinary letters in arousing mental images in the reader's mind—they stir their imaginations, and make them *see* or *feel* the things talked about.

If you take time to examine carefully the language of these letters, you will see that it is colorful but not fancy. The pictures painted with words are very vivid. The readers see themselves enjoying a benefit or suffering from the lack of it. Each of the letters *takes time* to build these mental images. Concrete examples are supplied to back up any generality. In many cases, they take a product or service and show the *romance* in it. Thus, they charm and interest the readers as might a good bit of fiction. They have no thought of stopping, because what they read is too exciting.

They are caught and held by the description of Gloucester fishermen; they are intrigued by the brief recounting of the history of paper; they are chilled by the thought of their own boys, lost like eight-year-old Billy in Union Station; they picture themselves on Island Lake, pulling in the big, fighting bass. Always, the experience is *personal*. The readers, themselves, are leading characters in the letter, enjoying or fearing what happens there. All of this is an imaginative process, started and kept going by the ability of the writer to paint word pictures that seem *real*.

But no one can stir the imagination of another human being unless he, too, sees and feels the thing he is describing. It takes imagination to create imagination. A lot of people say they lack the imagination to write the kind of letters that follow. What they mean is that they are afraid to

Figure 7-40

The Connecticut Mutual
Life Insurance Company

Hartford, Connecticut

Date

Mr. John Q. Prospect
Hartford, Connecticut

Dear Mr. Prospect:

    Will you accept with our compliments an attractive and
useful Dur-O-Lite pencil, rich in appearance, and precision built
for years of dependable service? It is yours for the asking.
Just return the reply card.

    We make this offer because we want you to see our new
"Insurance Indicator." The indicator has helped many of our
clients settle for themselves two questions which seem uppermost
in the minds of people when they consider their own life insurance.

How much should I own?
and
What kind?

    There isn't anything magical or complicated about the
"Indicator." But it will enable you to find out for yourself how
much and what kind of life insurance you should own.

    Just fill out the enclosed card and mail it to me today.

Sincerely,

Senior Vice President

RWS:hkop
(Enclosures)

Figure 7-41

Mary MacIntosh Services

The Allen Laundry
12TH AND ALLEN STREETS
ALLENTOWN, PENNSYLVANIA
HEmlock 5-9671

Dear Parents:—

CONGRATULATIONS!

We, at Allen, were very happy to hear that you have been blessed with a child. In this complex age of atoms, missiles, and ever more astounding scientific discoveries, the miracle of birth still dwarfs all man's knowledge and inventions.

As tangible proof of our good wishes, we enclose a free coupon which we sincerely hope you will feel free to use at no further obligation. Simply dial HEmlock 5-9671 and ask our Operator to have the routeman stop. Give him this coupon, together with the soiled articles, and they will be returned to you in 3 days looking like new.

This is our effort to lighten your burdens at this important time in your life.

Sincerely

Mary MacIntosh

- -

This coupon entitles you to your choice of the following:
EITHER
ONE COAT, SUIT, OR DRESS expertly cleaned and pressed without charge
OR
An average family's laundry for ONE WEEK FREE (up to 15 lbs.) processed in the famous Mary MacIntosh coin-op service. All shirts and linens ironed, everything else fluff dried and neatly folded.
FREE PICK-UP AND DELIVERY
This coupon must be attached to soiled work

Not Good After June 4, 19___
ALLEN LAUNDRY AND DRY CLEANING

let themselves go—to sit and dream of romance in their business—to put that romance on paper. Of course, it is always wise to keep our imagination within the boundaries of our own experience. Mr. Smith, for instance, was qualified to write of seafaring because of his close affiliation with it.

In the same way, Harold McQueen, long a resident of Chicago and a student of that city's early history, had the necessary background to write about John B. Sherman's mansion. And Mr. Voorhees' knowledge of Travelers Aid Society gave him the credentials to describe actual cases handled by the organization.

The lesson that we learn from these, and the other letters that follow is—*let your imagination run, but keep it on the highways you have traveled*. Write what you know; sell what you believe in—these are the keys.

Reeling in the romance of fishing. Perhaps the use of imagination in business correspondence seems a difficult skill to master. You might even feel that most merchandise is lacking in qualities that might strike an imaginative chord. Well, are you sure about that? At first glance, *fish* might seem to be unappealing to the sense of romance and adventure. We all know that fish are cold, dead and slimy in the market. But wait! What about the fish in the sea? Could there be any romance in a business that catches them for commercial purposes?

Yes, plenty of it. Putting the story in words has built a big consumer acceptance for the Frank E. Davis Fish Company of Gloucester, Massachusetts. Over the years, the letters written for that company by John A. Smith have sold millions of pounds of fish, and the emphasis in these letters has always been on the romance of the business. Mr. Smith has put "oomph" in the fish business. It was there all the time, but this sales letter-writer had to *see* it. Check the historical background, the methods of manufacture, the sources of materials, and you will usually find in any product enough glamor to talk about in an interesting and exciting manner. Figure 7-42 shows one of the fish letters.

There is much to appeal to the reader's imagination in the sales letters of the Frank E. Davis Fish Company. The one you have just read is personalized from "Dear Friend" down to the title under the signature of Mr. Davis—"The Gloucester Fisherman." Notice, too, that the pronoun *I* is freely used. The letter just *talks* to the reader—about early days in Gloucester—about folks and fish.

Capitalizing on historical background. People are naturally interested in the origin of things: in the battles, love affairs, ways of living of the human beings whose bodies long ago returned to dust; in any

Figure 7-42

Dear _____,

Way back in 1623, a small group of Pilgrims gathered in their small huts to name this fishing port Gloucester. They were a hardy lot of folks, living mostly on game and salt water fish. They built small boats and braved the treacherous waters off Gloucester to get fish for their families. In those times women folk helped too—for every hand meant more food for the cold winter months to come.

I remember, as a small boy, my grand father telling me about being lashed to the mainmast in a stiff blow, when his schooner was half buried in the plunging sea. It was a hard life. But still, Gloucester boys follow it year after year. It's in our blood. It's our way of living. Nature has located us close to the richest waters there are.

Have you wondered why Gloucester is one of the greatest fishing ports in the world? You see, we have many varieties of delicious fish landed here daily. More good fish come right in here to Gloucester than any other port in the world. That's why you can never say you've tasted fish at its perfect prime unless you get it direct from Gloucester.

So you won't mind, will you, if I ship some of my fish direct to your home? It won't cost you anything, unless you feel like keeping it. All I ask is that you try the fish at my expense, and judge for yourself whether it isn't exactly what you have always wanted.

On the enclosed cards you will find a full description of the *three special offers* I am making. If you are like most of my regular customers, you will choose my Special Get-Acquainted Assortment. I've made up this package to let people know how good all my fish are.

You see, I can tell people that I give them the first pick of the finest, primest catches. But the best way to let them know that my fish are exactly what I say, is to send a generous meal-size package of 14 different kinds of seafoods—to taste! That's just what you get in my Get Acquainted Assortment; 14 different varieties of delicious seafoods, that will tell you as no fine writing ever can, what a real treat it is to eat fish shipped direct to your home from the fishing smacks.

Then, there's my special deep-sea Lobster Offer! Each package comes to you with no shell, no waste, just the tasty, flavorous meat of a 2-pound lobster. And when you come to compare prices, you will find that my lobster—even though more tender than the ordinary kind—*costs less than half* for what you actually eat! And on the third card, you'll find dainty Sardines in Olive Oil—a new pack, delicious, and each package ready for instant use.

For 52 years we have been selecting the primest grades of ocean fish to be sent direct from the fishing boats to our customers. And it is real pride on our part to know that thousands of families have found our fish so much better than any they could get locally, that season in and season out they send us their orders.

Today, I invite *you* to join them. I want you to know the satisfying taste of fresh-caught, prime-grade seafoods. If you have never tasted anything but the kind you get in stores, there's a real treat awaiting you. Read the cards enclosed now, and see how you can get one, or all of my Introductory Offers, without sending a penny in advance. All you do is check the offer you want, fill in the card, and your seafoods will be on the way to you the very day I hear from you. You pay nothing, unless you are perfectly satisfied that my fish are really the best.

It is just this way that we secured our thousands of customers. So you know beforehand that you can send your order with full confidence. You know in advance that you will get the choicest, tenderest, fullest-flavored seafood that you have ever tasted. Check and sign the enclosed postcards and mail them to me— *today.* They require no stamps.

historical fact with which they do not happen to be familiar. This thirst for news of the past is often the basis of imaginative sales letters. Norman Alper in Figure 7-43 shows how effective history can be with the early history of paper making.

Figure 7-44 is another example of the ability to make words stir the imagination. Notice how cleverly Harold Pitcairn McQueen, a business letter-writer of Chicago, used the historical background of an old home in placing before his readers the services of landscape gardeners Swain Nelson & Sons Co. The lack of a strong Hook is explained by the fact that the purpose of the letter was to break ice for a personal call later.

Figure 7-43

Gentlemen,

More than 1,800 years ago Tsai Lun, a Chinese, first manufactured paper in the modern, beaten-pulp manner.

But almost 6,000 years ago—as far back as 3500 B.C.—the Egyptians were making a type of paper called *Papyrus*. The Egyptians peeled the thin, inner layers off the stem of the Papyrus plant. These strips were laid side by side on a hard, smooth surface. Then more strips were laid across—at right angles. The strips—now a mat—were soaked in Nile water, with some starch added. As a final step, pressure was applied to the Papyrus for hours, followed by polishing with hard stone or glass.

That was the beginning—in Egypt. The art of Papyrus-making spread. The Romans made more than 20 kinds of Papyrus. Some grades were used for wrapping goods. But for 4,000 years the process was done entirely by hand.

These old Egyptian Papyrus makers would surely marvel at the enclosed large Reply Envelope. For it was made of wood pulp. Huge machines changed the pulp into tough yet attractive paper—22 Substance, Ivory Kraft. And then...we at Equitable formed the paper into envelopes at an unbelievable speed. Printed at the same time, too, on a rotary press attachment of the envelope machine!

Check Equitable's low prices on the envelopes you use—28 and 32 Substance, Fawn Kraft, and 32 Substance Ivory Jute Finish (carried in stock) for *proofs*—a wide variety of papers made-to-order in minimum quantities of 25,000 for your *promotional mailings* and *job printing*.

Just write the quantity you usually buy on samples of your envelopes. Mail them to me in the enclosed Reply Envelope. An attractive Equitable quotation, samples, and money making suggestions, will be sent to you promptly.

Another sales letter—seeking to arouse interest in the British West Indies—is Figure 7-45 written by James Hawkins for agents Defoe & Stevenson, Port Royal, B.W.I. Here is a business communication that fiction could not excel: full of the names of pirates and buccaneers that excited our imagination when we were children; crowded with historical

Figure 7-44

Dear Mr. and Mrs. —————,

One evening, 16 years after a pioneer family had cleared a piece of forest land on Lake Michigan and built their farm house, they stood in their yard and watched the reflection of one of the greatest fires in history.

These folks lived a good day's journey from that swamp city of Chicago, which covered but 18 square miles of mostly mud. When Mr. Heinzen built his home in 1855, Chicago had but 159 miles of wood sidewalks and 27 miles of plank streets. Cobble stones had been tried—only to disappear in the mud. The Illinois Central had just laid its tracks along the shore, and the *Democractic Press*, one of Chicago's first newspapers, was telling the world to "Come West." George M. Pullman came—in time to raise our only skyscraper (the four-story Tremont House) on some 5,000 jackscrews; followed by Carter H. Harrison of Kentucky—whose son was to serve Chicago five times as mayor.

And so, from that time till this, the old farm on the lake has seen the rise of Chicago—from village to mighty city.

Now I hear this landmark is to be your home—and I'm interested because in 1856 this Nelson company came into being, growing with and serving the men who built Chicago, many of whose sons now live along the North Shore.

I wonder whether you feel we could help you to make your grounds an appropriate setting for your most interesting home.

facts that make the reader's heart beat faster. Emotionless, indeed, would be the person who could read this letter and not feel an urge to visit the West Indies. It is truly magnificent writing—as good as you will ever encounter in a sales letter.

Using characters the reader can visualize. As has been mentioned, generalities don't get very far in a sales letter. Any broad statement about the merits of a product or service must be proven with concrete cases. This ideology is the keynote in Figure 7-46 used by H.B. Voorhees to raise money for the Travelers Aid Society. He was not content merely to state that the organization does "good work" and let it go at that.

Figure 7-45, page 1.

Defoe & Stevenson - agents - Port Royal, B.W.I.

CODES: BENTLEY'S & A. B. C.

Howard Smith Paper Mills Limited,
407 McGill Street,
Montreal, Canada.

Dear Sirs:

PUNCH

If you took three puncheons of rum and two hogsheads of sugar;
dumped them in a well; then drew up the mixture in buckets: you would have
what might truthfully be called a magnificent punch.
It's exactly the kind British soldiers had when they landed on
Trinidad during the Napoleonic Wars and broke into a sugar-house and a
distillery.
I always liked that story. There is a grandeur and a magnifi-
cence about the business which seems so in keeping with the native grandeur
of our islands. The sea is so brilliantly blue; the flaming tropical
foliage so glorious. Hills blaze with the orange-red Bois Immortel; there
are giant trees and tree ferns, scarlet poinsettias, purple bougainvilleas,
golden poui, many-hued hibiscus ....

BUCCANEERS

When Defoe wanted a satisfactory island for his Robinson, it
was our Tobago he chose; when Jim and Long John Silver set out for Treasure
Island, it was here they came. Drake still lies beneath the Caribbean
waters, "waiting for the drum"; Raleigh came to Guiana in search of El Dorado;
Morgan, admiral of the buccaneers, ruled at Port Royal and Blackbeard in
the Bahamas; the little island called "Dead Man's Chest" is here, and the
old pirate harbour of Tortuga.

FOUNDER

All through the islands there are so many reminders of our tur-
bulent past, there are so many interesting historical events to recall, that
some of the most important are easily forgotten. For example: one of our
showplaces is our "Gibraltar", the fortifications on St. Kitts' Brimstone
Hill; while three miles from them is a practically unknown memorial of much
deeper historical significance -- the grave of a forgotten Maker of Empire,
Sir Thomas Warner. The first English settlement in the West Indies was
his establishment on St. Kitts, from which he sent settlers to colonize
Nevis, Antigua, Montserrat and St. Lucia. Briefly, this son of a Suffolk
yeoman was the founder of the Empire's oldest group of colonies.

Instead, he documents this work with a random sampling of true
stories. Accordingly, the readers imaginations are exercised; the people
they read about are there with them; they visualize themselves or some
person dear to them in the same predicaments.

Figure 7-45, page 2.

ACCIDENT

The first English foothold in the central Caribbean was obtained in more accidental a manner. Some, I suppose, would say "more English" a manner, more typical of the haphazard and absent-minded fashion in which an Empire has been built. Penn's "disorderly rabble", having been soundly beaten off from Santo Domingo, desperately grasped at the idea of getting something to show for their pains, so they landed on Jamaica. From that time on, English buccaneers had a headquarters in the very middle of Spain's dominions.

That's all ancient history now. The buccaneers have joined Columbus and the Conquistadores and the battle fleets of England and of France in our West Indian story. Modern Port Royal could hardly be called "the wickedest town in the world", and nowadays we don't see many "stately Spanish galleons" dipping past our shores richly laden from the Main.

TREASURE

A treasure remains, however: eternal sunshine and rest, beauty of land and sea, and the health-giving breezes of the Trades. No wonder West Indian cruises are popular, and that every year we welcome more visitors from Canada.

For you in Canada there is another, and a more practical, interest in our islands -- one more closely connected with pieces of eight and double castellanos. I refer, of course, to the question of Canada-West Indian trade.

TRADE

The complementary character of our climates and our products makes the development of such a trade seem natural, and much has been done to stimulate it. Did you know that your first Trade Agents, appointed under the auspices of your Department of Finance, were seht to the West Indies? Trade treaties have been negotiated assuring preferential treatment for each of us in the other's markets. Regular steamship service has been supplied. The Canadian-West Indian League has done magnificent work in strengthening business ties and fostering goodwill between you in Canada and us in the Bermudas and the British Colonies of the Caribbean. Indeed, this letterhead is one specific example of our trade, for, like many of our office forms and business communications in the West Indies, it is printed on your Progress Bond.

Much has been done for the expansion of trade and travel between us. I think even still more can be accomplished, and even greater advantage taken of the opportunities offered us to work together for our mutual prosperity.

You can easily obtain full information as to specific trade possibilities from governmental sources, or from the League, or from your various financial institutions interested in the West Indies; and you can count on their helpful co-operation in any matters promoting trade and travel between your great Dominion and these islands -- the Crown Colonies which lie closest to you.

Yours sincerely,

James Hawkins

P.S. I certainly like your Progress Bond, White, 40(m).

Perhaps you have received other letters from Travelers Aid. They are almost always fine examples of sales letter carpentry, supported by stories to set the reader's imagination on fire. The one you have just surveyed was reinforced on the inside pages with specific cases to turn the heart inside-out. Like this:

With a thin three-weeks-old baby in his arms, and two tear-stained children clinging to his coat, Joe Barnes timidly

Figure 7-46

Dear Mr. and Mrs. Olsen,

Clipped to one of the checks we received last December was a card bearing this message:

"For someone stranded on Christmas Day!"

I thought, as I held that card, of eight-year-old Billy, who had come to us that morning in the Union Station. The terminal was filled with a happy holiday throng—arriving travelers being met by smiling friends and relatives and packed off into cars and taxis—all except one lonely little boy.

Billy was not met. The Travelers Aid worker found him standing alone beside his shabby little suitcase, and trying awfully hard to be brave. Someone, he said, was supposed to meet him, but he guessed they "just forgot."

I thought, too, of young Joe Barnes, whose tragic story is told on the next page, stranded here in Chicago with his three small children, and the body of his wife. And of 20-year-old Jennie, incurably ill and going home on a stretcher—to die. And of barefoot Peter and John, stranded 300 miles from home because of careless planning on the part of some careless grownup.

And then I thought of the thousands of others who come to us throughout the year; some of them needing merely a sympathetic listener; others, in desperate need of the help that Travelers Aid alone gives to the traveler in trouble away from home.

Some of their stories are briefly told on the inside pages of this letter. We ask you to read them, and if you will, to make yours a happier Christmas by sharing it with these other less fortunate folk. Tear off the coupon and please mail it with your check to Travelers Aid today. Mark it, if you wish,

"For someone stranded on Christmas Day!"

approached the Travelers Aid desk at the railroad station. He was taking his wife's body to her parents, who had promised a home for the children.

Grief-stricken over the loss of his wife, Joe was on the verge of collapse, and the baby's sudden illness terrified him. He had very little money and had not eaten in 24 hours, but "It don't matter about me," he remarked, "it's the kids I'm worried about."

· · · · · · ·

"You see, my son's wife doesn't like me—and I can't stay where I'm not wanted"—Mr. Lane's voice trembled and his mild blue eyes filled with tears as he told the Travelers Aid worker why he was "running away" from home at age 87.

What have appeals for charity to do with *business* letters, you wonder? Well, in one sense, nothing; in another, plenty. The technique used in the Travelers Aid letter is one of the best for selling the product or service to which it may be applied. Support your claims with actual cases; let your reader *see* living people in what you say, rather than mere words about them. Personalities—not platitudes—stir the imagination.

Consider Figure 7-47—a sales letter used by the Robertson Paper Box Company, Montville, Connecticut. The writer (it is signed by the

Figure 7-47

Good Morning, _____ ...

...and do you know Walter Tiskey?

Well, he's a young fellow here at Robertson's who stands behind a drawing table with a rule, pencil, cutting knife, and a head full of ideas.

Everybody around here marvels at the way he snaps them out. Ideas, we mean. Ideas which our die-cutters take, pass on to our technical men and printers, who pass along to customers some of the most unusual Folding Display Boxes that this era of smart merchandising has known.

Robertson salesmen come to Walter with a handful of knives...a water bottle...shotgun shells...a new toilet preparation...a batch of noodles, biscuits, candy, or bakery products...sheets, pillow cases, blankets or lingerie...in fact, *anything* that needs a container—and Walter "sparks" a sample box (made by his own hands) which the customer falls for, head over heels.

In this day, when new *ideas* are so importnat to the winning of the customer's dollar—when *eye-appeal* is just about the most important essential to store selling, it's good to have a fellow like Walter Tiskey around.

The reply card enclosed is for your use—so that you may profit from Tiskey's help.

president) doesn't just say his company can supply an idea to meet any box problem; he talks about the man from whom the ideas come, and thus makes his message far more interesting.

Imagine the get-away. Letters that seek to arouse interest in vacation spots have a great opportunity to stimulate the reader's imagination. The things described are those that the prospects have dreamed about during the long work months when they have had their noses to the grindstone.

They are ready for any mental spree the letter may encourage, and if the place offered sounds at all interesting, the more facts presented the better. This is one sales letter-problem where the writer has no need to worry about length; the greater the array of advantages, the more likely he is to touch points of vulnerability in the reader.

Where would you like to spend your next vacation? Well, perhaps the letters coming up may lead you in the right direction.

Let's see what Ken Raetz has to offer us at Normandy Court (Figure 7-48). The folder that described the location has been lost, but as we recall, Normandy Court is located in Michigan—not too many miles from Chicago.

In that letter, you saw at work a master in the use of the English language. Many of the words are little barbs that prick the imagination. The tone is intimate and personal, but not "sticky." From one advertising person to another, the approach is perfect. The message is short, but long enough to make the reader feel that the writer is thoroughly sold on Normandy Court. Some of the phrases are extremely vivid: a pleasant lullaby or an exhilarating cocktail...enticed three beautiful Wall Eyes...luxuriate in your own laziness...to revel in the chef's gustatory miracles. Yes, this letter gives the imagination an exciting prod. Result—a strong urge to be off to Normandy Court.

But wait a minute—this workout of your imagination is not over. Perhaps you will prefer the cabin Hassenpfeffer, up in the North Woods (Figure 7-49). Rose Kreuser tells you about it—for the owner.

Well, there you have them—two sales letters out to do a similar job. Did they stir your imagination with their many interesting facts? Where would you choose to go—to Normandy Court or to Hassenpfeffer cabin?

Heightening the excitement of home ownership. There are a few families in the world that do not crave to own their own home; and many of those that have a home are dreaming of the day when they can own a better one. A home is not just a mass of bricks, lumber, or stone. It is a place where the owners may do as they please, where no landlord can tell

Figure 7-48

Dear _____,

Right now Mr. LeRoy is up at Normandy Court, the lucky stiff, and as a result, a part of my job is to try to whip up prospects into a frenzy of dissatisfaction with their present surroundings and give them positive assurance that Normandy Court is one place where "All's well with the world."

I speak from experience, too. Last Memorial Day weekend we crammed more fun into three altogether too short days than I had ever thought was possible. You'll recall that that weekend was a scorcher in Chicago, but up at Normandy cool breezes ruffling the pine trees were either a pleasant lullaby or an exhilarating cocktail...as you preferred.

I am not a fisherman, but one of the guides showed me a place where a No. 7 spoon enticed three beautiful Wall Eyes into my boat. You play hard or you luxuriate in your own laziness, but it's ten to one when nightfall comes that you sleep like a baby on your Simmons Beauty Rest. And food, Mr. Frailey! People actually come from miles around, and even from other lodges, mind you, to revel in the chef's gustatory miracles.

If Joe was literary-minded, we would call him Merlin, for it's my feeling that "Joe" is entirely too prosaic a name for a man as accomplished as he.

Quite a few ad men and others associated with the graphic arts have made the Court their stamping grounds. You will have a good time and I am quite sure that Ed LeRoy would enjoy meeting the man whose "Bulletins for Dictators" have been such a source of constant inspiration in our regular advertising work.

Figure 7-49

Dear _____,

Do you still feel yourself in the clutches of "Ole Man Winter"? Are you weary and tired of cold, sleet, ice—one sunless day after another? Do you have that listless feeling—just a casual interest in the things that used to seem so vital?

Man—what you need is a rippling lake full of fighting bass—a can of worms—a box of spinners and flies—a reel. You need a sun-kissed white sand beach and nights bathed in silvery, shimmering moonlight peeking through tall, imposing pines—short, bristling cedars—green, furry spruce.

Man—you need to rub the soles of your feet on a carpet of spongy pine needles—you need to hear the chatter of the chipmunk—the screech of the loon—the hoot of the owl—the "whippoorwill" of that odd night bird. You need the distant wail of the coyote—the sight of a frightened deer.

Man—you need the North Woods—the Land of Hiawatha.

North on M-94, just 11 miles from Manistique, Michigan, here in the heart of Hiawathaland, the "cure" awaits you. The doors of a big brown log cabin—the cabin Hassenpfeffer—are swung open to you. Here you'll welcome the sight of dozens of cottontails romping about the place—cottontails that gave Hassenpfeffer its name.

Hassenpfeffer is no ordinary cottage, such as you would expect to find in a near-city resort. It is a two-story cabin, constructed of hewn logs—logs felled on the very spot where Hassenpfeffer was built. It has a stone foundation, and the inside is finished in natural white birch, taken from wooded acres around the cabin.

A large, bright kitchen, a dining room with natural stone fireplace, and a rambling screened sun porch covering the whole front of the cabin, occupy the main floor. Up the stairs off the kitchen, the second floor is an airy, comfortable bedroom which will accommodate at least six people.

Hassenpfeffer is so securely built—so snug and warm in winter, it is an excellent hunting lodge. During open season, you can hunt raccoon, pheasant, duck, wild geese, bear, deer, coyote, fox, wolf.

Hassenpfeffer stands on a little hill, about 130 feet from the white sand beach of Island Lake. The cabin itself is literally hidden by pines, cedars, and spruce.

For decades, pine needles have been dropping to the ground, until now they have formed a spongy carpet over the whole territory. It is a delightful sensation just to step on Nature's own inimitable carpet—a sensation you will never forget.

Island Lake joins Dodge Lake about halfway across. Both lakes are full of big, fighting bass, trout, and pike—to say nothing of the thousands of game little perch, sunfish, bluegills. Here you fish at dawn—by day—at twilight—by moonlight. Some beauties are just waiting to be caught—there's never a dull moment.

Island Lake has a yellow sand bottom; the water is so clear you can see right down. It's perfect for diving and swimming.

If you wish to play golf, the Hiawatha daily fee course is just 2 miles from cabin Hassenpfeffer; the private club, 5 miles out. Both courses are in excellent condition.

When you start on your vacation, wouldn't you like to *know* that you are going to a heavenly spot in a movieland setting? A spot where you can have every vacation advantage? Where you will be really secluded—away from the noise and heat of the city? Where thrills and excitement await you? Where you will enjoy cool, restful nights?

Hiawathaland has all this. It can be yours not only this year, but every year, because we're selling cabin Hassenpfeffer and 5 acres of woodland for $_____. As you wish, you may make a downpayment of $_____, and we will arrange convenient terms—or you can purchase it outright.

Mr. Frailey, we promise you a vacation such as you never have had before. Come up for a few weeks—live in Hassenpfeffer cabin—see for yourself why you should own it.

The attached reply card supplies the details. Mail it right away, so that we will know when to expect you.

---

them they must move, where the children and their pets can play unmolested, where loving care can shape the grounds with trees and flowers and shrubs—so that everything more and more reflects the personalities of those who live there. There is so much about the thought of owning a home that stirs the imagination of a family that doesn't have one. Is it any wonder that many of the most colorful letters are those selling homes? Or selling something to make them more precious?

The letter in Figure 7-50 seeks to picture what a few trees, set in the right places, might do in beautifying the exterior of a home—hoping that the picture will grow in the reader's mind until action is impelled.

In the above letter there is no concealment of purpose. The writer says, "Dare I ask you to day-dream for a moment?"—he wants the reader to *imagine* the trees he talks about—to see them as they might stand next summer, if only he will start the ball rolling. And if successful in creating those mental images, the writer stands a good chance of transforming imagination to reality.

Figure 7-50

Dear Mr. —————,

Christmas—New Year's—and now the ever-welcome breathing spell. Dare I ask you to day-dream for a moment—about next summer?

It's July!

Once more the sun is bearing down in much too generous proportions for comfort. Around the rustics seat, we again wish those spreading Sugar Maples were making that spot more attractive. The bare corner of the house should be set off by the decorative Honey Locust we've spoken about so often. And our porch! For two years now our next door neighbors have used theirs every hot afternoon, protected by the cool shade of the Elms they planted.

Desires that come too late! "If only we had thought about them sooner, we would be enjoying them right now," you say to yourselves.

Now let's skip back again—to today—and suggest:

Whatever your desires for next summer may be, they can be fulfilled if you plant your trees *now*.

Moved best (and at less cost) when they are dormant—their lifegiving sap will start to flow weeks *before* the first signs of Spring.

A word from you on the enclosed card will start the ball rolling. Yes, come to think of it—a ball of earth—holding the tree you want in use next July.

In Figure 7-51, Irvin A. Blietz, Wilmette home builder, is offering one of his own houses, and he takes time to describe every point of utility and beauty. This is a very wise procedure for a letter of this type. Buyers want to know all the details that Mr. Blietz supplies. They may stretch the letter longer than might seem necessary, but time is not a worry of the average home-buyer. They want all the facts.

7. AVOIDING MISTAKES IN SALES LETTERS

A checklist of things the masters never do. Many of the costly mistakes made in sales letter-writing can easily be avoided. They are the

Figure 7-51. Letter to Create Mental Image of the Home

REALTORS, DESIGNERS, BUILDERS, MANAGEMENT, INVESTMENTS
2550 CRAWFORD AVENUE · EVANSTON, ILLINOIS · UNIVERSITY 9 · 1000 · BROADWAY 3 · 4080

Dear Mr. and Mrs. Frailey,

I have just finished a lovely home in the Williamsburg tradition at 1211 Chestnut Street, East Wilmette, which has been awarded the Good House-keeping shield for excellence in design and construction. Needless to say, I am mighty proud of the award and certainly would like to have you see this new home.

It has a massive, double-door entry with shutters on either side flanked by potted cedars; a circular staircase; a huge bowed picture window in the living room; a natural wood-burning fireplace with a marble-faced mantel; and a shuttered door screen between the living room and dining room. One entire wall of the dining room is a glass window.

The kitchen, if I say so myself, is a masterpiece of efficiency, beauty, and design, with its snack table, Dutch door, and serving pantry. The family room is paneled in pickled pine and opens out to an outdoor screen-ed porch. One side of this porch is in the new modern glass brick. A separate staircase leads directly to the servant's quarters.

There are three master bedrooms with two master baths, beautifully tiled (one bath has a glass-enclosed, tiled shower stall) -- in addition to a downstairs powder room.

The decorations throughout the house were selected by Mrs. Blietz, and I think she has done a beautiful job. Why not drive out this way some Sun-day soon and see for yourself? I'll be at the house every Sunday from two until six, and would really enjoy showing it to you.

Incidentally, I wonder if you saw the publicity that the Chicago metro-politan papers carried regarding the Connecticut Village of 39 homes that I am starting just one block south of the Kenilworth Station of the North-western and North Shore Railroads in East Wilmette (walking distance to the lake).

In this Village I will have winding streets, James River lamp posts, ever-green landscaping, and outstanding character such as made the Indian Boun-dary Park development so famous. The homes will all be in the better Colonial tradition and will range in size and price from 6 rooms, 1½ baths to 9 rooms, 3½ baths. I mention this village thinking that you or some of your friends might be interested.

If you know of anyone who is thinking of buying or building a home, I will be happy to send them complete details about this development, if you will furnish me with their names and addresses on the enclosed card.

Looking forward to a visit from you, and with my best wishes for the New Year.

Sincerely yours,

Irvin A. Blietz

DESIGNERS AND BUILDERS OF: KINGS COVE ON THE EAST FORK, CARRIAGE HILL ON THE WEST FORK, CONNECTICUT,
NEW ENGLAND, PARKWOOD, PINE TREE, PANORAMA, WILLIAMSBURG, SPRUCEWOOD, ELM TREE, HILLSIDE, LINDEN
VILLAGES, PEBBLEWOOD LANE, INDIAN HILL NORTH AND OTHER FINE NORTH SHORE HOMES AND APARTMENTS

result of ignorance rather than intent, as writers *never* want to lessen the chances of success for what they are trying to do. Consequently, it is well that we listen to the voice of experience and view with an open mind the tips the masters give us.

Although the work of these masters varies according to their respective personalities and beliefs, there are nevertheless certain cardinal points on which they all agree: things *to do* that will increase the pull of a sales letter; things *not to do,* that will decrease that pull—so much that it may not pull at all. Throughout the pages of this *Handbook,* you have seen what these principles are, and there are still others yet to be revealed. We have surveyed chiefly the positive side of the picture: devices and procedures developed because they are known to be helpful. Here, however, let them tell you about the negative side: traps to avoid; *don'ts* in sales letter-writing. They are all simple enough, and yet the frequency with which they are disregarded in business correspondence indicates they are not generally understood. Consider these errors carefully, for any one of them might easily cause a letter of your own to fail.

DON'T belittle your reader. Often sales letter-writers, in their eagerness to make the sale, come up with an assertion which tends to belittle, humiliate, or ridicule the readers or something about their businesses. The statement may be merely an insinuation, but it is likely to cause offense. Here are statements taken from actual business letters. Probably none of the writers realized the negative reaction set up in the reader's mind. Ignorance may be bliss, but it still doesn't pay off in sales letters.

> *From a letter offering detective services:*
> "We are of the opinion that there is something wrong, or that you suspect there is something wrong in your place of business." Even if true, this is an irritating remark. The reader may close his mind to anything else that is said in the letter. What right, he thinks, has any stranger to make such a bald accusation.

> *From a letter offering mailing lists:*
> "Your own mailings and those taken care of by so-called mailers, often reach the wrong prospects. That's the reason for your failure."

> Fighting talk, with two barbs to prick the reader! First, the writer takes a crack at his competitors, the "so-called mailers"; second, he uses the nasty words, "your failure."

> *From a letter offering wallpaper:*
> "Why do you depend on luck to increase your business?" This question is insulting. The reader is told that he is inefficient. He depends on luck.

From a letter selling boiler equipment:
"Don't close your eyes to changing times. Don't feel that you can continue to operate with inefficient and wasteful equipment."

First, the writer insinuates that his prospect is not up-to-date. Then he makes the plain accusation that the present equipment is inefficient and wasteful. The word "continue" does the dirty work.

From a letter selling glassware:
"These dealers are letting someone else go after the pennies—they go after the quality merchandise trade at a real profit. Why gamble with your future?"

The other dealers are smart but this one is dumb, insinuates the writer. Worse than that, this prospect doesn't use his head—he "gambles" with his future.

From a letter offering typewriters:
"Do you fumble the sales inquiries that come to the Doe Corporation?"

Pleasing question, isn't it? The writer doesn't exactly call his prospect a "fumbler," but he wants to know if it could be true.

This was the opening sentence. The man who got the letter—the president—doesn't know what was said later. He didn't read it.

From a letter offering accounting systems:
"There's mighty little fun in being robbed day by day, dollar by dollar, by antiquated accounting and collection equipment in your own office."

Since the writer is selling the "cure," it must be taken that he means his prospect's equipment is the antiquated kind. No doubt that is true, but some things are better not mentioned.

If you agree that the quotations just exposed were humiliating to the men to whom the letters were sent, then you are in the proper mood to inspect an even more horrible example of tactlessness. The writer is a business consultant offering his services.

Dear _____,

Insinuates the prospect has not been efficient In view of the economic situation, it has become imperative that you...operate more efficiently if you intend to show a proper return on your investment and effort.

Insulting questions	Do you know the facts about your business? Do you face them squarely? Because of our broad experience...we believe we can help you do that and more.
Ends with tactless question	The writer is frequently in the vicinity of your office. Are you sufficiently interested to extend him the courtesy of an interview? Your very truly,
Conceited implication; smart people value my importance	P.S.: Years ago, a similar letter went to a junior executive of a company, who referred it to the general manager. I served that company many years, more recently the second generation. This junior executive is now head of the institution.

The tragedy of the examples just reviewed is that the thought behind the belittling statements was well intended; at least, the writers had no idea they were handicapping their own efforts. The same thoughts could just as easily have been expressed in a tactful way. For example:

Negative	"Your own mailings and those taken care of by so-called mailers, often reach the wrong prospect. That's the reason for your failure."
Positive	"You know how it is with mailings. Unless they reach the right prospects, they are doomed to failure."

The negative sentence places the blame on the reader; states the failure as a fact. The positive sentence presents the problem impersonally—assumes the reader will agree how important it is that the right prospects are reached.

This is a very important point in sales letter-writing; *don't* put your reader on the defensive. *Don't* insinuate. *Don't* humiliate. *Don't* belittle.

DON'T exaggerate. The bridge-players who consistently overbid their cards soon lose the confidence of their partners; sales letter-writers who overbid their products soon lose the confidence of their readers. And that means, lose the sale! Truly, exaggeration is a poor weapon. Guard against it. You know the importance of sincerity in any contact with a fellow human being; you know that it is impossible to stretch facts beyond reality and at the same time be sincere. If letter-writers aren't fooling themselves, how can they expect to fool their readers? Of course, you may make a sale with facts you know are not true, but in the long run you are sure to lose a customer; never forget that in business there are ethics that must be respected.

However, much of the exaggeration seen in letters and advertising is not necessarily meant to deceive; the people responsible for it simply seem to proceed on the basis that those who read are very small children or morons. For example, a while back we were told in the national magazines that the easiest way to make a hit with the men is to make party sandwiches with a certain food preparation. That may be a good tip, but we doubt if many young ladies would endorse it. Another magazine advertisement showed a happy young couple driving down the highway, with this foolish dialogue beneath the picture.

He: Is that trooper following us with arresting intent?
She: He wouldn't give *you* a ticket, darling. You look too impressive in your new _____ hat.

You encounter a lot of that kind of piffle in modern advertising; you encounter far too much of it in sales letters. "Do you want your sales letters to produce the maximum number of orders?" asks one sales manager. "If your answer is *yes,*" he continues, "be sure to use our envelopes." Nonsense, isn't it? The envelopes *could* help, but there are numerous other factors that team to produce the maximum number of orders. The statement is pure exaggeration, and the reader is chilled rather than warmed by it. Note the exaggerated statements that follow—the words in italics that are overdrawn.

- Your last letter gave me the thrill *of my life.*
- John, I *won't be able to sleep* until I know you got this order.
- You know I hold your opinion *above all others.*
- *Nothing could please me more* than to grant this concession, if company policy would permit.
- We are *worried sick* about this mistake, and will *never* be so embarrassed.
- It *hurts us more* than it *could possibly* hurt you.
- You might *search the world over,* and *never find* an opportunity like this.
- Joe, there are a *thousand reasons* why you should not quit under fire.
- We appreciate your business *more than we can say.*
- This is the *biggest chance you have ever had* to double your sales.
- It's the opportunity *of a lifetime.*
- I am *amazed* that one in whom we placed *implicit* confidence should refuse to pay this bill.
- You are one of a *carefully selected few* to whom we are making this offer.

Remember as a sales letter-writer that facts need no stretching; exaggeration *weakens* your arguments, lessens your chances of success. Put your best foot forward—write with enthusiasm—but be sure it *is* your foot, just as you describe it. Exaggerated copy is only an insult to the reader's intelligence—it never pays. This is one of the things that all good letter-writers know.

DON'T try to trick the reader. Experienced and ethical writers do not hold feed bags in front of their readers, as may be done with a horse or mule to get him to move forward. Neither do they make statements not strictly true, in the effort to flatter or please them. As was said a moment ago, sincerity is the only foundation for a sales letter which will stand firm to the end. Notice how the following letter begins:

Will you accept a beautiful fountain pen and pencil—*with my compliments?*

With your permission, I am going to send you a big new fountain pen and pencil, oversized, self-filling, with 14 karat gold point—*free.*

And if you care to pay the small cost of engraving (only $1), I'll have your full name die-stamped on it in solid gold leaf.

The circular enclosed shows you this beautiful new pen and pencil in its exact size. It looks as good, and works as well, as the pens which sell in stores at $30 to $50, and the makers guarantee it to give satisfactory service. More than that, your name on it in letters of gold gives it a distinctiveness often lacking in high-priced pens.

Are there any strings tied to that offer? Not a one. Of course, the words "with your permission" tell any intelligent person that there is something fishy which has yet to show up. An extremely gullible reader might think he is about to get the pen and pencil free, as the letter plainly states, but the next paragraph in the letter destroys that dream.

I am going to send this fountain pen and pencil to you, just to get you to *try* our new letterheads and envelopes with your name and address on them in raised letters.

So the truth comes out. In reality this beautiful pen and pencil, the kind that sells in stores at $30 to $50 is not free. Here is what the reader has to do to get it:

The regular price of the 500 letterheads and envelopes, with monogram and address on them in rasied letters, is $29.95. If you mail the enclosed Reservation at once, you get them for the

$29.95—*and in addition* you get the beautiful fountain pen and pencil *free of charge.*

What does common sense tell you about such an offer? If the pen and pencil is worth $30 to $50 how can the company afford to sell the stationery and envelopes for $29.95. Either the reader will pay far more for the latter than they are worth, or the pen and pencil don't have the value described. Obviously, the company has to come out with a profit on both items—the reader is being deceived one way or the other.

The above is not intended to criticize the use of premiums, when offered as such and without any attempt to hoodwink the reader. But it does criticize the *way* the pen and pencil set was offered, and with the obvious impossibility that a $30 item could be given free in a sale amounting to $30. The value is simply too big compared to the price of the stationery.

Another form of deception, although it may be mild, is when a condition is described as an excuse for writing the letter—a condition that will hardly hold water in the light of human intelligence. It is something more than mere exaggeration, because the writers must have their tongues in their cheeks as they state the condition. Here are some examples:

> "Hundreds of letters have been received asking if our kits would be available as Christmas gifts. This national approval leads us to suggest to you the attractiveness of the Christmas wrapped..."

> "Although our Fifth Birthday occurred in October, we have been amazed at the requests we are getting for an extension of our remarkable combination subscription offer...so by popular demand, we are going to reopen this special offer to a selected list of old friends only..."

> "Many of my customers have written me, asking if I could quote a quantity price of my pipes and tobacco, to be given to friends, relatives, employees, and business associates at Christmas."

In all of the above letter introductions, the writers seek to convey the impression that they have been swamped by requests for the action later explained. "Hundreds of letters" cannot properly be interpreted as "national approval"—the number is too small. In the second question, it seems the writer was rather easily "amazed" and the idea of a "selected list" is extremely stale. It is also a fortunate coincidence that in the letters to the pipe merchant, all groups of possible prospects were mentioned—"friends, relatives, employees, and business associates."

These, of course, are the same groups the writer would have mentioned had the letter been written on his own initiative, instead of by popular request.

Neither can we swallow without a wink the introduction used by another circulation manager.

> This letter, coming to you in advance of any public announcement, is intended for your eyes alone. It contains information we ask you to regard as confidential. You will see why in a moment.

> We are sending this letter at this time to only a few of our old customers, because we feel that they are entitled to first chance at this remarkable offer.

Here the reader is given a little secret. For some reason not explained, only a few of the old customers are to have a shot at the remarkable offer—he is one of the chosen few. If true, it is easy to see why the matter must be a secret. What would the other old customers think if they knew they were not cut in? We could be wrong, but it seems more logical to think that *all* of the old customers who were in good standing with the company got the letter. If not, those left out certainly had cause to feel slighted.

Perhaps you have respected the memory of the famous violin makers of the past; certainly, you know how their violins are prized by the great players, and the prices they bring when sold. Well, maybe we have been deceived about violin-making. Maybe you or anyone else with a workbench can turn out a fine violin. That at least is the impression developed by a sales letter from a company which has all the "makings." Here are the bits that can be quoted:

> Dear Mr. —————,

> What a thrill to hear the rich golden tone of a violin made with your own hands in your own home! How you can amaze your friends! And this at a cost of only a few pennies a day.

> …Of all the hobbies today, violin making is easily beginning to take the lead with men and women who are eager to make things with their own hands that are really worthwhile. Things that were formerly considered impossible!…It is a most unique hobby—intensely interesting, yet actually simple enough for you or any home craftsman to master at once…. No wonder hundreds of people are now adopting this hobby, and other hundreds have already satisfactorily completed one or more technically perfect instruments.

...All of the materials in our Kits are of the very finest to be obtained, assuring you of a fine instrument—one that you'll be proud to play and to show to your friends.

...Don't deprive yourself of this supreme enjoyment another day. *Begin this fascinating hobby now!*

Yes, we think it would be fun to build a violin, but is the job as easy as the writer of this sales letter leads us to believe? How does he say it— "Actually *simple enough* for you or any other home craftsman to *master at once.*" Be still, old masters in the art! Don't turn over in your graves! This writer has just gotten carried away.

And what do you think of the conflicting statements in the following opening and closing paragraphs of another sales letter? The first one says, "Don't worry—I won't shoot." The second fires the shot.

Naturally you will think this another letter asking you to renew your subscription. It isn't. Your subscription has been canceled and I am writing now simply to ask some assistance from you....

If you have changed your mind and do want the subscription then I'll know my work wasn't so badly done. In that case, just put your initials alongside this paragraph, return to me, and I will see that a *new* subscription is entered to begin with the current issue.

Of course, the writer does leave himself one loophole, but one too small for squeezing through. He declares the *old* subscription has been canceled—all he wants is a *new* one.

DON'T be too flippant. The margin between cleverness and flippancy is sometimes rather thin. Some never have the ability to write in a light and nonchalant manner without irritating their readers; others try the same tactics, and arouse only antagonism. The difference is intangible, but real. Certainly, beginners who are not sure of themselves should not attempt to spread their wings too far.

In the attempt to lighten the tone of their letters, you often see writers using slang words or expressions. The attempt usually fails. Especially irritating are such words as "Gosh," or "Golly," or "Heck." They make the letter sound too juvenile; the writer, too immature. Also in the same objectionable class are such combinations as "Wotinhel," or "Damitall," or any similar form of disguised profanity. The use of slang and profanity was discussed in an earlier section of this *Handbook*—the suggestions to avoid such uses given there are especially important with respect to sales letters.

DON'T abuse your competitors or their product. A commendable trait in average people is their love of fair-play. They do not admire the people in business who run down their competition or another product or service. If people thus attacked were present to tell their side of the story, it might be different. But sales letter-writers who disparage competition orally or in writing are seldom received with favor. Read the following contrasting letters—written to customers by partners who had severed their relationship. Which of these letters do you think the customers liked best?

(1)

Dear President _____,

This is to advise you that I have bought the interest of my former partner, John Doe, in X-Y, Incorporated, and that he is no longer connected with the company.

I want to thank you for your many courtesies in the past, and for your loyalty to the company, which I hope will continue.

Our name, our products, our package, and our catalog are known throughout the Industry, and the business will continue to be operated as usual, and under the same high standards.

It is our aim to contribute everything possible to your continued growth, and we will be constantly seeking new ways in which to serve your business.

In grateful appreciation of your goodwill,

(2)

I hate to hang out
the dirty wash *but*

...my partner and I have split up...we're quite washed up... through...we've kissed each other goodbye...and now *he's* sole owner of X-Y, Incorporated (there I go giving him free advertising already).

So what? Well, I thought you might be interested to know that although my former partner bought *me* out, I'm by no means quitting the automotive parts business. Not by a long shot. After all, I've been eating...sleeping...dreaming...buying... selling...cataloging automotive parts for a good many years ...and people who should know have told me that I've done a pretty good job. Now, without any *encumbrances,* handicaps, etc., etc., I believe I can do a better job.

And that's exactly what I'm doing right now...building the finest automotive replacement parts business to be found anywhere.

Judging from the congratulations and good wishes I'm receiving from old customers, manufacturers, sources of supply, and many good friends, this new _____ Corporation will really and truly be worthy of your business.

I'm all set...in our own building...0000 S. Michigan Avenue. So won't you please try to save a little piece of an order for a guy who has always appreciated your business?

All kidding aside! I've got my sleeves rolled up and I'm earnestly going into the replacement parts business in a big way, and soon one of our representatives will be in to see you. When you happen to be in Chicago, I hope you'll drop in for a handshake and a hello.

It is impossible to decide from these two letters what caused the split in partnership and which of the two men, if either, had the greater reason to be provoked. But clearly the writer of the first letter puts himself in a far better position with the old customers. He says nothing at all to the detriment of his former associate.

To be sure, there is much temptation for sales letter-writers to compare the strength of their product with the weakness of another; to expose some deficiency in the other company's service; to play tit-for-tat with other organizations that have not been ethical. But an eye for an eye, a tooth for a tooth, is never a winning slogan in letters, or any other part of business. In the long run, writers who concentrate on the advantageous quality of their own product are ones who come up with the most goodwill from customers and prospects. Yes, of course, if they have a "point of difference," they can and should put the spotlight on it, because if the prospect cannot find this advantage elsewhere, they will surely come to the writers for it.

DON'T ballyhoo. Some sales letters call to mind the spieler outside the circus sideshow—big noise and fervor, nothing specific to back his claims. Plenty of ballyhoo, but no ballast! Merely to make a number of empty assertions about a product is the lowest degree of salesmanship. You have witnessed the value of *proof* in getting favorable action; you know that a generality is only a shell without the oyster. And yet how often you read in sales letters:

- "The astonishing performance of this razor will"...
- "You will appreciate the many modern refinements in this utterly different automobile"...

- "Right from the can, as good as mother could make, and yours without"...
- "With brilliant lines in the modern trend"...

Just a lot of ballyhoo! How shall the reader interpret it? *How* will he be astonished when he puts the razor to his face? What *are* modern refinements? How different is *utterly*? *Nothing* from a can could equal mother's cooking—at least, *prove* it. Just what *are* brilliant lines in the modern trend? Do any of these high-sounding phrases paint sharp pictures in the reader's mind? Absolutely not—no pictures at all.

Here's a sales letter from a laundry. The writer wants Mrs. Doe to try the "finest laundry service" in Cleveland. But any laundry could talk in terms of "finest." *Why* is it the finest? Where's the proof?

A hotel in New York wants Mr. Doe to stop there on his next trip. The writer says his hotel is "truly different." Yes, a lot of hotels are "different"—unpleasantly so. Anyway, if he means there are advantages in staying there not found in other hotels, just whay *are* they? Where's the proof?

"You should attend this annual banquet. The entertainment will be *unusual* and the speeches will be *outstanding*." Wonderful! But you said after the banquet last year, that you would never be hooked for another—$25 dollars for a tough steak, a boiled potato, and the inevitable apple pie; a couple of tap-dancers and a funny man who wasn't funny; a soap-box speaker who prattled about world affairs. Should you try again? Why? Unusual entertainment! Unusual in *what way*? Outstanding speeches! What does the writer *mean* by outstanding? Could this banquet be worth $25 dollars, and a whole evening of your time? Where's the proof?

Generalities need to be *explained*. They won't stand alone. "Save for the future—practice thrift while you are young, and you will be protected when you are old," says a sales letter-writer. The sentence sounds all right, but what is there in it to be remembered a half hour later? *Thrift* is an abstract word. So is *protected*. They are like drops of water—soon evaporated. Why didn't the writer *interpret* "thrift" and "protected": money in the bank when too old to work; travel, contentment, independence; not left destitute and unwanted when the sun of life begins to set.

Don't be a circus spieler in your sales letters. Come down from the clouds—put your feet on solid earth. If you have something *worth* buying, tell the reader *why*. Be specific. Give him proof.

So there you have the key points of the master letter-writers. Look at the checklist in Figure 7-52 often so you can avoid these six major

Don'ts in good sales writing. Disregard the experts' advise and you will sincerely handicap your sales correspondence.

Figure 7-52. A Master Checklist of Don'ts

1. **Don't** belittle your reader. The man humiliated is never your friend.

2. **Don't** exaggerate. A truth needs no stretching. The reader knows you are taking him for a ride. You fool only yourself.

3. **Don't** try to trick your reader. Don't put false bait under his nose. All of the cards belong on top of the table.

4. **Don't** be flippant. Buying is a serious matter to the reader, if not to you.

5. **Don't** disparage your competitors or their product. Show the reader what *you* can do for him. It doesn't matter what the other fellow *can't* do.

6. **Don't** ballyhoo. Thunder is only a big noise; a bolt of lightning gets attention.

8. DRAMATIZING SALES LETTERS

Blueprint for winning special attention. In Section 3 (pages 121 to 145), you have seen how business letter-writers may use some form of showmanship to make their message different. The idea is that it may capture preferred attention in competition with letters of the more conventional type. You have seen, too, the qualifications of a good dramatized letter, and the faults that may cause one to be ineffective. You know that the idea must not be farfetched or remote from the central thought of the letter, and unless it is really clever, it may do more harm than good.

When used with discretion and good taste, a dramatized idea may be especially effective in a sales letter. It tends to break down the readers' initial resistance, and to put them in the mood to continue the message. Psychologically, however, showmanship in selling faces the danger of being received as an attempt to "show off," so that the prospects feel they are being maneuvered into buying by clever people and must guard against them. The idea should never be so spectacular that it overshadows the rest of the letter. In other words, it should *aid* the general sales thought, rather than *compete* with it.

The very best of all dramatized sales letters are those that manage to sample the product. A fine example was the letter in Figure 3-7 on page 132 with the pieces of yarn attached—illustrating the difference between hand-made and machine-made yarns used in rugs. The purpose of the idea was to *instruct* more than to *impress* the reader, although the final result was as convincing as any sales message could possibly be. Perhaps in some similar way your own product can be dramatized for presentation to prospects. If so, go ahead and prepare the letter. It will probably outpull any of the conventional letters you have used.

The following dramatized letters will complete the collection started in the earlier section; you should be able to pick out from the collection a number of ideas adaptable to your particular type of business.

Using showmanship for dramatic sales... Here in Figure 7-53, is a letter used by *The Cincinnati Inquirer* to sell accident protection—probably as an inducement to subscribe to the paper. The letter does not attempt to complete the deal, but paves the way for a personal call.

With a large question mark, a note in script on the back of the bill, which is enclosed with the letter, hastens to cushion the shock— "Suppose this bill were *yours* —could your pocketbook stand this unexpected expense?"

Figure 7-53

Dear —————,

I'm writing to you about your husband.

If he were to come home with a broken arm, who would pay the doctor and hospital bills? Suppose he were hit by an automobile or fell down the stairs or was otherwise disabled by accident, would your income stop?

As long as nothing unexpected happens, your husband's income just about covers your living expenses with possibly a few dollars left over for savings.

But—accidents, like lightning, strike without warning. Every minute 17 persons are accidentally injured or killed! Suppose your husband were to have an accident today. The unexpected expense for doctors, hospital, drugs, etc. would seriously interfere with your income and might wreck your savings account too.

There's only *one* way to protect yourself and your family from the heavy expense of accidental injuries.

It will be a real pleasure for me to tell you how you can get this protection easily and inexpensively. I will call within a day or two to discuss this vital problem with you.

It will take only a few minutes and you will not be obligated or disappointed.

IN ACCOUNT WITH

CITY HOSPITAL

YOUR CITY,

FOR SERVICES RENDERED:

Room — 10 days @ $200⁰⁰ per day	$ 2,000	00
Medication	300	00
Laboratory fees	1,700	00
X-Rays	600	00
Physician's Consulting fees	750	00
Amount due	$ 5,350	00

TERMS: CASH

Of course, you noticed that this letter is addressed to the lady of the family, rather than to the husband. The dramatized idea should have even more appeal to women, than to men. Because of the implication of moderate income, it is also plain that the letter is slanted at wage earners.

Keeping the reader's name in large script. If it is true that individuals are most interested in themselves, then the sales letters that dramatize their names should have special attention value. Instead of the conventional address and salutation, Figure 7-54, written for *Tide* by Harry H. Costello, carried the names "Sutton & Peterson" at the top in

Figure 7-54

THIS LETTER IS GOING TO BE DIFFERENT.

I'm not going to start out by saying that just because 7100 busy executives read *Tide*—that is any reason why you should read it.

And, I'm not going to tell you how *Tide* keeps your mind refreshed and brings you the really significant news of advertising and marketing dished out in short, pithy paragraphs, piquantly flavored with anecdotes and personalities.

All I'm going to say to you is this:

> "Friend—*Tide* is a good magazine for you to read. It's entertaining and full of interesting news that might suggest a new business opportunity or a new slant on some problem in your work. It certainly is worth 32¢ a week. You ought to have it."

Tide is so good I read it myself. So, I know what I'm talking about. And, you'll like it too—once you read a copy. You see, *Tide* has an editorial style all its own—the newsiness and accuracy of *Time*, the compactness of *Reader's Digest*, and the whimsical flavor of *The New Yorker*—all put together in a way that makes business reading entertaining and interesting as well as useful and informative.

> *Tide* is published twice a month—costs only $16 for a full year's subscription. You can start your subscription now by simply filling out and mailing the enclosed postage-paid card. The modest fee can follow, later, when we send a bill.

I'm sorry I can't offer you a set of books or ten easy lessons on playing the Hawaiian guitar along with your subscription. It seems as though the boss got the crazy idea that people would buy *Tide*—because they wanted to read it—and so far more than 7,100 readers have backed him up. But, see for yourself what *Tide* is like—fill out and mail the card *today*.

---

red script. The letters were about an inch high and stretched across as much of the page as does the body of the message below. In addition to this attention device, you will admit that the letter is written with refreshing humor and frankness.

Another way of dramatizing a sales letter is to get a prospect's license plate number and display it, along with his name, prominently, in a letter. For example, if you were "Mr. Roberts," you would no doubt be pleasantly surprised to see a picture of a gasoline station attendant holding your license plate in his hand. This was done in a letter, shown in Figure 7-55, prepared by Harry Latz, which reads as follows:

Figure 7-55

THE LICENSE ON YOUR CAR, MR. ROBERTS!

Just for fun check up and see if we're not right...then drive to your nearest Gulf station and see for yourself that we have your number...especially at this time of the year!

Have you thought about the coming winter...ice, snow, hard starting, harder gear shifting...probably not...so we would like to recommend that you stop at the Gulf station right away for a Gulf winter lubrication.

You'll find a smiling attendant ready to serve you...ready to refill your crankcase with winter-grade Gulfpride Oil...the world's finest motor oil...100% pure Pennsylvania...Alchlor-Processed and free-flowing in any weather. He's ready, too, to drain the worn, heavy summer lubricant from your transmission and differential and refill with Gulf Transgear Lubricant winter grade...no more hard starting...grinding gears...worn parts.

Let him give your car a real Winter Lubrication...with lubricants that are made specially for winter temperature...rainproof, slush-proof, mud-proof. Then you'll be all set for the coming season...mild or severe. Be sure to use That Good Gulf Gasoline...it's kept in step with the calendar...refined to suit the weather...it'll be your guarantee of quick starting.

There's a Gulf station near you...drive in today and have your car prepared for winter...your local Gulf man appreciates your business. Visit your Gulf dealer and get acquainted.

GET HIS NUMBER

Using pictures to illustrate copy. A mild kind of showmanship in sales letters, and one that nobody can call out of place, is that where the copy is reinforced with suitable pictures. There is a heart-tug in Valentino Sarra's picture of a child's shoes. (See Figure 7-56.)

Figure 7-56

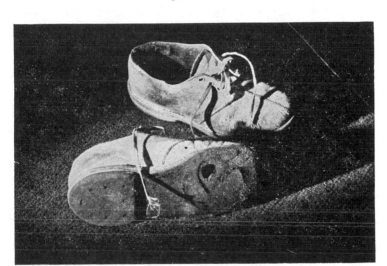

The letter was used by B. A. Roloff as Extension Secretary for the Travelers Aid Society in Chicago. You will concede that it puts appeal in the message.

A child is missing from his home tonight—and parents wait with anxious hearts for some word of reassurance.

It makes no difference that they are poor people and the child has probably not been kidnapped—he is their child, and he is gone, and his mother lies awake tonight wondering where he is.

Thousands of children leave their homes each year without parental permission and in Chicago alone last year 777 such youngsters came to the Travelers Aid. These are the cases of which you seldom hear, because in so many of them the nationwide chain of Travelers Aid Societies quickly intercepts the young runaways, learns their stories, and returns them safely to their homes.

This is truly a remarkable service and one of which the public knows comparatively little because it functions speedily, smoothly, and without publicity. Obviously, the value cannot be measured in dollars and cents. Just try to set a price on a mother's gratitude!

Wouldn't you like to help us continue this important work? Five dollars will mean a great deal to us and even one dollar will be mighty welcome. Your check in the enclosed envelope will bring happiness to grieving mothers through the return of their missing children.

Illustrations of this type are just as appealing in sales letters as in any other form of selling. The reader *sees* what he is urged to buy, and if the sight is pleasing, the urge is strengthened.

Blending simplicity and effectiveness. Showmanship in sales letters sometimes takes such an elaborate form that one wonders if the result is worth the effort; the expense appears so great that only a very high pull in orders would enable the idea to pay its own freight. For those who like now and then to get out of the rut and do something different, a simple idea of very little cost may be just as effective as one that is complex and expensive. The letter with the two pieces of yarn, Figure 3-7 on page 132, which rates as high as any, involved nothing more than the cost of the yarn and the time it took to staple the two pieces on each page. Anyway, it isn't the expense that counts; the result has little relation to it.

Figure 7-57 is the effective, simple Christmas sales letter prepared by Norman Focht for The Men's Shop in West Chester, Pennsylvania. To this letter is clipped a small tag on a red string—the dime-a-dozen kind used to identify gifts. On the tag, where the name of the recipient is usually written, are two words in longhand—"To myself." See how the tag ties in with the message.

Whether or not the psychology back of this appeal is sound, the manner of offering the suggestion is unique. Besides, the profit on one order probably would offset the cost of the tags and labor.

How to dramatize unseen quality. Somewhat similar to the sales letter idea comparing the two pieces of yarn, but doing a more difficult job, is Figure 7-58 that compares the two kernels of corn. Could you think of a better way to demonstrate how a product may have hidden qualities which make it worth more than other products that *appear* just as good?

Selling hidden quality was also the purpose of the yarn letter, but the comparison was more obvious. The reader could *feel* the red and

Figure 7-57

It's this way, ————...

...I don't believe in anyone being selfish and thinking of himself first. But I do feel as though it's all right for a fellow to give some thought to himself when he remembers others at Christmastime.

And here's why...there's no one more deserving of a gift than yourself. You plug along, like most fellows, for 365 days in the year, putting in a lot of hours of hard work. So, when it's time for Santa to slide down the old chimney, you are entitled to a treat as much as Aunt Emma, Cousin Ted, the cop on the beat, and all the others.

So for goodness sakes, don't skimp on yourself...give yourself something worthwhile. Tie a tag on a new suit, topcoat, or overcoat from Kauffman's...a gift that will bring you a lot of happiness and satisfaction.

Stop in and look over our new winter selection. It's a grand array of clothes that says "Merry Christmas" to you in no uncertain tones. And remember, we have a Budget Charge Account Plan which makes paying easy—if you desire to take advantage of it.

Merry Christmas!

blue strands—test their texture—and quickly tell the difference. But the two grains of corn are not so easily identified. One kernel is far more productive than the other, and worth a lot more to the planter, but the extra value must be proven in use.

Any company having difficulty in getting across to prospects the point of unseen quality can use advantageously this very graphic comparison of the two grains of corn. The idea carries a fact to the prospect that many pages of sales copy might not explain so effectively. It is just as good a demonstration for a service as for a product. In this particular case, the John C. Bowers Company seeks to make plain that not all property managers work with the same effectiveness; some are able to produce more income from given properties than others. There is no way of selecting the most skillful manager, however, until his services are tested in the various duties of management. Neither is there any way of knowing—at least by the layman—which of the two kinds of seed corn will produce the most bushels. But the difference in value is *there*, whether it can be seen or not.

Figure 7-58

JOHN C. BOWERS COMPANY
PROPERTY MANAGEMENT
APPRAISALS   REAL ESTATE SALES   INSURANCE
4628 BROADWAY, CHICAGO

Dear Mr. Ambrose:

In the little bag are two grains of seed corn. Look at them ever so carefully, and you still will not see anything that makes one grain different from the other. But there is a difference of great importance to the farmer who might put them to work in his own soil -- a difference in results. One of the grains is a sample of ordinary seed corn, the other of the hybrid variety. Hybrid seed produces from 6 to 35 bushels more per acre.

A lot of values are like that. They cannot be seen on the surface, but they are indisputable when comparative results are checked. It isn't easy, for example, to visualize the difference between ordinary property management and the scientific kind. It is only when the profits are counted at the end of the year that expert management proves its worth.

We cannot list all the attributes of a good manager but certainly they include executive ability, seasoned judgment, an open mind toward new ideas, capacity for hard work, a thorough understanding of human nature, and that rugged honesty which ensures conscientious service for every client. But how many of those attributes can be seen in a man as he walks down the street -- or in a company as you step into its office?

It has been more than twenty years since John C. Bowers entered the real estate business. During that period a lot of water has gone over the dam -- thousands of clients have been well served. Always receptive to better methods as they were discovered, always in touch with professional sources from which scientific facts could be drawn, the management services of the John C. Bowers Company have been steadily strengthened and refined. This is the inevitable result of experience -- accumulated power to serve -- but something, also, which cannot be seen on the surface.

In your building seeds of extra profit can be planted -- seeds which will be sure to bring you more "bushels" when results are weighed. This is no idle thought. We are making many other properties yield extra dollars. Why can't we do as much for YOURS?

If that's a logical question, then stick the enclosed card in the mail the very day you get this letter. Sending the card does nothing more than give us the chance to prove we are scientific planters -- ready and able to raise a bigger income crop for you than you ever have had before.

Sincerely yours,

JOHN C. BOWERS COMPANY

MEMBER OF
NATIONAL ASSOCIATION OF REAL ESTATE BOARDS
INSTITUTE OF REAL ESTATE MANAGEMENT
CHICAGO REAL ESTATE BOARD

The sales letter with the corn was one of a series by this Chicago Realtor—the majority of the mailings being of the dramatized variety. Last of the series was one of the "big" letters described on pages 139 and 140 in Section 3. It was enlarged to twice the size of the ordinary business letterhead. The copy is in keeping with the "big" idea, and is shown in Figure 7-59.

Figure 7-59

So we decided

to make it
BIG

Several times recently you have had letters from us in which we craved the privilege of talking to you about our ability to serve you in a very special and pleasing manner.

Thus far, that privilege has not been granted, and we think it must be our fault. Either we have been too bashful in explaining what we can do for you—or we failed to make our letters stand out in your mail.

So now we are coming to you in a BIG way.

Maybe we should always use BIG paper because BIG benefits should be called to your attention with BIG emphasis.

Anyway, we are making this message short, as we don't want the BIG point to be cluttered in your mind with a lot of puny words.

It all sums up to this. We are burning with a BIG desire to serve you with BIG satisfaction to yourself.

We want to hear you say, "Come on over with your BIG ideas about managing real estate—but they had better be BIG or you'll get a BIG invitation to leave."

To make it easy for you to reply, we are attaching a letter all ready for you to mail back to us.

The letter contains one BIG word—and when it gets back to us our thanks will be BIG too.

Yours for BIG profits,

The letter the reader is asked to return continues to emphasize the "BIG" idea. The one BIG word "Yes" does the job. This return letter is reproduced for you in Figure 7-60. Together—the letter to the prospect and the one he is supposed to return—they are an example of showmanship in sales letter-writing at its best.

Figure 7-60 Dramatizing the Important Word

John C. Bowers Company,
4826 Broadway,
Chicago, Illinois.

Gentlemen:

My reply to your BIG letter is,

Come on over, as indicated below. My mind is open.
Bring your BIG ideas for selling property. But don't
waste my time unless they are really BIG.

                                       Sincerely yours,

                               (Typist fills in name)

Come { Time _____
       { Day _____

A GUIDE TO SUPPLEMENTARY SALES LETTERS

6. SMOOTHING THE WAY FOR YOUR SALES STAFF

7. FOLLOWING UP THE SALES CALL

8. HELPING YOUR SALES FORCE SELL

A GUIDE TO SUPPLEMENTARY SALES LETTERS

1. HOW TO HELP INCREASE SALES

To have and to hold. In business, the strength and depth of the roots are proportionate to the goodwill content of the soil. If the amount is sparse, the company must continuously struggle to get new customers to replace the old ones that are lost; if the amount is plentiful, sales increase and the company prospers. Very few organizations neglect making the effort to get orders. The methods of one company may be better than those of another, but they all work hard and consistently to make sales. But that is only *half* the job; it is just as important to *hold* an old customer as it is to *gain* a new one.

Unfortunately, many companies concentrate most of their efforts on getting business. They blindly assume that customers once in the fold will continue to remain there. They leave the customers alone, except for the necessary routine contacts, the calls of the salesmen, and fervent appeals for *more* orders. They forget the little courtesies, the evidences of appreciation, that might build goodwill and make the customer less vulnerable to competition. In their sales program there are no planned letters to keep the customer conscious of a friendly business relationship; none to show appreciation; none to make the salesman's job easier. Occasional efforts along this line are spasmodic and ineffective—crumbs thrown to the customer in a hit-or-miss manner.

This emphasis on getting orders, with the lack of emphasis on holding goodwill, is in the long run a costly procedure. Often the sales expense on the initial order exceeds the profit; the company looks to repeat orders to place the account on the right basis. Repeat business is almost always more profitable than new business, and this fact would seem sufficient to encourage every possible effort to keep customers satisfied and loyal to the company.

It doesn't take long to dictate a letter thanking a customer for an order; a letter later saying that the order has been shipped; and a letter after delivery, asking "How do you like it?" All of these letter contacts, or any one of them, tell your customers that your company is interested in them as well as in their order; that the desire exists to follow through until it is known they are thoroughly satisfied.

Why more of these *supplementary* sales letters are not written is difficult to understand, for anything that helps to *increase* sales must deserve a place in the company program. "You are right in theory, but not in practice," says many a sales manager. "We are too busy to waste any time on unnecessary correspondence." Common sense tells us, however, that such an excuse doesn't hold water. The sales department finds time for other activities—why must this one be neglected? Why call letters that *help* the sales program *unnecessary?* Sales executives who see the need of one kind of selling, to the exclusion of another, are like horses that wear blinders. They can only see straight ahead. They don't know, or will not admit, that to either side there may be opportunities just as fertile as those in the direct sales program. What they should be after is a *whole* and *complete* program of sales activities, with *nothing* skimped or slighted that might contribute to the success. If there is no one in the sales department who has time for these supplementary sales letters, then someone can be hired for that purpose. The position will always more than make up its sale salary in the business that it *saves* for the company. To have is fine; to hold is wonderful.

Keeping your letters short but effective. Supplementary sales letters need not be long. The subject matter is not nearly so important as the fact that the readers have been reminded in a friendly way that they have not been forgotten. Customers do not want to be just a name in the records of the company with which they deal. They want to be recognized as human beings. The letter that they get accomplishes that purpose—makes them *feel important.*

How letters may do this job is illustrated by the following cordial contacts made, as the occasions present themselves, by a fuel oil company. None of these letters can be considered time-wasters, for they are only a few paragraphs long. Neither are they any more remarkable than many of the other supplementary sales letters you will see later in this section. No, they are just a valuable addition to this company's sales program—sensible, simple, and sincere letter contacts which, over a period of years, are certain to increase sales.

In one sense, they are form letters, but in a short time a typist can turn out a day's quota of originals so that the effect on the readers are exactly the same as if the message had been dictated solely to them.

(1)

Welcome to New Resident

Welcome to Bridgeport!

We know you are going to enjoy your residence in Bridgeport. Its many parks and boulevards are known throughout the world. It is a beautiful city with its magnificent Nelson Gallery of Art, its stupendous Municipal Auditorium, and its many other attractions, almost too numerous to mention.

You will be greatly impressed by Bridgeport's outstanding residential district. Beautiful homes for mile after mile! Bridgeport is warm in friendship, warm in cordiality, and we know that you will consider yourself a part of it in but a short time.

We cannot help but feel that we, in our business, have had some part in the warmth of Bridgeport, at least as far as winter heating comfort is concerned, because we have been rendering a service since 1914 in that direction.

When you are ready, we should like to serve you, too.

(2)

Letter to New Customer

It is indeed a pleasure to welcome you as a new customer of the Datona Wood Company. We hope to please you always.

We attempt to show our appreciation for the business given us by rendering a service which is just a bit more than is expected. We are constantly on the alert to handle only the finest of quality firewoods, so that no matter what price wood you buy from us, it is unquestionably the best in its class.

We sincerely hope that you are pleased in every respect in doing business with us. It shall be our endeavor at all times to see that you are entirely satisfied.

(3)

Thanks for Past Orders

When Spring rolls around, a firewood dealer either has something for which to be thankful or just the opposite. He either has had a satisfactory winter season, or things haven't gone quite so well.

We are privileged to be in the former group—we have reason to feel quite happy over the season that has just passed. We wish, however, to place our appreciation where it is most appropriate, and that is with you—our customer. We thank you for having given us the opportunity to be of service to you during this past season.

We want to extend to you our best wishes for an enjoyable summer, and a most pleasant vacation.

(4)

Thanks for Sending a Friend

Thank you very much, Mrs. Jones, for recommending our company to a friend.

It is indeed a real pleasure to know that we have pleased you to the extent that you have felt inclined to tell someone else about our service.

Many, many thanks for your thoughtfulness.

(5)

To Lost Customer

When we lose a customer at Datona, it is a serious matter.

We don't immediately fly off the handle and loudly exclaim, "What's the matter with those folks anyway?" We sit down and very seriously summon all of our thinking energy to determine what we have done here at Datona that was wrong. Why have *we* failed to please the Jones family?

We are of the opinion that we must have made a misstep somewhere along the line, and we want to ask the personal favor of you to write on the back of this letter, just what happened to cause you to end your business relationship with us. A stamped envelope is enclosed for your convenience in replying.

Will you do this, please?

(6)

Follow-Up of Letter Five

Some time ago, we wrote to you expressing regret that you had not done business with us recently. We asked you very frankly to tell us why. So far we have received no reply.

We realize that there are many reasons for discontinuance of business with a firm; however, if in any way it was our fault, we want to know it. If we are doing something wrong, we want to correct it.

Won't you reply by letter, or call me personally by phone and tell me just what happened? I will be ever so thankful to you for this favor.

The above six letters might all be called "unneccessary" by business-men who do not sense the importance to sales of cordial contacts with prospects and customers. But this opinion does not hold up in the light of the results obtained by companies who *do* use letters to foster friendly public relations. Nobody can say how many cords of wood the above six letters have sold, but enough, surely, to make a long trainload.

Has anybody seen Jones? You will recall that one of the basic methods of letter-writers is to visualize as nearly as is possible the person to whom they are writing. The mental image helps to bring out that person-to-person tone that makes the written words a conversation rather than a letter. The better the image, the closer the writer can come to using the right appeals for a particular reader or group. Names in a card file or on sheets of paper are cold and impersonal. When they stand for *real people,* they take on life and personality. This was the thought, of course, that motivated the rather remarkable letter shown in Figure 8-1. It is the brain-child of H.A. Lufkin, of the Newton Manufac-turing Company, Newton, Iowa.

In explaining how he happened to dictate such an unusual message, Mr. Lufkin said: "It's only once in a blue moon we get to know these men personally. Naturally, it is a tremendous help when we can know more about them. Finally, I hit on this semi-humorous tangent, and the replies came back nearer to 100 per cent than on anything else I ever hope to write."

Yes, it seems reasonable that a letter so unique should develop a large number of replies, and after Jones became a *person* intead of a mere *name,* it must have been easier to correspond with him. But the supplementary sales letter, in any of the forms it may take, does not need to be so spectacular. If it's just a pleasant contact with the prospect or customer, it may help to keep the human relationship alive. In doing that, it is a real asset to the sales program.

But what *are* these supplementary sales letters? What particular purposes do they serve?

Figure 8-1

Dear _____,

????????

Who is this man *Jones?* Is he fair, fat, and 40, or thin, dark, and 70? Does he live in one room, boil coffee on an electric grill, or does he have a fine family, a bull-dog, and old-fashioned friendly neighbors? Does he smoke big, black cigars and carry a cane, or is his weakness red neckties and chop-suey?

Does he sing in the choir, play the pipe organ, hunt ducks, or shoot pool? Is he an expert with a dry fly, a 30-30, a camper's skillet, and a cribbage board? Has he a wooden leg, a big, black mustache, and cauliflower ears?

These are some of the questions which run through our minds from time to time when we sit down and start a letter to a man we have never seen.

Writing to a name is one thing, but writing to a real, live, human sort of a fellow is quite another. Of course, we know we can't see every man personally, but if you have no objection, Mr. Jones, we'd like to know something about yourself, your family, your likes, and dislikes, so we can write to you a little more personally than has been possible in the past.

Here's a stamped envelope; we'll pay the freight. What do you say?

---

2. WE HAVEN'T HEARD A WORD

Choosing the best courses. When one or more sales letters have been sent to an individual or company without provoking a reply, and the chances seem slim, three courses of action still remain. The first is to lose your temper, and give the other person a piece of your mind. You can be very self-righteous and ask, "Don't you think we are entitled to the *courtesy* of a reply?" This is a neat way to blow off steam, but it also completely alienates the reader. Your chance of selling your product or service is consumed in the heat of your reproach. Number one course is good for those who cannot control their patience, but very bad for business.

The second course is to file the correspondence, and look for other game. This is better than the first, because no matter what you may think about impolite people who will not yield to your persuasion, they know nothing about it. Eventually, they may come through anyway, but it's not a good bet.

The third solution is to *try again*. If you really concentrate, a new approach may occur to you—something different, which may bring the rascals out of their shells. Of course, it usually isn't fair to call them rascals, for they may not have been under any obligation to answer. After all, who is at fault if a sales letter, or a series of sales letters, fails to get a response? It *could* be the writer.

Avoiding the pointed finger. A good example of the type of follow-up that scolds the reader for his failure to reply is the one in Figure 8-2. The company from which the letter was mailed doesn't matter, but it is interesting to know that it was signed by the president. You can tell he is no longer thinking much about getting the order, but he does mean to put the other fellow in his place.

Figure 8-2

Dear _____,

On December 13 we received a request from you for some prices on signs.

In your letter you informed us that the sign you had in mind would be used in a container made by the Doe Company.

We replied to your letter on December 15th, and when we did not hear from you, we wrote again to you on December 29th.

At the same time we wrote the Doe Company, and got the necessary information from them.

After getting the required information, we again wrote you, on January 19th, asking that you be good enough to acknowledge receipt of this information, and let us know if you were interested.

To date we have not had the courtesy of hearing from you.

Don't you think that when you ask for certain information, and a company goes to the trouble of getting it for you, then at least you should show some interest and repay them with a reply— even though it is to say that you are not interested?

To be sure, it is no fun to be stymied, and after so many vain attempts to get a reply, it is easy to understand why this president lost his temper. On the other hand, he sent his protest to the purchasing agent of a much larger company than his own, and presumably a company that he hoped to sell. But the one blast of temper killed that dream. The purchasing agent sent the letter to me with this remark, written with a red pencil: "Here's a dandy way to destroy goodwill—he'll get no orders from us."

The stinger in this follow-up is the insinuation of discourtesy on the part of the person who didn't reply. The latter might have swallowed the last paragraph, even though the implication is not complimentary, but that one sentence did the dirty work. One cannot accuse another of discourtesy and still retain the other's goodwill.

The temptation to scold a prospect who has not come through in the way desired is strong, but better judgment tells us that his goodwill is worth more than any satisfaction to be derived from hauling him over red-hot coals. Resisting the temptation is even more difficult when an expected order is lost, as had happened to the photographer who wrote the goodwill-buster in Figure 8-3.

In Figure 8-3, the writer fell into one of the traps described in Section 7—DON'T abuse your competitor or his product. It seems he had some cause to complain, but the tirade should have been mailed to the Secretary of his Trade Association, if mailed at all. It was of no particular interest to the wayward customer. Besides, she had to share his wrath, along with the unethical competitor. The insinuations in some of the things he said to her could not be pleasantly received—"In all fairness" (she isn't fair)…"You should know" (she is dumb)…"By one of ordinary social instincts" (She doesn't have them)…"If you had ever had any business experience" (dumb again). So, it isn't surprising that the woman's reply was brief but sharply pointed. In it the unsatisfied and insulted customer remitted the requested $18 and, furthermore, suggested that the photographer use the money to pur- chase some books on how to write business letters!

There is a great lesson for business letter-writers in this exchange of correspondence. Perhaps it should have been another "DON'T." Never scold your customers even though they may be wrong. Never let your anger toward a competitor fall on a customer's head.

Using the right kind of follow-ups. The tone of the letters which follow is good; the writers try in a friendly way to get the elusive replies. They don't insinuate, and they don't scold. They simply imply, "Come on, now. Be good and write that letter—just as I would do for you if our positions were reversed."

The first one goes all-out in making the reply easy for the reader. Copies of the previous letters are attached—an old idea involving some

Figure 8-3

Dear _____,

Your letter was a shock, I assure you. Business, in a chaotic condition anyway, would be in a much worse state if everyone were as unethical in their dealings as some photographers are.

"A competitive sitting!" That is just too much. This work is creative—it isn't like a piece of merchandise one can hold up and compare with something sold by another merchant. If we failed to please you in our attempt, in all fairness you should have given us another chance. You saw the type of work we do and should feel reasonably certain that if the first sitting did not please, another one would.

We went to you in good faith, traveled 160 miles, used our time and materials, and did not even ask for a deposit on our work. That is the confidence we had in you. Now, I am not really scolding. I am just telling you this because you are an intelligent woman, and should know that these practices are unethical and should not be shared in by anyone of ordinary social instincts.

Naturally, you were interested in getting the best possible picture of your child, but the point is *we could have* given it to you. If another photographer had come along after Z & Z and you had let him try again—then Z & Z would have had their work for nothing and you can see it is an endless chain of entirely *wrong thinking* and harmful practice. If you had ever had any business experience I would not need to tell you all this.

Now our minimum sitting charge is $18. On receipt of this we will mail you the usual three photographs, for we are unwilling that your money represent nothing. We will select the pose that we consider the best—and finish it for you. I am really sorry about all this—however, I do thank you for your very nice letter.

---

trouble for the writer's secretary, but not too much trouble if the reply is secured.

Dear _____,

Enclosed are copies of two letters written you. It will only take a moment to run over them again.

Won't you just make a notation on the bottom of this letter as to when you will be in the market, and for what?

No need to write a letter, just place your answer on the bottom of this sheet.

Thank you.

The next follow-up was dictated by Vice President Earl Hollingsworth of Fine Products Corporation. The location of the company is cleverly revealed in the message which appeals to a special interest of the reader. It would be hard to resist such a friendly contact.

Dear _____,

It was way back on a bleak day in February...on the 10th to be exact, when I wrote you and sent you a package by Parcel Post. Now Spring is here. The sap's rising, the trees are budding, and the flowers are blooming...still no word from you.

I have never seen the Dogwood more beautiful around Bobby Jones' Golf Course. Come on down to Augusta to see the Masters' Golf Tournament, which takes place the last of this month. It's a great show and I know you would enjoy Augusta at this season...and please bring an answer to my letter of the 10th with you.

The little questionnaire at the bottom of the following letter may help to draw the reply. All the reader has to do is scribble *yes* or *no* three times, and shoot the page back in the enclosed stamped envelope.

Dear _____,

Did you ever write a man about a matter you felt sure would interest him—and then wait and wonder why he didn't reply?

That's what I'm doing now.

When I wrote you my last letter I tried to make it easy for you to answer. This time, I'm not only going to make it easy, but I'm going to make it *profitable,* as well.

Just look below—take your pencil and write "yes" or "no" opposite the questions that apply in your particular case. Then return this letter in the enclosed stamped envelope.

Do this now—IT WILL PAY YOU.

> Yours sincerely,
> ALLEGHENY TUBE & STEEL CO.
>
> Sales Manager

Are our prices in line? _____

Are our couplings suitable? _____

Are you in the market? _____

A follow-up used by Cunard White Star Limited also encloses a copy of the previous letter. Unlike the previous examples, this one takes time to advance a strong sales argument for immediate action—do it now, or you may be disappointed.

> Dear _____,
>
> Do you remember the letter we recently wrote you on March 10th? For your convenience, I am enclosing a copy.
>
> You will surely want to go to Europe this year, and inasmuch as advanced bookings are so unusually heavy, I am calling your attention to the advisability of reserving accommodations as early as possible.
>
> If, by any chance, your plans or the plans of your friends include a trip abroad between June 15th and July 10, by all means make reservations now. There is a very strong likelihood that no space of any sort will be available during this period.
>
> The volume of travel this year is so great that it far exceeds available accommodations, and we do indeed want to see that you and your friends are provided with desirable space.
>
> Won't you let us know on the enclosed card if you or your friends are planning a trip abroad this year, so that we can be of assistance to you in securing just the type of accommodations you desire?
>
> Cordially yours,
>
> P.S. Even at this early date, there are a number of sailings for which it is already difficult to secure accommodations.

The repetition in the above letter seems to have been intentional. The writer had just one point to drive home—accommodations going fast—and he made sure that "Mrs. Booker" would not overlook it.

A follow-up by *Forbes* magazine, shown in Figure 8-4, is appealing because of the novel implication that the magazine will keep on working for the reader for a salary of only $28 a year instead of the usual $42. This idea carried throughout the letter makes the subscription cost seem very low. The question in script—"Are you firing me?"—helps to capture reader attention, too.

Figure 8-4

Are you firing me?

I've tried to do a good job for you.

I've kept you in touch with what's going on in business . . . given you new ideas, accurate forecasts of what to expect . . . shown you many ways to make or save money . . . told you of good investments and warned you of bad ones.

Are you going to take me off your payroll now . . . when my salary is so nominal . . . when you have so many problems I can help you solve?

I want to prove my worth. Won't you keep me on for the next three years at only $84? It saves you $42 on my annual salary . . . means a whole year's work for you FREE . . . insures no raises for the next three years.

I'll punch in every other week without fail and keep you posted on latest corporate developments . . . interpret them in terms of your career, your business, your investments . . . make certain you're "IN" on the inside story of business, investments and the money market.

How about it? I'll pull my weight! Simply check and return the enclosed order form now and I'll be back on the job bright and early.

Sincerely,

Forbes Magazine

5r
18-1076

3. HOW TO ANSWER INQUIRIES

Beginning with the Chain. When sales letter-writers answer an inquiry about a product or service, they are not faced with the problem of getting attention. It may be assumed that the readers are already at least mildly interested, or they would not have requested information. Hence, that part of the sales formula which we call the Star has already been accomplished—only the Chain and the Hook remain.

The purpose of the Chain, you remember, was to increase interest until it becomes desire; the purpose of the Hook, to impel action. The first—to increase interest—is the one immediately before the sales letter-writers as they sit at their desks with the prospect's inquiry about to be handled. What can they say to transform the casual interest to something more deep-seated and real?

Their position at the moment is similar to that of a retail store clerk, whose turn it is to meet and serve the customer who has just entered. The latter is enough interested to have stepped inside, but is far from being sold. The clerk's problem is to show the merchandise, explain its good qualities, and make the prospect *want* to buy. The fact that many clerks fall far short of this responsibility, and are merely order-takers and not salespeople, does not in any way change the picture. Merely to lead the way to a showcase, and pull out a few trays for the prospect to paw over, is not *selling*. And neither is it selling when a correspondent simply sends a booklet or some other form of advertising to the person who has inquired about a certain product or service. It may be a very good booklet, but it still lacks the personal touch that a letter can add.

Suppose you had written to a firm of nationally known manufacturing chemists for information about one of their products—what would have been your reaction to the following reply?

> Dear ————,
>
> Your request for a sample of Z———— is being given immediate attention.
>
> We gladly send you this sample and hope the results will convince you of its worth. You can replenish this supply from your druggist. Thanking you for your interest in Z————, we are,

A magnificent sales letter, isn't it? Yes, if the moon is made of green cheese. The man who wanted the sample is the head of the biggest business of its kind in the world. An order created by the sample and the letter would have been substantial. But on the letter, the interested executive wrote—"Why should I buy it from this firm?" Well, he shouldn't—and he *didn't*. A sales correspondent without any concept of salesmanship had destroyed a fine opportunity for the company. If the salesperson had any reasons *why* this executive should buy, they were kept hidden in the sales letter. This sales correspondent only "hoped" the sample would convince the reader of its worth. The correspondent couldn't be sure, or tell why—but this person did *hope*.

Unfortunately, too many inquiries are handled this way in American business. A booklet is tossed in the mail, a sample forwarded, a blunt letter with a generality or two about the product is dictated—and that's all. The tragedy, of course, is twofold. First, it costs money to develop inquiries, and it seems a pity not to make the most of them. Second, when the prospect's interest is cooled, it may never become warm again.

A time when facts are important. In general, the reply to an inquiry can be longer than the usual sales letter which goes unsolicited to a cold prospect. Unless the reply is very dry indeed, details about the product or service will not disconcert or tire the readers. They *want* the facts. They have asked for them. They are interested enough *at the start* to take all of the information that may help them in deciding whether or not to make the purchase.

Thus, the best replies to inquiries are crowded with *facts* the writer thinks his reader may want to know. He omits nothing that might help to gain the order, because he knows this is the one best chance he probably will ever have to sell this particular prospect.

Compare, for example, the weak effort of the writer who handled the inquiry to the chemical company, with the thorough, convincing reply in Figure 8-5. It was written by the Deltox Rug Company to a furniture dealer in Louisiana. Two fine features of this letter are the way the spotlight is focused on the reader's home state, and the attached list of other dealers who are already in "the Deltox family." There is an interesting story connected with the use of these lists in various states—but first read the letter.

It is a long way from Oshkosh, Wisconsin, to Louisiana, but the writer of the Deltox letter (Figure 8-5) succeeded very nicely in taking his rugs "close to home." Five times, the dealer's state is worked into the message. "For Deltox is the leading line...in Louisiana"—"Look over the attached list of Louisiana stores"—"Deltox is styled for the Louisiana...trade"—"Brown, Rust, and Green sell best in Louisiana"—"On his next Louisiana trip."

All right—now the story as told by George Hughes, then Sales Manager for the Deltox Company. Originally, lists of sold dealers in the

Figure 8-5

You certainly wrote to the right manufacturer, Mr. Doe, when you asked for our Catalog and Prices, for Deltox is the leading line of fibre and wool-texture rugs in Louisiana.

Look over the attached list of Louisiana stores selling Deltox Rugs. As a group, these stores sell more fibre rugs than all of the others combined. But why did they select Deltox Rugs in preference to others?

There is but one answer. Deltox is styled for the Louisiana and other Southern trade. Hence, Deltox rugs sell easily down your way. And because of this, you can be assured of a profitable season with our line.

A Catalog and Price List are being mailed you separately. The Price List is properly marked with your trade discount.

Mailed also are samples of our best-selling summer fabrics—Delfibre and Delweave. The color plates of patterns on these lines will be found in the catalog. And it makes no difference what patterns you select. They are all good. But the colorings of Brown, Rust, and Green sell best in Louisiana.

James C. Barr, our District Manager, will visit with you on his next Louisiana trip, but you will need rugs before he calls. We suggest, therefore, that you select the quantities of sizes in the patterns and colorings you want, and send us your order on the enclosed handy form.

various states were not attached to letters answering inquiries about Deltox rugs. You can understand why, as it takes considerable time and labor to compile such lists and keep them up-to-date. However, when the idea was finally given a workout, it was found to be worth many times the cost; the percentage of orders received was several times higher when the lists were used! There is no mystery in this fact. The reader could always find on the list names of other dealers he knew and respected. Thus, he had local testimony for Deltox rugs—a lot more powerful as a sales argument than a generality such as, "Over half the furniture dealers in Louisiana are handling Deltox rugs."

Backing up the booklet. Many companies use booklets to help sell their products; the idea is that they can be produced in more attractive form, and do a more complete job, than letters which might carry the same information. This may be true, but on the other hand, booklets lack the personal touch which is so important in making a sale. It is a mistake, therefore, to answer an inquiry with a booklet and nothing else—no matter how interesting the copy may be. The ideal procedure is to include a letter that will serve a double purpose: first, to arouse reader interest in the booklet; second, to put in a sales lick or two. This double job is done very well by Mortimer B. Fuller, Jr., in a letter for the International Salt Company (See Figure 8-6).

An inquiry for a booklet, or any other material distributed by a company, is also a tip-off that the time is ripe for the nearest salesman to call. These two shots, first the booklet and then the salesmen, often land

Figure 8-6

Dear _____,

Your request for a copy of "The Farmers' Salt Book" is appreciated. We welcome the opportunity to become acquainted.

Years of hard work of many experts gathering together the best practical experience on this subject have gone into the creation of this booklet. If it is as useful to you as we have tried to make it, we will be more than happy.

As in all businesses, farming in recent years has been tough. That's one reason we became so interested in helping farmers to know more about the correct use of salt.

It takes so little money in salt to return a lot of money in results. You're as welcome as you can be to all this information but we would like to be still more useful to you. We have a fine research bureau that knows or can find out anything you want to know about the use of salt on your farm.

So, if there is anything in this book that isn't clear to you now or at any time, you will please us if you will write us about it. If you are unable to purchase our Smoke Salt or Sausage Seasoning from your dealer we will forward them to you C.O.D., or upon receipt of money order. The prices are—10 lb. can Smoke Salt $ _____ postpaid, and 10 oz. can Sausage Seasoning, $ _____ plus postage.

Sincerely,

P.S. After you have looked over "The Farmers' Salt Book," if you would like us to send one to any farmer friend of yours, just send us his name and address.

---

the order. Pfaelzer Brothers of Chicago, meat packers, use this two-edged sword whenever possible. To make sure that the salesman is recognized when he gets to the prospect, his picture (about 1 inch square) is attached to the letter:

> Thank you so much, Mr. Billings, for your interest. The booklet, "Personalized Service," has been mailed to you separately, and it is a real pleasure to send it.
>
> You will enjoy reading this book because its contents conduct you on an interesting picture tour of our plant—at the same time, clearly pointing out the advantages of our service that reaches 50 states.
>
> To the many restaurants it serves, Mr. Billings, "Personalized Service" has a truly great value. You, too, will find it a source of greater satisfaction and increased profits.
>
> I also have taken the liberty of sending you a copy of our latest price list. You will find it complete and interesting because in it are displayed various cuts, qualities, and weights, so that you can easily find the best items for your needs.
>
> We have suggested to our representative, Mr. Sam Jones, that he call on you the next time he is in your vicinity. He should have an opportunity to do so in about a week or ten days. Meanwhile, the back page of our price list explains just how to order—the booklet tells how your order will be filled.
>
> A postage-free mailing card is enclosed for your convenience. Mail it today, and "Personalized Service" will begin working in your interests.

As indicated, this very friendly Pfaelzer reply to an inquiry does not carry the conventional salutations and complimentary close. Neither did the equally friendly Deltox letter you saw in Figure 8-5. In the section devoted to letter mechanics, it was pointed out that a considerable number of business organizations have discarded these rather unnecessary forms. While such firms are still in the minority, the trend seems definitely in that direction, because the omission does not detract from the personal tone that modern writers cultivate.

Facilitating coordination with a dealer. When the company does not sell direct, and this is usually the case, best results are not obtained from an inquiry *unless* the dealer or agent know about it. A copy of the reply, or some other notification, should be mailed to the distributor. This impresses dealers with the power of the company's advertising program, and gives them the chance to follow through locally. While some dealers may be remiss in taking advantage of these inquiries, the alert ones find them helpful.

Teamwork of this kind is illustrated by the next two letters: one the reply to the inquiry, and the other the notification to the local merchant. The letters were signed by Advertising Manager, Harold O. Leiser— pitching for the Walter Booth Shoe Company of Milwaukee. (See Figures 8-7 and 8-8.)

Figure 8-7

Reply to the Inquiry

Dear _____,

As you requested, we are immediately sending you the booklet, "Shoes from Authentic Fashion Sources."

In this little booklet you will find the type of men's shoes that gentlemen prefer. You will find shoes for all wearing occasions—for campus wear—for business wear—for sport wear— and for dress wear, all authentic reproductions of the kind of shoes that usually are much higher priced.

As the name of this booklet implies, the shoes illustrated are inspired from different fashion sources. The shoes themselves are not fantastic creations like one does find in certain lines, but they are the type of shoes that you will be proud to wear, as you will know that they are correct fashions.

The various models shown in this booklet retail at a price range between $30 and $75, so you can find in CROSBY SQUARE the grade of shoes you want, and we assure you that dollar for dollar you will receive a full measure of fine appearance, good fit, and honest material.

Below we are listing the authorized dealers featuring CROSBY SQUARE Authentic Fashions. Won't you drop in at one of their stores at your earliest convenience?

The above complete job (Figures 8-7 and 8-8) is worthy of imitation by all companies that advertise to create sales opportunities for their agents. It seems like half a job to reply to interested prospects, and not let the people most interested in on the secret.

Answering a customer who couldn't shop. The companies that sell direct by mail receive many out-of-the-ordinary inquiries; the majority are developed by the catalogs which are the backbone of their sales

Figure 8-8

Notice to Dealer

Dr. Albert Randolph,
3333 Main Street,
Your City,

wrote in for our booklet, "Shoes from Authentic Fashion Sources," advertised in *Time, Esquire,* and *The Saturday Evening Post.* This we immediately sent him and wrote him a letter, advising him that he could purchase a pair of CROSBY SQUARE shoes at your store.

Don't you believe it would be a good idea for you to get in touch with him by phone, or by dropping him a short letter, inviting him to your store?

Turn his interest into a sale for you.

---

program. Because they come from all kinds of people, from all kinds of homes, some of these inquiries are obviously not so promising as others; but to the credit of the companies concerned, it must be admitted that each letter from prospect or customer is handled as carefully as if it were the only sales opportunity of the day. In this respect, Sears Roebuck, Montgomery Ward, and most of the other big mail-order houses are doing a letter job comparable to any in American business. Every inquiry is answered completely, clearly, and cordially. The will to serve is conspicuous in every reply.

A good example of the care taken to give each inquiry the very best attention is this Montgomery Ward letter from my files. The circumstances provoking the letter were unusual. To this good company came one day an inquiry from an inmate of the New Mexico state prison. He couldn't very well go shopping for what he wanted, so he wrote:

Gentlemen,

Have you some person in your organization who can advise me as to the proper things to purchase for an elderly lady of 75 years, for Spring and Summer wear?

I wish to buy a Spring coat, hat, shoes, etc., and of the things you have listed in your catalog, I am at a loss to know what to choose. The lady in question is 5'1" tall, and weighs around 120; has dark eyes, with black hair turning grey.

I know the sizes of everything but would like you to advise me what is the correct thing.

Yours very truly,

P.S.: I have one of your general catalogs for the current season.

Here was a sales opportunity that some business correspondents might have handled indifferently, since it was rather obvious that the prospect was not in a position to question the advice given to him, and that he probably did not have a lot of money to spend. Yes, in some cases, it might have been pushed aside as not worthy of reply. But not by this outstanding Montgomery Ward sales correspondent; to her, the occasion was a challenge, and she did her best as the convict's shopper. A picture of a model, dressed in the described outfit, was included:

Dear _____,

Behold the charming little lady with the dark smiling eyes and black hair so generously sprinkled with silver! She's on parade for your inspection after a tour through the smartest shops in Chicago. From the top of her head to the tip of her toes, she is correctly attired wherever she goes.

The dress, as you'll see, Mr. _____, is of lovely acetate rayon crepe in soft beige color (light tan). The dainty lace trim and soft shirring at the neck gives it such a dressy look. Somehow, they always seem to be a necessary part of the elderly woman's costume. See how her medium brown, hand-woven straw hat, smartly trimmed with soft velvet ribbon and brightly colored flowers, blend with the dress, and the neat-fitting one-strap brown pumps. There is comfort as well as style in her Foot-Health shoes.

The most important part of her costume is the becoming polo coat of all wool, in the new treebark weave. The well-dressed woman, old or young, likes the new polo coat, as it is so becoming to every figure and can be worn for every occasion. Of course, no costume is complete without a purse and gloves to match the shoes and hat. The shaded brown steer-hide purse so easily carried on her arm, and the smartly tailored brown capeskin gloves add the finishing touch to her very practical and becoming, yet inexpensive, outfit.

Seventy or 17—the woman of today wears what is most becoming to her—the color and the styles that bring out her individuality, making her different from anyone else. That's just what this lovely costume I have chosen for your lovely lady will do.

One thing nice about it too, it can be worn the year around, with the possible exception of the coat and the hat.

The order blank is all filled in, ready for you to return to us with your check or money order. All you have to do is to fill in the sizes. New clothes and a new thrill, and a new interest in life for old or young. You, alone, know the happiness this will bring to your lovely lady. Can't you just see her in this costume now?

Perhaps, you are saying that the language of this letter was "over the head" of inmate Number 0000. But how can you judge except by results? The order blank came back to correspondent Ms. Lucy Young with everything specified exactly as she had suggested. Furthermore, the buyer wrote to her: "Please send me some idea of what to buy the lady in question for summer dresses." You see, there is no limitation in place or condition for a good sales letter—not when the writer is willing to do a complete and sympathetic job.

How to finally capture the reluctant sales. When several attempts to secure a reaction from the prospect have failed, it is good to have an especially strong point in reserve for the final approach. This procedure is illustrated in Figure 8-9 used by Pacific Manifolding Book Co. Ltd., and signed by Philip T. Farnsworth. The true story of the garage man who almost lost $2,900 for lack of an adequate recording system would be likely to make any businessman take serious inventory of his own methods.

The experienced salesman knows that not all prospects can be handled in the same way. Although in general it is better to serve milk and honey to the individual or company that has asked for information or prices, now and then a case develops where a firm and independent reply may get quicker action. This is true in the situation where the sales manager has reason to think that the inquiry has not been made seriously, and that the prospect has no real intention of buying.

The following reply, shown in Figure 8-10, deals with a company which year after year had applied for quotations—and year after year had ignored them. Finally, the sales manager decided the time had arrived for plain talking. The customer, a soft-drink distributor, was told *exactly* what the container had to offer.

Obviously, the writer staked all on his unusual reply, but he had nothing much to lose. After the experience of several years—price quoting and no sale—there was little to be gained by repeating the process. So he used an old appeal which often moves people to buy—the attitude of indifference. In other words, some folks are more impressed

Figure 8-9

Dear _____,

I've written to you before about the new Wiz Register. In looking over the copies I'm afraid they must have been pretty ordinary letters. They couldn't have been very good, because they didn't get a reply.

I want to tell you about something that happened to me some time ago. I was showing the machine to a garage man. The garage man didn't want to buy—thought his old sales books would do all right. He had used them for 12 years and didn't know of any mistakes. While I was talking a man dropped into the store and just stood there listening while I talked. Pretty soon he spoke up.

"That's what I thought too, Ed," he told the garage man, "but about a year ago I bought one of those machines and it saved me plenty." He went on to tell how one of his men had made a sale the day before leaving town for a vacation. In his excitement he forgot to file the billing copy. A month later, the man found the error when he looked over the audit slips in the locked refold compartment of his Wiz Register. The refold slip saved him $2,900, enough to buy two dozen Wiz machines.

That's a true story. I'll vouch for it. Naturally, things like that don't happen every day, but if you'll put a sample of your present sales slip in the yellow envelope, I will see if I can work out a Wiz System that will protect the records of your business.

when no effort is made to sell them. It is not the best approach under most circumstances, but in this case it *worked*. A week after the letter was mailed, an order for 30 carloads of the containers was received. As the writer of the letter commented, "It pays sometimes to shoot straight from the shoulder with customers and prospects who shop around."

4. SHOWING APPRECIATION FOR ORDERS

Impressing new customers. When we think of all the time and expense involved in getting a new customer, it seems only logical that every effort should be made to consolidate the victory. The position of new buyers are not as fixed or sure as that of ones whose names have been on the books for a long period. The new buyers still have their fingers crossed. They hope they have made a wise purchase, but they cannot be certain until later. Their mental attitude is that of doubt, and

Figure 8-10

Dear ――――,

In yesterday's mail we received a letter from you advising that on September 27th you asked for quotations. Our filing clerks have made a very thorough search for this letter and it seems that we did not receive it. We make a special effort to reply promptly to all correspondence.

We regret very much that our reply is not going to be just what you expect. For several years past, it has been customary for your company to ask us for quotations. We have always given you our very best. Our letter quoting you prices on our *superior quality L-25 plastic containers* has always been the last bit of correspondence between our companies for another year. At the end of each year we go through the same procedure. Our quotation letters have never been acknowledged and we have not succeeded in securing your business, all of which is evidence of the fact that your company believes in buying on price instead of quality.

We have repeatedly tried by correspondence and through the calls of our representative to assure you we could save you money because our wares would give you less mechanical feed problems and hence be cheaper in the long run. We have absolutely failed in putting this idea over with your company in spite of the fact that similar companies all over the country are using our containers exclusively.

Last year we quoted you on a 25-car basis and we note from your letter that you are interested in a 15-car contract. For that reason our prices would not be as attractive as they were last year, and since we were unsuccessful in securing your specifications then, we certainly would be this time. As a matter of fact, our prices have not changed since we quoted you last year.

We have been extremely anxious to secure your business, as we feel that we are particularly well-equipped to take care of companies like your own, that are big not only from the standpoint of size, but also with regard to quality of the goods demanded.

Our containers are sold strictly on their merit and not on a price basis. We believe that every manufacturer knows the real worth of his product and when other manufacturers cut under our prices to secure the business, we think it is significant and proves that the business could not be had on an equal price basis.

their company is strictly on trial both as to the goods sold, and the nature of its services.

During this preliminary time when your customers and your company are getting acquainted, any action is worthwhile that will please them and help them to form a favorable first impression. A little extra courtesy at the start may go a long way toward winning goodwill and the confidence that leads to repeat orders. Granted that this is just straight thinking, it is hard to understand how any company could fail to thank a customer for that first order. Futhermore, the letter of appreciation can do the additional job of *reselling* the buyer at the very moment when he is wondering whether or not he should have made the purchase.

A "thank-you" letter supplements the work of the sales staff and helps them on their next call; it puts the company in the class of those who *appreciate* business; it does a whale of a job compared to the small effort required in its preparation. In many circumstances, it can even be a form letter, although it should always be individually typed and personalized.

Saying thanks: examples from everyday business. To reveal how various types of companies do the "thank-you" job, the following letters are presented as typical. Most of them are fairly short, as thoughts of appreciation should be. Gratitude is not an emotion that can be stretched without creating an impression of insincerity. Letters thanking new customers are similar in this respect to Christmas messages—they are best when done simply.

(1)

Dear _____,

First of all, "Thank You" for your order calling for electrical supplies.

Then we want you to know that the quality, delivery, and prices which merited this order are also to be found in all of the other electrical supplies we carry; such as electrical devices manufactured by the Westinghouse Manufacturing Company, and other substantial organizations.

And as our acquaintance ripens, and you become more familiar with our stock, the feeling will grow that for anything and everything electrical, you can depend on Hyland as a sure and constant source.

Please be assured of our appreciation for this initial order. We shall strive to do all possible to cause it to be the first of many.

(2)

Dear _____,

Old friends are essential in any business, but one must get acquainted with new folks to grow and increase the number of old friends. Right?

This is a greeting from Weatherbest and a personal thank you for the recent order that we believe is the first you have given us.

We appreciate your thinking of us and frankly it is our hope that you will find the quality of the product and the service so satisfactory that you will feel it to your best interests to call upon us real often.

(3)

Dear Reverend _____,

We are indeed glad to say "welcome" and thanks for your order of the 6th, which arrived this morning. The shipping department is working on this order, and will send it to you within the next two days.

It gives us great pleasure to be able to write this letter welcoming you to Reliance, and we sincerely hope that this order will be just the first of many during the year.

(4)

Dear _____,

This letter is our personal representative to shake your hand and welcome you among us. For over 120 years we have been welcoming new customers and making new friends, and we look forward with pleasure to counting you among them, and to serving you with our best efforts.

Since 1841 we have been specializing in coffee; and during that time have learned many things about roasting, blending, packing, and selling. That experience is yours for the asking.

We are waiting to help you in all your coffee problems. Whether it is about bulk coffee, package coffee, or making coffee in a small restaurant or large one, please feel free to call us and see how much we can help you.

There are also many other items in our stock which you will find profitable. Let us be of service. We will do everything possible to please you, so that we may have many years of pleasant business relations together.

The close of this last letter might well be the key thought of any thank-you message—"We will do everything possible to please you, so that we may have many pleasant business relations together." Care should be taken, however, not to let too much emphasis rest on getting *more* orders, to the detriment of the main purpose, which is to show appreciation of the order just received. The goodwill letter that carries a greedy palm outstretched may do more harm than good.

The perfect "thanks-for-your-first-order" letter may accomplish the following purposes, although not all of them may be necessary in every case:

1. Shows appreciation of the order.
2. Welcomes the buyer as a new customer.
3. Tells when the order will be shipped.
4. Assures the customer of a wise purchase.
5. Mentions facts to build confidence in the company.
6. Expresses the desire to *merit* further orders.

Personalizing the sales staff. When new customers are being thanked for an order taken by a salesman or agent, it is good business procedure to work that person's name into the letter. In such cases, it is they who will continue to contact the buyer, and they need every assistance from the company. The mention of the contacting agent's name not only makes him share the appreciation, but it also helps to keep his identity fresh in the mind of the customer. The following letter, Figure 8-11, used by International Salt Company of Scranton, Pennsylvania, features the salesman in the very first sentence.

In a similar way, a letter used by the Lion Oil Refining Company, El Dorado, Arkansas, mentions in the last paragraph the names of the two men who secured the new dealer and who no doubt will continue to work with him.

Because this is your first association with us, Mr. Wiley, we want to thank you for the confidence you have placed in Mr. Hinds, Mr. Clark, and our company. We sincerely believe this is but the beginning of a long and mutually pleasant association between you and our organization.

How a master said "thank you." The business world lost one of its best letter-writers at the death, several years ago, of H.J. Cocking, then sales promotion manager of Quaker City Rubber Company. No matter what the problem, he always came up with a well-nigh perfect letter solution. See how in Figure 8-12.

Figure 8-11

Dear _____,

Our Mr. Walter has thanked you in person for your order of January 3rd, but I also want to thank you on behalf of the company. This is your initial order and I know of no greater kick a sales manager can get than the beginning of business with a new customer.

The signing of an order is an expression of confidence, and I want you to know that we recognize the responsibility we have in maintaining that confidence.

The most important thing to the buyer of any product is the character of the supplying organization; its resources; its facilities; its reputation; and its standards of service.

You have at your beck and call every facility of our company. We would like to be useful to you beyond the mere necessities of business transaction.

The experience and services of the International Salt Research Laboratory are freely available to you in any salt problem you ever may have. We would like to have you use them.

In any emergency when Mr. Walter may not be available, do not hesitate to write, wire, or phone us here at headquarters.

We appreciate your business. We want to continue to deserve it.

The language of Mr. Cocking's letter is simple, one-to-one talking; the spirit is sincerely friendly. No doubt you noticed, too, that he defied tradition with an ususual complimentary close.

The goodwill blitz. Once, a plan was devised by an automotive supply company to literally dazzle their new customers. Four letters—not one—went from the Bowers Battery and Spark Plug Company to welcome new dealers. By the time they had emerged from such a bombardment of goodwill, they must indeed have felt welcome, and about to be favored with unusual service.

The first letter was signed by C.P. Bowers, President. Mr. Bowers told how he personally made the first batteries by hand, and then personally took the trouble to talk to the buyers about them. He assured the new dealer that he was just as eager now to keep in touch with him.

Figure 8-12

Dear _____,

It was just fine of you to send us that nice order for Belting. Thanks a lot.

For the confidence you have place in Quaker and its products, we are very grateful. In return, we shall leave no stone unturned to justify a continuance of that confidence.

You'll always find the Quaker organization happy and ready to give you the fullest measure of assistance, so make your Mechanical Rubber problems ours. Don't feel you'll be putting us to any trouble, because besides selling quality rubber goods, it is our job to create satisfied customers.

Quaker will not forget you after this, your first order. No, Sir! It could not have carried on for 52 years—successfully weathering every business upheaval—were that its policy. This order will be the beginning of a long and pleasant business relationship. Anyway, that's what we shall try to make it.

So kindly think of us the next time you need Mechanical Rubber Goods, and if we can help you in any way, please call on us. Don't hesitate, will you?

Our one desire is to serve you faithfully. More is humanly impossible. Less, we will not tolerate.

The second letter was signed by Roy W. Shreiner, Sales Manager. He talks mostly about service, and how he was ready to help the new dealers make money.

The third letter was signed by John R. Dreibelbis, Production Manager. He tells about the people who worked in the plant, carefully making and testing the thousands of batteries and plugs that were shipped out every few hours. Then he invited the new dealers to visit the plant—see how things are done there.

The fourth letter was signed by C.G. High, Advertising Manager. He talks of the top-to-bottom spirit of service in plant and office; how he wants to help the new dealer by developing prospects. And he asks for suggestions, using the "Help-me—help-you!" approach.

With so much goodwill flowing toward them from important executives in the company, the new customers can hardly help feeling that they have indeed become part of an alert and friendly organization. Does this feeling impel them to push Bowers batteries and plugs? Well, why not? Especially, if some of the other companies happened to give their orders no special attention!

Appreciating old customers. If many companies fail to give proper recognition to orders received from new customers, the number is still insignificant compared to those that pay little or no attention—with never a word of thanks or appreciation—to the "old faithfuls" who continue to buy month after month, year after year. This is shockingly poor business procedure, for the customer neglected today may turn out to be the customer gone over to a competitor tomorrow.

It is human nature to take things for granted, and never to lock the stable until after the horse is stolen. Why worry about satisfactory old accounts which seem so safe and sure, when there is so much new business to fight for? But the sales manager who clings to that kind of thinking is frequently rudely awakened. The customary orders *don't* come in, the salesmen can't explain why they no longer seem welcome, and then the truth comes out—the buyers have simply been persuaded to give their orders to another firm. Of course, this will happen in spite of good sales strategies in a certain percentage of cases, for some turnover among customers in our highly competitive business markets is unavoidable. But if that turnover can be *held down* by some evidence of goodwill and appreciation on the part of the company, surely the effort is worthwhile.

The sad part, too, about the loss of business from lack of customer appreciation is that no company is really indifferent to the value of a good account. Far from it! The steady and consistent buyers who pay their bills promptly and never cause any trouble rate high in the minds of sales executives—but the latter just don't get around to expressing their appreciation in visible form until the fire in the buyers is out.

There is no set routine for showing order appreciation that could be advocated to fit all, or even the majority, of cases. It is very desirable and proper to send a thank-you letter for each order to the occasional buyer, but it would be a foolish waste of time to write a hundred or more times a year to the buyer whose orders are received every day or so. For the latter, a special note of appreciation, sent three or four times a year and signed by major executives, is much more effective. The general rules to follow are that (1) every customer must be contacted often enough to let him know that his orders are sincerely appreciated, and (2) the system be airtight enough to make sure no single customer is denied a share of company recognition.

The following letters thanking old customers for orders are typical of the better sort seen in business correspondence:

(1)

Used by Salisbury & Satterlee Co., Minneapolis

Dear _____,

Habit, custom, even the language of a people, may undergo great changes in the course of a lifetime. Yet one habit, one custom, one old phrase, continues unchanged into the fourth generation of our business.

Even today as we repeat it again to you, it has lost none of the sincerity and depth of responsibility that it carried when Tom Salisbury stepped out on the loading platform to say "Thank You" to that pioneer Minneapolis merchant, first caller at the new factory overlooking Saint Anthony Falls.

Your orders number among the newer and brighter links in that long chain of confidence begun back there in 1877—links which are the driving force of an organization whose responsibility it is to serve you to your complete satisfaction.

The shipment made to you today combines the up-to-date improvements in the bedding industry with the best workmanship our long experience can provide. May it be our privilege to continue to serve you.

Thank you.

(2)

Used by Nicholson File Company, Providence

Dear _____,

Probably at various times you have checked the orders that come into your plant—perhaps you do it every day. I find it interesting to go over the orders we receive—for a dozen files here, a hundred dozen there—every one representing faith in our products and our company.

Every so often, in looking over our records, I have the desire to write to those names on our books—to tell customers like you, Mr. Krueger—that every order for a dozen or a hundred dozen files is important to us, and that we are doing our best to deserve your business.

I hope that if you have any special problem or requirement in your use of files, you will let me know, so that we can give you all the help we can.

(3)

Used by Maurice Weiner, Reading

Dear _____,

Even though I did say it the other day here in the store when you made your purchase, I want to say it again...

"Thank-You!"

I want you to know that I sincerely appreciate your patronage. And remember...now that the sale has been made, Maurice Weiner just *begins* to serve you.

I won't feel that the sale is "closed" until you receive full wearing service and lasting satisfaction from your purchase...until you honestly feel that you have received full value for every dollar spent!

It is my earnest hope that behind this personal service our business relations may long continue.

When possible, it is desirable to tell the buyers exactly when their orders will be shipped or delivered. In some cases, this information can be given in the thank-you letter, in others a simple card or notice can be mailed separately. The procedure tells the buyers their orders are receiving special attention; also, it helps to complete the sale when the order has been taken subject to payment on delivery.

Following-up a sale or service. A business courtesy not extended often enough is contact with the buyers some time after their purchase to find out if they are thoroughly satisfied. Letters of this sort not only show that the company is interested *after* the sale, but they also may result in additional business. Sometimes, too, they unearth faults in the goods or service which need to be corrected. It is not good for business to have dissatisfied customers keep their troubles to themselves, since they are rather sure not to return to the place where they feel they were not well-served. Moreover, if the complaint is legitimate, the reputable company *wants* the opportunity of making things right, and of eliminating the chance of similar difficulties in the future.

From your own experience, however, you know how seldom these after-the-sale contacts are ever made. Perhaps you purchased a new TV a few months ago, maybe a new automobile, or reroofed your home. Last summer you may have purchased oil from a new dealer for your home or factory, had your basement waterproofed, or your yard landscaped. You can think of hundreds of things and services for which you paid out good money during the past year. But how many of the companies that benefited by your patronage took the trouble later to inquire how well you were pleased, or if there could be any additional service they could render? Very few, we'll wager. But if you *did* receive one or more follow-ups of that nature, you were pleased and no doubt said, "Now there's a *good* company."

Follow-up can be sent to companies as well as individual buyers. Here is an example in Figure 8-13.

Figure 8-13

Letter from Standard Register Company

Dear _____,

We are constantly striving to improve our products and service to our customers. This effort is justified because our business must be operated profitably if it is to grow.

I am writing, therefore, to a few customers like you who have installed a new Form Flow Register. We want you to know we deeply appreciate the confidence you already have shown in our company and our products. We believe in our Form Flow Register because we honestly feel that it will give improved service to the user. However, irrespective of how we may view it, we know that its quality can only be determined by the user.

Consequently, while I realize the request may be a little unusual, I am wondering if you would write me personally and frankly, expressing your viewpoint toward this new product. Tell me if it is serving you well, giving you satisfaction, and in general, exactly what you think about it.

Quite often our salesmen relate to us experiences of our users that we can pass along as helpful to other businesses. Possibly you have experienced some unique advantage in the system you are using. It's possible, too, that there may be further applications for registers in your business, or you may know where an application could be installed profitably in some other business—or possibly you would like our representative to make a complete survey of your record system.

At all events, Mr. Smith, I want you to know that I would deeply appreciate a letter from you commenting as has been suggested. May I thank you in advance for your cooperation?

Pressing an advantage in a follow-up. When you have what you feel is a clear advantage over your competition, don't miss an opportunity to press it for future business. One industry that does this type of follow-up extremely well is hotels and motels.

Note the phrases and paragraphs which call guests' attention to the advantages of returning to a particular hotel or chain.

The *Congress* in Chicago uses the opportunity to thank the guest graciously, and also acquaint him with other hotels under the same management. Since the letter is written in February, a special gesture is made toward the resort hotel in New Hampshire.

Dear —————,

Mr. George V. Riley, Manager of the Hotel New Yorker, wrote me urging that I get in touch with you and determine whether or not you enjoyed your recent visit there to the fullest extent. He earnestly hopes you did.

While writing you, I thought it a good opportunity to advise that I am prepared to make advance reservations for you if you are planning to return at any time in the future.

Some of the other fine hotels operated by the National Hotel Management Company, Inc. for which I will be glad to extend this complimentary service, are the Book-Cadillac, Detroit; the Van Cleve, Dayton; the Adolphus, Dallas; the Netherland Plaza, Cincinnati; the Nicollet, Minneapolis; and the Eastern Slope Inn, a fine winter and summer resort in the New Hampshire White Mountains.

I sincerely hope you will give me an opportunity to cooperate with you in this respect.

Cordially yours,

P.S.: Plan now for ski-larks in the White Mountains this winter. Details regarding the Eastern Slope on request.

The *Homestead,* Hot Springs, Virginia, in its letter to the appreciated guest includes a copy of their magazine— "for those of our guests who like to be reminded of us now and then."

Dear Mr. and Mrs. —————,

Every day it's proven to us that The Homestead is hard to forget.

Anyone who has once sampled the way of life which makes The Homestead what it is, who has once been here, can almost certainly be depended upon to want to come back.

And, sooner or later, practically all of them do come back.

You're one of them, you know.

And though your taste of the way of life here may have been brief, we wonder if you didn't catch at least something of its flavor; and if you may not feel, sometimes, that the memory of it is pleasant.

So we'd like to remind you of it; and we're sending you a copy of the little magazine we issue from time to time—in the hope that you'll recapture a bit of the "feel" of The Homestead. "The Spectator" is published for those of our guests who like to be reminded of us now and then—who have, they tell us, pleasure in having their memories of The Homestead renewed.

And in case you're of the same notion, we'll be happy to count you among them. Just send back the postage-collect card, and you'll get "The Spectator" from time to time—as frequently as we issue it.

With Homestead-y greetings,

In Section 4 an occasional urge on the part of a few writers to humanize the complimentary close was mentioned. We can see no objection to the example in the foregoing letter— "With Homestead-y greetings." It seems to fit the style of the message.

5. EXAMPLES FROM SUPPLEMENTARY SALES LETTERS

Inviting the use of other products and services. It is a strange trait of human nature that people may buy their hats in one clothing store, and their shoes in another; may have a checking account in one bank, and a savings account in the one across the street; may buy their letterheads from one printer, advertising booklets from a second, and office supplies from a third. This may be good for business in general, since it tends to scatter the plums, but any company offering a complete supply of products or services naturally wants to get all of the customers' orders.

The reasons why an individual or company passes favors around are numerous, but often the simple fact is that the buyers are not invited to increase the scope of their purchases, nor are they made conscious of opportunities to buy which have not occurred to them. The supplementary sales letter, shown in Figure 8-14 used by the Wilkinson-Grey Company, New York, had a calendar enclosure that listed commodities in which customers might have been interested. Even if the customers didn't know all the items this company offered, the very fact that they were put before them on the calendar might be an urge to buy them.

A similar letter (Figure 8-15) that goes fishing for a bigger catch is one used by the Kimball Laundry Co., Omaha.

Figure 8-14

GOOD MORNING, MR. _____,

As another year rolls around—it is just three years ago today since you made your first purchase—the following questions come to mind.

How can we do more for you? How can we render a better service or a more unusual one? What is there that we can do to make it easier or more pleasant for you to do business with us?

We appreciate your cooperation during these years a great deal and moreso than words can adequately express. May we take this occasion to thank you most sincerely and assure you of our continued effort to do our utmost in serving you to your entire satisfaction?

There are still a few items which we either have not sold you at all or have not sold you recently, and we are taking the liberty of indicating them on the pocket calendar enclosed for your use.

If there is anything further that we can do, Mr. Doe, to justify your placing this additional business with us, kindly do not hesitate to make your suggestions.

Figure 8-15

Dear _____,

You remember poor Oliver Twist, Dickens' little boy who dared to "ask for more," and was held up to the other inmates of the workhouse as a shining example of ingratitude.

In writing you this letter, I am emulating that unfortunate youngster, but hoping you will not visit his punishment upon my head.

To end more briefly than I began, I am grateful for the laundry business you've been sending us, but very, very eager that you should try some of our other services—dry cleaning, for example.

You know that our laundry work is distinguished by a more-than-ordinary amount of care and attention. Please believe that you will be equally delighted with our unusual dry-cleaning service.

Will you try it?

Figure 8-15 reveals the hand of a good carpenter. Even though short, it plainly follows the formula of the Star, the Chain, and the Hook. The reference to Oliver Twist gets *attention,* which quickly becomes *interest* as the story is applied to the writer's desire for "something more." Then to arouse a little desire, the reader is reminded of the quality service she is already getting—followed by the confident, action-impelling question, "Will you try it?" Just as expertly constructed is another try by the same company for more business. See Figure 8-16.

Figure 8-16

Dear _____,

Robert Bruce, hiding in a cave, watched a spider spinning and climbing a web. Time after time the web broke but always the spider began spinning and climbing again, until finally he reached his goal.

Watching this determined fellow, Bruce got renewed courage, emerged from his hiding place, and started his successful "comeback" to the throne of Scotland. Perhaps he or one of his followers coined the old copybook maxim:

"If at first you don't succeed—try, try again!"

Realizing you have a good reason for not giving us your laundry business right now, I don't wish to pester you about it.

But your circumstances may alter—you may need a first-class laundry service—and when you do, I want you to think of Kimball's.

That's why I keep reminding you with these letters—in the spirit of "If at first you don't succeed." I'll keep on trying until your need and one of my letters happen at the same time.

Meanwhile—thanks for the dry-cleaning business you are giving us. It is much appreciated.

Blueprint for getting additional business. A company may increase sales by getting more customers, or by getting larger purchases from those already in the fold. The letters you have just been reading were seeking the second objective—trying to get individuals interested in items they had not been buying. First Alabama Bank in Mobile, Alabama, had the same idea in the use of the three sales letters which follow. Each is directed to people already among the bank's customers, but each seeks to interest them in services of which they are not taking advantage.

(1)

Dear _____,

I was very glad to notice that you opened an account in our Checking Department recently, but we in the Savings Department are wondering if you will permit us to have the pleasure of serving you also. It might be that you could very conveniently use our Savings facilities.

While in the bank transacting other business, it would take only a few more minutes to step around to the Savings Department and make your deposits. These deposits need not be large, but if regularly made they will soon amount to a sizable sum.

For your convenience, First Alabama Bank issues, free of charge, your personal ALERT Card. This permits you to make most banking transactions 24 hours a day. As a member of ALERT, First Alabama Bank offers its customers access to over 270 offices in 31 cities. Further, your ALERT Card will be accepted at other major banks throughout the state of Alabama.

The personnel of my department are constantly working to make and hold friends, and I can assure you that we will do everything we can to make saving with First Alabama Bank a pleasure.

P.S.: Remember, the only thing we have to sell is *service.*

(2)

Dear _____,

You opened a savings account with us about three months ago. By now, we hope you are well-acquainted around the bank, and familiar with the services we provide for customers.

Just to give you a little of the history of the bank with which you are doing business, we were organized in 1901, employing five men. We are located in 31 cities with over 270 offices throughout Alabama employing hundreds of men and women. Your bank is at your service any time and will be glad to discuss business and financial problems with you. Don't think for a moment that you intrude on the time of our officers or employees when you ask for information or advice. They are here for the very purpose of working with you. Ask questions, get all the facts, make use of the facilities that are here at your beck and call, and we predict a better understanding between you and your bank.

Add systematically to the savings account you opened just 90 days ago, thereby building a surplus fund that will increase the joy of living, and make it possible for you to enjoy more fully the good things of life.

We want to see you in the bank often.

(3)

Dear _____,

Everyone has his individual problems, and today, on account of changing conditions, each of us is seemingly confronted with more financial problems than ever before.

You are a friend and customer of First Alabama and, therefore, are privileged to consult us about your banking or any financial business in which you are interested. If you have failed to capitalize on this service, we now invite you to take advantage of every source of information which has been provided for your benefit.

No one person at the First Alabama endeavors to specialize in all lines of banking and finance. But for virtually every problem in these fields, we have a group of fully qualified experts in each diverse area to take care of your requirements.

The savings account that you already have is the avenue to the solution of many difficulties that may arise. By adding to it systematically, and with frequent consultations with us about your financial affairs, a cash reserve fund can be established that will justify every effort on your part.

We are taking an interest in your progress and will assist in any manner possible. Our friendly, qualified, and dedicated people here at First Alabama Bank are always prepared to sell you our only product—*service*.

How to use the "partners in interest" approach. Making your customers feel that they are part of the company goes a long way toward *keeping* their friendship and support. One way to do this is to ask them now and then for criticisms and suggestions—not necessarily as they apply to their own relationships, but also to the company's operations in general.

When you mail a letter asking for suggestions and criticisms, you are accomplishing at least three things: *first,* you give your customers the definite impression that you want to improve your products and services; *second,* you appeal to their pride by the implication that their opinions are considered valuable; *third,* from the replies you will often get something of real value—the knowledge of a weakness you did not suspect, or a practical idea that is worth adopting. But even if the third accomplishment never happened, the first two more than justify the customer contact as a goodwill builder.

A supplementary sales letter of this type is one shown in Figure 8-17. It was used by Guthrie-Morris-Campbell, dry goods merchants of Charleston, West Virginia. Although the letter did not develop any criticisms, it did result in a vote of confidence for the sales staff and the company; there was also the good impression it made on the dealer, as was evidenced by a prompt reply from him.

Figure 8-17

Dear _____,

In looking over Mr. Wood's accounts, we are very glad to note the nice business you have given him, and want to assure you of our appreciation.

However, in view of the somewhat larger volume received from you last year, we are just wondering if any difficulty has arisen which is within our power to remedy.

If you have not received full satisfaction from us in every way, either in merchandise or service, we would deeply appreciate your letting us know about it; not only because of our earnest desire to serve you well individually, but to help us avoid disappointing other customers, if you have discovered a weakness in our operations.

Please understand that we appreciate your continued business even though it is of less volume, but we want to be sure that we are rendering the kind of service you deserve, and will appreciate a word from you as to whether or not anything may have gone wrong.

With fine regards,

A serious problem for many companies is how to control personal contacts made by employees who are working outside the office or plant. It is difficult to know whether or not the contacts are as cordial as the executives in charge want them to be. A very able effort to throw some light on this problem, is a letter used by C.L. Sullivan, head of the

Customers' Department of the Peoples Gas Company, Chicago. The letter is successful in avoiding any suggestion of a behind-the-back check-up of the meter reader. In fact, the reader is included in the request for criticisms after a fine tribute to his work.

> Once a month you are visited by a faithful representative of your gas company. He doesn't stay long because he has many places to go, and he must keep up with a stiff schedule. Day after day, in all kinds of weather, he goes about his job. Just as the actor clings to an old tradition that "the show must go on," so is this man taught that his service to you must be rendered.

> He may not wear fine office clothes, but in his heart he has the same spirit of cooperation that you'll find in all of our employees. He tries to meet you with a smile, to answer your question cheerfully. Not only must he be accurate in what he does for you—but we expect him also to be helpful and courteous.

> Of course, you know this man—the reader of your gas meter. Maybe, you've never given him much thought, but he really is a fine fellow. Some of the most important positions in the Peoples Gas Company are held by people who began by reading meters. And one of their best assets now is that they got to know our customers long before they became executives.

> But, of course, with more than 800,000 meters to read every month, there are many things to try the patience of our meter readers. Sometimes, they may be blamed for mistakes over which they have no control—sometimes, they are just physically tired from a hard day's work in rain, snow, and sleet. So being human, it is not surprising if one of them now and then gets "grumpy" —forgets for the moment that a customer's goodwill can only be earned by cheerful service.

> Once in awhile, we like to ask our customer-friends how they enjoy their contacts with these meter readers. Often, by doing that we get valuable ideas for improving this branch of the service—ideas which the meter reader appreciates just as much as does the company. Or, there may be small wrinkles that need to be ironed out—but we can't do anything about them unless we know what they are.

> So—please, as a favor—will you return the enclosed card and tell us about *your* meter reader? Give him a pat on the back if he deserves it—give him any help in the way of a criticism where you think it is needed.

Needless to say, the foregoing letter does not go in one mailing to more than 800,000 customers. The idea is to "sample" this particular feature of Peoples Gas Company service by contacting a fair cross-section of gas users—sometimes as many as 5 to 10 per cent of the whole number. Meter reading is not the only operation checked, as similar letters are mailed at regular intervals to develop suggestions and criticisms of other types of service. The idea has helped to build the unusually fine reputation held by this company among its customers—it should do the same for any other public-minded organization.

The request for customer opinions does not have to be in the form of a letter, although it may be the most personal. President C.J. Leonard of the M.B. Cook Company, Chicago, once did the job with a two-color double postcard to give the mailing a little added interest. One half of the card was used to invite suggestions and criticisms; the other half was for the customer to mail back to the company. The latter carried the company's permit number, and required no postage except that paid by the company if returned.

Quite properly, for a check-up of this nature, the customer's part of the job was made just as easy as possible; no lengthy questions to answer—just a few lines for him to write on as he pleases.

Putting the customer on the sales force. Another human instinct that the sales-letter writer may legitimately take advantage of is *pride* of possession. John Doe buys a cabin on a nearby lake, and the next day begins to sell his best friend on doing the same. The cabin happens to be equipped with a Jones pump, and that makes John Doe eager to give it a boost. When he cures his ivy poisoning with some Jones lotion, he is eager to tell any other sufferer about it.

It is just natural for any individual to flatter his own judgment by believing his own choices and purchases are best; therefore, it's a sensible sales procedure to ask satisfied customers for the names of friends the company might approach. To be sure, there is one limitation to the use of the plan—the assurance of satisfaction. The unhappy customer is just as quick to attack as the happy one is to defend.

The following two letters go prospecting in a quite capable and tactful manner. As fine examples of business writing, they are worthy of more then casual attention. Note their good points.

(1)

Dear _____,

Since 1919 hundreds of oil burners have come and gone. But Williams Oil-O-Matic—the oil burner that heats your home—has come through these years with its position of leadership stronger than ever in sales, in performances, in prestige. On account of this marked preference for Oil-O-Matic you are a member of the largest owner group in the entire oil-burner industry.

Back of every Oil-O-Matic installation is the world's largest factory devoted exclusively to the manufacture of devices for temperature regulation and control. Back of every Oil-O-Matic is the famous Williams engineering staff and their patent-protected features that you will find on *no other oil burner.*

Aren't these the advantages—the protection—you want for friends and relatives who are now discussing a change to automatic heating? Whether these friends and relatives are making this important change right now—or will in the future—they should know the facts about Williams Oil-O-Matic.

We shall appreciate your taking the time to write on the enclosed card the names and addresses of parties who might be interested in learning more about Oil-O-Matic. Your name will not be mentioned. Just fill in the card and mail—no stamp necessary. This generous cooperation will indeed be appreciated.

(2)

Dear Mr. Aspley:

Did you ever know an advertising man who wouldn't rather fish than work?

Neither did I.

But in order for me to do both I had to figure out a way to combine the two.

So I've bought Normandy Court, on Big St. Germain Lake -- which, according to Merritt Bacon, is the best fishin' hole in the state. Smith McLandress and Jim Whelan, agree that the beach, the woods, the cabins and the atmosphere are just about everything one could wish for.

Mrs. LeRoy, ably assisted, will be responsible for food and the complete comfort of the guests -- IF ANY. That is my job. Of course I'll get up there often enough to go fishing with you, I hope.

But to get back to the guests -- (and you can't run a resort without guests) -- here's where you can help! I want to build up a list of good people to whom I can send an invitation to spend their vacation, or a week end, at Normandy.

Will you trust me with the names of a few of your friends who like to fish or who go North on their vacation? I'll send them a guest card, like the one enclosed, and I'll not use your name unless you say so.

If it's O.K., please do it right now. It won't take but a minute and I can get my work started on time.

It is remarkable how a good letter-job always stands out among others of ordinary rank. Yet if you analyze the reason, it is usually because *all* of the factors that contribute to effective correspondence have been respected. And in this letter, that is what you find: pleasing appearance, natural language, expert carpentry, convincing argument; an interesting personality; and a friendly spirit.

6. SMOOTHING THE WAY FOR YOUR SALES STAFF

Blocking for the ball-carriers. It is much easier for the staff to work confidently with old customers with whom they attained a friendly relationship than to walk cold into new prospects' places of business and talk to them about a possible first order. Consequently, a letter of introduction preceding the call may help immensely in getting them off on the right foot. This letter may be mailed for the new person who has just been assigned to a territory, or it may simply be an ice-breaker for a veteran who is about to call on a prospect he has not met before. In the first case, the letter goes to all customers and live prospects in the territory; in the second, to individual prospects as the salesman personally may direct.

Needless to say, some letters of introduction do a better job than others; the good ones do such an interesting job that the sales staff are pleasantly remembered at the time when they appear on the scene and present their cards. The letter, as seen in Figure 8-18, gives one salesman, "Tom," such a fine build-up that some of the bankers who got it may even have looked forward to meeting him. If so, the effect on sales could hardly help being positive. The introduction was written by Carleton D. Beh, of Des Moines, Iowa, for the company that bears his name.

The part of this letter which is especially sound is that the spotlight is properly placed on the salesman, and not the company. The bankers who got the letter already knew about the Carleton D. Beh Co. and its services—they did *not* know Mr. Ray. Furthermore, enough facts are supplied about the man to make him a personality, rather than just a name. He is an Iowa boy, went to an Iowa High School, and then to an Iowa college. At the latter he played football, a fact that would carry weight in the mind of a sports-minded reader.

Equally successful in setting up a personality for the reader to contemplate is the letter found in Figure 8-19. The first paragraph is as deftly spun as one you might find in a bit of good fiction.

Using pictures to break the ice. Since one of the main purposes of the introduction letter is to get the sales staff and the prospects or

Figure 8-18

Dear _____,

May we introduce our new representative in your territory—Mr. Thomas L. Ray.

Tom is an Iowa product. He completed High School in his home town, Oelwein, Iowa, in 19..—graduated from Cornell College (and its football team), Mt. Verson, Iowa, in 19..—served a year and a half in the School of Hard Knocks—then apprenticed himself to us and the Iowa Municipal Bond business.

If you like industrious, ambitious young men of character, then you'll like Tom. He admits he doesn't know everything so he will be easy to get along with—except on Iowa Municipals—he's very enthusiastic about them. We are depending on Tom to get to know you as we know him, and are pledging our unqualified cooperation to him.

So when a rather tall, dark, and good-looking young fellow of about 24 summers' maturity appears in your Bank in the near future, a kind word and a little initial business will develop a friendship and trust with which we feel you will always be happy.

Figure 8-19

Dear _____,

A light-complexioned man of medium build is about to enter your life. He is not a figment of some fortune-teller's imagination, but a real, live man, who walks and talks. Incidentally, he talks about Smith's valves and he knows what he's talking about.

He's been with us about ten years now, and he likes his job as much as he does his golf. Because of his unusual knowledge of valves, and valve problems, we are putting him in your territory: where a man *has* to know valves.

Mr. Miller, may we introduce our new representative—Mr. J.W. "Jerry" Williamson.

You may expect a visit from Jerry next Thursday morning. In the meantime, you can reach him at Main 1-0123, should you need prices or information of any sort before his call.

---

customers acquainted as quickly as possible, the attachment of pictures help to make the presentation more effective. It doesn't need to be a fancy photograph—just an inexpensive "glossy" or a reproduction like those seen in trade or club bulletins. If the introduction of the person is to be used frequently by letter, it may pay to have a special letterhead made up, with a personal picture in one corner. It is best that the job *not* be too elaborate. The object of the idea is to let the reader *see* the person talked about before the call—it is not to promote a Hollywood star.

The United Autographic Register Co., Chicago, is responsible for the next letter of introduction. (See Figure 8-20.) A small picture of the salesman appeared in the upper righthand corner.

Figure 8-20

Dear _____,

Lately, we've told you a great deal about Uarco registers and manufacturing systems—but we haven't said much about Uarco's very valuable asset, the Uarco man who calls on you.

In some ways he's the most unusual salesman you've ever met. First, he's not a high-pressure salesman. He wouldn't sell you anything on a bet, if he thought for a minute that you wouldn't benefit by the installation.

Second, to use a slang phrase, "he knows his stuff." He knows records and record-writing machines thoroughly. He's trained and has had the experience of dealing with hundreds of different kinds of firms—especially manufacturing.

Third, he's the fellow who will service your registers. And when we say service, we really mean SERVICE. He'll not only help check your supplies, but he'll check your registers every call and see that they are working right. He'll oil them when necessary. And he won't charge a cent.

Finally, he's loyal to his customers and his "house." He's just as proud of Uarco as we are of him—and that's saying a lot. He's glad to be working with a human firm which has been the leader in its line for half a century.

So when Carl Nutter calls on you, please make him welcome. Listen to his story. See what he has to offer. Ask questions and answer his. You'll learn a lot from him—and he, of course, will learn much from you.

Will you please write on this letter, "Sure, I'll be glad to talk with him," and return it in the enclosed envelope?

When the writer of the introduction and the reader are already acquainted in a business or personal way, the request that the salesman be received can be put as a favor—always a difficult appeal to deny. William T. Summers, Jr., does this very well in the following letter written for Graham Brothers, Inc., Los Angeles.

Hello _____!

It has been some time since you and I exchanged greetings over the telephone. Frankly, I have missed hearing from you.

I just wanted to drop you a note to the effect that we have assigned Mr. George Tyson as our Ambassador of Goodwill to your office. George is a newcomer to our Sales Department after two years' training in other departments here at the office. In fact, one of his positions with our company was in our own Purchasing Department. From this experience he has gained a true appreciation of your problems and will give them proper consideration in his visits with you.

I will consider your giving George a pleasant reception a personal favor. Do not hesitate at any time to call on me for anything I can do to repay your courtesy.

Helping overcome sales resistance. Unfortunately, a salesman is too often regarded as a necessary evil—a pest carrying a gold brick and blessed with lungs that never wear out. The prospect who holds such a notion is always on the defensive and determined not to be high-pressured. It is a false concept, for the average sales staff is genuinely interested in the service they can render. Nevertheless, it's quite prevalent.

A letter which attempts to pass this barrier by displaying the salesman as a conscientious helper is one used by the Keystone Chemical Co., Inc., Cleveland. Notice, too, how the writer avoids a formal salutation.

When Paul _____ Calls on You—

Please don't feel that he's there to match wits with you and high pressure you into placing an order. True, his job is to sell Keyspray and other products in our line, but his first obligation is to anaylze your specific requirements and make intelligent recommendations.

We have found that this policy works to the advantage of all concerned. It has revealed and eliminated conditions that were a serious handicap to dealers' sales and profits. It has placed the purchasing and use of insecticides and sanitation supplies on a more efficient and economical basis. And in recognition of this helpful cooperation and the recognized value of Keystone products, it has favored us with preferred consideration.

So we say, when Paul calls on you, please feel free to take him into your confidence. He is a specialist in his particular line, sincere and conscientious, and will be only too glad to work with you if you will give him that opportunity.

How to facilitate changes in personnel. You could scarcely ask for better examples of customer relations, conducted tactfully and with the sincere will-to-please, than two letters written by H.J. Cocking to handle a common problem in business—the death of a popular salesman, and the selling of the man selected to take his place. Too often in this situation there is a loss of business during the period of transition, but in this case the loss is avoided.

Letters About Salesman's Death

Dear ⸻,

It is my sad duty to inform you that our Mr. John Doe, who has been calling on you for so many years, died very suddenly Tuesday night, February 13th.

Mr. Doe was with us for over 20 years and we are certainly going to miss him. His death will be a significant loss to the whole Quaker Organization.

He leaves a wife and daughter to mourn his loss, as well as a host of friends who will miss his regular calls and friendly cooperation.

You have done your job well, Mr. Doe, and the least we can do is to remember the thoughts of a brother worker, "God bless you, Mr. Doe…and happy landings."

But we must carry on. So may I ask, until we can replace Mr. Doe, that you kindly send us your inquiries and orders direct? You may rest assured we shall do everything possible to warrant a continuance of your friendship.

Dear ⸻,

Since Mr. John Doe's sudden death, we have interviewed several men to carry on his good work. Now we are glad indeed to tell you that we have engaged Mr. Edward Jones who will call on you on behalf of this company.

You'll find Mr. Jones a likable chap and I'm sure he'll leave no stone unturned to help you in every way he can. He knows the

Mechanical Rubber Goods line very well and has had a lot of hard selling experience.

At first, perhaps, you won't feel the same toward Mr. Jones as you did toward Mr. Doe...that's only natural. You knew Mr. Doe so well for so many years, and, like ourselves, had a world of confidence in him. But these changes cannot be helped, and we feel confident you will give Mr. Jones a break. You will help him all you can, won't you?

You know, it's pretty hard when a man first tackles a territory. A little encouragement goes a long way, so please extend him the glad hand. Breaking the ice is a bit tough, hence this letter.

I sincerely hope your business is good right now, and thanks a lot for the business you gave us through the late Mr. Doe. If there is anything we can do to help while Mr. Jones is getting into his stride, rest assured we'll be ever so glad to do it, and we mean every word of it, too.

Of course, there are many other reasons why it is necessary to change sales representation—inefficiency, insubordination, promotion, resignation, and all the rest. But whatever the circumstances, the primary purpose of the announcement is usually to win goodwill for the new salesman, and thus help him get adjusted as quickly as possible. Turnover is always expensive to business; the problem is to hold the cost down as much as possible. Figure 8-21 is typical of the sort that are satisfactory when no special problem is involved.

Figure 8-21

Dear _____,

Mr. Bruce Bell, our salesman who solicited your business personally, is no longer connected with us.

Mr. Bell has entered business for himself and while we wish him every success, we want you to know that your orders are appreciated and noticed at Brunner's. We intend to give you the same service, quality, and reasonable prices as we have in the past.

Mr. Walton Wilder, who is taking Mr. Bell's place, will call on you at regular intervals. Although Mr. Wilder is not entirely familiar with the printing business, I know you will find him always on the job, ready to be of service to you. Any favors shown him will be highly appreciated by me.

I want you to feel free to call on me at any time that I can personally be of assistance to you.

How to tackle tricky transitions. Whenever one salesman enters a territory or one leaves, there is always a ripple effect on your customers. In one case, they tell you they do not want Salesman A to leave and how can you, Mr. Company XYZ, be so stupid as to allow this travesty to commerce happen. In another instance, your salesman's leaving is greeted with applause (probably the reason you relieved him of the territory!) and 400 suggestions came in on who should now fill the position. (Their Aunt Mazie's second *oldest* boy heads the list.) There is one other case that arises—the territory gets a new salesman. This occurs through either replacement or addition. If replacement, your customers will give you feedback as to the wisdom or senility of your choice; in addition, you may wonder if the new salesman ever arrived because the customers are only talking about the veteran who has been in their territory for the past ten years.

All these Tricky Transitions can be smoothly handled by well-constructed letters of introduction. First, relying upon the power of a letter to be your personal contact with your customers, go right in their offices and *tell* them of a change and why you're making it. Be sure to let them know that you're only making the change to serve *them better.* Second, take the customers into your confidence by asking for their assistance in making the "New Kid" welcome. Always show your sales staff in the best light possible. In these memos you cannot criticize your past salesman, but rather, give the good points of the incoming one. (Caution—just because the salesmen are new to the territory, never let your customers think they are new to the business.) Give *all* of their qualifications in the first introductory letter.

In the next set of letters, let the new members of the sales staff speak for themselves. This permits a little more personal tone in the message, and, if the letter is carefully worded to avoid the appearance of conceit or flippancy, it can make a very good impression on your customers. The cap to this campaign to handle a tricky transition is the formal company announcement of Salesman A's arrival in Territory X. This may be in a letter such as the one shown in Figure 8-20, or an "announcement card" format as seen in Figure 8-22.

With these introductory letters to smooth the way for your sales force, your business will never be interrupted or your customers inconvenienced by necessary adjustments in personnel.

7. FOLLOWING UP THE SALES CALL

Keeping the gate partly open. Very few sales are consummated on the first call, nor is such a happy event to be expected. There are numerous reasons to prevent it. The prospect may have in stock adequate supplies of all the merchandise of the kind being offered; he may be tied to a competitive company by many years of friendly dealing; he may have been too busy at the time of the call to give the merchandise fair consideration; he may have had previous relations with the company that were not satisfactory; he may have been impressed the wrong way by the approach; any of these reasons or numerous others may have kept the gate at least partly closed.

But so what? If selling were so easy that one call would usually win the order, a good sales staff would not be needed. Closing a sale—especially with a new customer—is like winning a prize-fight. In the first round, prospect and salesman are sparring against each other: the salesman to discover what the opponent needs that matches what he has to offer; the prospect to form an opinion of the salesman and his line, so that he may know how to proceed in later rounds. The fight may be a draw for several rounds, but only a knockout can end it. The salesman may have to take considerable punishment for awhile; his chances of victory may appear hopeless. But if he is a salesman and not an order-taker, he keeps on plugging. The harder the fight, the more he enjoys it. Victory is sweeter when hard-won. A good salesman never throws in the towel—but his trainers back in the office *can* help him.

Sales managers of the better sort do not turn their staff loose to succeed or fail by their own efforts. Instead, they back them up with a barrage of sales helps direct from the home office. These helps include letters to the prospects that may add to the arguments already advanced by the staff or, at least win a little goodwill for their next call.

Of course, the obstacles encountered by the sales staff are never the same in two or more cases. They may report that the prospects were pleasant but noncooperative; that objections were produced which they were not prepared to answer; or that the best they could get was a flat refusal with the pointed implication that any further calls would be a waste of time for both parties. In other words, after the first call, the gate may be partly open or it may be closed tight—and the follow-up letter from the office is dictated according to whatever situation may prevail.

Thanking a prospect for the interview. The simplest follow-up letter to write is the one in which the chances of getting an order are still considered good. There are no special complications, and the salesman is optimistic about eventually making the sale. Some sales managers seem to think that in such cases follow-up letters are unnecessary, but this is not straight thinking. A friendly letter of thanks for the interview may go a long way toward making the second call more productive; certainly, no sale can be hindered by an expression of goodwill from the home office. Instead, such a letter tends to create in the prospective customers' minds the idea that they have been contacted by a well-organized company, alive to sales opportunities, and eager to cooperate with its salesman.

Let us look at a few follow-ups of the salesman's interview that may be called typical and satisfactory. The first of these letters, Figure 8-22, has the added advantage of an enclosure which is both effective and unusual: a "Taxicab Pass" the prospect may use for trips to the plant. This is factual evidence of company appreciation used to supplement the words in the message. The idea is that of the Central Pattern & Foundry Co., Chicago.

Figure 8-22

Dear ——————,

William Zint, our representative in your territory, has told us about the interview you granted him. He appreciated your courtesy a lot, and so do we.

Although new in your territory, Bill is by no means a new man in the aluminum, brass, and bronze casting business. He has been with our company for nearly nine years, in every department—through the factory, office, sales, and inspection units— and is thoroughly educated in the nonferrous casting business.

After you have met him a couple of times, you will realize as we do that you can rely on his knowledge of castings and their uses—rely on his promises. He's a dependable, regular fellow.

And Bill knows, as we want you to know, that "Central" will back up any promise he makes, and every casting he sells.

Why don't you let Bill or one of our staff show you around the next time you have a free afternoon. Please use the attached pass. We look forward to seeing you.

A second neat follow-up is shown in Figure 8-23. Here it seems the salesman didn't get very far, so his efforts are supplemented by the offer of a catalog. It could have been mailed with the letter, but the psychologists tell us that it is better to make people *ask* for things, instead of offering unsolicited gifts. The request assured a closer inspection.

Figure 8-23

Dear _____,

We are grateful to you for the courtesies that you extended to Mr. Rolfe when he called on you last Thursday.

He has told us of his talk with you and said that you were not quite ready to consider buying at the time of his call. It's not always possible for a representative to drop in at exactly the right time, but we want you to know that whenever you're ready, we're ready to serve you.

We have a new catalog that we shall be glad to send on if you wish. It lists many different styles of eye-protectors for every purpose. Lenses can be had for any and every need. Along with the catalog we can send you prices so that you would find it convenient to select items you might be in need of before Mr. Rolfe's next call.

Feel free to call on us at any time that we may be able to render you a service. We shall welcome the opportunity to serve you.

Writing follow-ups that sell. If you, in your follow-up, feel you want to confirm something your salesman told the prospect, you might want to emulate the style found in the following letter excerpt.

The courtesy and consideration you gave Mr. Hearst are sincerely appreciated. Thank you so much, too, for taking the time to discuss your requirements with him.

Mr. Hearst spoke very highly of your place and he also mentioned that you enjoy a very fine reputation for serving T-Bone, Porterhouse, and Sirloin steaks. The quotations he has asked us to confirm are as follows.

(Four items priced)

Figure 8-24. Smooth Follow-Up to Sales

Dear _____,

We were indeed pleased to learn that our representative, Mr. Oscar Meyers, had the pleasure of calling on you and of discussing our merchandise.

Apparently your stock was complete, but merely the fact that an order was not obtained on his first call does not discourage us; selling is not his entire mission. The important thing is that his visit brought Schuylkill Valley Mills to your attention.

As a keen buyer you know that hosiery retailing is gradually emerging from the destructive price market into which it had degenerated during the past few years, and is rapidly shaping into channels of carefully planned merchandising campaigns based on economically sound principles.

You know that profitable operation demands low stocks which turn frequently. Schuylkill has specifically designed its services to cater to the present-day requirement of the retailer demanding maximum turnover on a minimum investment.

There is probably nothing we might add to what Mr. Meyers has already told you about the exceptional and unvarying quality of our hosiery and its possibilities from a sales and profit standpoint. Mr. Meyers will call on you at regular intervals and an opportunity to convince you of our ability to serve you promptly and efficiently will be indeed appreciated.

Paving the way for another call of the salesman is a task easily handled by a well-constructed follow-up letter. Sometimes the prospect is not available when a member of your sales staff calls. Letters, such as the few excerpted below, show your continued interest in the prospects' business as well as letting them know your sales representative will return at a more convenient time.

> You were away from the store when our representative, Walter Manning, was there a few days ago.
>
> •   •   •   •   •   •   •
>
> Since missing the folks who do the buying is not an unusual occurrence in a salesman's life, James Griffen, our sales rep, left cheerfully with thoughts of better luck next time. But we'd like to leave just one thought with you, which perhaps will save some time for you and him on his next visit.

.   .   .   .

On such a beautiful day as we had last Monday, it wasn't surprising that our John Samson found you away at Grover's Lake doing some fishing. That's the difficulty we all have in the recreational equipment business; we can't wait to try out each new product. Next time, why don't you take John and our new X-12 Bass Tamer with you.

Remember, your follow-ups are actually sales letters so don't lose the opportunity to "sell." On this point, see Figure 8-24. It is a fine example.

When you learn from your sales staff that a large order is out just waiting for the right "close," a good quick note to the potential buyer can lend a helping hand. It should be friendly and sincere, not pushy or frantic, because you don't actually have that order yet. The letter shown in Figure 8-25 shows how to help a salesman over the high barriers of a major order.

Needless to say, no sales staff can sell *all* prospects, and no amount of supplementary letters can achieve that miracle for them. But like the steady drops of water that eventually carve a channel in hard rock, consistent sales effort may often land what seemed to be an impossible victory. The sending of just one follow-up to a sales call may be totally inadequate. The field and the office may have to make many attempts before they reach the sale, but sometimes they can and *do* get there.

The difficulty of writing the follow-ups to a specific prospect increases with the number that have to be mailed. The writer can't say the same thing over and over. This may be a good thing, even if it does add some worries, since the need of new approaches may eventually bring forth the one that does the job. There is a case on record of one businessman who wrote a sales letter once a week for 49 weeks—all to the same prospect—before he got an order. But the order was big enough to pay for all the trouble.

It is a strange twist of human nature that sometimes they may yield to some simple little appeal, although they couldn't be budged an inch by more elaborate and thorough prodding. For example, John M. Palmer, Sales Manager for the Lee Clay Products Company, Clearfield, Kentucky, strikes a new high in simplicity with the following successful gem of a letter.

Dear Mr. Andrews:

Did you ever know the source of that old expression, "an elephant never forgets"?

Somebody said it and it is a safe bet that in his spare time, apart from originating pat sayings, he was a Sewer Pipe Salesman.

Figure 8-25

Dear _____,

I certainly thank you for the courtesies you have shown Mr. Lester Leach, our sales representative, during his recent visits with you. Les has just recently been transferred to the Sales Department after spending two years in other work with our company.

Naturally, he wants to make good and your pleasant reception has done much to build up his ambition and courage. It is our sincere desire that his calls result in a profit to your company.

We have asked our friends in Santa Barbara to furnish us with prices for you on the job you are figuring there. Just as soon as we get this information we will ask Mr. Leach to bring it to you. This should be in your hands not later than Wednesday.

Just a word in passing about Grahamixed Concrete. We realize that you have a considerable investment in mixing equipment and that naturally you want to derive a profit from your capital outlay. However, there may be times when the moving of a mixer from one job to another might cause inconvenience or a greater expense than by the use of Grahamixed Concrete.

In these or any other instances we will be glad to give you the best price possible on the quality of concrete you need. As almost every job is different in nature, we prefer to figure each one on its individual merits and quote accordingly.

Just as soon as possible, I want to thank you personally for your courtesy to Mr. Leach and our company. Until then, I wish you the best of success in all your undertakings.

Dale Boyd is no elephant...doesn't even own a trunk...but he keeps writing me to remind you that for the past year or more he has been expecting an order from you like nobody's business.

Why don't you give Dale a break and send us your next order for a mixed car of Sewer Pipe and Flues?

Yes, that's the whole of it, and the appeal is in the one question, "Why don't you give Dale a break?" But it may be a stronger appeal than some businessmen imagine. Any thoughtful person welcomes the opportunity to help somebody else—call it the feel of power, if you must. However, you will find that most follow-ups to a stubborn prospect run long and factual. The writer tries to review all the major sales advantages in the hope of finding a new slant that may do the job better.

In a clear-headed, factual way, James Timmer, the Correspondence Manager for Federal Hardware & Implement Mutuals, replied to the objection which had cost one of their salesmen a sale—that the prospect had decided to stick with a local New York agent from whom he had gotten good service. (See Figure 8-26.)

As you can see, the tone is extremely good. At no point does Mr. Timmer seem to argue with the prospect, or to challenge her loyalty to the local agent. Instead, he begins by agreeing with her— "That

Figure 8-26

Dear _____,

I want to express my thanks for the courtesies extended to our representative.

C.C. Jackson tells us that you are staying with your local agency for the present, at least, because you feel that they have been giving you good service. That certainly is a very commendable reason.

The Federal Mutuals realize that there is no substitute for service. That is why no Federal salesman, regardless of previous insurance experience, is permitted to enter the field until he has been thoroughly trained in property insurance coverages. Properly written insurance results in prompt and satisfactory settlement of losses. Over 90 per cent of our losses are settled within two weeks.

Then, too, we have fire protection engineers who periodically inspect all of our mercantile and manufacturing risks. If any hazards exist, recommendations are made for their removal. This minimizes the possibility of loss and frequently results in lower rates.

So you see, Mr. Doe, we are equipped to give you as good service as any other insurance carrier. In addition, we can save you 30 per cent of the premium on your Fire Insurance and 40 per cent on your Windstorm Insurance, based on our present dividend schedule.

Before your next Property Insurance policy expires, we would like to demonstrate, with our Program Plan, what Hardware Mutual service is. The enclosed card will bring you this service without any obligation.

certainly is a very commendable reason"—and that is always sound sales psychology. Then, after stressing the services rendered by his own company, he plays his ace of trumps—the respective savings of 30 and 40 per cent, which it seems the prospect did *not* enjoy from her current protection. In the face of these circumstances, the average person would think twice before again renewing the old policy.

When the office and the field work together in digging for sales, the teamwork pays off in profits and volume.

Thanking the long-time customer. A very delightful customer contact is a letter of appreciation. The occasion is the fine treatment given a salesman by the customer, and the letter is a goodwill gesture that many a sales executive might easily overlook. The last paragraph especially should leave a pleasant impression not soon forgotten by the reader. This letter rates high as an example of the kind of customer appreciation which leads to more orders.

Dear Mr. Fredricks,

While Mr. John P. Sherman was getting ready to leave St. Louis for Kalamazoo and we were discussing the territory with him, we came across your name.

We told Mr. Sherman, of course, that you were one of the oldest and most faithful customers of ours in the entire southern Michigan district. He knew, therefore, that when he walked into your store for the first time, he could do it with the confidence that he would be meeting a man who thinks the same way we do about giving good values to his customers.

Mr. Sherman just reported his first visit with you the other day. He enjoyed it very much, _____, and we want to thank you for being so cordial and courteous to a stranger and making him feel at home in your city.

It is nice to have some occasion to write you without discussing shipments, orders, prices, etc. Incidentally, Mr. Fredericks, we hope you end this year with a mighty fine volume of retail sales that will show you a healthy net profit.

The keynote of the above letter is the first sentence of the last paragraph—"It is nice to have some occasion to write you *without* discussing orders...." A letter contact which has no motive except an expression of goodwill carries many times the weight of one where the writer is obviously seeking to feather his own nest. "Unnecessary" contacts of this sort build the friendship and respect that keep customers in the fold. Sales executives should take time to write more of them.

Following-up an executive's call. Now and then every alert sales manager likes to rub shoulders with customers and important prospects in the field. These personal contacts are of great help to the salesmen, and they also tend to give the office executives a broader perspective on sales problems.

The multiple advantages to the letters following the executive's calls were beautifully summarized in a letter addressed to me by George J. Hendricks, a divisional sales manager for a rug manufacturer. The different print highlights his prints and was not in the original.

Friend _____,

Sales managers, as you know, often make trips into the field to contact their salesmen, at which time important buyers are seen.

Good business policy suggests that the executive follow his visit with a letter to the buyer for the purpose of *creating greater goodwill.* Few of these letters, however, attempt to do a merchandising job.

I'm enclosing four letters which follow the executive's call on buyers which are far more productive than the usual kind. Note how *they credit the buyer with freshening the executive's viewpoint.* Note how *they praise the buyer for some one thing he has accomplished.* And then note how *they seek to tie the line into the store's activity.*

Most buyers, I find, have some pet business hobby. In retailing, it is usually some phase of merchandising, either sales training, store layout, display, or advertising.

A glance about the store, or a few minutes' talk with the buyer brings out the phase of selling in which he is particularly interested. *A few pointed questions will get the buyer to talk about it. It is no trouble to note down afterward the high points of the talk or to write on these points after the return to the office.*

Note that the paragraph of the letters are formed, except the third and fourth. This method reduces dictation time to the absolute minimum. A new form can be prepared following every trip.

I think that the effectiveness of the letter lies in these facts: Ask a man—point blank—to do a thing, and he balks like a mule. But *give him a pat on the back first—then ask him to do that very same thing—and he goes to work with a will.* Which just goes to prove that regardless of the size of our ego, we poor humans are starved for praise.

It's a shame, too, for it is easy to praise when praise is merited—and makes a man work so much the harder.

I hope you like the letters—also, the philosophy. With best good wishes,

Bravo to the comments of this sales manager! He knows the philosophical undercurrents of selling. Let the buyer know, he says, that something in which he is particularly interested has captured the visitor's attention. This places buyer and customer on the same side of the fence—makes the former more receptive to the latter's suggestions. Figures 8-27 and 8-28 are two of the four messages that Mr. Hughes mentions; form letters *can be personalized* by changing one or more paragraphs.

Although, as Mr. Hughes explained, the use of the semi-form letter in making these dealer follow-ups cuts dictation time to a minimum,

Figure 8-27

Dear Mr. Godwin,

I can't resist the impulse to write and tell you how much I appreciated the talk I had with you when I was in your store several days ago.

Somehow or other—a fellow grows stale sitting at a desk on a job like mine, and all too often loses the retailer's viewpoint. But your clear merchandising ideas did a whale of a lot in giving me a fresh grasp of up-to-date retailing policies.

These two paragraphs changed to fit the conditions met in the respective retailer's store.

I was particularly impressed with the artistry of your newspaper advertising. I can easily understand why your ads have pulling power, and why they pay for themselves many times over.

I cannot help but feel that a Deltox Rug ad, used whenever you offer a suite for less than $400, would help a lot in making your fibre rug sales more profitable.

I don't get away from the office very often, but when I plan my next trip, I shall do so with the thought of meeting you again.

With best good wishes,

Figure 8-28

Dear Mr. Webber,

I can't resist the impulse to write and tell you how much I appreciated the talk I had with you when I was in your store several days ago.

Somehow or other—a fellow grows stale sitting at a desk on a job like mine, and all too often loses the retailer's viewpoint. But your clear merchandising ideas did a whale of a lot in giving me a fresh grasp of up-to-date retailing policies.

The other letter put a finger on newspaper advertising. This one talks about furniture set-ups.

I was particularly impressed with your set-ups of furniture in the store to create the impression of model rooms. I can see why they would cause people to want to buy more things than they had planned to buy before entering the store.

I cannot help but think that a Delroyal Rug or two in those room set-ups would help a lot in speeding up the sale of Deltox Rugs.

I don't get away from the office very often, but when I plan my next trip, I shall do so with the thought of meeting you again.

With best good wishes,

they still give the impression of being completely personalized. In every respect they are personal and friendly, and the plug for Deltox rugs is made in a way that could not offend.

8. HELPING YOUR SALES FORCE SELL

Keeping the kettle warm. Keeping the sales and contacts of popular salesmen when they are off their beat always is an ever-present sales problem. The people who pitch for them during their absense cannot be expected to know the respective needs of the buyers, or be acquainted with their buying habits. But if they throw wild, much loss to the company can be the result. For example, let us suppose that a popular salesperson has become ill. Sometimes a buyer, looking forward to the time when the sick salesman will recover, holds up an order. This loyalty speaks well for the salesman, but a customer not buying is never too safe under the fire of competitors. A letter from the sales manager or president may be of considerable help to both the substitute salesman and the company.

The best appeal is one which instills sympathy for the incapacitated salesman. Assurance that, as before, full credit for orders sent directly to the office, or even given to the substitute, will be credited to the absent salesman's account will make the buyers feel they have retained their loyalty. A letter once used by Vernon S. Porter, a managing director, clearly illustrates this approach. (See Figure 8-29.)

Getting the best from letters preceding a salesman's call. All salesmen know that it is usually better to walk into a buyer's office or store at a previously announced date than to barge in on him without warning. An exception might be when the salesman knows he is not wanted, but in that case the call would probably be a waste of time anyway. Many salesmen handle their own announcements of future calls: some of them on their own initiative because they have found it worthwhile; others simply go as directed and announced by the sales

Figure 8-29

Dear _____,

We are very sorry to advise you of the indisposition of our representative, Mr. A.K. Jones, which has resulted in his removal from his home to the County Hospital, Oldborough.

It is still too early to give you any very definite news, except that the patient is relieved to be in the hospital with the benefits of specialized treatment.

Mrs. Jones is, of course, keeping us posted with bulletins, and inquiries can be made to her home address or to Miss Isherwood of our Telephone Department, Aldergate Street.

During his indisposition, Mr. A. Sutherland is traveling the territory on his behalf. Mr. Sutherland is young, but we think you will find that he makes up for this in keenness and enthusiasm. He has been in training in the House for some six months, and has a thorough groundwork in our merchandise.

We should like to explain that Mr. Jones receives full commission for all orders taken by Mr. Sutherland on his behalf. We hope you will be good enough to extend to Mr. Sutherland the courtesy always accorded the regular Maw representative.

We ask for your valued support during this period.

manager, or some assistant. Unfortunately, many companies have no routine at all for announcing the calls of salesmen and leave them to sink or swim without this practical sales help.

A very simple practice where salesmen call regularly on old customers is to supply them with postcards, to be mailed a few days ahead of their arrival. This works very well for salesmen who are detail-minded and can be trusted to carry out the assignment, but there are few sales forces blessed with men who can consistently do this. Another weakness of the plan is that the card serves simply as an announcement, and cannot serve also to point out a sales feature or two that might be pertinent at the time of the call. The last purpose is best accomplished by a letter from the home office, although it involves a more systematic control and coordination of the salesman's time than some companies are willing or able to supply.

A typical letter is the one shown in Figure 8-30, in which the salesman discusses the need of teamwork in selling, with a boost for himself and the way he plays the game.

When a sales manager knows a reader well enough to use a first name, he can write more frankly than to customers with whom no intimate contacts have been made. In a following letter, Figure 8-31, no punches are pulled, but the closing words, "Thank you, Roy" indicate a relationship to justify the tone of the body content. The mailing was made for printers Hederman Brothers, Jackson, Mississippi, by C.B. Bardwell, Supervisor of Sales.

Casting the die: letters to those who won't see the salesman. Some salesmen are more gifted than others in slipping around the barriers that are set up to keep them from the individuals who have the authority to buy. The difficulty, of course, varies in different companies, depending on the amount of red tape in the purchasing department, the disposition of the buyer, and the general attitude of the company personnel toward the public. As a rule, business executives do not like to go over the head of the person who may be blocking a salesman, because the act is sure to be resented and may cause additional trouble. When a buyer simply will not talk to the salesman, and the latter has repeatedly failed to gain an interview, a letter to the proper executive may unravel the tangle; at least, it is worth casting the die on the assumption that there is everything to gain and nothing to lose.

The writing of such a letter is not a job for the novice, but one for the good letter-carpenter. There is hardly any problem in business correspondence that provides a greater test of the writer's diplomacy. Figure 8-32 shows how H.J. Cocking, when Sales Promotion Manager of

Figure 8-30

Dear _____,

At the start of the football season, I was watching two West Coast elevens battle.

A back on one of the teams, a runt of a fellow, kept breaking through for long gains. The spectators were praising him to the skies—giving him all the credit for the yards gained.

But I noticed that this little fellow had very little to do with evading tacklers. His teammates opened the holes for him, and all he had to do was grab the ball and run.

As the score became topheavy, I lost interest. My thoughts turned to sales, but the subject of teamwork stuck in my mind.

After all, selling is a 50-50 proposition. When I sell you a bill of goods, you still have the job of reselling. Conscious of this fact, I reason things out this way:

> If I attempted to sell you certain merchandise knowing the goods would not resell easily, I would be a poor teammate.

> Yet, when other stores, similar to yours, are doing a good selling job in given lines, I feel I am practicing good teamwork in stressing these lines during visits with you.

In other words, when I encourage the purchase of items I have good reason to believe will resell easily, and discourage the purchase of others, I feel I earn the right to continue playing on your team. And we both gain more ground!

Incidentally, I shall be seeing you in a few days to show you a few things which will make me a better teammate of yours.

---

the Quaker City Rubber Company, Philadelphia, matched his wits against those of the stubborn buyer.

What are the appeals that might impress the buyers? Analyze the letter, Figure 8-32, for a moment.

1. Mr. Cocking tries to arouse a little sympathy for the salesman—"He seemed a little hurt, too"—with the added compliment that the reader knows how salesmen are.

2. He refers to Bill as a good fellow, and as one who knows his line thoroughly.

Figure 8-31

Dear _____,

Down on the corner, just a block from where I am sitting, is a grocery store. Next Saturday, if you will send me the money, I'll step down there and buy your groceries for the next week, and then send them up to you.

What? You say that you have a grocery store in your own town, and that you prefer to buy at home and help your grocery man instead of the one in my town? I can hear you say "No" from here; and you are telling me that your first interest is to buy what you can where it will help build up your own community. That is exactly as it should be. Since your first interest is in your local community, then your next interest must be in the welfare of your state.

Our salesman has been calling on you regularly every five or six weeks and the records show that we have been favored with only a small portion of your business. We want you to know that we appreciate the portion that shows on our books, but we would like to have more. Our equipment is as good as money can buy, our product is as good as can be made anywhere, and our service is clicking with other customers. They buy regularly, so it must be good.

Mr. Walters is going up to call on you about November 5th, and before he gets there, what about looking over your stock, and jotting down a list of all the special ruling, lithographing, and other jobs that have been going to out-of-state firms? Just hand the list to Bob when he gets there. We'll get it in the next mail, and we'll do the work.

Thank you, Roy.

---

3. He compliments the reader again with the words, "a busy executive like yourself."

4. He plays the trump card—you want *your* salesman extended the same courtesy.

5. He announces Bill's next call with the confident tone of expectation that he will get his interview.

6. He says that Bill's story will be short, and adds another compliment—"He realizes your time is valuable."

Figure 8-32

Dear _____,

Bill Robinson, our salesman in your territory, was at my desk this morning and told me he has never been able to get your ear for a single moment. He seemed a little hurt, too—you know how salesmen are.

Bill is a good fellow and a hard worker—knows the Mechanical Rubber Goods line as well as any fellow I know—so I told him I'd write to you to try to break the ice, as it were.

Of course, I explained to Bill that it isn't always convenient for a busy executive like yourself to see a salesman, especially when he drops in without any previous announcement.

I also told him that most officials are very liberal in granting interviews—because they expect the same courtesy to be extended their own salesmen—which is only right.

So with this little kink ironed out, Mr. Robinson will call on you November 10th, and if you can conveniently do so, I will certainly appreciate your giving him a few minutes. His story will be brief and to the point. He realizes your time is valuable.

Under another cover I am sending you a catalog. Should you desire samples and prices on anything listed, please use the toll-free 800 number which appears on the cover.

For the courtesy extended Mr. Robinson, please accept our thanks.

7. He thanks the reader for his courtesy—again implying it will be forthcoming.

8. At no time does he appear to be angry, nor does he insinuate the reader has not been playing fair.

Measured by results, the letter was completely satisfactory; the salesman got his interview, and came out of it with a sizable order. Another letter to smoke out the recalcitrant buyer, with the added appeal that the reader cannot afford to disregard something important to his company, is one dictated by W.T. Quimby and shown in Figure 8-33. Instead of setting a definite date for the interview, however, the writer says that the salesman will telephone for an appointment. This may be more tactful, but it gives the buyer another chance to dodge the issue.

Figure 8-33

Dear _____,

I have before me a sales report from our Mr. R.R. Roberts, who has tried several times recently to talk to you on the subject of screw pumps.

While we realize that an executive in your position is a very busy man and one whose time is exceedingly valuable, we also are confident that you would be one of the first to want to know if there were changes which could be made in your plant which would reduce maintenance and upkeep and save you money on your pumping equipment.

Mr. Roberts reports that he has been very courteously received by your employees. He feels, however, that the message which he has is of sufficient importance to justify your personal attention, and I agreed to write to you on his behalf for an appointment so that he can lay the facts before you.

In order not to inconvenience you, Mr. Roberts will call your office the early part of next week, and if you would leave instructions with your secretary as to what day and time is best for you, it will not be necessary to disturb you until the time of his arrival.

A sales director at Prentice Hall uses rather different tactics. The letter, Figure 8-34, is a summary of the reasons why the teachers were missing important help by not being allowed to see the salesman. Of course, he realizes that his reader is the man who refused the interview, but he is careful never to express that thought. The primary purpose of his message is to get a more favorable reception for the salesman on his next regular call.

Letter aids for salesmen, and for other purposes, are by no means limited to these illustrations. It is important that those responsible for sales in any company be continuously on the alert for special opportunities to contact customers and prospects. The effort must be made in a hit-and-miss manner, letting the chips fall where they may. A routine must be set up for the use of supplementary sales letters, and one or more persons delegated to make sure the schedule is carried out.

Figure 8-34

Dear _____,

Our representative, Mr. Stokes, has reported a most pleasant visit with you recently. Although I am sorry that it was not possible for him to meet your commercial teachers, I fully understand your inability to arrange a meeting at the time; increased enrollments have made many teachers' programs more than full.

However, our representatives come to you with a two-fold purpose—both service and sales. They are carefully chosen for their classroom teaching and supervisory experience, and their ability to present teaching martertials.

In their daily contacts with hundreds of schools, they observe the latest methods in teaching procedures. Therefore, they come to you with both the newest and most up-to-date teaching aids—Prentice Hall publications—and a sincere desire to present helpful teaching suggestions. With the present crowded schedules and bulging classrooms, your teachers need the best and most efficient aids in order to carry on.

Mr. Stokes plans to visit you again in about three months. He can help you and your teachers. Feel certain that the time you can afford to spend with him will prove worthwhile to your school.

PRACTICAL LETTERS TO REGAIN LOST BUYERS

PRACTICAL LETTERS TO REGAIN LOST BUYERS

1. WHY DO CUSTOMERS STOP BUYING?

Taking inventory of sales. As has been pointed out, the tendency in most sales departments is to place more emphasis on getting new customers than in holding old ones. This is understandable, as there is no greater thrill for the sales staff than to land a new account, especially if the struggle for it has been long and difficult. Getting new business is one way to increase sales volume, but not the only way. Volume can also be increased by helping old customers to sell more. Remember, there is no gain at all if the amount of new business is offset by the *loss* of old business. Hence, the ideal sales program is the one that pays equal attention to both objectives—making new advances, but holding the ground already captured.

Certainly, the executives of any company should want at least an annual inventory of customers. For example, what percentage of sales last year went to newly acquired buyers, and what percentage went to customers carried over from previous years? They should want to know how many old customers stopped buying, *why* they stopped buying, and what can be done, if anything, to bring these lost sheep back to the company. Have the lost customers gone out of business? Not usually. Are they buying from other companies? Obviously. But what happened? Why *do* customers leave one company for another?

When sales managers are reasonably sure of the answer to the last question—why customers run away—they are better qualified for two jobs. First, they can take steps to eliminate the faults which may have caused dissatisfaction; second, they can decide intelligently how to go about reclaiming some of the business.

Indifference: the sales slayer. To find out *why* customers quit buying, one of the nation's well-known retail stores selected a cross-section of 100 representative charge accounts that had not been active for more than one year. Personal calls were made on the 100 lost customers, and they were asked to state frankly what had happened. The answers, tabulated in percentages, were most amazing.

Do customers leave a company because they are angry, because they can buy at a better price elsewhere, or because they have been influenced by friends or relataives? You would expect, perhaps, that those were major reasons, but none of them rated high in the survey just mentioned. In fact, more than two-thirds of the 100 inactive customers had *no special reason for not buying*—the retailer had simply *let them drift away*. Here are the figures:

68 of the hundred had no special reason

14 had grievances which were not adjusted

 9 were lured away by lower price or better service

 5 had been influenced to shop elsewhere by friends

 3 had moved and were shopping in other areas

 1 could give no answer—he was dead

To be sure, the figures just cited would vary for other groups of 100 among customers of the same store, and in greater degree among customers for other types of business. But it seems fair to assume that the *indifference of the company* is the leading reason in the great majority of cases. People stop buying because they are *allowed* to stop. The company favored with their patronage forgets to show appreciation or does little or nothing to hold their goodwill. Often, the only check made of accounts is for credit purposes; no one bothers to notice that certain accounts are going stale; no one bothers to even ask the customers *why* when they stop buying. So they just drift away, and *nobody seems to care*.

This is not true of all companies, for some watch their customers as a hen watches her chicks. But it is surely true of more companies than the simple principles of good business procedure seem to warrant. Of course, the company with strong field representation, and salesmen calling regularly on customers, has a more favorable opportunity to keep customers in the fold than the one that does a lot of business by mail, or the one in which personal contacts by salesmen are limited in number. Nevertheless, *no* company, irrespective of salesmen and their calls, can afford to overlook any form of office cooperation which might help to keep customers satisfied and assured that they are considered *important* to the organization. And there is no better means of doing this office job than with letters!

The fact that customers have stopped buying does not necessarily mean that they cannot be induced to buy again. A small percentage of the lost sheep may even wander back on their own initiative, but a far greater percentage need just a little encouragement—perhaps only the question, "We've missed you, where have you been?" It only takes a postage stamp, a piece of paper, and a little time to ask that question, and the payoff in revived business makes the effort worth many times the cost.

2. HOW TO APPROACH INACTIVE BUYERS

Rekindling a fire. One fact that makes neglect of inactive customers lamentable is the comparative ease with which many of them can be induced to buy again. There is no way to prove the figure, but some sales analysts maintain that a company spends 20 times as much getting a new customer as it takes to regain an old one. If that difference seems too large, at least it must be conceded that the cost of getting the old customer back is considerably less, whatever the exact figure may be.

Mere prospects are strangers to the company. They know nothing of its services, and little about its products. They may have been buying a long time from a competitor, and have no reason for wanting to buy elsewhere. It takes hard, intensive effort to get their first orders—when that happy end is finally reached.

But the old customers know all about the company, its products and services; three-fourths of the usual sales program is already completed with them. The one-fourth that remains may be to adjust a complaint, or simply to give them a little attention—the attention that was lacking when they drifted away. We have already seen from the retailer's survey of 100 lost customers that more than two-thirds of them had no real reason for leaving, and the ease with which they left suggests the ease with which they may be brought back. Of course, inactive buyers like to be *noticed*, and probably will *never* return if the company remains aloof. Not to be asked to buy again is damaging to their ego. Why should they go back to a place where they have not been missed? Remember, it takes less effort to rekindle a fire than it does to gather twigs and start from scratch.

But suppose *you* were the inactive customer, and you got a letter like the one shown in Figure 9-1—what would be your reaction?

That letter was used with considerable success. The approach is simple— "We appreciated your orders…Why have you stopped buying?" The story gave the letter length, but it was a good story and helped

Figure 9-1

Dear _____,

Away back in the early days of this business, I learned a very valuable lesson.

In those days we depended more on footwork—and less on headwork!

Well, here's what happened.

One day I was traveling through the territory with one of our staff, and we called on a long-time customer who had suddenly stopped buying. After exchanging the usual greetings I asked why we weren't receiving any more orders. And this was the reply.

"There's really no reason at all. I just happened to give a couple of orders to another salesman who had been calling on me for a long time. Nice fellow, and I wanted to give him a break! But you folks have never made any effort to re-sell me so I just thought you weren't interested in my business. Never even got a letter from you asking why I quit, so I've been going along with this other firm."

Well, *we are* interested in *your* business.

And to prove it, we're writing to ask why we haven't been getting any of your orders. We don't want to make the same mistake we made years ago. We want you to know that your account is really valued, and that we'd like to keep it. If there's anything *we* can do to restore our relationship, we'd appreciate it a lot if you would let us know.

Will you?

Thanks!

to convey the writer's thought. Here are three quite short contacts of the same sort.

Dear _____,

Do you realize that it has been all of six months since you and Hotel Fontenelle got together?

We enjoyed having you with us. When'll you be back? We miss you.

Watchfully yours,

Dear _____,

Just a short note to let you know that we have missed your coming in for service. The last time you were in was last July.

Anything wrong? If so, tell us, because you know we want to please in our service to you.

Won't you come in? Or better still, phone—the number is 000-0000.

Thank you.

Dear _____,

Can you spare me two minutes?

One minute to read this—and one minute to say: "We haven't sent you our order for Nipples, because—

_____

_____ ."

Please fill in your answer and return this sheet to us in the stamped envelope enclosed.

This won't obligate you in the least and we'll surely thank you for your two minutes—and your courtesy.

The light, humorous touch can help you get the inactive customer back in the fold again. The letter having this touch will be read and enjoyed by its recipient, and it will certainly go a long way towards re-establishing a favorable image in the customer's mind. The Plaza letter (Figure 9-2) is an excellent example of this type of correspondence, and it is one that continues to be used most effectively.

How to recover lost sheep. When you reach the end of this section, you will have read many letters to inactive customers, letters actually used by business executives during recent years. Most of them can easily be adapted to the needs of any other company, although there is considerable variation in treatment and content. Some simply express appreciation of past business, and say the customer has been missed; some ask casually what is wrong; some assume a grievance, and lavishly promise to make things right.

These differences bring out the question of just how far the letter to lost sheep should go. For example, there are certain points that these contacts may develop; the use of one of them is a moot question among business-letter writers, as you will see momentarily.

Figure 9-2

WESTIN HOTELS

Jeffrey Flowers
Managing Director

Dear Mr. Harris,

We looked in the Palm Court and the Terrace Room and at the best table in the Ballroom. We even sent our best chambermaid to search the closets of the State Suite.

You aren't here.

We haven't seen you this year, and, frankly, we're worried. Several disastrous things could have happened to keep you from our doors. Perhaps our laundry starched your handkerchiefs on your last visit... it actually happened twice last year! Or maybe the Oak Bar was temporarily unable to supply your favorite champagne...there is such a demand on the very great years! Worse yet, you may have been lured into another hotel, and they've lost your credit card, and you can't check out. A prisoner! We shudder. You can understand our concern!

Seriously, though, you may not have returned to The Plaza simply because you haven't returned to New York. If this is the case, don't hesitate another day. There are lots of new things to do here. The theater this year is superb. Avery Fisher Hall is open at Lincoln Center. And, of course, The Plaza has added something since your last visit. You may have heard about it. Limousine service is now available to any theater in Manhattan -- compliments of The Plaza, of course.

Please hurry back to New York and The Plaza. Or at least tell us how you are. We hate to lose touch with our friends!

Sincerely,

J. Philip Hughes

Here is a checklist you may follow:

1. Tell your customers their past orders were appreciated. If the fact was not mentioned when they were buying, perhaps there should be some form of mild apology for the oversight.

2. Tell them how much they have been missed. *Don't* say you noticed their absence while going over the records. No one is really missed if the fact is called to attention by a *record*. They want to be missed as *individuals;* not as names on the books.

3. Tell them you want to *serve* them again. That's better than asking them to *buy* again.

4. Tell them you are keenly interested in knowing *why* they stopped buying. Merely asking that question is *not* an assumption of dissatisfaction; it might be for some other purely normal reason.

5. Tell your customers anything new and beneficial in service or product; things that have happened since they stopped buying. Or, mention some other inducement that might be interesting; a gift you want them to write or call for; any special thing you can do for them.

6. Tell them you think something may have happened to displease them, and how eager you are to make things right.

It is point Number 6 that is questionable. Unless the writer has a guilty conscience and *knows* why the customer stopped, why invite trouble? Perhaps the mistake was inconsequential, and already has been forgiven if not forgotten. There is an old saying, "Let sleeping dogs alone." If something serious did happen, the customers will probably mention it in their reply; and remember, in the check made by the retailer of 100 inactive customers, only 14 had grievances. The odds, then, are better than 8 to 1 that the customers have no complaint to voice. Is it smart to play a long-shot?

No—not in the majority of cases. Let the storm clouds form as they may. Don't worry about them while the sun still shines. Go as far, if you think it wise, as to ask, "Why did you stop buying?" But don't do it fearfully, leaving the plain impression that you expect an unpleasant reply.

Of course, there are exceptions to all rules. A letter that handles the possibility of complaint in a very casual and adroit way is one dictated by C. W. Giller for the Shelby Salesbook Co., Shelby, Ohio (Figure 9-3). It demonstrates what has been mentioned so often in this *Handbook*—it isn't so much *what* you say, as *how* you say it.

With such careful attention to detail, the inactive buyers can easily become re-interested and active ones. In fact, because their business has been so sought after, you may be surprised at the *increased* orders they place with you.

3. CHECKING ON FORMER FRIENDS

Making use of the casual approach. You have now read a few letters that either made no reference to the possibility of the former customers being angry, or else did it so casually that they pay little attention if in a

Figure 9-3

Dear "Old Customer,"

Have you heard the saying, "Old friends are like the ticking of a clock"? You get so used to hearing the tick that you rarely notice it until it stops.

We get used to doing business with Old Customers, too. So much so that now and then we assume that everything is running along smoothly and we sometimes fail to express our appreciation as often as we should. And then—suddenly the clock stops and we find that an Old Customer has stopped buying.

That's just the position in which we find ourselves with you. Your orders have stopped and we are wondering if you would tell us frankly just what the trouble has been—whether there is something we did not do that we should have done, and whether there is anything we can do *now* to get you back on our list of regular customers. If there is, we surely want to do it.

If there is anything wrong with the works of our clock, let us see what is out of kilter. Of course, accidents will happen at times, and if one has happened in this case we hope you will tell us about it. We think we can fix it up the very day we receive your reply.

Like any successful business, our progress is largely dependent on satisfied customers. That's why we want you satisfied and that's why we earnestly request you to fill in the attached business reply card.

Let's see if we can't get the old clock to ticking again.

---

good humor. This, as we have agreed, is probably the best approach in the majority of instances. The purpose of the more casual letter is chiefly to remind the lost buyers of the company, and to make them feel they are important enough to be missed. Their reactions are likely to be much the same as when a friend of former years calls them on the telephone and invites them out to dinner. If they have no reason to hold ill will against the friend, they are likely to accept.

The letters that follow are typical of the more or less casual group. Because of the importance to business of this form of correspondence, the number of examples is not stinted, and you may derive from them a reasonable concept of how various companies have seen fit to handle the problem.

The first, shown in Figure 9-4, consists almost entirely of a story which is both interesting and timely. Godchaux's of New Orleans, who used the letter, have had ususual success in reviving old accounts by this and similar methods—one mailing had the remarkable return of 45 per cent.

Figure 9-4

Dear _____,

The day was warm and the milling crowd at the political rally stirred restlessly as the speaker left the platform. In an effort to swing the crowd, one of the candidates, a former General, had recounted his long experience.

His opponent arose and, laughingly addressing the crowd, said: "My fellow citizens, what General Smith said about having bivouacked in yonder clump of trees on yonder hill...is true. It is also true, my fellow citizens, that I...stood guard over him while he slept. Now all of you who were generals and had privates standing guard over you while you slept vote for General Smith, and all of you who were privates and stood guard over the generals while they slept vote for Private John Jones."

And so Private John Jones launched himself on a long and brilliant Congressional career.

At Godchaux's we have our "Generals" and we have our "Privates" too. We feel it to be an achievement that each account, large or small, receives the same meticulous service, the same prompt, efficient courtesy that 107 years in retail business have schooled us to give.

Recently you have not used your charge account. We hope that it was through no fault of ours. But if it was, won't you let us know. Meanwhile, your account remains open. When next you are in the store, won't you say "Charge it"?

The sending of a stamped envelope with any kind of a sales letter should increase the chances of a reply; this is especially true of the more or less personal messages that reach out a hand to an old customer. Not many people will throw a stamped envelope away, and it doesn't seem honest to keep it.

Two special plays for attention. Just as for any other type of business correspondence, a good start in a letter to lost sheep may help to secure a happy ending. For example, consider the letter used by the

Container Corporation of America with the rubber-stamped "CREDIT O.K." This message, too, shuns the mention of a possible grievance, and simply asks *why* the customer has not reordered. The extra cost of time in using the rubber stamp is inconsequential, and the idea does give the letter an effectiveness it would lack if the same words were merely typed in the line.

```
Dear Mr. Hanks:

When your first order for containers was received and passed to
this department for CREDIT O.K. I commented that our salesman,
Dunford, had landed a worthwhile new account -- the kind to whom
we'd like to sell lots of containers -- just the kind that our
business needs.

Our opinion was correct -- you discounted our invoice!  But, as
anticipators -- did we overrate ourselves?  We haven't had a re-
peat order as yet, and we're wondering why.

You know how it is in your own business.  There are many good
concerns who ought to be doing business with you.  Their credit
is good  and they buy frequently and in good volume.  Maybe you
sold them once and they never came back for more.  You wish they
would  -- but you don't know why they don't.

That's the way I was thinking about your account today -- just
that ONE order --


Yours very truly,
```

The next appeal to lost sheep has no mechanical device to attract attention, but it does start with a question of interest to almost any individual. In just the first paragraphs we can see the cleverness of this letter. Who does not remember his first door key, or how his mother always seemed to be awake when he got home? The letter did a reclaiming job for Anabolic Foods, Inc., Chicago.

Dear Doctor,

You remember that your mother always rested more comfortably after she heard the sound of your key in the lock? While you—proud in your possession of your first door key—laughed and told her there was no need to worry.

The Anabolic family is large and far flung. Yet we too feel better when all of the family "is in." Then we know we are successfully doing our part—that there is no call for any member "to leave home."

Since we have not heard from you for two months, we'd feel more comfortable if we heard you "come in" this month. The enclosed order blank is your key.

Now, let's look at a set of three letters with quite an impressive pull record. The record first, then an analysis.

	Recipients	Replies	Sales
Letter 1	70	8	$308
Letter 2	62	12	$607
Letter 3	50	26	$74

Of course, deductions made from one limited test are not to be trusted completely, but insofar as these three letters are concerned, the second did a better job than the first. These two mailings together got most of the money, although the third letter developed far more replies. Probably a fourth letter would have been wasted. Three seems to have been exactly the right number. See how these letters worked together to go after those reluctant lost buyers.

(1)

Dear ―――――――,

We know that you will agree that old friends are the best friends. If an old friend suddenly seems to forget you, you're going to want to know the reason.

That's just the situation we are up against with regard to your company. Several months have passed since that last order, so, of course, we would like to know the reason "why?"

Won't you use the back of this letter and tell us why we haven't heard from you recently? It is our experience that a firmer friendship arises with a clearer understanding, and that is the reason we are asking you to write us today.

(2)

Dear ―――――――,

We are still wondering why we seem to have lost an old friend in you. A short time ago we wrote to ask why we aren't receiving your orders recently, but as yet we have had no reply.

This matter is of great importance to us. Frankly, we want to keep the business of old customers like you, and we are sure it can't be too late to restore the pleasant relations that we formerly enjoyed.

So once again we ask—won't you please take just a minute to jot down on the back of this letter the reason we haven't been hearing from you? We are enclosing a self-addressed envelope and will appreciate your reply.

(3)

Dear _____,

It has been my experience that a frank discussion of any problem is the quickest and best route to a satisfactory solution.

Our problem right now is that we have not been getting your business, and I am greatly interested in finding out why. After all, we are dependent on firms like yours to distribute our products if we are to retain the place we enjoy in the field of competition today.

We want your business; we need your business; and if there is any complaint, be it a matter of service, policy, or quality of product, we want to know what it is so that we can make an honest effort to correct it to your satisfaction.

I would appreciate a personal note from you stating frankly why you are not buying our products, and what we can do to make you want to buy them.

The first and second of the above letters were mailed on regular company stationery, and the signature was identified with the Sales Department. The third letter was signed by the president, and reproduced on his personal stationery. The added pull of the president's name evidently caused the large number of replies, although the sales volume was very low. Evidently, the Sales Department had extracted most of the juice from the lemon before the president was allowed to squeeze it.

The letters you have just been reading tried hard to shun the possibility of a dissatisfied customer. They merely asked the former buyers where they had been; why had they been away; why didn't they come back home where the fatted calf was waiting for them. This is a fine approach to the customer who has wandered away for no particular reason; why look for trouble where no trouble is known to exist? However, many sales correspondents have taken other roads that lead to the same objective—we shall now see how.

4. ADMITTING POSSIBLE FAULT TO SAVE SALES

Making an offer that's hard to refuse. Directly opposite in psychological appeal to those that assume *no* grievance, are the letters that carry the assumption of a mistake or fault, and ask the former customer what needs to be done to make things right again. The strategy, of course, is good when it happens to hit the truth; it may be so straightforward and sincere that even the readers who have no chip on their shoulders are favorably impressed by a company so eager to play fair. The approach, however, is often grossly misused, so that the writer seems too apologetic, too conscious of weaknesses in service or product.

Few would criticize the tone of a letter used by the Dennison Manufacturing Co., Framingham, Massachusetts. The writer frankly admits that something might have happened to displease the former customer, and appears very sincere to make reparation—but doesn't overplay his hand or grovel at the feet of the reader.

Dear _____,

Probably you have found yourself in the same position as I am now.

You have wondered why folks you had been doing business with stopped abruptly and you heard no more from them. It caused you some concern. You began to wonder why you lost their business, because you did your best to keep them satisfied.

It is possible that something we may have done—or did not do—has disturbed you, because we haven't had an order from you for a long time. Often it is just a misunderstanding, though I might make a thousand guesses. So all I can do is ask you "What happened?"

In this old world we can't get anywhere by ourselves. We've got to have someone else's help, so won't you be good enough to tell me just why we haven't heard from you? Be absolutely frank. Don't be afraid of treading on anybody's toes—facts only can iron out a troublesome spot. Your goodwill is worth much to us, and we want to keep it.

Please use the enclosed envelope for your reply.

P.S.: Is there any service I could perform for you at this time—a catalog, prices, or just information?

Equally pleasing is a letter (Figure 9-5,) by Lowe & Campbell Athletic Goods Company. The very first sentence established the thought of a possible fault—the rest of the letter to make up for it.

Figure 9-5

Dear _____,

Is it our fault? Are we to blame? You bought athletic equipment from us last year—so far this season we have not heard from you. We are naturally wondering why this should be. If we have mishandled any of your orders, we want to hear from you about it—a statement of the fact will enable us to correct any error we may have made, and to remove any misunderstanding that may now exist.

New customers are, of course, welcome at all times—but it is much more satisfying to know that our old friends are re-ordering. Will you not also look upon us as friends, and think of us as being here to see that you get immediate and satisfactory service on all your orders for athletic supplies?

Sincerely, Mr. Rich, we are anxious to find out why we haven't heard from you this year. Has our Fall Catalog failed to reach you? Have we fallen down on a previous order—or does it just happen that you haven't needed anything in our line this year?

Won't you use the back of this letter and the accompanying envelope in telling us just why we haven't heard from you? Better yet, just use the enclosed order blank.

A very clever letter idea is the one that leaves half of the page vacant for the readers to fill in their side of the story.

Dear _____,

We are anxious to adjust whatever complaint you may have, or to know why you have ceased to order from us. But we can really do little until we hear *your side* of the story.

That's why we've arranged this letter to make it convenient for you to tell it.

Our side of the story	Your side of the story
The space on your order card is as white and clear as new-fallen snow.	
There is always a reason why a good customer stops buying, a reason we should like to know so we can remedy the difficulty if we have been at fault.	

That's your side of the story,
the side we want you to tell us.
Will you meet us halfway?

Will you fill in and mail to us
the other half of this letter in
the enclosed postage-paid
envelope?

I will consider it a personal
favor.

While the foregoing letters have varied in style and content, they all
have contained the assumption of a fault that needs correction. Deltox
Rug Company, in one of its follow-ups, goes even a step farther by
attaching a questionnaire for the reader to check "Yes" or "No." You
might also call it a disguised order blank, as the last two questions
definitely probe for facts that could lead to sales. See Figure 9-6.

Dear _____,

You will agree that it is poor business to permit a good, paying
customer to stray away.

So, as good and successful merchants, you follow old customers
when, after a reasonable time, they do not return to buy again.

There is sound thinking behind such a practice. So sound, in
fact, that we follow it ourselves.

Now it happens that we haven't had an order from you since
early last year. A copy of our last invoice to you is enclosed. And
for some reason we feel that this absence of your business is due
to some fault of ours. If this is true we wouldn't be fair to you or
to ourselves if we didn't take steps to remedy the situation.

So, will you do this for us? Look over the attached sheet.
Answer the questions that have a bearing on the condition that
keeps you from buying from us. Just a check-mark will do. And
we invite additional comments if you feel them necessary.

But please answer. A stamped air-mail envelope is enclosed to
make this very easy.

With best wishes.

Giving letters strong personal appeal. It is hard to hold ill will
against an individual who says "I am sorry" as if he *means* it, and then
asks for another chance. Explanations and apologies may help in some
cases, but usually they only intensify the ugly situation, and the writer
finds himself securely chained in the well-known "dog house." But
regret, sincerely and simply expressed, is a great disarmer.

Figure 9-6

Checklist of Questions From

Doe Furniture Company,
El Dorado, Arkansas.

1. Did you find our merchandise unsatisfactory in any way from a quality or workmanship standpoint? Check which:
   Yes ( ) No ( )

2. Did our merchandise fail to sell satisfactorily for you? Check which:
   Yes ( ) No ( )

3. Have you had customer complaints regarding our merchandise? Check which:
   Yes ( ) No ( )

4. Did our salesman fail to call on you regularly? Check which:
   Yes ( ) No ( )

5. Will you be in the market next Spring for summer rugs, such as fibre rugs? Check which: Yes ( ) No ( )

6. Are you in the market now for 100 per cent wool rugs that you can sell at $360–$475 in the 9 × 12 sizes, with smaller sizes selling for less? Check which: Yes ( ) No ( )

ADDED COMMENTS _____

_____

_____

Some of the best letters to inactive customers are those that use the person-to-person approach—just one person talking to another. There are few people who will continue to hold a grudge against the writer or company that seems concerned about any shortcomings, and eager to make things right. The letters that follow are good examples:

(1)

New friends...new accounts and so-called big business deals are very alluring...but after all...the old friends of yesteryear are the ones who count...*those who made the grade with us*...in good times as well as through the dim, dark days.

It becomes almost a habit to look for their business. In fact, we actually grow to expect it. Then...when one of them suddenly stops sending in orders, it's a severe jolt and we wake up to the fact we haven't a God-given right to the business of any concern.

But it isn't altogether a matter of dollars and cents...there's something deeper...*something below the surface*. Call it sentiment or whatever you will...I just can't explain it, but *you know what I mean.*

So...in this same spirit...*if we slipped up or displeased you...we are sorry. Tell us about it*...don't send your business elsewhere...*give us another chance*...we'll do the right thing by you. We can't do more than that, can we? Less...we will not tolerate.

Our new bulletin just off the press is a humdinger...both interesting and helpful. Your copy will be mailed...just the very minute we know you want it.

There's a prepaid envelope attached for your reply. If you can slip an inquiry or order in it...well..."bully for you." Anyway, *let's get together again*...please.

Just for "Auld Lang Syne." Thank you.

The thoughts expressed in the foregoing letter are not easy to resist. We all like to give people a break when they seem to deserve it. Note the impelling language in the letter.

In the number (2) letter there are references to past deficiencies, but also reminders of the other times when the best of services was rendered. The result of this approach—the asking for another chance— was that the customer *did* return to the fold.

(2)

Dear Steve,

Do you remember some of the truly great boxers of the past? Personally, I believe that most of them could knock over most of these stiffs posing as top-notchers—if their legs would hold up. However, sooner or later, they are all bowled over by old-man age.

Strange as it may seem, the rock, sand, and cement business is something like the prize fighting game.

I like to remember these "old time" boxers as real guys. True, they were licked a few times, but that's no reason why I should admire them any the less. Is it, Steve?

We were champions in the service with you for a long time. It is true that the "legs" we used failed to come through a couple of times. However, we often came out winners on tougher battles than those we lost.

Our experience on those two jobs of yours taught us a good lesson. Those trucks we had were champions in their day, but that day had passed. None of those "old boxers" could buy a new pair of legs—but we could and *did* buy new trucks. As you undoubtedly know, we have invested about a quarter of a million dollars in new delivery equipment, which again puts us on the winning side, and minimizes chances for delay to our customers.

Steve, we have really staged a successful comeback on our service. We are as near as your telephone, and will welcome your placing another bet on us like money from home.

The same strong personal appeal is found in a letter used by the Gates Rubber Company. This letter never failed to bring back either an order or an explanation. A letter that pulled 100 percent *must* have been good.

(3)

We have always tried to look on our customers as friends as well. We want you to feel that we are every bit as much interested in serving you as we are in selling you. That is the idea upon which this company was founded.

But in spite of high ideals, we are all human—we *can* make mistakes, and we know that we sometimes do. Perhaps that is what has happened in your case, for it has been a long time since we heard from you, and we can not help wondering why.

If we have made a mistake, handled an order in a way that did not meet with your full approval, inadvertently sent you merchandise that wasn't up to the standard you have come to expect from us—then please give us a chance to make amends. You have our word that we will do everything humanly possible to prove that *you made no mistake* when you gave the Gates Rubber Company your business as in the past.

On the other hand, if there is some other reason why we have not heard from you, won't you please write us a letter and tell us about it? We want your business certainly, but if we cannot have it at present because of factors neither one of us can control, we still want your friendship. And with no word from you— neither orders nor letters—in the past six months, we have no way of knowing just exactly what has happened.

So please write to us—or better still, send us an order. Then we'll know everything is all right. We have missed you, and there is nothing that we would welcome more than the opportunity to take care of your automotive accessory requirements again.

We will be looking forward to hearing from you.

5. TELLING YOU WHAT WE'RE GOING TO DO FOR YOU

Appealing to readers' self-interest. So far, the letters we have been surveying have gone after inactive customers by recounting the friendly relationship of the past, and asking why it cannot be renewed. The readers have been told how much their orders were appreciated, even though the company may have neglected to say so sooner. "We miss you," most of the letters have said, "and if we were in any way at fault, we want to make things right."

You might say the major appeal in these letters has been to the human beings to forget grudges when others meet them halfway; to the intangible urges to return to old places when they feel sure they are wanted. Few of the writers so far have offered any *special inducement* for the homecoming beyond general references to quality of products and services. Few of them have plainly and specifically asked for an immediate order. The writers tried instead to awaken the goodwill that once had existed toward the company; the assumption was that if that could be accomplished the orders would be forthcoming later.

The following letters use different tactics. In each some benefit the readers and will be achieved by doing what the writers have asked. In the first, the bulk of the message is devoted to points that are shown by enclosures.

(1)

Remember when you were a kid—when you were absent from Sunday School someone sent you a card telling you that you were missed? We are not accusing you of playing hookey but we have been doing a little checking up. Your name hasn't appeared on our order register for quite a spell. You have been away much too long.

Since you last ordered from us we have made three important improvements in our envelopes that mean more sales and bigger profits to you.

All the curl has been taken out of the flaps, which means up to *20% more production in your printing department.*

The gum is being applied to the flaps by means of a rubber roller. This means that there will be no dry lumps of gum to smash your type. No smashed type, *more profit to you!*

The paper is watermarked. While this doesn't mean that the paper is better than it was, it does peg the grade as a definite standard. We find that our customers like it, therefore we believe this feature will *help you sell more envelopes.*

You will find a sample of this cracker-jack envelope enclosed. You have our price list, so just write your order on the bottom of this letter if you like, slip it into the enclosed business reply envelope that requires no postage, and shipment will be made the same day your order is received.

In similar fashion, H. N. Fisdale sought to bring lost customers back to the Chocolate Products Company of Chicago, Toronto, and London. Mr. Fisdale did not talk about missing the readers, or how much their business was appreciated in the past. On the contrary, his message was used to point out a benefit—the money to be made by buying a certain chocolate syrup. In effect, it is strictly a sales letter slanted at inactive buyers.

(2)

Spring is in the air! Birds singing, flowers sprouting, soft winds sighing, employees sleeping, and you—well, what are you doing? You should be *getting ready for a bigger chocolate drink sales season.*

Are you?

If you are, *let's get started NOW.*

You haven't ordered any Stillicious Vitamin B Chocolate Syrup from us in a long time.

Maybe you're figuring on waiting until the hot weather actually hits us before ordering.

Don't wait.

Like everything else in this world, if we want anything, we have to get out and work for it. The same with chocolate. *Right now* you should be paving the way for *a big summer business* on chocolate.

Start putting it on your routes now; get your driver-salesmen enthused; let your customers know you are selling the best and richest chocolate drink on the market—STILLICIOUS.

Use the enclosed envelope to send in your order. Overcome spring fever by *acting at once.* We'll be waiting.

The above letter was mailed to 86 inactive buyers, and 24 replied with orders! Spring is also the motive of a Pfaelzer Brothers letter that took a firm stand with its readers. They are told to order, or at least reply; otherwise, their names will be removed from the mailing list. Of course, we wonder what the writer intends to do if the inactive buyers say, "take it off." It is not good sales psychology to pull an unloaded gun.

However, the letter reads very well, and may have cleared the one hazard.

(3)

Spring Cleaning Began Here At—

Pfaelzer Brothers today, and among the many things that had our attention was our mailing list.

When we found that your name was among the few that had not ordered for quite a long time, we were confronted with two alternatives: one, to remove your name right away; the other, to drop you a line to find out just what the trouble seemed to be. And that explains this letter.

There must be a good reason for our not having heard from you—and surely, if it is important enough to keep you from sending us an order, it is worth our trying to find out what it is.

That is why we ask you to *do us this favor*. Look over the enclosed price list, *use the postage-free blank* to send us your order for 50 lbs. or more (beef, lamb, veal, corned beef, etc.)—or else use it to tell us to keep your name on our mailing list.

With the market as high as it is now, you will find our price lists even more interesting than before—because not only will they *enable you to study the trend* of the market, they will also help you to adjust your menu to meet current conditions. Our "Specials" which appear in every issue are *timely and long on profit*.

An order will be appreciated. Your reply will be most welcome. Either way, we'll know you are still interested. *We'll be happy to hear from you again.* Mail the blank *today*.

Searching with the Bjornson touch. It is never possible to draw an exact line between active customers and inactive customers. *How long* must the company wait for an order before the customer can be called a lost sheep? The answer to this question depends partly, but not entirely, on the nature of the business. Certain products are sold more frequently, and must be ordered more frequently, than others. If Mrs. Flanigan has appeared almost every morning over a long period of time in Ryan's Grocery Store, and then does not appear for several weeks, the chances are she is buying her groceries at some other place. But the fact that Grocer Ryan has not bought paper bags for six weeks might mean nothing at all to the jobber that supplies him. He may have acquired a six-month's supply on his last order.

Nevertheless, it must be taken for granted that customers have been lost when they buy nothing for a period of three years. That would seem to be true of almost any kind of business. Furthermore, the longer an individual or company has gone without buying, the less can be expected of a letter that seeks to regain their business.

The letter in Figure 9-7, written by master letter-writer N. Bjornson, went to customers who had not bought anything for three or more years, and yet 26.9 percent replied! Because of this remarkable pull, the letter is worth our special study.

What *did* make the letter pull? First, it starts with an interesting quotation that is peculiarly fitted to a letter to former customers. Second, it asks tolerance for any mistakes made in the past on the grounds that the reader himself probably has similar troubles in his own business. Third, it requests a reply as a favor to the writer—always a good appeal, for people like to feel they are able to do favors. Fourth, it renounces personal responsibility for past errors by referring to the new management. Fifth, it lists new facilities for serving the customer. Sixth, it asks for an order in a polite and casual way that is far remote from high-pressure. Seventh, it makes the reply easy. So you see, because of these seven points, the message has considerable persuasive power, and from start to finish is tactfully worded so as not to offend the reader.

That the results attained by Mr. Bjornson were not accidental, or a "one-time" stroke of fortune, is proved by a similar pull attained by the letter in Figure 9-8. This attempt to revive inactive business was mailed to 560 firms and produced 184 replies—a return of 32.8 percent. The replies included several orders, and four prospects for new machines, as well as many assurances of future business.

To furnish a motive for the letter, a penciled note on scrap paper was attached—a copy of a memo which Mr. Bjornson had received from his superior officer.

The main argument in the body of the letter is the reminder that no company should be as well equipped to service a Dexter Folder as the one that made it. Again, we find the same technique in closing as in the first of Mr. Bjornson's letters—he simply asks that the readers scribble their answers on the back of the same sheet, and furnish an addressed envelope to facilitate a reply.

Trading gifts for replies. A very common device in letters to lost sheep is to offer a souvenir or gift as an inducement to those who will reply. The thing given away varies in value; the cost depends on what a customer is worth to the particular company. At least, it needs to be appreciated, or the effect is undesirable. Here are some letters of this type:

Figure 9-7

Dear _____,

One of the ancient philosophers said that whenever he lost a friend he died a little.

We could not, I am sure, express our feelings at losing a business friend in a more appropriate manner. Nor need we try, for everyone of seasoned business judgment knows that in the press of everyday duties, at times complicated by conditions beyond their control, things that should not happen sometimes do happen, and matters that should be taken care of are not always attended to.

In your case, was it something we did or was it perhaps something we did *not* do which caused you to drop out of sight as one of our business friends? Will you do me the favor of giving me your answer to that question?

I have a very definite and, in a sense, a personal reason for asking this favor.

In the first place, we have new management here, and frankly, we don't know all the facts about many former transactions. Secondly, we have now completed a thorough study of production costs and markets, and we believe we are fully equipped to meet all competition from a quality-service-price standpoint.

Besides that, we have fully improved facilities for research, much new equipment, several new lines, well-scheduled service, and plenty of technical skill back of every job. And if I may add the personal angle, here it is: It is a part of my job to find out how we rate with former business friends, and what we can do to regain their confidence.

If you happen to be in the market right now, an order for even a roll or two of our materials would excite us, and so would a request for a quotation; but if that isn't in the cards, I shall just look forward to your answer to my question with sincere appreciation of your thoughtfulness.

There is no need to dictate a letter. Just jot down your reply in a word or two on the other side of this page. The enclosed envelope saves you further bother.

Figure 9-8

Dear ————,

Someone has said that excuses are but shabby patches with which people try to cover up their mistakes.

I should have known the answer to the question on this note—should have made it my business to find out *before* the Boss asked me—but I didn't. That was my mistake, and I had no valid excuse, nor did I try to invent one.

But now that the question is in my lap, I can think of no better way of getting the right answer than to rely on your generosity in helping me out.

Was it something we did or was it something we did *not* do which caused you to stop buying your machine parts from us? Or am I simply on the wrong track—am I assuming that you have bought parts elsewhere when in reality you may not have been in need of any?

Whatever the answer, I would warmly appreciate a brief reply. As you know, all Dexter parts are made to precision standards, and we feel that "the doctors" that brought your equipment into the world are better able than anyone else to supply the needed remedy in case of a strain or breakdown! We want your Dexter equipment to keep on making money for you as long as it is possible to keep it running fast and smoothly with the highest quality parts—the only kind we have to offer.

An order, no matter how large or small, would make us very happy—prove beyond any doubt that we're not in the "dog-house." But if that just isn't in the cards, I'm going to look hopefully for your reply telling me why we haven't enjoyed any parts business from you for several years, so that I can pass the answer to W. S. R.

No need to bother dictating a letter! Just jot your reply in a word or two at the bottom or on the other side of this sheet, and return it in the enclosed envelope.

(1)

Dear ————,

Here I come again, but wearing a new suit. About a year ago, we offered you a souvenir for an order. Several hundred of our good customers took us up and sent in orders.

Not a single one complained about the souvenir, but a lot of you folks asked for, and received, another one.

Well, here I am again with a new gift. It's a great little gadget that you can use at home or in your office. You'll like it, and it doesn't cost you a penny. Just an order for something you need...anything at all!

You're our friend and we'll give you service, and good value, as well as the souvenir. So mail the card within 15 days...that's giving you time enough to really need something.

And thanks a lot for what you have already done for us.

Needless to say, the above letter went to regular customers as well as to those who had fallen by the wayside. The desire to get something for nothing has no limitations.

(2)

Dear _____,

You know, I just caught our file clerk throwing your old order card in the waste basket. Here's about the conversation which followed.

"What are you doing that for?"
"Oh, they haven't bought anything from us for three years, and probably never will again."

Maybe the first is true, but I certainly don't believe the last part. If you're still in business, there must be some reason why we haven't had more orders from you.

Would you like a copy of this year's ABC Stationery Catalog? I'll tell you what. If you'll write a short note about you and us on the back of this letter, and ask for a catalog, we'll send it to you pronto, and include a personalized memo cube as a present.

Do it now, and send it back to us in the enclosed business reply envelope. O.K.?

In that letter, the inactive customers were told *what* they were going to get—a memo cube. But in the next one the readers are left guessing. Only the psychologists could tell us which is the better procedure.

(3)

Dear _____,

I have a very useful and attractive gift for you.

You don't have to purchase a penny's worth of merchandise in order to get it...we're not trying to get you in the store to sell you something. But we ARE trying to get you in just to have you say "hello" and tell us that you still think of Ruttenberg's as "your furniture store."

You see, we've *missed* you. My brother Lou and I have spoken of you several times since you were last in to see us and we certainly would hate to think that you were staying away because you were dissatisfied with either our merchandise or our service. And we're more than anxious to have you come in and have a friendly little chat with us.

Remember—you won't have to stay more than a minute; just as long as we see you again we'll feel satisfied. So call at the store on Thursday, Friday, or Saturday of this week and ask either one of us for the little token of appreciation which we've put aside for you. If you can't get downtown during the day stop in on any of these three evenings. We'll both be here at the store working until around nine o'clock, and we'll gladly give it to you then.

It will seem good to see you again, so don't disappoint us...please.

The gift offered does not need to be something different from the usual item of sale. It can be an extra case free if a certain number of cases are ordered, a special discount for the one purchase only, or some other inducement equally attractive.

6. REVIEWING SHOWMANSHIP AND PULLING POWER

Guidelines for regaining attention. Dramatized letters are especially effective for rousing inactive customers, and especially so when they are mailed to long-dormant customers. In the latter case, the problem is not greatly different from writing a sales letter to a prospect who has never purchased—and we have seen in Section 3 how showmanship, properly restrained and appropriate to the content, can win quick attention.

The principles, of course, in preparing a dramatized letter to inactive customers are no different than in preparing one for any other business purpose. No doubt you remember that they are...:

1. The idea used must be really clever.
2. It should be fresh and original, as even a good idea grows stale when it has been used too often.
3. The point made should be the same as that in the body of the letter; otherwise the readers are likely to think you have tricked them into giving their attention.

4. The best ideas are those which do not involve a lot of expense or trouble. Remember the two strands of yarn in the rug letter. (See Figure 3-7.)

Putting principles into powerful practice. With those simple but important principles in mind, we can now see how certain companies have used showmanship in letters to lost sheep; particularly, as to how well they meet the requirements. As nearly as possible, the examples in Figure 9-9 have been reproduced in their original form, although several of them were made more attractive by the use of two or more colors. However, this need not handicap your inspection, because you are interested in the *ideas* they contain, and how they might be adapted to your own correspondence.

An unusual idea that contains considerable showmanship was used in a letter saying the readers were missed. It was attached to a partly typed reply which they are supposed to complete and mail back.

The letter

Dear _____,

On the attached sheet, we have taken the liberty of *starting* a letter written by you to us.

Will you finish it?

The reason for this unusual request is that we've missed you. And we'd like very much to know whether this is due to causes beyond our control—or to some situation which can be adjusted if we get together and talk it over.

There is another reason, too. We are eager to show you some really exceptional values for all your Fall requirements. Skilled buying at the right time is bringing us a lot of new customers. But, it's old friends like yourself whom we are much more concerned about satisfying.

Won't you, therefore, tell us frankly why you haven't been in to see us lately by finishing the letter we started? A business reply envelope is enclosed for your reply.

While the letter was engineered in the sales department, it was signed by Louis Wellinghoff, Credit Manager—proving once again that in business there is no reason why the sales and credit departments cannot work together. In later sections of this *Handbook* you will find other examples of cooperation on the part of credit managers—the answer to the myth that there is an unavoidable split in interests between credit managers and the sales force.

Figure 9-9a.

In Mourning for the Departed

Figure 9-9b.

Cartoon Follow-Up to Lost Sheep

Now look at the showy attachment:

Reader's Reply

Dear —————————,

When a friend of mine—business, professional, or otherwise—passes me up, I always want to know why, just as you do in my case.

I believe as you do, that if customers will give you their reasons frankly, it's often possible to adjust the situation with satisfaction to all concerned.

Therefore, I am willing to tell you why I have not used my charge account recently.

The reason is—

(Balance of the page left blank, for the customer to complete a reply.)

When talking about sensational pulling jobs executed by finely crafted letters the following four are all bellringers of their type. The first had a total cost of mailing of about $100—a trifling sum compared to sales amounting to $9,760.

(1)

About the most interesting feature of my job is the writing of letters to good friends and customers like yourselves, from whom we haven't heard for some little time. Those who have fallen by the wayside, as it were! They bring forth so much sentiment and expression of goodwill.

Besides, most of the replies I get are very interesting and encouraging. Many renew their acquaintance by sending me a nice order or by telling me when they will be in the market. So you see...it's worth the effort.

Of course...once in a while...a great while...someone registers a "kick," but you know that's to be expected in a big family of 12,000 like ours. Anyway...we always manage to iron out satisfactorily any little difference that may exist. No halfway measures are tolerated. On that score my Company is adamant.

Now...it's so long since you sent us an order that I am wondering if anything happened. If it did...which I hardly think is the case...then we'll make it right. Can't do more than that, can we?

So, I'm going to bank on your giving me a break...just as I'd give you, were you in my position. Mind you...the enclosed prepaid envelope doesn't in any way obligate you, but I'd certainly appreciate a word from you. It will help me a lot. You'll do that much, I'm sure.

And for your courtesy...one million thanks.

The following letter, brought back far above average results.

(2)

Ever had a customer suddenly stop buying? If so, what did you do? You asked him: "What, if anything, is the matter?"

If his complaint was a just one and you made a mistake, or had been wrong, you did your level best to make amends.

That is just the attitude in which I am writing you this morning. We haven't had an order from you for some time and I would certainly appreciate it if you told me why not. If any department of this business has failed you I want to know it.

The fact that this business isn't perfect is surely not due to any lack of effort on our part, or because we aren't trying to make it so. Changing conditions have not as yet found us unprepared to take care of our trade. And, furthermore, never have we lost sight of our customers' interest.

I am looking forward to hearing from you with the keenest anticipation.

For a follow-up of lost business that makes no effort to do more than to contact its readers in a courteous way and ask why they have not been buying, you could hardly find a more effectively worded letter than this one.

(3)

Did you ever bump into an old friend on the street—one you hadn't seen for years? It's a real thrill, isn't it?

Something of that sort just happened to us. We were browsing through our old records when up popped your name. It was mighty nice to see it again—brought back old times—and incidentally started us to wondering why we had lost track of you.

Things have been going along pretty nicely with us—we've a lot of new products, and a lot of new customers—but somehow it's the old friends that we have made in our 75 years of business that really count. We don't want to lose them. And, if in some manner we have not served you properly, we'd certainly appreciate the opportunity to square ourselves.

The Wrisley Company is better equipped than ever to supply you with quality soaps and toiletries—we're extra proud of our

Bath Crystals—and you'll be interested in the profit possibilities that every item in our "Complete Line" offers.

The envelope we're enclosing is to make it easy for you to turn this sheet over and write us—

to have our representative call,

to send you price lists,

or, to say just what you think of us.

We hope it's good, but if it isn't—don't hold back; we can best correct our faults when we know exactly what they are.

And for sheer simplicity—courteous, friendly, to the point—this last one rates a blue ribbon.

(4)

There surely must be some reason why we have not received your bundle lately, and since it is important enough to cause you to stop using our service, it is certainly more important that I find out just what the reason is.

It may be that the service you were getting was not exactly suited to your laundry needs. In this case, one of our other "Seven Superior Services" outlined in the enclosed pamphlet may appeal more strongly to you.

At any rate, whatever the reason may be, won't you please tell me about it on the special form enclosed for your convenience, and send it back to me in the self-addressed, stamped envelope, also enclosed?

Thank you, very much.

From the letters you have read in this section, perhaps you have gained a better idea of how wayward customers may be brought back to buy again. The cost of the effort is so small compared to the sales that may be gained. It is not nearly so difficult to revive an old customer as to get a brand new one. Most of those who stopped buying from your company had no special reason, except, perhaps, because nobody seemed to appreciate their patronage.

No company can afford to omit letters to lost sheep from their sales program. Doing so is a foolish waste of a sales opportunity and that means waste of profit. Contact at least twice a year the old customer-friends who have stopped buying. Tell them you want them back. You may be surprised at the number who accept your invitation.

CREATING LETTERS TO WIN GOODWILL

SECTION 10

CREATING LETTERS TO WIN GOODWILL

1. EXPLORING THE IMPORTANCE OF GOODWILL LETTERS

It is doubtful if any group of successful executives would discount the importance of goodwill to sales. We can't think of a single company that could get along without goodwill. There is no substitute for goodwill in business, and the company that fails to recognize its necessity is surely headed for failure. This poem sums up the thought quite well.

> The most precious thing a man can have
> Is the goodwill of others.
> It is something as fragile as an orchid
>   And as beautiful;
> As precious as gold nugget—
>   And as hard to find;
> As powerful as a great turbine—
>   And as hard to build;
> As wonderful as youth—
>   And as hard to keep.
>
> —Author unknown.

In the broadest sense, everything that happens in business should be planned and carried out in a way to win and keep the favor of customers, prospects, and the general public. Wide awake executives know this to be a fact, and much of their thinking is directed to the promotion of what is rather loosely called "friendly public relations," and to the creation of a "favorable public image." Unfortunately, however, in many cases the effort made to gain goodwill is of the hit-

and-miss variety, and many opportunities are either ignored or over-looked. This is particularly true of the letters that *could* be written but never are. Because the writing of them is apart from the actual operation of the business, they are not included in the planned sales program, and are pushed aside as something relegated to "time-permitting" status, but not strictly necessary.

It is conceded that the "necessary" things in the operation of a business must claim first attention. Goods must be manufactured, sold, and shipped. Advertising must be planned and prepared. Credit terms must be established, and money must be collected. People must be hired, trained, supervised, and motivated. To these few examples, you can add many more—the things that must be done regularly, and under strict control, day in and day out.

Obviously, too, the *manner* in which these things are handled helps or hurts in the winning of goodwill. Prompt and efficient service, products of uniformly satisfactory quality, routine contacts conducted courteously in person or by mail—they all contribute to friendly customer and public relations. In this *Handbook* you have already seen how these routine matters, when handled in letters, can be made pleasing and helpful to the general sales program. You know that *every* letter written for business should do everything possible to win or hold goodwill. Making the contact a pleasant experience for the reader is one of four primary obligations as a letter-writer, no matter what the news in the letter may happen to be. Under no circumstances, under no provocation, should you be anything but a friendly human being trying to do your best to serve your reader. Every business message can reflect your company's goodwill, even if it denies a customer request, or talks about the lawyers who are going to sue for an unpaid bill.

The difference, then, between all company letters and those you will see in this section is not so much in spirit as in purpose. The regular letters accomplish a double job—they sell, they collect, they adjust, *and* they win goodwill. But the winning of goodwill is the *only* job performed by the letters in this section. They can be ignored, and the routines of the business will continue. For some they may be "unnecessary," but you can be sure it is not a mistake not to use them.

Goodwill letters receive special attention. Regular buyers are accustomed to getting certain types of letters from their supplying companies about their orders, their payments, and other routine matters. Even though the letters are friendly and help keep the buyers satisfied, they are still more or less taken for granted. But when special letters, written for no other purpose than to carry goodwill are received, these are certain to gain special attention. Imagine the effect if, for example, one customer is complimented about his election to some civic office, others get a letter of appreciation on the anniversary of their first purchase, or a letter of sympathy goes to another because some member of her family is in the hospital. None of these goodwill contacts would be expected; in a strict business sense none of them are necessary. But the mere fact that any one of them came in the mail one day would surely win special favor for you and your company.

The expression of goodwill does not need to be lengthy; it may or may not contain something more tangible than words—the effect is still a pleasant surprise to the reader. For illustration, here is a short note sent by a Kansas City rental company, to new tenants. With the note went a box of stationery, imprinted with the tenants' name and the address of the property into which they had just moved.

Dear Mr. and Mrs. _____,

Our sincere wish is that you find your new home as comfortable as you hoped it would be.

This writing paper is with our compliments, and we trust it will help establish your new address with all of your many friends.

Among those who think that landlords are hard to get along with, the receipt of such a goodwill gesture would be sure to soften their opinion toward at least this one firm. Furthermore, the favor created would help to smooth future landlord-tenant relations. Thus, the "unnecessary" letter and gift render a service to management that could well be worth many times its cost.

If the importance of the box of stationery in the idea just described seems greater than that of the message, consider next a letter mailed to customers by the Republic Engraving & Designing Co., Chicago. Here the message stands alone quite successfully:

Dear _____,

One of the greatest assets of life, as I see it, is its true friendships. A friend is a valued possession.

What is true of our personal lives is also true of our business lives. We like to have our customers feel that there is a warmth of friendship underlying each business transaction and that friendship in business is something more than just receiving your order.

I have given this quite a bit of thought recently, and feel that those who respect their obligations promptly and abide by fair business ethics should have a word of praise now and then, and here it is—

"Thank you good folks for allowing us to serve you, and for your loyal support in using our Readco Republic Rubber Printing Plates, and most of all for your friendship and the pleasant business relations which we enjoy with you."

From the point of view of necessary business operation, the writing of the above letter was a pure waste of time; from the point of view of giving a good customer a pleasant little surprise, it may have been the most productive letter mailed that day by the Republic Engraving and Designing Co.

No matter the cause given by your letter, your true purpose is added goodwill and regard both for and from your customers. Every bridge between you will eventually reap a reward as both your image and your income soar.

Here's something "interesting," friend! Speaking of the good that can be accomplished by letters with no business purpose other than to carry a little goodwill, R.W. Baxandall once said: "For building goodwill and overcoming sales resistance, one of the best ideas we ever have used is to send the customer or prospect some idea or information he can use in his own business, saying that we are sending it with our compliments, and hope that he will find it useful. Such thoughtfulness, *with no strings attached*, is appreciated by the recipient. It shows that the writer knows his problems, and is interested in helping him."

After the above introduction, Mr. Baxandall illustrated his thought with a number of pertinent examples.

- A bank sends business firms a reprint of a timely speech on current financial problems.

- A college sends to high school principals a "school calendar" with spaces for filling in the social and athletic activities for each day of the school year.

- A printer sends a football schedule for colleges in the state.

- A jeweler sends an inexpensive "Memory Book" to high school graduates.

- A department store sends a "Baby Book" to parents of newborn babies.

- A manufacturer sends his customers a mimeographed list of government publications which may be helpful to them.

- A popcorn company in Iowa sends its customers ideas on how others are getting business—the best locations, etc.

- A company sends to customers and prospects copies of current legislation which might affect them.

The key words in Mr. Baxandall's comments are "With no strings attached." Goodwill letters are not dictated to ask for orders. The best ones ask nothing at all except the privilege of a friendly contact with the reader; the chance, perhaps, to do him a little favor—something apart from the daily grind of business.

Goodwill works two ways. When the right relationship exists between public and company, goodwill flows back and forth on a two-way circuit. Athough we are primarily interested in how a company may do its share of the job, the letter in Figure 10-1, written by a customer of the Southwestern Bell Telephone Company, Kansas City, is the type that any company may expect to receive now and then if its own program for winning goodwill is in order. In business, as elsewhere, a company usually gets what it gives.

There can be no problem in customer relations when the people served feel toward a company as did the mother who wrote that letter.

Figure 10-1

Dear ———————,

The joyousness which I feel this morning is boundless. I would be ungrateful, indeed, if I did not make some expression of thanks to your company—meaning more specifically the personnel from executive to operator; from cableman to local technician—for the part they played in producing this state of mind.

Perhaps you have guessed. My son, whose voice I have not heard since he left the United States two years ago on a voluntary overseas assignment, called me and talked to me just a little while ago from London, England.

I do not know what the charges for such a call are. What it meant to me cannot be expressed in monetary values.

I am grateful for American industry and the American way of life—the "can-do" that surmounts all obstacles and makes possible the luxuries we enjoy, and such things as spanning half a world so that a son and mother may say "hello" to each other.

I know an infinite number of people contributed to making this call possible. To each one of them I want to say with the warmth of personal friendship—

"Thanks for a job well done."

Moreover, the organization that receives few or no letters of appreciation from customers can well afford to examine its own efforts to build goodwill; it is almost certain that lack of friendliness on the one side of the business relationship indicates a similar lack on the other side. On the other hand, cordial contacts with customers—beyond the mere necessities of taking orders, shipping them, or collecting money—will build a reserve of respect and loyalty that tends to increase sales, reduce customer turnover, and eliminate misunderstanding. The letters you are going to examine in this section required no great outlay of time or money—just a little appreciation of the human equation in business, and the thoughtful application of the law which says that others will give to us what we give to them.

Blueprint for goodwill letters. It would be an endless task to try to list all the kinds of letters than can be used in business to win and hold goodwill. Although the examples that follow do not begin to cover them all, they do reveal friendly letter-writers at work; they show how easy it is to express the little courtesies of life in business as well as in social relationships. Executives who might question the value of these goodwill contacts would simply expose their own failure to keep in step with the modern tempo of business.

Modern letter-writers go out of their way to share (within reason) the experiences of those who favor the company with their orders. They seize every opportunity to win the friendship of customers, along with their patronage. They let them know that their buying is appreciated. They write letters of congratulation when good things fall their way; they write letters of sympathy when they suffer a business or personal loss. They remember them on special occasions such as Christmas and birthdays not with old platitudes, but with sincere expressions of goodwill. They treat them as members of the family; explain new policies so that they will be understood; invite suggestions and criticism. It all sums up to a concept of mutual dependence on each other—of the recognition that in every transaction *human beings* are involved. This is the modern trend of business—and it is good. Customers are not mere names on file in the order department. They are *people* whose friendship can be won for a company as easily as for an individual. Without that friendship, they are merely buyers—here today and gone tomorrow—with no ties to keep them in the fold.

Goodwill letters may be "unnecessary" in the narrow sense of routine business operations, but when viewed in the true perspective of helping to build faith and loyalty, they become of great importance to sales.

2. SHOWING APPRECIATION *IS* GOOD GOODWILL

Rendering unto Caesar what is Caesar's due. In this *Handbook*, you have seen many letters that let your readers know their support is appreciated. This recognition of what the customer means to the company seems to be a logical business procedure, although it has been too often overlooked until he has gone elsewhere to shop. As we discovered in Section 9, locking the stable after the horse is stolen is costly; it's much easier to hold than to regain a customer's goodwill.

The hardest customers to keep are the ones you sell or service only infrequently, or so efficiently that they are not apt to be aware of what you do for them. For example, if you are a fuel company and arrange with your customers to deliver oil to their homes, they may take good service for granted after a time. Your delivery truck probably arrives without having to be called, and there may be only a very few deliveries made during the entire heating season. When the next heating season comes around, another fuel company might not find it difficult to get your customers to switch—unless you have made an effort to keep their goodwill.

A good letter can be just the thing in this situation. For example, a fuel company prepared the following three letters for their dealers to use in maintaining customers' goodwill. They were made available to each dealer, imprinted with his name, at cost.

(1)

Dear ————,

In a few weeks memories of bitterly cold days, howling snow storms, and all the other untoward things brought us by this coldest of many a winter will melt before gentle spring breezes and a friendly, ascending sun.

But before this happens, we want you to know that we are happy to have been able to serve you with the finest fuel we know of—always-dependable ABC Double Grade Fuel Oil.

It is just such a winter as the one we've passed through which brings to mind the great importance of having fuel that delivers ample comfort and protection under all conditions. It makes us happy to be associated with a business which means so much to the families of our community.

So thank you heartily for permitting us to be of service. May the pleasant months to come prove to be a period of productive work and happy recreation for you.

(2)

Dear _____,

Many a day we write letters asking for this and that, but this note asks nothing but that you accept our sincere thanks for the privilege of serving you.

It has been an unusually trying winter. There were times when we found it difficult to make deliveries. There were days when there were unavoidable delays. If you experienced any delays, we hope you'll not think of us too harshly. We did the best we could under the circumstances.

On the other hand, we are happy that we were able to supply you with the best fuel we know—comfort-packed ABC Double Grade Fuel Oil that can always be depended on to release an abundance of warmth whenever needed.

We hope this spring and summer will be pleasant seasons of work and relaxation for you and your family.

(3)

Dear _____,

The old fashioned winters grandfather told us about came back to haunt us in this most modern of all years.

It was not pleasant for anyone, but we are happy that we were equipped to provide you with the one thing that kept them out of our homes—good fuel.

We were not always on the ball, but we tried hard, and so far as I know, no one of our customers actually suffered from lack of fuel.

We are grateful for having been able to give adequate service, and we thank you warmly for the privilege of supplying you with ABC Double Grade Fuel Oil—the ever-dependable, heat-rich fuel.

Now that we can once more smile a bit about winter's vicious onslaught, and look to pleasant months ahead, we ask you to accept our wishes for a happy spring and summer season of work and play.

You noted, no doubt, that in none of these three letters did the writer ask for future business. Instead, the letters were content to thank the customers for the privilege of serving him—and on the goodwill thus created, they were willing to stake their chances of getting the next year's order. Had the writer, that consistent master N. Bjornson, *asked* for the future business, the message in any of the three cases would have been just another sales letter, and much of the effectiveness would have been lost.

When appreciation stands alone. Telling customers how much they are appreciated, and then putting the bite on them for more business, is not the best way to impress them with your sincerity. It is too much like using one hand to pat them on the back, and the other to reach for a favor, all the time saying to yourself, "If I say something nice to these people, maybe they will come across with another order." The customers recognize the real purpose of the gesture, and it may do more harm than good.

In the following oustanding, well-crafted appreciation letters, no ulterior purpose is revealed. While they may ask for the goodwill of the reader, no strings are attached to the request. Sincerely, and without exaggeration they thank the customers for their business favors and hope they may continue to merit their friendship. Naturally, any individual or group reacts favorably to a message which comes out of a clear sky—with no particular motive or necessity except the desire to say "Thanks."

(1)

Dear —————,

In the month of March, in the year 19—...

A young man set out in the earnest quest of earning a living. In the type of business which appealed most to him, he cast his lot.

It took but a very short time for this young man to learn that earning a living in terms of dollars and cents was not the primary requisite of employment.

He found in rubbing shoulders with a world of realities, that other things mattered far more—unselfishness, consideration of others, conscientious service, and above all, honesty.

He learned, too, that his most valuable asset was not his bank account, nor his worldly goods, nor things material, but rather his loyal friends.

Having personally played the role of this young man, I have learned these things, and learned them well.

I therefore want to express to you my sincere thanks for your loyal friendship and your genuine cooperation in these past years. They have made it possible for me to pass the milestones—one by one—and have contributed largely toward making my tenth anniversary in the insurance business possible.

(2)

Dear _____,

It is in a civic-minded mood, rather than a boastful one, that we point to our store's attainment in becoming "First in St. Louis...Fifth in America."

We offer you our thanks and grateful appreciation for the role you have played in enabling us to reach this high place in the department store world. Your loyalty and confidence in our merchandise and service have contributed greatly to our success.

It has been a real pleasure to serve you, and we shall strive constantly to merit your friendship and patronage.

Please feel free to call on any of us whenever we can be of assistance, for we all will welcome an opportunity to further express our gratitude in terms of helpful service.

(3)

Dear Mr. and Mrs. _____,

This is the kind of letter that I am most happy to write, because I am taking this means of thanking you for your constant choice of the Palmer House as your home in Chicago.

Your names rank high among those of our loyal and distinguished "repeat" clientele who, year after year, give us definite proof that we are setting the pace of hotel leadership in Chicago. It is to friends like you that we owe the success of the Palmer House.

And so I wish to express my sincere appreciation of your patronage, and to assure you that we shall continue to do everything within our power to maintain our present standards of service, cuisine, and furnishings.

Thank you again.

A little gift for good measure. The use of gifts with appreciation letters is more common at Christmas than at other times of the year, but the Miles Kimball Company of Oshkosh, Wisconsin, did *not* wait for any special occasion to present a goodwill token. In fact, as their letter, shown in Figure 10-2, tells us, the offering was made in the month of May.

In another letter, the first "birthday" of the thing purchased furnishes the motive for the goodwill gesture. To make the appreciation more tangible, a gift in the form of free service is offered.

Figure 10-2

Great morning, Dr. _____,

There's something about a May day like this one up here in Wisconsin that gets into the blood of even an overweight letter-writer like myself.

I got to thinking on the way to the office, ten minutes ago, how I spend most of my time trying to *get* business, and precious little of it saying "thank you" to good folks like you who keep the wolf at our doorstep from having cubs.

So this letter isn't to sell you a darned thing. It's just to tell you I appreciate your account, and that I'm sending you a little book I've enjoyed and think you may like.

It's a sort of calendar—a timetable showing when and where to look for the various birds, flowers, and other actors in the pageant of nature. It isn't generally known by the cutthroats with whom he plays poker, but once in a while our Mr. Kimball likes to take himself a lone hike. This guidebook has made such occasions more interesting to him.

It's coming in a separate wrapper. I'm hoping you will find it a little useful.

Happy Birthday to you!
Happy Birthday to you!

Well, maybe it isn't your birthday, Mr. Doe...but have you forgotten?...It's your car's birthday!

Yes, just one year ago we delivered that smart, sparkling new automobile to you. We hope it's given you a full year of driving enjoyment and comfort...and that it will continue to.

It seems fitting that today—on your car's first birthday—we should say "Thank you" once again for buying it from us. And because we are still just as much interested in your car's performance as we were the day you bought it—we have a birthday surprise for you.

Drive in within 30 days, and we'll give your car a thorough factory-specified 20-point lubrication...FREE!

It won't cost you a cent. Just bring this letter along. We'll be looking forward to seeing you roll into our driveway soon.

The token sent with a goodwill letter does not need to be expensive, but it should serve some useful purpose. At one time or another, most people are bothered by the breaking of a shoelace, with no spare handy for replacement. Clarke's, of Tulsa, Oklahoma, use this annoyance as the basis for an appreciation message. Although at the end of the letter a play for another sale is made, it is not done in a way to offend the customer, or to detract from the cordiality of the contact. This letter is also very short, proving that appreciation can be aptly expressed without a book full of words.

Dear _____,

Some morning soon, when you are dressing at a mile-a-minute rate, a shoelace might s-n-a-p. So we're sending you a new pair with our compliments.

We sincerely appreciate your patronage and want your purchases to be 100 percent satisfactory—even to the laces.

It was a pleasure to sell you the shoes you're wearing now, and we hope for an "encore" when you need another pair.

We all like presents, particularly when they are unexpected and we're told we deserve them. We'll remember who gave us these "surprises" and so will your customers.

Extending goodwill toward the departing customer. Granted that those of cynical mind may question the motive behind a goodwill letter to customers—attributing to it the thought of future sales—the charge could not be made against a friendly expression of goodwill to the customer who has just been *lost*. Such a message is the one sent to those who have just sold their stock in the General Foods Corporation:

Dear Mr. and Mrs. _____,

In a family of many thousands of stockholders, some new names appear and some drop out each week.

I have learned recently that your General Foods account has been closed. Possibly this may be due to a change in name or address, or to transfer of your stock to the name of some broker or other individual.

It is also possible that you have relinquished your General Foods stock. In this event, we sincerely hope to retain your friendship for General Foods, despite our regret in the loss of one of our family of stockholders.

Your frank comments would be sincerely appreciated if there has been any dissatisfaction with any of our products or policies.

If you would like, during the next year, to have us keep you on our mailing list for descriptive material about General Foods, such as we include in mailings of our dividend checks, please let us know.

As we have seen there are many ways to send goodwill letters of a general nature. When used with sincerity, and not as a "plug" for more orders, they can be a powerful help to any company. The best of the lot are those which are written for no special reason, except to let the customers know their business is appreciated. The cost of an occasional "Thank You" is small; the return may be abundantly large.

Now, let us look at some special occasions when goodwill letters provide just the right personal touch to your business letterwriting.

3. DESIGNING APPRECIATION LETTERS FOR THE HOLIDAY SEASON

Mastering that difficult Christmas letter. Contrary to popular opinion, it is not easy to dash off a letter of appreciation for the New Year or Christmas. One difficulty is in making the message different from the many others the reader is likely to receive; another is conveying a sincere thought without having it take on the form of sentimentality. There is probably more pencil-chewing by business writers at Christmastime than at any other period of the year. Many writers would like to get away from the expression, "A Merry Christmas and a Happy New Year," but nobody seems to come up with anything adequate to take its place. In view of these obstacles, the following checklist may be helpful:

1. Don't try to be clever or spectacular in the preparation of a Christmas letter to customers and others.
2. Wait for a quiet moment when you can relax and write the message without interruption or pressure.
3. Think of something you would like to read if you were getting the letter instead of writing it. Then say that something in the simplest possible language.
4. Remember you can be a little more personal in a Christmas letter than in almost any other kind. People *expect* sentiment in a Christmas letter; they are in the mood to accept it at face value.
5. There is no limitation in length for a Christmas letter, but *as a rule*, the shorter ones seem best. At least, avoid too many adjectives, and try hard not to repeat.
6. Don't ask anyone else to write a Christmas letter for you. The sentiment you wish to express is *yours*—it suffers a loss of effectiveness when offered second-hand.

Writing a yuletide message is not a job that can be done by any set of rules or any formula. A good Christmas letter comes from the heart, and beyond the few simple suggestions already offered, no person can tell another *how* it should be written.

Instead, for your inspection and study—so that here and there you may find an adaptable idea or thought—some holiday messages have been chosen for this *Handbook*. They represent a fair cross-section of the *best* letters of their type as used in American business during the past several years. You will find all of the letters sincere in tone—couched in simple language. They express appreciation in a way that would be accepted as real and genuine. They serve the purpose for which they are intended. They are *goodwill builders*.

(1)

Merry Christmas, folks!

Guess what! This gift-giving all started with a Saint named Nicholas throwing a purse of gold through a window each night for three successive nights.

It happened that Saint Nicholas knew a poor nobleman in Lycia, Asia Minor. The fellow had three lovely daughters and he worried about their future, so Nick threw a purse of gold through their window, and returned the two following nights to do it again.

Well, you can imagine how happy that made them. And the news got 'round and folks all over Europe decided to make each other happy by giving gifts on a night called Saint Nicholas' Eve. For economy's sake they cut it down to one night, and dropped the gold purse idea—they just filled shoes and stockings with candy, cookies, and handmade toys and trinkets.

And that's how we got hold of the swell idea of giving dolls, scooters, trains, toasters, fur coats, and neckties during the grandest season of the year.

All I wish is that I could be the original Saint Nicholas this year—that I could be everyplace at one time. Then I'd be sure to visit *your* home, and I'd bring along that gold purse, too.

Anyway, I hope Santa brings you and yours all you want for Christmas, plus a New Year filled with all of the things that make life worth living.

(2)

Dear _____,

MERRY CHRISTMAS—What other phrase can start the heart strings singing more quickly or more gladly than those two words? In them are wrapped all the best human emotions of the ages.

It's useless to try to improve on them for they form the perfect thought.

And so, as another year draws to a close, I want to say thank you for your part in making it a pleasant one, and again let me say right out of my heart—MERRY CHRISTMAS to you and yours!

(3)

Dear _____,

"Christmas" means a lot of things, but to our Organization this season centers chiefly around two of the finest things in life...home and friends.

Looking back over the years and thinking of Christmas Days gone by makes us realize just how empty life would be without the proper home life and good, true friends.

So at this season of the year we are thinking of you and your associates whose friendship has helped us along the way. We hope this will be a truly Merry Christmas for you and everyone at your house, and that the New Year will bless your home with all of the good things in life.

(4)

Greetings, friends!

> Once a year we drop things material,
> Turn to matters even ethereal;
> Wishes to all here and there,
> Christmas spirit fills the air
>> New Year's coming
> Just around the bend.
> May good luck
>> Happiness
>>> Be yours
> No end!

You can see that it is difficult but, certainly, not impossible to structure a Christmas message with just the right blend of sentiment and honest goodwill.

Using showmanship in the Christmas message. Because so many holiday messages are likely to be received by the same individual or company, and because the things to be said are limited, any idea to attract special attention—if appropriate and in good taste—may give the

Christmas letter an advantage over others of regular form. On the other hand, sentiment and showmanship are not easy to blend, and anyone using a dramatized mailing should be sure it is in keeping with the spirit of the season. Another factor, of course, in determining the fitness of the idea is the character of the group who will receive it; some firms are more conservative and critical in their reactions than others.

Advertising people, for example, would probably react favorably to a message which appeared in one of the business magazines a few years ago. It went like this. Be sure to read it aloud:

VROLIJKE KERSTMIS	BOAS FESTAS
SARBATORI FELICITE	FELICE NATALE
JOYEUX NOEL	CHRYSTOVJNA
FROELICHE WEIHNACHTEN	WESOLYCH SWIAT
TIN HAO NIAN	GLAEDELIG JUL
KINGA SHINNEN	FELICE PASCUAS
ICHOK YILARA	VESELE VANOCHE
GLAD JULEN	SRETAN BOZIC

BOLDOG KARACSONYI UNNEPEKET

All of which is by way of saying
Merry Christmas, and (to which we
add) a most excellent New Year.

Another Christmas message which gets out of the groove had on the outside of a small folder a drawing of a jewel box, and attached to the center an imitation diamond. The caption said: "WE DO NOT ASK FOR DIAMONDS." Then on the inside of the folder appeared the following message:

As we pause in sober contemplation of the millions of people in other lands who do not have happiness this Christmas, we are humbly grateful for the privilege of living in a country where spiritual values have not been subordinated to material things.

So, on our Christmas list we do not ask for diamonds or other worldly possessions. Instead, we want only your goodwill—to so serve you that you will continue to think well of us, as surely we do of you.

That you and yours will find happiness on Christmas Day—that you will have good fortune during the coming year—is the sincere wish of myself and of all my associates.

One of the cleverest ways to send dynamic holiday greetings can be found in Figure 10-3; it was used by the Rylander Company. Note the exceptionally effective personal touch of applying actual employees' signatures to the message.

Much thought must go into your decision of whether or not to use the element of showmanship in your holiday letterwriting. Just remember, good taste and integrity will always stand you in good stead.

Guidelines for other holiday letters. Messages of appreciation need not be confined to Christmas and New Year's, although they are days which may come first in the company goodwill letter program. Certainly, a company is rather stingy that remembers to thank its customers only once a year. A letter mailed in connection with some

Figure 10-3

THE RYLANDER COMPANY

December 31, 19___

Dear "Customer" --

This letter is one of the very last to be mailed by our firm in 19 !

We hope it will be one of the first that you open in 19 so we can be among the first to wish you a Happy New Year.

Please accept our sincere thanks for our pleasant association together during the past year. Your orders have been most welcome and your many acts of cooperation are appreciated. We will strive hard to merit your patronage and good will for many years to come.

Sincerely yours,
THE RYLANDER COMPANY

(signatures) - at your personal service to help you with your direct-mail and letter service requirements.

B.E. Heitmann

Marilyn Mills - the "voice" who answers our phones.

Clara Rietroch - who writes up your orders.

Lillian E. Stroud - she is our bookkeeper.

H. C. Black - who ships and receives.

Cecil B. Smeeton - our auditor, C.P.A. of course!

Charlotte Lewen - who are responsible for our good-
Esther Fait - looking (plug!) mimeographing.

H. Henning - Printing Department Supervisor

Ed Norman - the "harmony" boys who multigraph
Ed McEvoy - your letters. They sing while they work.

Walter Relz - Mailing Supervisor

Wilbur A. Robinson - Typing Supervisor

Adeline Dolojuch - Addressograph Supervisor

A.H.C. Stroud James A. Troyer - our dependable messengers.

And a couple of dozen other capable and friendly folks who are here to serve you.
(Wish we had room on this sheet for all their signatures too!)

other national event or day may carry the advantage of having less competition, too. Not uncommon in American business are goodwill gestures to tie in with Thanksgiving, the Fourth of July, Mother's Day, Father's Day, Easter, the birthdays of Washington and Lincoln, and other times held high in public esteem.

For certain types of business, the above days are particularly significant, and letters may be used either to gain goodwill or as sales helps. A florist naturally takes advantage of Mother's Day; a clothing merchant is equally interested in Father's Day; a sporting goods dealer finds the Fourth of July one of his booming sales periods. The Lincoln Life Insurance Company would hardly overlook Mr. Lincoln's birthday. And of course an expression of gratitude to customers is appropriate for any organization on Thanksgiving Day.

It doesn't matter so much on what occasions the goodwill letters are mailed; the important thing is that every company should use *enough of them* to keep the fire burning. Merely to mail a Christmas letter or card because the act is customary is a sad reflection on a short-sighted company. Customers need more attention than any one annual contact could possibly give. It is just as logical for customers to *buy* only once a year, if that is as often as their purchases are appreciated.

4. VIEWING LETTERS OF CONGRATULATION

How to recognize a good opportunity. The individuals who do not like to have good deeds noticed are a rarity. The desire for praise when praise is due is a basic human craving. People are proud not only of the honors they win, but also of anything outstanding done by a member of the family, or associates in their businesses. They are thrilled when their sons or daughters earn a scholarship to college, when a child marries, when they first become a grandfather, or for no bigger reason than building a new factory or moving into more pretentious quarters. Anything that pleases them becomes doubly sweet when it is recognized by some other person or company. A letter of congratulation makes them feel important; adds a personal touch to a business relationship; can hardly fail to win a bit of their goodwill.

Hence, astute executives are ever on the lookout for *any opportunity* to write a letter of congratulation. They keep in touch with the personal activities of customers, and even of important prospects that they hope to sell someday. Their sales staff are instructed to report back to the home office about the honors and happy events incidental to the lives of customers; if a good dealer has recently been elected Mayor, a letter of congratulation is forwarded promptly. If a purchasing agent is promoted to the rank of Vice-President, he is quickly commended. If a merchant has moved into a new and bigger store, that fact, too, is recognized.

It takes only a few minutes to dictate a letter of congratulation; the goodwill created may endure throughout the years. The company that ignores an opportunity to render a word of praise to a customer is both thoughtless and negligent. It is not a form of hypocrisy to write these letters of congratulation—not when there is a sincere interest in the good deeds of others. To be sure, if the readers feel that their backs are being scratched only in the hope of getting their orders, the result is negative; but average business executives are really sincere about liking their customers. Naturally, they are glad to see them prosper.

A quick reference list. It is futile to attempt naming all the circumstances that might prompt congratulatory letters. The activities of mankind are too numerous—and interests too wide—for tabulation. Instead, see the list below for opportunities you can use to extend your company's goodwill.

- Some form of promotion in business, in civic office, or in a social organization.

- Any type of service which is of value to society, and for which the worker gives of his/her own time without recompense.

- Some personal accomplishment: the winning of a golf tournament, the making of a speech, the writing of a magazine article, the solution of a business problem, or any similar achievement.

- Some business accomplishment: the building of a new plant, the opening of a branch office, the acquisition of another company, the announcement of a new product, the substantial increase in sales volume, the offering of a new service which will be of benefit to the community.

- Milestones reached in progress: the fiftieth anniversary of the company, a personal birthday, the anniversary of the opening of an account, the tenure of years in a business position.

- Honors won by members of the family: the winning of a varsity letter by a son, the election of a wife to some civic or social position of leadership, the graduation of a son or daughter from college, the winning of a scholarship.

- Some happy event in the family circle: the birth of a baby, marriage, recovery from illness.

- Some material advancement: the acquisition of a fine new home, the winning of a blue ribbon for "best dog in the show," the gaining of control of some business enterprise.

- Some spiritual circumstance: the joining of a church, work done as Scoutmaster of a troop of Boy Scouts, the donation of a large sum to charity.

- Achievement in some personal hobby: acting in the little threatre, singing in a chorus or choir, public display of an oil painting, a poem published in the local newspaper, a display at a flower show.

You see, when such a list is started, there is no place to stop it. But no matter what the reason for the congratulatory letter, it is sure to win goodwill; not only because it flatters the ego of the reader, but also because it tells him that the writer takes a personal interest in what he is doing. We know of one business executive—tremendously popular and successful—who for 30 years has made it a point to start each working day with the dictation of a congratulatory letter. Each day, his secretary appears with her notebook, and asks the question: "Who is it today?" And surprising as it may seem, he has never once lacked a candidate.

Examining typical letters of congratulation. While every situation must be personalized, a close look at some well-prepared congratulatory letters will help us catch, perhaps, the proper spirit. Let's look at this first letter:

Dear _____,

I take this opportunity to congratulate you on your letter announcing you have moved to larger quarters. This letter came to my attention through Dartnell Publications. It is a very interesting letter and worthy of the favorable comment which was given it.

An extra tingle made a round trip on my spine when I read the fifth paragraph wherein you mention letterheads, envelopes, and invoices, because I am keenly aware of the many fine envelope orders which we have had from you the past few years. The business is appreciated, I assure you.

When I was a youngster I spent my summer vacation on a farm and my early recollections are closely associated with a pair of overalls which had conspicuously displayed across the shoulder straps, "Oshkosh B'gosh." However, in more recent years I find the name Oshkosh more closely associated with Direct Mail and envelopes than with blue denim and wide open spaces.

I wish that I too might be in a position to climb up and inspect your new quarters. Naturally, I am interested in that sort of thing, and besides I have never had the pleasure of meeting up with one of those St. Bernard dogs.

When you come to St. Paul, climb up and see us sometime. Our office is on the second floor.

In that one letter, there are at least four things said that must have pleased the reader: *first*, the congratulations for the move to better quarters; *second*, the favorable comment about the letter in Dartnell Publications; *third*, the appreciation for past envelope orders; and *fourth*, the reference to a hobby, St. Bernard dogs. Then, at the end, comes the cordial invitation to call when the reader happens to be in St. Paul. You could not ask for a more generous, effective expression of goodwill.

It is only natural that a businessman of long experience should take pride in anniversaries, especially when they date back many years to the time of the company's founding. Using this pride as the basis for a goodwill letter-contact is both logical and appropriate. Following is the way the Deltox Rug Company recognized the fifty-sixth birthday of a retail furniture store.

Mr. —————,

What a thrill it must give you, Mr. Perez, to look back over your many years in the retail furniture business. For each and every year testifies that you treated your customers fairly and squarely, and gave them full value for the money spent in your store.

Established 1888. That's a long, long time. And we'll gamble your records show that the children and the grandchildren of your original purchasers have bought from you.

There's something mighty comforting in a long record of service to the public. And we know that you are going to find, on the day that your business is 76 years *young*, that this spirit is particularly heart-warming.

As a comparative youngster, with only 37 years of business life behind us, we congratulate you.

Do it with style! To illustrate further how businessmen of our time are building goodwill by letters of praise, a few more examples may be helpful. None of them offer much of a problem in the writing—a stylish, friendly hand extended in sincere commendation, and the job is done. The mere fact that the honor or deed *has been noticed* is more important to the person receiving the letter than the form in which the praise is worded. It takes so little time to dictate one of these goodwill messengers compared to that necessary for other kinds of business correspondence that it is difficult to understand why more of them are not written. Just be yourself and use a style which suits you and the situation. Here are a few letters which show each writer's personality came through.

(1)

Dear _____,

It was a real pleasure to read in this morning's paper of your selection yesterday to be the next president of the Association of Retail Merchants. I can think of no one better qualified for this important position, and you have my heartiest congratulations.

Knowing, as well I should after the many years you have been a loyal customer, how thoroughly you have managed your own business, and what a great inspiration you have been to your employees, I am sure you will lead the Association in a way that will benefit every member, and be a real credit to yourself.

Please remember that all through the year while you are carrying the ball for many a touchdown, I will be up in the grandstand, rooting for you.

Style: *Mildly reserved and formal.*
Situation: *Writer may not know reader personally; good when reader is in a higher position than writer.*

(2)

Dear _____,

The fact that the Community Chest Drive has reached its quota two days before completion is only another evidence of your leadership ability and willingness to accept any obligation for the good of our community.

I have attended most of the noonday luncheons, and could tell from the first day that we had a Chairman who would direct the Drive successfully. It is not an easy job to control the efforts of so many volunteer workers, or to keep them happily united throughout the campaign.

Truly, you have held the torch light high all the way, even though there must have been times when other men would have faltered.

There is little material reward for social or civic service, but I know you must feel amply recompensed by the thought of the good you have created for the unfortunate people in our city.

You have my sincere congratulations, added to all the others that you must have been receiving.

Style: *Warm and companionable.*

Situation: *Writer and reader have shared an experience; good for either equal or different stratum communication.*

(3)

You old rascal!

Somewhere along life's way, you have discovered the Fountain of Youth—but you have never told me where it was. Is that the way to treat an old business friend?

I, too, was once a fairly good tennis player, but it has been at least ten years since I gave up the game because the old legs wouldn't take the punishment. But you are as old as I am, and now I read that you won the City Championship.

Today, I am going to ask for a new credit report on you, because I think you have been operating under false colors. Your name can't be _____ as it stands on our books. It must be Connors or Becker or Noah.

Seriously, I am both amazed and delighted about your victory. You have reminded me of something I forgot too soon—that a man is only as old as he *thinks* he is. Maybe I should have that racket of mine restrung.

Do you need a doubles partner?

Style: *Light and breezy.*

Situation: *Writer must know reader well; good for equals or when writer is higher than reader.*

(4)

Dear _____,

Congratulations—from all of us here at Armstrong's.

It is good to hear that you have been made Manager of the Jefferson. In a way, it's just like having one of our own family promoted, because all of these past ten years you have helped make so many of our conventions run smoothly.

According to the newspaper account, you started 23 years ago as a night clerk at the Jefferson. Somehow, it makes us feel good to contemplate the careers of ambitious young men who start from scratch and rise to the top—that can't happen in any other country.

Style: *Kindly and mildly solicitous.*
Situation: *Writer is acting on behalf of a group and may or may not know the reader; good for company-to-employee letters when writer has superior position to reader or when one company writes to its suppliers or customers.*

(5)

Dear _____,

I was deeply concerned a month ago when Tom Turner wrote that you had gone to the hospital for a major operation. While you and I have not met personally, the many letters we have written back and forth have developed a feeling of friendship which I know is mutual. It didn't seem right that you should suffer this misfortune.

But this morning word came from Tom that he saw you in your store a couple of days ago, and that you had set some kind of record for quick recovery.

This is indeed good news, and I congratulate you for being in such good physical condition after such an ordeal. Maybe I am like an old hen mothering her chicks, but I do hope you will take things easy for awhile, and not bother too much about business.

Style: *Friendly and ingratiating.*
Situation: *Writer may or may not know reader; good for mutual relationships either with companies or individuals.*

(6)

Dear _____,

Welcome to our eventful world!

They tell me you arrived by air day before yesterday, via Stork Transcontinental. This, you know, is the oldest airline, and it has an unblemished record for safe transportation.

We could have written to your father—an old and loyal customer of ours—but no doubt he is too busy handing out cigars to even read his mail.

And of course your mother is just as proud and excited as he is. When you get older, _____, you will better understand what joy you have brought to your parents, and why we have hastened to congratulate them.

In the meantime, so that all the things now happening will be properly recorded, you are getting with this letter a Baby Book which we know you will cherish in the years when you become a grown-up.

Until then, best wishes to you, _____.

Style: *Clever and humorous.*

Situation: *Writer may or may not know the parents; good for any new baby's arrival.*

     Note: The inclusion of a small but very thoughtful gift is an added bonus with this list of letterwriting brilliance.

(7)

Dear _____,

She was a shy little girl with big blue eyes, and lovely blonde hair. It took a little while for her to accept me as a friend, but finally she climbed on my lap and we had a lot of fun together.

It's *your* little girl I am talking about, and the event was the night you had me up to dinner, after you gave me that first very much appreciated order. It seems only yesterday, but of course we both know that many years have passed over the dam since that pleasant evening.

If I had any doubt about that it would have been removed when I heard from Al Gray, our salesman, that the little girl with the big blue eyes was married last week to a Captain in the United States Army.

This must have been both a sad and a happy occasion for you. It isn't easy to give up a daughter, and I know how devotedly you have worshipped her. But to have her marry so well must have been some compensation.

Congratulations? Why, I have a great store of them—for you, for your daughter, and especially for the lucky young man.

This morning I had the extreme pleasure of spending an hour in our Gift Department—trying to find that one rare thing which might give the newly wedded couple something they would really cherish in future years together.

I think I made the right selection. At least, it is on its way to them with my best wishes.

Style: *Reminiscent and familiar.*

Situation: *Writer must know reader very well and for a significant number of years; good for any milestone such as graduation, engagement, marriage, new baby of the child of the reader or Mayor's anniversary or birthday of the reader personally.*

Note: Remember to adapt the recalled shared experiences to your own relationships with your reader/friend.

(8)

Dear _____,

Tomorrow will be an important day in your household, and I hope this letter arrives in time to include my congratulations with all the others you are sure to receive.

I have a friend who says he never wants to be reminded of a birthday. To me, that seems very foolish. It is not a misfortune to grow older, year by year—not when, as with yourself, each milestone represents additional progress.

More and more with the passing of time, you have become a vital force for good in your community. And that means more friends, more prestige, more to be thankful for each birthday.

It has been a great privilege to serve you these past 30 years. We have no customer who deserves more of our appreciation.

So a Happy Birthday to you tomorrow—and many, many more in the future.

Style: *Sincere and respectful.*
Situation: *Writer may or may not know the reader; good for all levels of correspondence.*

As you can see from these examples, congratulatory letters are not difficult to write. They generate exceptional goodwill when they are used properly. People want to believe that when good things happen to them and their family, other people are happy for them. Not all events in the life of a customer or friend are happy, however. There are times when condolences are in order rather than congratulations, and then the letter-writer faces a much more difficult job. Still, the effort to keep the personal touch in your business correspondence is well worth the efforts.

5. HOW TO WRITE COMPASSIONATE LETTERS OF CONDOLENCE

Sympathy: a real evidence of goodwill. The old saying, "A friend in need is a friend indeed," has great significance in customer relations. Probably no business letter is so much appreciated as the one that expresses sincere sympathy for a reader in distress; in no other way can a few short sentences go farther in offering comfort and building goodwill that lasts long after the shock of the misfortune has eased.

Businessmen generally recognize the importance of this fact, but the majority approach the writing of a condolence letter with considerable dread. Their mental attitude in such cases is much the same as yours is likely to be when you visit a funeral parlor to console a friend. Your heart beats faster in sympathy, but you just don't know *what* to say.

The difficulty of the message varies, of course, with the nature of the misfortune. It is not nearly so hard to talk to a customer about an accident to himself or someone in his family, when the chances of recovery are promising, as about the death of a close relative. If the loss is material, the problem is comparatively simple; especially, when sympathy can be accompanied by some tangible help. But death is something nobody likes to think or talk about, perhaps because we instinctively fear it.

Unfortunately, this dread of writing the condolence letter too often leads to the omission of the task. We *mean* to express our sympathy, but put it off until the time has passed when it would be appropriate. Or, if the job is finally done, our thoughts are so frozen by the inhibition of not knowing what to say that the final form of the message is either too blunt and cold, or too "flowery" and exaggerated. In neither case is the result what we intended.

A blueprint for benevolence. True sympathy is not an emotion that can be expressed by following specific directions—as a woman may knit a sweater or bake a cake. The formula of the Star, the Chain, and the Hook, has little or no value in composing a message of condolence, and anyone who thought to use it for such an occasion would surely come out with a monstrous example of insincerity. However, a few flexible suggestions may be helpful to those who find the condolence letter a perplexing problem. Do *not* take them too literally, as the last thing you want to do is to make your message so mechanical that it lacks warmth.

1. Place yourself in your reader's position—
   What if *your* business had been wiped out by fire?
   What if *your* loved one were dangerously ill in the hospital?
   What if *your* brother had died?

2. Say what you would if you were there—
   What words go along with that first handshake?
   What would you say as you make your exit?
   Remember: Be yourself.

3. Keep the language simple and brief—
   Resist the temptation to quote scripture or poetry, especially when talking about death.

Do not deliver a sermon, your reader is in no mood to hear one. Do not wax eloquent and effusive, the message will seem insincere.

4. Be sure your sympathy is *genuine*—
Don't be hypocritical.
You have no moral right to write the letter if your motive is merely to gain goodwill for yourself or your company.

5. Offer tangible aid—if help is possible—
Can you give material assistance to one who has suffered financial loss?
Does the reader need to be taken somewhere?
Can you provide temporary housing for a fire victim's records?

With the foregoing suggestions in mind, the best way to learn *how* to write an effective letter of condolence is to see how other businessmen have done the job.

Examining expressions of sympathy. All letters, even when death and sympathy are involved, can be adapted from the efforts of master letter mechanics. Look at these examples and see how they have followed the blueprint, kept their own style, and fulfilled this most difficult task of written goodwill. They are representative of the better sort commonly seen in modern business correspondence.

(1)

Dear _____,

I have heard through our mutual friend, Frank Smith, about the big loss sustained by your family during the recent floods.

At a time like this it is hard to find words to express one's thoughts. But you must believe me when I tell you we, too, feel your loss.

To lose your home is sad. No matter how elegant or how humble it may be, it's always "Home Sweet Home" to you. The kindly thoughts associated with that home—especially, those of your boyhood days spent there—will linger long in your garden of memories. It can't be otherwise.

Yet, out of this catastrophe—from the mass of debris and ruins—bigger and better towns will arise. They generally do, you know—so don't despair.

Do you remember that Latin phrase, Mr. _____? "Dum spiro, spero"—"Whilst I breathe, I hope." You know it's hope that pulls one through many a crisis.

It will pull you and yours through this one. As hard as it may seem, keep your courage, and don't lose faith.

(2)

Dear _____,

Our salesman, M. W. Prince, tells us you are in the locality most seriously affected by the flood. We realize there is very little help we can offer, but do wish to express our sympathy, and the hope that you have not suffered too great a loss.

If your envelope supply has been destroyed, we offer the complete facilities of our plant at Cleveland to rush supplies to you.

A letter outlining your needs will be given emergency attention. We shall also bend every effort to see that the most speedy delivery possible is made.

Note: Here is an offer of tangible aid.

(3)

Dear _____,

As I stood and looked at your father yesterday, I thought of you and his immediate family and their natural sorrow in losing this man who had been father and counselor for so many years.

But as I looked around me at the family and friends who were there, I knew that beneath your sorrow you were proud of your father and rightfully so.

He has left behind him a fine heritage in sons and daughters, and in loyal friends. You will miss your father but you will never be entirely without him, for his spirit is incorporated in every one of you.

So in this inadequate letter, I tell you, Malcolm, that I am sorry you lost him. Please do not hesitate to call upon us if there is anything we can do.

(4)

Dear _____,

The Quaker Organization was deeply moved upon hearing of the untimely death of your father, and hastens to extend its deep sympathy in this, your hour of trial.

While the privilege of knowing your father personally never fell to our lot, we realize the extent of the loss you have sustained.

At a time like this, mere words are empty and shallow, but yours is a suffering which is universal...which belongs to every human being in every corner of the world. A deep anguish which, sooner or later, cuts into every human heart...strong and weak.

Death is the inevitable goal, and there may be some small degree of consolation in the thought that death is but a narrow starlit strip between the companionship of yesterday and the happy reunion of tomorrow.

May this thought help you to carry on.

(5)

Dear _____,

Cynthia Brown tells me you went to the hospital a week ago for major repairs; that everything turned out fine, but you will be in bed another two or three weeks.

Knowing how strong you have been physically, I think you may fool these doctors, but just in case time passes slowly, I am mailing you today some books which I have read and liked.

The best of wishes for a quick recovery!

Note: A small gift makes a great impression.

(6)

Dear _____,

Word has just reached me of your husband's passing, and I am both deeply shocked and saddened at this tragic news.

Throughout the 20 years I knew John, he had the respect and admiration of everyone who came into contact with him. Too few are granted so warm a personality and so fine an intelligence.

Please accept my deepest and sincerest sympathy for you and your family in your bereavement.

(7)

Dear _____,

I heard yesterday the true story of the incidents that forced you out of the business you worked so hard to build. Don't worry about what the newspapers said. You still have friends, character, and ability.

When your plans are made to re-establish yourself, remember this company will go the limit to help you.

(8)

Dear ——————,

I see the critics have had you on the fire. Forget it. The concert was splendid, and you deserve better treatment. Most of these critics think they must tear everything apart to prove how smart they are.

Rubbish! The concert was good. You are good. And we are proud that you come to our store for the things you need and in what you are doing for the community.

Strive for simplicity in writing your messages of sympathy. Use short words. Use them sparingly. *Feel* what you are trying to say. You are not making a speech, writing an essay, or showing how kind you can be. You are just offering a friendly hand to a person in distress. Sentiment plays the part best when the stage is void of scenery.

6. REVIEWING MISCELLANEOUS GOODWILL LETTERS

Hi folks! We've moved. Naturally a business leader feels good when he can present tangible evidence of growth or improvement—and the customers to whom he tells the story will share his pleasure, IF the progress is presented as a *benefit to them*, and not just something to crow about. For example, on page 560 you read a letter from an executive of Curtiss 1000 Inc. to Miles Kimball. It was a reply to an announcement of new quarters for Mr. Kimball's company, Direct Mail Associates, Inc.

Now you will see in Figure 10-4 the announcement that impelled such a friendly letter. It must have developed considerable goodwill, if results are any measure. Mailed to a list of less than 200, the letter motivated many recipients to climb to the 19th floor to pay the writer a visit, and many more mentioned it to him later. And still better—the kind of replies included were what everyone loves—*orders.*

Dealers, too, can use appreciation letters to smooth relations with sources of supply. The one in Figure 10-5 was written to make the writer's company seem appreciative.

Goodwill and style—perfect partners. When you can catch your reader's attention and promote their goodwill at the same time, you have found the secret to powerful letters. Some examples will show how much can be generated from the stylish letter-crafter.

A clever letter that attracted a great deal of goodwill was written by Walter J. Tuohy, then president of the Chesapeake & Ohio Railway, a part of the CSX Transportation. It was sent in answer to an equally

Figure 10-4

Dear _____,

Won't you eat a hearty breakfast some morning soon and make the climb up here (albeit by elevator) to our new quarters?

It's a bit breathtaking (the lack of oxygen above the 19th floor, you know) but the true adventurer won't mind that. Besides, we'll have our trusty St. Bernard Alpine rescue dog out on the stairs, with a cask of the best about his neck.

We're proud of our new home and want to show it off to you. There's more than twice the room we had where we were born and spent the first 18 years of our life. It's worth the climb just to see Joe Bubasta, our production manager, reveling in the increased efficiency he's getting now.

Then, too, when you visit us we'll have a chance to cough politely and call your attention to all the new equipment we've bought these last few months: the printing multigraphs, automatically fed, which deliver 7500 letters each hour...the new high-speed Baum folder...the nine new computypeprinters and processors...the new automatic Gordon printing presses with Miller air feeders.

We'll hesitate—artfully—in front of these presses, because when you see the genuinely excellent color printing we're doing, you may make a mental note to call us in the next time you need letterheads, envelopes, invoices, or any other sort of printing. The man in charge of this department is a master printer in the old Guild sense of the word. Enclosed is a sample of a job going through one of the presses today.

Then we'll take you to my own turreted office, where—immodestly enough—the bookcase is decorated with the silver cup presented to us (the cup itself says) "for excellence of letter copy," and with the gold medal we got last fortnight for another DMA letter.

Whereupon we shall realize at long last that these things which mean so much to us, couldn't possibly be quite *that* interesting to you...and for the rest of your stay we'll be well-mannered. We do want you to come. If there's a hurry-up job you need now, of course telephone us—at (123) 456-7890.

But plan to visit us soon.

Figure 10-5

Dear _____,

We're pretty busy these days, getting ready for the formal opening of our remodeled store. And it would take something pretty important to make us pause in these preparations.

But that's what we think of your generous cooperation with us in the publicity for this event. It's important to us; has made us feel very good.

But then we're not surprised, for in the period we have been doing business with you, we have found you always willing to go out of your way to be helpful to us. We might as well acknowledge, here and now, how much that spirit has been appreciated, and helped us enjoy our work.

We, at this end, shall strive constantly to merit that consideration in the future. We think that your shoes are now in one of the finest stores in the state—anyway, positively the finest store of its kind in the city. We only wish that you could be with us Friday of this week for our formal opening.

Again, thanks sincerely. And now we'll resume trimming our windows.

---

clever letter written by a young girl, Judy. Both letters are reproduced in Figure 10-6, A and B. Attached to the letter was a check for $50 marked "Food for Fido."

It was hard to resist Warren Piper's invitation to see the "Famous Crown of the Andes." In the letter even Mr. Piper's postscript adds a personal touch that is interesting and amusing. (See Figure 10-7.)

The art of the artful introduction. Although frequently used in business, letters of introduction are usually cold as ice, and far too formal. Obviously, this lack of warmth is a detriment to the people being introduced, since the success of their mission partly depends on the interest of the person who reads the letter.

The adequate letter of introduction should accomplish at least three things: first, give the full name of the person being introduced; second, give a satisfactory reason for the intrusion; and third, make the party who gets the letter really *want* to meet the person talked about. It is in the third of the purposes that the letter of introduction often falls short.

Figure 10-6

A

Mineral, Va.
December, 19___

Mr. Walter J. Tuohy
President
Chesapeake & Ohio Railway
Cleveland, Ohio

Dear Mr. Tuohy,

We lived beside the railroad,
    In a cottage small and white,
We loved to watch the trains go by,
    At morning, noon and night.

We waved to all the engineers,
    And called them all our friends,
But now there's been a tragedy,
    That brought that to an end.

We had a dog we loved so well,
    She was a big Great Dane,
We found her Monday by the tracks,
    Killed by your speeding train.

We know you couldn't help it,
    But she was our only pet,
If we could have another dog
    It would help us to forget.

He wouldn't have to be so big,
    Just one to love and feed,
A little fluffy puppy
    Is all that we would need.

My daddy says that Santa
    Is awfully poor this year;
There's five of us already
    And another almost here.

But if he digs around his pouch,
    And finds a little pup,
And leaves it here at our house,
    We'll never give it up.

I'll love him, oh, so very much,
    And keep him off the rail,
So please, if you see Santa,
    Won't you tell him our tale?

Very truly yours,

Judy Mahone

B

THE CHESAPEAKE AND OHIO RAILWAY COMPANY
TERMINAL TOWER   CLEVELAND 1 OHIO

WALTER J. TUOHY
PRESIDENT

December 16, 19 ___

Dear Judy:

We're sorry that you lost your dog,
    Your one and only pet,
But we have talked to Santa,
    To see what we can get.

At Christmas-time it's not so nice,
    To suffer such a loss,
Just when you should be happy,
    You're saddened and you're cross.

We know how much a pet can mean,
    Because we have one too,
A kitten we call "Chessie",
    A little one like you.

Our Engineers are very sad,
    They didn't see your Dane,
They didn't mean to hurt him,
    And cause you all this pain.

So we have talked to Santa,
    And told him what we did,
He said he'd look inside his pouch,
    To see what he had hid.

We're sure he has a puppy,
    (He hinted one was there)
We told him where to bring it--
    To your cottage, white and fair.

To all of you at Mineral,
    A Christmas full of cheer,
To your brother and your sisters,
    To your Dad, and Mother Dear.

Judy, Merry Christmas,
    Stay bright-eyed and dewy,
Take good care of the puppy,
    Sincerely, Walter Tuohy.

Miss Judy Mahone
Mineral, Virginia

Figure 10-7

·WARREN PIPER & COMPANY·

Importers of Diamonds
Manufacturers of Platinum Jewelry

31 NORTH STATE STREET
CHICAGO

September 21, 19

To my Friends, Patrons, Neighbors,
      Rotarians, Club Mates . . . and to You in particular:

It is possible that you already know from the newspapers, radio or movies, that I have finally succeeded in buying the famous Crown of The Andes which contains the oldest and largest collection of emeralds in the world. I hesitate to place three superlatives in one paragraph, but it happens to be the largest jewel transaction in history.

I want my friends to see the famous Crown in all its glory while it is still in Chicago, because it is so magnificent that it is impossible to describe or illustrate its beauty. Also I am afraid it will be necessary to dismantle the lovely diadem and sell the jewels separately. The new owners are money-minded men who can hardly be expected to know that we who handle precious jewels are in the calm and proud possession of eternal things. There are 453 emeralds of superb quality in the famous Crown, and they have been offered $250,000 for one single stone.

I am enclosing two complimentary tickets for the exhibit of the Crown and other treasures which are now being shown on the 8th floor of The Fair Store, State and Adams Street corner, as a personal compliment to Mr. D. F. Kelly. The exhibit will be open from 9 A.M. to 5 P.M. daily until September 30th.

I hope you will enjoy the exhibit as my guests.

Sincerely,

Warren Piper

Please don't try to find me on September 24th, because that is my red-letter day, my forty-fifth birthday, my fifteenth wedding anniversary, and the twenty-sixth anniversary of my business. All three on one day, and the doctors have me on the water-wagon!

How personal the introduction may be depends on the relationship between writer and reader. If the two parties are friends, or if they have known each other in a business way for a long time, the tone of the message can be much more intimate than if they are comparative strangers. Here are three examples:

(1)

Dear ⸺,

On the train returning from the National Convention, you will remember that we talked about the cold and lifeless letters commonly written by employees of insurance companies. We both thought something should be done to correct this condition.

Accordingly, we hired an outsider to conduct a Better Letter Course in our company. In a way, we stole a march on you, for the man in charge is a resident of your city.

His name is William Watson, and I am giving this letter to him with the suggestion that he present it to you personally. I am doing this as a sort of favor to you, because from the results gained here, I think you will want this man to do a similar job in your own company.

He is strictly okay, and approaches the job from a business point of view, rather than that of a college professor.

(2)

Dear _____,

If you have ever doubted my appreciation of your many orders, here is proof of its reality.

During the past three years we have had a salesman who has been highly satisfactory in every way. Now he is forced to move to your part of the country. You know, where men grow big and strong, and have plenty of hair on their chests.

Since we cannot use Jimmy Ware in Colorado, I am asking him to contact you. You'll like his red hair, and the way he brings in orders.

(3)

Dear _____,

One of the drawbacks in the size of our business family is the inability of many of our office men to get acquainted with dealers in distant territories.

Nevertheless, when one of them does get out on a trip, he tries to meet as many customer friends as possible. And that's what Russel Smith is going to do next month.

The name, of course, is already familiar to you, for he has written to you many times about matters pertaining to promotion and advertising. For example, he arranges the repainting of your signs, and often sends you reprints of ads, new promotional material, and other sales helps.

Russ and his wife are driving from here to Seattle and should pass through your city about the tenth of September. He won't have a lot of time, but you can be sure he'll spend an hour in your store, just to say "hello" and give you a preview of the new product you will hear a lot more about after the first of the year.

Don't plan any entertainment for Russ and his wife. They really won't have time for it. But it is good that you two should get to know each other personally.

The simplest forms of introduction are those written on the back of business cards. They serve the purpose when both parties are rather well acquainted, but are not appropriate if the relationship is more formal. The message on the card cannot be long, but it can at least say something to arouse interest in the person being introduced.

Any of the following might be adequate:

- Joe: If you have wished for a really good secretary, wish no more. Introducing Virginia Browne. She's tops.

- Hello, Ms. Palmer, I want you to know Jack Smith. He has helped us no end—can do as much for you.

- Bill, shake hands with Henry Wilson. He has a story you will want to hear.

In several of the sections that follow, you will find many additional illustrations to prove that goodwill may be woven into the fabric of all kinds of business correspondence. There is no reason for dividing letters into two groups, saying: "These are goodwill letters, and these are not." *All* letters should reflect a spirit of friendliness, irrespective of what they talk about. In this section, you simply have seen types of correspondence in which the emphasis on goodwill may be somewhat stronger; so strong at times, that the gaining of it was the only purpose in their mailing. Many of them could be ruled "unnecessary" from the viewpoint of actual operation of the business; but not from the viewpoint of cementing the bond of loyalty between company and customers. These so-called goodwill letters are *important*, and deserve most serious executive consideration. *Their omission is a direct loss to sales.*

IMPROVING HUMAN RELATIONS IN LETTERS

IMPROVING HUMAN
RELATIONS IN LETTERS

1. HOW TO EXPRESS PERSONAL REGARD

Extending the extra courtesies of business. Apart from company purposes, there are many letters written that represent nothing more than good fellowship, and the will of the writers to be nice to those with whom they are acquainted. Indirectly, they may facilitate the transaction of business, but they are not mailed with that intention. Charles Hanson Towne's poem, "Around the Corner," perhaps points to the motive behind these letters. Do you remember it?

> Around the corner I have a friend,
> In this great city that knows no end;
> Yet days go by and weeks rush on,
> And before I know it a year has gone,
> And I never see my old friend's face,
> For life is a swift and terrible race.
> He knows I like him just as well
> As in the days when I rang his bell
> And he rang mine. We were younger then,
> And now we are busy, tired men—
> Tired with playing a foolish game,
> Tired with trying to make a name.
>
> Tomorrow, say, I will call on Jim,
> Just to show that I'm thinking of him,
> But tomorrow comes—and tomorrow goes,
> Around the corner, yet miles away...
> 'Here's a telegram, sir'... 'Jim died today!'
> And that's what we get and deserve in the end—
> Around the corner, a vanished friend.

The letters in this section were written by people who take their human relationships seriously. They like to pause now and then to dictate a personal letter to some business friend: sometimes, to reply when no reply is needed; sometimes, to comment on an incident of credit to the recipient. Without these human relationships business would be cold and uninviting, as indeed some people try to make it. But the ones who get the most out of their business life do not agree that everything they do must be connected with the making of money. They *do* "remember Jim."

From the writing of these personal letters you can derive much enjoyment, and the replies that come back to you will more than make the effort worthwhile. Of course, they too are goodwill letters, if you want to call them that; but the writers speak not so much for their companies, as for *themselves*. For example, when Tim Thrift dictated the letter shown in Figure 11-1, he was replying to a compliment that had been paid to a booklet he had prepared for circulation among his business friends. He had written the copy, and set the type with his own hands, not for any special reason, except that it was his pleasure to keep in touch that way with those he knew and liked. Thus, the letter to Tim, and his reply, represented an *exchange* of mutual regard, and both men were warmed by the thought of it.

The format of this letter is also worth your attention. Most business executives have their own private stationery for use on semi-personal occasions. You would expect one of the masters of the letter-writing world to have something especially attractive, and Mr. Thrift does not disappoint you. The paper, a heavyweight, is buff color, with a deckled edge at the bottom. It is trimmed slightly smaller than the conventional 8 ½ X 11 letterhead size. The two large t's are printed in a lively red, the rest in a solid black. The typist of the letter completed the perfect whole with a new job of blocking. The signature is bold and interesting. In its original colors, you could not imagine a more attractive ensemble.

Of course, a cordial letter contact does not need to be as formal, as this sample. Personality and warmth may be just as conspicuous when offered in smaller doses. Note how one business executive made just two paragraphs interesting.

Dear⸺⸺,

I have tried various means of putting myself in an Oriental mood in order to more fittingly accept your kind invitation for Thursday, June 28th, at 6:30 p.m.

However, my attempts have all been in vain, probably because my Honorable Ancestors have imbued me with only an Occi-

Figure 11-1

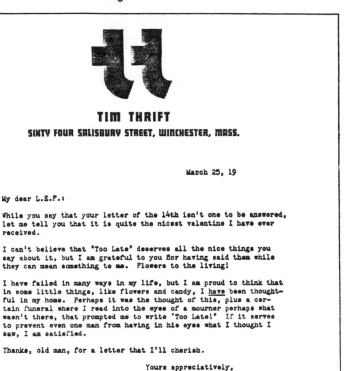

TIM THRIFT

SIXTY FOUR SALISBURY STREET, WINCHESTER, MASS.

March 25, 19

My dear L.E.F.:

While you say that your letter of the 14th isn't one to be answered, let me tell you that it is quite the nicest valentine I have ever received.

I can't believe that "Too Late" deserves all the nice things you say about it, but I am grateful to you for having said them while they can mean something to me. Flowers to the living!

I have failed in many ways in my life, but I am proud to think that in some little things, like flowers and candy, I <u>have</u> been thoughtful in my home. Perhaps it was the thought of this, plus a certain funeral where I read into the eyes of a mourner perhaps what wasn't there, that prompted me to write "Too Late!" If it serves to prevent even one man from having in his eyes what I thought I saw, I am satisfied.

Thanks, old man, for a letter that I'll cherish.

Yours appreciatively,

dental background. Therefore, I shall simply say "thank you" for including me, and I shall join you at 7 Mott Street at the appointed time.

Jack Carr, one of the small group who helped blaze the trail to better business letters has always seemed at his best when writing to a friend. Following, you have a sample of his friendliness, and the light, humorous way in which he handles a more or less serious subject. Incidentally, in the longest paragraph, he pleads for more letters in business of the type we are considering in this section.
Presenting Jack Carr!

- There seem to be so few people in the world like you—fine folks who will take the time and trouble to write a little letter like yours of the 11th.

- I wish I had Tom Dreier's gift of expressing my emotion when I read your marvelous message. Imagine what a wonderful thing is the mail...capable of conveying across a continent a warm, human handclasp like you put into that letter.

- We've never met personally, I don't believe. And still as I read your message here on my desk I feel we've got much in common...besides tonsils.

- Here's an idea! Let's start this New Year with a resolution to write more letters like yours. Do a little more verbal backpatting. God knows the world is hungry today for a bit of sympathy and understanding and encouragement.

- Billy B. Van has the right idea. As a spreader of sunshine that man merits a monument. There's a place in the sun, under my Palm Tree, any old time he's ready to sit there. And if you'll just say the word, we'll move over and make room for you too.

Any of these genuine kudos would be welcomed by you or your readers, would they not? So let us turn our attention to uncovering the ways to produce what was called "verbal backpatting."

Strategies for the unexpected "pat." The absolutely best characteristic of letters of personal regard is their unexpected and, therefore, spontaneous natures. Your readers should be pleasantly startled by your taking special notice of *them*. The more unexpected the "pat" the higher the goodwill lift. No opportunity should be missed for this friendly sparkler. Not long ago, the papers carried the story of the 100th birthday of a well-known and greatly loved State Street merchant in Chicago. Hundreds of letters were sent by business friends to celebrate the occasion. The recognition of service anniversaries is a much appreciated act of business courtesy, especially when the event represents a great many years in the harness.

The letter in Figure 11-2 was mailed to the head of a Midwest company on this 50th service birthday. The writer was a former employee. You can almost imagine the smile and warm glow on Mr. Crawford's face when he read this "pat."

Sometimes a letter of appreciation may give the recipient an opportunity to reply in the same spirit. When one "pat" leads to another, the business relationship has definitely taken a step upward to becoming a personal one. As we have seen throughout this book, people talking to people is the goal of every successful letter-writer. Figures 11-3 and 11-4 are fine examples of this personal contact.

Figure 11-2

Dear Mr. Crawford,

I don't know of any letter I would rather write than this one about your 50th service birthday. And yet it seems impossible to put in words how I feel toward you and the company which you have led to so many victories. You know how it is with the thoughts which are deepest in the heart—like people caught in a burning building, they all rush out together.

So often we hear it said, "If I could only live my life again, how different it would be." I, too, have wished I could do that, but there is very little I would change in the ten years I spent in your company.

All that I have managed to do since dates back to what *you* gave me—the will to work with enthusiasm, to plan ahead, to make every accomplishment only the beginning of another step forward, to encourage others to make the most of their opportunities, to live for God, and *with* God, realizing that this earthly stay is only a preparation for His kingdom.

All of these precious values you gave me, and I shall ever be grateful. A lot of water has passed over the dam, but not a day comes that I do not feel the influence of your inspired leadership.

God bless you on this 50th anniversary. You will never really grow old, Mr. Crawford, for yours is the spirit of youth, and all that you have taught others will live on eternally.

With regard for time spent together. Some people are more thoughtful than others in writing a thank-you or appreciation letter after personal contacts in which some service or courtesy was extended. The situations that call for such letters are numerous—failure to take advantage of them means loss of goodwill that easily could have been salvaged, and in some cases, an act of rudeness. The speaker who has been well-treated by a business organization, the executive who has been the guest of a friend at the latter's golf club, the traveler who has been taken out to dinner by a business acquaintance in another city, any recipient of a business courtesy, should take time to send a little letter of appreciation. (See Figures 11-5 and 11-6.)

Figure 11-3

Dear _____,

Among the letters in my possession is one written by a merchant in Florida to a credit manager "up North." He said, "I don't see why you pester me about a bill which is only two months past due—down here in our state that's considered about the same as cash."

I thought of that a minute ago when, after working all day on a pile of unanswered letters, the one you wrote to me a month ago came to the surface. It looks as if replying in 30 days is considered about the same as by return mail—by yours truly.

Nevertheless, I can't ever remember getting a letter which I appreciated so much, and I shall always prize it highly.

Of course, what you said wasn't the whole story, because everybody knows (unless it's you) who is responsible for the progress in your Department—who trained and inspired all the fine people working there.

But it's nice to know a man like you who takes the praise that rightfully is all his own, and says to a friend, "Come share with us lest we be selfish." It's been a long time—too long, Henry—since I have read the Bible, but I think it talks a lot about sharing our honors with others.

I don't know exactly how to say it—maybe I shouldn't even try. But I think you are the salt of the earth, Henry, and I am very grateful to have had your friendship.

Figure 11-4

Dear _____,

Always at this time of year I take inventory...

...not of merchandise on dusty shelves or in gloomy store rooms, but of friends.

I seat them before me in a comfortable group and through clouds of smoke from a much used pipe, I look them over carefully and ask myself, "What have I done to make their lives happier—and what have they done for me?" For friendship is a two-way road.

And I see that I have received much—and given but little!

Sweet people, these, for their hearts are molded to the proposition that it is better to give than to receive.

Are some outstanding? Yes! For some men hand out priceless gifts like encouragement and inspiration. They stimulate the mind. They help tremendously in smoothing over the rough spots...with no thought of reward.

And I pause—to gaze upon a kindly countenance—the smiling face of one of my outstanding friends. I would chat with him. The group withdraws—and I am left alone with this one man. I offer him my pouch and point to a glass. We drink a toast, of my proposing...to "My friend, _____!"

Figure 11-5

Dear _____,

One of my most enjoyable evenings was spent with you folks in Chicago. It will always be a pleasant memory to me, and all along I shall be hopeful that you will make the trip to Mexico, and arrange to spend some time here with us in Fort Worth.

Gosh all fishhooks! It's hard for a country boy like me to find words to express myself properly. Not having the command of the English language like you do, it's possible that in such a case the less one tries to say, the better off he is. Silence would, no doubt, be golden, but I just can't help talking, even in a business letter. So I must say that I am grateful to you for your hospitality.

Here's one of those long-distance handshakes from down in Texas, and although you may not hear from me very often; I want you to remember throughout the year that I will have pleasant thoughts of you two.

My love to both of you!

2. APPLAUDING PERFORMANCE OR SERVICE IN YOUR LETTERS

Recognizing good work. As we go through the daily grind of business, now and then we are favored by exceptional service or a special courtesy on the part of some workers. They may be the gas station attendants who take particular pains to wash the windows and

Figure 11-6

Dear _____,

Here I am back home again after a day which was really tops for fellowship and interest. I could see that you have built an unusual spirit among the members of your association.

That is no exaggeration. You know a speaker compares and rates audiences, just as audiences compare and rate speakers. I don't know when I have talked to a group as "ready, willing, and able" as yours.

Particularly, did I enjoy the trip to the Zales' farm. From now on I'll get more pleasure out of watching the horses run— because I can bet on their stable. It may cost me some money, but it will be worth the gamble. I saw one black colt that should win a big race someday. I'd like to *see* it happen.

Here's hoping our paths cross again, my friend—until then, get plenty of that old sunshine.

Sally Kimball

check the oil, clerks who make helpful suggestions, ushers in the theatre who try to make their ticket-holders comfortable, or any other individuals who give to their jobs that "something more" which the average worker never even thinks to give. The executives who stop to write a letter of appreciation for such outstanding service are not only performing an act of courtesy but they are also helping to encourage the kind of public relations we all want, but seldom encounter.

A bouquet of orchids, then, to Vice-President H. Clay Jackson, of the Southwestern Petroleum Co., Inc., who took the trouble to commend the good work of a telephone operator in Fort Worth, Texas. Evidently, Mr. Jackson was well acquainted with the executive to whom he wrote, for he addresses him as "Dear Ed." (See Figure 11-7.)

It is true that letters of this variety take a little time to write, and when they are not written nobody knows the difference. However, it seems that the bigger the people in business, the more thoughtful they are likely to be in passing along such courtesies. Perhaps the reason is that the leaders in business best know the importance of praise in motivating employees. Just as they appreciate a good word for one of

Figure 11-7

Dear Ed,

It is a long cry from that curious instrument exhibited by Alexander Graham Bell at the Philadelphia Centennial in 1876 to the intricate and marvelous System of today; from that first New York exchange, noisy as the Board of Trade in a Bull Market to the almost noiseless automatic service. Truly the history of the telephone is the history of the Nation.

Before we hear the last "number please," due to your mechanical gadgets that will rob us of that lull where we might put our feet up on the desk and wait for "her" to do the work, let me take time out today and pin a bouquet on the lapel of one of your splendid operators whose willing service is appreciated very much by the writer.

A few days ago, I was trying to locate one of our salesmen traveling in Ohio...this young lady in your office worked very hard on the call, and though we did not locate the party, it was not her fault. She stayed right on the call for at least half an hour, and it was a very pleasant visit for me to listen to her as she had Chicago, Detroit, and many other large cities helping her with her work.

I do not know her name, but I did get her number (30)...and I know this fine girl is writing her name in kindness, love, and mercy on the hearts of thousands with whom she must come in contact year by year. Her name and her deeds are building a monument for The Southwestern Bell Telephone Company that storms of Time can never destroy.

I have "kicked" about telephone service when I thought a kick was coming. Not many kicks, however, on your Fort Worth service...and since this was a most unusual case of service well-performed, I most heartily commend this young lady to you, and would appreciate your conveying my good wishes and thanks to her.

their own workers, they try to speak favorably for those in other companies that serve them well. An outstanding example was the late L. A. Downs, president of the Illinois Central System, whose letters helped in many ways to develop friendly public relations for his railroad. When Mr. Downs consented to an article about himself in *American Business*, he had no further obligation to either the editor of this magazine, or the author. Nevertheless, he took time to write the following note of appreciation:

Dear _____,

Mr. Whitmore has sent me a copy of *American Business* for March, and I have read with more pleasure than I can possibly express here your exceedingly generous article about my letters.

Please accept this note as a sincere statement of my deep appreciation.

With the kindest regards,

Later on, you will have the opportunity of reading more of the goodwill letters written by L. A. Downs. How he found time to write them was a puzzle to his associates, but thousands of individuals in all walks of life were favored with his cordial, human messages.

Giving a pat for retirement. Retirement most likely comes to everyone in business. Along with letters of congratulations upon reaching this august age, the most treasured ones are the "pats" from colleagues, customers, and other concerned well-wishers.

Here are the examples of retirement sentiments. The style of each one is different, but there can be no doubt the feelings expressed are genuine:

(1)

Dear _____,

As I contemplate your resignation as Vice-President, my emotions are split two ways. I know how abundantly you have contributed to the reputation of the _____ Company, and certainly 50 years is a long time to remain steadfastly in the service. For all of that you have my sincere congratulations.

And yet, as I think of the company *without* your quiet, rugged leadership, there comes a feeling of great loss, and the wish that you could always be there in your office; ready as in the past to help the staff when in distress, or to share the joy of their good deeds.

Knowing the modesty of your personality, I doubt if you realize how much the staff have leaned on you—or how often they have spoken your name to me with genuine appreciation of the interest you have taken in them. You may be sure, Mr. Gable, that your name has been written too deeply in their hearts to ever be erased by the passing years.

I do not know what plans you have made for the future. I only know that I wish you a period of great happiness, and perhaps the opportunity to do some of the things you have been denied under the pressure of work obligations. I can think, too, of no greater pleasure than to pause at the end of 50 years to review old accomplishments—to take inventory of your many friends.

And so, old friend, I salute you! May God bring you many more happy years—the reward for all that you have done for others.

(2)

Dear _____,

To me, the 40 years you have spent with this organization have been like a perfect day. I see you leaving with the same feeling I would have when I am sitting on a bluff watching a beautiful sunset. My heart is full of thanks for all this day has brought me, but I am sad to see its end.

The day to come may not be as long as the day gone by, but it may be enriched by the memories of my association with men like you.

(3)

Dear _____,

I was indeed sorry to read of your retirement from the United States Supreme Court. During my studies at Harvard Law School and thereafter in the practice of law, I followed your opinions carefully. I have always admired your sound reasoning and the excellence of your decisions.

Your retirement will be a great loss to the country. It will be difficult to replace the dignity which you lent to the Supreme Court.

With all best wishes,

Since these letters are so welcomed, business correspondents would be remiss in not taking this last opportunity for showing their personal regard for their readers.

Promotion, praise, and partners—a letter for all. Recognition of good performance includes the friendly "amen" for the individuals who have just climbed a step higher on the business ladder. They may be business associates of the person who writes the letter, or connected with some other company. In either case, congratulations in writing are likely to be more appreciated than those extended on the telephone or even in person. A letter may be taken home for family inspection, or filed for safekeeping. You may think that average businesspeople attach no importance to the compliments they may receive on "the way up," but this opinion is contradicted by the many successful executives who keep scrap books, or some other record, to mark the pleasant incidents in their careers. One business leader, known from coast to coast and often quoted in the newspapers, has two letter files to which he alone has access. One is labeled "Bouquets," and the other "Brickbats." These two collections, he claims, have helped to keep his ego in proper adjustment.

Be that as it may, a letter like that in Figure 11-8—sincerely motivated, and so accepted—is a certain goodwill builder.

An idea that seems unusually good for the commpany that can use it is tendering of appreciation for good work to the family of an employee. It is illustrated in the following letter. The purpose is to win as much goodwill as possible.

Dear Mr. and Mrs. _____,

Your daughter, Marjory, has just completed a short term of employment in our Transcription Department.

I thought you would like to know that we were well pleased with her work and attitude, and we were sincerely sorry to see her go. When she again looks for a position, I hope we will have something which will appeal to her.

Marjory has been a credit to your home, and I know you must be proud of her.

The idea of paying tribute to *someone else* who has had a hand in the success of an individual can be adapted in many ways, and since this other person is usually left in the background, the goodwill created by an unexpected letter of praise is sure to be more than worth the effort. Here are two examples:

(1)

Dear _____,

It was very nice to see you at the sales banquet on Thursday night. You looked so proud sitting there at the table of Champions with your husband.

And you had a good right to be. An increase of 68 per cent in volume over last year is something to brag about. I am proud of Harvey, too.

Figure 11-8

Dear "Vice-President"—

It was a great pleasure to hear of your promotion. At the banquet where the good news was announced I tried to congratulate you personally, but I cannot resist the urge to place in print how I feel about your good fortune, which surely you so much deserve.

It must be a challenge to take the place of one who has been both your leader and your friend. I know that you have prayed for the strength to carry on his good work—and to add, as you surely will, to all that he accomplished.

It always has seemed to me that you and _____ were like brothers united in one common purpose. I know how often the two of you were mentioned by employees in your company—as if you were a team pulling them over a rough road.

Now, my friend, the load is yours to pull alone, and we who know your power have no doubt of the result.

It must be, too, a great satisfaction for you to start this new responsibility with the hearty approval of those in the ranks, as well as that of the board members who selected you for the job. You have always gone out of your way to be decent and helpful in contacts with workers—now the seed you planted is bearing fruit. There isn't a man or woman in your company who isn't glad to see you made Vice-President.

In the mental image of the many who are pleased over your promotion, look at the man in the back row, second from the right. Yes, that's *me*. The old boy is tickled pink.

But the purpose of this personal note is to let you in on a secret. It concerns *you*.

One of the biggest reasons for Harvey's success is the cooperation and encouragement which he gets from his *wife*. I know this is true, because he, himself, has told me so.

You know, as a sales manager I have seen some salesmen held back by wives, and others pushed ahead. You are one of those that *inspires*.

Harvey and I are very grateful for your fine understanding of a salesman's problems—for all the help in making him a success.

I thought you ought to know.

(2)

Marjorie,

Since I saw _____ _____ this morning, I have been thinking about the many years you have been my efficient secretary.

The reason is that _____ _____ was very complimentary about the report you typed on the new Training Plan. He said it was not only logical in content (my part) but the best looking report, and easiest to read (your part) he had received in his 40 years with the company.

You see he wanted it to be a perfect job, because now it goes to the Chairman of the Board.

I could have told you all this, but it occurs to me that I have been thoughtless in not always giving you credit for your loyalty and good work. This time, I wanted to make my appreciation a matter of record.

We have worked together as a team for a long time. You really have done a swell job, although many times I must have tried your patience.

A letter such as this last one, if the writer wanted to think of it selfishly, should be worth many times its weight in gold, for surely the person who got it would be inspired to extra effort. And the same is true with respect to any down-the-line employee, whose work is too seldom given proper recognition.

3. EFFECTIVE METHODS FOR BETTERING HUMAN RELATIONS

Weaving an intricate pattern. As you no doubt realize, the threads woven and embroidered into the cloth of human relations run in many directions. The letters you have been reading touch only a small number of the activities common to business. They do, however, have one common attribute—the reflection of the writers' personalities, and their feelings of brotherhood with other human beings. No one can be properly trusted with human relations unless they have a genuine *liking* for people—all people, irrespective of their station in life, or their work level in the business world.

The letters that follow were obviously written by individuals who enjoy human contacts. Always you see a person *talking* sympathetically to the reader—understanding the latter's emotions and eager to share them, good or bad. Every company needs workers of this calibre, for the goodwill they win is an asset too great for calculation.

(1)

Dear _____,

I won't give you any excuses for the delay, except to say I am sorry. But with this note, you are getting the booklet, and I hope it proves worth waiting for.

Also, kind sir, I thank you for the privilege of doing this work for you. I trust your client appreciates the bargain you engineered for him, as I really spent more time than I had anticipated. But Grandma always said it is more blessed to give than to receive—and who would argue with Grandma?

Until the bell rings again,

"Begging to remain,"

(2)

Dear _____,

Thanks for your impatient letter. I don't blame you for wondering about the book. But really, I'm helpless.

I spent one afternoon last week with the printers, but they are in an awful mess, due to labor pains. The situation in the whole Chicago area is lousy. If fist-fights would help, we would be in there swinging.

At least while out there, I saw the plates coming through. And I promise to keep after everybody who has a hand in the job.

(3)

Dear _____,

Isn't it a doggone shame when some nice guy drops into your office to say "hello" and finds that you are out on a Welfare, Chamber of Commerce, Y.M.C.A., Boy Scouts, or what-have-you Drive? Apparently that is what I was doing last week. I am so sorry I missed you.

I did check on your speech to the Ad Club, and am told you did yourself proud.

Now please do not forget the address, and when you are in town again, drop in for a good chat.

My best wishes to you and Mrs. Smith.

With the warmth generated by these letters, the glow of goodwill can leap to great heights. But not all letters can be happy and light, some must be sad. Yet, as we will see, the glow can linger.

Writing personal letters about death. The difference between the following letters and the others in Section 11 is in the relationship between reader and writer. Here, the letter is more personal—quite separate from business affiliations. The nature of the problem, however, is the same—what can be said that might bring some comfort to a person so saddened by death?

(1)

Dear _____,

I was shocked to hear of Bill's passing. Mrs. Smith and I wish we could do something to make things easier for you.

You and Bill were so nice to us at the Charlotte Convention. It will always be a pleasing memory.

On December 31, Bill wrote to me that he had just returned to the city from a fishing trip. I think this must have been one of his last letters to a friend. I shall prize it highly.

Should you and your lovely daughters ever come to Cleveland, please remember our home is your own.

(2)

Dear _____,

A letter came from Jennifer Jones yesterday, with the word of your wife's death. I was deeply saddened.

Probably others would expect me now to know what to say that might help a little bit to soften your sorrow. Instead, it all seems so futile, there being experiences in this patch-quilt world of ours that simply will not yield to words.

You know, however, my good friend, that I feel deeply for you in this time of adversity, and the many miles between us cannot lessen my feeling of being *close* to you—or the wish that I *could* help.

All human relations can benefit from these "pats." Let us now look at some widely divergent situations, each aided by warmth of goodwill.

Ambassador of goodwill—Lawrence A. "Larry" Downs. Throughout his business career, Mr. Downs never lost interest in human relations. He did everything that might be expected of a business executive to win and hold the friendship of those who even remotely had any contact with his company. His own circle of friends reached far and wide into all walks of life. He had an uncanny sense of human relationships, and could talk with sympathy and understanding to any individual, on any subject.

In his letters, Mr. Downs practices the principles and spirit which are upheld in this *Handbook*. You saw one of his shortest messages earlier in this section; now you are going to see more. He is our choice as the typical executive among many who use letters to win goodwill and to maintain public esteem. Thousands of people in and out of the Illinois Central System remember the sincere friendliness of his personality; thousands have been touched by fellowship, which was neither forced nor limited to a select group. Mr. Downs *liked people*. He went out of his way to extend those little extra courtesies—usually by letter—that are so often overlooked in business life.

You will like the letters of "Larry" Downs; you will be sorry that his last message has been typed. He proved beyond any question that friendly letters can be an asset to any business. From even the few examples of his work that follow, you may gain a better concept of human relations—ideas for your own use.

These letters were orginally printed in the magazine, *American Business*. They were taken almost at random from the many carbon copies available. It would have been wasted effort to try to cull the "Best," for Mr. Downs wrote on the same high level of friendly effectiveness, day in and day out. He wrote no letters that held any reasons to offend. He was what every business letter-writer *can* be—an Ambassador of Goodwill.

To a Fellow Executive

The one purpose of this letter is to tell you how well I think you deserve the splendid compliment that is paid you in the N. W. Ayer & Son brochure, "Who Are the Leaders?"

If I were asked to name one man to represent what I consider the finest and best in our American tradition, whose life and work would stand as a refutation of the abuses that are heaped upon American business by some social and political agitators, you would be the man.

I am proud that the railroads can be represented in this fine tribute to America's industrial high command by one of its own leaders, and one who so well deserves that honor.

With assurance of my genuine affection and esteem,

About the New Baby

The announcement of the birth of Larry Downs Cavender on May 24 was received some time ago. I have delayed acknowledging the very nice compliment you pay me in giving the baby my name until I could secure a little gift for him. It is being forwarded today.

My wish for the boy is that he grow up to be a fine young man, a useful and worthy citizen, and a joy to his mother and dad.

With kind personal regards,

Appreciation

Your letter pays me the finest compliment that one in my position could receive. I want you to know that I very much appreciate the sincerity and frankness of it.

Looking backward, it does not seem like 40 years since I started working for the Illinois Central at a spot which I can see from the windows of my office.

However, the calendar tells me that it has been 40 years, and my heart tells me that they have been happy years, notwithstanding the disappointments which have been an inevitable part of the difficult times we all have experienced recently.

I thank you most cordially for your letter and your good wishes.

To a Customer

On Saturday morning, I received your letter and answered it immediately. I suppose you got my answer on Monday.

On Saturday evening we received your car of lumber from our connection at Winona, Miss. At 7 o'clock Sunday evening we had it in Robinson, 500 miles away.

If I do say so myself, that was pretty good service. We are always glad to look after our friends.

Loss from Fire

As a neighbor, the Illinois Central is mighty sorry over the loss which your company suffered through fire yesterday. I hope that the property destroyed was fully protected and that you will soon be able to rebuild.

With kindest regards,

To Retiring Director

Your decision to retire as a director of the Illinois Central has been received by the directors and also by the officers of the railroad with very keen regret. For myself, I regard your retirement as a deep personal loss.

The ties of nearly half a century are not easily broken in any case, and in the case of a man of your accustomed vigor and devotion to duty I know this decision was a hard one to make. As compensation for the sacrifice, however, you have the knowledge of an extraordinary length of responsibility conscientiously performed. Your service as a director has covered more than half the history of our railroad, and you have participated in decisions which have more than doubled its mileage, and have multiplied its capacity and efficiency many times.

Your faithfulness in attendance upon the annual inspection trips has endeared you to the many members of our organization, few of whom have rendered longer service than your own. They, too, will regret your retirement.

My own work as officer and director has benefited from the example and counsel derived from your seniority in years and experience. For that I thank you. It is my earnest wish that the relinquishment of the cares which you have borne so faithfully may result in your improved health.

To Another Executive

I do not undertake to read everything Arthur Brisbane writes, but I do not miss what he writes on any subject of as much interest to me as your birthday.

I read the piece about your birthday while on the train, and this is my first day in the office since then, and the first opportunity to send you a personal word of greeting.

I hope that you have a great many more anniversaries and that all of them will be happy ones.

Apology for Mistake

I don't know how to answer your letter. Our error was a piece of bad work, the like of which has never before occurred in my experience and I am sure will not occur again. Our people feel keenly over it; so much so, that they unburdened themselves to me, and I was told about it immediately.

I feel now that this is a belated apology and expression of regret—nevertheless, it is sincere.

To a Young Employee

It is true that my first job with this company was in the position of rodman. I was a graduate of Purdue University, having completed the general academic work and also the course in civil engineering.

While I was a rodman the thought never occurred to me that I might some day be president of the railroad. My immediate concern was to be a good rodman, and after I had mastered that job I began figuring on what I might do next. The usual line of promotion in that department is from rodman to instrumentman, so I began to prepare myself to be an instrumentman.

After awhile my chance came, and I was promoted. With each advancement in the organization, I went through the same experience—first endeavoring to do my immediate work thoroughly and later undertaking to prepare myself for the next step.

There are several thousand employees in our organization, and only one of them can hold my present position at any one time. However, every position in the organization is worth any man's best efforts.

Of course, the same is true of every other organization.

I send you my best wishes. Perhaps we will meet in the Board Room someday.

To a Fellow Official

The years pass swiftly. It seems only yesterday that we first met, when you and I were youngsters in the service. Today marks your twentieth anniversary with the Illinois Central. I am happy to present you and your wife with lifetime passes.

On such an occasion, I could say much regarding your splendid record, your faithfulness to the railroad, your loyalty as a personal friend, but I need not do so.

You know what is in my heart. It is my earnest wish that you and those dear to you will have many happy years together.

When you meet an executive interested in people, writing friendly letters to them, extending out-of-the-ordinary courtesies, you are almost sure to discover also that he is motivated by enthusiasm for his company, its products, and its personnel. Enthusiasm is not a quality that can be bottled; instead, it flows in ever-widening circles. Naturally, the person who *enjoys* his business connection is better able to scatter goodwill in his letters than the one who goes about with a long face and is at heart a malcontent.

Certainly, in all of the letters written by L. A. Downs, you catch a feeling of enthusiasm for the Illinois Central. He wanted others to respect his company as much as he did; perhaps, subconsciously, he felt a connection between his own goodwill contacts and the reactions of his readers to his beloved railroad. We do not think for a moment that friendly letters are written for that ulterior purpose, but we *do* believe that goodwill is a thing that inevitably bounces back to the individual or company that expresses it.

4. BLUEPRINT FOR LETTERS TO MOTIVATE EMPLOYEES

Executing an obligation of leadership. In the small company, with just a handful of workers, the president or manager can keep in touch with each employee personally. This, of course, is the most desirable form of supervision and motivation, but it is not practical in the larger corporations. The president of a flock of 1,000, for example, seldom knows all of his workers by name, and he couldn't possibly sit down and talk to each one of them at necessary intervals. To be sure, part of this leadership responsibility is delegated to department heads, but the head of a company is properly reluctant to lose all contact with those he should, by right of office, be the most qualified to encourage and direct.

In this predicament, the majority of chief executives and other leading officials usually fall back on personally dictated messages in which their thoughts for the mutual good of company and personnel are set forth. In some cases, the distribution takes place at regular intervals; in others, only when business leaders have something on their minds which they consider worth passing down the line. No matter in what form, or how often, the letters are sent to employees, it is highly important that they be written in simple language every employee will understand, and in such an interesting and convincing manner that they gain favorable acceptance. To make their messages effective, chief executives obviously need acquaintance with the principles of letter construction; they are no more immune to improvement than any humbler correspondent.

Unfortunately, some of the executive letters you may have seen or received do not do the job intended. The cause may be just one fault or a combination of several. The writers may forget that they are talking to folks of less experience or knowledge, so that what they say goes "over their heads." They may lack the ability to unbend and talk the language of the average person; or they may "preach" instead of point the way. They may write with the false notion that anything coming from an executive is sure to be carefully read, and therefore make no attempt to use interesting words or impelling suggestions. In the latter case, they ignore the formula of the Star, the Chain, and the Hook, although what they write is an attempt to influence human behavior. In that sense their message is just as much a sales letter as the one sent by the sales manager to the customers or prospects.

A personal letter to employees of the Jewel Tea Company, Barrington, Illinois, is shown in Figure 11-9. It was written in a way that wins attention and respect.

Figure 11-9

Dear _____,

I am about to celebrate my thirtieth Thanksgiving Day with Jewel. And I am happy. A question is on my mind; it is one which may interest you as well as me. What profit for a man to spend 30 years in one occupation, while his youth slips away?

Youth is impatient. Things, it feels, must happen and happen quick. If they don't happen in one spot, the urge is to try a new spot, and then maybe another. Natural, yes. But what youth possibly does not yet know is that the only happenings which can really count are those which happen within.

Luck, youth says, I must have; I must place myself where I will get the best breaks. It has not yet learned that it makes its own luck. It does not realize that in shifting about in search of *breaks* it may actually be applying *breaks* to its career; so that when youth is gone, it's just where it started.

So I think these years have been well spent. And as for the vanished youth—I wonder. Health I still have; it has been a healthy life. And I wonder if, when we speak so yearningly of vanished youth, we do not really mean that bodily health which, largely through indifference or ignorance, we so often abuse. For true youth is a thing of the spirit. And in spirit I do not feel a day older than I did 30 years ago. That, I think, is my grand Good Luck; that and the friends I have made these many years in this one spot. And I am thankful.

But you should be interested in my life only to the extent to which you can use the fruits of my experience to guide better your own course in your life. Here are a few simple suggestions of things worthwhile which I have learned, and which may appeal to you as good.

I have learned that one is laying up trouble for himself if he neglects the simple things that make for good health. Yet men are prone to do just that—and regret it later. Moderation in all things, and immediate heed to danger signals, will preserve that priceless possession of good health, the lack of which is a most serious handicap. Never forget it.

Teach yourself to like people and to like work. Take your job seriously—but don't take yourself too seriously. Believe that *how* you work is more important than *where* you work. Cultivate a sense of humor—laugh. To keep young you must play and you must have fun; make your job and your life a game—and play the game to win. Learn to get entertainment out of your work and out of your contacts with people. Be a good loser, but never quit.

Read—and keep an open mind. Just as stiff joints mark an aging body, so fixed ideas mark a mind in its dotage. Question your own opinions continually, and invite new ideas. You will never be old as long as you can say truthfully: The only thing I really know is that I don't know—but I propose to learn.

And quit worrying about yourself and your success. The people the world remembers best are those who forget themselves—and work for their fellow men. Center your interest not in yourself, but in your job, your family, your fellow workers. Study and strive for their success—and you will wake up some morning to find yourself a success.

Good health; interesting work; the satisfaction of accomplishment; the respect and love of your associates. For these be thankful.

Making the worker a partner. Another message full of "meat" for any employee with a serious attitude toward himself and his career appears in Figure 11-10. You feel that this executive is full of fight, and that his spirit must penetrate throughout the organization. Strong emphasis is placed on the position of each employee as a *partner* in the business. Also, the fact is made quite plain that the idea of partnership is not a mere slogan—each worker is expected to make a contribution to the team.

Figure 11-10

Dear Partner in Progress,

I have always been tremendously proud of the high type of men and women who represent this Company. That you have dedicated March as National Colborn month is but another indication of the splendid loyalty and cooperation with which you have always backed me up.

March closes the fiscal year, and all of us are naturally anxious to have it represent the best year by far in the history of our organization. I greatly appreciate the extra effort you are putting forth to make this month outstanding.

During periods of economic readjustment, many people in business blame their lack of success on "conditions." I know, however, that the real Century Crusader is much like Napoleon. When asked how he intended to combat seemingly insurmountable circumstances, he replied: "Circumstances?...I *make* circumstances.

General business conditions today mean little to a wide-awake salesforce. They capitalize on them, whatever they may be. Remember—when people are most interested in conserving money, "Silver-Seal" offers a real investment in economy.

Time and time again in the early days of this business, when others were spending their time "harmonizing the blues," my Fighting Partners were proving the old saying that "Good pilots are made in stormy waters." These fighters doubled their efforts; did some constructive thinking; and made their own circumstances. *They* GOT THE BUSINESS.

Although there is absolutely no comparison between *then* and *now*, some salesmen are licked by a few newspaper headlines. We remember, however, that this business enjoyed a successful inception during the toughest times this country has ever seen. We are privileged to draw aside the curtain of economic "fog" and look forward to personal prosperity and continued success. We, of Century, have never made a compromise with "conditions"—we never intend to. We are concentrating our efforts. We *are* getting the business.

During the coming year, I want to see you keep in step with the progress of the Company by being prepared to take ever-increased responsibilities. More first-rate men and women are joining our organization today than at any other time in our history. New opportunities for advancement are arising daily for those who demonstrate their ability to lead.

The outlook for the coming fiscal year is exceedingly bright. Brookmire's forecast of consumer incomes—the best index of future business activity—places the estimated consumer income for the next six months at 6% *over* the average for the past three years. Capitalize on this *fact*. Shove aside all negative influences with POSITIVE THINKING, POSITIVE ACTING, and POSITIVE SELLING.

Now is the time to act. Get going—and keep going, with

Your fighting partner,

Before his courageous spirit finally yielded to Death, Carl Wollner had several periods of illness. Returning from one of them, he dictated the following message found in Figure 11-11 to his employees.

Figure 11-11

To All My PANTHER Friends
In Office, Factory, and Field—

As I return after an absence of more than six months, my thoughts for you all can best be expressed in the words of a poet...

> A rose to the living is more
> Than sumptuous wreaths to the dead;
> In filling love's infinite store
> A rose to the living is more
> If graciously given before
> The hungering spirit is fled.

Let me thus hand a rose to all Members of the Panther Organization who have so nobly carried on, and have done such a fine job during my stay in the hospital, and subsequent convalescence out West. It was all along a wonderful inspiration to me to watch from the background how well the Panther Organization kept on functioning.

Space does not permit individual mention of those whose work has been particularly outstanding during this year. Fact is, everybody must have done a good job for the *result* to be so gratifying. I wish I had the command of words to express adequately my gratitude to each and every one of you.

Things are topsy-turvy in the world across the seas. We are mighty fortunate to be AMERICANS—let us all be proud of that. Let us realize anew what the grand old American Way of doing business and the matchless American Way of living has done for us all. Let us appreciate it enough to be willing to do our part to always keep this country sane and safe, as it has been.

Above all, let us pledge ourselves once again to do our part, to the utmost of our ability, to continue to make good on our respective jobs, so that the Company we love may continue to prosper as an important part of the greatest country on earth.

Amazing as it may seem, it's only 110 days till Christmas, and those days will pass rapidly. With them the year will be gone. There is still much work to be accomplished between now and the dawn of another year. We'll all have to get busy to find ourselves in anywhere near as good position as we hoped to be by Christmas.

Again, Heartfelt Thanks to all of you for the good work you have done—and every good wish to you all.

The employees of one company received the Christmas message in Figure 11-12 a few years ago from their president. It is one of the many pages from the philosophy of a business leader, a philosophy never smeared by the thought that money is the only thing to be derived from business.

Figure 11-12

WHAT A CHRISTMAS GIFT!

A Christmas in my early youth still remains the most memorable one to me.

It was made so by a gift received from a businessman and a good woman at a Sunday School Christmas Service.

This good man came up to me, squeezed my hand, and with a hand on my shoulder, said, "My boy, I perceive that God will make of you a force for good in the world. Never refuse an opportunity to take part in all such services!"

The woman came up and said, "Jacob, you said your piece beautifully!"

These were the sweetest words I have ever heard. I did not sleep that night. Something happened inside of me. My candle of hope was lighted—and ambition sprouted. It wasn't true what so many had said to me—"You are just a dumb, good-for-nothing kid."

My heart still beats fast with a profuse gratitude for the Gift of those two good folks.

It lies within our power and will to create such a memorable Christmas for many a poor soul—discouraged, hope and faith burning low, possessed with an inferiority complex, and ambition waiting to be lighted.

> Maybe just a word or a friendly glance from you or from me will make this Christmas a most important and joyous one. I know it will be to the giver, as well as to the poor soul who is in need of inspiration.
>
> My wishes for this year are that every day will be Christmas in Spirit. Now and forever!

Sometimes the precepts for getting ahead in business are more acceptable when presented in story form. Here, in Figure 11-13, the readers are left to make their own deductions, except for one short paragraph near the end.

Figure 11-13

> To the Thoroughbreds in our Company,
>
> Sportsmen the world over will never forget Black Gold, winner of the Kentucky Derby in 1924. In size, he was little more than a pony, but there never ran a horse with a heart so big.
>
> And yet, it isn't his victory in the Derby that gave Black Gold immortality. Many years have passed since that chunk of black dynamite went to the post for the last time, but strong men who were at the track that day were not ashamed of tears when they told you what happened.
>
> A true thoroughbred never quits. His body may be broken, he may even be matched against unconquerable Death, but his spirit still laughs, and his brave heart carries on. And so it was that last day in the life of Black Gold.
>
> They took their places and soon they were off—a fine field of blooded horses—and many in the grandstand had placed their bets on Black Gold. But somehow, they didn't mind losing those bets—it was like paying tribute to the great soul of a noble friend.
>
> You see, coming down the stretch Black Gold stumbled—some said he was kicked by another horse—and his leg snapped. The other horses thundered past him, and he was left helpless in the rear.
>
> But the race wasn't over for Black Gold. Long after the others had gone under the wire, he came hobbling home—finishing his last race on the three good legs that were left to him. No Victor's Wreath for Black Gold when that race was done—only

a bullet to end his life. But bless that little horse for teaching us what it means to be a thoroughbred.

We need thoroughbreds in this business, too—products that will stand and test, salesmen who will finish each day's work as that horse finished his race, workers who will face the public with an honest will to serve.

"_____, Thoroughbred"—better to possess that title, than to be called a king.

At the beginning of each new year, most people decide they are going to do better; some of them wisely set specific goals to be accomplished. Naturally, good business leaders encourage this practice; a gain for the individual is a gain for the company—if they want to look at it selfishly. The person who wrote the letter in Figure 11-14, however, knows how easily New Year's resolutions are forgotten. The hope was that this follow-up would help keep them alive.

All these letters to employees show them that you regard them as valued human beings not just interchangeable parts in a piece of machinery. The goodwill engendered by these messages will see tangible results not only in the working relationships of your company but in the year-end fiscal report as well.

5. DYNAMIC HUMAN RELATIONS WITH THE PERSONNEL DEPARTMENT

A delicate phase of human relations. When people apply to a company for a job, they expect to be received in a courteous manner, even if their application is rejected. The employment manager who simply says "no," or, worse yet, says nothing is not functioning in a way to win goodwill for their company. Neither is it considered good business practice, to have the secretary of the personnel director or the receptionist turn away applicants. Everyone who comes to a business office looking for employment is entitled to courteous *attention*. They are offering what they have to *sell* to a company that *buys* personnel. If the sale is not made, it is still possible to retain the applicants' goodwill, and surely from the point of view of public relations, the goodwill of one person may not be as important as that of another.

Human relations with respect to employment are usually pretty well organized in the larger companies, and letters play their part in the program. In these companies a Personnel Manager or Director con-

Figure 11-14

"Those Grand Resolutions!"

Along with the rest of you, on New Year's Day I made a few resolutions. I felt good about them too—kind of satisfied with myself. But here it is the end of January, and some of these resolutions are already beginning to crack. And I looked for the reason.

I think I found it. We can't create new habits—destroy old ones—by simply resolving. Only indomitable persistence, trying and failing, trying again and failing not so soon, will make resolutions a reality.

I have certain tasks to accommmplish—a contract with myself. I will eat moderately, play moderately, save more money—I will have a passion to overcome every influence that keeps me from being my *best*. I won't be a flower that blooms on January first, and dies a month later. Not for a few days only, but all through the year, I'll fight to make my life really count.

Get out your resolution, your aims, your quota, or whatever you said to yourself that you *would do*. Then say, "I'll make the flame of my resolution just as hot today as it was on January 1. I set myself a goal, and by the Eternal, I'm going to *make* it."

ducts the interviews and writes such letters as are considered necessary or desirable. Of course, there may be one or more assistants, but they all work toward the same end—to make the applicants feel that the company appreciates their interest, and to handle the applications in such a manner that goodwill is created.

Naturally, people looking for a job are more or less on the defensive, and if they have been rudely received other places, they are quite likely to have a chip on their shoulder. To handle them tactfully is a delicate job for which some people are better qualified than others. This is especially true of the letters written to the applicant, as there must be nothing in them that might cause ill will, or bring trouble back to the company. On the other hand, if these letters are friendly and encouraging, they may win goodwill that could prove fruitful at some later time.

Checklist of kinds of personnel letters. The personnel department has a great responsibility for fostering good human relations for your company. Your sales department sells your company's products/ services. It is supposed to keep your customers happy with what you can provide. The personnel department sells your company's working conditions. It keeps your work force happy to be in your employ.

The personnel director should have a plan to follow so that no opportunity for increasing goodwill is overlooked. Look at Figure 11-15. This checklist will be used extensively during this section. It represents a dynamic, usable, and practical guide to a personnel department letter campaign.

The first of the letters used in connection with employment is quite often written by the applicants—either in answer to an ad, or because they have selected the company as a place where they would like to work. Strictly speaking, the application letter is not a form of business correspondence, although it may serve the purpose of benefiting business by bringing applicant and company together. In many cases, however, the job-hunter simply calls at the employment office, and the contact begins with the interview.

If the first interview develops the certainty that the applicants are not to be hired, the employment routine stops right there. Tactfully but plainly, the applicants should be told that the decision is unfavorable. It's an injustice to let them go away thinking they have a good chance of getting the job. However, this still permits a business courtesy that will help to retain goodwill: Step One.

Dear _____,

Thanks for calling on us yesterday about employment. It was nice of you to think of our company as a place where you would like to work.

We are sorry that we could not offer you any encouragement, but this is no reflection on your attitude or ability, and we are sure that you will find a place where you can demonstrate your worth.

You know the work needs of different companies are never the same. Your problem is to find the place that *fits* your combination of experience and training—as of course you will.

The best of fortune to you, both in finding the right job, and in making the most of it.

Assuming that the applicants pass the first interview, the second step is usually to have them fill out the company form that supplies information needed, a record of past jobs, and the names of people to whom the company may write as references. Very few employment managers hire "on sight." There may be others that they hope to interview for a particular position, and they wish to guard against the dangers of a first impression. A valuable opinion of the applicants may be gained, too, from the neatness and accuracy with which the form is filled out. Hence, with the question of employment not settled, another form of business courtesy may be rendered: Step Two.

Dear _____,

We appreciate the time you took yesterday to fill out our application for employment. The fact that you were asked to do so is evidence of the good impression you made in our little visit together.

Of course, you realize that filling out the blank does not mean for sure that you will be hired, but it does mean that we will give you every possible consideration. Also, if the job does not work out this time, we still have a record of your experience and training when something else turns up.

Because of the importance of the position for which you are being considered, and the fact that other applications must be studied along with yours, it will be about two weeks before we can give you the final decision.

In the meantime, thanks for coming in to see us.

There is no problem at all in dictating a letter like the one you have just read, and the reaction of the recipients are sure to be good. It tells them that the filling out of the application was not a mere formality, or an excuse for getting rid of them; also, they learn that the company is systematic in handling details of employment. Another purpose accomplished is paving the way for a possible rejection, so applicants will not feel so discouraged in the event they don't get the job.

Figure 11-15

PERSONNEL DEPARTMENT LETTER CHECKLIST

Send a Letter When:

1. The application has been rejected.

The Letter Should:

A. Show appreciation that your company was considered.

B. Wish the applicant success elsewhere.

2. The applicant is still under consideration for a position.

    A. Show appreciation for interest in your company.

    B. Promise notification as soon as possible as to employment status.

3. Another person has introduced an applicant.

    A. Express appreciation for their interest in your company and the applicant's career.

    B. Assure the advocate that the candidate will receive special consideration.

4. The applicant's past performance is to be checked.

    A. Be addressed to an official of the last places of the applicant's employment.

    B. Ask for a frank opinion of the applicant's abilities and character.

5. The applicant has given references.

    A. Tell the references that the applicant has used them as a reference.

    B. Ask for as impartial an evaluation as possible.

6. School records are needed.

    A. Ask for transcripts and an objective report of activities.

    B. Ask for a subjective opinion of conduct and affability.

7. The applicant has been accepted.

    A. Convey congratulations.

    B. Give information concerning when to report, to whom to report, etc.

8. The applicant has been rejected.

    A. Not discourage or offend the applicant.

	B. Give at least one objective reason for rejection.
9. Applicant arrives at work.	A. Welcome the applicant.
	B. Give all pertinent information needed to make the new association easy.

Often it happens that the people applying for work have brought letters of introduction from some other businessman, from a teacher or minister or from some other individual who thinks they have an in with the employment manager. In such a situation, common courtesy again comes to the front with a suggestion: Step Three.

If the applicants brought letters of introduction, the personnel officers now have another letter to write. They usually have several versions already prepared to fit different situations, as the introductions may have come from a friend, a business or professional acquaintance, a dealer, or just from some other company. Here is what might be said in several of these cases:

(A)

Dear Colonel Murry,

It was good of you to send Bill Perkins in to see me. Many of our best employees owe their jobs to people like yourself who take a friendly interest in our company. You can be sure that, with your stamp of approval, this youngster will receive very special consideration.

In the event that we are unable to find an opening now that would challenge your protégé, we will surely keep his application in mind for a future possibility.

Thanks again for your cooperation, which we are very happy to regard as evidence of your goodwill.

(B)

Dear Colonel _____,

It was good of you to send young Perkins in to see us. Many of our best employees owe their jobs to people like yourself who take a friendly interest in our company. Please always feel free to recommend any person of whom you approve, as we value your judgment highly.

As it happens, we had nothing to offer Mr. Perkins yesterday, But we did make some suggestions that may lead to his employment elsewhere.

Thanks again for your cooperation, which we are very happy to regard as evidence of your goodwill.

(C)

Dear _____,

A lad named Perkins called on us yesterday, saying you had given him a list of good companies to check about employment. We consider it a fine compliment that you included us in the list.

Mr. Perkins told us he had held a temporary position with your company, and he seemed quite eager that we should investigate his record while with you. Of course, we would have done this, except that there just wasn't any job open for which he could be considered.

Nevertheless, it speaks very well for the good feeling between our two companies that you tried to give us a new employee. We thank you for doing this, and shall do as much for you when the opportunity develops.

With the application form on file, the next step is to make use of it. Certain information is required from the persons whose names were given as references, and from the companies listed as previous places of employment. The problem in either case is to get *all the facts,* and not a build-up for the applicant with the worst side of the story withheld. The letters written for these purposes are not special business courtesies, but the way they are worded may decide the result. Anyway, two jobs are at hand: Steps Four and Five.

The letter sent to companies where the applicant has worked is more difficult to write. Even if an employee has been discharged for some good reason, the average personnel manager hates to tell the truth—it goes against the grain to "kick a fellow when he is down." Unless the letter can in some way break through this barrier of compassion, the reply is quite likely to be noncommittal, and of no value to the company that wants the facts.

Certain companies send out a questionnaire, and sometimes request a letter, too, but the reception is not always favorable. It seems an imposition to ask someone in another company to take the time and trouble to answer a lot of questions. Since no two people are likely to interpret a questionnaire in the same way, the answers to a specific question are hard to compare. A short letter that puts the shoe on the other person's foot and asks for frankness is more likely to produce a fair and impartial report.

Dear _____,

John Doe, a former employee of yours, has applied to us for a job in our bookkeeping department, and we will greatly appreciate your frank opinion as to his ability and conduct.

Probably, what we are after all adds up to answering one question: Was your experience with Mr. Doe such that you would be glad to hire him again?

Knowing by reputation the high standard of your personnel, we think anyone considered good enough for your organization is plenty good enough for us.

On the other hand, should there be some reason why this applicant is not likely to make good with us, it is far better for him not to start out with us, as nothing is more damaging to a man's morale than to fail on a job.

So, as a favor to him as well as to us, won't you please give us the information you would want if you were now in our shoes? Anything you say will be held strictly in confidence, and we shall be very happy to do as much for you when our positions are reversed.

If the preceding letter is tough to write so that the truth will be obtained, the one for securing full information from a character reference is even tougher. Obviously, the applicants have offered only names of people they are sure will say nice things about them. They have probably gone to the trouble of finding out if the opinions will be in their favor *before* they supply the name. This, indeed, puts the writer "behind the eight-ball," and for that reason many personnel managers do not even bother to follow up these character references, unless they have some friendly relationship with one or more of the references.

The chief hope, it seems, in this predicament is to put the request in such a way that the reader feels he would be unfair to the applicant and himself by giving a distorted report.

Dear _____,

It seems that Michelle Ortiz leans heavily on your judgment, for she has given your name as that as one who will help me decide whether or not it is best for her to go to work for our company.

First, I will place my cards on the table, and then ask for yours. Michelle strikes me as a young woman who may make a name for herself in some company, and in fairness to her I would not want to employ her unless what we have to offer *fits* her pattern of abilities, her disposition, and what she really *likes* to do.

It is a great injustice to hire a young individual with some doubt of her making good, and then have to let her go later. I know you wouldn't want that to happen to Michelle.

Now, that's how I feel—and I very much need to know what *you* can add so that the right decision will be made.

Will you do me the favor—and Michelle the favor—of telling me what you know of her? Particularly, will she be happy working on a routine job? Is she dependable? Are her friends a *help* to her? Would *you* hire her if you were in my place?

Please be assured that everything you say will be considered confidential. All we are after is to put our two older heads together and come up with what is best for Michelle.

Thanks, _____, for your help. I shall hope in some way to have the privilege some day of doing as much for you.

There are, of course, other sources of information personnel directors can use, and they may turn to them if the position to be filled is considered important: Step Six.

A much easier letter for the personnel manager to write is the one to an individual *not* named by the applicant as a work or character reference. In this situation, the man to whom the letter goes has no personal obligation toward the applicant, although he may still be reluctant to give a detrimental opinion. Here, for example, is how a letter might be written to a former teacher or principal of the applicant:

Dear _____,

I know you must be busy with the new school term just starting, but I have a favor to ask which I hope is not too great an imposition.

Sally Smith, who graduated from your fine high school two years ago, would like a secretarial job with our company. You can help me a lot in deciding what our reply should be.

I can't think of any individual so well-qualified to know the real ability and character of Miss Smith as the Principal of her high school. You have watched her in and out of the classroom for four long years, and indeed your opinion should be absolutely impartial.

Of course, there is also the question of her work as a student, although we are not so narrow-minded as to think high grades are all that counts in determining the fitness of an applicant.

_____, I don't want to hire Sally Smith unless the association will work out right for her and our company. I very much need your impartial judgment. Won't you please drop me a line during the next few days, telling what you think we should know about this young lady?

It will all be treated in confidence—and my appreciation will be great.

Once the decision is made—to hire—the applicants should be notified. If they are to be hired, the word may reach them by telephone, or by letter. If not, the letter is adequate. Here, unfortunately, is when Courtesy usually stubs her toe. The applications are left in the file, and the applicants are left in doubt. Eventually they realize that they are not getting the job, but the fact that they were kept in the dark is irritating—goodwill is lost. In keeping with good human relations, the Employment Manager has another obligation: Steps Seven and Eight.

When the final decision is made, only one of two letters is needed. The applicants get the job, or they do not; but in either case, they should be told. There is no doubt about sending the good news if the decision is favorable; but even if it's negative, the company owes the applicant the courtesy of a letter.

Dear _____,

Thanks for calling on us yesterday about employment. It was nice of you to think of our company as a place where you would like to work.

We are sorry that we could not offer you any encouragement, but this is no reflection on your attitude or ability, and we are sure that you will find a place where you can demonstrate your worth.

You know the work needs of different companies are never the same. Your problem is to find the place that *fits* your combination of experience and training—as of course you will.

The best of fortune to you, both in finding the right job, and in making the most of it.

The aim of a letter such as the above is two-fold: to remove any resentment applicants might have toward the company, and to offer the encouragement that they may need. That second objective is not so much a business necessity as a moral obligation held by any person who handles employment. Of course, if the applicant is left feeling good toward the company, a benefit to human relations is also gained.

Dear ——————,

You win. Your application for the position in our Advertising Department has been accepted. Can you report for work Tuesday morning at eight-thirty, September 17th?

It will interest you to know that you are getting this job in competition with 38 other applicants, a vote of confidence which I know will challenge you to prove we picked the right person.

Dear ——————,

I promised to let you know when a decision had been reached about the position in our Advertising Department. This happened yesterday.

Picking the right person out of 38 applicants was not easy, and I want you to know that you were one of four after all the others had been eliminated. However, the final choice was someone who had had considerable experience in writing our type of copy.

Otherwise, everything about your application was fine, and it would please you a lot to read all the complimentary things that some very important people said about you.

With your permission, we will keep your application in our active file, looking forward to some other opening that may develop.

Thanks, ——————, for your interest. I predict considerable success for you in the business world.

You might think that the cycle of employment letters is now complete, but there remains at least one more important step. The first day on a new job is always the hardest, with new people to meet, new policies to learn, new methods to master. One thing may help to cushion the adjustment: Step Nine.

The last letter of the series is the all-important message of welcome received by the applicant the first day on their new job. The length may vary according to the setup of the organization. There is certain information about the rules and policies of the company that the new employees need to know. It may be given to them personally by the Personnel Manager—the best way when expedient—or included in the letter of welcome. But the primary purpose is to make the individual feel at home—to ease the shock of that first difficult day when everything seems strange, and the simple things appear complex.

Dear _____,

As president of the company of which you are now a very important part, I extend a hearty welcome and the hope that you will like all of us as much as I am sure we are going to like you.

Today will be the hardest you will ever spend in our organization. I know that is true, because I still remember my first day on my first job. Things will seem strange, and some of the work you are asked to do will seem much more difficult than it really is.

However, there isn't a worker in our office who doesn't want to be your friend, and help you get adjusted to the job. If you have questions to ask, see Gary Jones. He is a lot more interested in you now as a member of our business family than when he hired you.

You are going to enjoy your work here, _____; more, I think, than you can possibly realize as a beginner. Our company is the biggest and best of its kind in the world, and that's something for you to be proud of. We work as a team, and not as individuals, and everybody in your department *wants* you to make good.

So congratulations, and my best wishes! There are lots of others who wanted your job. I know you feel challenged—and will give your best.

A letter such as this one signed by the company's president, is a great morale-builder, and it arrives at a time when the new employee most needs encouragement. The attitude of workers thoughout the whole period of their employment may be influenced by their experiences the first day. They read the letter, and they take it home to the family. It is a simple, easily tendered business courtesy that should never be omitted in the letter program.

The above, then, are some of the most important letters the Employment Manager may write as his contribution to friendly public relations. Some are necessary to the handling of the application; others are just acts of courtesy that help to win goodwill.

Understanding letters of application. Whether or not *Handbook of Business Letters* should pause to discuss the letters written by individuals seeking employment is a question of some doubt. Businessmen do not write these letters—they *read* them. On the other hand, the application letter does serve a business purpose, because it brings together the company which may need a worker and the worker who does want a job. For the benefit of those in business who are not employers, it will do no harm to pass along a few helpful suggestions.

1. Do not waste the time of a business executive—or your own—answering an ad about a job, unless what you have to offer the company *matches* the specifications listed.

It may be tempting to the person badly in need of work to disregard facts mentioned in the ad, in the hope that a letter may make the sale in spite of these deficiencies, but the chances of success are not one in ten thousand. If the advertisement reads, "Man not over 30, with college education," it does not open the gate to a person 40 years old who didn't finish high-school. Unless the individual fits the pattern of the job, the finest letter ever written would no doubt be futile.

2. The application letter is one evidence of the writer's ability. It is a *sample* of their work, and they are sure to be judged by the care and intelligence with which the job is done.

This fact seems to be overlooked frequently by job hunters. They don't put their best foot forward. The letter asking for the interview is dashed off with an inane disregard of appearance, spelling, and correct English. Sometimes it is written with a pencil on soiled paper—with fingerprints for added decoration. How any person could expect to make a favorable first impression with such a letter is difficult to understand. A letter asking for a job is a *sales* letter—perhaps the most important ever to be mailed by the writer.

3. Application letters should be typed. If the applicant is forced to use a pen, great care should be taken to write plainly. A letter hard to read goes into the wastebasket. That's where it belongs.

If you feel inclined to argue about the last assertion, consider the position of the executives in the big company who get letters asking for employment. At times, they are literally beset with them. They swarm in upon them in every mail. Why should they extend the courtesy of trying to read a sloppily prepared letter, when the writers themselves were discourteous in making it so hard to read?

4. The problem of attracting special attention is very great in the application letter. If the writers are able to make their letter favorably different from the others, they have given themselves a tremendous advantage.

Anyone who handles application letters knows how much they follow the same old groove. They start with "The writer would like to apply for a position with your company," or "With reference to your advertisement in this morning's *Star*, the writer wishes to apply for said position." Then they follow with a monotonous description of personal characteristics, jobs previously held, education institutions attended, throw in some references, and end with, "Hoping to receive the courtesy of an interview," or something equally as colorless. Naturally, any executive is bored with reading these letters, and turns with relief to one which is done in a more interesting style.

5. As is the case in all types of sales letters, the person applying for a job should avoid generalities, and try to advance specific points to build credibility.

Just to state that you graduated from the University of Illinois means nothing. The fact becomes more interesting if you say, "During my four years at the University of Illinois, my lowest grade was B. I won varsity letters in football and track, was captain of the debating team my senior year, and the president of my fraternity, Chi Psi." Those are *reasons* why the reader of the application letter should be interested— actual *proofs* of outstanding accomplishment.

6. Attaching a picture of the writer is a good way to attract attention, since it helps the reader of the letter to visualize the individual and catch some idea of his personality.

The picture used need not be an expensive or large photograph; a small snapshot in some informal pose is much more effective. It costs very little to have "glossies" made from a negative, and one attached to the letter will surely be a point in its favor.

7. Don't try to describe your history since birth; concentrate on a few points especially in your favor, and leave the rest of the story for the interview.

A good way to avoid the necessity of a long two- or three-page letter, is to prepare an information sheet that gives the details of education, age, experience, and the like, and save two or three of the strongest points about yourself to include in the letter. Thus, the letter first wins the attention of its readers after which they can turn to the information sheet for additional details.

8. The principles of good letter-carpentry are just as important in the preparation of an application letter as in any other form of written salesmanship. The old formula of the Star, the Chain, and the Hook, is the one to follow.

The foregoing suggestions are by no means the whole of the story, but the people who try them will soon find that their application letters are having a better "pull" than before. Employment managers are human and react like anybody else to an approach that is interesting, convincing, and different from the daily run-of-the-mill. Actually, there is no reason why any individual should have a feeling of inferiority or dread in asking for a job. The one who reads the letter is a buyer of work hours; the one who writes it has work hours for sale. It is a fifty-fifty proposition, like any other business deal.

Checking the strategies of a few good examples. Each of the following application letters won an interview for the writer. That is all that any similar letter may hope to accomplish. It has done its job if the writer is called to the company office to meet the employment manager.

Here is an application letter written by a young lady in Atlanta, Georgia, to a paper mill. It won an interview—and she got the job!

Dear ————,

I figured it out this way:

(1) Every firm uses one or more stenographers. They are, so to speak, "Standard equipment" in every office.

(2) Most firms have occasional use for a commercial artist to illustrate a product, to design a label or package, to sketch an attention-getter for a sales letter, etc.

(3) A stenographer who can do commercial artwork should be valuable to her employers in a number of ways, especially in connection with sales work.

So I learned shorthand and typewriting, and combined this with commercial art training.

For some two years or more I have done most of the art work for the Blank Rubber Company of this city, filling out my time by writing sales letters.

I could continue to do their work, but the fact that my father is one of the department heads places me at a disadvantage so far as advancement is concerned. Also, I believe that a connection with another firm would broaden my experience and make me more efficient.

I am 21 years old.

I am what might be called an "experienced beginner," and have no exaggerated ideas as to what I should expect as a starting salary.

If you believe it possible that you could find a place for me in your organization, I will appreciate an opportunity to show you samples of my work, and to give you any information you may wish.

Please do tell me when I may see you.

The foregoing letter is in no sense remarkable, but it does reveal an individual intelligent enough to plan her education to fit a specific business purpose. Furthermore, it does not bore the reader with a long, drawn-out exposition of details. It is certainly a far better application letter than the average ones received by those who "hire and fire."

The next letter was sent by a young man to the managers of 25 large hotels. It produced several interviews—and the job he wanted. It is done in a simple, natural style, sure to impress more favorably than the typical stilted messages frequently mailed by job-hunters.

Dear _____,

My name is Smith—William Smith. I am itching to work in your hotel.

I am 23 years old, 6 feet tall, and run to the lean side with a weight of only 150 pounds. For the past four years I have been connected with the Blank Feed Company. General office work, advertising service, and some selling have taken most of my time there.

My record is okay plus. You can verify that. Telephone Mr. A.B. Jones, Personnel Director, at (123)-456-789 and he will tell you it is so.

I have had considerable training in connection with conventions and much of my life to date has been spent in hotels. I know the atmosphere. I know people. What I don't know about the hotel business is plenty, but it is nothing that hard work and study will not supply.

I am not afraid of hard work. I like it.

All my life I have had the secret desire to be in the hotel business. All I want is a toe-hold. I'll do the climbing after that.

I have no high-hat ideas about salary. I wouldn't be worth much at first. A man must *prove* his worth as he goes along. I want to start on that basis.

Will you dig up some place for William Smith to hang up his hat, roll up his sleeves, and show his stuff? Give me just that chance, and you have my promise you will never be sorry.

Tell me when I can come and talk to you. It's the biggest favor I have ever asked.

The young lady who prepared the following application letter understood the formula of the Star, the Chain, and the Hook. She gets quick attention, using a beloved name as the lure, arouses interest and desire, and then closes with a positive, confident request for action. Attached to the page in the upper righthand corner was a small picture.

Dear _____,

Why did Abraham Lincoln win rail-splitting contests so easily?

You've heard the reason: He knew exactly where to place his wedge to give his blows the most power. The scene of Lincoln's youth—Springfield, Illinois—is where I was born, where I lived through the school years. When Lincoln won these contests, he was the same age as I am now; and I, too, want to enter a log-splitting contest.

I have a good, strong wedge and a sturdy hammer, but I need a log.

In the first place, I want to get into dress designing or any allied field of women's ready-to-wear. I have creative ability which has been fostered by art courses—water-color, life, art appreciation, clay modeling, stage and costume design—and one summer at the Traphagen School of Dress Design in New York City. I taught stage and costume design for one year.

I received a degree in English from the University of Chicago. Since college I have been molding my wedge: working as a stenographer until I am now capable of answering letters independently.

This, then, is my wedge into the field of women's wear: to be a stenographer to a buyer, to a designer of clothing or window displays; to the art staff, or to an advertising director. Your store and its opportunities can be my log.

Will you let me enter the contest?

You may reach my by calling (123) 456-7890. Or, just jot down the time you'll see me on the postal card I'm enclosing, and toss it in tonight's mail.

A very appealing letter asking for work is one written by an older man who refused to accept the verdict that he was ready for rocking chair and slippers. His problem was one faced by many a senior in business. Perhaps this letter may suggest a way out for someone else whose "gray hair tops gray matter."

Dear ——————,

Will you give work to a man aged 52?

In December, I lost a job as Advertising and Sales Promotion Manager. The reason did not concern my ability or character.

A shock came when applications for other positions were turned down with the comment "too old."

A man in perfect health, with 25 years' experience and a very special ability for advertising and sales work was to stay idle and watch the "cubs" go by—perhaps to become a shabby down-at-heel, cadging nickels and chased by cops.

I was beginning to see *red* and then I saw the truth. No real advertising man need ever be out of work. He certainly should be able to sell his services.

That is why I am establishing my own business, to supply real, honest advertising, sales promotion, and research service to nonconflicting clients for a reasonable monthly retainer.

This service covers every phase of sales publicity and research. No assignment is too small or too large to be given proper attention. I can work with your executives, advertising agency—or alone.

And as far as age goes, what does it matter as long as gray hair tops gray matter?

I ask *your* help. May I have a talk with you?

You can leave a message at (123) 456-7890, or write—and I'll come running.

The application letters you have just read have at least two common characteristics: first, the approach is out-of-the-groove, and therefore interesting, second, they reveal the personality of a pleasing person. The writers just *talk* to their readers about their problems and their ambitions, and that is the secret of their pulling power.

DEVELOPING SALES MANAGER LETTERS

DEVELOPING SALES MANAGER LETTERS

1. UNDERSTANDING THEIR IMPORTANCE TO BUSINESS

Struggling between the devil and the deep blue sea. Since the assumption is that the sales managers know more about the company products and how to sell them than the sales staff, it must follow that they should be able to give them more help personally than by mail. But sales managers can't spend all their time out of the office, and even if this were possible, only a small part of it could be spent with any one of the salesmen. Thus, they are forced to do most of the job with letters.

In facing this fact, however, many sales executives find themselves between the devil and the deep blue sea. They must either furnish the sales staff with more letters than they will want to read, or take the chance of letting them run amuck for lack of proper motivation and control. One fact that adds to the problem is that average salesmen get a vast amount of mail from other departments and individuals in the company. After a hard day's work, they are expected to open a bulky envelope and wade through a lot of correspondence that they often feel has little connection with sales; and sometimes, unfortunately, they are correct.

The person who has never worked as a salesman probably does not realize how many letters flow from the office to the field, and apparently some sales managers are just as much in the dark or they would do some constructive streamlining. This does not mean that necessary letters can be omitted; it means that the salesman should not be bothered with details which could be handled just as well in some other way.

In an effort to find out just how many letters the salesmen of his company were expected to read, the vice-president of one large corporation had them counted for one week. The actual figures were as amazing to him as they probably will be to you:

Number of salesmen receiving mail....................900

Letters sent to them in one week 23,405

Most letters received by one person......................87

Fewest letters received by one person.....................19

Average number per person that week...................26

Whether or not the above figures furnish a fair estimate of what goes on in other companies we do not know, but for the organization with this large a sales staff they no doubt come close. Hence, we must concede that a serious encroachment is taking place on time that could better be devoted to selling.

Obviously, where the problem does exist the solution seems clear. First, some form of control should be established over the staff's mail to keep the amount of it no greater than is reasonable and necessary. Members of other departments should not be allowed to write to the sales staff unless the necessity is understood and approved. Second, writers in the sales department should take pains to make sure that their own letters are necessary, and promote the general objective of using the staff's time to the best possible advantage. Third, letters used to motivate them—inspire them to greater effort—should be so constructive and interesting that they *want* to read them.

Sales Managers who assume that this third point does not apply to their own letters and bulletins might very easily be fooling themselves. It is no exaggeration to say that many people in the field—perhaps the majority of them—do not look with special favor on the word-lashings they get regularly from headquarters. They are meant to inspire but they only *tire*. They call on the sales staff to give the old college "try," but they don't include *"how."* They may quickly scan the message to see if it contains any fact they must know, but that's about all the attention it gets. Too often, the reaction is something like this: "Another shot in the arm from the Boss! Must think I need a sermon a week."

Of course, these disparaging remarks do not, by any means, apply to all sales-manager letters meant to inspire. None need wear the shoe unless it fits. But let's face it—anyone knows that the staff in general looks with cynicism on some of the letters they receive. For this attitude they are not entirely to blame. They are tired of "pep" talks when what they need are solid, workable sales ideas. They have been getting the sauce without the meat. The sales manager who supplies *both* is the one whose letters are read.

How to classify the letters. Practicallly all of the letters mailed to salesmen serve one of two general purposes—to challenge or to control. From the point of view of better business correspondence, you are more concerned with the first group than the second. Letters to control include all the matters of a routine nature that must be planned and supervised—in them, the staff is told what to do and how. Letters to challenge are just what the word implies. If successful, they inspire greater effort—produce more sales. They include letters of constructive criticism, since a person may be challenged to correct a fault as well as to multiply a virtue. Of course, some sales manager letters do a double job; they tell the salesmen what to do, and make them want to do it better than ever before.

As we have discovered in other sections of this *Handbook*, there is nothing about a generality to impress or challenge the reader of a business letter. This is perhaps even more true with respect to letters to salesmen than of any other type. Contrary to general opinion, average salesmen are not thin-skinned nor overly sensitive. They are fighters with plenty of scars. If they were squeamish and highly imaginative, they would listen to the objections of their prospects, and be swayed by them. Instead, they override objections. They live only one point of view—their own. The prospects should buy. Their egos are strong, as they must be or they could not sell. They appreciate a compliment when they think it is sincere. They are *not* responsive to inspirational patter that merely says, "You can do it, old sod,—you can do it."

The most effective letters to salesmen are written by individuals who have been through the fire themselves. The people who have rung doorbells, walked the streets with a sample kit, pleaded with merchants for orders, are the people who can talk the language. They know from experience what they are talking about. They too, have gone to a hotel room at night, sat on an uncomfortable chair, and opened the inevitable brown envelope from the home office. They know the difference between real help and platitudes.

This is not a treatise on personnel procedure, but it must be evident that the best-equipped sales managers come up from the ranks. There are exceptions to this rule, but they are only exceptions. The person who has actually sold is best able to tell others how to sell.

For example, the sales manager who wrote the letter in Figure 12-1 did not deal in generalities. He wanted to drive home one sales point— that every sales call cost the company money. He gave the exact figure to prove his point, but he didn't preach to his readers, or exhort them to "do better." He presented the facts and let the sales staff draw their own conclusions.

Figure 12-1

Dear J.D.,

Suppose every one of your dealers had a ticket booth and cashier at his front door and required you to purchase admission. And suppose that admission cost you $8.85 plus 10 per cent tax, or a total of $9.74.

If it were an actual cash outlay out of your own pocket, I'll gamble you would insist on your money's worth. "Buyer out," "Come back tomorrow," "Stocked," "Too busy," "Haven't received last order," "Turnover too slow," would fall on deaf ears. And, further, I'll gamble you would have a very definite message someone would have to hear; you would have a real proposition ready before you opened your pocketbook.

I am not putting a premium on the number of calls you make. But I do emphasize the necessity for making as many productive calls as possible—making every call count. A dealer sold today does not require your time later.

It costs this company just $9.74 to put you in a dealer's store; not for each order but for each call; just *your* salary and expenses.

Our only possible dividend is an *order.*

Selling the need for letters. Sales managers sometimes have to take a moment and sell their staffs on the importance of written communication. Some may fall into a scattergun approach and can aim generally at this potential problem. Two sales managers we found, however, had rather unique strategies.

The first had humor as an ally. The letter in Figure 12-2 was sent to each member of the sales force of a large fur company. Each letter this letter-craftsman sent was not only read, but anxiously awaited.

The second sales manager did not write a "communication" letter until there was a specific reason. In Figure 12-3, we see the reason was an almost lost, and certainly lessened, sale.

The most important sale each of these sales managers made dealt with their future letters. They would be *read.*

"Don'ts" when writing to salesmen. One of the Sales Letter Bulletins distributed by the Dartnell Corporation of Chicago, listed ten

Figure 12-2

My fellow pavement pounders,

I am sending you the latest safety information. As you know our company sells the best line of chinchillas that can be found anywhere in the U. S. of A. It is vitally important that our sales force know how to protect themselves as they sell these friendly little creatures with their oh-so-sharp teeth.

Here, then, is your first lesson. Before setting out on your sales call, take   then put your foot   . By the time you get to   the chinc babies.   Don't touch   bite.

Well, folks, that was informative, wasn't it? No? Sorry about that. When I write you I always want to give you the latest poop on everything. I want nothing left out or misunderstood. You don't want to be bitten, either, do you? Of course not.

Well, I guess I will just have to do better next time. You will hear from me soon.

"don'ts" for handling salesmen by mail. They are worthy of your consideration.

1. Don't pick on your sales force. If you must write unpleasantly, put it all in one letter.

2. Try to make the letter that your people will receive on a Monday morning as cheery and helpful as possible. Give them a running start for a big week.

3. Don't preach to your staff. Teach as though you taught not.

4. Don't write unnecessary letters about trivial things and ask salesmen to answer them.

5. Don't keep talking about what some other company's sales staff did or is doing. It's counter-productive.

6. Insist that every letter going to salesmen should pass over your desk. Otherwise, some sour message could send everyone into a dither for a week.

7. Don't keep telling them what you used to do when you were a salesman. They don't care.

8. Praise for doing something well is usually more effective than

Figure 12-3

Dear _____,

Sometimes, I wonder if you fellows in the field really read all of the letters I write to you. I'm not kidding myself about the answer, for I spent ten years of my life doing exactly what you are—and two of them in *your* territory.

Anyway, let this be a lesson to you, my buckaroo!

Two months ago, I wrote to you about a company, Blank & Blank, which seemed to be doing a lot of business, and I suggested that a call might land you a nice order.

When none of your daily reports showed that this call had been made, I wrote again—and a third time just two weeks ago.

I wouldn't for the world want to jump to wrong conclusions, but there were only two things that might explain why you didn't see Blank & Blank; either you didn't read my letters, or you had lost faith in my nose for orders.

Anyway, we got an order yesterday from this company by mail, and it totalled $505.50. Of course, you'll get commission on this order, but a personal call—with all your persuasive power—might have doubled the size of it.

Yes, I know. Letters are a nuisance after a hard day's work. But it could cost you real dough not to read them carefully, as I'm sure it did in the case of Blank & Blank.

All of this is said in the best of spirits, old fellow. You know I appreciate your efforts, and anything I suggest is for your good as much as the company's.

P.S. By the way, did you read *this* one?

---

bawling a person out for doing something wrong. This is especially true in correcting faults.

9. Don't write cold-blooded letters to warm-blooded salesmen. Put some pep and vinegar in them. Write to your people as though they were sitting across from you at lunch.

10. Whatever else you do, don't write when you are mad. Madness is a mild form of insanity. If you write at white heat you will surely regret it. Give your anger a chance to cool.

Although the above admonitions are quite sound, one fact needs to be remembered—and all great leaders recognize it. No "don't" or "do" can be made broad enough to cover all individuals. What can and should be said to one salesman, may be the wrong thing to say to another. Not that there is any logic in the notion that salesmen are different from other human beings—that they have to be coddled and handled with gloves. This is nonsense. Once in a while, one meets a salesman who seems to enjoy the pose of being temperamental, but it is only a pose. All human beings differ in mental stability and emotional reaction. Salesmen are just humans who sell—not a separate species.

2. HOW TO OFFER SPECIFIC SALES SUGGESTIONS

How to keep current and concrete. The best letters to salesmen are those that do more than root for better performance; they carry to their readers specific information, ideas, or suggestions that can be *put to work*. We have small liking for the message that merely prods the salesman without showing one or more ways to "run faster." Surely, one of the obligations of the managers is to show *how*. No staff in the field is assumed to know as much about selling as their manager. Why, then, should the latter not pass along the benefit of their knowledge and experience?

In the letter in Figure 12-4, the importance of getting new accounts is given the spotlight, and then the salesman receives a *concrete suggestion* for doing the job—*concentrate on brewing demonstrations.*

One of the most frequently used words in business is *service,* and nobody questions its right to that prominence, but *service* is merely a generality unless explained and interpreted. You might write to ten salesmen about giving dealers better service, and no two of them would come up with the same notion of what you meant by service, since every individual defines a generality according to his own inclination and thinking. Sales manager H. N. Fisch knew better than to fall into that trap. Here's his letter—Figure 12-5—with *service* so clearly explained that no one could mistake his meaning.

In Section 9, we put our heads together to see how lost business might be regained. We agreed that it is sometimes easier to revive an old customer than to get a brand new one. The truth of this contention is demonstrated in a sales bulletin once used by the Sinclair Oil Company.

The Lost Legion

Business is a battle. During the past year you have called on a lot of accounts from whom you secured no business. They are

Figure 12-4

Dear _____,

You are running first in the current campaign, but I hope you won't let that go to your head. From what I hear from many of our other men, they are out to get your scalp. It won't surprise me if some of them start climbing up very close to first position. You'll have to work doggone hard to hold first place, but I'm counting on you to be there when the campaign is over.

New accounts are going to play a big part in winning, because additional new customers will help push up volume. Of course, converting split business into exclusive accounts will help tremendously too, but in the final analysis, you cannot deny the importance of those new accounts.

[Now comes the concrete suggestion]

Most of the men who have been doing exceptionally fine work in securing new business tell me they are making demonstrations frequently because they find that it helps not only to secure orders but to build steady business. I am passing this along to you because I believe that you, too, should be able to use this suggestion to good advantage.

Why not run a little two weeks' campaign of your own in which you concentrate all your time on brewing demonstrations? Instead of trying to sell by mere words, simply brew coffee with every prospect possible; emphasize that there is no obligation involved, and that you just want to show the kind of blends we are now producing.

There is no doubt in my mind but that the results you will secure will be beyond your own expectations. Try it and see.

---

the lost soldiers of your industrial army. Why not make a list of each of these accounts which might again be open for business during the coming year, and go after it?

The sales manager of a large concern tells of a salesman who had made a splendid showing during a sales contest. After it was over, he wrote his manager, "I have scratched the bottom of the barrel to make a showing in this contest. There simply isn't any more business in sight right now."

No sooner had the letter been mailed than a prospect called the salesman, asking him to come and see him. The salesman had tried hard to sell this prospect during the contest but had

Figure 12-5

Dear _____,

Walking down the street with Abe Davis, who operates one of Fort Worth's finest exclusive men's stores, was Bill Morgan, (not his real name.) Abe said to Bill: "You know, Mr. Morgan, I have my house insured with your organization, and ten days ago that heavy wind we had blew several tiles off the roof. I've been forgetting to notify your office."

Bill said, "That's too bad."

Then Abe sort of stuttered a bit, and finally asked, "Well, whom should I call down there about it?"

And Bill replied, "Just call the complaint department."

What a splendid opportunity Morgan had to render a real service to one of his customers! And how he muffed it! Abe left an opening for Bill to say, "Well, Abe, let me make a note of that right away. Don't worry about it. I'll take care of it just as soon as I get back to the office."

But what did he do? He simply referred Abe to the complaint department—after Abe had already said he had been forgetting to report the damage.

That is what we mean when we talk about service in selling. Service isn't giving a dealer an extra discount. It isn't giving him 30 or 60 days extra dating. It's doing the things for him that are *not included* in the regular duties of selling. Service is the first car in the train of modern selling.

To increase your sales, _____, observe and watch for every opportunity for *Service*.

---

been turned down so emphatically that the account seemed hopeless.

But the prospect had been thinking over some things the salesman had said. Now he had gotten around to where he gave the salesman another hearing, and an order.

That gave the salesman an idea. He called on all the prospects who had turned him down during the contest and soon had a nice month's business booked.

One of the oldest and most successful oil companies used the following plan for years. Every six months the accounting department made a list of all accounts who hadn't bought anything for two years. Then the salesmen went out and tried to get them started again.

Because an account was lost last year, or turned you down on your last call, doesn't mean that it may not be available in the future.

Perhaps, because of your former experience, you can play your cards a little more intelligently this time—and present just the argument that will land him.

On entering her building the other day, an executive said to the doorman, "Good morning, and how are you today?" The elderly doorman, with a broad smile and a twinkle in his bright eyes, replied, "Well, I feel mighty good. The Lord has given me a *new* day, and I mean to make the most of it. Yes, sir, old Tom has a new day for himself, just the same as everybody else."

In his remark was a suggestion often used by sales managers in letters to their sales staff—forget the past, take the time that is yours, and plan your work to make every hour as productive as possible. It's a good suggestion, too, for many salesmen jump around like grasshoppers—"Good on distance, but hell on direction." If the salesmen are willing to profit by good advice, the letters below bring them constructive help.

(1)

Dear _____,

How would you handle your deposits in a bank that goes broke every day?

If you put $864 in a bank every morning, and if every night when that bank closed its doors the president took whatever amount you had not used during the day and put it in his own pocket...

WHAT WOULD YOU DO?

Why, you would draw out every cent just before time to close, wouldn't you?

Well, you have just such a bank and its name is the "Time Bank." Every morning the Time Bank credits you with 86,400 seconds. Every night it takes away from you every second that you have not used during the day. It carries over no balance—it accepts no "I'll do it tomorrow" checks. Each day it opens a new account for you with a deposit of 86,400 seconds.

IF YOU FAIL TO USE THE DAY'S DEPOSIT, THE LOSS IS YOURS. There is no going back. There are no leftover seconds to be credited to your tomorrow's account. You've got to use up all the 86,400 seconds on the day they are deposited for you.

BUT HERE IS WHAT YOU CAN DO—

You can begin to draw out and use your 86,400 seconds on any day that you wish. Even though you have wasted yours—even though you have never cashed in on one cent's worth of time—still you can start tomorrow and you'll find the cashier of the Time Bank ready and willing to pay you money for each and every minute you give him in exchange.

DON'T WASTE TIME, FOR TIME IS MONEY.

(2)

Dear ―――――――,

Ever since Tuesday I've been happy.

For it was on Tuesday we received your first orders of the week—which proved that you had knocked Old Man Slump for a row. And the several orders you secured since then show that you have what I said in my last letter—a winning heart.

What pleased me more than anything else was that the dollar value of the orders you secured was far above the average. For that you get a hearty congratulations—and an invitation to get yourself a big Italian dinner in that old New Orleans restaurant we both know so well.

You remember the place. I certainly shall not forget it. The place where the waiter, when I asked for more dressing for my salad, told me: "You eat that salad the way she is fix. The chef he know better than you how to fix a salad." Remember?

Well, I remember the time we were in the midst of a seller's market, and could talk to buyers in much the same way.

Today, though, the better plan is to counsel with buyers. Show them why we feel certain lines will sell well for them. And indicate by everything we say and do that our sincere purpose is to do for them what we, were we in their shoes, would do for ourselves.

Tonight, ―――――――, when you return to your room, get out your book of customers and qualified prospects—and *plan for tomorrow*. Make a list of all the well-rated stores in New Orleans, and then decide on the order in which you will contact them tomorrow. This process—which I have mentioned many times before—will help you get a quick and profitable start in the morning.

Lay this letter on your dresser, so you won't forget.

More power to you!

While each of these managers wanted to "fire up" their salespeople, they did not have to deal with some specific shortcoming that the salesperson had shown.

Strategies for winning sales, salesmen, and satisfied customers. All salesmen have problems from time to time. Sales managers, if they are truly interested in their people, will sense when a "letter from home" is in order. Some everyday, but nonetheless bothersome sales blocks were handled by these caring sales managers. Note the concrete suggestions each offered.

(1)

Dear ————,

I have just finished writing three pep letters, and have just finished tossing them all into the waste-basket.

I figure that soft soap and smooth talk from me won't help to pull you out of your sales slump. That's something you ought to talk over with yourself. And if you feel you need a lecture, then start in on yourself right away, because I don't want to lecture you—I want to help you.

Really, this should be our best season—but like any other time, we'll have to go after the business in order to get it. We know people are eating popcorn—we know it takes machines to pop the corn—we know someone has to sell the machines. That's our job. And we are going to do it.

You know, ————, we have a successful distributor who says he never yet has failed to make a sale when he picked out, called on, and conscientiously worked on, ten good prospects.

So here is my suggestion. Every day, without fail, pick out ten good prospects, put the sales kit under your arm, and go after the orders—and remember that neither you nor I is going to be satisfied with anything less than that—-ORDERS.

There is plenty of business waiting for us—let's *get* it.

(2)

TO THE SALES STAFF

An old plainsman once taught a young chap a lesson that would do a great many agents some good if they applied the principles of that lesson to their daily work. As the story goes, the young chap became anxious to hunt sage-hens after he noticed that the veteran of the plains returned with a full game-bag each evening.

Granting his request, the plainsman gave the enthusiastic but inexperienced youngster a gun the following day and directed him to one of the best hunting spots. Nothing was heard of him until he came plodding back to the ranch-house toward evening—tired, hungry, and empty-handed. He complained that he saw no game, salving his disappointment with what he considered a good alibi.

The experienced plainsman listened patiently, and then explained that the young hunter was at fault because he had showed a lack of intelligent aggressiveness. The young man was told to go out the next day and try disturbing each clump of sagebrush by walking through it.

Those directions were carried out, and the next evening found the hunter proudly exhibiting his game.

Of course, not every clump of sage walked through disclosed the presence of a sage-hen, but being a known haunt, it was merely a matter of *walking through enough of them* before finding a fowl.

Just so it is with prospects; see not just a *few* people, but *lots* of them. You can't walk through the sagebrush without finding a hen. And the more brush—the more hens.

(3)

BE SURE THAT YOU UNDERSTAND EACH OTHER.

A clear-cut understanding in a business deal saves both time and money. Definiteness and frankness are necessary to conclude any sale in the right way.

We are constantly forced to write to salesmen asking them what was their understanding regarding certain deals. We constantly get letters from customers saying, "Your salesman told us we could do so-and-so."

The best salesmen know that the worst thing they can do is to assume a weak attitude with a buyer. There's nothing that creates confidence so quickly as to snap right out what your price is, what the terms are, and what your house will and won't do.

You don't have to take an apologetic attitude about anything. You are rendering your customer a service by making the call and bringing your goods to his attention. Every sale must bring a fair profit. There must be terms which must be respected. Get your profit. Your trade knows you are not giving away goods.

When your customer mentions cheaper goods, tell him we can make them at half our price, if he doesn't want *quality*. If he makes a general statement about other prices, get something *specific*. Don't take generalities about prices, complaints, or anything else.

It's the easiest thing in the world to speak in generalities. Many a complaint or opposition to your proposal fades away when you ask for *facts*.

Never leave a customer in doubt as to what you or the house proposes to do. Never leave any part of a transaction up in the air.

Lay every card on the table. Be definite. Be frank. Be thorough. Be prepared for the inevitable sale.

(4)

Dear _____,

A new member of our sales organization was "talking shop" with me when I was spending a day in the field. "It's my first week out, and I haven't done so badly; but there's one thing that stumps me. What do *you* reply when the prospect says, 'I'm not interested'?" This is a problem that has floored many a veteran. Well, what *do* you say?

The prospect who says, "Not interested," may really mean that *you* are not interesting. You have failed to dramatize your approach in a way that commands consideration.

"Not interested" is really no answer at all. That's why it is the most difficult of all responses to combat. It may be a cloak to disguise any one of a dozen more or less valid objections, such as, "I haven't the money," "I don't need it," or "I don't believe it will do what you claim."

"Not interested" is always an indication of weakness. The prospect is *afraid* to reveal the *real* reason for fear the objection will be broken down. Always counter with a question that can only be answered in the affirmative.

Aren't you interested in having your business under complete control?" or "Wouldn't you like to know how to get the highest percentage of profit from your business?" have always proven effective for many of us in this business.

But, of course, the very best solution of the problem is to make your talk so *interesting* that the prospect will have no chance to say, "I'm not interested."

Try out the suggestions I have given you. They have worked for me, and I am sure they will work for you.

(5)

Dear Fellow-workers,

I found this story in an old mazagine. Its truths are so current, I felt I had to pass them on to you.

KNOW YOUR POTATOES

The farm wagons stood in a public market. Both were loaded with potatoes in bags. A customer stopped before the first wagon.

"How much are potatoes today?" she asked the first farmer's wife.

"Two-fifty a bag," the wife replied.

"Oh, my," protested the woman, "that is pretty high. I paid only $2 for the last bag I bought."

" 'Tators has gone up," was the only thing the farmer's wife had to say.

So the housewife went to the next wagon and asked the same question. But the second farmer's wife "knew her potatoes." Instead of treating her customer with indifference, she replied:

"These are Wisconsin white potatoes, Madam. They are the best potatoes grown. In the first place, we only raise the kind with small eyes so that there will be no waste in peeling. Then we sort them by sizes. In each bag you will find a large size for boiling and cutting up; a medium size for baking. The baking size cook quicker and are all done at the same time, which means a big saving in electricity or gas. Then we wash all our potatoes clean before sacking them, as you can see. You can put one of these bags in your parlor without soiling the carpet— you don't pay for a lot of dirt. I'm getting $3 a bag for them— shall I put the bag in your car or deliver them?"

This smart wife sold *two* bags, at a higher price then her competitor had asked, in spite of the fact that the customer had refused to buy at the first wagon because she thought the price was "too high."

All of which proves that a customer's idea of price depends entirely on *ideas in his own mind*. When *you* put the right ideas there, the sale is not far way.

The more you know about what you are selling—regardless of whether it is some highly technical product or just potatoes— the better able you will be to overcome price objections. Customers should not be allowed to think that a price is too high. They won't think so if you know the fine points of what you are selling—as well as the farmer's wife knew the good points about her potatoes.

Study your product—then you can *sell* it.

(6)

Dear _____,

After calling on a butcher five or six times, a salesman selling a special meat-cutter decided to give him a demonstration. The following conversation took place.

Salesman: It's a nice machine, isn't it?
Butcher: Yes.
Salesman: It saves time and labor, doesn't it?
Butcher: It sure does.
Salesman: Do you like it?
Butcher: Yes.
Salesman: It will be easy to keep clean.
Butcher: I think you're right.

The salesman continued to slice the meat without saying anything further. The butcher became impatient and asked if he might try to work the machine. The salesman let him do so, but was at the end of his rope. He felt no further on with the sale than when he had started his demonstration.

Finally, he asked, "If you like the machine, why not let me have the order?" To this, the butcher frankly replied, "You haven't asked me."

How many salesmen go out and call on prospects day after day, giving one talk after another, and never mention the order? You'd be surprised. Salesmen time and time again wail about the merits of their products—and never once ask for the order. The prospect listens politely and finally the interview ends with the salesman asking permission to come and tell his little story over again another day.

Fellows, the business is here. Somebody is going to ask for the order if you don't. When you tell your story and forget to *ask for the order,* you are giving your competitor a chance to walk in on what is to him a "Cold Turkey Prospect," and he gets the order on his first call.

Beat him to it: ASK FOR THE ORDER.

So much for the sales manager letters that try to pass along specific help in getting the order. Of course, hundreds of other examples could be added to those you have just read, but the purpose of them all is to hand out tools with which the sales staff may do its job better. Whether it is to plan time, overcome some kind of resistance, or, finally, get that all-important sale, the sales manager should be there with aid for the staff. This is done through good letters. They are not emotional in their appeal. They simply say, "Here is a good idea—*use* it."

3. WRITING INSPIRATIONAL LETTERS TO SALES STAFF

How to insure they are interesting. A great many letters to salesmen are purely inspirational in nature. The managers who use this type of letter are content to leave more specific facts about selling to instructional bulletins, to sales meetings, and to personal conferences in field and office. In these particular messages they want to get under the staff's skin, to appeal to their better self, to challenge them to greater effort.

The tone of an inspirational letter must obviously be quite different from that of a factual letter. The former aims to stir the emotions of the salesmen; to make them alert to their shortccomings, and eager to do better. The factual letter aims to make them think more intelligently about their efforts and provides them with actual ideas they can use to improve them. Both types can be effective, but the inspirational letter has one special obligation to meet. It *must be interesting.*

We have discussed the natural tendency of average salesmen to look with a cold and critical eye on their mail from the home office. They feel, sometimes rightfully—that much of it could be omitted, and it is an imposition on their time to clutter their evenings with unnecessary correspondence. There is always the danger that a purely inspirational message will not be taken seriously—that it will be pushed aside as just another "pep talk."

The mention of this danger is not meant to imply that inspirational sales messages should be discarded. Not at all; but to do the job they must be bright and interesting, so that the sales force will really look forward to getting them—never fail to read them. This puts a premium on the skill of the sales managers which is not nearly so evident when they compose a brass-tack idea or a practical suggestion memo. In the latter case, they can be prosaic and still get attention. But not so in writing the inspirational letter. If dry and dull, it is tossed aside with a yawn or a shrug.

Some sales leaders have the gift of writing topnotch inspirational copy, just as some ministers are better able to inspire their congregations; some coaches better able to inspire their teams between halves; some politicians better able to inspire their listeners. There is hardly any way that the "gift" may be explained or copied. The people who lack the personal magnetism, the imagination, or whatever it may be, to challenge others should simply not attempt this type of motivation. They may try very hard, and mean everything they say, but the message just won't play on the heart-strings, or accomplish its purpose. The result is "pip," not "pep."

As a rule, it is not a wise practice to set up a routine under which a challenging letter must be mailed at regular intervals, weekly or otherwise. The obligation of coming up, week in and week out, with an inspirational thought that really clicks, is far too heavy a burden on sales managers? Often they are busy and cannot get to the writing of their "Saturday Sales Special" until shortly before it must be sent to the printing department for multigraphing. Working under pressure, and lacking a really good idea, they are likely to dictate a message that *drips* more than it *drives*. When not forced to meet a mailing date, they may wait until something really worth talking about turns up—and the message is sure to be better.

A guide to some excellent examples. Because the nature and purpose of the inspirational letter to salesmen is easily understood in the reading, it is hardly necessary that we comment on any of the following examples. Instead, they are presented as typical of the better sort that you encounter in sales correspondence. Their individual effectiveness you may judge from your own personal reactions. If *you* were a salesman, would these letters, some or all of them, inspire you to greater effort? The answer to that question is probably the only index to their value.

(1)

The Best People
in the World!

The other night, after seeing the show at the Hollywood Theater we went over to Drakes Deli before going home. While seated there, I noticed a large sign over the door on the inside of the store. The words impressed me so strongly, I wrote them down.

> "The best people in the world pass through
> this door—*our customers*"

I wondered then, as I often have before, if these clerks realize that their customers are to them the best people in the world.

And I wonder today if Panther folks everywhere—out on the Firing Line, in the Office, in the Mailing Room, in the Order Department, in the Bookkeeping Department, at the Factory, everywhere—realize that the best people in the world to us are our customers?

If we realize that, we can't help doing our jobs better.

With a heart full of appreciation to our customers for their goodness to us, how can we help treating an Order with even more care? Filling a drum over at the Factory with thought of the customer's needs, to make that package look prettier than any that ever left the Panther factory? Rush the credit information with double care that we might give this customer, our best friend, better Service than ever? To write that letter to the customer with every consideration due him, yet carry out our purpose? And if we're in the field, realizing that the best people in the world are our customers—sell each and every order so that there be no misunderstanding, no friction.

In the retail field throughout the country, there's a pronounced scarcity of genuine Salesmanship. Everybody will admit that. While it isn't true in the wholesale end of business generally, yet here too, there's need for more *expert salesmanship*, so that the *best people in the world* may be served still better.

Do *we* realize that *our* customers are the "best people in the world"?

Yours for the *best people* in the world,

(2)

Good Morning, _____

"Do you know what I consider the secret of successful accomplishment?" a prominent executive once asked me, supplying the answer himself: "It is singleness of purpose."

Since then I have thought of that a good many times. I have found myself starting enthusiastically to develop one idea, only to leave it half carried out, while I turned to another. On the golf course, for example, I have driven from the first tee, determined that day to concentrate on keeping my right elbow in. But by the time I reached number 9, I found I was directing my attention to keeping my left arm straight, or to keeping my head down or my eyes on the ball. I did not continue to work to one end, and therefore I did not improve in any direction.

The father of a brilliantly successful financier once said to his son, who had applied again and again for admission to graduate business school: "The dog waiting at the door to get in always in the end gets what he wants. His one thought is to get in, while people's minds cannot continually be concentrated on keeping him out."

It is almost a certainty that business executives of average intelligence can accomplish just about what they set out to accomplish, if they will concentrate all their efforts on that *one thing* and stick to it, working for it, and believing in it.

If there is one prospect you particularly want to sell, one company or family whose business you are anxious to get, concentrate on that one and *persist*—and you will, almost inevitably win that patronage. If you are right there with the persistent SINGLE PURPOSE, you will one day find resistance weak—and the door will open to you.

All of these examples are grand, but they are designed to fit rather general incidents in a selling career. Let us look at the impact you can make if you can connect your inspirational letter with a special occasion/event.

Exploring letters for special occasions. Messages to motivate salesmen are sometimes more effective, and probably easier to write, when connected with some special occasion—a holiday, a campaign, an anniversary, or some similar event to which the salesmen already attach importance. This is particularly true of contests, since the staff are already urged by the incentive to win and are thus in the mood to accept encouragement and suggestions. In Figure 12-6, the sales force get a good "shot in the arm," plus the fact that they are supposed to state definitely what they will accomplish the following month. A question that must be answered increases the pull of such a letter.

To take advantage of the spirit of competition that most human beings seem to possess, sales managers hold sales contests frequently; usually they last from one to three months, and are accompanied by many devices to keep interest at a high pitch. One of the common features is the use of special letterheads that tie in with the idea on which the contest is based. The aim may be to see which of the salesmen can score the most runs in an imaginary baseball game, cover the most miles

Figure 12-6

What NEXT?

You have just passed the halfway mark in the Campaign. In March all previous records were broken. You have every reason to be proud of your efforts.

But in April...WHAT NEXT?

There is always one danger in a good beginning—the temptation to "coast" to the finish. Once a person lets down, it is almost impossible to regain the same high level. What seems to be sure victory slumps off to defeat.

You have seen this happen in football games, in tennis matches, and on the baseball diamond. Sometimes you see it happen in business. "The time I bear down the hardest," says the world's greatest golfer, "is when I'm several holes up on my opponent."

Neither you nor I want to lose any of the momentum already gained in this sales contest. We can't afford to look backward, or feel too satisfied over what has been done. There's plenty of hard work ahead—no time to waste in a too-hasty celebration.

Records are made to be broken. March was good, but April comes as a new challenge. This contest is as important to you as to the company. It's your bread and butter. As you help to increase sales, you strengthen your own security.

Congratulations? Sure. In all sincerity, you have them. But again...WHAT NEXT? By how much in April will you *exceed* your March record?

Knowing you as I do, I am not afraid to ask that question. You are not the kind to dodge a specific question. Jot down on the bottom of this page the answer—and send it back to me in your next report to the home office.

Make it worthy of the best you have to give. By how *much* will *your* April sales beat those you made in March? Ten percent? That's too little. Twenty percent? Fine enough, if that's your level.

Come on now—seriously—because you mean to DO it...

In April, WHAT NEXT?

in a trip around the world, or win the most rounds in the padded ring. In each case, the letterheads are designed to fit the motif of the contest.

The letter shown in Figure 12-7 is an example of this form of

Figure 12-7

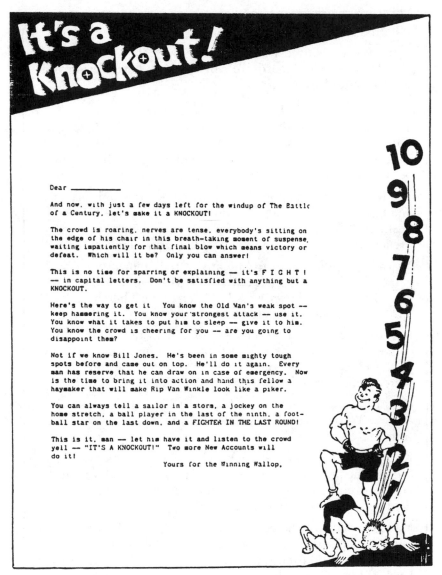

showmanship. In this contest, they are striving for a "Knockout." While such games may seem childish to certain individuals, sales managers know that they help to stimulate sales, but their success depends considerably on the originality of the idea and the way it is promoted. Merely to announce a contest, and say nothing more about it until the winners are decided, would be a very foolish procedure. Letters, bulletins, standings—frequently distributed—are necessary to keep the salesmen interested.

Material prizes are not the only incentive to better sales performance. The joy of winning, if properly applauded, may be just as potent a reward for the average person, and many a successful campaign for orders has been based on nothing more tangible. Sometimes, too, people may be induced to work harder just to honor someone else. One of the best examples of this style of letters follows:

Dear _____,

On the night of August 12, 55 years ago, a big, raw-boned youngster swung off of a Michigan Central train at Kalamazoo, and for the first time in his life, set foot on United States soil. There was no band to welcome him; no one to give him the keys to the city. Even the taxi drivers hardly gave him a glance. They knew there would not be enough money in the boy's pockets to make it worthwhile...he was too obviously "from the country."

And they were right about that. The smell of the cow barns was still on his clothes and his hands were covered with the calluses that come only from the handles of pitchforks and the "faucets" of cows.

Early the next morning found this boy trudging along a dusty road to a spot 3 miles north of Kalamazoo where, in the middle of a corn field, another immigrant boy was dreaming and sweating—trying to make a little converting plant into a gigantic paper mill. The boy had heard there might be a job. And that is how Doc Southern, at seven o'clock in the morning of August 13, met Jacob Kindleberger and went to work for KVP.

I think you know much of what happened before...how, discouraged by two years of looking for work in his native London and not finding it, he borrowed money and sailed by steerage for Canada...landed in Halifax...was sent to Leamington, Ontario, by an employment agency with the promise of a job waiting...found it a false report...hired out to a farmer the next morning although he had never had a farm tool in his hands before...milked cows and tended tobacco crops for two and a half years.

Then the trip to Kalamazoo on the hearsay evidence there might be a job. First, a job as a clerk...but that was only a title. In those days, everyone from J.K. down pushed trucks, shoveled coal, tied bundles...did whatever had to be done. Next, a road job, selling ice blankets. Before long, production. Then a hand in sales, General Sales Manager and Third Vice-President, First Vice-President and Director, and now CEO and Chairman.

That's pretty sketchy, but it gives the high spots—some mighty low ones, too, for that matter.

Fifty-five years of Doc's kind of Hard Work and Loyalty call for some real recognition. Now don't reach for your checkbook...this is something a darned sight more important than golf bags and loving cups...something that will please him a thousand times more.

Just send him some *orders*.

Don't think I'm crazy. I know just as well as you do that you have orders in here since last May that are unshipped...that you are afraid to face some of your customers without a bodyguard...that you are scared to call on others for fear that they will make you take an order.

That condition, however, does not apply on two lines—*parchment* and *specialty*. We can still handle *big* increases in both. And both can be highly profitable.

So what we are asking is this...will you go out every day between now and Labor Day, determined to make the next five weeks the greatest for *parchment* and *specialty* orders in the mill's history?

You will? That's great. Not that I had any doubt about it...in fact, I was all prepared. For in this mail, you should also find a packet of stickers like the one attached...ONE FOR DOC. Put a sticker on every *parchment* and *specialty* order you send in between now and Labor Day. Put one on the envelope, too.

Let's pile them in until the bloody h'Englishman yells for 'elp!

ONE FOR DOC,

P.S. He started work on the morning of the 13th. I'll bet a little personal note arriving that morning (it's on Friday) would make him feel like a million...yes, *two* million.

This idea works effectively in proportion to the popularity of the individual being honored; it may backfire if that popularity is not a reality. In the case of Doc Southern, you can tell the affection was genuine. The letter-writer incited the best efforts of the staff through warmth and personal sentiments. One feels anxious to know how many orders came in to honor him.

4. HOW TO RECTIFY WRONGS

Criticism: the supreme test of leadership. It is much easier to praise members of your sales force in a letter than to point out one of their faults. Criticism, even though well-intended and constructive, is often taken in the wrong way, especially when directed to a person whose general record is good, and whose connection with the company covers a considerable period of time. There is hardly any kind of letter writing that requires more tact—more sympathetic understanding of the particular individual—more knowledge of human nature. Nevertheless, letters of criticism must be written, for it is a function of leadership to *improve* as well as to *inspire*. In the larger sense, the overlooking of a weakness for fear of hurt feelings is not doing anyone a favor. If the fault is pointed out and corrected, the offenders have benefited as much as their company. But the problem of making them believe that is not simple. Many good salesmen are lost to their companies because of tactless letters of criticism.

As every capable sales manager knows, no two salesmen are likely to react in the same way to the same treatment. Some skins are thick; others are thin. One person discounts a criticism as only an attempt to push up sales; another magnifies it so that a mole-hill becomes a mountain in his mind. One person knows he must have faults, and appreciates help in correcting them; another thinks he is just about perfect, and that anyone correcting him must be prejudiced.

How various sales managers do the job. For writing to salesmen who have faults needing correction, one sales executive of national reputation has a formula that is both simple and interesting. "When I face the problem of pointing out a weakness to my people," he says, "I do three things. First, I build them up by saying something true about their work which is a compliment. Second, I tear them down by pointing out the weakness. Third, I try to build them up again with another complimentary remark, or some words of encouragement." This plan, the executive says, is used invariably, whether the criticism is presented in personal interviews or in letters. How the plan would work for others, we cannot testify, but it seems logical in principle:

> Build them up,
> Tear them down,
> Build them up again!

Other sales executives, equally well-known for success are not so considerate. Their philosophy is much more rugged. They state "I am willing to work hard with the salesman who can take my suggestions in the right spirit. I will overlook mistakes, hang on to them longer perhaps than would the average sales manager; but when I find out they are super-sensitive to criticism, I am through. Selling is a tough game. There is no room in it for people who are soft and can't take the bad with the good."

The letters that follow have been selected as representative of those being written in modern business, and to show how different sales executives handle criticism. In each case, the person who has dictated the letter is a tested leader. It is well to remember, however, that each letter is for a particular individual; a different approach might have been used for someone else.

(1)

Look Here _____,

Sit square in your seat for a few minutes and keep your shirt on. You're going to hear a few things that maybe you won't like to hear. And the more you resent them, the more I'm going to say, "fine."

I *might* start off by telling you that you're good, and we like you fine, and you're doing a good job. But what good would it do you if I did tell you that? It would just flatter you into a favorable opinion of yourself and you'd continue to knock along, getting about as many orders as I could put in my eye, and without making any money for yourself or the company.

> So...brace yourself. You're going to get mad. So what?
> So you're going to get that torpid liver stirred up and
> break into more action than you've shown in months.
> Results? You're going to do yourself some good.
> Now...here goes.

You are doing too much *negative thinking*. You know what I mean by that. I mean that even before you call on a prospect you're thinking up an excuse for not getting the order. You've got a first-class array of "if's, and's, and but's" that never did get you anywhere...never got you one signed order. You're not even running around in circles—you are just leisurely *walking*.

Does this make you mad? Okay, keep your seat. There's more coming.

You're wasting more time and energy thinking about how poor times are, and what you would do "if," than is good for you or your pocketbook.

Yes, I know. You and I were successful back in the old days when we had time for leisure, and could sit for three hours over lunch and gossip. But that method of living went out with the De Lorean. We can't mess around like we used to.

Nobody gives a hoot whether you or I like the present day's speed. We've got to keep pace with it or fall behind. For my part, I have no intention of falling behind, and ultimately getting into a rut. And *you're* not either, if I can do anything to jar you out of your rut.

To begin with, you're a salesman. If you weren't, you couldn't get *any* orders. You have sold merchandise, and therefore you can sell more. What's the reason that you're not doing it? You haven't a salesman's personality? We know that's the bunk. People aren't buying like they used to? Other salesmen are getting plenty of orders, without much trouble. Your personal worries are getting you down? Skip it. We all have personal worries, but we don't have to let them whip us.

So, it all adds up to this, _____. The bugaboos that are keeping you from being a success exist only *in your own mind.* And what's more, you're going to get rid of them. Starting right now, you're under doctor's orders. You're going out to make more effective calls before ten o'clock in the morning than you have been making in two days.

You're still mad, aren't you? Good! That's fine. When you get up in the morning, read this letter again, and get mad all over again.

And when the 15th rolls around with the biggest commission check you've enjoyed yet, we'll see who is right. Hold off writing that nasty letter you're planning on sending me—until we see who *is* right.

(2)

Dear _____,

It's easy for me to appreciate just how you feel. The big Eastern houses are jittery. That's the reason they are only talking about lower prices but haven't really issued a new price list. Of course, that has caused some of your customers to wait—to lose confidence, and make you the goat.

The very same thing that is happening to your customers is happening to *you.* You are commencing to *lack confidence.*

Don't overlook that you are not in direct competition with these folks—in product, price, or quality. You are like a runaway horse headed in the wrong direction. Jerk yourself back just as you would the horse if you got hold of its bit. Give yourself a good, hard yank.

You have been basing your sales arguments on price, and price alone. Naturally, that has always been a weak argument. Today, it's worth less than ever. If you, yourself, are afraid of the price situation, how the devil could you inspire prospects to put their names on the dotted line?

Mine is just a hunch that you are trying too darn hard to sell your goods. I say this because I've noticed how you report calling on this or that good customer, not getting an order, and then calling on a half dozen poorly rated, slow-pay fellows in the same town.

Some guy a whale of a lot smarter than I am said: "THE GOLD MINE of any company is its list of present customers." That's truer now than ever before. These customers *know* that your price has ALWAYS been right, and they *know* it's right NOW. It's to them you want to go with CONFIDENCE. Be at ease, be friendly, and leave the impression you are there to serve. To check up on stock! To suggest needed sizes and new styles! To stimulate HIS customers' interest in what HE has to sell! Not in what YOU have to sell.

For crying out loud, _____. You can't let this thing get you down. You are just as good a salesman as anyone I know. You've got personality, a heart, a soul, a body, and your Creator endowed you with plenty of brains. Is there any reason under the shining sun why you cannot sell?

Don't forget that there are plenty of WANTED goods. It's your job to demonstrate to your customer that your company makes these wanted goods. Plenty of people have money. Just look at the people who haven't lost a day's pay in years. In any community, no matter how small, you can point them out to your prospect by the dozens.

All you need, _____, is a good shot of CONFIDENCE that will restore in you mountain-moving FAITH in yourself.

Suppose tomorrow morning while you're getting ready for the day, you memorize this little creed, and then, each morning as you pick up your order book, repeat it.

I believe in myself.
I believe in my work.
I believe in my company.
I believe in the quality of the goods I am selling.

I believe my goods are priced right.
I believe I'm going to have a good day.

It's been a long time since I mentioned the "third shirt button." There's something in it, though, so I'm suggesting that TOMORROW when you have picked up your brief case, after reciting the above creed, you STICK OUT YOUR THIRD SHIRT BUTTON, square your shoulders, get that fighting light in your eyes—and you know, _____, you just can't help but sell.

(3)

Dear _____,

I have read your letter, and think the one giving you the most trouble in your territory is a bird by the name of _____. Until we either regulate its liver or clear its mind, it will continue to bother you a lot.

Now, in talking this over with you frankly, _____, I don't want you to get the idea that we don't realize that you have had a hard proposition over there. Neither do I want you to feel that we have been critical about your work. We think you have been doing fine, and the fact that we gave you a better contract this year should convince you that our feeling is sincere.

The experiences you have been having are not much different from those of many other salesmen in your Division. For instance, I consider the territory north of you, the one held by Brown, harder than your own. The same applies to Smith's territory, east of you. South of you is Jones. He took the worst scolding of any man in our Division for the first six months he was in that territory, but he is now sitting on top, laughing at conditions.

Did you check the standings at the end of the last quarter? If you did, you know that Brown, Smith, and Jones got over the quota line. So did White who was in a territory that looks about as prolific as the desert of Sahara. Now, get me right, _____. This isn't a criticism, but simply a comparison of territories and people. These are results brought about by people who have been absolutely determined that nothing on earth is going to hold them back.

The reason I am making this point so strongly to you is because I am sincerely convinced that your territory trouble is really trouble with yourself. If you are absolutely sure in your own mind that our proposition is not profitable for your dealers and consumers, then I would have very little respect for you if you continued with the work. Salesmen never become gifted enough to make a success selling goods in which they do not believe.

Of course, you'll always have some trouble. There are some consumers that will insist our price is too high, that other products are better. But don't let that kind of talk get your goat. You can't please everybody with one recipe for stew, or any one kind of car. Neither will you ever be able to sell and satisfy every prospect. But the breaks are in your favor. Also, here is a little secret I will let you in on. If our competitors are having such a walk-away, why do I have seven applications received this week from salesmen now selling competitive lines?

You know, _____, it's a mighty good thing for us that we do have these conditions that build up sales resistance. Otherwise, there would be no need of salesmen. Most sales conditions, however, are a matter of mind, and our most successful salesmen are the ones who generally make their own conditions.

Now, as for your resigning, _____, it's entirely up to you. You are over 21 and you know your own business. What we want you to understand is that we have found no fault with the work you have done. We'd like to have you stay if *you* think you are the person for the job. I am willing to back any of our people to the limit as long as they "think they can." When they tell me they *can't,* then it's time for them to quit.

We are going to stay in your territory, and we are going to build up a real business there which will be mighty profitable for the dealers who stick with us. Some salesman is going to collect on this business. You have the first chance.

I expect to be up in Smith's territory next week. If you want me to drop off and talk this matter over with you, I'll be mighty glad to do so. Just tell me where you want me to meet you.

(4)

Dear _____,

Is length of service an asset or a liability?

Practically all of the people in our division have been with the company over ten years. The average is 11 years, and you are the Dean of Service College with 20 successful years behind you.

What a wonderful asset this should be for you. On the other hand, it could be a liability. Twenty years of service in the same sales organization is a tremendous asset only if it has built a rich background of broadening experience. If it has deepened the rut of personal satisfaction—lulled you into a false feeling of security—then it's a great liability.

Regardless of how the company may feel about you or me in a personal way, they would be unfair to allow this feeling to have any influence in their judgment of future value. When we get down to brass tacks, _____, it is *future* performance that will determine your progress—not the victories of past years.

What brought this up? Well, I will tell you.

Yesterday, from the statistical department, I received an analysis of the sales for all the salesmen in our division, starting from the first year of their employment. If you could see your own chart, I think it might surprise you.

No, your sales volume hasn't dropped sharply in recent years, and your commissions are still running better than $600 a month. But the curve *is* dropping, _____, and the decline began four years ago, just after you were crowned champion of the division.

I know that good salesmen don't bother a lot about figures, or to compare them one year with another. So maybe you didn't realize that each of the last four years your monthly average has been a little less than the one before.

This wouldn't worry me if you were an old man—but if my record is straight, you are only 44, with at least another span of 20 years ahead of you. Right now, you have one boy in college, and another soon out of high school. The three girls are younger, but in the years coming up they, too, will need to be educated.

In other words, you just can't afford to let your income gradually slip downward, and the time to reverse the direction is while you are still making good money.

I'm not sure *why* your sales curve has been going down, but the reason *could* be the one I mentioned in the beginning of this letter. Success breeds self-satisfaction—sometimes too much of it for our own good.

Please, my friend, don't think I am preaching or criticizing. You are one of our best salesmen, and you know how much I admire all that you have done, and are doing. But that sales chart with your name on it...well, somehow, it made me think about the both of us, and how easily it would be for success to become a liability.

One thing I am rather sure of. Your curve has dipped as low as it will ever be. You are smart. You'll see the common sense in what I've said. You'll be on the way back to the champion's spot for the rest of this year, and for all the years to come.

I'll bet my last shirt on that, _____. And you know it wouldn't look so good for me to go around the office without a shirt.

In the foregoing letters, you have witnessed various sales managers in more or less critical moods. Some spoke bluntly; some tried to correct the fault with gentle reasoning. Each letter was slanted at a different individual, which helps, no doubt, to explain the variations in tone and content.

Of course, there are other situations that would require sales managers to reprimand members of their sales teams; for example, an instance in which a salesman had an argument with a customer, or the case of one who turned in excuses and alibis for not making good, rather than bringing in revenue from closed deals. However, the illustrations given above seem to apply to the most common situations in this area, and will serve as a valuable reference to any sales manager who finds it necessary to stir action and to keep them moving at a profitable speed.

KEEPING EVERYONE HAPPY WITH ADJUSTMENT LETTERS

KEEPING EVERYONE HAPPY
WITH ADJUSTMENT LETTERS

1. HOW TO CORRECT AND AVOID MISUNDERSTANDINGS

Adjustments—an overview! No company can be expected to attain perfection in production, performance of personnel, or in any of the other parts which together we call a *business*. Even if such a state ever did exist, misunderstandings would surely occur now and then between company and customer. Hence, in any well-regulated organization, you will find experienced "trouble-shooters" whose job it is to investigate, adjust, and even anticipate any interruption in pleasant customer relations. One of their primary qualifications is the ability to write courteous, satisfying, persuasive adjustment letters.

Meeting this obligation is often a difficult and exacting problem, for angry people are seldom in the mood to listen to reason, or to accept any explanation which conflicts with their own preconceived ideas. It is not easy to apologize in such a way that a mistake will be understood and forgiven; to refuse a special request from an old and faithful customer without incurring displeasure; to make an impatient buyer understand why the shipment of an order has been delayed; or to handle tactfully any other of the thousand and one situations which complicate customer relations.

Fortunately, the majority of the complaints received in the routine operations of a company are not so serious that they cannot be pleasantly and quickly adjusted. One company, for example, after analyzing several thousand complaints in an effort to discover the causes, came out with some rather surprising figures. The percentages would probably vary for other individual companies, and for business as a whole, but there is no reason to doubt their approximate correctness.

This company found that:

- 22.5 per cent of all complaints they received were sincerely made, and with just causes.
- 41 per cent were motivated by impulse rather than deliberate reasoning.
- 23.7 per cent were pretended abuses: usually a defense for lack of funds, or some other inability to go through with the purchase.
- 12.8 per cent were totally unwarranted, and caused by perversity.

Insofar as the above percentages are accurate, they lend considerable encouragement to those who wrote adjustment letters. With proper tact and understanding, they may hope to handle with reasonable success all customers with chips on their shoulders except the last group. The latter *know* at heart that they have no just cause for complaint, and for that reason will resist to the last ditch any attempt to smooth their self-ruffled feathers. No amount of reasoning or fair play will change their attitude, since they are *looking* for trouble and are not to be satisfied unless they get it.

The troublemakers, of course, deserve no special consideration; letters to them may be short, firm, and courteous. The others *mean* well toward the company, even though their claims are unwarranted. With a little tact and patience, letters may be devised which will restore their goodwill and leave them still friends of the company. To show how these unhappy customers are handled by the experienced "trouble-shooter," is the purpose of this section.

Understanding when complaints are blessings. In spite of the trouble they cause, complaints are not resented by modern business executives. Instead, they view them as a means of finding out what things are wrong in the operation of their businesses, in the quality of their attitudes, and performances of their personnel. It is seldom pleasant to discover a fault, but much better than to let it continue unsuspected.

The proper reaction toward customer misunderstandings is very adequately presented in the bulletin in Figure 13-1. It was sent to Montgomery Ward's correspondents.

Understanding the customer's point of view. Success in handling angry or dissatisfied customers depends partly on the correspondents' ability to look on the letters of complaint as if they, themselves, had written them. Then, and then only, are those in the Adjustment Department in the right position to reply. From the correspondent's point of view, the complaint may be just another worry, and the letter, an unreasonable tirade which deserves to be answered, tit for tat. From the customer's point of view, the complaint represents something that was

Figure 13-1

HOW DO WE REGARD A COMPLAINT?

In answering complaints, sometimes I wonder just what the correspondents think—what their attitudes are when they start to write.

There are two ways to look at complaints—the right way and the wrong way. If we, as correspondents, take the attitude that each letter is just another complaint to be handled, and tackle it in a routine way without regard to the thoughts and feelings of the customer, is it fair to Montgomery Ward or to us that we stay on the job? We are not fitted for adjustment work or any work that puts us in contact with customers, if we think that way.

The real correspondents are the ones who deep down in their hearts are thankful to the customer for having made the complaint, because it may show us where we are weak in our merchandise or service. And it also offers us a splendid opportunity to prove that Montgomery Ward is really anxious to please.

It is seldom that a complaint is wholly unjustified—there is usually some ground for the customer writing, and the "kicks" we receive should not be considered as an annoyance. Few are from grouchy old customers who are trying to get something for nothing—90 percent of them are legitimate complaints which we should welcome with open arms.

They open the way for an investigation. And we must all admit that if no one complained about our merchandise, or the handling of an order, Montgomery Ward would have been out of business years ago.

These remarks are made to give you a little better idea of what complaints really mean to Montgomery Ward. Let's adopt the right attitude. Let's show more tolerance and a sincere effort to run complaints down. After all, they are a barometer because they point out our weak spots.

We should be glad customers write to us instead of remaining silent or broadcasting their complaints to their neighbors and not giving us a chance to make things right.

---

paid for but not received. The letter is a warranted appeal for justice. Just what the complaint really is—what the letter stands for—depends on the circumstances of the particular incident and the honesty of the individual. But right or wrong, the customer must have first consideration, and the letter needs to be interpreted on behalf of the *customer,* not the correspondent.

Another important point made in the bulletin above is the necessity of *investigating the facts* before attempting to write the adjustment letter. Several workers in a Chicago store did *not* take time to know the facts, or the following customer's letter would not have been necessary.

> Dear _____,
>
> Enclosed find check for $6.63 to settle balance shown on your books as due you. Of this sum, $3.50 plus 13 cents postage is for one copy of O. Henry. That's okay. I ordered the O. Henry. I now pay for the O. Henry.
>
> The remainder pays for the second of two cigarette cases, satin-covered, initialed E.T.
>
> I ordered one cigarette case in December.
>
> You sent two.
>
> I returned one.
>
> You sent it back to me.
>
> I wrote to you, saying I'd ordered only one.
>
> You wrote to me, saying I could send it back.
>
> You returned it, saying that on account of the initials you couldn't accept it... I'm tired of paying postage on the doggone thing... so here's your money.
>
> But that isn't the last straw. My wife ordered an egg poacher. You sent a cookie-dough squirter. We have a cookie-dough squirter. We don't have an egg poacher. We don't want a cookie-dough squirter. We do want an egg poacher. I hesitate to return the cookie-dough squirter lest it start on a series of travels similar to those of the cigarette case.
>
> Now personally, I like to buy from your store, but if there is any more of this monkey business, I'll trade somewhere else. After all, a customer likes to get what he ordered—no more, no less, no different.

The mystery of the second cigarette case! The cookie squirter that turned out to be an egg poacher! What a mess of trouble for the correspondent before he can qualify himself to answer that complaint letter. But he can't do it adequately until he finds out what happened. And finding out may bring to light faults in the store's routine for handling mail orders. But that's not the only benefit to be gained. There's a customer at stake. He likes the store, but he doesn't like the "monkey business." His wife still wants an egg poacher—not a cookie squirter. Here's a customer to be saved or lost by what the adjustment correspondent says and does. It's a chance to render a service to customer and company—nothing to be annoyed about.

Strange as it may seem, customers do want what they ordered—no more, or less, no different. Maybe they shouldn't be so finicky, but they want what they want. Here's another letter that proves it.

> Nuts to you!
>
> I received a letter from you (initialed JD) which started with this sentence, "I would like to send you a copy of the *March* issue for free examination." And then it read, "Simply sign the enclosed card, include $1, and we will mail you the *March* issue."
>
> So I sent a dollar. Did I get the March issue? No. Instead I received a postal card telling me the March issue was no more, but that you were sending a copy of the April issue.
>
> Now that isn't what I wanted. I was willing to pay a dollar to read the articles in the March issue, and then decide if I wanted to be a subscriber or have my dollar returned.
>
> The March issue is what you offered. The March issue is what I wanted. If you can't supply it, return my dollar and I will return your new 64-page book, "Answers to Health Questions."
>
> Maybe I am unreasonable, but I am rather tired of being offered one thing in a mail solicitation, and then being disappointed by receiving another. I feel that I have had enough.
>
> Either I get what you offered and I ordered or there is no sale.
>
> Phooey from me to you,

If you like to know how stories end, you'll be interested to know that the above letter was a success. The writer got the March issue.

Blueprint of writing the adjustment letter. It is foolish to say that all letters answering complaints should be prepared in the same mold. The proper procedure depends on the nature of the particular case and the personal inclination of the correspondent. However, there are certain steps that seem logical, and unless you can improve on them, it is better to follow them rather than to write in a hit-and-miss manner.

1. Say something in the beginning to make the customers feel you are really glad to know about their complaint...*thank* them for telling you.

2. Tell them in a friendly way what you can do, or can't do, to make things right with them.

3. Justify the decision. Don't argue, if it is not favorable, but lay the facts on the table, so they will know *why* you are refusing.

4. Try to regain their goodwill—perhaps, by doing something else that might please them.

5. Assure them they are appreciated as customers—imply confidently that they are *still* buyers.

When a clash is inevitable between customer and company points of view, and the writer of the adjustment letter faces the necessity of a complete turn-down or of a compromise which he knows the customer is not likely to approve, there is always the grave danger that the continued correspondence exchange will develop into a first-class dog-fight. That means, of course, the end of the business relationship. Hence, no matter how incorrect the customer may be in stating his side of the case—no matter how insistent and argumentative—the company representative cannot properly let himself be drawn into a heated argument.

Benjamin Franklin once gave some sage advice on "How to win an argument," which some business letter-writers could follow to their own advantage. Here it is:

> The way to convince another is to state your case moderately and accurately. Then scratch your head, or shake it a little, and say that is the way it seems to you, but of course you may be mistaken about it; which causes your listener to receive what you have to say, and as like as not, turn about and try to convince you of it, since you are in doubt. But if you go at him in a tone of positiveness and arrogance you only make an opponent of him.

It may be a little difficult to scratch your head in a letter, but you can go along with the idea of not being too aggressive or arrogant. Winning an argument at the cost of a customer is hardly a good investment. A famous football coach always said, "We aim to win but not humiliate." Deny the customer's request if you must, but in a way that says, "I know exactly how you feel, and I wish we could do as you wish, because there is a lot to be said in your favor."

How to avoid major mistakes. Before we examine actual letters used to handle complaints and special requests from customers, a few *Don't signs* will be useful guides to those who aspire to success in this important field of business correspondence.

1. When the customer is right, admit the fault frankly. Don't try to cover up or alibi.

2. Say you are sorry, but don't cry all over the carpet. Profuse apology is a sign of fear and weakness. Sincere regret is all that the customer expects.

3. In general, it does no good to explain all the gory details of an error. The customer wants to know that the error will be *adjusted;* not how it happened. Keep that skeleton in your own closet.

4. Never grant a concession or make an adjustment with an air of condescension—as if you are doing it merely out of the goodness of your heart, and not because it is the right thing to do. This belittles the customer—and causes resentment.

5. Never refer to the "complaint" of a customer as such. Not when writing to *him.* Call it a "request" or a "misunderstanding." Complainers are not liked in this world. The customer is asking for justice—not making a *complaint.*

6. Avoid the use of any word or phrase which might imply suspicion of the customer's integrity or truthfulness. For example: "We have your letter in which you *claim* one case was missing."

7. Never delay the reply to the customer's letter. If it takes time to investigate, write and thank him immediately—tell him how soon he may expect your final decision.

8. Never go back at a customer in a spirit of anger, no matter how unjust or unreasonable or discourteous he may have been in his letter to you. A business letter-writer is an Ambassador of Goodwill. He may never play any other role.

9. Never try to dodge responsibility by placing the blame for a mistake on some other party. People do not admire buckpassers. Above all, protect the sales staff if you can. They need the respect and confidence of the customer.

10. Never repeat the details of a fault. For example: "We have your letter about finding two dead roaches in one box of our flakes." Let the customer forget such things as fast as he can. Make the adjustment, but talk about something more pleasant.

11. Never pretend great surprise over a mistake. This implies you doubt it really happened. For example: "Never in all our 30 years in business, has such a mistake been made in our factory." Who will believe you?

12. Don't hide behind the word "policy" in refusing a claim or request. The customer has the right to know *why* he is denied.

13. Treat a complaint with just as much respect as an order. Let the customer know you are just as eager to serve as to sell him.

14. If the matter at hand seems important to the customer, don't try to change his opinion. Join *with* him. Attach an airmail stamp to your reply or send it special delivery. For the cost of a few pennies, you may make your company stand first for service in his mind.

15. If the customer addressed his letter to you, never turn it over to someone else for reply unless company organization makes it necessary. In that case, write to him anyway, and tell him he will be hearing from the other party.

To the above cautions might be added one trite but very true axiom—"An ounce of prevention is worth a pound of cure." A certain number of errors is unavoidable in any company, but there is little reason why the *same one* must happen over and over again. The individual handling a complaint should be sure that a report is made to *all* departments and workers who may have been involved. A faulty routine can be changed; an inefficient employee can be fired. Certainly, the salesman in the area should get news of the complaint, and how it was handled. This is also true of any request made by the customer which requires special decision: a variation in regular terms, permission to return goods not selling as anticipated, or any other dispensation apart from the usual custom or policy.

Classifying types of adjustment letters. The most logical way to classify adjustment letters, so that each type may be considered as a separate problem, is to think of them in relation to the action which the company intends to take. This action is influenced by several factors: the circumstances which provoked the customer's complaint or request, the determination of responsibility if an error has been made, the relative importance of the customer as a buyer of the company's products, and other conditions which make it impossible to set up a rigid, unbreakable policy. For example, a company may insist that all customers are treated alike, and an honest effort may be made to live up to that intention, but the brutal fact remains that, for the sake of keeping goodwill, a big buyer is more likely to receive special concessions than is the small buyer. Be that as it may, these company letters that seek to smooth out the wrinkles in customer relations may be grouped in the following ways:

1. Letters of regret and apology—chiefly used in situations where the damage has been done, and the main objective is to salvage as much goodwill as possible.

2. Letters in which the answer to the customers is "Yes"—they get what they want, completely and without reservation. In the case of a mistake, a letter of this type means that the company is assuming full responsibility.

3. Letters in which the answer to the customers is "No"—they get nothing that they want, or a compromise which may or may not be satisfactory. This type of reply places the fault in the laps of the customers, provided a complaint has been filed.

4. Letters in which objections are *anticipated* and explanations are offered *before* the customers have had the chance to complain or be displeased. Thus, one of these letters may announce and justify a change in policy, an increase in price, the discontinuation of a service or product, or some other step the customers might be expected to resent. The above classification demands a broader interpretation of the word *adjustment* than when it is used merely with reference to customers' complaints about orders, or how they have been handled. But all of the conditions covered in the broader interpretation need to be "adjusted" if pleasant customer relations are to be maintained; in that sense, the letters which talk about them *are* adjustment letters.

2. DEVELOPING LETTERS OF APOLOGY AND REGRET

Attempting to salvage goodwill. Things may happen in business which interfere with cordial customer relations, but by the time they are brought to the surface it is too late to repair the damage. You can think of numerous illustrations: a dealer wants some goods for a special sale on a specified date, but they are shipped to Jackson, Mississippi, instead of Jackson, Michigan; the president of a trade association makes much ado about the luscious steaks to be served at the annual banquet, and they turn out to be very tough; a gift shop orders goods for the holiday season and they arrive after Christmas; an important guest is treated rudely by the night clerk, and the fact does not come out until the former takes an important convention to another hotel. These and many other slips occur in business; their number and kind defy count or description. Sometimes, a partial reparation may be made; usually not. The only adjustment left is a letter of regret and apology, which may or may not heal the wound.

Inspecting examples taken from business. There is, of course, no *one* way that a correspondent may best write a letter expressing regret when some service or product has gone sour. It is useless to offer a lengthy explanation which to the reader is only a confession of weakness, an alibi for something that never should have happened. Instead, it seems better to just express the regret—simply and sincerely.

Here are three examples:

(1)

Dear _____,

There is a saying that "Even a monkey falls out of a tree once in a while."

But we certainly have gone the monkeys one better by making a mistake twice on your order. We're having the printer try again today, with instructions to "double-check the imprint." Shipment will be rushed tonight.

We surely appreciate your good nature under these exasperating circumstances. We hope you will believe that our printers are usually not so confused.

(2)

Dear _____,

Thank you for your card which reports the second dish broken. I don't blame you for saying what you did about us. If I were in your shoes, I'd probably say a lot more.

This premium business is very new to us. We are still experimenting, but hope to find the right way to pack these refrigerator dishes so that they will arrive in perfect condition.

I am sorry you have been put to so much trouble, but another dish is being mailed, and we have made some further changes in the way of packing.

One thing you can count on, _____. We will see that you get a dish all in one piece, if it takes all winter.

(3)

Dear _____,

Filbert's Department Store sent us the overalls which pulled out at the seams, and we wrote and told them they did the right thing by replacing them immediately. Of course, we have made good with Filbert's.

Whatever you do, don't blame Filbert's for your trouble with this pair of overalls. It really wasn't their fault. We are the ones to blame, and you can be sure we regret the unpleasant experience you have had.

What we want now is to know if the new garment proves to be all that you have the right to expect. The people down at Filbert's would like to know, too. Will you please tell them?

Thank you.

Now that you have some critical experience under your belts, let us look at some exchanges and how they were handled by the master letter-writers.

Looking and learning from both sides. After reading, here is an opportunity to test your skill. Read each customer's letter of complaint. Based upon what you have seen so far, mentally reply to them. Then, carefully read the answers that the experts crafted. Compare what you have written with these actual letters.

All right, let's begin:

SET 1

Letter from Customer

Dear _____,

I am a customer of long standing—my home being almost completely furnished with your appliances, such as electric refrigerator, washing machine, etc. I have always felt that your merchandise was thoroughly reliable, and still do. But unless the mistakes that have been so common in my orders lately are eliminated, I will be forced to take my business to some other concern.

The nuisance of having to send things back is getting to be just a little too much. The last three orders have all had mistakes made in articles sent.

The first was a coffee percolator instead of a coffee warming pot. This I sent back, and it was corrected. The second was a 3-quart Corningware casserole dish in place of the 2-quart I ordered and paid for. I needed the casserole dish, so I gave you the $14.98 rather than wait for the adjustment. The last mistake was sending two jigsaw blades instead of the two sabre-saw blades ordered.

These were three successive shipments. Your percentage of error seems to be too high.

For your own information, you have already lost several accounts in this region because of similar mistakes. So it might be wise to eliminate the cause of these mistakes, and save more of your customers—including *me*.

The Reply

Dear _____,

It would be a great disappointment to lose your business but an even keener one to lose your friendship and faith in our firm. So I want to thank you for your letter which I feel was written in friendliness to give us another chance.

It is a bother to send things back, _____, and I am sorry you had to do this. I don't wonder that you didn't return the casserole dish when we sent the wrong size, but even though the amount involved is trifling, we want to make it right. Here is our check for the three-quart casserole dish you didn't receive.

If you wish the saw blades exchanged, let me know the article number you selected. The correct blades will be sent at once, and then you can return the others when convenient. A check will be sent for postage, as we certainly don't want you to have extra postage expense because of our mistake.

Your orders should all be filled promptly and completely, and I am going to see that a more careful check is made to prevent those things you bring to our attention. You see, letters like yours have a real value—they help us to know just where we are slipping.

You have been a good customer for a long time, _____. From past experience, I am sure you know that our aim is to please—both by our goods and our service.

SET 2
The Customer's Letter

Dear _____,

I used to think that the Doe House was a good hotel. I have changed my mind.

Not that my opinion matters much to you, because one customer won't make or break the Doe House. And not that the Doe House matters much to me, either, because there are a lot of other hotels in Gotham. But when one of your employees is unnecessarily antagonizing customers, you may like to know it. So here's the story.

My wife and I drove to Gotham on a business trip on the morning of October 16—a trip of only 200 miles. We intended to drive back the same evening.

While I was having a conference at a studio on Erie Street, my wife spent the afternoon at Field's. I met her there shortly after five o'clock. She announced that she was short of actual cash. I checked and noticed that I was, too. It was too late for the bank. However, I had a government check for $74.25 in my pocket, which I thought would be as good as cash. So I said, "We will turn in this check at the Doe House when we go there for dinner."

When I presented this check, your cashier asked if I had a rating card, and if I was registered at the hotel. I told him I had no card, and was not registered, but that we had stayed at the Doe House many times. I gave him the date of our last visit (in August) and suggested that he look up the card I signed then.

He refused to take any further interest in the matter. I then went to one of your assistant managers, and she stated she could not go over the head of the cashier.

So there we stood in your lobby, 200 miles from home, embarrassed, angry, hungry, and with 85 cents in our pockets. We didn't even stop for dinner—we headed home before it got any later.

At a gas station near Middletown, we stopped for gas. We told him about our problems and our fears about being on the road with no cash available. He said he would see what he could do for us and took the check inside. A passing policeman even asked if he could help.

The officer looked at my auto registration card, and made a telephone call. He came out and said the check was O.K. We got the gas *and* our check cashed. Quite a contrast, wasn't it, with the helpfulness at the Doe House?

Your cashier either lacked the resourcefulness to know his business or the desire to be of service—and I feel sure that the desire to be of service is what he lacked. I realize that hotels are imposed on, and must have rigid rules, but that is no reason for treating old customers like crooks.

Don't bother to answer this letter. We are all through with the Doe House.

The Reply

Dear _____,

I am grateful for your letter. You have done the Doe House a big favor in telling me of your experience.

Our cashier, the assistant manager you speak of, and I have just had a talk—a serious one. I did most of the talking.

Thanks to your thoughtfulness, other guests of this hotel will not be treated with the same heedlessness. Of that I am sure.

Somebody has said that excuses are shabby patches with which we try to cover our failures; so rather than try to explain away our conduct, I prefer to rely on your generosity.

My associates and I are genuinely sorry. We ask you also to convey our apologies to Mrs. _____.

I said no excuses. I shall try to stick to that. But may I leave this thought with you? We are all human. A sleepless night, or some personal worry, can at times throw the steadiest nature off-balance. Has that ever happened to you or someone close to you?

I suspect that something was amiss with my associates the day you were here. However, neither tried to excuse their mistakes, and for that I give them credit. Can you—will you—look at it in that light?

When you folks are again in Gotham, I will be happy to have you step over to the Doe House and have dinner with us. Your consent will show me that you have decided to overlook the incident, and this simple gesture on our part may help to let you know how sorry we are.

Drop me a line when you are coming, and a table in the Gold Room will be reserved for you and your party. Of course, there will be no check.

How did you make out? Did you refer to the checklist at the beginning of this section? With the help of those tips, it is a certainty that your trial "mental" letters would have been as successful as the ones presented. The letter-writers paid particular attention to calming their puzzled and/or angry customers. Did you wonder how the incidents actually came out? Both letters were worth the efforts taken on them; the appliance store got another order, and the couple came in for their "apology" dinner.

One last series of exchanges can show how valuable a good adjustment letter can be. Look at these.

1. Complaint

Dear _____,

On February 3, I sent your truck driver, A.B. Smith, a repair bill for $150.89, the amount of damage he did when he collided with my auto in front of the school house on E. Chapman Ave. I had signalled a left turn, which he admits.

Up to now he has ignored the bill. If not paid in five days, I shall begin suit in the small claims court, to recover same with costs.

2. *Adjustment*

Dear —————,

Needless to say, we sincerely regret that your claim for damages in the amount of $150.89 has not been adjusted to your satisfaction before this time.

During the 27 years we have been in business we have been extremely jealous of the reputation we have acquired for courtesy, not only from our office executives but from our drivers as well.

We are sorry the accident occurred but hope that our driver conducted himself in a courteous manner. We have instructed Mr. L.B. Long, manager of our operations at Orange, to pay you immediately the $150.89 in full settlement of the claim.

Again we apologize for our delay in taking care of this matter and will appreciate your not holding this unfortunate experience against our record for carefulness and courtesy.

If at any time we can be of service to you, you have only to let us know.

William T. Summers,
Adjustor

3. *Appreciation*

Dear —————,

Your most courteous letter was received, and Mr. Long gave me his check for $150.89 in full settlement for the damage done to my auto by your truck driver.

I owe you people an apology for my hasty action and hope you will forgive me. It has been many years since I received so courteous a letter. It has impressed me greatly, and my wife and I often speak about it....

It must be conceded "a job well done" when one short letter such as Mr. Summers' can change an angry man threatening to sue, to a smiling one who says, "I owe you people an apology."

3. TELLING THE CUSTOMER "YES"

Dictating the easy ones. It requires no particular skill to grant customers' requests or to adjust misunderstandings their way. The big thing they are after is satisfaction, and if they get it, the letters telling them so are comparatively easy to dictate. However, there are two things the correspondents should keep in mind so that the situation may be turned to the best advantage of the company.

One, as already noted, is taking care to grant the requests or make the adjustments cheerfully, without implying that the customers are getting something to which they are not entitled. A favor extended grudgingly or with an air of patient condescension is little better than a favor denied. The recipients naturally resent the insinuation that they have been unreasonable, or that they are being humored as a matter of policy.

The second is the complement of the first. If the implication of coddling is carefully avoided, and the adjustment or concession is offered in the light of a *service* which the writer and his company are happy to render, then the time is propitious for the winning of considerable goodwill. Usually, the people filing complaints or asking for some special services are on the defensive. They may even present their cases more belligerently than the circumstances warrant, hoping in that way to force a favorable reply. If money is involved, they fear that an argument may develop, and worry about a possible loss. Then back come letters from the company—sympathetic, agreeable, cheerfully accepting the customer's viewpoint, and asking only the *privilege* of making things right. Under such circumstances, the customer's reactions are highly favorable: they feel that they are dealing with a fine, dependable company; their attitudes are filled with goodwill. Many a lasting business relationship dates back to a complaint properly handled. The individuals who write adjustment letters can be *salesmen* even though they never leave the office.

Making it a big YES. There are a lot of words in our language that people especially like to hear, and surely one of the first ten is *yes*. Of course, it can't always be used in business letters, but when it is possible its use is sure to please.

Yes, _____, you can have another 30 days to pay this bill, and we are very glad to do you this favor.

· · · · ·

Yes, you are right, _____. Distributors cannot always anticipate the exact volume of their Christmas sales, and we certainly don't want a fine customer like yourself to be without any of our goods when he has the chance to sell them. We stopped taking orders four weeks ago, but don't worry. You'll get your five cases not later than Wednesday of next week.

· · · · ·

Yes, _____, what you say in your letter is true. We were late in making the shipment, and we are sorry.

Yes, _____, your July bill for gas used in your home is somewhat higher than ususal—but did you notice that the two preceding bills were averaged?

. . . . .

Yes, indeed, _____. We will be glad to exchange the sizes, and we consider it a privilege to render you this little service.

Yes is a fine word, isn't it? Well, then, as a business correspondent, use it at every possible opportunity. Readers smile when you *agree* with them; they frown when you do not. Even if you are not going to do all that they have asked, it is usually possible to say "yes" about some little part of it. If that is so, *start* with the part that says *yes;* then, reluctantly, swing to the *no.* Even a turndown letter can be dictated in such a way that the reader feels you are sorry it couldn't be otherwise. *Be happy to say yes—be sorry to say no.* The writer who takes pains to follow that simple slogan will make many customers friends.

Consider, for example:

(1)
A Happy Yes

Dear _____,

Yes, of course. It makes us feel right good to have this chance to give you a lift. You have been a loyal customer for many years; why shouldn't we do something for you once in a while?

Jack Smith, during his call next week, will help you pack the china and see that it is shipped. In the meantime, the numbers that you want will be rushed right out to you.

Best regards, _____, and thanks for putting this problem of yours where it belongs—in our lap.

(2)
A Sour Yes

Dear _____,

It seems a little unreasonable that you should ask us to take back china which you have had in your store for almost a year. We urge our buyers to anticipate their sales carefully, and not to overstock, and while we are pleased to grant you this concession this one time, we must go on record that we are not setting any precedent to follow when you find yourself in a similar predicament in the future.

We might say, also, that several dealers in your territory have been reordering the same numbers you wish to exchange, and if they can sell them, we believe a little push would do as much for you.

Please pack the china very carefully, as we will not be responsible for breakage.

(3)

A Sad No

Dear _____,

Yes, how well we know what a good customer you have been, and you have every right to ask any favor within our power to grant. We do appreciate your business, and like to prove it when we can.

The candy business, as you know, is difficult. We try hard to package our line in the best possible way to withstand the condition you describe. We think you must have found that our candy *does* stay fresh longer than any other brand.

But when we ship an order, and it is accepted by the buyer, about all we can do is sit back and hope it sells within a reasonable period of time. We just couldn't guarantee it to keep fresh indefinitely—if we did, we would soon be out of the candy business.

The lot you mention has been in your store eight months, and that is a long time for any candy to stay in the condition it left the factory. Of course, as an experienced candy dealer you know how true that is.

There is one bright side to your problem. You bought 144 of the 1-pound boxes, and have sold 123. On the latter you have made a substantial profit, and more than enough to offset any loss on those still unsold.

Please understand, _____, we feel very badly that we can't take the 21 boxes back. But some other time, we surely will go out of our way to do you a favor—something that the conditions of our business will allow.

I think you know how hard it was for me to write this letter, for we are proud to have you sell our fine candies, and surely wish you well.

(4)

A Sour No

Dear _____,

As a good businessperson, and one who has handled package candy for many years, we think you must understand how unreasonable it is to ask any maker to accept the return of goods which are eight months old.

You know that no other firm would do this for you, and you certainly can't ask, in any spirit of fairness, that we be the exception.

Another time, we suggest that you give our packages a better display on your counters and push them harder. Also, it may sound strange for us to say so, but we would much rather you ordered in smaller quantities, than to overshoot the mark and then ask us to hold the bag.

Our answer has to be no, _____. We cannot, and will not, allow dealers to return candy which they have accepted and found to be in good condition. We make it—you sell it. That's the only way we can both realize a fair profit.

Special tips for saying "YES." As was stated earlier, writing letters when the answer to the customers' complaints is "yes" are generally easy. There are, however, special tips to keep in mind as you begin:

1. Say "yes" without quibbling. Nothing is flatter or less satisfying than letters that tell the customers that they will get what they want, but, first, they will have to listen to the company's excuses.

2. Satisfy the customers' specific requests. For example, do not say "yes" to a customer who wants roses instead of daffodils in a *bouquet* and then expect great joy when you add that you will send out the desired *corsage* of roses immediately.

3. When offering compromise, be certain that it alleviates the customer's problem. For example, a restaurant wanted 75 pounds of chicken parts. A meat supply house had 30 whole chickens ready for immediate delivery. The compromise was actually in the customer's favor, and comments about extra meat, bones for stock, etc., further warmed the customer's feelings toward the company.

Using these hints, a business correspondent can always say "yes" effectively.

4. PRACTICAL LETTERS THAT MUST SAY "NO"

Avoiding misunderstanding and bad precedent. When the customers' requests must be denied, completely or in part, the writers telling them so face a rather difficult situation. The only bright side of the problem is that in many cases the customers' requests are based on a misunderstanding of the circumstances, and being fair-minded, as most people are, they may listen favorably to reason. If, however, the appeal to reason fails—from lack of tact on the part of the correspondent or stubbornness on the part of the customer—future business may be wiped out.

Certainly, the job of refusing the customer should not be left to an inexperienced clerk, or to one not well-regarded as a writer of friendly letters. It is a task requiring the highest type of diplomacy, and should be delegated to one of the best letter-writers in the company, and of course, one who is closely allied to sales.

The letters which follow cover a few of the circumstances in business which involve trying to deny the customers what they want and at the same time keeping their goodwill. The number of these situations is almost countless, but the method of handling them is pretty much the same. They all seek tactfully to make the customers *understand* why the company cannot go along with them—they appeal to the customers' sense of fairness when they are acquainted with the company's point of view.

In many cases the causes are worthy, but if the bars are let down in one instance, a precedent is established for similar action in all other instances of the same type. For example, one of the thorns in the flesh of business are the requests from customers who think a big order should bring them a concession in price. Often, they are difficult to refuse, because an order may be lost, but most executives are agreed that price-cutting is a practice which does not pay in the long run. The one who can write the letter which makes the order stick without any concession is favored in the company—and Figure 13-2 shows how one person did the job.

Refusing to sell direct. We don't suppose a day passes in the life of the average manufacturing company that one or more letters are not received from people who are trying, either from ignorance or intent, to bypass authorized distributors. No company of reputable rating, however, will compete with its own dealers by selling direct to a consumer; in fact, no company would long have any dealers if it followed such a practice. Under such circumstances, the logical procedure is a friendly letter to the ambitious buyers which holds their interest in the product, but sends them to their nearest distributors to get it. A very good letter to handle this situation is the one in Figure 13-3. It uses the line of thought which would fit almost any similar need.

Using the letter as a reference, here is an outline which can be

Dear _____,

John Smith submitted to us your order for 10 dozen of our style No. 190 at $12.50 each, and I am forced to grip the arms of my chair with super-strength to resist his arguments, which are the embodiment of logic and common sense.

But the man whose example I want to follow—the man whose business principles I admire and try to emulate—is none other than yourself. I know for a fact that the steady customer who is standing in your fitting room buying five suits is paying the same as the first-timer who is buying one, despite the fact that the selection of your clothing by the "regular" could influence countless others to trade at your store.

If your business had not been built on the principle of *one price to all,* your store never could have achieved the success it has, nor would it be recognized today as *first* in your city.

By no other policy could it have won the confidence of your community, and what is just as important, even the confidence of your competitors.

And the same principle of one price for all, Mr. _____, is the one that can build also for me. So you need only to look into your own heart to know why I must at all costs adhere to the same policy on which your own store's business was built, for if I waive I should surely be a failure.

I know that you, above all, will give me credit for this desire to succeed in the right way. I am also sure you will be the last one to refuse to give me business simply because of my determination to stick to the path you, yourself, have followed.

I enclose a little booklet which explains style No. 190 fully, and I wish there were some way by which I could have you know, just as well as I do, that every statement in this booklet is a correct statement of facts—with nothing "dolled up" to make it sound good.

Should you care to compare our No. 190 with any other competing number, you can easily get the facts by having a pair of each tested by a reputable testing firm. We have had tests made of all the numbers that compete with ours and we can say with honest conviction that we have not found its equal yet.

Figure 13-3

Dear _____,

Thank you very much for your order for one of our new ELECTRA electric irons.

We sincerely appreciate this evidence of your interest in the new ELECTRA, and wish that we could fill your order. However, as manufacturers, we sell through retail dealers, and our arrangement with the dealers throughout the country does not permit our selling direct from the factory.

We regret, therefore, that we must return your check with the request that you either visit or telephone the ELECTRA dealer in your city, who will be glad to deliver your iron at the price advertised. In buying from the dealer, you will have the advantage of choosing from a large stock and will avoid the annoyance of possible delay in shipment.

The name, address, and telephone number of the ELECTRA dealer in your city is:

Polk Electrical Supply Company,
4422 East Main Street,
Telephone, (123) 456-7890

Every ELECTRA is guaranteed by us, and also by the dealer, to be in perfect condition.

We hope that you will soon be numbered among the many thousands of women who have found that with the new ELECTRA ironing is no longer a drudgery. The ELECTRA is very easy to handle. It saves 30% of the time needed when you use any other electric iron now on the market.

To bring an ELECTRA to your home, simply pick up the telephone and call:

(123) 456-7890

followed by any person faced with the same problem of telling a would-be direct buyer to see the authorized dealer.

1. Start by thanking the buyer.
2. Explain that you sell only through dealers.
3. Say that check is enclosed.
4. Give name, address, and telephone number of dealer.

5. Mention guarantee of the product.

6. Resell the product to hold the buyer in line.

We think the above outline might contain two more points. These would be:

2½. Explain *advantages* of buying from a dealer.

4½. Notify dealer of a prospective customer in his town.

When *true,* as it may be of certain products and services, point 2½ can be made quite convincing in the turn-down letter. The person buying from a local dealer or agent can conveniently turn to the latter for repairs and get quick attention for any justified complaint. People who buy automobiles at the factory, for example, sometimes have more trouble in getting them serviced than do those who buy their cars "at home." An alert dealer would appreciate point 4½—the *service* from the factory, the customer-lead.

Explaining damage in transit. A considerable number of the complaints that must be adjusted in business are based on customer dissatisfaction with the *condition* of the delivered goods. Some of these causes for complaint are purely imaginary, and must be handled with a firm but polite *no.* An example was the case of the merchant who wanted to return candy which had been in the store eight months (See letter (3) on page 680.) Other times, the damage claimed is so slight that the buyer is only looking for trouble in mentioning it. Even if the trouble is so slight as a tiny scratch on the leg of a chair, no company can afford to brush it off too brusquely. The concern of the buyers may seem petty and foolish, but it is still important to them.

In the great majority of damage claims, the common carrier is at fault and not the company. The goods are carefully packed and delivered in perfect condition to the carrier, and the damage occurs between that time and delivery. In such cases, the carrier is responsible, but not unless the condition is declared before the goods are taken away and stored or displayed in the buyer's place of business. Not all claims may be approved by the carrier, and when one isn't, the shipper is likely to feel the full blast of the buyer's displeasure.

Experienced buyers—retail and wholesale—understand the obligations of the carrier, and how to handle claims for damage in transit. All the seller has to do after learning of the damage is to supply the date of shipment, the bill of lading number, and the name of the transportation company. With this information, the buyer is content to present the claim direct to the carrier; this is the procedure usually followed.

However, as a goodwill service some companies prefer to adjust the buyer's complaint and look to the carrier for compensation. This plan is especially favored in dealing with small or inexperienced buyers who seldom get a shipment and do not understand how to present a claim to a carrier. It involves trouble and some small expense for the company, but both are more than offset by the goodwill to be won by the special service. A good illustration of such service is found in Figure 13-4. You will agree that any person who received a letter like the following one would feel cordial toward the company sending it.

The person who dictated the above letter demonstrated both a keen knowledge of human nature and a fine spirit of service on the part of the company. First, it was made plain to the customer that the company's responsibility ended with delivery of the desk to the carrier. Hence, the company was going out of its way to make the son's birthday a pleasant one, and to spare the customer the necessity of filing a claim against the railroad. In other words, the writer made sure that the goodwill services rendered by the company would be understood and fully appreciated.

Figure 13-4

Dear Reverend _____,

We are very sorry to know from your letter of March 15 that the mahogany desk you ordered as a birthday gift for your son arrived so badly marred that you cannot accept it.

As the Borderland Railroad gave us a receipt acknowledging that the desk was received perfectly crated, it must have been damaged in transit. Although our responsibility ends when the railroad has accepted the desk, we know how much interest you have in this beautiful and useful gift for your son. We are, therefore, sending you today, by prepaid express, another desk exactly like the one you ordered. It should reach you promptly.

If you will please telephone the express company to make a special delivery immediately on the arrival of the desk at their receiving station, you should have it not later than the day of your son's birthday.

Please leave the damaged desk in the hands of the railroad. We shall enter a claim with them, so that you will not be troubled further.

We thank you for writing promptly, and assure you that our only desire is that you receive the desk promptly, and in perfect condition.

5. FORMULATING LETTERS THAT DEAL WITH PRICE ADVANCES

How to announce higher prices. Naturally, no individual or company likes to hear that the price of a commodity or service has gone up. Unless the news is presented tactfully, the buyer may turn to other sources of supply in an effort to escape the increase, and even though unsuccessful, may place an order with another firm. Businessmen do not like to see their customers in a shopping mood, and they realize the importance of making the announcement of a price increase as painless as possible. Unfortunately, this objective often tends to make the announcement letter too apologetic, as if the writers *feared* an unpleasant reaction from their customers. Note the almost guilty tone of the opening paragraph of a letter used by one sales manager.

> For months, against a steadily rising market, we have stoutly battled to maintain our present price levels, but we are now reluctantly forced to advise increases which we hope you will accept as necessary, and without any loss of your valued business.

It is obvious that the writer of the above paragraph was trembling in his boots, and fearful that the reader would resent the increases and take the next orders elsewhere. Because of his own mental attitude toward the price changes, the very thing he fears is likely to happen. The customer says mentally: "The writer of this letter must know his company is taking advantage of a higher market, or he would not be so apologetic—he isn't pulling any wool over my eyes."

Of course, it is also possible to make the announcement of higher prices too blunt or casual. No doubt you have seen letters of this type, in which the writers seem to gloat over the fact that at last their company can reap a greater profit. They make it plain that business is brisk, and that the orders are not especially needed. For example:

> We are pleased to send you our new price list, with the understanding that all of the quotations are subject to change without notice. We might add that our factory is now operating around the clock, and orders on hand are ample to keep us on that schedule indefinitely.

There is plenty to irritate the customer in such a tactless announcement. The writer is "pleased" to send it. It states in a rather domineering way that the quotations will be changed at the will of his company. Next comes the boast about the number of orders on hand, and how the factory is running 24 hours a day. The implication is plain: "Here are the new prices. You may take them or leave them. It makes no difference to us." In assuming such a devil-may-care attitude, the writer forgets that the time may come when the company will again be begging for orders. The letter creates a spectre of ill will which later will come back to roost with devastating results.

One of the simplest ways to announce higher prices is to send the new list without special comment, while trying to put into the letter something else that may be encouraging to the buyers. The latter are well aware, usually, of any general trend in the market, and they are not likely to be surprised when a particular company follows the trend. If the buyers are merchants; their own sales prices have been advanced, anyway.

When it seems best to *explain* the price changes, figures carry much more conviction than mere generalities, such as "in keeping with the advancing cost of raw materials," or "because of the stiffening market in all lines of business." The figures used in the following excerpt make the price advances seem quite necessary and reasonable:

> Today we are paying 40 per cent more for burlap bags than we did a year ago. Of the more than 100 ingredients that we mix to put in them, not a single one has failed to advance in cost to us. The range of these increases runs from 20 to 160 per cent.

Sometimes writers can actually turn rising prices to seem to be in the buyer's best interest. Look at this gem:

> So, to keep in step with these widespread improvements in business conditions, we have had to change our own prices accordingly. Probably you have had to do the same thing in your own business.

The psychological approach used in the above announcement is particularly good. In a rather casual way, the increase in prices is connected with something pleasing to the dealer—"improvements in business conditions." Then the idea is pleasingly advanced that the dealers have also advanced their own prices. Thus, the customer and the company are placed in the same boat, and the chance of mutual understanding is good.

Although it is not possible to set forth any "one right way" to announce higher prices, certain general principles seem to emerge from the comments already made:

1. Don't apologize. Prices must go up and down with the business market. The seller is always entitled to a reasonable profit.
2. On the other hand, don't be callous or indifferent if the announcement happens to be made when orders are easy to get.

The customer is entitled to as much courtesy and consideration in good times as in bad times.

3. In a general rising market, it is usually unnecessary to *justify* the advance. Don't weaken your position with explanations.

4. If, for some special reason, an explanation does seem desirable, be specific. Figures that prove increased cost of production are far more convincing than generalities.

5. When possible, accompany the announcement with some comment or fact that points to more favorable business conditions. Make the buyers realize that higher prices are only an indication of better times for *them.*

Breaking the news optimistically. The letter containing the announcement of higher prices should never indicate fear or doubt as to how the news may be received. The tone of the letter needs to be confident, unconcerned, and as optimistic as it can possibly be made. This is the tone in Figure 13-5. First, it talks about the many new "specials" brought out for the benefit of customers, and then it minimizes the extent and number of the price increases—it makes *good news* of the fact for the customers.

In another letter, Figure 13-6, the edge of higher prices is dulled by reminding the jobber of the extra profit to be made from stock already on hand, or that ordered before the advance. The emphasis is placed on sales to be made, and the mention of prices is secondary.

Using price advance as a sales lever. An old sales stimulator—and it works, as you know—is the offer to accept orders at prevailing prices until a given date, when an advance is to be made. In fact, salesmen frequently are accused of dating orders back in the misguided attempt to get the old prices for their customers; but when the company makes the offer and adheres to the announced date, there is nothing unethical in the practice. In the following message to customers who have not ordered, one writer used the lever to pry up business like this:

Dear _____,

This morning the robins were chirping at a great rate—so loud, in fact—that I got up half an hour earlier than usual.

Now—if you ever saw any person uneasier than a commuter in the morning with more than five minutes to spare—I'd like to meet 'em. That's what the robins did to me.

Five minutes to kill! "When the robins come, the lawn must be sprinkled." So down to the cellar I went and pulled out the

Figure 13-5

Dear _____,

Your copy of the OTC Hand Tool Catalog is in the other compartment of this envelope.

Because of new machinery design, you now require many more special tools than ever before, and we are happy to tell you that over 100 of these "specials" were brought out for you during the last year. They're all in this pocket edition catalog, along with the 800 other items in the OTC line, so look it over carefully. (If you hurry, you might skip a page which shows just what you have been wishing for.)

Since the cost of everything from soup to nuts has been skyrocketing, you'll be surprised when you see that not all of the items have been advanced; that many were raised only a little; and that some are still the same. We had to scratch our heads to do it, but conditions like we are going through are good for all of us because we keep on our toes.

One thing you can be sure of is: OTC quality is still tops. So, when you need anything, shoot your order in to us on one of the postage-free cards, and we'll see that you get what you want, when you want it.

Thanks for readin'.

---

hose—a 50-foot section of Wonderful Garden Hose—that had already seen 10 seasons' service. It may last another!

That's the kind of hose we want you to be selling. Quaker Garden Hose makes and keeps customers. We missed your order greatly this year. Kinda nice to fill it last year—we want to do it again.

And here's the offer—

Prices are advancing! If you will send us your order before May 1st for shipment as soon as possible, we will accept it at the before-the-advance price. A clear-cut saving of 10 per cent to you. Sorry—but orders for future delivery cannot be accepted.

You know Quaker products—Quaker goods have a margin that is interesting. The order form is for your convenience. Fill out NOW—insert in envelope and mail—no stamp necessary.

Alerting customers of long standing. Raising prices is a touchy

Figure 13-6

> ## COLD CUT TIME IS
> ## KABNET WAX TIME
>
> And, with temperatures ranging from 70 to 100 degrees, THIS IS COLD CUT TIME!
>
> Butchers everywhere are appealing to jaded summer appetites by featuring luncheon meats and other hot weather foods. Most of them are wrapped in a waxed paper. To help your salesmen make it KABNET WAX, a full page ad is appearing directly inside the front cover in the August issue of *Meat Merchandising*, the Business Paper of the Retail Industry. Reprints will be mailed to your salesmen in a week. Cash in on this KABNET WAX season.
>
> More good news for you is the fact that your present inventory of KABNET WAX, plus any orders placed prior to August 2nd, will make you some extra profit. Attached are the slightly higher prices effective as of that date. Higher retail schedules are also attached. Regardless of what floor stock you may have, may we ask that you advise your sales force of these new prices and put them into effect with your trade at once? We are making this request of all KABNET WAX distributors.
>
> Your cooperation in capitalizing on the summer KABNET WAX season, and in putting these slightly increased prices into effect at once, will be sincerely appreciated.

problem that faces most businesses. When letters are sent out somewhat impersonally and across the board, one tack can be taken. However, when the writers must break the news to important distributors with whom they are well-acquainted after years of business relationship, it's a different matter. In the latter case, the letter goes to *one* person, instead of a group, and the plea for understanding should be made in a personal way, as one friend talks to another.

A very fine example of this kind of business writing is the letter in Figure 13-7.

The letter follows the line of thought suggested earlier in this discussion. It is not in any sense apologetic. The writer, Jim Shirreffs, simply puts his cards upward on the table and asks for cooperation. His letter is friendly and convincing. It accomplished its purpose.

Answering price objections. There is considerable difference

Figure 13-7

Dear _____,

Everywhere we go, we notice that prices are increasing. It makes no difference whether this is soup or nuts—in the average meal we eat, shoes, clothing, or perhaps the price of liquor. Inasmuch as you read the newspapers, it will be no news to you that the price of labor and materials has advanced rapidly and consistently.

Higher labor costs have increased material costs, or vice versa. In any event, finished goods are commanding higher figures today than they have for many months. These higher wages mean more prosperity for the workers, which in turn reflects back to the capital goods industry, and sooner or later affects you and me.

All of which means that, effective June 15, there will be an increase in the price of finished goods for your company. This increase is not very material, and no doubt can be easily absorbed without making any change in your cost setup, at least temporarily, and can later be passed on to your dealers and consuming public.

I am outlining the various items which we make for you, with a comparison of your old cost and the new. This is covered by the attached sheet. You will note that in three cases there have been no changes. The sum total, considering all these items as component parts of one unit, shows a net increase of 11 per cent. This covers labor and material.

As you know, _____, material and labor costs have been advancing. We have preferred to absorb these costs for the past several months, rather than to pass them on to you, but it can't be done any more—hence, all new shipments are being billed at these new prices, the first batch of which are covered by the enclosed invoices.

I look for these prices to be stable for some time to come, but in the present labor and metal market, anybody's guess is good.

Best regards from Bill and "Yours Truly,"

Yours for "Better Lite-ing,"

between *announcing* a higher price and *defending* it when some customer files an objection. The reply to the latter must take time to answer every point, and to change the unfavorable opinion. Unless this job is fully performed, the danger of a breach in the business relationship is present.

The writing of such a letter is not to be taken lightly. Great care must be used not to *argue* with the customers, or to scoff at any reason they may have advanced in support of their opinions. On the other hand, the writers must firmly support their own positions, and prove the price is *not* too high. Obviously, the job requires both skill and patience; it is one of the most difficult in the field of business correspondence, as well as in the field of personal selling. Let us look at excerpts from master letter-writers' work to see how they handled the "too high" objection:

(1)

In fact, Mr. _____, we are paying 10 per cent more, on an average, for our raw materials.

Considering the cost of our raw materials and labor, our prices are fair. Our overhead is the lowest in the industry. The only way we could reduce prices, and continue to make normal profits, would be to cheapen the product. If we did, it would destroy our good name as a manufacturer, and yours as a merchant, if you continued to sell our line.

Do you believe that either of us can afford to do this?

(2)

But you know, Mr. _____, *quality* is an odd commodity. The sincere manufacturer buys it by the pound and by the hour; he builds his factory with it; he makes his engineers use it to design his products; he surrounds his salesmen with it; and lastly, he stuffs it into his products until it reaches the bursting point. Gates products are built that way.

It would have been very easy to leave that 5 per cent out of our manufacturing cost, Mr. _____. I don't think anybody could ever detect a 5 per cent loss in quality. However, if we did leave it out, Gates Vulco Ropes wouldn't be the *best* we could manufacture—not by 5 per cent they wouldn't.

We didn't like raising our prices, but *every single item* that goes into our belts has gone up in price during the last few months. We *had* to.

(3)

Our advertising is like those ten suits of clothes. We don't advertise to preen ourselves. We do it because advertising is necessasry—vitally necessary to our business.

Years of careful checking have shown us that we are on the right track. After all, the million dollars we spend annually for advertising represents only a small percentage of our sales cost—a few cents per tire. But it is these few cents per tire which keep up our volume and hold down our costs. We are building a better tire today than we have ever built, and we're selling it to you for less money.

Advertising has done it. We pre-invest a few cents in each tire to guarantee its sale so that you save dollars when you buy. If we didn't advertise at all, our sales would drop to the point where production costs would increase—and up would go our prices. Eventually we would be out of business.

These excerpts show that there are four main points to overcoming the objection of "too high" prices. First, there should be a word of appreciation for the customer's letter. You will never know what your customers are thinking unless they write to you. No matter how abusive a customer's letter may be, you may not show any irritation or resentment. Nothing is to be gained, and much can be lost by such peevishness. Next, be sure to compliment your customer on being a high-grade merchant. This tactic pulls the fangs of most irate customers. When you tell them you are using the best and consequently your prices have gone up, you have effectively overridden their objections to using your fine products. Obviously, they do not sell or use cut-rate material, do they? Also, ask questions which need to be answered "yes." No matter how far apart you and your customers seem to be, if you can get them nodding in agreement with your points, you have also made them comfortable with your prices.

All reasons for ever mentioning price are not to be avoided—its just a part of business. Indeed, price has been defined as: a relative condition, determined by prevailing cost of materials and labor, plus a reasonable profit for the seller. Assuming that methods of production are efficient, there seems to be no way to reduce a price except by the sacrifice of quality—surely a death-knell to any business. Let these thoughts be reflected in your letters.

A fair cross-section. The things that may cause complaints or misunderstandings in business are as numerous as the people who are bothered by them. In this section, you have surveyed some of the more common irritation points, but far from all of them. A fair cross-section of the *causes* which make adjustment letters necessary has been presented with actual samples taken from business to show *how* the letters may be written. Behind the writing of any effective adjustment letter, there must exist on the part of the writers and their companies a genuine desire to meet the customers halfway and, if possible, to make the adjustments that will retain their goodwill.

Viewed in the right perspective, complaints are a blessing to the company that receives them. They bring to the surface errors and faults that need to be corrected, conditions of which the company has not been conscious. Mistakes cheerfully adjusted may lead to a long and pleasant relationship with satisfied customers. Even if your customers are at fault, and their complaints must be denied, it may be possible to put the company in the right light, and still retain customers' friendship.

A great many of the misunderstandings—the causes of friction between customer and company—are connected with credit or collection incidents, and their adjustment falls properly into the hands of the Credit Manager. What they are, and how they may be handled, you will find out in the next section of this *Handbook*.

WRITING PRODUCTIVE CREDIT AND COLLECTION LETTERS

WRITING PRODUCTIVE CREDIT AND COLLECTION LETTERS

1. UNDERSTANDING COLLECTION LETTER PRINCIPLES

Correlating collection to sales. To do the job completely, a collection letter has two objectives to reach. The first is to get the money; the second, to retain the customer's goodwill. Some credit managers seem to concentrate so hard on the first objective that they overlook the second. If we remember our premise, however, that all the individuals in a company are members of the sales department, and that everything they do may help or hinder order-getting, there remains no other conclusion except that credit managers must do everything possible to build customer friendship.

The actual attainment of this ideal is not as easy as it may seem. The matters discussed in a credit or collection letter are often irritating and controversial, and no amount of diplomacy or understanding on the part of the writer can make them otherwise. Sometimes, credit managers are poised like people on a fence between two pastures, with a bull on either side. No matter which way they jump, they may be in trouble. If they are too lax in approving credit or collecting a bill, the company may end up with a sour account and an angry treasurer. If they reject doubtful applicants for credit, or insist on the payment of a bill, a customer could be lost and the sales department may accuse them of lack of cooperation. Even the average customer looks suspiciously on their best efforts and is ready to fly off the handle on the slightest provocation. No business correspondent requires a greater sense of diplomacy, or a greater knowledge of human nature, than does the manager.

In spite of all the difficulties, writers of credit or collection letters that meet company obligations must be able to coordinate their activities successfully with those in the sales department. They are not expected to ask for orders, although some of the letters in this section do that very thing, but they are expected to *sell* goodwill—to make the news in their letters as painless as possible. In other words, they should be order-minded as well as money-minded, not to the extent of being too lenient, but always remembering the value of the customer.

Nothing can be worse for business than rude, threatening, and pompous letters on your company's letterhead. Look at some of these statements with which some credit managers in the past have saddled their company's good names.

- We refuse to have further expense writing you letters. (*You're not worth our time and money.*)
- You promised if you did not pay for the goods within ten days you would send them back to us. You have not paid for them and you have not returned them. (*You're a crook.*)
- Therefore, be advised and informed that we have definite legal rights in a matter of this kind. We assume you are aware of the action we can take if this matter is not completed at once and by return mail. (*You're incompetent.*)
- We are not interested in any excuses. We demand and insist that the matter be completed at once. We will expect your remittance within one week of the date of this letter. If we fail to receive it we will reserve our legal right to take further action WITHOUT ANY ADVANCE NOTICE being sent to you. (*You're a liar.*)
- We have been fair. We have been reasonable. In return we have not received what we consider proper consideration from you. If the condition were reversed, how would you like to be treated as you have treated us? (*You're crass and uncouth.*)
- We are marking in our records that the matter will be settled within one week. We will not assume responsibility for any action that may be taken if there is a delay beyond that time. You will therefore see to it that remittance is sent to us at once. (*You're stubborn and childish.*)

While bad manners in any business contact is inexcusable, spoken errors can be forgotten in time! The written barb, however, remains sharp and injects its venom with each reading. Even worse, it can be passed around, and the ill-will grows in ever-increasing spirals. How much better to never create such a monster in the first place.

But, let us leave the unpleasant land of the "never-do's for the carefully crafted home of courteous carpentry.

Crafting courteous collection letters. The principles to be followed in the construction of a collection letter vary little from those that apply to other forms of business correspondence. You have surveyed these principles in the section devoted to Business Letter Carpentry. The purpose of a letter may be to sell goods, to adjust a misunderstanding, or to collect money, but in any case the main objective is to gain a favorable reaction from the reader. The attempt is to *influence human behavior*—to plant in the reader's mind a flow of thought which passes from *Attention* to *Interest* to *Desire,* and finally to the *Action* wanted. This formula of the Star, the Chain, and the Hook may seldom be disregarded.

Particularly important is the *planning* of the collection letter and using the steps with which you are already acquainted. Form letters are not too effective in persuading people to pay their bills, since the circumstances holding up the payment are rarely the same wtih different customers. The best appeal to use in one situation might well be the worst in another. Only by careful analysis of the accounts, their histories, and present conditions, and of the particular individuals, who may be acting for themselves or for their firms, can the writer of the collection letter select what seems to be the most promising approach.

Another factor influencing the letter is the *credit policy* of the writer's company, to which of course, there must be adherence. In some companies, and in certain types of business, the terms may be more lenient than others; but whatever they are, the credit managers must be governed accordingly. No policy is so inflexible, however, that it cannot be bent a little to fit the need and inclination of respective customers— in method of handling, if not in change of terms.

In his *Handbook of Modern Retailing,* Sidney Carter supplied a useful analysis of customer paying characteristics. In all, he listed 18 different types of buyers—any one of which might be visualized by the credit correspondent while handling a particular case.

1. Pays promptly and takes pride in it.
2. Takes all the time possible because there are other uses for the money.
3. Buys the limit on credit, then pays cash—sometimes to other merchants.
4. Easygoing—needs to be reminded a number of times.
5. Hates to let the money go or likes to keep it in the bank as long as possible.
6. Sickness or other unusual circumstances prevent prompt payment.

7. Will pay to keep with a good credit standing.

8. Will pay only when convinced it will avoid trouble.

9. Unfortunate or indulgent; wants to do the right thing but cannot control buying.

10. Withholds payment because of a grudge against the store.

11. Thinks because business is given almost exclusively to the company it should extend more time to pay.

12. Never did intend to pay. This buyer does not succeed so well in getting credit established because of the organization of the modern credit structure.

13. Lives in the future, post-dates checks, thus buying on "cash-credit."

14. Reckless.

15. Installment contracts make it difficult to pay on due date.

16. Poor financier. Honest enough but simply cannot get affairs untangled. Always more or less in "hot water."

17. Has old debts which interfere with prompt payment of current obligations.

18. Carelessness or oversight. Not systematic. Forgetful, interested in other things, does not keep records.

Having listed his 18 types, Mr. Carter said: There may be other kinds of people. It is important to understand them before sending out collection letters. It ought to be possible to figure out the reason why the money has not been paid. No one with a bad temper should be in the credit business, just as no one who is too easy and sympathetic can succeed in making a deadbeat pay promptly. The essential thing is that each account is to be treated as a special case and should have individual attention."

Foremost, then, in the carpentry of a collection letter is *analysis* of the particular customers and their accounts—what are their personal characteristics, and how have they previously paid their bills? With this concept formed, the selection of the right approach is simplified.

The spotlighting of analysis does not, however, mean that any of the more general factors in letter construction may be overlooked by credit correspondents. You will remember these factors as they are set forth in the Rating Scale for business letters. Each has something to say about the effectiveness of a letter, no matter what the purpose. A neatly typed message on an attractive letterhead will always be regarded with more favor than one which looks cheap and shoddy. Natural language—short words—will always make a better impression than ancient, stiff, and stilted expressions. People who owe money are just as receptive as any others to other people who can "Relax—be natural—just talk." Letters which reveal the personalities of the writers and reflect the spirit of their companies, will out-pull ones of the cold, colorless, conventional sort.

From first reminder to notice of suit. Until now, the collection letter has been mentioned as if it were a single unit expected to do the whole job. But you know better than that. In many cases, it takes more than one request to get the money—and sometimes, a pack of lawyers. Most credit managers, therefore, have a series of letters ready to fire at the customers as long as there is a reasonable chance that they may be induced to pay their bills. The first of the series is merely a gentle reminder based on the assumption that the customers have overlooked the mailing of their checks. Each letter thereafter increases the pressure, and various appeals are used in the hope that one of them may rub a soft spot.

Naturally, all collection efforts begin when the payment is due, although a short period may be allowed before the first shot is fired. The same efforts end—if they stretch that far—when legal action is filed. Between these two points, the credit managers' feelings about the account also pass through a number of changes. At first they may only be mildly concerned, and the tone of their first reminders are casual. As time goes on, and successive letters fail, they begin to worry, and to talk more firmly to their delinquent customers. It is during these later stages that some credit managers break down and begin to say things which only cause more trouble. This loss of control is understandable for the provocation is great; nevertheless, it is not in keeping with the goodwill objectives of the company, and it seldom helps in making the collection.

The actual number of letters in the series varies among companies and industries. One company may attempt to make the collection in a short span of time; another may not turn to legal action for six months or even a year. Despite these differences, the appeals used seem to travel over about the same course. One sequence may consist of a dozen letters, another of only six, but the same ground is covered up to the unhappy day when defeat is conceded and the file is sent to the legal department. In Figure 14-1, the sequence is shown in graph form. The days involved may change in your company, but it is an average picture.

A psychological procedure seems to have been developed among credit managers for the collection of past-due accounts, and almost any collection letter that you encounter can easily be placed somewhere in this established procedure. This is what happens:

1. The customer is simply reminded that the bill should have been

Figure 14-1

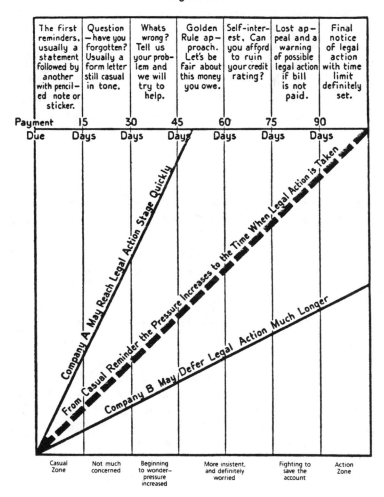

The first reminders, usually a statement followed by another with pencil—ed note or sticker.	Question —have you forgotten? Usually a form letter still casual in tone.	Whats wrong? Tell us your prob—lem and we will try to help.	Golden Rule ap—proach. Let's be fair about this money you owe.	Self-inter—est, Can you afford to ruin your credit rating?	Lost ap—peal and a warning of possible legal action if bill is not paid.	Final notice of legal action with time limit definitely set.

Payment Due — 15 Days — 30 Days — 45 Days — 60 Days — 75 Days — 90 Days

Company A May Reach Legal Action Stage Quickly

From Casual Reminder the Pressure Increases to the Time When Legal Action is Taken

Company B May Defer Legal Action Much Longer

Casual Zone	Not much concerned	Beginning to wonder— pressure increased	More insistent, and definitely worried	Fighting to save the account	Action Zone

paid on a certain date. The reminder may be a statement, or a short letter very casual in tone.

2. The first reminder, unheeded, is followed by another; perhaps a second statement with a pencil notation or sticker to gain special attention. Or, it may be a letter, still friendly, but not quite so unconcerned.

3. With two ineffectual attempts washed out, the approach stiffens considerably. The writer of the letter no longer suggests that the customer has forgotten to pay; now the question asked is *what's wrong*. The customer is told that in the event of some difficulty

which is holding up the payment, the company will do its best to help, but can't do anything if left in the dark.

4. Now the attack shifts to a new front. The writer knows the account is in danger. Some special appeal is sought that may arouse the customer's better self. *Fair play* is asked for and perhaps a note for the customer to sign.

5. Since the customer has not responded to the Golden Rule, the writer tries to touch *self-interest*. The customer is reminded of the importance of a good credit rating. The legal clouds are forming—a hint of court action may appear in the letter.

6. The sand is running out. It is time for the final appeal. It may be written by the credit manager, or by a major executive. The customer is reminded of the expense and embarrassment if a suit is filed. The company still wants to be cooperative but it cannot let the matter drag out any longer. It is what you might call the *last resort* letter.

7. Success now hangs by a thread. There remains the one hope that the customer may be frightened into action. A specific number of days is given to pay. There will be no more letters; either payment is sent or the suit will be filed.

Logically the above psychological process blends with the reasons why people do not pay their bills. It is not hypocritical for credit managers to ask in the beginning, "Have you forgotten to pay this bill?" Lots of people are careless about money matters. They do forget to pay, and only need a reminder to be spurred into action. Others are poor managers. They are honest, but frequently find themselves burdened with financial problems. Why isn't it natural for the managers to ask, "Is anything wrong? Can we help?"

Then there are those irresponsible people who do not take their financial obligations as seriously as they should. They write a few checks this month, and some more the next. At heart, they mean very well, and sometimes are governed by a sense of sportsmanship. Some of these folks may respond favorably when the managers ask, "Don't you want to play fair with us, as we have played fair with you?"

You see, each of the appeals used in the collection letter series may smoke out a different class of buyers, and when in turn they are all applied to the customer the *right* one may induce payment. Finally, as the series runs its course, the credit managers are forced to the conclusion that they are dealing with a very selfish individual—one who has no intention of paying unless forced to do so. Such a person may value a credit rating, and the mention of it is worth trying, but the chances are that nothing will happen until the letter stating "Pay or be sued" is sent. Payment, if possible, will be sent if only to escape the lawyers. If not, there is nothing left for the credit manager to do personally to save the account.

Later in this section you will inspect letters that illustrate each step on the chart; meanwhile, there are certain common faults in collection-letter writing that need to be avoided, and you should know what they are.

Avoiding stumbling blocks to successful collections. Writers may be guilty, though unintentionally, of one or more of these faults, and that their efforts have been frustrated.

Customers' reacting to those faults are purely psychological. They may be left indifferent, humiliated, or annoyed, but in any case the results are the same—they are *not* to pay their bills. Thus, we remind ourselves once again that a letter of any sort is a *personal contact,* and to make it pleasant and effective, the writers must rely heavily on their knowledge of human nature. Only when we are able to subordinate our own emotional reactions to those of our readers are we able to win their confidence, and have some chance of getting what we want from them.

The first of the faults that you should recognize, so that it will never handicap your own efforts, is the use of an *obvious* form letter. Even if the message is going to a large group of poor-pay customers, it can still be personalized in such a way that all recipients think it was specially written for them. This involves perfect interface typing and very careful work on the part of the typist. No doubt you have seen many collection letters where the fill-in of name, address, and salutation did not match the body of the letter. To such an apparent form message, the average recipients are likely to be indifferent. They say: "The writer of this letter isn't really worried about my account, because the same thing is being said to a lot of others." So they push the letter aside, and don't pay their bills.

We are not advocating that all collection letters should be personally dictated and typed, although that would be a fine practice if the cost were not too prohibitive, but the same effect can be attained by intelligent planning to avoid give-away insertions, by the use of the right equipment, and by perfect secretarial cooperation. The personal letter will always out-pull the form letter, and since the purpose is getting the money, it seems foolish not to use the best possible method.

Overcoming the faults of insincerity and poor taste. It is never smart for letter-writers to say anything they do not really mean. Average readers are not easily deceived by flattery, extravagant statements, or any other kind of insincerity. They consider an attempt to pull the wool over their eyes as a reflection on their intelligence, and rightfully they resent the implication. For example, how would you have reacted to the following collection letter in Figure 14-2?

It is difficult to comprehend how that writer could expect such a conglomeration of insincerity to fool his reader, or how he could forget his own self-respect in taking the pose of a friend when he obviously intends to have his pound of flesh. "Goodbye" is a good thing to say to him.

Almost as unwarranted as insincerity in a collection letter is the unsavory, and equally ineffectual, use of ugly names and insinuations which humiliate and anger the reader. In this connection, we are reminded of a description in verse of a mythical credit manager.

> Now John Itellum was a hard-boiled baby,
> He respected neither man nor lady;
> His letters were sharp and to the mark,
> No roaming dog could claim a better bark.

> At collecting money he was truly great,
> He made them pay on the discount date;
> He boasted with pride no payment was lost,
> Itellum could collect at any cost.

> "This son of a crook," he'd snort and roar,
> "Would take an inch, and then want more,
> I'll mince no words in letting him know
> No monkey business with me will go."

> "So come, Miss Green, and take a letter,
> We'll make it sizzle, the hotter the better;
> He'll settle in full, and within ten days,
> Or the Judge will cure his dead-beat ways."

> Thus every day, and hot under the collar,
> Itellum chased the almighty dollar;
> But here's the truth, and it isn't funny—
> 'Twas customers he lost instead of money.

It seems a queer and perverted kind of reasoning that motivates letter-writers to bully and scold their readers, when their purpose is to win cooperation. Why should the humiliated customers be expected to run for their checkbook? Aren't they more likely to defer their payment until the last possible moment, or even endure a lawsuit rather than favor credit managers who goaded them so unmercifully? What would be *your* reaction to the following choice sample of business discourtesy?

It is now obvious to us that you will never pay the money you

Figure 14-2

Dear _____,

Out of the thousands of people who have taken my course, only a few have ever attempted to beat me out of the payments. My crew are a mighty fine bunch, as a whole. You are one of them and I can't help but feel that you are as honest and proud as any.

If you didn't get that last letter I wrote, or those before, you couldn't answer them. I'm sure you haven't been getting your mail. Someone must be opening it, and I want you to make an investigation. I am really getting worried and if I do not hear from you soon, I will ask the Postal Authorities why mail is not being delivered to you.

As I said before, 97% of my students are honest. It is only once in a while that some little weasel-faced skinflint, smart-aleck, sneaky crook, tries to get my course and not pay for it. I don't care to know such folks, and I let the law take care of them.

It would be mighty hard to prove to me that you don't want to treat me fair. I know down deep in my heart the reason why you haven't answered is that you have not received my letters.

But even if you are hard up when you get this letter, don't be afraid or ashamed to tell your old friend. I, too, have gone through the leanest kind of poverty. I had to wear cheap suits, cheap shirts, cheap shoes—everything I wore had to be cheap. That's why I take such an everlasting joy in helping young people like yourself to better things in life.

But remember that if you do remain silent—if you let the next ten days go by without choosing the path of friendship between you and me—I shall feel the same way toward you. I shall feel that you have misunderstood me, that you have chosen to go into a lawsuit with your eyes open, in spite of my kindly efforts.

Of course, I shall stand up for my rights under our agreement. Even you wouldn't think of me any more as a *man*, if I were to back down now. No. I must ask that you pay as agreed.

But I repeat, when our attorney sues you, it will only be because you left me no other way out. I'll still want you for a friend, just as much as I ever have.

Goodbye,

owe our firm until we have resorted to court action. This is after all the only way to deal with people who shirk their obligations.

We have given you more than a reasonable time to settle this bill; we have been fair to you every step of the way. Unfortunately, it is useless to be decent to a stinker.

In three days we shall begin legal action. Be assured that this will cost you far more than the amount of our bill. Wouldn't it be much easier for you to begin acting like a responsible citizen and pay us what is rightfully ours?

One of the best tests of a collection letter is the customer's reply, especially if it contains a smile and a check. However, the reply may turn out to be embarrassing. It is hoped that few credit men are forced by their own mistakes to read a reply such as this:

You must be a very lucky man indeed. It's not every company that will hire such a blockhead as you for a credit manager. Such stupidity in business is rare these days.

Two days after I received goods from your firm, you began dunning me. Before the end of two weeks, I had received no less than three statements from you. Had you checked my credit record you would have noticed that for the past four years I have been paying my bills to your firm promptly on the first of each month. Now you can pay the penalty. You may either wait one more month for your money or enter suit.

We assume the customer whose letter you have just read had cause to be angry; at least one could assume he or she had not been handled tactfully by the credit manager. Right or wrong, most credit managers manage to keep their boats on an even keel. With a sympathetic understanding of the customers' problems, they perform their collection duties without arousing resentment, even though at times they may have to demand payment of delinquent bills.

In earlier sections of this *Handbook,* you have encountered principles of letter writing which apply with equal force to the work of the credit correspondent. The old-time "whiskers" may deaden and defeat a collection letter as easily as they do one which seeks to sell or accomplish any other business purpose. The best collection letters are friendly and personal in tone; they reveal the human qualities of a person who merely asks and expects the money due. Such a tone is, of course, impossible in a letter couched in formal, stilted language.

Resisting the fault of self-pity. Especially obnoxious are the collection letters which whine for cooperation. In them, the writers appear as very much abused people. They paint nice halos around their own heads; and then try to shame their ignoble readers into paying their bills. The latter resent the injured tone of the messages and the inference that they are most unreliable compared to the paragons with the haloes.

It is true that good business relations depend on mutual understanding and cooperation. The appeal to fair play is often used adroitly in collection letters, but the result is opposite to that intended when the writers wear their hearts on their sleeves, and reproach the customers. Sad, sweet souls are never popular in business correspondence. Listen to this one:

> I think you know that I'm your friend. And now because I was your friend, because I went to bat for you many times, I find that I'm in trouble.
>
> When you said last year that you needed the goods, I saw that you received them even before I was able to see your credit report. When you were late with your payments on several occasions, you received no dunning from me. I went out of my way to show you that I wanted to help you all I could. I wanted you to see for yourself that all credit managers aren't callous to other folks' troubles. Some of us have a heart. But your last bill is now six months overdue, and they are asking me here why I let you alone for so long. They are blaming me for being too easy on you.
>
> I know that you will agree that one favor deserves another. There is no better way you can show your appreciation for what I've done for you than by paying this last bill immediately.

The avoiding of certain insinuating words which imply deficiencies of character in the reader—red-pepper words which dig in and sting—is also important. You know what these words are—neglect, failed, ignore, claim, should, and others innocent enough in the dictionary but troublemakers in a business letter. These words are just as destructive in a message asking for payment of a bill, as in one with some other intent. The second purpose of a collection letter, you will remember, is to retain *goodwill*. Insinuating words irritate—they are never goodwill-builders.

Dated action also has an important part to play in the construction of a collection letter. When a specific time is set for payment, the chances are increased that it will be forthcoming. This is a tested fact, and you may prove it by using *dated action* in your own correspondence.

Avoiding the divided urge is another plank in the platform of good collection letter-writers. When people are given their choice of several things to do, they are likely to do nothing. Don't say:

> We ask that you send us immediately a payment on your account of not less than $100, or if you don't feel able to do that now, send us a post-dated check for the same amount. Certainly, the very least you can do is to write and tell us when we may expect our money.

The credit manager should decide what *one* card is most likely to do the trick, and not mention any others The customer is then impelled to action with greater force than he is when offered several choices.

> So that you may begin to get your account with us in better shape, we must ask for a payment of not less than $100. Please mail this payment to arrive at our office within five days, which means by Saturday.

The *divided urge* is a serious fault in any collection letter. Do not use it.

2. PRODUCING CASUAL REMINDERS

How to do what the name implies. As a matter of routine, most companies mail a casual reminder to their customers a few days after they have failed to pay a bill on the agreed date. This is the first in the sequence of collection letters, and of course, if the payment is made, the last. The period of time allowed before the first reminder is mailed depends largely on the nature of the business, and the judgment of the credit manager. Irrespective of the number of days before the reminder is sent out, its tone is almost always casual and gentle. No attempt is made to put pressure on the customer, since the implication is that the payment has been overlooked, and that it will now be forthcoming. The credit manager is not worried about the account; it's understood that for one reason or another people and companies do put off the payment of their bills.

Instead of a letter a billing statement is often used, but in either case the purpose of the mailing is the same—to bring to the customer's attention the fact of nonpayment. If the nature of the business is such that a rather long time is allowed before any pressure is applied, a second and even a third statement or short letter may be used before the credit manager shifts into high gear and makes a more determined effort to collect the bill.

Because a bare statement showing the date of the purchase and the amount due is at best a cold and impersonal contact with the customer, some credit managers personalize one or more of the statements—usually the second—with some special device to gain attention. It may be a hand-written notation, a typed one on the statement in red ink, or by using a rubber stamp to highlight a word such as "Please."

Another rather common idea used to attract special attention to a statement is to attach a sticker, often of a semi-humorous nature. To avoid repetition where statements are mailed several times to the same customer, the company may have several on hand—adding new ones at regular intervals. This is a necessary procedure, as no sticker is likely to attract as much attention when exposed to a customer the second time.

As with any other idea to gain attention, the success of a sticker on a statement depends on how clever or unusual it may seem to the recipient. For example, John T. Heyward, of the Michie Company, Charlottesville, Virginia, has used a number of out-of-the-groove stickers, and reports a better return with them than from the more conventional letter reminders. The one on the opposite page (Figure 14-3) was especially effective in bringing home the checks.

Perhaps you think a reminder in verse is far removed from the dignity of business, but Mr. Heyward tells us that numerous customers sent friendly comments about the sticker along with their checks. Some of them were in the same humorous vein, and one came back with another verse.

> Here's a check for $18,
> Never mind receipt,
> My bills come so thick and fast,
> They're hard as h—to meet.

We recommend the use of stickers to add pull to billing statements. Many credit managers will testify that the combination of sticker and statement does a better job than the statement does alone. Some users, however, save the sticker for the second mailing. The procedure which works best for you can only be determined by test and comparison over a considerable stretch of time.

Guidelines for the first reminder letter. Whether or not statements are used as reminders, the time eventually comes when letters become necessary. In either case, the tone of the letter is usually casual, although a little pressure may be found when one or more statements have already failed. You will see from the following examples that letters of this type fall into one of three classes.

1. Those which simply tell the customers that the bill is past due.

Figure 14-3

Slowly, with great feeling

If a bod-y trust a bod-y

And fail to get prompt pay.___

May a bod-y ask ___ a bod-y

Please re-mit to - day.___

2. Those which "save face" for the customers by suggesting that no doubt they have overlooked the payment.

3. Those which advance some reason why the customers should not be indifferent to their obligations.

Letters of the third class are commonly used where collection of the account is pressed to a conclusion in a comparatively short period of time; only a few requests are made before talk of legal action is heard. The credit manager in this case is anxious to hasten the payment, and does not propose to wait very long before cracking the whip.

The following letters fall in the first class—simply telling the customer that the bill is past due. Each can be adapted for your use.

Dear _____,

Just a friendly reminder that your check for $25 will be warmly appreciated.

If your check is in the mail..."thank you." If not, will you please give this account your usual prompt attention?

Dear _____,

It isn't going to take much to balance your account—you owe so little.

That's why I'm so sure this reminder will bring us your check by return mail.

Am I right?

Dear _____,

Will you please do us a favor?

Our annual audit will take place this month. Can we count on your cooperation in making sure your account will not appear among those showing past-due balances?

If your check is already in the mail, please disregard this reminder.

If not, your cooperation in mailing your check by return mail will be appreciated.

Here are some examples of reminder letters of the second class—those that "save face" for the customers by suggesting that they have overlooked their payments.

Dear _____,

IT'S SO SMALL...

we wouldn't be surprised if you had forgotten all about the balance due on the attached statement.

But as a lot of these small accounts can add up to a truly sizable sum, won't you please take a minute right now to send us your check. Then we won't have to trouble you again.

Dear _____,

You are usually so prompt in sending your payments that I wonder if you realize your account is past due. Since this is undoubtedly an oversight, won't you please send us your check to cover the overdue balance of $54?

We appreciate the splendid cooperation you have always given us and shall look forward to hearing from you soon.

Gentlemen,

May we remind you in a friendly way that your payment of $101.50 is past due?

We are not in the least worried about your account—test us with another order—but it does take money to pay *our* bills.

You can help us by sending your check.

Dear _____,

With all the things you have to do, it is easy now and then to forget to pay a bill.

We know that; also, that you won't mind our asking for the check which is due us.

Just slip it in the enclosed envelope which needs no postage. And at the same time, why not send us another order?

The third class of first-reminder letters consists of those in which some reason is given the customers why they should not be indifferent to their credit obligations. Unlike the first two groups, these letters contain a little pressure.

Dear ―――――,

You surely know...

it's not HOW MUCH a person owes that determines his credit rating...but rather HOW PROMPTLY he pays his bills that really counts.

Take the amount you owe us. It is not large. But is *is* long overdue and should, for the above reason, be given your immediate attention.

Won't you send us a check today?

Dear ―――――,

The privilege of serving you is certainly our pleasure. For this, we extend our sincere thanks.

However, the enclosed statement of your account as of the end of last month lists an amount that became due some time ago.

We feel certain that you understand how important and necessary it is that every successful business organization keep its receivables up-to-date, and you can help us in this respect by sending us your payment within the next week.

If this is not possible, will you kindly tell us at the bottom of this letter the approximate date on which we can expect payment and return the letter to us.

Your cooperation will be greatly appreciated and will, above all, enable us to continue to give you the high type of service to which you are entitled.

Dear ―――――,

Enclosed is a statement showing how your account stands on our books.

It has always been your custom to pay such accounts promptly, and we wonder if there is some confusion about these items which causes you to delay making payment.

If these charges agree with your records, will you please send your remittance by return mail?

Dear _____,

It is always a pleasure to do business with a customer who meets his obligations as you have done. We like to see you earning for yourself the 2 percent discount, which over a period of time amounts to quite a saving.

We are wondering, therefore, why we have not received your check. No doubt it was an oversight and needs only this reminder.

It is always difficult to get back to a normal paying basis once you have let a month's purchases go over into the next—and of course the result is a real loss to you.

We shall be looking for a check by return mail. We hope you will not disappoint us.

With these examples to follow you can now write all kinds of casual reminders. Remember, each has a specific purpose and a specific time, when it has the most effect. Use them wisely and perhaps the quest for the illusive payment will be ended.

3. ISSUING FOLLOW-UPS WHEN FIRST REMINDERS FAIL

Ending the first stage. The common approach in the letters you have just been reading was the assumption that the customers had overlooked paying their bills. While this may be said (with reasonable doubt in the mind of the credit manager), it is still a strong enough possibility to preclude the charge of hypocrisy. Besides, it is only a form of courtesy that the customers should have the benefit of the doubt.

But when the casual first reminders have been mailed and several days later the customers still remain silent, the credit managers face the probability that the accounts are not in as good a shape as they hoped, and that it is going to take more pressure to make the collections. They may try again to probe gently for the money; or perhaps they may attack and go more bluntly at the customers. Usually, the decision of which approach to use depends on the type of business, the trade customs in the field of operation, and the credit managers' analysis of their particular customers.

Certainly, when a second letter is necessary following the first and one or more statements, stage one in the bill collection procedure is nearing an end. It is no longer reasonable to assume that the customers have forgotten to pay their bills. There may be some cause, unknown to the credit manager, which is holding up the remittance. It may or may not be a serious obstruction, but it does exist and dilatory collection letters are no longer advisable.

If the requests for payment continue to be mild and casual, the customers may take them too lightly. They must be jarred loose from the complacent attitude that they can wait as long as they wish, or that the company will continue to dance as long as they want.

Thus, while we may call the letters which follow "Second Reminders," or "Follow-Ups" of the first letters, they are written in a far more serious mood, and with a far different psychological background. The credit managers are no longer viewing the account with unconcern. They may hide their doubts for the sake of policy, and try to keep the second letter on the same friendly plane as the first, but inwardly they are probably looking at the customer with considerable suspicion.

Examples from credit correspondence. In the letters below, you will sense the change which has taken place in the attitude of the various credit managers who wrote them. Some exert more pressure than others, but they all begin to tighten the screws which, with the last turn, will lead to talk of the lawyers, and finally to court action. The latter stage in the collection sequence may still be several letters ahead, but the stagehands are beginning to set the scenery.

Dear _____,

A DOLLAR WON'T DO AS MUCH AS IT ONCE DID...because people won't do as much for a dollar.

That's pretty descriptive of these modern, so-called easy days. But it hasn't been easy for us to induce you to part with some of those "WON'T DO AS MUCH DOLLARS."

What we're trying to say is that we've been patient and friendly in asking you to send us your check for the amount above.

Once again, then, please send your check by return mail. The enclosed addressed envelope will simplify matters.

Dear _____,

It's hard to believe, but another 30 days have gone by and still no check from you for the overdue charges on your account.

As you have not questioned any of the items on our monthly statement, we assume our records agree with yours. Won't you, therefore, let us have your check to bring your account up-to-date?

We'll appreciate your prompt cooperation. May we hear from you by return mail?

Dear _____,

NO NEWS IS GOOD NEWS...

doesn't always hold true. Especially so when we have sent you a number of reminders about your past-due account, and have received no response.

And certainly not, when the absence of any word from you could adversely affect your CREDIT STANDING—ONE OF YOUR MOST VALUABLE ASSETS.

It is our earnest wish to cooperate with you in every possible way, but you make it difficult to do so by not answering any of our reminders.

May we expect some good news...by return mail?

Dear _____,

At the outset...

we want you to know that we appreciate having the pleasure of numbering you among our many thousands of satisfied customers.

However, as the several reminders mailed to you have brought no response, may we again call to your attention that your account became due for payment some time ago.

You'll agree, we feel certain, that our request for payment is not unreasonable. Won't you respond to this friendly reminder by sending us your remittance by return mail?

Your cooperation will, in all sincerity, be appreciated.

Dear _____,

I've been playing a game with you, although you didn't know it. The game was who could keep silent the longest.

You win.

May I have a remittance of some kind on your account?

Dear _____,

Reluctantly, I must once again bring to your attention the $472.50 open on your account, and 45 days past due. I say "reluctantly" because I dislike writing letters like this as much as you must dislike receiving them.

Your check will give me a chance to write you a letter you'll enjoy receiving, and one that will be a pleasure for me to write. Won't you send the check today?

Follow-ups using the story approach. In the past it was probably true that credit and collection correspondence was the driest and dullest of all the letters written for business purposes. One of the reasons may have been the great importance attributed to money matters, with the resulting notion that anything said about money must be in the most austere and dignified manner. Be that as it may, many credit managers of the modern school have discovered that sometimes more money can be collected in a shorter time with an *interesting* letter than with one which bores the reader with rigid formality. Many a collection letter has clicked in a big way because of a story or an unusual approach which would not have been tolerated in the past.

In this *Handbook*, you have already discovered that it is quite all right to use a story to gain *special* attention provided it does not backfire for want of any logical connection with the main thought of the letter. The story idea must add emphasis to the thought content which follows; if not, it merely gains temporary attention. It may even distract the readers from the central theme of the letter. In some way, perhaps subconsciously, the readers are made to feel that they were *tricked* into giving attention, and so their initial interest is turned into resentment.

Another thing worth remembering about a story introduction is that it must be *really* as interesting to the readers as the writers think it will be. In speech or writing there is nothing less likely to attract favorable attention than a story which falls flat in the telling.

When contemplating the use of a story in a collection letter two "musts" need to be remembered: first, that the story is not too shopworn; second, that its connection with the central theme of the letter is not too thin. In short, it must be a good story appropriate to the occasion. People do like stories, there can be no doubt of that. Otherwise, why are they told so frequently at all the places where folks get together? The use of one which is to the point and interesting may add life and pulling power to a collection letter. But don't drag one into the message unless it *fits*.

The story approach is usually more suitable for letters in the early stage of the collection sequence. Later, when the tone can no longer be so chatty or casual, a story may tend to soften the seriousness of the situation, leaving with the customers the impression that they may continue to dilly-dally about the payment. The letters which follow were mostly second reminders—the writers were still trying to maintain a warm and human tone without too much pressure.

Dear _____,

Thousands of people sit on the porch of the Inn at Yellowstone National Park watching for the eruption of "Old Faithful." The traveler is never disappointed. "Old Faithful" spouts with the regularity of the sun, moon, or tide.

Credit managers at their desks are not so fortunate. Payments are not always made on agreed terms. Perhaps there should be a little elasticity to terms, but to stretch them on and on indefinitely is merely to place a burden on the company that must base sales prices on anticipated sales revenues.

So, how about playing "Old Faithful" to us today by placing a check for the above amount in an envelope and starting it on its way.

Dear _____,

Once when Lincoln was poor and hungry, a stranger approached him and requested change for a $20 bill.

Being without a cent, and seeing the humor of the situation, Lincoln stooped down and confided: "Sorry, I can't oblige you stranger, but I thank you for the compliment just the same."

Some of our friends pay us the same compliment that this stranger paid Lincoln. They let their account stand on the books, thinking no doubt that we don't need the money. But we do. You would be surprised.

So won't you please give this little account of yours the necessary attention, and let us have a check for $620 within the week?

Dear _____,

Here is a good story they tell of the Speaker of the House.

One member, making his first speech in the House, found its members listless under his oratory. After adjournment, he sought out the Speaker and asked him what he thought of the speech.

"Well maybe what you said was all right," replied Mr. Speaker, "but it seemed to me that you did not make the most of your opportunities."

"My opportunities?"

"Yes. You had several chances to sit down before you did."

Lest we be accused of making too long a speech about the $50 you owe us, we will make just one remark, and then sit down to wait for your anwer.

PLEASE SEND US A CHECK.

Now, we're sitting.

Dear ⎯⎯⎯⎯⎯,

Very few persons, even those in the country, know whether a cow's ears are above, below, behind, or in front of her horns. Others do not know whether cats descend trees head-first or tail-first.

Very few people can distinguish between the leaves of the various kinds of trees in their neighborhood, and comparatively few are able to describe their own houses, beyond the most general features.

Persons who pass the same traffic signals every day cannot tell whether the green light is at the top or the bottom.

It's fascinating to notice and analyze the things you see and hear in your daily routine; to notice the faces of people, their walk, their characteristics. If you look for interesting and odd things, you will find them.

Incidentally, have you misplaced our bill covering charges of $54, dated September 20th?

Dear ⎯⎯⎯⎯⎯,

"What do you do with your beard when you go to bed at night?" a little girl asked her grandfather. "Do you put it on top of the covers, under the covers, or in your nightshirt pocket?"

Grandpa had never thought about his beard at night, so he couldn't answer the little girl's question. But when he went to bed that night, he tried putting his beard on top of the covers, under the covers, and in his night-shirt pocket. But no way seemed right.

All night long, Grandpa tumbled and tossed. He lay on his back, he lay on his side, and he lay on his stomach. He couldn't get comfortable with that beard—he couldn't go to sleep.

You see, the little girl's question had made him beard-conscious. I wonder what question I could ask you to make you *check-conscious?*

Your account is long past due, you know—since June 10th.

These stories no doubt brought a smile to the lips of their readers. Because of the gentleness of the letters in which they were included, we can be reasonably sure that both the customers' goodwill *and* payment were forthcoming.

4. ENTERING THE MIDDLE STAGE—USE OF SPECIAL APPEALS

Increasing the pressure. Assuming that statements and reminder letters have failed to collect the delinquent account, credit managers now step into the middle stage of the collection procedure. They can no longer afford to regard the situation lightly, or to continue with more or less casual requests for payment. They know that something has happened which is keeping the customers silent, or that the latter are simply the kind who will not pay until they feel lawyers breathing on their necks? The managers still hope that the money can be collected without recourse to legal action, and wonder what appeals, they might use to stir the customers into meeting their obligations.

From long experience in dealing with human beings, the credit managers know that unless the customers are totally without funds they may be receptive to some special reason for paying, but the managers also know that different appeals vary in effectiveness with different individuals. Thus, in the effort to collect a particular account, they may use a sequence of letters, each one going at the reader in a different way. In one, they may in a person-to-person fashion encourage the customer to tell what is wrong, and stress the desire of the company to *help* solve the problem. In a second, they may appeal to the customer's sense of fair play—the Golden Rule approach. In a third, they may talk about the value of good credit rating, and how the customer cannot afford to lose it. In each case they are probing for a "soft spot"—the one reason for paying which may have greatest weight in the customer's mind.

This is the middle stage, and it may drag out or be very short, depending on the willingness of the credit managers to match their wits against the stubbornness of their customers. In any case, the casual tone of the reminder letters is gone. These new letters may still be friendly, and should be, but they must be more insistent. The screw is being turned—the pressure is increasing.

Appealing to reason—what's wrong? Credit managers realize that all customers cannot be expected to pay their bills regularly and when due without an occasional slip. When the emergencies are real, and the customers' intentions are honest, the average company is more than willing to *help* the customers solve their problems. But no help is possible when the latter keep their troubles to themselves, as frequently they do. The reason, of course, is pride. Individuals are usually embarrassed when they get in financial jams. They want to keep up appearances. Instead of placing the facts before the company to which they are indebted, they ignore the collection letters which come to them hoping for a turn in fortune that will permit them to pay.

Experienced credit managers understand difficulties, so they seek to write letters which will break down the reserves and produce facts. The letters have to be tactful, with nothing in them to injure the readers' pride, for if the latter feel humiliated or belittled, they are not likely to reply. The appeal is to *reason*—how can we help unless we know what's wrong? Hence in Figure 14-4 is a very good example of the appeal to reason. The desire to *help* the customer is strongly stressed. We think almost any honest-minded customer would appreciate the letter.

Figure 14-4

Dear _____,

In an experience of more than 50 years, we have found that when people do not pay their bills promptly there is usually some good reason for it, such as sickness, dearth of funds, disagreement about terms, dissatisfaction with the goods, or failure to receive them.

Therefore, it seems very probable that there has been some such reason for your failure to pay the amount below.

But why do you keep us in the dark?

We do not want you to feel that we are inconsiderate if there is good reason for nonpayment, but we cannot know the reason for your failure to pay unless you tell us.

So will you not, as the very minimum of fairness to us, write on the back of this letter just what the trouble is? Or better still, if the amount is correct and it is at all possible, send us your check and have this matter off your mind and ours.

There are several approaches that credit managers can call upon in the middle stage. As each point is mentioned, check the excerpts given to see how some letter experts led into each one.

APPROACH 1: "We can't help unless you tell us."

If you will only acquaint us with details of your apparent difficulty, you can be assured of our wholehearted cooperation. Just let us know what we can do to help you.

If we only knew the facts, no doubt some arrangement could be made that would relieve your mind of the worry of an overdue debt, and satisfy us, too.

Whatever the problem is, please do not keep us in the dark. Let us help. Why don't you call Thursday and we can talk out this snafu together.

APPROACH 2: "Why haven't we heard from you?"

Continued silence on your part makes us uneasy that something has seriously gone awry with you or your business. Since your payment is also way past due, we are on tenderhooks wondering what's happening. Write or call and tell us.

From experience we know that when we haven't heard from you something is wrong. Drop us a line. Your late payment is no reason for your constraint in sharing with us your needs.

The thing that does bother us, however, is that you have not at any time written, explaining the reason for the delay. I know you will understand that it will be a lot easier for us if we did have an explanation, and it would make us feel that you had as much confidence in us as we have had in you.

APPROACH 3: Saving the customer's "face" and calling for a response to this goodwill.

Normally we would be concerned if an account was overdue as long as yours, but you and I have been through the "hardware" wars together—I know we can count on a good explanation: In view of the manner in which you've always handled your bills before, I don't have a care about your coming through.

Every business, large or small, meets with some difficulties at some time or other. If we weren't for the assistance of business associates—if the business world operated on the principle of everyone for themselves—none of us would survive long.

All of us like to see the checks rolling in regularly, and when a customer gets behind, we wonder why. Usually there is a good reason for a delay in payment, and our company has always tried to see the other side of it as our own.

APPROACH 4: "Do we need a lawyer?"

Our ability to help delinquent customers has its limits. We must necessarily conserve it for the benefit of those who show a willingness to clear their accounts. Please let us hear from you.

Collecting long overdue accounts leads to many problems, most of them unpleasant for us and for you. If you'll tell us your situation now, perhaps we can still settle amicably. Certainly we'll do what we can to make it as easy as possible for you.

Won't you please send us some word *before your account passes out of our hands?* This postage-paid envelope is for your letter, or, preferably, your check.

APPROACH 5: "If you were in our shoes, what would you do?"

Sometimes the person who makes the biggest howl is the one who gets his money first, but this plan would work with us, and we are placing you in the position we would take, taking it for granted you feel as we do. Instead of worrying you with "duns" we just want to appeal to your sense of fairness.

If our positions were reversed, and we owed

you a bill like the one enclosed—two months overdue—how would you feel, and what would you do? Wouldn't you feel justified in writing a sharp demand for your money? We do...*almost*.

We were glad to cooperate with you and grant extra dating on a number of invoices covering shipment of your Fall requirements, as listed on the enclosed statement. In all fairness, don't you believe that you in turn should reciprocate by taking care of the past-due items now?

Each of these approaches will be valuable additions to your tool chest of letter carpentry. However, sometimes even the very best intentions are rebuffed.

Applying the approaches successfully. Anything to which credit managers can continuously turn for those missing monies owed their companies is, of course, invaluable. Such are the approaches just discussed. However, the actual meat of a letter fashioned upon these skeletons should also be shown. Each of these letters did precisely what they were intended to do—they got the check. (The number above each letter corresponds to the Approach number it represents.)

(1)

Dear _____,

May I ask a favor of you?

Your account for September has not been paid, and we have had no explanation or reason. Will you please check the blank below, and return it to us in the enclosed envelope?

This will help us no end to cooperate with you.

I have not paid my account because:

1. Of oversight _____
2. Of the rush of work _____
3. Of error or overcharge _____
4. Of disagreement as to price or terms _____
5. I will remit in _____ days
6. Payment is in the mail
7. Check is enclosed

(2)

Dear _____,

I wish I were able to sit down and talk to you for about ten minutes about your account. I would like very much to know the circumstances that have caused you to delay your payment of January and February charges.

Without this information, I have to sit back and look at such factors as past experience, ratings, and credit information, in such effort to determine why your account has not been paid. Now the surprising thing is that all these factors point to your having a very satisfactory credit standing. For some reason or other we have been waiting five months for even a partial payment or an explanation of the delay.

I know you will understand that it would be a lot easier for us if we did have an explanation, and it would make us feel that you are not abusing the confidence we have in you.

To avoid the possibility of any misunderstanding, we will appreciate your either making immediate arrangements for taking care of this overdue balance, or dropping us a note today telling us just what we can expect. Surely, you will agree that we are entitled to this consideration.

(3)

Dear _____,

I know you will take this letter in the friendly spirit in which it is meant. Here's what it's all about.

Due to my desire to be as helpful as possible during these recent years, I have extended the credit privilege until now I have thousands of dollars outstanding. Some of you, no doubt, feel that you could pay me something, but would rather wait until you could send me a substantial amount.

However, small sums paid regularly from many sources would make a total which would be of real assistance to me.

So I am asking you to let me have a little every week if possible to apply on your account, which I know you are just as anxious to whittle down as I am. I don't want you to feel embarrassed over this request. I know you will do the best you can.

With best regards, I promise you the same faithful service in the future that I have tried to give in the past.

(4)

Dear _____,

Is it worth it...
to jeopardize your credit standing—one of your most valuable assets—over the amount shown above? If you will give this question the serious consideration it deserves, we believe that you will agree with us that it isn't.

The last thing we want to do is to take any step which would impair your credit standing, but the amount you owe us is long overdue, and we have received no response to our many reminders. So unless we hear from you promptly, we'll have no choice but to turn your account over to our attorney for collection.

Neither of us will gain from this action—and the needless expense and embarrassment can be avoided. But only if you send us a check for the full amount within the next ten days;

We shall expect your prompt reply,

(5)

Dear _____,

If someone owed you $150 and seemingly made no effort to pay it, how would you feel?

But now suppose you had put yourself in the place of the customer, assumed that perhaps he had been hard pushed for money, and had decided to wait rather than appeal to the law to collect your money.

Then later, suppose you wrote him a friendly letter, asking him to treat you fairly as you had treated him. Wouldn't you feel certain that you could expect a prompt response?

Although there are laws that regulate business, Mr. _____, the biggest reason that almost all business transactions are completed smoothly is that most people believe in the square deal. Business would go to pieces if we couldn't depend upon the sacredness of an agreement.

That is all we ask from you—a square deal. You believe in that just as we do, don't you? Then let's settle this matter. A check from you by return mail will keep us friends.

You have now examined representative letters taken from American business showing how collections are handled in the first and middle stages. The approaches and letters have run the gamut of techniques available to innovative credit managers. They can be as clever as they like as they try to find "missing" payments. They can, through short but interesting letters, appeal to the customers' sense of fair play, their common desires to maintain good business reputations, and to keep their good friends (the credit managers) from having to use collection agencies and lawyers.

Goodwill maintenance through this section has been of paramount importance. It is hardly consistent to talk about fair play, while at the same time calling the customer ugly names. Nor does it arouse goodwill to assume an attitude of smug holiness, the inference being that the writers are very fine people, and the readers are skunks. On the contrary, the success of the letter appeal depends on a sincere person-to-person assumption that the customers are upright and the company still has faith in their good intentions. This assumption cannot be created by insincere exaggeration, or by statements that humiliate and anger the readers.

Finally the sand runs low, and the credit managers are forced to admit reluctantly that nothing is left to do but bring the threat of legal action.

5. LETTERS PRECEDING LEGAL ACTION

Reaching the end of the rope. Credit managers do not reach the last stage in their collection efforts without considerable regret. They wonder what they might have said in their previous letters that would have secured favorable results. Although the circumstance may have been beyond their control. They feel deeply the responsibility of having accepted an open account which is about to sour, with both the loss of profit and the expense of legal action. They therefore try one final plea which might avert the catastrophe.

Obviously, this last collection letter in the series must be firm and positive. But no matter how the writers may feel toward the customers who have given them so much trouble, they must still be courteous and considerate. Nothing should defeat the purpose of this last important effort to get the money. Sarcasm, reproach, ugly names—all are futile in a collection letter. There is nothing to be gained by browbeating a wayward debtor.

In the writing of this "last resort" collection letter, one fact needs to be remembered. It is a serious mistake to cry "Wolf" unless the wolf is there. To tell your customers that they are getting the very last chance to pay before you turn the account over to the lawyers, and then later write them again with the same threat, is an indication of weakness and insincerity which their customers will be quick to sense. There is no point in pulling a gun unless you mean to shoot exactly as and when promised. The custom of trying to frighten the customer with one letter after another that merely *talks* about legal action is common enough in certain types of business, none too savory or reputable, but good companies of established reputation do not stoop to such methods.

Usually, three letters are considered adequate in this last stage. The first is a plea that the customers pay the bill and save themselves the trouble and expense of legal action. The latter is mentioned as impending, but no date is set. The second sets the date, but still leaves a period of time during which the payment may be made. The third is more of a notice than a letter, and sometimes is omitted. It simply tells the customers that the lawyers have taken over.

Analyzing the right and wrong way. There is no accepted formula to follow in dictating the final-stage collection letters. Some credit managers make them short, the assumption being that it does no good to rehash circumstances or to repeat arguments advanced in previous messages. Others plead their case at greater length, repeating freely in the hope that a spark might cause fire even though it failed the first time. Then, there are those who seek an entirely new approach—a last minute mailgram or express letter, a dramatized idea, or a story which is particularly appropriate.

Whatever the method or content, the only true measure of effectiveness is the percentage of success—in 100 cases, how many times does the letter induce the customer to pay and thus avoid legal action? There is one way, however, that a collection letter of this type may be tagged "right" or "wrong" without argument or equivocation. This is the distinction between the letter which disregards courtesy, and the one which still approaches the customers as business friends.

The Wrong Way

You do not answer our letters. What is more serious, you do not pay your bills.

Matters of courtesy and honor are important to us, if not to you.

You will either pay this bill, or take the consequences. If the latter, it's your fault, not ours. We at least have acted like gentlemen in this transaction.

In ten days, we shall send this bill to our attorneys for collection. You will not find them as easy and lenient as we have been.

The Right Way

Our collection department has just sent a statement of your account to my desk; they were about to send it to our attorney. I have asked them to postpone action for a few days, because I don't want to collect money in this manner if I can help it.

It will be much easier for both of us if you'll simply send your check today.

Let's get this matter straightened out in a spirit of mutual consideration.

No doubt the difference between the above letters is plain enough to require little explanation. In the "Wrong" letter, the writer is petulant, sarcastic, and insulting. In the "Right" letter, the writer is a decent person who doesn't want to take legal action, but will if left no choice. Notice the tone of the letter. It's frank, but friendly throughout. The letter shows a willingness to assist the customer in whatever way possible.

Here are five examples of "Right" letters. They are stronger letters than the foregoing, but they manage to make an unpleasant point without being rude.

(1)

Dear _____,

Unfortunately, we have not received a satisfactory reply to our many requests for the payment of the account mentioned below. As you know, this account is now considerably overdue.

We are sure you understand that at our present wholesale prices we cannot afford to allow accounts to remain outstanding for a long period.

Therefore, if we do not receive a remittance within seven days from the above date, we shall be reluctantly compelled to place the matter in the hands of our attorneys without further notice to you.

We sincerely hope that this will not be necessary and that you will send us your check by return mail, so that we can continue to be of service to you.

(2)

Dear _____,

Your balance is many, many months overdue, and we've had no

answers to any of our letters. Therefore, unless we hear from you within the next ten days, we'll have no other choice but to turn your account over to our attorneys for immediate collection.

It is our sincere hope that this will not be necessary, since it would cause us both needless expense and embarrassment. To avoid this unpleasant action, do let us have your check by return mail.

Dear _____,

It is with regret that we find it necessary to send this fourth letter, our last REQUEST that your forward a check in payment of your note.

This obligation was incurred a considerable time ago on the basis of its being paid when due, and it seems reasonable to believe that ample time has elapsed for you to comply with the terms mutually agreed on when you purchased your policy.

If your remittance for the full amount of this note is not received within the next week, we shall assume that it will be in order for us to take such steps as circumstances warrant.

(3)

Dear _____,

Although we have written you a number of times about your December 16th bill amounting to $1237.48, we have received no response whatever.

Your references spoke well of you and we were glad to give you the benefit of the regular 30-day accommodation. However, further correspondence now seems to be useless, and we have decided to place the account with our attorneys for collection unless it is paid in full by May 1st.

We urge you to take care of this account without further delay.

(4)

Dear _____,

Ninety percent of the accounts we collect through attorneys are handled that way because the customers will not answer our letters.

We are forced to sue because friendly requests bring neither payment nor explanations.

Your account of $407.98 is long past due. We must assume that the amount is correct, for you have never questioned it.

We both want to keep away from the courts if possible. So before sending the account to our attorney, we will wait ten days for your letter and check.

(5)

Dear —————,

Do we sue?

Indian summer has turned to winter. Winter has dissolved before the warm spring sun. Now summer is about ready to take over where spring leaves off...and we still have heard nothing from you since that November day when you authorized us to place your $250 ad in our paper.

We published that ad in good faith, and you know how patiently we've been waiting for our money. At first we thought our turn hadn't come around as yet. Then we wondered if anything had gone wrong that prevented you from paying. We even offered you a small gift and told you how nonpayment of this small debt would hurt your credit standing.

The time for further warnings is now past. You really have left us no other course but to turn your account over to our attorneys for collection.

We really don't want to do this, —————, so we're giving you three more days of grace. This is your last warning, however. Your account is *scheduled for the attorneys on May 5.* Save it by doing the right thing and mailing us your check today. A handy envelope is enclosed. Use it at once.

Viewing letters seasoned with humor. You might think that nothing but a serious tone would be appropriate for the final stage of the collection procedure, and in general this is true. However, some credit managers have had considerable success with letters that talk in a lighter vein, even though the news in them may not be so pleasant. In using this approach, the writers skate on thin ice, for if what they say seems too superficial, the customers may not take the message seriously. Humor has power to influence human behavior, but unless it "rings true" it tends to do more harm than good. For example, who would be favorably impressed by the following letters?

(1)

Dear _____,

The lawyer said, "The question is immaterial, irrelevant, and irregular," and because the witness did not have to answer the question the case had to be dismissed.

You have been sent five notices requesting payments of $365.40 which is due us. The notices were sent to you on the following dates:

> January 5
> January 10
> January 15
> January 22
> January 29

Now, we are sending you the final notice. If we do not hear from you, we will have to place your account in the hands of a collection agency. Let us hear from you, and please send your check so we can dismiss these letters as "immaterial, irrelevant, and irregular."

(2)

Dear _____,

Slick Johnson was sentenced to the gallows for the excessive use of an exceedingly sharp razor.

Sitting in his cell, he struggled to find words that would explain his predicament to the Governor and win a pardon. The next morning the Governor received this message in his mail:

Dear Guvenor

They are fixin to hang me friday and here it is tuesday.

Respectfully
Slick Johnson

Like Slick, we too are in a predicament. Our collection department is fixin' to "kill" your policy next Friday because the payment hasn't come in.

One of those printed forms in your check book is ideal for arranging a prompt pardon for a friend, who for only $43.82 a quarter can serve you both faithfully and well.

(3)

Dear _____,

An interesting story is told of Benvenuto Cellini, the celebrated 16th Century goldsmith.

It seems that Cellini, after months of painstaking labor upon a cunningly wrought gold vase which he had been commissioned to make for the Bishop of Salamanca, was unable to collect his fee. Exasperated and in need of funds, Cellini called on the debtor and pointing his pistol at him cried, "Pay or I shoot!" The Bishop paid and Cellini went his way rejoicing.

This simple and direct method of collection is not used today, but there is a similar one that has similar characteristics. When every other friendly means of getting our money has been used and our customer, like the Bishop, simply refuses to pay, we say, "Pay or we'll shoot."

And we are serious about it. We have no pistol, it is true. Our "gun" is the Cooperative Adjustment and Collection Service— and it has a mighty fine reputation for hitting the mark.

Don't make us unlimber this weapon to collect your account. We don't like to shoot it off because it makes a big noise and scares everybody—and you know how it is, there is always the likelihood that someone will get hurt.

It is possible to season a collection letter with a sprinkling of humor, and at the same time preserve the dignity which is expected of business relationships.

Pinch-hitting for the credit manager. A common practice in collection procedure, when the time for legal action is near, is to send the customer a final appeal signed by some other important executive— the treasurer, a vice-president, or even the head of the company. Such a letter not only carries the weight of coming from a top executive, but it may also have a new approach which gets better results than those already used by the credit manager. At least, the game is worth the effort, and sometimes it does the job.

A check was promptly gained with the following letter written by the late Carl Wollner, then president of Panther Oil & Grease Manufacturing Co. You will note that the customer is handled without gloves, although the spirit of the message is summarized in the complimentary close, "Still Friendly." The letter was hand-written on a memo page with "Office of Carl Wollner, President" in the upper lefthand corner. The effect was startling.

Dear Mr. Lloyd,

Doggonit! Have I lost my ability to write a customer a letter friendly enough to get an answer? You got my letter—didn't you? Why the heck didn't we get an answer? That account of yours is old enough to have whiskers on it and we really need *our* money. You've got no right to keep it.

Maybe the credit manager was right after all when he said you wouldn't answer my *friendly* letter.

Do I have to pass the buck back to him and let him get the money any way he can—friendly or *otherwise?*

Before I do, here's postage and an envelope to mail that check *right* now, please sir!

Still friendly,

Here are five other "last resort" collection letters in which top executives pinch-hit for their credit managers.

(1)

Dear —————,

The effort of Mr. Clark to bring about a friendly settlement of your long overdue account was referred to my attention this morning along with the file of correspondence for review and decision. As you know, there is an unpaid balance of $96.43 and this has been explained in our many letters and statements. I feel sure that if there were any question regarding it you would have taken it up with us some time ago.

There comes a time in the collection of a long delinquent account when it seems that there is nothing left to do but to place it with our collection attorney. When that happens we both lose something. We lose your goodwill and the opportunity for a continued friendly business relationship, and you lose your valuable credit reputation. Isn't that worth your serious consideration?

I have instructed Mr. Clark to delay action on this for ten days, which will give you time to get your check to us. You will be glad, I know, if you take this opportunity to prevent an unpleasant situation. We have tried to be considerate in handling your account and any action that we may be forced to take will be your responsibility.

(2)

Dear —————,

Our credit manager has just handed me the enclosed statement of your account, with the recommendation that it be referred to our attorneys for collection. After carefully going over our Collection Department records, it looks as though you have ignored the terms of your agreement.

Invoices covering your rental installments have been sent to you promptly each month; letters written to you requesting payment have not resulted in settlement.

Nothing can be inferred from your inaction save a violation of the terms of your subscription, to which we invite your attention. There is no question as to the validity of your contract. There is no question of our good faith in carrying out our part of the agreement. The next step is up to you. What do you intend to do?

If for any reason settlement will be delayed longer, I suggest that you wire me immediately. If I do not near from you promptly, I shall be forced to assume that you are prepared to defend the action that will be started immediately, involving the entire amount of your contract, plus attorney's fees.

(3)

Dear _____,

Our collection manager has placed before me a statement of your long overdue account and informed me that his repeated efforts to collect have had no effect.

He also asked for my instructions as to whether he should place your account with our attorneys for collection. I have instructed him to hold this matter in abeyance for five days until I could write to you.

If you cannot pay the full amount overdue, send me half of it at once, and tell me when you can pay the balance.

If you fail to answer this letter promptly, I will be forced to conclude that it is best for the Collection Department to proceed with legal action.

I am enclosing a stamped envelope, addressed to me, and I ask that you let me hear from you by return mail.

(4)

Dear _____,

Our collection manager tells me that we must take legal action against you. He says that you owe us $73, that the bill was past due after September 15, that he wrote to you without reply on September 25, October 10, October 20, November 1, and November 15.

I have asked him to hold the law in check for a few days. Speaking as a friend, I don't want to get our money by force. As a business person, I don't relish the idea of paying out money to collect an account. This, in my opinion, is a step to be taken only when the other party refused to sit down at the council table with me.

I have been frank with you, _____. Won't you be the same with me? Write and let me know what is the matter. Even though your account has reached the ultimatum stage, I may be able to help you.

Just sit down now. Write that letter. Use the enclosed envelope which has been addressed to insure my personal attention. The Golden Rule that you and I learned in school may be considered an outmoded, overworked idea by some people, but I believe, if we both apply it, we can straighten out this matter to our mutual satisfaction.

(5)

Dear _____,

This morning our collection manager suggested to me that we turn your account over to Dun's. Five letters have been mailed to you since April 5.

I do not wish to authorize such action before taking up the account with you personally. You understand that I want to give you every opportunity to settle your account without reporting it to Dun's.

To speak frankly, I am inclined to think you have some good reason for not writing to us. I shall retain this correspondence on my desk ten days to give you an opportunity to send your check, or to tell us what to expect.

You must realize that this debt is a matter of real importance to you. Please let me hear from you.

Handling the breach in very old accounts. An especially difficult problem for credit managers is how to handle old and honored customers who for some unknown reason have recently stopped paying their bills. Naturally the managers do not want to throw over the business which might still be salvaged, but any account old or new reaches the stage of legal action when all other collection efforts have failed. Nevertheless, the tone of the "last resort" letter to one of these older customers is usually less stringent than if sent to customers not deserving the same consideration. The writers want to get the account back on the right basis if they possibly can. Consider these examples.

(1)

Dear _____,

Frankly, we are reluctant to send your account to our lawyer for collection. You have done business with us for some time, and we believe in your good intentions. After all, lawyers do have a way of getting the money, but in the end it costs you more and often leads to many unpleasant consequences. So, we are going to give you every chance to avoid outside collection of your account.

It will be necessary, though, for you to do your part. A payment of a part of the account by March 10 and satisfactory assurance on the balance is what we consider your part now.

It is entirely up to you.

(2)

Dear _____,

Isn't there some time during the day that you have a few moments to spare? Will you do me this favor? Use a few of those moments to sit down and write a letter about your present financial condition and how things will be for the next few months.

We dislike to talk about such a delicate subject as payments and credits, but it has become necessary to be very frank with you. I know that you will be equally frank with us.

We have had to delay shipments because of the condition of your account, which has always been past due during the last few months. Balances, and rather sizable ones, too, have been carried forward to the next month. That, considering that you have an opportunity to make your sales before we require payment, is a condition that should not exist.

And so, I am asking you, as I believe you would ask me, to tell us the whole story. You have been a customer of ours for a number of years, and we want to continue serving you. Taking legal action on this account is really the very last thing we want to do.

You will find us ready to work with you on any plan that will help you to get on a better basis.

We want to see you earn the 2 percent discount we allow for prompt payment. With billings the size of yours, this would amount to quite a sum over a year's time.

So, won't you do me that favor? Just tell me the story. And, with your letter, can you send me a check?

(3)

Dear _____,

Your balance is still $123.90, and our patience is still holding out. We have enjoyed our business relationship with you for several years, and we are reluctant to end it in unpleasantness. However, your silence is putting us into an uncompromising position.

The problem is simply that we have been unable to collect by our usual, friendly methods. Good business policy demands that we do collect. The solution, you see, is squarely up to you.

We must ask now that you remit a substantial payment on your account immediately. Unless you do, we shall have no choice but to turn the account over to our attorneys ten days from now.

Let's solve this problem today, and stay friends.

In these last letters you will note there were no angry words, only simple and polite statements of the situation. The writers were anxious to be helpful and to give their longtime customers special consideration. The solutions were left up to the customers.

Curtain...end of the play. When the final appeal fails, the credit managers have reached the end of their personal efforts to collect the past due accounts. They may or may not send a final note, saying that legal action has started. It doesn't matter so much—the customers soon find out that they are in hot water.

Throughout the many preceding pages, you have watched this three-act drama.

• In Act I, you saw the letters used in the first stage of the struggle—nice, easygoing letters containing no pressure. They were mostly reminders—nobody was too worried.

• In Act II, the plot thickened. Doubt was beginning to form. The letters were longer—more intense. Various appeals were tried to stir the debtor into action—the plea for cooperation, to fair play, to pride, to self-interest.

• In Act III, came the climax. By then all in the audience knew the customer's intentions were not good. Would the debtor be driven to pay by threat of legal action? In the wings, new characters waited for their cues—the lawyers. One last appeal. Unhappy ending. Curtain!

So now we turn from the precise and controlled letters used in the collection procedure to those that serve special purposes, and are out-of-the-groove.

6. BUILDING OUT-OF-THE-GROOVE COLLECTION LETTERS

Evaluating the pro and con of showmanship. You're well aware by now that the dramatized letter may sometimes out-pull others of more conventional style. The reason is that people tend to give special attention to things which are *different*. This is a psychological fact. If it were not true, all automobiles would probably still be painted one color, and the various makers would not try so hard to bring out new, more strikingly designed models. Few of us like to do the same things in the same way; we seek different forms of entertainment: we buy different types of clothing; we rush to try a new cereal for breakfast.

Hence, there can be no logical argument against the use of an occasional collection letter based on a different approach, or prepared in some special way to gain attention. The dramatized collection letter is okay, provided it conforms with the rules for showmanship in any other kind of business correspondence. The idea must be original and really clever and it must be appropriate to the purpose and thought of the message in the body of the letter. As you know, it is a mistake to gain attention by some spectacular device, only to have the reader realize later that there is little or no connection between the idea and letter-content. In such a case, the showmanship turns out to be an insult to the reader's intelligence, and does more harm than good.

Certain disadvantages limit the extent to which the dramatized collection letter may be used. If a special letterhead has been prepared, the readers know that the message is not for them alone—that it is a form letter sent to numerous customers who have not paid their bills. A form letter is seldom taken as seriously as one pointed directly at a particular customer. Moreover, a dramatized message must sacrifice some dignity for effect, and may not be regarded too favorably by conservative readers who never wander from the conventional path. Highly original collection letters are not for general use, although we know that they often out-pull the cut-and-dried ones.

Collecting with clever copy and clip-ons. A collection letter may get out of the groove merely in thought-content or the way it is typed. It may travel on the regular company letterhead, and not involve the expense of a separately printed form or of some special gadget that has to be attached. Figure 14-5 is one that displays an unusual bit of typing.

Figure 14-5

Dear _____,
Regarding the ALMIGHTY $.

There i$ a little matter that one of our cu$tomer$ ha$ $eemingly forgotten entirely. $ome make u$ promi$e$ but do not keep them. To u$ it i$ an important matter—it'$ nece$$ary in our bu$ine$$.

We don't like to $peak about $uch remi$$ne$$. NUF $ED.

Very truly your$

Ordinarily, letters in code are not effective, because it's an imposition on a reader's time to expect him to decipher such a message. Figure 14-6 however, is simple enough to offset the objection.

Because business letters are commonly written in prose, it is obviously a form of showmanship when a collection message is put in rhyme. These attempts can be very good or very bad, depending largely on the quality of the verse—and since business people are not poets, the result is usually not so good.

Often you encounter collection letters with some attachment or clip-on which dramatizes the thought of the message. Such a letter can be very successful if the point is not too far-fetched and the gadget not too elaborate. One popular letter had a feather attached. The letter read: "A feather is not very heavy, but have you ever carried a feather-bed upstairs? One small unpaid account does not burden us, but

Figure 14-6

Good morning, _____,
Here is a little Secret Code Writing. Can you solve it?
rof kcehc evah ew yaM
stnec evlewt dna srallod owt-yteniN
?liam nruter yb

Please let us have your answer immediately. Thank you.

Yours very truly,

P.S. Solution: Just read it backwards.

hundreds of them can make a tremendous load." Obviously, the feather itself adds a little punch to the message and is quite appropriate.

Unfortunately, the idea is sometimes overdone. An illustration of how far from the path of common sense a writer may wander is a collection letter on which was attached a small cigar in a cellophane bag, a safety match, and a small strip of sandpaper. The idea, of course, is: "Have a cigar on us, and please send your check." But you can imagine in what shape the cigar arrived after its journey in the mail. Furthermore, any female recipient would have been appalled even had there been no damage in transit. This type of attachment is plainly in very poor taste. The credit manager who uses this kind of gimmick succeeds only in offending the customer.

On the other hand, some very effective collection letters have been built around attachments selected for their interest value and with good taste. Shown in Figure 14-7 was the idea used by Vic Knight in the Dartnell Business Letter Service. It was both amusing and original. Across the top of the letterhead in big type is the caption, "WE'RE GIVING YOU THE WHOLE WORKS." Clipped on was a packet of seven miniature letters. The normal eye would need a magnifying glass to read them, but this doesn't matter as they are intended only to dramatize the copy.

The packet of miniature letters attached to Figure 14-7's message recalls another written on a small letterhead about one-fourth the usual size. The copy reads: "Your overdue account is so small that we are using as little space as possible to write to you about it. Please send your check today. Thank you." Then, of course, you think of the "BIG" collection letters—blow-ups four times as large as a standard letter, with the copy reading: "Since all of our regular-sized letters have somehow escaped your attention, we think this BIG one may do a better job."

There is much truth in the agencies saying that one picture is worth a thousand words. You know how profusely advertising agencies use illustrations and color to enliven their copy—in magazines, in booklets, on billboards, and in other forms of publicity. In the same way, a business letter may gain favored attention because of a colorful letterhead or an interesting picture or heading.

The easiest way to illustrate a collection letter, although it may not be the most effective, is to attach a sticker. A number of the companies offering business services carry a wide selection of stickers designed for use in sales, collection, and other forms of business correspondence. An advantage of these stickers is that one may be used for a short while and then discarded in favor of another before repetition has destroyed its interest value.

Figure 14-7

Dear _____,

Once upon a time we thought we could write good collection letters. They started off with the mild hooey of, "Perhaps you overlooked last month's statement, isn't it lovely weather, and how are all the folks?"

Then they worked up to a grand finale, and in the last letter, we said something like this: "Now see here, you yellow-livered deadbeat, if you do not lay the cash on the line by day after tomorrow, we will have you clapped in the hoosegow—if not sooner."

For quite a while, we thought that was about the world's best series of collection letters. Then it just so happened there came a time when we were slow about paying one of our own bills, and we began getting that same bunch of letters back—one every ten days.

That experience cured us of the notion we could write collection letters. Our best efforts are reproduced above—not so you will waste any time reading them, but so you won't feel slighted. Yes, with this letter you are getting "The Whole Works."

But all we are now attempting to do is to keep some cash coming in by telling good customers like yourself the truth. We need the $67.95 that you owe us, and it will please us a lot if somehow you can manage a check.

Special letterheads for collection letter purposes also may be obtained, which means that any credit manager may have a fling at showmanship without too much trouble or expense. Although we do not recommend these special letterheads as a standard item, there is no question but that now and then, if inserted in the regular run of letters, one of them may do a surprisingly good job in collecting unpaid bills.

Focusing collection letters for specific days. If we assume that *anything* out of the ordinary may be called of particular interest to mankind, we can agree that a collection letter may successfully get out of the groove even *without* the use of special letterheads, cartoons, gadgets, or any of the other devices we have been reviewing. In the examples that follow you will see how various credit correspondents have written effective collection letters in connection with certain days or events to which the average man attributes importance.

The reasoning that prompts such letters is that the customers' respect for the day will in some intangible way make them receptive to a letter that talks about it. To what degree this reasoning is sound, no one knows, but we cannot deny the prevalent emotional reactions displayed at certain times of the year—a feeling of good will and tolerance during Christmas week, of patriotism on the 4th of July, of renewed ambition at the start of a new year. Hence, a collection letter which touches one of these impulses often has a better chance of success than the usual run-of-the-office variety.

In connection with the use of these special-day letters, however, one caution needs to be mentioned. Writers must guard against insincerity and exaggeration; unless they, themselves, feel the same emotional reaction which they are trying to arouse in their readers, the message will fall flat. With this reservation in mind, examine the following examples:

(1)

When the holiday season comes around, we do not like to change the atmosphere of pleasant tidings...so we won't.

We are postponing further correspondence about your account until after the first of the year, when we will review all accounts again.

In the meantime, we would like to wish you a joyous holiday season.

(2)

We take this opportunity to extend our sincere wishes for a Happy Holiday Season.

We sincerely hope that your sales during this season will far exceed those of previous years.

We realize that you are busy at this time, but our calendar year is drawing to a close and we are anxious to have our receivables as up-to-date as possible.

Won't you please take a few minutes to send us your payment now, as your account is considerably past due.

Your cooperation will be greatly appreciated.

(3)

We should like at the outset, to extend our sincere wishes to you for a most successful New Year. And we thank you for having granted us the privilege of serving you during the past year.

Judging from all reports, most businesses enjoyed a substantial increase in holiday sales as compared with the same period for the past several years.

We hope that you, too, shared in this increase and that the added sales will enable you to start the new year right by bringing your account as shown on the enclosed statement up-to-date.

We will appreciate your cooperation.

(4)

For a special reason we make this request now. Inasmuch as this is the last month of the year, we are anxious to have our accounts paid up-to-date before we make our annual reports.

On the enclosed statement, we list your purchases that are past due, and the months in which you sent us these orders.

Since part of your account has been extended quite a while, we feel certain that we can depend on you to send us your payment in the next few days.

(5)

IT'S AN OLD CHINESE CUSTOM!

In China, the celebration of New Year's is a great event. The custom is to go among their creditors and settle their obligations.

This starts a chain because with the money received, one man pays another and the second pays a third, and so it goes—*then* they all celebrate with a lot of noise, the burning of redfire and the shooting of fireworks.

If you could start the chain, we could close our books with our obligations paid to others. Just an old Chinese custom, but a pretty good way to start the New Year in *any* country.

You'd be surprised, too, how loudly we can shout—

"HAP...PY NEW YEAR-R-R!!!!"

(6)

This coin is only a penny. But the character of Abraham Lincoln is an inspiration worth millions to any American.

When he was an Illinois country storekeeper, Lincoln once innocently overcharged a customer a few pennies—then walked 3 miles through rain and mud to refund them.

Deep down inside of us, we all want to be as fair as Lincoln was. His birthday is a good time for you to show your fairness. And what better way than by paying your overdue account?

That's fair, isn't it?

(7)

One hundred and fifty years ago this month, Washington's troops suffered untold hardships at Valley Forge because the Colonies couldn't raise the money to feed and clothe them. Their credit was mighty poor.

We may not be walking over the snow with bare and bleeding feet like Washington's soldiers, but like the Colonies, you do owe us some money.

Don't wait for warmer weather to get into action. Unlimber that pen and fire us a volley of $274 while you grin and bear it like the boys at Valley Forge.

Duty calls!

(8)

If some mysteriously powerful individual stated to do a good turn for business, as Saint Patrick did a good turn for Ireland, do you know what he would do first?

He would drive the past due accounts out of your business and ours.

Now, it is our duty to ourselves and to our customers to keep the past due accounts from accumulating on our books. As there is no chance of our being visited by a patron saint, we have to call on you to assist us.

Won't you please send a check for $341 remembering how much better we'll both feel in celebrating March 17?

(9)

The Pilgrim Fathers *came across* in the Mayflower.

Of course, your account isn't quite as old as that, but you'll admit it's a long time since you "came across" with some cash.

Suppose you have your bookkeeper look into our statement of charges *now*. (I'll wager you'll find it O.K.) Then the next thing to do is to instruct him to fix a check for you to sign and send it to us *today*.

In other words—do as the Pilgrim Fathers did.

COME ACROSS.

The number and kinds of these out-of-the-groove collection letters are limited only by the imagination of those who write them, but those you have seen are fair samples of the run. And just for good measure, here are 12 "shorts"—one for each month of the year.

January

Well, the little fellow arrived on time this year. Sorry we can't say as much for your check that was expected in our office on January 5.

February

February, the month of holidays! Lincoln's and Washington's birthday...and Valentine's Day. We hope that your check for $25 has not taken a holiday. You know it was due on the 10th. What's that—it's on its way? Thank you.

March

March, they say, comes in as a lion—goes out as a lamb. Not roaring like a lion, but gently reminding you, comes this little notice to tell you that your payment of $40 was due last week.

April

April showers bring summer's flowers. But not yet, alas, your payment of $15 which was due on April 3. In anticipation...thank you.

May

Now comes the merry May.

When shines the sun each day...

Not much as poetry, I realize, but then poetry is not my line. What I really want is to remind you that your payment of $10 was due on the 14th.

June

Summer—time for vacations—jolly, blossom-scented days, moonmad nights...No wonder, perhaps, that your payment of $55, due the 21st, is A.W.O.L.

Won't you send it, please?

July

Month of the 4th—much noise! Thoughts of shade, ice-cold lemonade, a fishing trip in the North Woods. And no thought at all, it seems, of your payment of $32 which was due on the 8th.

Too hot to worry much...but won't you send it, please?

August

There once was an old country legend named Pete? He weighed a good 400 pounds. Then along came August. Up went the thermometer and with each degree of heat Pete got thinner. Seemed like he just began to melt. And as it got colder, Pete actually faded away. Poor old Pete.

September

Throughout the land the school bells toll. Well do we remember the way we ran to avoid getting in after the late bell rang. Maybe that payment of yours for $105 hasn't been to school, and didn't try to beat the bell.

Before we send for the truant officer, we'll try again. There. Did you hear it?

October

Boooo-oooo-oooo...

'Tis the month of Ghosts, Witches 'n' Goblins—time of Halloween! But we don't really mean to frighten you; only to remind you that your payment of $20 was due on the 10th.

November

Ye olde Thanksgiving is almost at ye hande. Yea, verily, all folke rejoiceth. We hopeth.

May there be bounty at thy home and much feasting—without ye stomach-ache to follow.

And many thee please hurry thy payment of $44, due on ye 17th...so that we too may rejoiceth.

We thanketh thee.

December

'Twas the night before Christmas...

And as you well know, throughout the house no one was stirring. To your house, we hope Santa Claus will come, making all your dreams come true.

But desolate is our house, for to it your payment due on

December 3rd has *not* come. Play Santa, won't you please, and see that we are not forgotten any longer?

The merriest Christmas to you!

These apt, if short, messages along with other examples of out-of-the-groove letters can go a long way with keeping your customers' goodwill *and* getting those delinquent accounts paid up.

7. KNOWING HOW THE CREDIT MANAGER HELPS TO SELL

Teamwork makes money. It is not unusual to find a company in which the credit and sales departments stand apart. Of course, this is understandable since the nature of their work may often cause differences of opinion. However, there is no basic reason why the sales force should not be interested in the financial security of an account, or why the credit department should not be interested in helping the account to grow as much as possible. Both conditions contribute to the customer's value to the company, and as the company prospers so do all its employees.

Consequently, the credit correspondents who think only about money matters are not making the most of their opportunities to serve and help their company. Granted that their major responsibilities are to extend credit privileges wisely and to make sure they are not abused. They still have another responsibility, that of maintaining goodwill and helping as best they can in the general sales program.

Note, for example, how all these responsibilities are well met in this short letter:

Thank you for bringing your account so nearly up-to-date. Another small check this month, and you'll be current again.

With the spring rush coming up soon, wouldn't you like to stock our new line of gardening tools now?

The credit managers who write letters like that one deserve a master rating: first, because it firmly asked for the money due the company; second because it did it in the nicest possible way; and third, because it also asked for another order. Thus, the letter served as a business-builder as well as a money-protector.

There are many ways in which the alert credit and collection letter-writer can help to win goodwill and increase sales. In Figure 14-8, the customer had allowed his account to fall so far behind that he dared not send in any more orders. This meant a double loss to the company until the money could be collected. Accordingly, the collection writer sug-

Figure 14-8

Dear _____,

Your orders have been missed. For many years you have sent in each month a number of orders which have been appreciated, and have had our prompt attention.

You have not told us the reason why you have not favored us with any business recently, but we are inclined to believe it is because you owe us a past due account.

We want your business, and we want to provide as convenient a manner for handling payment of your account as is possible. There is no reason why it should be necessary for you to turn to some other source of supply, for we are sure you have been well pleased with the quality of Menasha merchandise.

Let's start out on a clean slate again.

Attached are two notes of $112.81 and one of $112.80 dated today, and falling due on November 20, December 10, and December 30. Will you kindly sign and return the notes which will take care of the balance on your account? Then, having deferred the charges now outstanding, you undoubtedly will be in a position to handle current charges promptly. In fact, you can take advantage of the 2 per cent which we offer for payment in ten days.

Your consideration of the settlement that we have offered will be appreciated. Why not sign the notes and send them along with a nice order for merchandise to be billed on our regular terms?

gests a solution to the problem—as a salesman he invites additional purchases.

As so often stated in this *Handbook,* the only dependable test of a particular letter is whether or not it does the intended job. The customer who got the letter you have just read promptly complied with both of Mr. Pope's requests. He did sign and return the notes. He did include an order.

When merchants do not pay promptly for a shipment of goods, the reason is sometimes that they are not selling as they anticipated. To offset this possible objection, the writer of Figure 14-9 comes up with specific sales suggestions. Thus, it not only functions as a collector, but also may accomplish a double purpose for the sales department: first, to

Figure 14-9

Dear _____,

So far we have not received your check for the ten 24-count cases of Shelby's Seasoned Croutons delivered on June 10.

When you bought these croutons, you didn't intend simply to add merchandise to your inventory. You bought them to increase your sales and your profit—and you selected the ideal brand for that purpose.

"Make it special" is the advertisement we've been running nationwide for the past month. The thrust is that when unexpected company comes, how can the everyday meal become "special"? When leftovers are served, how can it be assured they're eaten?

How many people in your area have company coming today? How many have leftovers in their refrigerators? How many will come into a store in a quandary as to what to serve? And what will you do to help them solve their problem?

Every one of these people is a golden opportunity for you—an opportunity to make suggestions, to make sales, to make profits. We want to help you to make these suggestions. We want to help you increase your sales not only of Shelby's Seasoned Croutons, but also of other things as well. If you are at a loss as to what to suggest, please contact us and we will send you a supply of recipe leaflets that will help you do the job. If you would like further assistance, we can arrange for a store demonstrator to come and distribute samples and suggestions directly to your customers.

For your own good, for your own profit, we urge you to use these suggestions. It takes more than just a store with a stock of merchandise to make a successful and profitable business. Your success depends upon the salesmanship you put behind the merchandise—and salesmanship is largely suggestion.

Shelby's Seasoned Croutons, plus *your* salesmanship, equals profit. Try it. You will find that it works.

In the meantime, won't you please send us your check to cover our invoice on June 15?

---

help move the stock now on the merchant's shelves; second, to pave the way for another order.

Figure 14-10

Dear _____,

It is not only because we want to see this account paid that we ask you to send a check today, but also because we want to do more business with you, and we're afraid that the overdue account, amounting to $35.67, is keeping you away.

The popularity of our new ELECTRA model warrants your stocking it. A circular is enclosed. Although introduced only two months ago, the ELECTRA is already demanded in preference to all others. It is advertised in all the leading magazines.

We have not received an order from you for several months, and doubtless you are now in need of some of our line.

Just add ELECTRA to your next order, and, at the same time, let us have your check.

Thank you.

Introducing a new product or service. Because many letters are written by credit managers they can be a useful means of spreading the news about new products and services.

To remove any doubt with respect to the effectiveness of a combined sales and collection letter, we hasten to tell you that high percentages are often reported with both payments *and* orders coming in. Figure 14-10 is a collection letter which takes time to sell a new product while Figure 14-11 sells a service.

Thanking those who pay promptly. A growing tendency among credit managers, and one sure to win goodwill, is the occasional recognition of those to whom it is never necessary to send collection letters. This, we think, has been in the past a too-often neglected courtesy. The customers who never cause any trouble deserve applause—for the selfish purpose of holding their favor if for no more commendable reason. If you concede the connection between goodwill and sales, you will agree it is no exaggeration to call the following messages of appreciation *sales* letters:

(1)

Dear _____,

When you send us an order, we receive it with appreciation and try to fill it promptly with the highest quality merchandise.

Figure 14-11

Dear _____,

Many of our customers call at the yard for their own supplies. To speed our end of the affair, we have just installed the very latest loading equipment, and also have put extra men in the warehouse. Your trucks can now reduce their loading time here by from 30 to 50 per cent—a very substantial saving.

We haven't seen any of your drivers for some time. We hope, however, that you will soon give us an order, and test for yourself the efficiency and economy of our new loading system.

Stop in at our office some day next week, and we will be glad to show you the new equipment. At the same time, we would like to talk over your account, $77.65, now past due. We think that you will want to give us at least a substantial payment.

Please do drop in next week. We will be glad to see you.

Then we send you an invoice or statement and you promptly send us your check. We also appreciate that. But sometimes we forget to tell you about it.

We just want you to know that we genuinely thank you for your orders, and I, in particular, thank you for your prompt payments.

(2)

Dear _____,

Your account with us in now paid up-to-date.

If, in the course of transactions, we have left some doubt in your mind as to the policy we have maintained, please be assured that our deepest concern has been to strengthen our business relationship.

The personal touch is too often overlooked in the handling of large volumes of correspondence; therefore, if we have not thanked you for your cooperation, let us do so now.

We will look forward to the opportunity of serving you once again.

(3)

Dear _____,

Did you ever have the feeling that you were failing to do something important, and could not think what it was? I have—but today I thought of it.

The writer who is responsible for collections has spent most of his time with a list of names that does not include such good agents as you. The most familiar names are those to whom we write many letters. When we glance at your account, we pass on with a genuine glow of satisfaction, knowing that your remittances follow from month to month like clockwork without even a reminder from us.

When we consider all the letters we have been compelled to write during the year, it is a pleasure to write one voluntarily to an agent who has, even in this present day stress, maintained such a high standard. Perhaps it has never occurred to you what a joy such an account as yours is to the credit department.

Now my conscience feels better. With sincere appreciation and cordial good wishes to you,

(4)

Dear _____,

The play has ended and the stage is dark.

This does not mean, however, that the memory of a good performance is forgotten, or that the principal actors, whose work made the play a memorable thing, are unappreciated.

On the contrary, we do appreciate the fine manner in which you paid your notes on the fan account, and it is with real pleasure that we return the original note and mortgage to you, cancelled with recorder's release.

This one play is over. That is true, but the show of business continues and we want to have a part in that big performance by helping you either with our equipment or suggestions.

Again that word of thanks for your choice of our equipment, and your promptness in making the payments. We hope, too, that we shall soon rise to the curtain call for serving you again.

There are many thousands of people who never fail to make their payments regularly until the obligations are cancelled. These conscientious customers are a joy to the companies that deal with them—but this joy is seldom expressed in a letter of appreciation as it should be.

While these letters only take a couple of minutes to dictate and a stamp to place them in the hands of the customers, they go a long way toward building goodwill and increasing sales.

8. HOW TO WRITE LETTERS TO SOLVE OTHER CREDIT PROBLEMS

Emphasizing the need for judgment, skill, and diplomacy. So far, most of the letters in this section have revealed how various credit managers, or their assistants, go about the job of collecting money from customers who for one reason or another have not paid their bills as agreed in the terms of sale. These letters are of great importance since no company can afford to treat collections lightly. There are, however, many other situations connected with the allocation and control of credit which the credit manager usually handles by mail, and some of them may require the highest degree of judgment, skill, and diplomacy.

Ordinarily, people expect to be reminded when they have not paid their bills. They are not as "touchy" about a collection letter as about one that asks for a financial report, one that refuses to allow an unearned discount, or one that insists on cash in full before the shipment of an order. Any one of these or other similar problems may turn out to be as difficult for the credit manager to solve as the collection of a troublesome account. It is not easy, for example, to write the letter which tells a prospective customer that available information does not justify credit privileges, and which nevertheless tries to salvage both the order and goodwill. But this is part of the credit managers' job, and he or she must know how to go about it with a reasonable percentage of success.

Another bothersome angle to these special credit problems is the natural tendency of persons in the sales department to resent the loss of orders which the credit managers will not approve for credit. As a result, the managers are accused of lack of cooperation when they are really only performing their duty to the company by not taking on dangerous accounts. They stand on the point of a needle, wanting to please both customer and salesman, but still mindful of the fact that they will be held responsible for errors in judgment. At best, they can only play their cards as they see them, trying to make the customer understand the *reason* for any action considered necessary, and being always as friendly and tactful as is humanly possible.

Asking for credit information. Obviously, any decision with respect to the credit privilege depends on the information which the credit manager is able to get about the customer. It may come from one of the agencies that furnish credit reports, from other companies that have had experience with the same party or firm, or from any other source considered reliable. Supplementing this assembly of facts, the credit managers in many cases also request the buyers themselves for a financial statement. All this takes time, and if the order-shipments are held up pending the final decision, the credit managers quickly find themselves in hot water with the new customers. That such a situation can be handled tactfully is illustrated by the following letters:

(1)

To me the high spot in any business day is the arrival of the first order from a new customer, and I want to tell you personally how much I appreciate your order.

Concerning the rather delicate question of terms and credit, I do not like to see a new customer receive the usual cold and formal request for credit information without some personal word from me on the subject.

It is our policy to extend every possible accommodation to our customers, and we realize that a friendly credit policy is just as important as the maintenance of quality in our product. These two services make for a permanent and happy relationship between manufacturer and customer.

Will you, therefore, kindly send me some information on which our credit manager can base his records? The name of your bank, together with the names of several suppliers with whom you have already established credit, will be satisfactory.

There will, of course, be some delay in our receiving this information. For prompt delivery, perhaps you would prefer to send a check for the first order so that we can make immediate shipment.

Please accept my thanks once more for this order.

(2)

It was a pleasure to receive your recent order which was entered for immediate shipment at our regular 30-day terms.

To enable us to extend the line of credit you may need, will you send us the usual credit information? For your convenience, we enclose a simplified financial statement form.

Thank you again for your order, and we hope that this is the beginning of a long and mutually pleasant business relationship.

(3)

Our representative has just written to us the good news of your decision to distribute our products. He tells us to expect your initial stock order soon.

We want to be sure that you will receive your stock without delay, and, as our credit department requires that we furnish them with information on all new accounts, we ask that you assist us by filling in the enclosed form.

Then, with the O.K. of our credit department, we can ship your order as soon as it is received.

(4)

We have just received the order you gave our sales represent-ative, Mr. Jones, for 10,000 cartons. It is a pleasure to welcome you cordially to the rapidly growing number of our customers.

Mr. Jones has asked us to ship your order on a "RUSH" basis. We would like to do so, for we want you to have the satisfaction of using our cartons at the earliest possible moment.

We and all other reputable members of the cardboard carton industry follow the practice of making a credit inquiry about new customers to confirm their good credit standing. This inquiry will take about a week to complete.

To avoid a delay on your first order, will you authorize us to ship it immediately on a C.O.D. basis? If you will send us a wire collect to that effect immediately upon receipt of this letter, your order will be on its way to you before the close of business tomorrow. If we do not receive a wire from you, we will ship your order on regular terms as soon as our credit records are complete.

Will you help us complete our inquiry by filling out the enclosed financial statement form and mailing it back to us at your earliest convenience?

The letters we have just inspected were by no means final with respect to credit classification. The writers were simply trying to save the initial order and at the same time secure information to guide them in handling future business. But a much more serious problem confronts credit managers when finally they have to *refuse* the credit privilege. When they can do that and still make the order stick, they are at their best.

Using finesse to refuse open terms. When the financial picture of a new customer does not warrant buying on credit, it is indeed difficult to say so and still retain goodwill. Some credit managers do not seem to worry much over this problem, for their letters are displeasingly blunt. Others, more salesminded, try nobly to break the news gently, and to make the order stick on cash terms. The latter is frequently possible, as many of the best credit managers will agree. In fact, they say it should be the rule rather than the exception.

Consider what one prominent credit manager says about salvaging orders in spite of credit obstacles. The speaker is C. G. Beardsley, of the Taylor Instrument Co., Rochester, New York.

We do not turn down orders. We accept them.

Then, we try to sell the customer on our terms instead of his. Moreover, the job cannot be done with a form letter. The reply must meet each case and show a thorough understanding of the buyer's problem. If that can be done then our proposition is half sold. We discuss the matter frankly, though politely.

We approach the customer by saying that since he is a newcomer, or is not rated, it is only natural that we should make credit inquiries, which we have done. We then discuss with him what the reports show, always making allowances for the fact that the reports may be wrong, and that there may have been improvement in the customer's business not reflected by the reports.

We tell the customer the reason why we must have our bill paid promptly, or why it would not be wise for us to supply him with added credit, and why we must have cash.

That this plan works is proved by the fact that we rarely have to cancel an order for credit reasons.

A disputed question among credit managers is how far the letter should go in telling the customers exactly *why* they cannot enjoy the privilege of buying on open terms. Some think the truth only tends to anger the customer, and so they do as little explaining as possible. Others, as in the case in Figure 14-12, put the cards face-up on the table.

The circumstances seen in Figure 14-13 are perhaps somewhat special, making it possible for the credit manager to suggest alternative means of obtaining credit. All the same, the writer has made a commendable effort to be particularly polite and gracious even while refusing. A less tactful credit manager might easily have alienated a customer of long standing.

Figure 14-12

Dear _____,

Thank you for sending us your business statement and references so promptly. All your references spoke very highly of you, as a businessman and as a member of the community. We feel sure that you are going to make a very profitable business out of the Arcade Shop, and we want to do everything we can to help you do so.

We have studied your business very carefully, and we want to make one or two friendly suggestions. We do not believe it would be to your advantage for us to fill your order on the open terms you asked for. Frankly, Mr. _____, you are somewhat undercapitalized, and for you to assume additional current liabilities just now might seriously jeopardize our prospects. If you possibly can, you should obtain at least $3,000 additional capital. With your personal ability and your favorable location, you should have little difficulty in doing so.

We also recommend that you allow us to halve your order and ship to you on cash terms. You will save the 2 per cent discount, which will mean a lot to you right now. We can ship the other half of the order on a moment's notice if you find you need it, and you will avoid tying up more capital in inventory if you do not.

Very soon—in a few weeks, perhaps—you should be in a position to command our most favorable credit terms. We hope that our suggestions will help you to do so. We will ship the first half of your order the moment we get your approval.

In contrast, what would have been your reaction had you received the following goodwill-buster? "Dear Sir: We cannot do business with you for obvious credit reasons. Perhaps one of our competitors will not be so particular, as we do not lean backward when it comes to risking questionable accounts." Decidedly, that is *not* a good way to refuse the credit privilege.

Knowing what to say when credit is approved. Although no problem confronts the credit managers when they tell a customer that a charge account has been approved, they have an excellent opportunity to win goodwill by making the letter something more than just a cut-and-dried confirmation. In other words, the credit privilege should be extended cheerfully, and with a hand of welcome. It may also explain

Figure 14-13

> Dear _____,
>
> I do wish we could arrange a time payment order for you, but owing to our small margin of profit, our requirements for credit are quite strict. To qualify, one must have a regular, established income.
>
> This being the case, there isn't any way in which we can fill an order in your son's name alone. I regret this more than I can say, for we always like to help our customers, especially the old friends of our firm.
>
> You mention that your son is leaving for college soon. Perhaps you could order the things he wants in his name. Or he might sign the contract with you and guarantee you the payments. We would be glad to ship his items right to his door.
>
> If so, the order should be sent in the usual way on one of our order blanks that you'll find in the back of our catalog. All questions should be answered carefully, and the contract signed as specified, so we can make our regular credit investigations and establish the proper credit rating.
>
> I do hope you will understand the reasons behind this decision. We want you to know you are one of our valued customers, and we want to continue serving you.

the credit policy of the company in order to get the new account off on the right foot, and to discourage any infractions which the customer might be tempted to make later. However, such explanations tend to mar the friendly tone of the letter, and usually they have been clearly made at the time the application was taken. We like best the type of letter which simply welcomes and thanks the customers and promises to serve them well. Here are several examples:

(1)

Like making friends, there is a real satisfaction in adding your name to our growing list of charge account customers.

We hope that this may be the beginning of a long and pleasant business relationship—profitable to you and to us—and that we may enjoy one another's confidence, friendship, and respect.

Please call on us at any time. We look forward to serving you.

(2)

It is our pleasure to notify you that a charge account has been approved in your name. We will constantly endeavor to serve you courteously and to your complete satisfaction.

Arrangements have been made to place at your disposal credit amounting to $250. When you wish to exceed this sum, I will be happy to discuss the matter with you.

Bills will be rendered on the first of each month, and are to be paid in full by the tenth.

An identification plate is enclosed, and a booklet that tells you how to use it. We know that you will find this new charge account a great convenience.

(3)

When we cashed a check for you the other day, it occurred to us that you might enjoy the convenience of a charge account with us.

This credit privilege does away with the need of paying for each purchase separately, and allows you to order by telephone when you are too busy to call at the store. It also brings to you the news of special services that we arrange from time to time only for charge customers.

We will be very happy to extend our credit service to you, and for the time alone saved you will find it a real convenience.

Just fill out the enclosed credit card and return it in the enclosed envelope which requires no postage. Twenty-four hours after the card is received, your charge account will be cleared and ready for you to use.

In many types of business, charge accounts—properly controlled—are considered a real asset: First, because customers are more likely to consolidate their purchases where they enjoy the privilege of credit; second, because they tend to create goodwill. Thus, the charge account encourages more spending and keeps it in the same store. It is, therefore, not uncommon for the credit manager of a company to *offer* the credit privilege to those who have been buying with cash and are thought to be dependable.

Putting the brakes on a charge account. One thing that makes credit managers' lives interesting is the way seemingly stable accounts will all of a sudden begin to turn sour. Over a long period of time, for example, customers may promptly discount their bills, so that the credit managers never have the slightest worry about them; then, month-by-month the unpaid balances carried over get larger and larger until finally it is necessary to suspend the credit privilege.

It is not easy, as all credit managers know to tell old and loyal customers (as in Figure 14-14) or brand-new ones (as in Figure 14-15) that future shipments must be made C.O.D., even though the change in terms are presented as a temporary means of helping the customers to get their accounts in order. If the letters are not extremely tactful, the writers may bring two evils on their heads: first, the complete loss of customers' business; second, the problem of having to fight for the collection of the unpaid balances.

That credit managers are not so hard to get along with as some people suppose, is proved by the next two friendly letters. In both cases, the customer has already placed the facts on the table—an act of frankness which would eliminate a lot of credit troubles if only carried out more frequently. Credit managers, as a rule, are willing to go along with a customer who seems honest and sincere; it is lack of explanation—continued silence—that forces them to be "tough."

> I want to thank you personally for your very frank letter. Everybody is up against it at one time or another. We have been ourselves. And that is exactly why we are going to help you.
>
> Don't worry about the account with us, even if it is past due. Forget it for 90 days. We are going to ask you to sign a note covering that period. By that time, things will undoubtedly look better.
>
> We wouldn't do this for everybody, but from your letter we get the idea you are strictly all right. We want you to build up a good business, and we will help you all we can. It's a pleasure to have folks know that we sell service as well as quality.
>
> Just sign the note and return it to us promptly.
>
> . . . . . .
>
> We are glad to read of your intention of paying as soon as possible our bill of June 3, amounting to $77.63. We realize, of course, that the farmers have been having a difficult time. But that, of course, makes hard sledding for us, as a large share of our merchandise goes to farmers.
>
> Now, we try to make things easy for everyone, but we have to ask our friends to pull with us—not against us. For this reason, we are enclosing a note for the amount due. This note is dated August 1 and is due September 1—in other words, in two months.
>
> Just please sign the note, and return it to us.

Figure 14-14

Dear _____,

Your recent letter of explanation about your past-due account and your order amounting to an additional $400 forces me to write to you frankly, as I would want you to write to me if the conditions were reversed.

Of all the companies who have accounts with us, there is not a one in which we have greater confidence than yours. But like yourself, we too have allowed many of our old accounts to become much larger than we would have in less trying times. However, we cannot continue to be so lenient, and we must watch collections closely if we are to stay in business and continue to offer quality services and merchandise.

In substance, _____, this means we are in the same boat with you—our creditors depend on us to keep their business solvent, just as we depend on you, and you in turn depend on your customers. It's a sort of moving chain of credit, and no link can be broken without injury to all.

In view of the fact that the amount of your account has steadily increased during the past 12 months (with a present balance of almost $3,000), we believe you will understand why it is best for both your company and ours that your last order be shipped C.O.D.

In fact, we are so sure that you will be in sympathy with this decision—it being the same that you will have to make with some of your own customers—that we are going ahead with the shipment so as not to delay the customary prompt service.

A substantial payment on your account will in the meantime be a great help. We can ask our manufacturers for more credit when you and other good customers are able to reduce the total of their past due payments. And this means eventually we can resume shipments to you on the old basis.

For the present, you will realize why your own account must be considerably reduced before any more credit can be extended.

With our very best wishes,

The same plan of getting notes signed was used by the letter-writer in Figure 14-8 when he wrote to his customer, although the amount involved was somewhat larger.

Figure 14-15

Dear _____:

You ask, "Why C.O.D. terms?" Here is the explanation, and we want you to see it our way, so that we may work together to make the C.O.D. basis only temporary.

Back in August we approved credit terms for you although reports indicated that your obligations were not always promptly settled. We told you then that we did not want to be guided entirely by records, and that we would do our best to assist you in rebuilding a credit rating. That is why open account terms were approved, and we expected you would promptly discount our various invoices.

Since you did not do this, the past-due account raised the question of continued credit, for such delays in payment often point to business difficulties. Consequently, in order to collect this old account and prevent invoices from piling up, we had to suspend credit terms.

This necessity is regretted by us, but we honestly believe that you will gain by our action. You now have the opportunity to catch up on the past-due account, to clarify this credit problem, and to earn your 10 per cent discount on current shipments—all by paying C.O.D.

We do not want to stress the 10 per cent discount too much, but, after all, the purpose of any business is to make money—and discounting bills is one of the easiest ways. There is no need to tell you that competition is very keen nowadays—generally, your margin has to be small, and it is important that you use every possible advantage to put yourself ahead of your competitors. When you earn a cash discount and your competitor loses it, you strengthen your business and he weakens his.

Past-due accounts are expensive—for both of us! It costs you money because you lose the 10 per cent discount and jeopardize your credit rating. It costs us money because of additional bookkeeping work, collection costs, and extra office time.

So that's the answer, _____, to your question—"Why C.O.D. terms?" and we think you must understand we have tried to do the fair thing, in the right way.

Explaining the value of discounts. In many sales contracts a special discount—usually 10 per cent —is offered the customer who pays the bill within a stated period, commonly ten days from the date of invoice. This "bonus plan" can be either a blessing or a curse to the credit manager—the former when it speeds collections as it of course does in many cases, the latter when it leads to an argument with some customer who thinks he should have the discount even though the stipulated date is past. On the whole, the good of the plan undoubtedly outweighs the bad, although the proportion may vary in specific companies or types of business.

When buyers do not take advantage of the discount privilege, one of two reasons is likely to be the cause: first, they do not understand how much money could be saved: or second, they simply haven't enough liquid cash to meet all obligations promptly. There isn't a lot that credit managers may do to offset the second reason, but they can educate the buyers who don't realize what discounts may amount to over a year's time. Here are a couple of examples to show how this educational job may be done:

Yesterday we uncovered something that we think will interest you.

On last year's purchase, you neglected to earn discounts amounting to $1,270.80.

It occurs to us that perhaps you are unaware that it is possible, in a year's time, to save 10 per cent on your average monthly purchases from us by deducting 10 per cent from the face amount of our monthly bill, providing you pay it by the 10th of the month following delivery.

No, there's no trick to it. Suppose your average monthly purchases comes to $500. If you send us your check in full payment by the 10th of each month following your purchase, you can deduct 10 per cent, or $50 from the total bill. By doing this every month, your annual savings will amount to $600, or 10 per cent of your average yearly purchases of $6,000.

Isn't that surprising? It's a grand idea if you can do it. And that brings us to the point of our letter. We don't want to seem to be telling you what to do. It's your business and you know best what can be done, but we do hope that in bringing these facts to your attention, perhaps you can finish the year with a sizable "discount earned" account.

We hope that you will buy frequently from us and that it will be possible for you to discount your purchases when you do. However, please be sure that discounting or not, we have enjoyed doing business with you and will continue to do so.

•   •   •   •   •

This is an explanation of how we can help your profits. Some of our dealers do not know that we give them a discount of 10 per cent if they pay their accounts within 10 days.

Six weeks ago, you gave us a $206 order. Had you paid this bill in full within 10 days, you would have saved $20.60. In other words, by waiting the full 30 days to remit payment, you paid, in effect, an interest of $20.60 on $206 for 20 days. Since there are eighteen 20-day periods a year, this is the equivalent of paying an annual interest rate of 180 per cent.

This savings is so important that many of our customers who are pressed for cash find it profitable to borrow from a bank—at 6 per cent—to take advantage of this service.

It's entirely up to you, of course, whether you avail yourself of our discount privilege. I just want to make sure that you know of this savings we offer our customers—a savings that means many vital dollars to you in a year's time.

Letters such as these just read present no particular problem. They really have a strong point to develop, and credit managers can write with the good of their customers at heart. But the negative side of the picture is not nearly so pleasant.

Discovering the art of saying "no." It may seem very simple to say that no discount will be allowed after the stipulated date, but *getting the money back* from customers who have abused the privilege is not as easy as it sounds. Particularly, if the amount of the sale is large, and the customers are old friends of the company, the credit managers are up against it when forced to write: "Since the ten-day period expired before your check was mailed, may we ask that you kindly forward the amount of the discount which you inadvertently deducted?" They may say "inadvertently," but they are not fooling either themselves or their customers. And the latter, called on the carpet, are quite likely to fight back. The temptation, of course, is for the credit managers to yield, but this is not fair to other customers who play the game according to the rules.

Possibly business would be better off without the discount privilege which came into being during a period of depression, and merchants said: "Send us the money which we need badly and in return for the favor you may deduct a percentage from the face amount." They probably had no thought of starting a custom which now exists in most lines of business.

Be that as it may, here are three letters in which credit managers of today sought to say "no" to their customers who had improperly taken discounts:

(1)

Terms of sales should be considered more binding than seems to be common these days, *"Let the seller beware"* is apparently the policy under which many payments are mailed out.

Some concerns evidently have one policy for payment of their purchases and quite another and different policy which they expect their customers to follow in paying their bills, but they cannot justly take unearned discounts and generally ignore the terms of the houses they buy from and expect their own customers to do anything different.

It is time that every business house of standing and reputation started a housecleaning in this regard and spread the word along the way that the present looseness and disregard of terms is a thing of the past, and that buyer and seller must "eventually" conform to a high standard of practice—*"so why not now?"*

In calling your attention to this situation we have in mind the fact that several payments have been returned to you because of the expiration of the cash discount period before the check was mailed. In each case a letter has been written to you explaining the matter and requesting your cooperation. Nevertheless, we do not seem to make any headway; so we request that you give proper attention to this letter and to this subject, advising us at your earliest convenience of your cooperation along these lines.

(2)

Although you say that you will quit doing business with us if we insist that you pay the unearned discount deducted from our invoice of April 10th, I honestly believe it would be the other way around. I say this because few of us have any respect for those who do not stand for their rights. And we are within our rights, else I wouldn't write.

Let's suppose a firm came to you and bought a bill of goods. Upon buying, it asked for the cash price and the term price. Then, suppose it waits until long after the term period had expired, and then pays you the cash price. Wouldn't you go to the firm and say it still owed you the difference? I believe that you would.

Now, that is our position exactly. When we offered our proposition, we, in effect, said to your buyer: "If you pay our invoice within 70 days, you may deduct 4% as a cash discount. But if the bill is not paid after 70 days, then the invoice is net. The discount privilege is lost!" This term proposition was accepted when you bought $4,683.50 worth of rugs on April 10th. The last day for discounting was June 20th. But your accountant didn't mail the check until August 6th—or 47 days after the last discount date. When he did, he deducted a discount that was no longer available.

What would you do were you in our place? Would you ask for the $187.35 erronesouly deducted? If you would, then you will know what to do with the stamped envelope I enclose.

With best wishes.

(3)

It is not a crime to take unearned discount.

Our only purpose in writing at all is to remind you of our terms, which are 10% in 10 days, net 30 days.

The last letter, written to you on March 18, mentioned the amount of $1.29 which was charged against your account. This meant, to our way of thinking, that you still owed that small amount.

However, while we would like you to pay what is due us, nevertheless, we realize that in demanding it we might cause some ill feeling, and we can assure you that no discount is large enough to cause us to do that.

So we're leaving it up to you. Pay it if you think we are right— don't pay it if you think we are wrong. But above all, let us remain good friends, both of us remembering...

It is not a crime to take unearned discount.

Thorns in the sides of credit managers everywhere are the customers who make what appears to them a sensible request, although from the points of view of the sellers these are exceptions to establish routine and cannot be granted. A policy not adhered to strictly becomes no policy at all, and there is no reason why one special favor should be allowed unless the company is prepared to do as much for others. For example, a common request is that the discount be conceded if bills are paid on the tenth of the month, instead of within the ten days following date of invoice. Or the customers have some other time of the month when it is more convenient for them to pay their bills, and see no harm in the practice provided the date is understood and they adhere to it faithfully. But no matter what the request, or how reasonable it may seem to the customer, it is still an exception to the established credit policy and only under very special circumstances can it be considered.

Saying "no" to these requests is, of course, a task requiring considerable diplomacy. Credit managers must take time to explain the company point of view, and do their best to make the customer accept it as fair and necessary. This job is done rather well in the following two letters:

(1)

Mildred Wiley of our Cleveland office has referred your letter to us regarding our regular terms of sale. We certainly appreciate the opportunity to discuss these terms with you.

In your position as purchasing agent, you no doubt have a much better understanding of terms than does the average person. Consequently, you know that the best terms are those which permit the retention of working capital for the longest period of time. Conversely, it is also true that from the selling standpoint, it is best to have short terms which will bring in working capital within the shortest period of time.

To get a balance between these two is indeed difficult, particularly when one considers that he buys from hundreds of different concerns and perhaps sells as many different ones.

Our terms of sale are 10% tenth prox., net 30 days. These are standard in the Rubber Industry, and we like to think that we treat all of our customers alike. Obviously, if a good customer like yourself said that you would not give us any more business unless we changed our terms, it would be foolish to think that we wouldn't give you the terms you wanted, but our experience has been that customers are willing to cooperate and as a rule do not ask for special preference.

We think of you as being like that, and we would appreciate very much your adhering to our terms of sale. We don't want to be arbitrary and we assure you we aren't. But if at all possible, we hope you will buy from us in the future on our regular terms.

(2)

We refer to your letter of May 30, in which you suggest a change of terms on our merchandise from 10 per cent 10 days from date of invoice, to 10 per cent if paid prior to the 10th of the calendar month.

We can see a great deal of justice in your request that some change be made in the discount period. From our standpoint, however, we are in somewhat of a dilemma because we are anxious to accede to the view of our customers, and while leaning in that direction, our sources of supply have tightened up their terms, as against becoming more lenient.

Thus, we are somewhat in the position of a tight-rope walker trying to maintain a balance—trying to favor our good friends on one hand, and take care of our invoices within the terms as laid down by our sources of supply.

As I have intimated, our sources of supply, instead of becoming more lenient, have tightened up on us to the extent that instead of giving 10 per cent for remittance in 10 days from date of invoice, it is now 7 per cent, and on some commodities, such as pig tin, of which we use a lot, we must pay upon receipt of shipping document. So, there are times when the goods have been paid for many days before we receive them.

With this explanation, I know you can see our position, and that you will be willing to pay our invoices according to the terms which for so long a time have prevailed.

Believe me, this cooperation on your part will be greatly appreciated.

We think the extremely pleasant tone of the two foregoing letters could hardly fail to strike a receptive chord in the mind of the customers. Thus, as this section comes to a close, you have seen two credit managers meeting fully their obligations to company needs, but at the same time approaching their customers with courteous appreciation of their viewpoint.

These examples may be accepted as the one and only basis on which sales-minded and sincere credit managers may handle their responsibilities completely, and with credit to themselves. There are, of course, any number of situations not illustrated which may from day to day confront the "watch-dogs" of the company's money. But so long as they continue to adhere to company policy without causing unnecessary friction in customer relations, no situation can be so difficult that no satisfactory solution can be found. The credit managers are very important executives in the average company. On the whole, they are doing their jobs in ways that deserve our commendation.

Now that you have come to the end of this *Handbook,* you are ready to construct all the different types of business correspondence needed by today's executives.

Nothing is too difficult for you to handle. You can speak the language, build with the mechanics, and use your personality to advantage. No type of written customer relationship is beyond your ability to perform. Products can be sold, personnel can be transferred, and accounts can be settled—by *you,* the business letter-carpenter.

Good luck to you all. Remember, a good writer is an example to others—pass it on.

INDEX